# The People
## v.
# Lee Harvey Oswald

# The People
## v.
# Lee Harvey Oswald

*Walt Brown*

WITH A PREFACE BY MARTIN GARBUS, ESQ.

Carroll & Graf Publishers/Richard Gallen
New York

First Carroll & Graf/Richard Gallen edition 1992

Carroll & Graf Publishers, Inc.
260 Fifth Avenue
New York, NY 10001

Library of Congress Cataloging-in-Publication Data is available.

ISBN: 0-88184-869-7

Manufactured in the United States of America

THIS BOOK IS DEDICATED TO MY IMMEDIATE FAMILY—
JILL, ANNIE R. AND GULLIVER

FOR MORE REASONS THAN THERE
ARE THEORIES ABOUT THE ASSASSINATION

"The only thing necessary for the triumph of evil is for good men to do nothing."

—Edmund Burke


"I hereby appoint the Warren Commission."

—Lyndon B. Johnson

# SOURCES AND ACKNOWLEDGMENTS

A study of the assassination of President John Kennedy involves careful scrutiny of a variety of sources, which, not surprisingly, has created a variety of theories over the years.

The primary sources for this work were the *Hearings Before the President's Commission on the Assassination of President Kennedy*, published in twenty-six volumes (1964) and the twelve volumes of published testimony of the House Select Committee on Assassinations (1978). The House Committee essentially rubber stamped the Warren Commission's evidence and findings, yet concluded that there was "probably" a conspiracy behind the murder of the President. The twenty-six volumes were read first, with the second set read to see how witnesses (perhaps "survivors" would be a better term) recounted their stories fourteen years later. This allowed me to get a clear sense of the witnesses' testimony, a necessary factor, because the attorneys in the narrative that follows often ask pertinent questions that were never asked by the government, and answers had to be shaped from existing sources.

This process was greatly aided by the hundreds of monographs available on the events of November 22, 1963. Dedicated researchers have studied the event, and, collectively, have asked questions, whose answers have added far more than twenty-six volumes to the literature.

Having been trained as a historian, it was my job in this narrative to be as fair as humanly possible in weaving together all these sources. The process begins with primary sources—published testimony and documents—and then moves to unpublished material. The usefulness and veracity of testimony is weighed and compared against subsequent interviews and testimony in secondary sources. From all of this emerges a coherent whole.

Some witnesses explain their reasons for saying one thing to the President's Commission and something quite different to subsequent researchers and do so in a way that makes the difference believable. Other people consistently tell the same story. Still other witnesses gave testimony that was not at all credible. You will not read that testimony in the pages to come.

Media accounts required the same scrutiny. With such an historic event, it is not surprising that editors and program directors of 1963 placed speed ahead of a slower, "get it right" approach. They are not to be condemned for the way they responded. While much of the reporting was accurate, some needs a skeptical reevaluation. Where media sources are used reporters are identified by whom they worked for at the time.

So when Jim Marrs, in *Crossfire: The Plot that Killed Kennedy*, suggested that the reader avoid placing complete trust in his book, or any single source, he was stating a concern shared by many people who would like nothing better than for "the truth" to emerge. To Marrs' credit, and despite his disclaimer, he wove an excellent narrative in which a reader *can* place trust.

In sorting out this tangled web, so many people were helpful that generic acknowledgments are necessary. To the librarians, archivists, and out-of-print book dealers whom I hounded for information, please know that your labors are not unappreciated. To the witnesses, medical specialists, and legal theorists with whom I spoke, I thank you for your time. To the many dedicated authors who have preceded me in publishing their quests for the truth of what transpired on November 22, I owe a double thank you: first for persevering when the public had more pressing business than an unsolved 1963 murder, and also for aiding me in the process of contacting those with knowledge of the case.

On a personal level, I would like to thank a few close friends who discussed the case with me. They include Jack Kabral, Jim Clarke, and Dave and Karen Richards. Doctors Stephen Jacobs and Terry Tuchin gave of their time to study medical evidence and helped me reach conclusions. A special note of indebtedness must go to Harold and Lillian Weisberg. Mr. Weisberg was patient enough to listen to the concepts of this book, and gave me some needed direction. I am also grateful to the people at Richard Gallen and Company, especially David Gallen, as well as the staff at Carroll & Graf.

Closer to home, my students and colleagues at Village School in Closter, New Jersey, have been a constant source of support. In the wake of the movie *JFK*, they posed many challenging questions and combed newspapers for articles that would help me. Special thanks in this regard go to Alan Deroian, principal, Laura Clinton and Sidney Schwartz, computer specialists, and Brian McTigue and his family.

Lastly, the book would not exist without the support, loyalty, and understanding of my family. Jill Brown has been my toughest and best critic. That's what best friends are for. My thanks also go to Ray and Ada for that lifetime editor. Finally, there's Gulliver, who slept through most of the research and some of the typing.

To all these people, and to anyone inadvertently omitted, "thank you." This is a story I've been carrying since November 24, 1963. Now it is yours.

—Walt Brown
June 1992

# PREFACE

A Ph.D. in History, a former FBI agent and a courtroom buff who even watched traffic court trials as a child is a good combination to create a factually and historically "accurate" criminal trial of John F. Kennedy's alleged killer. Walt Brown is all of these as well as a man who wanted to be a lawyer, a criminal defense lawyer, and, when Kennedy was shot, wanted to be the lawyer who would defend Lee Harvey Oswald at trial.

This book gives Oswald the belated defense he never had. From the Warren Commission and its defenders, we know the prosecutor's point of view. From the movie *JFK*, and hundreds of assassination and conspiracy books, we know what is supposedly wrong with the Commission's conclusion. But, Dr. Brown, setting the prosecution against the defense, in a courtroom with a "real fictional" judge, prosecutor, and defense lawyer, focuses and dramatizes the collision of the opposing views by placing the evidence in an adversarial setting. By skillful use of imagined direct and cross examination of fact and forensic witnesses, he highlights the questions that are still unanswered twenty-nine years after the event.

Dr. Brown creates testimony to show how the prosecution can best present its facts. It is an artful blend of fact and fiction. He does not let the fiction that is necessary to write an explosive and exciting courtroom drama set back his search for the truth. And he chooses how to ask and answer questions about Oswald's motivation; how and where to arouse in you, the juror, the reasonable doubt that Oswald is not the killer. And then, Brown asks you, the reader, now a jury of Oswald's peers, to determine your view of the trial's outcome even as he gives you his own.

At the end of the day, the problems with the Warren Commission are the same as with most commission-type investigations. Governmental commissions by their very nature and structure are sharply limited in their ability to accurately determine guilt or innocence, truth or falsity.

But so, too, are criminal trials limited in their ability to give us irrevocable clarity. The Oswald trial, vividly created and described by Dr. Brown, is not a search for guilt or innocence. The question with Oswald, as with every other criminal defendant, is whether or not he is guilty *beyond* a reasonable doubt. An acquittal does not mean Oswald, or any other defendant, is innocent; it only means that the trier of fact, whether it be a judge or twelve jurors, did not have sufficient reason to convict.

Nearly every trial, from a traffic case involving running a red light, to a simple assault, to the killing of a President, has many disputed facts which, in the hands of a skilled lawyer can be used to create reasonable doubt. Oswald's trial, involving so many witnesses and so many disputed facts, would make any jury hard pressed to conclude there was no doubt.

This trial, even if it had occurred, and irrespective of the result, would show both the strength and weakness of our unique legal system—a system with many flaws but one much better than ever existed elsewhere. A trial is not a good place to get at all the facts of a complex, fast-moving event, the motivation of the main characters, Oswald's ties to foreign governments, or facts about the CIA and FBI. Here, as in so many other "political" trials, we could anticipate that Oswald's lawyers would have had to battle our government to get at all the "facts" of that day in Dallas.

Dr. Brown functions here as a skilled writer, historian, and lawyer as he gives us both drama and an advocate's viewpoint. Dr. Brown walks a tightrope as he peoples his Texas trial of Oswald with fictional lawyers and a judge. He fully reveals the events of November 22, 1963: the Dallas motorcade, the shooting, the death, and the aftermath. But, he never lets the words used to create a fictional setting for his true story impair his credibility as he writes the trial of the century.

As I read his, and history's creation, I marvelled at his work while, at the same time, I was ever more saddened by the fact that the event he describes never came to be. So many questions could have been answered if the trial had taken place.

But even if Jack Ruby had not killed Lee Harvey Oswald on that November day, forty-six hours after the President was killed, and even if a trial had resulted in a clear acquittal or a clear conviction (an unlikely event given both the facts and the absence of facts), we still probably would be debating many of the vague and ambiguous facts with which the case leaves us.

Of course, if some of the questions that still plague us had been better answered, America might have been better able to move on and deal with the political and social crises that face us today.

Dr. Brown has done us all a service and whether we agree with his conclusion or not, we all are in his debt. I applaud his prodigious effort.

—Martin Garbus, Esq.

# PROLOGUE

On Friday, November 22, 1963, shots were fired in Dallas, Texas, at the motorcade carrying President John F. Kennedy, his wife, Texas Governor John Connally and his wife, and two Secret Service agents.

President Kennedy died as a result of massive trauma to the brain. The massive trauma was caused by bullet wound(s).

One of a dozen or more suspects picked up in the case was charged with the murder of the President roughly twelve hours after Mr. Kennedy was pronounced dead.

Almost forty-seven hours after the President was shot, his alleged assailant, Lee Harvey Oswald, a former marine who had defected to the Soviet Union and returned in 1962, was mortally wounded while surrounded by seventy police officials in the basement of the Dallas Police Department. He died two hours later in a quiet room across the hallway from the trauma bay where President Kennedy had been pronounced dead two days earlier.

Twenty-nine years after the events just described, the paragraphs above contain all of what we know for certain about those events. Anything more, be it "official" or "critical," is speculative.

Unfortunately for the peace of mind of many Americans, the Friday to Friday time continuum which began tragically on November 22 ended equally tragically on November 29, when newly installed President Lyndon Johnson, in the face of potential congressional, Senate, and Texas inquiries into the dual murders, appointed a blue-ribbon panel, headed by the chief justice of the Supreme Court, to investigate the crimes.

Ten months later, under great pressure to conclude their labors before the imminent presidential election, the "Warren

Commission" issued a *report* which concluded that Lee Harvey Oswald, acting alone, had killed the President.

The nation's fears were put to rest.

Forty days later, Lyndon Johnson won a landslide election.

Between November 1964 and January 3, 1967, Oswald's alleged killer, Jack Ruby, ably described by author Henry Hurt as "a pimp for all seasons," was convicted and sentenced to death, only to have that verdict overturned as a result of flagrantly unfair court procedures in obtaining the conviction. While Ruby was awaiting retrial, the world learned, on December 29, 1966, that he was ill with cancer. Five days later, the disease silenced him. The suddenness of it made little impression on an America bogged down in a war ten thousand miles away.

What it did mean, however, was that in a strictly legal sense, no one was ever found guilty of either of the historical murders committed in Dallas, Texas, between November 22 and 24, 1963.

Ruby was presumed guilty, and reasonably so. After all, a crime with sixty million witnesses is *not* likely to cast "reasonable doubt" on any jury. His motives, however, were less obvious than his deeds, and they, like the alleged deed and motive of Lee Oswald, lay shrouded in mystery three decades later.

The American system of justice has guaranteed, in the vast majority of cases, that the accused individual be tried in a reasonable amount of time, and be judged by a jury. This was true in the case of John Peter Zenger; the "Boston Massacre" trials of *Rex* v. *Preston* and *Rex* v. *Wemms,* et al.; Dred Scott; the Lincoln conspirators; Sacco and Vanzetti; the Rosenbergs, and, more recently, in trials involving a host of serial killers and other low-light sociopaths. The trials cited also suggest that verdicts are often reflections of their historical epochs and not "justice" in the purest sense.

Lee Oswald never had a trial. He was convicted in the media, and subsequently by a presidential commission, without the benefits guaranteed in the Constitution, and, in the latter case, with the only truly damning evidence coming from his widow, someone who would never have given such evidence if a trial had been held.

What follows is an attempt to give Lee Oswald, and, by indirection, others as well, a day in court. This work, which was begun in 1963, assumes that all events occurred as generally described in the media until that moment at 11:21 A.M., C.S.T., when Jack Ruby fired at Oswald. In this narrative, the bullet failed of its ultimate goal, although Oswald lay comatose and under heavy guard for many months. As the presidential commission was nearing the end of its labors, Oswald began a slow, painful recovery, and was able to stand trial in late December 1964. Once jury selection, not included here, was completed, the opening arguments began on Tuesday, January 5, 1965, in Lubbock, Texas, 320 miles from Dallas. The change of venue was granted for reasons of security and publicity, and because Ruby's 1964 conviction had been overturned in part because of the absence of a change of venue.

Because the sources in some cases are more recent than 1965, the testimony, while valid, is occasionally kaleidoscoped: some witnesses were too frightened to come forward then, others were given orders *not* to reveal what they knew, and still others were ignored. This book lets them, too, have their day in court.

Some of the witnesses will be familiar to the reader, while others may be new. The selection was made with two foci: first, to put new commentary into a subject that has been well covered, albeit by different literary vehicles; second, for the sake of space. The roughly fifty prosecution witnesses in this book issue tens of thousands of words, which are regretably old wine in *old* bottles, while the defense calls over 125 witnesses, many of whom add to our knowledge of events. This material in itself is unusual: dozens, perhaps hundreds, of people have come forward with new data since 1965; virtually 100 percent of them exonerate the defendant. In terms of volume of witnesses, it is clearly a diminishing returns proposition for an attorney, and more so for an author, to have fifty people testify to grassy knoll shots when the point can be made with ten.

In a good mystery, the reader becomes the detective. In this work, you have the right to become juror, irate prosecutor, judge, or, if the evidence so convinces you, executioner.

Ultimately, what this book is trying to say is that, for the record, Lee Oswald's side of the events was never heard, and the "official" version was never cross-examined. That will change in the pages to follow. And while what you read may not sound like a good Hollywood movie or your favorite legal TV show, that is because trials don't always work like Hollywood events. At the same time, the narrative as presented was designed to keep readers' interest and not bog them down with Latin legalese that can make trial transcripts positively soporific. The prosecution's case is the rock-solid mass of evidence collected by the Warren Commission. The defense will attempt to demonstrate the circumstantial nature of that evidence, and the nonchalant way the evidence was dealt with by both local and federal officials. In so doing, it raises the question, "What were federal officials doing with that evidence in the first place?"

The murder of John Kennedy was a crime committed in Texas and was punishable only under Texas law. Technically, when Secret Service agents, allegedly acting to spare the President's family further anguish, removed Mr. Kennedy's body from Parkland Hospital to *Air Force One*, there could never have been a murder trial, because in Texas there must be an autopsy performed within the stated jurisdiction. So although we may disagree philosophically with Dr. Earl Rose, coroner of Dallas County, who claimed he had to perform the autopsy to maintain the chain of evidence in what amounted to him as an officer of the court as "just another murder," he was legally correct, although his plea fell on deaf ears. Fortunately, the murder of Oswald prevented the legal technicality of no Texas autopsy from becoming a matter of great public concern.

On the other hand, a peculiarity of Texas law in 1963 made this "trial" vehicle possible. At that time, if part of a conversation was admitted into evidence, the entire conversation could then be included. Without that, much of this narrative would be one lengthy, "Objection. Hearsay."

John Kennedy was President of the United States, not just President of a liberal elite or of the downtrodden southern black. As such, he was a federal official, but his murder occurred in Texas and was a Texas legal concern. As you read, notice the nature of the federal interference, and how it affected the immediate perception of events, and how it has affected our perception of those events since. When Lee Oswald was arrested, he was carrying multiple identifications, so the Dallas police, not to be confused with Scotland Yard or Interpol, did not know who he really was for part of that Friday afternoon. But Dallas confusion did not prevent FBI Director J. Edgar Hoover from telling insiders that the killer of the President was a Communist named Lee Oswald. No wonder the Dallas police did not seal airports, bus stations, or train depots! No wonder the new FBI headquarters was named for the prescient Hoover!

The only fictional events in this narrative are the survival of Oswald past November 24, 1963, and the fact that he would have had a murder trial without a Texas autopsy of the President's remains. No witnesses are invented; alas, about two hundred with interesting stories to tell were subpoenaed but had to be sent home.

If you disagree or agree with the findings herein, please feel free to write to the author in care of the publisher. Before you become too vocal, however, buy the twenty-six volumes of the Warren Commission *Hearings and Exhibits* and read all 17,740 pages. Be warned: about 95 percent of it is droll and has nothing to do with the case at hand; the seven Warren Commissioners should have read the remaining 5 percent before they affixed their names to the *Report.* The nonessential 95 percent will be the centerpiece to a companion volume to this work, which will ask one central question: did the Warren Commission cover up what they found, or did they simply fail, intentionally or through ignorance, to uncover the truth? America may get a partial answer to that question when (and if) existing sealed files are released in the months or years to come. If they are anything like the evidentiary claptrap already published, save your eyes and peruse the enclosed bibliography for some outstanding scholarship that has been published. Some may give you a sleepless night or two, and some may point you towards a solution to the crime of the century that you are satisfied with. But remember, you are seeking truth in a forest of obfuscation.

Two further comments need to be made. In the face of public doubt greatly aided by Oliver Stone's *JFK*, apologists for the official version seem to parrot two parallel ideas. The first is that if the Kennedy assassination were either a conspiracy or a cover-up, it must have been of incredible magnitude to succeed. Who said it succeeded? If you are reading this book, or have read others like it, the cover-up has *expired*. Secondly, allow yourself the momentary hypothesis that two young, eager reporters named Woodward and Bernstein, in haste to make a Watergate deadline, had been killed in a traffic accident. If that had happened, would the world have learned much of the truth of Watergate? No. The conspiracy/cover-up would have succeeded until scholars went back, scrutinized events, and published the truth.

Secondly, on a related plane, apologists will vehemently deny that the many curious deaths which followed the Kennedy assassination are anything but coincidence. Yet within a few years of the event, many—too many—key witnesses were dead, and from odd causes. Relate that to Watergate, now twenty years past. The Mitchells and Mrs. Hunt are dead. Everyone else in that caper is still pulling down six or seven figures a year, except the security guard who found the taped door in the Watergate complex. Compare that thought to the JFK obit file.

And what, finally, of Oswald? Is this book an attempt to make him the injured party, or to give his widow reason to sue the government for the kind of huge money earned by a mediocre major league shortstop?

No. Definitely not. The author has neither love nor sympathy for one of the title characters in this work. However, the other title character, "The People," is of great concern, as they are the essence of justice, and in a crime of the magnitude of the one committed on November 22, 1963, "The People" received either justice or a very miserable, three-decade judicial hangover. From Oswald's behavior on that morning, when he left behind his wedding ring and $180 at the Paine residence, coupled with his somewhat hasty departure from the Texas School Book Depository, it can be inferred that, if nothing else, he was, as he admitted in captivity, "a patsy." If that's true, it means he allowed himself to be the patsy for those who pulled the triggers that were pulled that day, and for that alone, no day in court will ever wash the remaining blood off his hands. For if he had not been the patsy, the history of this nation might be very different.

# One

Tuesday, January 5, 1965. An inch and a half of snow had fallen during the night on Lubbock, Texas, but had drawn far less attention than the trial that was about to begin at the County Seat of Lubbock County, 320 miles from Dallas, Texas, where the crime had happened.

The sidewalks and driveways in and around the courthouse square were equally devoid of lingering snow and civilians: state troopers from Oregon, Wisconsin, and Vermont had swept them of both. Only a handful of individuals, clearly identified to those officers, would be using those sidewalks and driveways in the weeks to come. Future snow would have to take its own chances.

A few minutes before ten o'clock, prosecuting attorney Raymond Matthews, a heavy-set, thinly-haired man in his mid-fifties, sat at the prosecution table conferring with his two assistants, men in their thirties who could have passed for brothers, which they were not.

Across the way, at the defense table stood four chairs. On the left a strikingly attractive reddish-blond young lady sat conferring with an older, graying man who was impeccably dressed. At the far right, in silent contemplation, sat the attorney of record for the defense, Edward Barnes, a youthful-looking thirty-eight year old with chestnut brown hair, brown, penetrating eyes, and Hollywood good looks and appeal. The empty chair awaited the defendant, Lee Harvey Oswald.

The remainder of the large, high-ceilinged courtroom contained three individuals: the bailiff, the court stenographer, and a uniformed Vermont state policeman seated at a tape-recording apparatus. The jury box and the visitors' gallery were empty.

At precisely ten o'clock, Bailiff Carl Carson gave a light rap on the door to the judge's chambers and then announced to the relatively empty chamber in a softer voice than usual, "Attention, all who have business in the courtroom of the Honorable Franklin W. Davis. All rise." Judge Davis, a mid-sized yet fragile-looking man in his early sixties, entered, took his time to mount the few steps to the bench, shuffled papers in a large folder, occupied himself for a moment, then said in a friendly manner almost as an afterthought, "Please be seated."

Having scanned the nearly empty chamber, Judge Davis nodded to Carson to have the prisoner brought in. Carson crossed in front of the bench, passed between the stenographer and the tape-recording apparatus, and knocked on a reinforced security door. A moment later, the door was opened, and the defendant entered the room with his arms cuffed behind him. In a dialect that somehow mixed both Texas and Louisiana, the judge told the Vermont officer that the cuffs should henceforth be removed as soon as the defendant cleared the security door. Lee Oswald was then freed of his steel restraints and led to the defense table.

Judge Davis then read from a thick, multi-page stack of eight-by-fourteen foolscap. "For the record, we are here today to begin the proceedings in Docket number F-154. I see here the arraignment for this case took place shortly after one A.M. on November twenty-three, 1963, and,"—drawing out the word "and" as pages were turned—"the grand jury returned a true bill of indictment on September twenty-four of 1964. Mr. Matthews, is the Prosecution ready to proceed?"

"The Prosecution is ready, Your Honor."

"Mr. Barnes, how say you?"

"The Defense is prepared to begin, Your Honor."

"For the record, Mr. Barnes, the defendant entered a plea of not guilty at the time of his arraignment. Since we are in a different jurisdiction, perhaps we should have a plea entered once again. Please explain what this means to your client."

Barnes briefly conferred with Oswald, and then all four individuals at the defense table rose, more or less in unison. "Mr. Oswald would like to plead not guilty, Your Honor." The attorneys were again seated.

The judge then lifted his gavel and rapped it lightly, more from habit than to get anyone's attention. "We are then ready to begin case F-154, *The People of Texas* v. *Lee Harvey Oswald* in which it has been charged that the defendant did, with malice aforethought, kill John Fitzgerald Kennedy by shooting him with a gun." There was a lengthy pause in which the judge seemed lost for words, but he nevertheless returned to his task with clarity. "The charge in this case is an enormous one, so let us have no doubt on that score. Although all of us except Miss Jeffries were here for the jury selection phase of the trial, I will repeat the introductions for her sake." The judge then removed his reading glasses and pinched the bridge of his nose almost reflexively.

"The bailiff is Mr. Carl Carson," indicating a Texas uniformed officer whose girth extended over his belt, but who moved well. "He has worked in my courtroom now for fifteen years, and when I say 'Carson,' he's there to do what has to be done. He knows my idiosyncrasies and prevents them, in his way, from becoming courtroom ritual. To my left over here," gesturing with a wave to the woman at the stenography machine, "is Mrs. Anita Martinez, who has been with me almost as long as Carson, and believe me when I tell you, even if several of us are speaking at the same time," and with that thought the judge swept both legal tables with a questioning eyebrow, "and of course I hope that doesn't happen, but if it does, you can all relax in the knowledge that Mrs. Martinez will record—accurately record—every syllable.

Now," the judge's voice rising slightly, "to my far left we have something new to my court and my courtroom experience, and that is a collection of recording devices—fancy tape recorders that will make a permanent record of our voices as we speak. Currently at the controls over there, according to my records," followed by a pause as the judge's glasses quickly went on and off, "is an officer from Vermont named Marvin Bryant."

"Martin Bryant, Your Honor."

"Forgive me, Officer. For the record, Martin Bryant. Over here," gesturing to the prosecution table, "the prosecutor of record is Raymond Matthews, who has served in that capacity in my court before. His assistants are Eaton Graves, to his right, and Earl Vincent, who have assisted him in legal matters in this court. Neither has ever been the attorney of record in a proceeding over which I presided. At the defense table, the attorney of record is Edward Barnes, the public defender in the state court in Minneapolis/St. Paul in Minnesota. He is here because the defendant indicated he would prefer a public defender and several were proposed to Mr. Oswald before he chose Mr. Barnes. Mr. Barnes was then extended 'temporary' reciprocal privileges, making him a member of the Texas Bar Association for the duration of this proceeding. At the far end of the table is Miss Carolyn Jeffries of Mr. Barnes's staff in Minnesota, and similar reciprocity was extended to her. Miss Jeffries, I welcome you on behalf of the state of Texas at this time, inasmuch as you were not here when Mr. Barnes and Mr. Matthews selected the jury from December twenty-six to December thirty-one."

"Thank you, Your Honor, and please extend my sincere thanks to the Texas Bar Association for the help they have provided me since Mr. Barnes and I were requested to serve on this case."

"I shall do that, Miss Jeffries. The final attorney of record is a man who has been in this courtroom on many occasions, and his courtroom dignity has always equalled his legal scholarship. To Mr. Robert Bennett Dean III it was not necessary to extend reciprocal Bar Association membership, as I believe he's been in this courthouse about as long as I have." The last statement was made almost as a question.

"Finally," the judge said slowly and with a sense of gravity, "we come to the defendant, Lee Harvey Oswald. Mr. Oswald, it insults my sense of pride in the state of Texas that you were nearly murdered while in the custody of officers of the court in this state, but you may rest assured that every—and I mean every, security measure has been taken to guarantee your safety, and secondly, your right to a fair trial. I must now ask you, Mr. Oswald, is it your desire to be represented by Mr. Barnes and his assistants, and before you answer, understand that if the answer is 'Yes,' we're not going to change our minds about that down the road. Are your attorneys acceptable to you?"

Oswald rose and looked squarely at Judge Davis. "Mr. Barnes and his assistants are acceptable to me, sir."

"Thank you, Mr. Oswald. You may be seated. Lastly, and I say this as a caution as I would to any defendant in this courtroom, Mr. Oswald, if a witness makes a statement which you believe to be untrue or which does discredit to you as a person, oral utterances by you are *not* the way to arrive at the truth. You need only lean over and whisper to counsel and leave the matter in their hands. Is it understood then, that there will be no outbursts of any kind during these proceedings?"

Oswald did not rise, but rather pursed his lips and nodded to the judge, a tacit indication that silence would be forthcoming.

"Lastly, I want two more matters on the record before we bring in the jury. First, due to those regrettable breakdowns of security in Dallas, first on November twenty-two and then on November twenty-four, it has become necessary, and again, this wounds my pride in the state of Texas, but it has become necessary to have security provided by state officers from Oregon, Wisconsin, and Vermont. This came about through briefs submitted originally by Mr. Barnes and agreed to by Mr. Matthews apparently after he got a couple of phone calls which he did not care for. I, too, have received such calls and they also wound my sense of pride in the state of Texas, assuming that is where they came from. Either way, the officers from Wisconsin will provide security between midnight and eight A.M., followed by officers from Vermont, such as Mr. Bryant at the taping machines, from eight A.M. until four P.M., and then the Oregon officers will take over from four P.M. to midnight. That means that if we go beyond four o'clock in the afternoon, and we may have to do this to prevent this proceeding from becoming endless, a Vermont officer will deliver Mr. Oswald to us, and an Oregon officer will escort him from the courtroom.

"These officers have security—security of this building, and of all its occupants, which, I assume you know, is only us until this trial is over. This building will be used by nobody else and will be accessible to nobody until the jury has delivered its verdict. Also for reasons of security, and so that news of the trial is not leaked to witnesses who have not yet testified, there will be no spectators, no press, and no photographers at this trial. Just as I will instruct the jury not to discuss the case amongst themselves, I will say this just once to each of you: what is said here, what we see here, and what is done here, *must stay here.* Naturally, as legal counsel, you will need to confer amongst yourselves or rehear testimony from witnesses. However, if I read any items in the newspaper that I deem to be beyond the scope of editorial guesswork, believe me, I'm going to find out the source of that information and hand down a contempt of court sentence that will make page-one reading in bar association journals." The judge swept his gaze from the prosecution to the defense table and allowed himself the suspicion that his message had been received.

"All right, Carson," Davis continued in much more upbeat tones, "bring the jury in."

Bailiff Carson then walked to the rear of the courtroom, exactly in the opposite corner from where the defendant had been brought in, opened a door, and briefly disappeared. Before he was seen again, fourteen men, whose approximate ages were between twenty-eight and fifty-five and who generally were dressed casually (although there was an occasional tie), took the seats they had been assigned during jury selection.

Judge Davis let them settle in and get another look at the defendant before he addressed them. "Members of the jury, I hope you had a comfortable weekend, and I sincerely hope, since you are now sitting on a jury, that there was no heavy wagering on the football games." The judge waited for a chuckle at his joke, which never came. "More seriously, Mr. Foreman, can you report to the bench that this case, to your knowledge, was not discussed by jury members over the weekend?"

The juror in the front row closest to the witness stand, a tallish, rugged man in his early forties—a livestock worker as Barnes recalled—rose and answered, "To the best of my knowledge, Your Honor, there was no talk like that." He then took his seat again.

Judge Davis swiveled slightly to his right so he could face the jurors directly. His tone was straightforward, candid, and certainly carried a sincerity that kept his listeners' attention. "Members of the jury: you are here in Lubbock County, in the Courthouse in and for the County of Lubbock, to hear evidence in case F-154, *The People of Texas* v. *Lee Harvey Oswald,* a charge which specifies that on November twenty-second, 1963, Mr. Oswald did, with malice aforethought, kill John Fitzgerald Kennedy with a gun. This charge carries with it the death penalty if you find the defendant guilty." The judge then paused to let his words sink in. "Having provided you the trial citation, there is very little more I can say to encourage you to take seriously every word spoken by the attorneys and the witnesses, and take seriously every exhibit and document brought before this court—even," he hesitated, "even if it means taking the court's time to view the document or the exhibit yourself. That is the reason these items are introduced by the attorneys—for me to rule on their legality, but ultimately, for you, the jury, to be assisted by these documents and exhibits in fairly rendering a verdict.

"We have, in addition, a unique distinction with respect to documents and exhibits, as you may be aware, for while Mr. Oswald was comatose following the attempt on his life, a blue-ribbon presidential commission, headed by the chief justice of the United States, gathered together a great deal of evidence with respect to this case. Now, while it is still your job and will always be your job to assess the validity of that evidence, you must realize that there is a great volume of it

. . . twenty-six volumes, in fact, which provided for the grand jury's returning of a true bill against Mr. Oswald when he began to recover his health. In any other case in the land, grand jury proceedings would not be admissible in this court. But these proceedings undertaken by the chief justice and his staff, while not drawing any specific conclusions, are here, they were made public, and I'm sure much of the material is going to be introduced into our record by either the prosecution or the defense.

"Now, why are we discussing all of this in Lubbock, Texas, three hundred twenty miles from Dallas? We are involved because of a process called a 'change of venue,' and it is done to guarantee further that the defendant receives the fairest possible hearing of the charges against him. Had this trial been held at the scene of the crime, perhaps inflamed passions would have operated against Mr. Oswald in securing a fair trial, or perhaps a bit of sympathy would have been extended to him for his near brush with death, also preventing what is most needed: a fair trial to determine if he is innocent or guilty. Now, as you can probably count, there are fourteen of you. This is so that if one or two of you, and God knows I hope it's not more than that, but if one or two of you become ill or face a family crisis during this trial, we will still have twelve people, as the law demands, to deliberate the verdict. If all fourteen of you are present for the entire trial, twelve of you will be chosen at the end of the proceedings to deliberate, and it will be my duty to thank the other two jurors for being literally confined for a lengthy trial for what may seem to them to have been for no purpose. I assure you that when that day comes, nothing I say will make up for the time away from your families, your jobs, your friends, and the lives you had before you were chosen to sit in that jury box. But your participation in this trial is essential, and you must all understand that, understand the sacrifice involved, and understand what is expected of you.

"The process begins today. The prosecutor and the defense attorneys will make opening statements to you, possibly lengthy ones. In these statements, they will tell you, in a general way, the nature of the evidence they are going to present, and they will tell you why they believe you should accept their evidence and not their adversary's evidence. These opening statements will prepare you for what is to come. Then the prosecutor, Mr. Matthews, will bring before you his witnesses—people who will support the state's contention that Mr. Oswald committed the crime he is charged with. In the case of each witness, Mr. Matthews will elicit direct testimony, Mr. Barnes will cross-examine the witness to see if any inconsistencies exist in the narrative, and then the witness will be subject to redirect by the prosecutor and recross by the defense, if necessary.

"It will also be at this time that the prosecution will enter into evidence its documents and exhibits, which, as I suggested a few minutes ago, you should familiarize yourselves with. Now, a caution. Many times in this courtroom, I've seen the prosecution finish their half of the case—and that's just what it is—half the case, and the jury is sitting in your chairs there with what I call their 'guilty face.' That's not your job. Your job is then to hear Mr. Barnes's witnesses, peruse his documents and exhibits, and only then, when twelve of you are selected, then you deliberate the case. Before that happens, there will be closing arguments by both counsel, restating ideas, reminding you of witnesses whose testimony may be getting stale in your minds—essentially, rearguing their cases one more time.

"Then it is the job of the judge to 'charge' the jury. At that time, I will give instructions to the chosen twelve, based on what I have seen and heard, giving you the benefit of my legal training and bench experience. *But you—the jurors*—must then make the ultimate decision: is the defendant *guilty* beyond a reasonable doubt? and if so, you must find him guilty. *If*, however, reasonable doubt exists, you must find him *not guilty.* I must also remind you at this point that, as you no doubt know, the defendant was charged with two crimes on November 22. It must be fully understood by you the jurors, as it has come to be understood by the attorneys and the court, that we are here to pass judgment only on the death of Mr. Kennedy, and that any considerations of the other alleged action are totally irrelevant to this proceeding and have *no place whatsoever* here.

"This task, with this man's life riding on your decision,

cannot be an easy one. The court has tried to make your task easier in several ways. First, we have tried to keep you away from security breaches which could create a miscarriage in the judicial process. Toward that end, if anyone—and I mean anyone—if anyone somehow manages to get a message—or threat—to you, beyond the occasional phone calls you will be allowed to your families it must be reported *immediately* to this court. Your identities have been withheld, but your neighbors will miss you eventually, or your poker buddies, and your employers, who have been notified, can only be counted on to remain silent for just so long.

"In the event you need to rehear evidence, that can be done through your foreman, and you can hear the evidence read back by Mrs. Martinez, our court reporter, or you can read her prepared transcripts, or you can hear the actual words after they have been tape recorded by the officer at that console to my left. In addition, you may have noticed several television sets in the courtroom. These have been 'networked' I believe the word is, so that a document or exhibit can be called up and will be displayed on all of the televisions at the same time, so that both sets of attorneys, the witness, the bench, and you, the jury, can see the evidence at the same time. Remember, then, your instructions: listen to everything that is said, and weigh each new idea and believe what you choose to believe as the truth; keep your own counsel on these matters; and if you are chosen to deliberate the verdict, deliver unto this court an honest and true verdict that all twelve of you can agree upon. No judge, attorney, or defendant—or nation, for that matter, can ask more of you. This is a murder case, and one which involves the death penalty. I cannot ask you to overlook the identity of the victim, but that does not, in and of itself, condemn the defendant. Only the evidence can do that.

"Turning to less weighty matters, it is incumbent on me to introduce the personnel in this proceeding," the judge continued, although probably only the jury and the minor players, for whom it was a major event, were paying attention.

At the prosecution table, Ray Matthews tuned out the judge's words, as he knew the players. He had been here before, and although he had a distinguished record as a

prosecutor, he was painfully aware that many of his colleagues earned far greater money and recognition than he
did, and he was equally aware that this trial would forever
define his legal reputation. Despite about a 90 percent conviction rate in his thirty-plus years in the prosecutor's office,
this was the case every lawyer in America would have
sought, and rightly so, as no less than seven very distinguished Americans, sitting on the President's Commission,
had literally handed him a conviction with a bow on it. That
conviction, with the attendant publicity—and no doubt the
execution of the defendant, would somehow offset successes
Matthews felt life had cheated him out of: his two sons were
both corporate attorneys, which in Texas meant oil and
monthly salaries greater than a public prosecutor's yearly
salary. The oldest son, Ray Jr., could still boast that he went
to school with one of Lubbock's more famous—if only fleet-
ingly—citizens, Charles Hardin "Buddy" Holly. Ray Sr., only
met famous people when he prosecuted them. But all of that
would change when he marshaled his forces, bored in on the
jury with the facts provided by countless investigative agencies, and won the conviction.

It would also no doubt increase his standing in the eyes of
his wife, who was third generation Texas money, which
meant pure-bred conservative, politically connected, and
anti-Red, a political philosophy posture Matthews planned to
make a great deal out of in this trial, both at home and in the
afterglow of the conviction, which could lead to . . . who
knew? But Matthews knew in his heart that the "defector"
about fifteen feet from him was his ticket to fame.

Across the aisle sat Eddie Barnes, the antithesis of Ray
Matthews: youthful enough in appearance to be Matthews's
oldest son, athletic to Matthews's paunch, and with a full
head of hair compared to Matthews's thinning hair. Barnes
had breezed through a local law school in the north woods of
Minnesota, and after three largely unproductive and frus-
trating years in the Federal Bureau of Investigation, where
he had learned to follow orders and never, but never, embar-
rass the bureau, had been wined and dined by the corporate
world, and had equally quickly come to hate that existence.
Where he had been the corporate libertarian always willing to

do *pro bono* work, corporate elders were far more eager for billing hours, and only a modest inheritance parlayed into a stock bonanza had allowed Barnes the option to leave the world of power lunches and high-priced torts to defend the less fortunate.

Even then, it hadn't been easy. With a wife and a young son and daughter, mortgage payments and a new car, the stock dividends only cushioned the economic fall from the corporate tower to the public defender's office. And then this opportunity, if Barnes wanted to call it that, knocked. The recovered accused presidential assassin had wanted legal counsel from a public defender, not a "hired gun," and Barnes had been one of ten selected for a screening process by the defendant. He was chosen precisely because he was *not* overly knowledgeable of the events of the weekend of November 22 through 24, 1963, as he had spent those days buried in law books preparing an appeal for an indigent, and, to Barnes, innocent client.

He had never been to Texas before, and although from a large, underpopulated wilderness state, he was still struck by the enormity of Texas. By contrast, when he walked over Dealey Plaza to try to obtain a sense of the crime that had occurred there, he was equally struck by how *small* it was. That had stood out: in all his phone calls to family back home, to reporters with angles on the case, or just to friends, everything that he had acquainted himself with about November 22 did not prepare him for the relatively small triangle that had been the killing zone.

This case, he thought, as the judge droned on, could be his killing zone, for in sheer volume of evidence, it was weighted against him. And he knew Ray Matthews was no slouch. He might not exude charisma, but he'd won his share, as Barnes had read a few of his cases when not poring through thousands of pages of FBI reports, local Dallas police or sheriff's department paperwork, and media accounts. It seemed to Barnes that six seconds of sudden tragedy had generated a lot of words—perhaps too many, and that might be to his advantage if the sheer preponderance of the evidence against his client could be used to generate some confusion.

In the meantime, he planned to give his esteemed adversary a good fight, his client a good defense, and then get back home to the people who meant so much to him.

"Having impressed upon all of you the extreme urgency of the task before us, I thank you for your attention," Judge Davis concluded. "Court will recess for ten minutes."

# Two

During the recess, there was quiet but animated debate at the prosecution table, as Eaton Graves, in strident whispers and with accompanying body language, was clearly trying to convince Matthews either to make his opening statement stronger or drop something from it. Earl Vincent occasionally stuck his nose into the fray, more as a referee than as a contributor.

At the defense table, Carolyn Jeffries and Robert Dean tried to make light banter with Oswald, hoping to keep his mind off the anticipated verbal onslaught from Matthews. Barnes went to the bathroom, and after washing his hands, splashed water on his face, catching a glimpse of himself in the mirror and reminding himself of the phrase "It wounds my pride in the great state of Texas," as it might come in handy later. Upon returning to the courtroom, he found the judge and Carson engaged in some topic that both apparently found humorous, so he rehearsed the strategy he had been through at least twice before with the defendant.

"Hear this and hear this good, Lee," he said in low but firm tones, "the next few minutes will be as bad as it gets. This is the firestorm. Matthews can say anything he wants about you, especially your, shall we say, changing political values, and you have to know that the jury is going to be hearing him, but looking at you to get a reaction. That means you can't sit here and wring your hands and have 'guilt' written all over you, nor can you pretend that you're listening to the weather report. Be yourself—a human being who is accused of a crime done by somebody else. And no outbursts whatsoever, or you're going to put yourself in a hole that nobody will get you out of.

"Remember, we went through this a week ago. I walked back and forth in front of you and accused you of everything up to and including carrying Black Plague. And what I didn't say, Bob Dean drilled you with. So what? The bottom line, or the good news, if you want it that way, is that I really hope he goes out there and shoots his mouth off and tells the jury all kinds of things about you. The more he says, the better—'cause everything he says, he has to prove. And there's nothing he can say—he's got no surprises—that I can't deal with. So you just bide your time and ride this one out—looks like the judge is about ready. Have some faith in the people at this table, Lee. When Matthews is done, I'll tell you honestly how much damage if any, he did. Meantime, hang in there, shut up, and be a stoic. Here we go."

Judge Davis gaveled the court back into session just as Officer Bryant was reseating himself at the tape recording console. "Mr. Matthews . . ."

Matthews rose, buttoning his suit coat as he did so. It struck Barnes that Matthews wore clothes very poorly, and it was off-the-rack stuff anyhow, Barnes concluded, musing that Matthews, if not a prosecutor, would be the kind of lawyer that gave out business cards at social gatherings.

Concluding what must have been the longest thirty-five-foot walk in his life, Matthews leaned on the witness stand as he began to speak: "Gentlemen of the jury; Judge Davis has spoken to you of the need to listen to the words, and see the documents and exhibits; that is his job. My job is to put before you the evidence gathered by many investigative agencies: the Dallas Police Department, the Dallas County Sheriff's Office, the Texas State Police, the Texas Rangers, the

United States Secret Service, and the Federal Bureau of Investigation. Those people just mentioned put in hundreds of thousands of hours to accumulate the evidence that you will be presented with. My job in one sense is made more difficult by the incredible weight—the sheer mass of material—that points to the defendant's guilt, but, on the other hand, that same sheer mass of incriminating evidence will guarantee that you will return the only possible verdict . . . guilty."

Oswald squeezed Barnes's left arm, causing Barnes to lean over and whisper, "Relax, kid, he hasn't fired a shot yet. He's still peeing into the wind and hoping he hits something. Wait until he drags out the heavy guns."

Matthews had let his last word, "guilty," sink in with the jury, and then he continued.

"So, members of the jury, if it is evidence and documents you are to see, so shall you see them. The prosecution will show you *the rifle,* which fired the fatal bullets, to the exclusion of *all other rifles.* One gun, all the bullets—no more, no less. You will handle, and see for yourself, the cartridges that fell from the rifle to the floor of the Texas School Book Depository as the assassin, Lee Harvey Oswald, performed his deadly work. You will see and handle, if you dare, the whole bullet and the fragments recovered from the bodies of the late President and the governor of Texas. And it may, I regret, be necessary for you to view the horrible pictures of the President, showing the wounds he received—from behind him and above him."

Matthews interrupted his narrative to walk to the jury box, place his hand on the rail and walk along the length of it, eyeing each juror to make sure he still had their complete attention. All three attorneys at the defense table were making notes, and Eaton Graves at the prosecution table was wearing a mask that indicated he had lost the debate with Matthews.

Matthews completed his walk and did an about-face, coming at the jury from a new angle, physically as well as literally. "You will also see and handle the order forms, as well as the money orders, used by the defendant, to the exclusion of every other human being on this planet, to purchase and pay for the assassination weapon and the gun taken from his person at the time of his arrest. You will see the simple, plain brown paper bag found in the sniper's nest—a square yard of paper so fashioned that it would conceal the gun the assassin carried into the Texas School Book Depository at eight A.M. after having been driven there by Buell Wesley Frazier, a coworker. You will further see and handle palm prints, taken from the boxes in the sniper's nest. You will hear, or better still, *read* a letter, mailed in January of 1961 from ten thousand miles away in Minsk, in the Soviet Union, where the future assassin sought, but ultimately was denied refuge, as the Bolshevik Communists did not even want this vermin in their midst—you will see or read this letter threatening John Connally, then secretary of the navy, now governor of Texas and almost fully recovered from the wounds inflicted by the man who killed the President of the United States."

Matthews turned his back on the jury briefly and walked to the railing at the far end of the defense table to continue. "And, lastly, you will see photographs—clear black and white exposures—showing the assassin with both guns used on November twenty-second, and in his other hand, you will see two grossly anti-American Communist publications . . . These things you will see with your own eyes, and, in such cases as you desire to do so, handle and pass them amongst yourselves as you intensely scrutinize the deadly capabilities of one man in a few seconds of Communist inspired hate-filled rage."

While Dean wrote "Know your audience" on his legal pad, Matthews walked towards the jurors, concluding, "These things you will see . . .

"And what will you hear? Oh, Lord, if there was only an easy answer to that question," and as Matthews let it sink in, Barnes whispered to Oswald that they couldn't put God on the witness stand. Much of the strain seemed to go out of the defendant.

After a pause Matthews resumed his narrative. "The best answer I can give you, as an attorney *not* qualified in psychiatry, is that you will hear the story of a pathetic life, a soul who never had anything and one which hated those who did. An orphanage awaited the defendant at age three, and by his teens, he was facing psychiatric counseling and the recommendation of institutionalization. If only that recommendation had been carried through!" Matthews attempted a dramatic gesture of raising his hands in the style of an evangelical preacher and came off looking like he was signaling a touchdown. "*If* only that recommendation had been carried through," he repeated for dramatic effect, "we would not be here now, and two young children in Hyannis Port, Massachusetts, would still have their father.

"The defendant then dropped out of school, joined the U.S. Marine Corps, achieved the rating of sharpshooter, and gorged himself nightly reading the likes of Karl Marx and teaching himself Russian, looking ahead to the day when he would betray his country.

"Through lies and deceit, he received a hardship discharge from the Marines—a hardship discharge because his mother needed him. So what did he do? Let me tell you. He visited his poor, sick mother for a couple of days, and then, on the pretext of going to Switzerland to attend Albert Schweitzer College—an interesting thought for a high school dropout— he sailed to Europe, flew to Finland and crossed the Russian frontier to begin a career whose goal was the destruction of democracy.

"In pursuit of that goal, he rudely told American consular officers in Moscow that he desired to renounce his American citizenship, a necessary duty inasmuch as his Russian citizenship was pending before the Supreme Soviet, and he told those same American officials that he would give the Soviets everything he knew about the United States military—literally the security of this nation, including his radar expertise acquired at Atsugi, Japan, where it was his radarscope that plotted the courses of the then-secret U-2 aircraft."

Prosecutor Matthews was clearly warming to his task. He was more animated, and certainly less wooden than he had been at the outset, and as Barnes read jurors' reactions, especially one middle-aged man in the back row, Matthews was scoring some points. Now he was moving, speaking individual thoughts to individual jurors: "And what were the results? He was given a common factory job in Minsk, where his salary was higher than that of the plant manager. American top-secret codes, from the defendant's days at El Toro

Marine Headquarters in California, had to be changed for security reasons, and, of course, on May first, 1960, a few short months after Mr. Oswald's arrival in Russia, the Russians shot down our U-2 reconnaissance aircraft."

As Matthews indulged in yet another orchestrated pause, Oswald told Barnes that he flat-out had nothing to do with the U-2. Barnes, already a skeptic about his client's pronouncements, brushed it off in a whisper: "Forget it; you're not on trial for that." Barnes wanted Oswald to know that he was not 100 percent sure just exactly who or what his client was.

Matthews, now back at his comfortable perch astride the witness stand, pressed on: "He had done his work well in the Soviet Union—but there was so much more to do. So home he came, married to the niece of an intelligence colonel— someone who is not going to be allowed to leave Russia easily. Yet she was. Was she vital to his mission? Was she the 'domestic cover' he needed? We'll never know, and it's not urgent, but what *he* came back to do *was*. He became a fanatic for Castro's Cuba, passing out leaflets and making radio appearances, and all at the cost of neglecting his Russian family.

"Then, after John Kennedy had humiliated Nikita Sergeyevich Khrushchev, Mr. Oswald's lord, patron, and master, in the fall of 1962, we find him purchasing guns a few short months later, in March of 1963 to be exact—and then he waited—waited to use his marksmanship skills on the person who had humiliated Khrushchev and the Russian power elite—the elite that had given him a life of luxury in Minsk.

"And what will we hear of 1963? We will hear that he became fascinated by weapons, and we will hear expert testimony as to his ability with weapons. We will hear of his hostility toward the FBI, who were merely doing their job to keep an eye or two on this 'former defector,' and keep America safe from the likes of his kind.

"We will hear of a series of meaningless jobs, and of a life that possessed no material belongings and no emotional sustenance. And on that day, that fateful tragic Friday in Dallas, we will learn that he carried a long paper bag into the Texas

School Book Depository with him; that he was not regularly seen that day; that several people saw a rifle extruding from the sixth floor window, southeast corner, of the Texas School Book Depository, at a time when the defendant had no alibi; we will learn that he—and he alone—was discovered missing from the Book Depository and his description was broadcast, although he had already escaped by bus and taxi, both of whose drivers will positively identify him."

Matthews came forward to the jury box to conclude with a glare he equated to the severity of the crime: "Then, in a continuation of his deadly rampage, he lingered briefly in his seedy rooming house, just long enough perhaps to change clothes and provide himself a new look—as well as a pistol, and within forty-five minutes was in police custody, where paraffin tests were taken which proved he had fired a weapon that day; where fibers from his shirt matched fibers found on the rifle; where his palm prints were taken and shown to be a match to prints found on the boxes and the rifle, and where, finally, he sat, told a host of lies to the authorities while a ballistics examination of the rifle and the bullets proved—demonstrated overwhelmingly—that the weapon that belonged to that man, *Lee Harvey Oswald,* had fired the bullets on November twenty-second, 1963, to the exclusion of all other weapons.

"That evening, an autopsy confirmed that the President had been killed from above and behind, and as the doctors in Bethesda Medical Center were concluding their work, that man, *Lee Harvey Oswald,* was charged with the premeditated murder of John F. Kennedy. And only the intervention of a crazed citizen—well meaning in his own mind but clearly deluded, prevented this trial from being held six months ago or more"—Matthews's voice began to rise to a crescendo— "and if it had, that jury would have—just like this jury must —find the defendant, *Lee . . . Harvey . . . Oswald guilty as charged . . .* and will demand that the court hand down the only sentence it can: death."

More calmly, the laconic dirge ended: "You will see, and you will hear; and in the end, your choice will be obvious— guilty. I thank you for listening so patiently to me. Thank you, Your Honor."

On the way back to the prosecution table, Matthews couldn't resist the temptation to patronize Barnes. Leaning over so only Barnes and perhaps Oswald could hear, Matthews quietly boasted, "Well, I didn't fry him for killing the cop . . ."

Barnes couldn't resist the temptation either: "Ray, you haven't fried him for killing *anybody* yet."

Matthews returned to the defense table with clenched fists, while Dean assured Oswald that minimal, if any, damage had been done. Miss Jeffries also leaned over and told Oswald that "Eddie" would cut Matthews's opening argument to shreds. Barnes had the last word, however, telling Oswald that the prosecution was fishing and would sooner or later have to find some real, not circumstantial evidence, or cut bait. In the meantime, Oswald would have to continue to be on his best behavior. Privately, to Dean and Jeffries, Barnes would later say that Matthews's opening argument had great power, and would have swayed him if he'd been on the jury. "But that's why there are two tables in this room," he concluded, "and we've got about an hour to be prepared to rebut, line by line."

Judge Davis removed a watch fob from within the folds of his judicial robe and wondered aloud if it would be the better course of wisdom to postpone the defense's opening argument until after lunch. Barnes thanked the court for its courtesy, admitting he foresaw a lengthy rebuttal.

# Three

As soon as Carson had escorted the jury in for the afternoon session, Judge Davis made a few remarks to make them feel comfortable, the most noteworthy being that in addition to the lunch just completed, it would be a day in which they would probably have a great deal more to digest.

Barnes could find no fault with that assessment, as he knew he had a long afternoon ahead of him and that what he had to say would consume much more time than Matthews's opening statement. He was also rethinking the wisdom of his flippant remark at the end of Matthews's opening statement, as having measured his opponent, he had found him to be worthy of good combat.

Matthews, to his credit, at least had a pleasant "good afternoon" for Barnes when he returned from lunch, but inside, he was still smoldering from Barnes's morning remark. "Time will tell," he thought, as the judge's gavel brought him back to business.

"Mr. Barnes?"

"If it please the court, Your Honor," he began, as he strode toward the jury with rehearsed, fluid, economy of movement that he owed to one law professor who always reminded students that the jury could see as well as hear lawyers.

Standing ten feet back from the center of the jury rail, with his feet slightly apart and his left hand in the front trouser pocket, he allowed a moment of silence to create anticipation among the jurors. "Members of the jury . . . what you have heard this morning from the prosecutor is essentially the framework of a case, just as a novelist might create an outline before writing a murder mystery. But just as no one is going to purchase that outline at their local bookstore, no jury can convict a defendant on the kind of thin, circumstantial, 'use your imagination' scenario that you heard this morning, which was frankly more intriguing for what it didn't say than for what it did say."

Barnes now walked slowly to the jury rail, placed his elbows on it, and clasped his hands together, almost creating a posture that said, "Trust me, we're in this together." Having surveyed the faces with sincerity, he spoke calmly, "Before I discuss Mr. Matthews's allegations point by point, let me just make perhaps the most important observation: in all that he said to you this morning, and that includes the references to witnesses who saw a gun in the sixth floor window of the Book Depository, there was no mention—*none whatsoever*—repeat, no mention—of one witness who is going to sit right over there,"—pointing an accusatory finger at the witness box—"and tell us that yes, a gun was seen in the window, and it was the defendant and no one else firing it. There is no such witness, period. And, gentlemen, without that one witness, if I'm sitting on that side of this wooden railing,"—rubbing a hand on the wood finish—"I am unable to vote for conviction—because the absence of that one witness—out of hundreds we may hear from—the absence of a witness that will come forward and swear before God that he saw Lee Oswald pull the trigger on a rifle on November twenty-second guarantees that I will have much more doubt than just reasonable doubt. There were hundreds of witnesses to the event; several will tell you about that sixth floor window; none will point to Lee Oswald.

"I already have respect for this jury for the attention you

paid to Mr. Matthews this morning, because I will be discussing his remarks, as I said, in detail, but did you get the
feeling, as I did, that except for the Kennedy name, and some
Joe McCarthy-like rhetoric, it almost sounded to me like we
were just discussing another homicide, and here's the facts,
let's get it over and go home to the folks. Maybe you heard
that like I did, and I have to comment about that.

"When I was brought to Texas to handle Mr. Oswald's defense, it was understood that I would be paid my regular
salary, not a whole lot, from the state of Minnesota. It was
also explained to me that I could not sell the rights to a book
or a movie about this trial for a period of three years, and
when that was mentioned, I have to tell you, it was the farthest thing from my mind. But Mr. Matthews's remarks this
morning, which said a lot and proved nothing—his witnesses
will have to do that, and they can't—but those remarks, coupled with my initial thoughts about the case must serve to
remind us all that this is not just another homicide, docket
F-154. This is the single . . . most . . . important . . .
trial to be held in the state of Texas, and it may be years, or
decades before a jury just like you, decides another case with
the importance of this one. This was more than a crime committed against one person's body; it was a crime against the
body politic; it was not a man, or an elected man, or even a
President that died in Dallas; it was a little of each of us, and
a lot of what America meant." Barnes paused and softened
his tone as he moved slowly to the witness box. "In a sense, it
was more than a homicide; it was patricide."

Barnes quickly removed his wire-frame glasses and wiped
a lower corner of one lens on his breast-pocket handkerchief,
a subtle way to let the jury ponder his last statement without
his having to just stand there silently. His voice resumed its
normal tone as he spoke again: "And just for the record, before I get to my real agenda,"—he paused and turned to both
Judge Davis and the prosecutor so they would not miss his
next thought—"aside from the single most important fact of
no witness who can place the rifle in the defendant's hands
at 12:30 on November twenty-second, there is the matter of
an autopsy. Gentlemen, Texas law requires an autopsy, performed by the medical examiner in the jurisdiction where the

homicide occurred, in order to have a homicide complaint issued or subsequent indictment occur. So at approximately 1:45 P.M. on November twenty-second, when Secret Service agents knocked Dr. Earl Rose, coroner in and for the county of Dallas, to the floor of Parkland Hospital and literally stole the President's body, they might have been acting in what they thought were the best interests of the Kennedy family, but they were also obstructing justice.

"So if I turned around right now, on January five, 1965, in Lubbock, Texas, and made a motion to Judge Davis for a dismissal of these charges because there was no lawful autopsy performed in Texas, the Judge would be impaled on the horns of a dilemma. He could do as the law demands and dismiss this case, and we'd all go home; or, less likely, and I don't mean to presume on his decision-making authority in this building, but he could also rule that the trial would go on, at huge expense, only to have the whole thing thrown out somewhere down the road on appeal. I know that. Mr. Matthews has no doubt dreaded that. Judge Davis certainly knows the law. And now you, the jury, know it."

Barnes slowly walked to the defense table, opened a Texas law book to a page indicated by a bookmark, then closed it and put it back on the table. "Your Honor, I would like to digress from my opening statement to tell the jury and the court that no such motion will be made at this time, or at any time in the future. The defendant has instructed me as his counsel that I am to try this case on its merits, *not* on the kind of loophole that would have left this case open for generations to come, and wounded, to use the bench's phrase, 'pride in the great state of Texas.' "

Both the judge and the prosecutor nodded to Barnes in tacit acknowledgment of the concession that he had just made. Barnes wanted both feeling sympathetic as he reapproached the jury to launch his counterattack.

"So, members of the jury . . . enough preliminaries. What can I tell you about this case that the prosecutor has not? As I promised you, I'm going to have some comments about Mr. Matthews's opening statement, so we can take a look at it from a little bit of distance and see it for the contrived set of circumstances that it is. In that regard, we are going to look very strongly at the medical evidence, which will shock, if not amaze and befuddle you. We will also discuss not only the evidence found, but the evidence that should have been found, and wasn't, and the evidence that was found and not discussed.

"In addition, since he told you about Mr. Oswald's life story, I thought I'd fill in a few, well, call them 'gaps' if you like—but whatever you call them, know full well there is *nothing* simple about the life of Lee Oswald. There is a complexity here that is going to demand that we find out just who he was and what he was, from the day he enlisted in the Marine Corps to the day he was arrested. Whatever went on before the Marine Corps is largely irrelevant—let's face it, lots of children have less than ideal formative years, and of all of them out there today, only one is on trial for his life for the murder of the President. And I think it's foolish to make an issue of the fact that Mr. Oswald did not complete high school, for as you shall see, he had more high school credits than most of the police that dealt with him in his all-too-brief captivity in Dallas, and I find it shocking that Mr. Oswald spent more time in high school than Mr. William Greer, the driver of the presidential limousine on November twenty-second. So let's not talk of orphanages or English I; let's talk real, hard evidence. Let's examine his life and find out if he was, in fact, a defector, or was he, in fact, a *spy?*

"From there, we must also consider Mr. Oswald's 'confession.'" Barnes paused to allow the jury to whet their curiosity as to what that was about. "We must also address the issue of motive—the real motive behind the killing, which was not addressed this morning. We must also try to discover if this political assassination was an isolated event, or was consistent with a pattern of threats against President Kennedy." Barnes could see the jurors leaning just a bit forward, and he felt comfortable that his statements were being given a fair hearing, or possibly generating serious interest.

"We must also discuss something called, for want of a fancy legal term, 'consistency of evidence,' and I can assure you that you will find that discussion both fascinating and very confusing. But take heart: in your confusion you shall also find reasonable doubt.

"That consistency of evidence will either exist or not exist when all the witnesses have been heard. And how many will the defense call? I cannot tell you that in exact numbers. But I can guarantee you this: there are scores of people who have reasonable, relevant testimony to give which will lead you the jury, and everyone else in this room, to the truth. *And they will be heard.* If the number of those witnesses is, for example, three hundred, and Mr. Matthews calls eighty of them, the defense will call the other two hundred twenty. It's as simple as that: there is no witness that can convict Mr. Oswald. There are many who can acquit him. There is no honest person that the defense will not welcome to that witness stand in pursuit of the truth.

"We must also turn our attention to the attempt, by person or persons unknown, to plant incriminating evidence against the defendant. You will hear from witnesses who will tell you that on a certain day and time, Lee Oswald was at a certain place. The next witness will say, 'No, he was at home.' And there are just too many of these incidents for us to ignore as coincidence. Taken together, they form a clear pattern that someone wants us to think that the defendant was someone that he was not.

"We would certainly be remiss if we did not ask reasonable questions about the other . . . twelve . . . individuals taken into custody by the Dallas Police in the twenty-four hours after the death of President Kennedy. Who were they? Why were they arrested in the first place? Why were they released so fast in such secrecy?" Barnes almost did a double take at the jury's surprise at this information. "You didn't know this? Stay tuned—it gets better.

"You will also learn of the destruction and the omission of evidence vital to the process of getting at the truth here. While this evidence will not be necessary to convince you of the defendant's innocence, it would certainly have helped us arrive at the truth of the matter. In the same vein, it's hard for me as an attorney not to be aware that some of you have looked over at the evidence table at the material published by the presidential commission on the assassination. Please, do not at any time confuse quality with quantity. Much of what is in those published volumes are the most meaningless cartloads of manure ever shoveled in the history of publishing. Allow me one example for now, and I'll have reference to others later."

Barnes walked to the defense table, opened a folder and took out a one-page document. Holding it for each juror to see, he concluded, "I hold before you Exhibit CE 2199, an FBI interview with Mr. David Lutenbacher, who was the school principal when Lee Oswald's older brother was in second grade. I've lost sleep at night worrying that this incredible document might somehow fall into the hands of the prosecution." Barnes then dramatically walked back to the defense table, replaced the document, and passed the folder to Miss Jeffries, with gestures to her, for the jury's benefit, that indicated that the prosecution must never see the document.

"Then we shall call our witnesses, or, actually, truth's witnesses, because they'll give us a pretty good read on what really happened in Dallas, Texas, on November twenty-two, 1963. Since they fall, for the most part, into categories, let's quickly list them, and then you'll meet them when Mr. Matthews—*and I*—finish with his folks.

"You will meet several people with information regarding various aspects of the case: those whose knowledge of the defendant before November twenty-two has a bearing on the case, particularly those who will tell a different story about his marksmanship abilities; those who were in Dealey Plaza on November twenty-two and saw and heard what happened; the medical team in Dallas, all two dozen of them, who will tell you a very different story about Mr. Kennedy's wounds than those classroom clowns who botched an event at Bethesda Naval Hospital that evening that does not even qualify as a legal autopsy; a group of people in the Texas Theater, where the defendant was arrested, who have some curious things to tell us; the Bethesda medical personnel— not just the government hirelings who signed their names to a totally worthless pathological examination, but other people present who will raise some incredible doubts—and perhaps a few fears, amongst us all; some people who are going to tell us about guns—especially that cheap bolt-action piece of junk on the evidence table that no rifleman would be seen

with; people with testimony about more than three bullets—
an interesting concept in itself; people who will help us clear
up the riddle as to whether Mr. Oswald was a defector or a
spy; people who saw the defendant where he was not—but
where they would like you, the jury, to believe he was; we'll
also hear from the defendant's alibis. Mr. Matthews told you
he didn't have one for 12:30 on November twenty-two, and
perhaps that's so because the defendant had no reason to
think he would need one for that time."

Barnes caught a deep breath and pushed ahead. "We shall
also hear from several people—several—who will tell you that
they delivered significant evidence to the Dallas police . . .
and never saw it again. We won't see that evidence, unfortunately, but when you are told the nature of it, that nagging ol'
reasonable doubt will worsen.

"Then, unfortunately again, we'll have to put some expert
witnesses on the stand. I hate to do this, but if the prosecution does, I have to. It's no fun playing 'my expert against
your expert,' but that is somehow the way this procedure has
to be. I can tell you this: my experts are *the* experts, not some
government lackeys dusted off and shuffled in here to blow
smoke at fourteen respectable jurors. In the same vein, we
will call witnesses who have knowledge with respect to evidence that does exist, and they too will have some very interesting things to tell you." Barnes edged back toward the railing by the defense table, concluding, "Those are the people
you will hear"—and then, with an intense promisory look at
the jury but a lightness of tone—". . . plus a few surprises.

"Now, to the prosecution's case." Barnes walked to his
place at the end of the defense table and used it as a prop as
he worked from notes taken during the morning session.
"First of all, I'm not here to call the prosecutor a liar. He was
telling the truth this morning, at least when he said there
was only one verdict you could consider. Unfortunately, he
was inaccurate when he used the word 'guilty.' Then he told
you of all the agencies that gathered evidence. So what? It's
the nature of the evidence, not who found it, that matters.

"The discussion this morning then turned to the rifle, this
rifle," Barnes continued, picking it off the evidence table and
walking towards the jury. "This, gentlemen, is a surplus Ital-

ian piece of garbage, which sells wholesale for the vast sum
of three dollars. It was considered a weapon of peace by U.S.
servicemen in World War II—its origin—because it never hurt
*anyone.* And this particular one, with serial number C2766,
was from a batch lot that was the subject of court proceedings on the very day of November twenty-two, because the
jobber who purchased the lot which included this pathetic
specimen claimed they were all *defective,* and he was suing
in court to get his money back. Look at it—it defines the word
'cheap' and some other words best not used in this court.
You have heard that people saw a rifle in the sixth floor window of the Texas School Book Depository, and I fully accept
their testimony that there was one there. But there's no
proof, other than the 'circumstance' that this gun was found
on the sixth floor, to suggest that this was the gun seen in
the window. The sheriff's deputies who found a rifle in the
Depository that day described it as a seven point sixty-five
Mauser, and signed affadavits to that effect. But a five second inspection of this weapon reveals the words 'Made in
Italy' and most folks that know anything about guns know
that Mausers are made in Germany—and far superior weapons, I might add. Those same sheriff's deputies, in their
statements and sworn affadavits, gave no indication of any
proof that the gun—whatever gun—they found, *had been
fired recently.*

"Testimony and documents will cast equal or more serious
doubts about the authenticity of the cartridges, the whole
bullet, and the fragments. In particular,"—Barnes's voice
tailed off as he replaced the rifle on the table and picked up a
small glassine envelope—"is a question regarding Exhibit
543, this expended cartridge. Look at the lip of that hull,
gentlemen: it's *crushed.* Each of you knows enough basic
gun lore to know that no bullet could have fit in that cartridge on the day it was found. What does that tell us? If
nothing else, it tells us that the prosecution, hopeful that if
we believe that this hull could have held a bullet, we will then
be gullible enough to swallow the yarn that an intact, pristine bullet, which originally weighed possibly as much as 161
grains but weighed in at one hundred fifty-eight point six on
November twenty-two, went through President Kennedy,

then smashed into Governor Connally, shattering ten centimeters of rib, shattering the radius bone in his right wrist, and embedding itself in the femur bone in his left leg. Three bones and seven layers of skin; a good deal of metal removed from the governor; some metal still in the governor; a nearly perfect bullet found somewhere in Parkland Hospital devoid of blood, tissue, or fiber striations. Not even the three so-called 'autopsy surgeons' would consider the possibility that one bullet could have done that damage and emerged intact. Their reasoning: there's too much other metal.

"In a moment of high drama, the prosecutor bemoaned the possibility that you would perhaps have to view photos of the late President. With all due respect to the privacy of the President and his family, those photos, X rays, and films are vital evidence, and we will spend much time viewing them and deciding what they show . . . and what they hide.

"Mr. Matthews also spoke of order forms and money orders for the guns in question. I'll make it easy for all of us: Lee Oswald ordered a rifle and a pistol through the mail—from the places Mr. Matthews told you and in the manner he described. However, we must remind ourselves that the ordering of those weapons is in no way a violation of any law whatsoever. We must also consider that an assassin is not likely to publicize his purchases—it would be hard to imagine a person being more obvious about buying guns than the defendant in this case, and that's a curious fact. We know that in Texas, there are hundreds of gun dealers and pawn shops where a total stranger can walk in and purchase a firearm without any documents *ever* being written or signed; yet short of taking an ad in the paper, it seems that Mr. Oswald —or someone else—went to a great deal of trouble to publicize the purchase of a cheap rifle and a mediocre pistol. Also, offered for your consideration as a passing curiosity, the order form that Mr. Matthews so desperately wants you to handle is for a gun that is thirty-six inches long. The gun over on that table is forty point two inches long.

"And in a plain, simple brown bag, he carried the weapon into the Book Depository. Says who? The coworker mentioned by the prosecutor? He will testify that Mr. Oswald had a bag two feet long. When I asked him to show me, by spreading his hands apart, he did so, and I measured twenty-six point eight inches. The only other witness to this event spoke of virtually identical numbers. Yet that rifle, even when taken apart, is between thirty-five and thirty-six inches long. You Texas gentlemen, like this Minnesota trout fisherman, know the difference between two and three feet, and so do witnesses.

"And a threat letter to Mr. Connally. The letter said, in fact, that the writer, presumably Lee Oswald, would do whatever was in his power to get a dishonorable discharge from the Marine Corps changed to its original 'honorable' status. If that's a life-threatening letter, we all better handle very carefully the Valentine cards we receive next month.

"Without making a mountain out of a molehill, forget all this Bolshevik-Commie nonsense. The defendant has made public statements that he is a Marxist, which makes him a believer in an economic theory developed in London. He is not now a Communist, and he never was; and he never considered becoming a member of the Communist Party. If there is anything whatsoever incorrect in those statements, I'm sure the prosecution will show us the signed documents. As for his Russian language ability, the prosecution can suggest, but not prove, that Oswald was self-taught, however unlikely that may have been, considering there were over thirty mistakes in spelling and English grammar in that so-called threat letter to Mr. Connally. On the other hand, the defense will present documents showing that the defendant was given a Russian test at the Army Language School in Monterey, California. Since when are Marines—buck privates at that, tested in Russian? And why? Now *that's* the question. Certainly *not* so he could become the traitor the prosecution wants you to see before you.

"And what of Lee Oswald, the sharpshooter? On December twenty-one, 1956, almost seven full years before the murder of the President by a person or persons very well skilled in marksmanship, the defendant, after repeated tries, fired a score of two hundred twelve, two points above what was necessary to qualify as a sharpshooter, in a ranking which began with marksman, went up to sharpshooter, and topped out at expert. In subsequent but different firearms tests, he fired scores of thirty-four and thirty-eight, when forty-nine or fifty was considered *average.* Then on May six, 1959, he was barely able to fire a one hundred ninety-one, one and only one point above marksman, the lowest designation you can achieve without disqualifying yourself from Marine Corps duty. After May six, 1959, there is no evidence whatsoever that the defendant engaged in rifle practice, nor that he ever acquainted himself with the weapon over there on the table which is similar to the one he ordered but quite different from the Mauser said to have been found at the crime scene. So, ultimately, you are being asked to believe that this December 1956, 'sharpshooter,' using a piece of cheap Italian junk, fired shots that FBI experts could not duplicate, and he did that on November twenty-two, 1963, two thousand five hundred twenty-seven days after he qualified as a sharpshooter. We know better, don't we?

"Mr. Oswald's alleged defection, as well as the time spent in the Soviet Union, will be the subject of testimony by many defense witnesses. What is of immediate importance, considering the picture painted by the prosecution of all the dirty deeds done, and secrets passed, is that at no time did the defendant renounce his citizenship, and when he asked to come home, the United States government *loaned . . .* loaned! . . . him the money to do so. Do we treat traitors that way, or do we treat U.S. government employees that way? You, the jury, must judge that. You must also judge the events of June 1963, when the defendant petitioned the State Department to have his passport reissued. It was done the next day, according to Passport Office documents, because they had FBI documents showing that Oswald was not in any way suspected of being a Communist.

"We then jump to November twenty-two to learn the stunning revelation that the defendant's palm print was found on book cartons on the sixth floor of the building in which he was employed as a stock boy. It would be far more revealing if a search of the area *failed* to reveal his prints. We are also told that a paraffin test showed he had fired a gun that day. But we were not told the whole story. A paraffin test measures the presence of certain nitrates, nothing more, nothing less. A positive reaction, such as the test showed, indicates the presence of nitrates, but the defendant worked around heavy construction paper, cardboard, and printer's ink. But there's more. The defendant was arrested at 1:51, and brought to police headquarters. Documents were taken from him, some of which turned up on a subsequent property inventory and some didn't, and then he was questioned. We are told, 'he told a host of lies to the authorities,' by the prosecution, but can they produce a transcript or recording of what the defendant really said? No. None was made. We can wonder for the next two centuries why not, but that is all we can do.

"We then skip ahead to 4:05 P.M., when the defendant was taken to a lineup. He was searched there by two officers, who found a bus transfer and *five live bullets* for the pistol. Talk of incompetence? The most important prisoner in Texas history is interrogated for two hours with five bullets in his pocket and the police are totally ignorant of it. Then, five additional hours later, at 9 P.M., the defendant was fingerprinted *for the first time*, and after having his hands and palms thoroughly inked, he is then given the paraffin test on his hands and his face. Of course his hands would test positive; but his face tested negative, despite the prosecution's desire to have you believe that he fired three shots in quick succession and stood in the resulting cloud of nitrate-filled smoke as it happened. In a further interesting twist to the prosecution's fabled paraffin test, the paraffin casts of Mr. Oswald's hands were subsequently sent to Oak Ridge, Tennessee, to be subjected to something called 'neutron activation analysis.' This is a highly complicated test which yields extremely precise results. The results in this case: there was no hint of any rifle related materials on the casts made on the defendant.

"Finally, you were told that the defendant would have been convicted months ago except that a 'deluded' citizen prevented that. The prosecution deftly overlooked the fact that the very same citizen had an interesting track record: in 1947, he was a Senate racketeering witness in hearings conducted by then Congressman Richard M. Nixon; subsequently, he was a paid FBI informant, giving up his mob connections to the highest bidder. And on November twenty-two, 1963, he owed the Internal Revenue Service forty four thousand four hundred thirteen dollars and eighty-six cents in back taxes. There is a great deal of information in there that demands our attention and points up the sheer fantasy of everything you heard this morning which was supposed to compel you to dash out and return with a guilty verdict."

Barnes pushed his legal pad aside and poured himself a drink of ice water, as much for his voice as to allow his words to settle on the jury before he dropped his next bomb.

"Enough, for now, about the razor-thin evidence the prosecution has. What don't they have, besides the eyewitness, that might make their case believable? Since they told you about the rifle and its mail order forms, as well as cartridges and bullets, why are there no order forms for the cartridges and bullets? Why was the FBI unable, after canvassing over seven hundred gun shops, totally unable to locate anyone who ever sold a rifle cartridge to the defendant? And, since three hulls were found and one live round was in the rifle chamber, even if we assume that the defendant, in some clandestine, covert operation, was able to purchase cartridges and keep it a secret from the FBI, where are the rest? They aren't sold like licorice sticks, one by one. They are sold in box lots—fifty, one hundred, and not one matching or even similar cartridge appeared despite thorough but incredibly unprofessional searches executed at two separate addresses.

"Also not found at those two sites were any materials for maintaining a rifle, even if it was a cheap one. Nor was any gun oil found—raising very serious questions about the prosecution's evidence. Not only was no oil found, the so-called paper bag contained no oil, and it's difficult to imagine a well-oiled rifle being bounced around on the back seat of a car without losing *one drop of oil*. And that gun, without oil, would have broken the shooter's chin, as FBI experts, using the weapon in a well-oiled state, had difficulty with both the bolt and the sights, which were way off. And just one more passing thought," Barnes said, approaching the jury with a document handed him by Dean, "this, gentlemen, is Exhibit 2560, an FBI memo relating tests done on the rifle at Aberdeen Proving Ground. And I'll quote from the document so as not to spoil the flavor of the original: 'The gunsmith observed that the scope as we received it was installed as if for a left-handed man.' " Barnes allowed for that to sink in for a moment. "It also must have been fun to have been an FBI man in the Dallas region then, as they combed through every rifle range they could, looking for other hulls fired by that junk," Barnes added, hoisting a thumb over his shoulder toward the rifle on the evidence table, "and although they found over thirteen thousand similar, only eighty of them turned out to be Mannlicher-Carcano hulls, and none were fired by the rifle on that table.

"So," Barnes wondered aloud as the document was returned to the defense table, "what is missing? Motive; eyewitnesses to the crime itself; proof that the gun was fired; proof the defendant possessed, maintained, or delivered the Italian rifle—not the Mauser—to the Book Depository; proof that after almost seven years to the day when he got lucky on a Marine slow-fire qualifying course, he used the cheapest gun, with a misaligned, left-hand sight to make shots over trees at a car disappearing down an incline and score two near perfect hits that FBI rifle experts *could not duplicate,* in conditions far better. That's all that is missing—a few mere details.

"So who was this Lee Oswald that joined the Marines, learned secrets—and the Russian language, left for Russia and treason, if you believe that, and had his way home paid by your tax dollars, and when he got here, there were no questions asked. In fact, he got a job at a defense-related contractor where his expertise with the Russian Cyrillic alphabet was a valued asset and where he fine-tuned his ability to doctor photographs. Well, who or what was he?

"I'm not going to pretend to tell you that I know," Barnes said with some resignation in his voice. "All I can do is try to ask the right questions to each and every witness and hope that the clear judgment of the jurors will tell us who Lee Oswald was between 1956 and 1963. We know he joined the marines, but lots of teenagers do that—his brother and half-brother did, so that part came natural. But then the plot thickens. He's learning Russian, answering other marines in Russian, calling them 'comrade,' receiving Russian literature in the mail, and posing for all the world to see. Some of his marine buddies questioned this behavior with their superior officers and *nothing* was ever said or done. Twice in the marines he was court-martialed, and subsequent to both events he was separated from his unit for a few weeks. Nobody saw him in captivity. What was he doing and whose orders was he following? Even more amazing, if not amusing, is what must be considered a unique event in marine and U.S. Military history. We learn from Donabedian Exhibit number 1, Oswald's service record, that he was treated on September sixteen, 1958, for acute urethritis, due to gonococcus number 0303, 'origin: in line of duty.' *Lee Oswald contracted gonorrhea . . .* in the line of duty?

"Then there's the hardship discharge. The question then becomes, did Oswald request it, as a traitor, or did the government grant it, to a spy? The true nature of the activities we can only guess at, unless the CIA wants to share some of the thousands of documents that they have on the defendant with us. But we can indulge the thought that Oswald did walk into the U.S. embassy and say all those bad things about America, knowing that he was talking right into Russian microphones, thirty-four of which were discovered in an electronic sweep of the embassy a few weeks after Mr. Oswald's essentially unproductive visit. 'I want to give up my U.S. citizenship,' "—Barnes gave the jury a big wink—"I'll tell the Russians everything I know," another wink, "and so it goes. If he was the traitor the prosecution would like you to convict and electrocute, just tell me why the United States government gave him four hundred thirty-five dollars and seventy-one cents to return home, and when he got here, he wasn't even questioned. Also ignored was a lengthy inventory of equipment commonly associated with espionage work found at the Paine residence on November twenty-two. Several sophisticated cameras, including a miniature Minox, and several equally small pairs of binoculars. Incidentally, those items had a value, on November twenty-two, of more than all the money Oswald had earned at his jobs since returning from Russia. Think he was using them to smuggle out information about American textbook sales?

"And what of the Russians? At the time Oswald was there, it is a known fact in intelligence service that the Russians were desperate—there's no other word for it—for any—*any* information about the American military. They would pay a drunken sergeant off-base somewhere a tidy sum just to learn the name of the lieutenant who commanded him, or how many rounds were issued to the bazooka team in a given company. And here's a U-2 radar genius that just drops in their laps and says 'Have I got a story for you.' Sorry, but it won't work—he was sent there by us, after we taught him Russian, put down a false trail, and played out a cute scene in the embassy. But the Russians aren't that stupid. They tucked him away in Minsk making radios and when he got tired of eating cabbage every night, he gave up a charade they never bought in the first place.

"That is not to say, however, that we have seen the conclusion of Oswald's intelligence career. We're told he handed out Cuban leaflets—and he did, just long enough to get photographed, punched, and arrested—in other words, *noticed*. He's tossed in jail *for being punched*, and, at his request, is interviewed by the FBI. Do they interview every subversive facing a ten dollar fine for disturbing the peace? Of course they don't. And where did Oswald operate his pro-Cuban 'Fair Play for Cuba Committee'? Out of 544 Camp Street, New Orleans, Louisiana, a building almost wholly rented to the most virulent right-wing groups and individuals in the state of Louisiana, whom Oswald met, conversed, and operated with as he established this silly Cuban posture. And then we're told by the prosecution that this was done, 'to the neglect of his Russian family.' Neglect, indeed. We won't know about neglect until we see Oswald's tax form for the year 1962, and that just isn't going to happen, although you can be assured it has been subpoenaed. In Exhibit, uh, excuse me, Exhibit 1141, another interesting FBI memo, agent A.O. Fonville of the Internal Revenue Service 'advised' and this is a quote, 'that no income tax return was filed for 1961 or 1962 by Lee Harvey Oswald.' 1961 is not surprising. Oswald was in Russia. 1962, however, is another matter, because Oswald cashed the refund check he received, and I don't think anyone in this courtroom is going to receive a refund check from the IRS without at least going through the formalities of filing a return."

Barnes again stood in the center of the court and scanned

the jury, focusing on the one juror in the back row that seemed most impressed with Matthews's opening remarks. "I ask you again, who is Lee Oswald?" Barnes walked around the defense table to give the jury a moment of reflection.

"We shall also consider Mr. Oswald's confession." This statement from Barnes caused jurors' expressions to change, some shifting in chairs, and curious looks from everyone in the court except the people at the defense table. "Oh, yes. He confessed. If needed, the defense will play both the radio recording and the televised recording of Mr. Oswald being moved through Dallas Police Headquarters at 7:55 P.M. on November twenty-second, when he told a reporter, 'I'm a patsy.' Now, I'm sure some of you read in the papers that I was employed for three years by the Federal Bureau of Investigation as a Special Agent before becoming a public defender in Minnesota. Well, gentlemen, I'm going to tell you that there isn't a police officer anywhere in this land who has a suspect in custody for killing the President of the United States who makes the statement 'I'm a patsy' without that officer reacting. Any—and I mean the lowliest, most raw trainee in Skunkville, Montana, is instantly and forcibly going to get that defendant in an interrogation room, get right up to his face and say 'Patsy for whom?' But the question was never even considered. The Dallas police had Lee Oswald, and although twelve other people—notice I did not say 'men'—were taken into custody—*arrested* on November twenty-second, we know almost nothing about them. Oswald confessed to being a patsy, and nobody cared. Meanwhile, twelve other defendants breezed through a revolving door and disappeared from the pages of history.

"We must also consider motive, because it is a fact known and accepted by all of us that people commit crimes because they have reasons to commit them. Many individuals did not like the policies of President Kennedy—he was changing America faster than it was prepared to cope with change. Some just didn't like him. One theater marquee in Georgia, reflecting their dislike for Mr. Kennedy's liberal civil rights program, showed the movie *PT-109* with the subtitle, 'See How the Japs Almost Got Kennedy.' Lee Oswald did not own that theater.

"Mere days before his death, John Kennedy, after meeting with his Cabinet advisors, signed an executive order which would have totally disengaged the United States from the Vietnam War as of January one, 1965. That order was rescinded by the new President, to the joy of the military and the war contractors, within seventy-two hours of Mr. Kennedy's murder. And look where we are now in Vietnam. We're stopping the Red menace, but if Mr. Oswald were the Communist that Mr. Matthews pictured him to be, he would have never removed the President whose ending of the war would have guaranteed Communist domination by today, and replaced him with a man who escalated advisors into combat soldiers. Lee Oswald wouldn't have done that.

"Mr. Kennedy was planning the repeal of the oil depletion allowance, a tax loophole which, in 1962, allowed oil companies not to pay taxes estimated at *twenty-seven billion* dollars. A lot of people will think about killing another human being for that kind of money—oil money. Lee Oswald doesn't even have a driver's license.

"Mr. Kennedy was deeply upset with the failures of the Central Intelligence Agency, which had botched the Bay of Pigs, and had, on November one, 1963, been suspected of aiding in the execution of Vietnamese political leaders less than friendly toward what were perceived as United States' interests. The President has spoken of 'scattering the CIA to the winds'; on November twenty-two, the right hemisphere of John Kennedy's brain was scattered to the winds. Even if, as is darkly hinted, Lee Oswald was on the CIA payroll, he was the designated, self-confessed 'patsy'; real CIA killers never get caught.

"Under Robert Kennedy's guidance, the Justice Department was waging a war on organized crime—the mob, the Mafia, whatever you want to call it—but a group whose very existence was denied by none other than J. Edgar Hoover; then Joe Valachi went before the Senate and made a fool of my former employer, Mr. Hoover, and Robert Kennedy stepped up the prosecution of mob leaders. That campaign died on Elm Street, in Dallas, as prosecutions of mob leaders and organizations *declined* eighty-three percent in Lyndon Johnson's first full year in office. The mob knows how to kill very efficiently; they don't need the defendant in this case to do that.

"So, the military, their contractors, oil companies with more money than we could imagine, the CIA, the Mafia, the ultra-right-wing hate groups who had trouble with the policies of an Eastern liberal—all these groups had a serious vested interest in the quick, nonelectoral replacement of John F. Kennedy. A major, vested interest—not something that is going to be entrusted to a would-be cloak and dagger trainee armed with a gun which, if fired straight up into the air, had only a fifty–fifty chance of the bullet coming down. It's just this simple—if this political assassination had failed —if John Kennedy had lived, you can bet your Texas pride and all it means to you that Robert Kennedy's Justice Department would have been all over this case with manpower you can only imagine. *They* would have found the *group; they* would have found the shooters; *they* would have punished the guilty. No group with serious motive is going to risk that on the abilities of a dollar-twenty-five per hour bookstore stock boy, who, just for the record, rarely spoke, but when he did, and it was politics, had high regard for the late President."

Robert Dean motioned to Barnes at this point, by prearranged signal, and Barnes then listened to Dean tell him that this was the time for a quick recess, which Barnes requested. A five-minute recess was granted. It was Barnes's and Dean's belief never to go too long. One juror with a full bladder can lose his concentration easily.

At the defense table, Graves asked Matthews, "Did we know all this?" Matthews, with a look that could have killed, indicated that no, *we* didn't know all this. "But," he told Graves and Vincent, "we're going to have to deal with it, somehow. Those fools in Dallas made this sound open and shut . . . and unfortunately, so did that pompous s.o.b. from Minnesota."

Following the recess, Barnes again approached the jury, and almost tried to create the image that this was their presentation. "Well, now, let us consider the concept of consistency of evidence, for it will make everyone's job a lot easier in the long run.

"Basically, it amounts to this: you're going to hear from many witnesses, as in any major case. Some will say one thing, others will directly contradict them. Some of this is basic human nature, or confusion, or the idea that what you believe in overshadows everything else and it colors your perception of truth. But certainly in a case like this one, an event that took, by the defense's best estimate, five point seventy-nine seconds, there should be a reasonable consensus as to what happened. And if that happens, then you, the jury, make your judgment, innocent or guilty, on that consensus. But what happens in the total absence of consensus, as is the case here?

"Let's look at a few examples. Many, many people heard shots in Dealey Plaza on November twenty-second. Oddly, a great number of them—certainly enough for us to suspect they're reporting accurately, suggest a strange pattern. First, they tell of hearing what sounded like a firecracker, but then they realized it must have been a shot, because the next sound they heard was a shot. Several will speak of very contradictory sounds and equally contradictory locations, and that means we must allow for the possibility that they're correct—and if they are, somebody should still be looking for that other gunman, or those other gunmen.

"Now, naturally, most of those people in Dealey Plaza were just plain folks, there to see the President. In my closing argument, I'll tell you about the dozen or so who were there for other purposes, but for now, let's stick to the people watching the parade. They expected to see the President of the United States, his lovely wife, the governor of Texas and his wife, and the vice-president and his wife, along with other dignitaries. They didn't expect to witness the carnage that occurred, so we cannot expect precision of them. They weren't standing there with stopwatches, surveyors' equipment, and recording devices, so if they say the shots took five, six, or even ten seconds, we cannot fault them. They may be right. The defense calculation of five point seventy-nine seconds is based on the bullet impacts shown on the film made by Mr. Abraham Zapruder. But what do we do with a witness who says, 'Well, I was there, and I know the shots lasted for just about two minutes'? Simple; we pass educated judgment on that part of his testimony and delete it.

"But what do we do when experts fall out? What do we do when two dozen eyewitnesses, trained doctors, surgeons, and emergency room technicians and nurses, tell us that the President had a gaping wound in *the back* of his head, and a neat, round entrance wound in the front of his neck? We can't ignore it; these are experts at what they do, and they were just doing their jobs and telling us exactly what they saw, with nothing to gain and no story to sell. But eight hours later, at Bethesda, Maryland, other doctors report no gaping wound at the back of the head, and no entrance wound in the throat; then *they* all sign papers saying that they promise to remain silent and know they will be court-martialed—and have their careers ruined—if they talk. Now we have something very, very wrong. So we read the 'autopsy' —which it wasn't—report, and we find many inconsistencies at Bethesda, where essentially there was none in Dallas. And we find the autopsy surgeon telling us that the President's wounds were so horrible and extreme that they taxed satisfactory verbal description. Sorry, Doctors, but that's your job at autopsy: verbal description. Were the doctors even permitted to see the photos? The answer is no, and we have to ask, 'Why not?' And then there's the matter of the President's brain—not an easy topic, but evidence nevertheless. Witness after witness will testify to the tremendous loss of brain tissue resulting from the fatal bullet, yet the supplementary autopsy report, dealing with the brain, tells that it weighed fifteen hundred grams—the weight of a full, undamaged brain—the weight of someone's brain who might have died from pancreas failure!! These problems, members of the jury, demand our attention, and if these reports are inconsistent, you must first make a judgment on what the truth is, then relate that truth to the defendant and make your judgment on him."

Barnes tried to continue to project to the jury a studious, deep-in-thought look, which was theatrical, as he knew what he wanted to say next. "Okay, enough about the President's brain: let's try now to use our own brains and focus in such a way that we can all look at the various evidence—the prosecution's, the defense's, and that which has been subpoenaed and may not appear, and let's find a way to approach the bottom-line truth in this trial. If Mr. Matthews were allowed to interrupt my presentation right now, he'd no doubt warn you with respect to what I just said about consistency of evidence. He'd tell you something like, 'Don't let the defense fool you on this one; they may plant the seeds of more than one gunman, but that doesn't let Mr. Oswald off the hook.' And, of course, he would be correct. You will get a wealth of evidence of multiple gunmen, none of which will guarantee that the defendant was not one of them. That's not my job. My challenge is to remind you that the prosecution *must* prove that Oswald *was* one of the multiple gunmen. If all you leave this courtroom with is the notion that it was three or more shots from the sixth floor window and/or other sites, then your verdict is obvious—since you don't know the identity of the shooter, and to be accused of a crime does not, and will never, make a person guilty of the crime.

"Let's consider what we think happened on November twenty-two, at least the basic events. The defendant awoke, had coffee at the Paine residence, left his wedding ring and one hundred eighty dollars behind, and carried roughly fifteen dollars and a package to work with him. The fifteen-dollar figure, by the way, is arrived at because when arrested, the defendant had thirteen dollars and eighty-seven cents, and he had spent one dollar for a cab ride, plus change for a coke and bus fare, which, for the record, was twenty-three cents. Once he reached work, the package was not seen again, and he spent the morning doing his job, while a large group of Book Depository employees were engaged in laying new flooring on, of all places, the sixth floor. It was they, by the way, as testimony will show, who moved boxes from where they were replacing floor boards and created the screen which has been called the 'sniper's nest.' Except for the promised presidential motorcade, it was a routine morning, although it would *not* have been if past trends had prevailed. The building in question rents space to book companies who sell textbooks to schools. Usually the 'fall rush' is over by the fifteenth of November, and layoffs occur, and as the new kid on the block, Lee Oswald should have been out of work at that location by November fifteenth.

"Mr. Oswald was seen and positively identified, sitting alone, in the lunchroom, *after* 12:15 that day by one clerical employee. I stress 'after 12:15.' A few minutes later, shots were fired, the President was fatally wounded, a motorcycle officer quickly entered the building, confronted the defendant, put a pistol in his stomach, and then continued onward. The defendant then left the building, walking eastward and catching a bus heading *back* to the scene of the crime, then departed the bus in traffic, catching a taxi almost adjacent to a bus depot. He then went home to change clothes and get a pistol."

Barnes returned to the jury rail and leaned forward, speaking softly. "Now, the fifteen of us have work to do. Let's think this thing through logically and ask ourselves, are these events the behavior patterns of an assassin, or, to use his own phrase, 'a patsy'?" If Lee Oswald's intentions, when he awoke on November twenty-second were to kill the President, would he have left behind one hundred eighty dollars and gone off to commit murder and finance an escape with fifteen dollars? I think we can agree about that being unlikely. Would he have been so obvious about the package, if, in fact, it contained a gun, or would he have gotten it to the stock-cluttered upper floors of the Depository sooner? I think the answer is again obvious. Would he have been seen in the lunchroom *after* 12:15, when the presidential motorcade was due at 12:25, and had a fifty–fifty chance of being either a few minutes late or a few minutes early? Of course not. He would have had to have been in place, with the rifle assembled, absolutely no later than 12:05–12:10. And then, would he have hailed a taxi parked *next to* a bus depot, when that depot was in fact an unguarded escape to all points of the compass? Consider the obvious, gentlemen."

Barnes turned to the bench and addressed Judge Davis: "Your Honor, would it be possible to test out the television system for the sake of viewing the next exhibit? If it works, then we know it won't break down when the exhibits are being introduced under oath."

"Any objections to that, Mr. Matthews?" Judge Davis asked.

"No, Your Honor," Matthews answered in upbeat tones.

Barnes turned back to the jury. "So far, in the last few minutes, gentlemen, we have examined the events of November twenty-second not strictly from evidence, but from the point of view of what makes sense. Now I'd like to continue that kind of deliberation with a look at six photographs." Barnes walked a few feet to a temporary microphone affixed to the side of the bench near the witness stand, knowing he could talk from anywhere in the courtroom and be heard by the microphone, but this was his idea of dramatics.

"Could we please have CE 877, 878, 879, 884, 886, and 890, in that order, for about ten seconds each, and then go back to 884 and hold on that exhibit? Thank you."

The jurors looked at their monitor with mixed curiosity and fascination, not knowing exactly what they were seeing, but knowing also that it was nothing they had seen in any newspaper which described the assassination. When the minute or so was up, and Exhibit 884 was redisplayed, Barnes resumed the initiative. "What you have seen, gentlemen, is a re-creation of the motorcade route through Dealey Plaza on the day of the assassination, viewed through a camera lens mounted in a telescopic sight on a rifle." The picture you are now seeing depicts what is believed to have been the view of the gunman, whoever that was, in the sixth floor window of the Book Depository at the time of the first shot. You can see that it shows a spacious automobile, but not the actual presidential limousine, just as it emerges from beneath foliage. Eight hundred eighty-six, please. This picture, from the re-creation timed and lined up with Mr. Zapruder's film, shows what the assassin would have seen, at the time of the second shot. And the last one, if we could have 890 please . . . this one shows the position of the car, reasonably easily fixed,"— and here Barnes's voice assumed a temporary tone of anger —"because the car was right in front of Mr. Zapruder and *virtually stopped.* Burn those three pictures into your minds: you'll see them again, and possibly more than once, as the experts tell you whether the shot is possible or not. Keep in mind, though, that no matter how many experts tell you it *could* be done, no expert is going to sit in this witness box and tell you he did it. Now let's change the perspective. 877, please."

Barnes moved down to the far end of the jury box, to create the sense of a disembodied voice speaking from behind the jurors. "This photo, gentlemen, and the next two as well, were also taken by the same camera, in the same rifle sight, from that same window. FBI Director Hoover wrote a letter to the President's Commission saying that the assassin fired at the car as shown in those other pictures, because before that 'his view was obstructed by trees.' Do you see any trees in that picture? Does anybody see any trees? Does anyone see one leaf? Does it look like an easier shot than those other three? Eight hundred seventy-eight, please," Barnes requested with a sense of urgency, as he knew he was making points. "Now, the re-created target is just a few feet away, and I still don't see any trees. Do any of you? Eight hundred seventy-nine, please. There it is, exhibit 879—*this* is the picture that should have been on the cover of *Life* magazine, entitled 'the shot not taken.' I've been very critical of the potential of the alleged assassination rifle, but it might have been able to make that shot, because that's how easy it is. If you look at that treeless picture—and remember, we're talking logic here, you've got to say to yourself, 'If there's one fella by himself up in that sixth floor window, why didn't he shoot at the close target in these three pictures, making a slow, wide turn in a spacious open limousine?

"There's only one answer, and there's only one reason: something called 'triangulation of fire.' If that pathetic amateur sitting at the defense table *was* guilty as charged, he would have fired the easy shots—like the one you are looking at right now. The tougher shots were taken because this event involved more than one individual. And that means conspiracy, but more importantly, it means *professional*. And Lee Oswald never was and never will be a professional anything, least of all a professional killer for hire.

"Let's get back to our narrative, but before that, I would thank the court for the opportunity to try out the new technology and show the jury how the system works," Barnes said, looking at the jury but speaking to the judge. "The next event in our scenario, after the shots, is the encounter with the police officer very shortly after the last shot was fired. Consider again the logic. Several people on both the fourth and fifth floors ran for the stairs after the shooting ended, and heard no one on the staircase. The elevators, ungainly and loud, never moved. If the weapon in question *was* fired, it was wiped clean, and hidden, and wiping a gun clean means not just a swipe, but a thorough polish job on small areas like the bolt and the trigger guard. So nobody heard an assassin escaping on the stairs, yet the defendant is accosted by a police officer on the second floor. And the police officer was reacting with the first shot, so he had, in essence, a head start on the shooter, who had to finish his deadly work and tidy up the three empty hulls, one of which could not have contained a bullet. How could Lee Oswald have done that, short of having flown out an upper floor window and reentering in the second floor lunchroom to have a gun pointed at him by Officer Baker? *How?*

"Oswald left the building shortly after. Other employees never even returned to the building, by the way, but their absence was somehow overlooked. But Oswald left. Because he committed the crime? No; *no, no,* and *no.* If he had done it, he would have been excused within the hour like all the other employees were. He left because he suddenly realized *that he had been set up and plucked.*

"Let's just back up briefly, then we'll move ahead. That morning he left behind his ring and one hundred eighty dollars; leaving behind the ring suggests to me, at least, that the defendant was expecting some kind of difficulties in the hours ahead. But the one hundred eighty dollars says that escape was not considered a priority. And did he try to escape? Again, *no.* Lee Oswald's actions, from 12:30 onwards, suggest a motive totally different than escape: self-preservation. He boarded a local bus and then a taxi, when he was within one hundred feet of the bus station, and gentlemen, believe it or not, there was never an alert issued to watch the bus stations, railroad terminals, or airports. Oswald, even with his miserable fifteen dollars, could have gotten out of Dallas and Texas before anybody knew it. But he didn't have to escape, he had to survive. So he passed up an easy ride out of town and went home—*to get the pistol."* Barnes paused and established eye contact with every juror.

*"To get the pistol,"* Barnes repeated. "Not to get a bus out of town, or even to walk behind the Depository and get lost in the crowd and eventually catch a boxcar going who cares where. *To get the pistol.* And then, ultimately, to come back into town, without ever having even attempted an escape. Now, gentlemen, what does that tell us? Well, for one thing, it seems obvious to me, as it should to you, that if Lee Oswald had any plan or thought whatsoever that he was going to aim and fire a rifle at the President of the United States that day, he would have had that pistol with him. No question—none whatsoever. If he was able to bring a rifle into the building, as suggested, a pistol would have been no problem. *But he didn't.* He had to go home to get it, and not to escape, remember. This makes it very clear that whatever planned event caused him to leave his wedding ring home was much smaller in scope than the event which caused the defendant to panic, go home, get a gun, and go to a theater, where, as we shall see, some strange things happened.

"So what has our exercise in logic taught us?" Barnes asked rhetorically, pacing, head down, in front of the jury. "Well, it seems clear that the defendant was unprepared for the events of the day as they came to pass, and when he realized what had happened, he took steps to protect himself. But none of the actions discussed in the last few minutes are the behavior patterns of an assassin, be he an amateur one or a professional killer. He could not have expected to shoot his way out of the building with the rifle, particularly since there was only one more bullet, and rifles tend to be noticed. So the pistol would have been vital—but at eight A.M., not at one P.M. So we have studied, using common sense and logic, both of which will be bolstered in the weeks to come with evidence, the actions on November twenty-second of a 'patsy,' exactly what he confessed to being on the evening of November twenty-second.

"Now, finally, I'm going to ask you to listen to all the subsequent testimony, both prosecution and defense, and ask yourself a couple of questions again and again. The first question is obvious: does that evidence prove that the defendant is guilty? Not 'does it suggest guilt?' or 'could it be stretched to guilt?' but just simply, does it prove the defendant guilty? Because I don't think you'll hear much of that. And the more testimony you hear, and the low quantity of guilt that is contained in what you're hearing, has to point you in a certain direction.

"The other question is one intended to arrive at the real truth here, because to me, Lee Oswald, whatever else he did on November twenty-two, and I'm not telling you he should be 'Man of the Year,' but I can tell you that you will *not* hear one sentence that says he did it. The other question is, does the evidence point in the direction of the defendant's guilt, *or* . . . does it point in the direction of a setup? Does the evidence boldly announce, 'Lee Oswald did it' or does it, in the manner of props on an elaborate theatrical stage, all in place so you, the audience, arrive and pretend that you're watching Hamlet happen in Denmark five hundred years ago, does it announce to you 'set up'? Mr. Matthews will show you all the props and costumes, and even some of the cast, but you're still seeing a fourth-grade class play, not a consistent pattern of evidence that says, 'Guilty beyond a reasonable doubt.'

"So, forgive my ramblings, but sit back and ask, does the evidence convict or shed doubt? Does it point at him, or at staged, carefully orchestrated theatrics? I'll certainly remind you of all of this in my closing statement, sometime down the road, but in the meantime, remember the questions. And remember the prediction I am about to make to you. When this is done, twelve of you will go into that room over there,"—with Barnes pointing a stern finger at a rather common looking door—"and you'll return *not* with the usual little folded slip of paper, but with an agenda. That agenda will suggest to the prosecution that the events of a good number of people in this episode be presented to a subsequent grand jury, either for perjury or obstruction of justice, or both. You will probably also make the suggestion that certain individuals in responsible law-enforcement agencies have behaved shamelessly and that it was your duty, in this media-free atmosphere, to bring those thoughts to light. And finally, at the bottom of that sheet of paper will be two words written in large, bold print: *not guilty.*

"Thank you, gentlemen."

The court seemed to catch its collective breath after the final few thoughts, unorthodox as they were, in Barnes's statement, but Judge Davis rapped once, lightly, a good sign to Barnes. He then asked Prosecutor Matthews if he would be prepared to begin testimony the following day and was told that the prosecution was ready to begin. The judge then told the jury that he imagined that they had heard quite a bit for one day, and hoped they had a good meal and got sufficient rest for the days ahead. He also gave them the obligatory reminder not to discuss the case amongst themselves. The proceedings were then adjourned for the first day.

A Vermont officer arrived to lead Oswald away, after Dean had had at least a few moments to tell him that without any major surprises, they were in good shape. Once Oswald left, Dean had very high praise for Barnes, which he had not wanted the defendant to hear for fear that he would take the proceedings lightly. Across the aisle, the optimism of the morning session, based on Matthews's clear and logical opening statement, had lost some of its bloom. "There was a great deal in there that we didn't read from the FBI or the Dallas folks," Graves told Matthews.

"I would hate to think of that as a harbinger of things to come, Eaton," Matthews responded.

Barnes had a quick, whispered conference with Bob Dean, and as the attorneys departed, Barnes and Jeffries quickly, Dean taking his time, Matthews commented, "Long day, Bob."

"You're right about that, Ray," Dean told him, "and you made it a lot longer for us with that opener. I was ready to vote for conviction when you finished, but, well, you know, I thought I'd stick around for the remainder."

"You'll vote Oswald guilty the same day I cast my vote for Barnes for governor of Minnesota," Matthews answered, good-naturedly.

"Stranger things have happened, Ray," Dean added, "and some of them occurred in Dallas, Texas."

"Mr. Barnes did hint at that, didn't he?" Matthews concluded. Dean and Matthews, with Graves and Vincent in tow, then left the courtroom together.

# Four

Wednesday, January 6, 1965: a raw, bleak, windy day, but not totally unlike that which was expected in Lubbock in January. To Barnes, whose wife had phoned the night before to say that it had been below zero in the northern suburbs of Minneapolis, it was almost springlike, albeit without sunshine.

To Ray Matthews, it was just raw and bleak—typical Lubbock. He and his staff had worked well into the night, and it was not the most productive time he had ever spent. While Earl Vincent and Eaton Graves had touched base with other Lubbock prosecutors in nonrelated cases, Matthews had shared the first day's events with his wife Barbara. She was hopeful that Oswald had been "painted with the reddest brush around," but she had to settle for an assurance from Matthews that Oswald's politics were made an issue, with the caveat, "But the Fifties are over, dear; some people allow for Communists to be around now; besides, there are so many of them, we can't convict Oswald purely for being one." When Graves and Vincent arrived at Matthews's ranch on the outskirts of Lubbock, they spent a few minutes venting at the volume of new evidence that they had been subjected to in Barnes's opening to the jury, but they then had to grapple with a difficult question: whom do we call first? Matthews put the issue in perspective: "Barnes was right when he said there was no witness to i.d. Oswald with a smoking gun, but there are still a lot of evidence and a lot of people to hear from. He added that he had expected a lopsided victory, not a standoff, in opening arguments, but reminded his assistants that it could have been worse: "Barnes made no mention of the Secret Service agents being out late drinking the night before Kennedy was killed, nor, apparently, did he review the Dallas police duty rosters for November twenty-two, which would have shown that the Dallas cops and detectives usually off on Friday still had the day off; reserves were protecting Kennedy in Dallas. If the jury had heard those two facts, our opening statement would have lost most of its impact."

Thinking back on the debate, Matthews remembered how he ended it the night before: "We've got to put a shooter in the Texas School Book Depository. If it wasn't Oswald, it's almost up to Barnes to tell us who it was. So that's our best approach, and that's where we start."

Now, as Judge Davis had the jury brought in, Matthews was rethinking his plan, but that was about all he could do, because the witnesses planned for this day could not be changed too radically at the last minute.

"Mr. Matthews, Mr. Barnes," Judge Davis began, "is there any business to deal with before the Prosecution begins its case?"

"Not from Defense, Your Honor."

"The Prosecution is ready to proceed, Your Honor."

"Call your first witness, Mr. Matthews."

"The state calls Buell Wesley Frazier." A Vermont state officer stationed at the center doors of the courtroom then left, to return shortly with a young, dark-haired, lanky individual. He was sworn in by Carson, and took his seat a bit nervously, suspecting that he was the first witness called.

Matthews approached the witness stand, and asked the witness to state his name and occupation, which he did, and in the process got a little shock value out of the exercise when the words "Texas School Book Depository" were mentioned.

"Were you employed at the Book Depository in October and November of 1963, Mr. Frazier?"

"Yes, sir."

"Did you have any reason to come to know Lee Oswald, the defendant in this case?"

"Well, he was one of the boys that filled orders, just like I did, and there was, oh, maybe fifteen all together, so it wasn't difficult to know all of them."

"I see," Matthews slowed down. "Now, Mr. Frazier, just for the record, do you see Lee Oswald in this courtroom today?"

"That's Lee, right over there," nodding toward the defense table.

"There's no doubt in your mind that the individual in the dark sport coat is the man you worked with?"

"Well, he doesn't look exactly the same, you know, bein' shot 'n all, but that sure looks like the fella."

"Very well. Now, did you ever have occasion to drive Mr. Oswald anywhere in your automobile?"

"Yes, sir. I drove him out to Irving a few times on weekends, and brought him back into work on Monday morning. Rest of the time he lived in a boardin' house, or rooming house . . ."

"Objection," Barnes interrupted. "The witness has no personal knowledge where Oswald lived the rest of the time."

"Sustained."

"Mr. Frazier,"—Matthews pressed on with irritation in his voice—"in the course of your driving Mr. Oswald home on weekends, did he ever tell you where he lived the rest of the time?"

"Not the address, no; but he did say he rented a small room over in Oak Cliff."

"Thank you. Now, you said you drove Oswald 'out to Irving' on weekends. Tell the jury about that, please."

"Well, his wife and daughter, first, and then the second daughter, lived with a lady named Ruth Paine, just down the block from my home in Irving. And Lee used to like to visit the children on the weekends, and it was no trouble for me."

"Was there ever a time, Mr. Frazier, when you drove the defendant *to* Irving other than a Friday?"

"Yes, sir. It was the Thursday before the President was coming to visit."

"And did you drive him to the Book Depository on Friday, November twenty-two, 1963?"

"Yes, sir."

"Did he have anything with him that morning?"

"Well, not exactly with him. When I got in the car, I noticed a package, a brown paper sack, on the backseat of the car, and shortly thereafter, I asked him about it."

"What did you learn from your question?"

"Lee told me the package contained curtain rods, and reminded me that he had asked me for the ride the day before so he could get them for his little room over there in Oak Cliff."

"When you arrived at the Depository, did the defendant take the package with him?"

"Yes, he did. He got it out of the backseat and walked off ahead of me."

"No further questions. Your witness."

Barnes dropped a pencil he had been doodling with and took his time getting up and heading for the witness stand.

"Well, Mr. Frazier, how are you doing today?" he began.

"Okay. A little nervous, I guess."

"That's normal, I can assure you, so just relax and try to remember as best you can the events that I ask you about. Now, this brown sack, did you get a good look at it, or just a glance?"

"I'd have to say a good look, 'cause I seen it clear when I opened the door to get in my car—it was just laying there on the backseat, and then I seen it again when Lee took it out of the car and carried it."

"Mr. Frazier, and I'm asking you this even though the prosecutor should have, I show you Exhibit 1304, the bag that was found near the three cartridge hulls on the sixth floor. Do you recognize this bag?"

"No, sir."

"Is there anything that you can tell the court that prevents you from saying you recognize it, much less being able to make a positive i.d?"

"Well, it just doesn't look like it, and besides that, it's much too long."

"How long was the bag you saw?"

"I told the police then, and I'll tell you now—it was about two feet long. I can still see it, over on the passenger side of the backseat, taking up a small amount of space."

"Mr. Frazier, what kind of car do you own?"

"An old Chevy. Fifty-three, I b'lieve."

"Would you characterize it as a roomy car?"

Matthews objected. "Calls for a conclusion, Your Honor."

"I think a person can make a reasonable statement about the size of his car without giving an opinion, Mr. Prosecutor; I'll allow it."

"It's not a real big car. It's a sedan that'll hold three in front and three in back, but it's tight."

"And the bag did or did not take up a lot of room in that backseat?"

"No, sir. It did not."

"Mr. Frazier, did you and I measure your backseat?"

"Yes, we did, sixty-two inches," Frazier answered, while Graves whispered to Vincent, "This guy doesn't miss a trick. He's wasting his time defending winos in Minnesota."

"Now, Mr. Frazier. For the Mannlicher-Carcano rifle that Mr. Oswald allegedly owned to be in a bag, even if dismantled, would require a bag of thirty-five to thirty-six inches. Did you see a bag, thirty-five to thirty-six inches, that took up fifty-eight percent of your backseat?"

"No, sir. What I saw didn't fill half the seat."

"Do you have any other reason to say that the package was not longer than two feet?"

"Well, before Lee walked away, he waited for me, while I revved the engine a little to charge the battery, and while I did that, he took it out of the back, put one end in the palm of his hand—his right hand, and he put the other end under his armpit." Frazier reached across his chest with his left hand to show that the end of the package pushed up the right armpit.

"Are you saying that he had this package, which the prosecution would like us to believe was the assassination rifle,

and he patiently waited for you so you could walk in together?"

"Yes, sir."

Barnes walked behind the defense table and took a two-
foot long two-by-four beam, and a ruler, and reapproached
Frazier. "How does this board compare in size to the package
you saw being carried by the defendant?"

"It's about the size I saw."

"Please measure this piece of wood for me, Mr. Frazier."

Frazier did so, announcing, "Twenty-six inches."

"Let's write 'twenty-six inches' on this board, and Mr. Frazier, suppose you sign your name on it with this marker, and
then let's go see how it fits the defendant's armpit."

Matthews was on his feet. "I must object to these irrelevant
theatrics, Your Honor. This proceeding is not about boards
being carried into the Depository."

"Mr. Barnes?"

"Your Honor, if the prosecutor can take the Mannlicher-
Carcano rifle, serial number C2766, apart so its largest piece
is twenty-six inches long, I'd be happy to substitute that for
this simple board. But this man, Buell Wesley Frazier, is the
only person who can demonstrate—or disprove that the defendant carried a large or small parcel into that building. For
that reason, he has given us his recollection, his best recollection, that the package fit the defendant in a certain way.
This test, and a similar one with a board the size of a disassembled Mannlicher should tell the jury what they need to
know. Furthermore, Your Honor, I think we should see CE
2009 at this time," Barnes added, before pausing for the
screen to come up, which took a little time.

"Could we have page two of that document, please?" After
another pause, Barnes drew the court's and the jury's attention to the first full paragraph, which indicated that Buell
Wesley Frazier had shown the FBI where the package began
and ended as it rested on his backseat. The FBI measurement of the area was twenty-seven inches. Barnes asked that
the document be kept handy.

"Objection overruled as to this board, Mr. Matthews; if
you'd like to substitute the broken down Mannlicher, as best
evidence, in the subsequent test, that is your choice."

On cue, Oswald stood and was escorted to the front of the defense table by Robert Dean. Frazier walked slowly, carrying the board. Barnes then gave instructions: "Please place the board as you remember seeing the defendant holding the package on November twenty-second."

Frazier, saying nothing, took one end of the board and skittishly gripped Oswald's right hand, which the defendant, on Barnes's instruction, had already cupped. Then Frazier put the board along Oswald's ribs and fitted it snugly under his armpit. Barnes then asked Frazier to take a few steps back, and instructed Oswald to make one full but slow rotation. He then took the board from Oswald and held on to it, making it a very visible evidentiary prop. "You may sit down again, gentlemen." Then, to Frazier: "Is that what you saw on November twenty-second?"

"It's very close, but it wasn't a board," he answered.

"No, you told us, it was a bag—a small bag. Yet in this FBI report, Mr. Frazier, on the bottom of page one, it says, 'Frazier glanced back and noticed a long package.' Did you tell the FBI it was a 'long' package?"

"I don't know why I would have."

Barnes turned to the prosecution table and addressed Mr. Matthews. "Mr. Prosecutor, do you have a preference for the second test?"

"The assassination weapon," Matthews sniped, trying to plant a seed in the jury's mind.

Barnes glared at Matthews, then turned to the bench: "Your Honor, I did not leave my family in Minnesota and give up all this time, nor do I believe the state of Texas invested a great deal of money to see justice done here, only to have the whole process undone by a remark like that, which would cause most attorneys to ask for a mistrial."

"Are you petitioning for one, Mr. Barnes?"

"No, Your Honor. Perhaps, though, passions could be moderated . . ."

"The jury is instructed to disregard the remark which suggested that the weapon on the table was the 'assassination weapon'; the prosecutor is put on notice that the court will *not* tolerate such remarks."

"The Mannlicher, then," Barnes went on.

"As you will," Matthews muttered.

Barnes quickly fetched a screwdriver from his briefcase, and while working on the rifle, he continued to question the witness. "Mr. Frazier, just as a curiosity, in all the times you delivered Mr. Oswald to Irving, do you have any recollection that he carried paper and tape with him?"

"Police asked me that too, and lots of times, and I know for a fact that he never brought anything with him. First couple of times it was warm enough, he didn't even have a jacket. Amazed me, sometimes, him going out there for the weekend and didn't even have a change of clothes. So I noticed, and there wasn't anything."

Barnes had completed the quick breakdown of the rifle. "Now, Mr. Frazier, let's take this largest piece, the stock—better still,"—Barnes's voice rose for dramatic effect—"let's put this large stock of the alleged,"—dragging out the word "alleged"—"rifle in the alleged bag. Why don't you do that, Mr. Frazier, and pack it tight."

When Frazier completed his work while Barnes stood behind the defense table, he was requested to reposition the bag in Oswald's arm. Robert Dean again accompanied the defendant to a point where he could be seen by the jury, and when Frazier put the rifle and bag in Oswald's arm, the end of the bag came to his right ear. Oswald again made one slow turn. Frazier returned to the witness stand, and Barnes moved into position near Oswald. "Does this look like what you saw on November twenty-second?"

"No, sir. Not at all."

Dean saw to it that all exhibits were restored and replaced while Barnes paced briefly, seemingly lost in thought, then asked, "Did you see Mr. Oswald, on November twenty-second, actually take the bag into the Depository?"

"No. He had gotten ahead of me. I'm not one to hurry to work."

"Did you see him during the A.M. hours of November twenty-second *after* he entered the building ahead of you?"

"Oh, sure. We all work in kind of close quarters there, and several of the boys was laying wood on the sixth floor, which meant fewer of us to fill orders. Lee was around regularly."

"Mr. Frazier, prior to November twenty-two, how long had you been employed at the Depository?"

"I was hired in September of 1963."

"Full time or part time?"

"Full time."

"The reason I asked that is there is a persistent rumor that the defendant was 'placed' at that location when in fact there were no jobs there—was it reasonably common for new employees to be hired?"

"Well, I got the job, and they needed Lee."

"Mr. Frazier, did you have any previous employment where you worked regularly with curtain rods?"

"Yes. I worked in a department store that sold curtain rods, and I packed plenty of them."

"To the best of your knowledge, did Mr. Oswald know that fact?"

"No. We never discussed it."

"So when he told you the package on the backseat—the one he carried away from your car toward the Depository, but not necessarily into it—contained curtain rods, even your own experience did not tell you that he was lying?"

"No. He said curtain rods, it looked right to me, and he had not lied to me before."

Barnes knew he had scored points, but it was clearly time to change direction: "And where were you, and what did you observe during the presidential motorcade?"

"I must object, Your Honor. There was no foundation laid for this cross-examination in direct examination."

"Mr. Barnes?"

"May we approach, Your Honor?"

"Come ahead."

Barnes spoke in hushed tones. "With all due respect, Your Honor, Mr. Matthews, if I can't ask these questions now, I'll call Frazier as a defense witness, and that's fine with me, calling the prosecution's first witness as a defense witness. Won't look good, but it will be done." Matthews was deflated. "I withdraw my objection, Your Honor." Barnes thanked him. Matthews kept an expletive under his breath.

"Would you like the question repeated, Mr. Frazier?"

"No. I remember I was in front of the Depository, and after

Mr. Kennedy went by, well, he had hardly gotten by, I heard a sound and if you ever been around motorcycles you know how they backfire, and so I thought one of them motorcycles backfired. Then there was commotion and I realized it was shots, and I heard two more of the same type. And from where I was standing, it sounded like it was coming from down by the railroad tracks, there, you know, down where that underpass is."

"So, if I understand you correctly, you heard three shots, although you did not identify the first report immediately as a shot. And they came from well down the street, not directly over your head."

"That's right."

"What did you do, Mr. Frazier, let's say within one minute of the last shot you heard?"

"Well, I seen some of the commotion, then I went back into the building."

Barnes almost pounced, because he had heard what he wanted, and he didn't want it lost on the jury. "Indeed you did. You went back into the building! Would you have done that if you had the slightest hint or inkling that the shots originated there?"

"Objection. Calls for a conclusion."

"Sustained." Matthews gave Barnes a grin.

"Just one more thing, Mr. Frazier. On the evening of November twenty-two, did you spend any time with the Dallas police?"

"Yes, I did."

"Please tell the jury what occurred."

"Well, first off, I told them basically what I said a few minutes ago, that Lee used to ask me for rides out to Irving on Friday and back to Dallas on Monday. I also told them about Thursday, going out, and Friday, coming in, and the package. And then, well, it got kind of ugly. They asked me the same question over and over, and I told them what I knew to be the truth. I told them how long the package was, and how it fit under Lee's armpit. But they just kept asking."

"Were you asked to take a lie detector test?"

Matthews slowly rose, preventing Frazier from answering.

"Your Honor, I fail to see any relevance in this line of questioning."

"Mr. Barnes?"

"Your Honor, not only was Mr. Frazier asked to take a lie detector test, but he took it. In addition, I show you part of Exhibit 2003, a receipt number 11064 for, and I quote, 'Confiscated, Evidence,' to wit, one Rifle, British Enfield, therein described, and ten Rounds British R P 303 Ammo; Tag Date, 11/22/63; arr: Frazier, Buell Wesley. Your Honor, the prosecution's leadoff witness was a suspect in this case, however briefly, or his belongings were seized in order to make him more responsive to the questions being asked. Lastly, my pretrial interview with the witness led me to believe that all of this was done with no regard for legal representation for this witness. There's clearly a relevance here, Your Honor."

Judge Davis affected a pained expression, swiveled from facing Barnes and leaned to his right to have maximum eye contact with the witness. "They make you take a lie detector test, young man?"

"Yes, sir."

Davis continued to ask the questions, "Is there any other item that defense counsel just mentioned—the gun, the bullets, no lawyer—that all accurate?"

Frazier was becoming unnerved. "Yes, Your Honor," with his voice cracking.

"Mr. Matthews, your objection is overruled. Mr. Barnes?"

"One last question, Mr. Frazier. Since the Dallas police were kind enough to establish that you own an expensive, foreign rifle, I want you to reconsider what you told us about that bag—as you saw it on the backseat—and as you saw the defendant carry it in the manner you described. I want you to tell the court if there's any thought in your mind that the package you saw could have contained *that rifle* over there, that we took apart."

Frazier looked down at the floor, and Matthew suppressed a desperate desire to object, but did so knowing he had taken a huge beating on this witness and couldn't afford another technical defeat. Frazier lifted his head, and spoke deliberately, "Judge, Mr. Barnes, Mr. Matthews, I don't know, and it has haunted me and will haunt me, what was in that bag.

But I can tell you one thing—I refuse to believe it was that gun over there unless it comes apart a whole lot smaller."

"Thank you, Mr. Frazier; no further questions. Move to admit CE 2003 and CE 2009, Your Honor."

"So moved. Redirect?" Judge Davis asked.

"Nothing further," Matthews answered, upbeat, with a stiff upper lip.

"You're excused, Mr. Frazier. I thank you for your testimony today—I'm sure having personal belongings seized was not easy for you. I must ask you, however, not to discuss your testimony with anyone—newspapers, other employees who might testify. I realize you may need to share this with your wife, but if you do, ask her to keep silent. Thank you again, sir."

As Frazier left the witness stand, he avoided looking at either Matthews or Barnes, and seemed relieved that perhaps, finally, the ordeal was behind him. Barnes was deep in conversation with Dean, whose assessment was that the first prosecution witness had been neutralized. On the prosecution side, the debate raged between Matthews, Graves, and Vincent as to whether to call Frazier's sister, Linnie Mae Randle, the only other Oswald-bag witness. It was finally decided to hold her, but Matthews was not convinced that they had, in fact, put the bag, much less a bag containing a rifle, into the Depository, nor was he thrilled with the next witnesses, the three "colored boys from the fifth floor." He knew they would be decent witnesses, but he knew Barnes could turn their stories to his advantage. To Matthews, however, it was moot; he had no choice.

"Mr. Matthews?"

"Your Honor, the state calls Harold Norman."

While the young, black youth was escorted into the courtroom and sworn in, Carolyn Jeffries handed Barnes a folder marked "Jarman, et al." Barnes was a little surprised that Matthews called "et al." first.

Matthews approached the witness and spoke with a sense of renewed confidence. "Mr. Norman, where were you employed on November twenty-two, 1963?"

"Texas School Book Depository, Dallas, Texas," the witness answered, in something of a monotone.

"Would you please tell the court where you were when the presidential motorcade passed by?"

"I, uh, well, they was three of us—myself, Bonnie Ray Williams, and Junior Jarman, and we were in the corner windows, facing Elm Street, on the fifth floor of the Book Depository."

"For the record, Mr. Norman, would the person you named as 'Junior Jarman' also be known as James Jarman?"

"Yes, sir. But everybody call him Junior, you know."

"Thank you. Now, I am going to show you an affidavit, Exhibit CE four hundred ninety-three, which is a statement made by you, and signed by you, to Special Agent William N. Carter of the United States Secret Service. Your Honor, I would like this admitted into evidence at this time." Judge Davis nodded, made a few notes, and indicated the prosecutor should continue. "Do you recognize your signature on this document, Mr. Norman?"

"Yes."

"Now, to the sixth paragraph. Would you please read the highlighted portion of the statement you signed."

"This here?" Norman asked.

Matthews did not want to prompt his witness, but had little choice.

"Just after the President passed by, I heard a shot and several seconds later, I heard two more shots. I knew that the shots had come from directly above me, and I could hear the expended cartridges fall to the floor. I could also hear the bolt action of the rifle. I also saw some dust fall from the ceiling of the fifth floor and I felt sure that whoever had fired the shots was directly above me."

"Thank you, Mr. Norman. Now, that statement was made some time ago, uh, December fourth of 1963, to be exact. As you remember that terrible moment now, Mr. Norman, are you still convinced that the shots were being fired from above your head?"

"Yes, sir."

"No further questions. Your witness."

Barnes knew he had to make the best of a no-win situation, so he walked to the far end of the jury box and spoke to the witness from a distance. "Mr. Norman, you stated that you believed on November twenty-second that 'the shots' had come from above your head. From all the evidence I've seen in this case, I would certainly agree with you that some shots were fired from the window you suggest. Do we agree with each other so far?"

"I think so."

"Good. Now, can you say for certain that 'the shots'— meaning all the shots, were fired from above your head?"

"No. But the ones I heard were above my head."

"That's fine, Mr. Norman. I only want you to testify to what you heard. By the way, when you were called to testify before the presidential commission on March twenty-fourth, 1964, did you not *deny* that you told the Secret Service agent that you knew the shots came from overhead and did you not also deny the way the statement was worded about several seconds later?"

"Yes."

Barnes wanted to drive the point home: "Yes, you did testify that those parts of your signed statement were incorrect?"

"Yes, I did."

"Help me out, here, Mr. Norman. Was it you, or the Secret Service agent who was confused on December fourth?"

"Musta been him, 'cause I know what I said."

"Then why don't you tell us what you said."

"I said I thought the shots came from above, but I didn't see any dust falling on anybody's head."

"Fair enough. Then why would this Secret Service man lie?"

"Objection."

"Sustained." Barnes didn't care; the jury heard it.

"Were there any other government or official documents that have not told your story accurately?"

Norman looked nervous. It was not a comfortable feeling to be so far from home and to be making liars out of the government's high-priced policemen. "Well, when I talked to the President's Commission, they asked me about another interview, but that was with an FBI man."

"Please tell the jury about that."

"I wish I could give you the exact details, but the best I

remember was they said, 'Did you tell the FBI what it says in this report?' and I said, 'I didn't say or remember anything like that.' And then they said something else, and I told them 'no' to that too. It was something about me leanin' out the window to look up."

"Then, Mr. Norman, how does your signature get on these documents if they are—according to what you're telling us under oath today—incorrect?"

Norman stared at Barnes with a look that could have killed. "What's yo' name, lawyer?"

Barnes was taken aback. "Eddie Barnes. I apologize that we weren't introduced, but now that we have been, could you answer my question?"

"Eddie Barnes, when a FBI or Secret Agent puts a paper in front of you and says 'this is your statement, would you read it and sign it,' he's saying, 'sign or you one dead colored boy.' "

Matthews wanted to explode but found it difficult to be faced with another one of his own hostile witnesses. He let it pass. Barnes pressed on. "Okay, Mr. Norman, but you did hear some shots, and you thought they came from overhead, right?"

"That's right."

Barnes now walked over and picked up the rifle on the evidence table, then walked as far behind the prosecution table as he could, to be at about equal distance from the witness and the jury. "It's 12:30, November twenty-two. A presidential parade is going by. Hundreds of people are cheering. Eighteen motorcycles are within one hundred fifty feet of you, and you *heard . . .*" Barnes worked the bolt on the rifle three times and then planted a seed in the jurors' minds. "I could tell the jury had trouble hearing this bolt clearly in this virtually empty courtroom, yet you had your head inside the window, and you heard it?"

"That's what I said." Barnes knew he had heard the perfect answer.

"And this empty cartridge, which weighs a fraction of an ounce," Barnes was now at the jury box, his back to the defense table, "I repeat, a fraction of an ounce, all that noise outside, and you heard this hit the floor of a warehouse built to hold hundreds of tons of books?" Barnes then dropped the cartridge.

"That's what I said."

"Subsequent to the shots, did you hear the elevator?"

"Not for several minutes at least."

"Subsequent to the shots, where did you go?"

"To the west end of the building, to see what was going on in the railroad yards."

Barnes spoke softly, hoping for jury, if not witness sympathy. "Here again, Mr. Norman, I have a problem. You said you heard shots right over your head. The President has just gone by. Now if you said, 'I hid out' or some such, I could believe that. But I have difficulty with someone going to the other end of the building when the potential assassin of the President is right over his head. It casts doubt in my mind that at the moment of the event, you believed it. Maybe later, you thought, 'hey, that was right above me,' but at that second, if you had believed that, based on that statement you made to me before—which was defiant, but was made *by a man with principles who believes what he's saying,* I think you would have gone to those stairs and caught that fellow. Did you hear anyone come down the stairs?"

"No."

"Was the defendant, Lee Oswald, the person on the sixth floor firing the shots?"

"I have no idea."

"So, we've got a loud parade, a shooter over your head that you ignore to go sightseeing, you can hear a bolt work and cartridges fall amongst the confusion. That about it?"

"That's what I said."

"You also said, 'Sign or you one dead colored boy.' " Barnes walked slowly to the defense table, flipped through a meaningless folder to allow his statement to sink in, then, almost as a casual afterthought, concluded, "Oh, no more questions; thank you, Mr. Norman."

Before Graves could even speak, Matthews told him there would be no redirect, to prevent a recross. There was discussion, however, about calling Junior Jarman, whose story was inconsistent, but Matthews insisted they had to put him second, and finish strong with Bonnie Ray Williams. To avoid one of the three would have planted too many suspicions.

"Your Honor, the state calls James 'Junior' Jarman."

A more dapper, slightly older black man walked to the witness stand with confident strides to be sworn, pronouncing the "I do," with vigor. Barnes wondered why to himself, then very quietly asked Oswald, "Did you know these guys were down there?" trying to catch him off-guard. Oswald replied with the silent look that the Dallas police had come to dislike strongly.

Matthews interrupted that sideshow: "Mr. Jarman, were you on the fifth floor of the Book Depository with Harold Norman and Bonnie Ray Williams when the presidential motorcade went by?"

"Yes, I was."

"Please tell the court how many shots you heard."

"Three, although the first one, what I think was the first one, sounded like a backfire."

"Did you do anything to make your knowledge available to police authorities?"

"Yes, sir. When I left the building, I told the officer that I believed they came from inside the building."

"No further questions."

Barnes knew contrived questions and answers when he heard them, so this didn't seem to pose a great challenge. "Mr. Jarman, along with Mr. Norman and Mr. Williams, did you testify before the President's Commission last March?"

"Yes, sir."

"And when they asked you where the shots came from, what did you tell them?"

Suddenly, much of Jarman's entering confidence faded. "I told them at first I thought the shots came from below and to the left. That is what I thought."

"Let's get directly to the point. You were in the same room with Harold Norman and Bonnie Ray Williams when they testified last March. But let's hear your story. What, exactly, did you hear above your head—that is, on the sixth floor of the Depository? What did you hear happening up there?"

"Absolutely nothing."

"Where did you go when the shots ended?"

"To the west end of the building, where the new flooring was going. We was watching the police and what all going on over there."

"While you were there, was there discussion among the three of you—you, Williams, and Norman, about what had happened during the shooting?"

"Well, Norman said the shot came from above us, inside the building. And somebody, and I can't say which one it was, talked about hearing the shells hit the floor."

"But you heard no shots overhead, nor bullets hitting the floor?"

"No, sir."

"You testified you heard shots from left and below. Yet you told police it was inside the building. It could have been below, in the building, but not below and left. It is important that you give us your best recollection on that."

"Well, I remember hearing left, and low, like maybe a lower floor on the building across Houston Street on Elm, but that's a dim recollection, and maybe it's just a guess based on the low and left feeling I had. But then when we talked, I guess they sort of convinced me—I know they believed it, that it was in the Depository."

"Let's try to jog your memory. Do you recall a pattern to the shots?"

"Well, I thought the first one could have been a backfire—I didn't think it was a shot at all, but then there were two that were shots, for sure, and the third shot was fired right behind the second."

"Last question, now that your memory's heated up: did you hear anything above your head to cause you to have any suspicion whatsoever that an assassin was shooting at the President from that location?"

"No."

"Thank you, Mr. Jarman."

"No redirect, Your Honor," Matthews announced, hoping to sound as if he'd carried the day.

"Not much 'direct' in the first place," Dean told Jeffries. "But then again, we suspected what they gave the prosecution was weak, so we can't say Matthews has let us down."

"The state calls Bonnie Ray Williams."

Barnes got Dean's attention, telling him five would get him ten that Matthews would regret his choice of witnesses, concluding, "He doesn't know it, but this guy's going to do him more harm than good."

Matthews approached the young witness in a sort of down-home neighborly fashion. "Mr. Williams, we've heard testimony this morning that you were on the fifth floor of the Texas School Book Depository, in the windows in the southeast corner as the presidential motorcade came by. Is that correct?"

"Yes."

"For the record, will you tell the court whom you were with?"

"Harold Norman and Junior Jarman," he replied, keeping his answers clipped.

"Will you tell the court what you heard with respect to the number and location of the shots fired?"

"Well, I think three. First is vague. Second and third, though, I remember. One behind the other. Quick. And the second shot, it sounded like it was right in the building, the second and third shot. And it sounded—it even shook the building—the side we were on. Cement fell on my head."

"Are you testifying that there was a connection between the shots and the cement falling on your head?"

Williams chuckled. "Well, if it was from the floor beneath me, I doubt the cement would have jumped up into my hair."

Matthews was not amused. "Please answer the question as stated."

"Well, at the time, the noise, the vibrations, I felt that something up above caused the cement to fall on me, and the only thing that seemed to be happening was the shots."

"Thank you, Mr. Williams; no further questions."

Barnes was hoping once again for an end run that would allow questions not covered in direct examination, but first he had to do a damage-control operation on this latest batch of testimony. "Mr. Williams, you've indicated that what you think were the second and third shots were fired quite close together, is that correct?"

"One behind the other."

"How close—one second? two seconds? three . . . four
. . . five—to the closest you can come."

"Maybe not one, but pretty likely less than two. Nobody
was countin', but it was quick. Bang . . . bang."

Barnes sidled over to the defense table, casually asking,
"And cement fell on your head?"

"Yes, sir."

"Mr. Williams, I'm not going to try to either bore or confuse
you with meaningless physics equations. It's enough to know
that the scientists who reach the conclusions understand
them. But I'm going to tell you this. If you fired a blank from
that rifle over there, four inches away but in direct line with
your everyday window, the glass would not be affected. And
you want this jury to believe that the building vibrated, and
cement fell on your head?"

"Something had to cause it."

"Indeed," Barnes answered, figuring that might just confuse the jury and win a point or two. "Well, Mr. Williams, you
viewed the parade from the fifth floor. What time did you
arrive at the fifth floor window?"

"Twelve-twenty, approximately."

"And where were you before that?"

Williams had hoped it would not get to this. "On the floor
above, eating lunch."

"Directly above?" Barnes asked. "In the area where it vibrated a few minutes later?"

"Yes, sir."

"How long did this lunch take?"

"I can't say exactly, though I sure wish I could. It could
have been five minutes, and it could have been more than
ten."

"For your comfort while you ate your lunch, did you create
a makeshift seat or anything like that out of book cartons?"

"I didn't sit on the floor, I know that."

"Did your lunch consist of fried chicken and a bottle of
pop?"

"Yes."

"For however long you were on the sixth floor, did you see
the defendant, Lee Oswald, or anyone else there during that
time?"

"I didn't see anyone there while I was up there."

"What had your work consisted of that morning?"

Matthews rose slowly, unbuttoning his suit coat as he did so. "I have to object, Your Honor. I fail to see relevancy in Mr. Williams's lunch, and as for how he spent his morning, we know when the shots were fired."

"I see a very clear relevancy in the fact that Mr. Williams was on the sixth floor until approximately twelve-twenty, Mr. Matthews. Now, Mr. Barnes, are you going to show the court relevancy on this other matter?"

"I believe so, Your Honor."

"Overruled."

Barnes wanted this point driven home to the jury, so he repeated the question. Williams matter-of-factly replied that he was putting down new flooring on the sixth floor. "Did that require you to move any of the book stock?"

"We had to move quite a lot of them boxes—put them over in the southeast corner—made quite a pile when we were done."

"Where was this pile of cartons?"

"Right behind there where I ate, the area where they said the shots were fired from."

Barnes feigned amazement: "Are you telling us that the flooring crew, and not the assassin, built that shield of cartons around the southeast corner window?"

Williams seemed defensive: "Had to; they were in the way. We didn't know somebody was gonna hide in there."

"Of course you didn't," Barnes said to calm him down. "Of course you didn't. Let's get back to the shots. Did you hear anything falling to the floor?"

"No."

"Could you identify the sound of a rifle—the bolt action—being worked—not the firing, but the sound of the bolt?"

"No."

"I've asked Mr. Jarman and Mr. Norman this question, so I need to ask you. When the shooting ended, where did you go?"

"To the other end of the building, to see what the commotion was in the railroad yard."

"Did you at any time in those few minutes, ever think that

maybe you could have done something about what had happened on the sixth floor?"

"I know my answer, and that's 'no.' Harold and Junior and I talked about it since, and we've said to each other that it just never occurred to us at the time."

"Very well. Just one more area to explore. When you moved those boxes to get them out of the way, to put down the flooring, did you pick them up, one at a time, and carry them down to the southeast corner and gently place them down?"

"Well, we sure didn't carry more than one, 'cause they are heavy. If there was a dolly, maybe one of us used it, but some of us carried. And we didn't exactly gently place them down. Pick them up, put them down."

"Mr. Williams, I have a letter written by J. Edgar Hoover, Director of the FBI, dated September fifteen of last year, which indicates that the FBI had determined that the average box of books weighed fifty-five pounds. Sound about right to you?"

"I won't argue it."

"Now here's the point, Mr. Williams. You've testified that you, and others, moved an awful lot of boxes to replace flooring on the morning on November twenty-two. 'Pick them up, put them down,' you said, when I asked if they were gently placed. Now if a falling cartridge, weighing less than one ounce can bring cement down on your head, Mr. Williams, how many complaints were there from fifth floor employees that day that cement was falling on their heads from fifty-five-pound boxes?"

Matthews was up and vocal: "Objection, Your Honor."

"Sustained, and the jury will disregard the last question."

No, they won't, thought Barnes. I'm praying they don't. "That was the last question, Your Honor," subtly reminding the jury of it. "Thank you, Mr. Williams."

Matthews felt like the ceiling had fallen on him instead of his witness, with the equally uncomfortable feeling that he was nothing for four on the first day of testimony. "Could we have a moment, Your Honor?"

"A moment, Mr. Matthews," Judge Davis answered, while Dean leaned past Oswald to tell Barnes that their concerns about the three men in the window under the sniper's nest had been unfounded.

And what a moment it was. While everyone at the defense table remained as low-key as possible, a vigorous debate raged at the prosecution table, as Graves and Vincent tried, without success, to convince Matthews that the case would be seriously weakened in the first day if they didn't put on somebody—anybody—who had something solid to say, and was unimpeachable. The veteran Matthews calmed that debate by reminding them of Barnes's opening statement: "The jury already knows that we don't have *the witness,* and for all purposes, we don't. Beyond that, who do we really have, to grab out of sequence, that has something solid to say and is unimpeachable? Humes? Roy Kellerman? Frazier, the FBI firearms expert, who will testify that the shot was easy but his shooters couldn't do it? Please, spare me that. We'll have to go with them, but later. For now, we build slowly. The jury isn't going to convict or acquit at this point—we know that. If we had three rock-solid, unimpeachable eyewitnesses, we could put them on and then coast. But they don't exist, and we've known that since day one. So, since we don't appear to have quality, we go for quantity. We just have to gradually let them know that the event happened from the window and let the evidence point to Oswald. Otherwise, our best chance is that Barnes will change Oswald's plea to 'guilty.' You s'pose that's going to happen?" Graves and Vincent accepted Matthews's logic.

"Thank you, Your Honor. The state calls Amos Lee Euins."

Graves and Vincent recoiled as soon as they heard Matthews's choice, for while they accepted his logic, they knew instinctively that another young black boy, hard on the heels of Norman, Jarman, and Williams, would prove less than valuable to a Texas jury.

Matthews sidled over to the witness stand after the young boy was sworn in. "How are you today, young man?"

"Fine, I guess. Nervous."

"Well, don't worry. You just tell the truth when I ask you questions, and, of course, when Mr. Barnes asks you questions. To start with, how old are you, Amos?"

"Sixteen. Be seventeen this Sunday."

"So you were fifteen on the day the President was killed?"

"Yes, sir."

"Okay, Amos. Now, to refresh your recollection, I show you Exhibit CE 367, a voluntary statement you made, and signed, to the sheriff's department, county of Dallas. Would you look at this and tell the court if that's your signature?"

Barnes interrupted: "Your Honor, could we have that on the screens, please? Perhaps the jury should see these exhibits."

"That's what they're for," the judge agreed.

A miffed prosecutor handed Carson the document and then had to stand at the witness stand amidst dead air while the screens came to life and the document appeared. Matthews then resumed, "Is that your signature?"

"Yes, it is."

"Now, Amos, even though everyone can see it, why don't you read the part after where you tell how you waved to the President and he waved back."

"It says, 'I watched the car on down the street and about the time the car got near the black and white sign I heard a shot. I started looking around and then I looked up in the red brick building. I saw a man in a window with a gun and I saw him shoot twice. He then stepped back behind some boxes. I could . . .'"

"Thank you, Amos. Does it say further along anything about the man?"

"Uh, here. 'This was a white man, he did not have on a hat. I just saw this man for a few seconds.'"

Matthews decided to take a gamble. "Could it have been the second man from the end at that table over there?"

Euins didn't flinch. "It could have been anybody in this room, for all I know."

Matthews made the most of the testimony. "I understand, son. I want to commend you for finding a police officer on that day, and for making a prompt statement. And thank you for coming here today. I have no more questions for you. Your Honor, I'd like CE 367 admitted, and it's no longer needed."

"Oh yes it is, counselor," Barnes reminded him, walking toward the witness stand. "You read very well, Amos. Suppose you read the part of that statement you signed that is between the other parts you read to the jury."

"Okay. Uh, yeah 'I could tell the gun was a rifle and it sounded like an automatic rifle the way he was shooting. I just saw a little bit of the barrel, and some of the trigger housing.' That's the part I didn't read."

"It certainly is. 'Automatic rifle,' " Barnes repeated for emphasis, pacing in front of the jury. "What gave you that idea?"

Matthews remained seated, but objected. "Your Honor, he's only a boy. All weapons will look sinister and menacing to a child."

"Mr. Barnes?"

"Mr. Euins is Mr. Matthews's witness, and he wanted CE 367 put into evidence. All I ask is an equal chance at it."

"Sounds reasonable. Overruled."

"Tell me about an automatic rifle, Amos."

"Well, some of the shots was real close . . . bang, bang, you know."

"You said 'Some of the shots,' " Barnes continued. "How many did you hear?"

"Four."

"All by the person in the window?"

"Two from there that I saw. The rest, I don't know."

"Okay. You *saw*. You said you *saw* a little bit of the barrel and the trigger housing,"—reaching for the rifle—"so you saw this much [indicating] of the gun. Did you see this telescopic sight?"

"No."

Barnes moved in close. "Amos, take this rifle and show me what you saw." The witness then took the rifle, put it against his right shoulder, and put his left hand near the end of the stock. Then he leaned a bit out from the witness stand to depict the rifle out of the window. "That is the way you remember it, Amos?"

"Yes, sir."

"What shoulder is the weapon against?"

"My right one."

"Yes, your right shoulder. It's just odd that the gun was sighted for a left-handed person."

Matthews objected. "He's making his closing argument."

"Sustained."

Barnes retrieved the gun. "Amos, I'm curious about something." Matthews cringed, having already heard this tone in Barnes's voice enough for one day. "You testified before the President's Commission last March. Do you remember that?"

"Yes."

"Amos, I read what you told them, and I'm concerned because it conflicts a little bit with what you've told us today. Did you tell them last March that you saw a white man with the rifle?"

"I told them I didn't get enough look at the features to know if it was a white man or a colored man."

"What did you tell them about the head of the man with the rifle?" Barnes was now taking the gamble.

"I told them I seen a bald spot on this man's head. He had a bald spot on his head, and that was what I remembered most in those few seconds."

"So how does that exhibit on the screen come out white man, and no hat—can you tell us about that?"

"Objection, Your Honor. Calls for a conclusion."

Barnes seized the opportunity: "Your Honor, I ask the court to let the boy answer. If it is a conclusion, then it should be stricken. But I think he can answer without an opinion."

"Answer the question, son."

"Well, when I told them, a couple times, about the bald spot, then they said, 'Well, then he wasn't wearing no hat.' Then they asked me if a bald spot would be easier to see on a white man or a colored man, and I said, 'Probably easier on a white man.' But I never said it was no white man."

"Amos, you were asked a few minutes ago if you could identify the defendant, and you indicated that you couldn't. Would you look carefully at him now and tell us if he has the kind of bald spot you saw?" Barnes then turned to Oswald and told him to lean his head forward so the witness could view the top of his head.

"No bald spot there that I can see."

"Thank you, Amos. Have a good birthday Sunday."

"No redirect, Your Honor. The state calls Geneva L. Hine."

Barnes did a double take and looked over at Dean with one eyebrow raised, inasmuch as the prosecution was clearly not hauling out its "big guns" yet. As he did so, a prim, thirtyish young woman entered the witness box and was sworn in.

"Miss Hine," Matthews began, "please tell the Court where you were employed on November twenty-two, 1963."

"I have been employed at the Texas School Book Depository since 1956."

"Objection," Barnes said, without looking up. "Nonresponsive."

"Sustained. Miss Hine, please answer the question as asked."

Giving Barnes a holier-than-thou "go suck an egg" look, she replied, "On November twenty-two, 1963, a Friday, I was employed at the Texas School Book Depository." Barnes wrote "touchy" on his pad and showed it to Oswald.

"Thank you. Now, where were you when the President's motorcade passed the Book Depository?"

"I was in the office area of the second floor, facing out onto Elm Street so I could view the parade."

"Did you hear shots, and if so, how many?"

"Leading, Your Honor, but as long as Mr. Matthews doesn't mind if I ask an identical question down the road, I won't object," Barnes interrupted. He knew this nonessential witness was just a nuisance and he wanted to send a message to Matthews that he could be just as much of one.

"Mr. Matthews?"

"Agreed, Your Honor. Miss Hine?"

"I heard three shots."

"Could you say with certitude where the shots came from?"

Barnes stood up and dropped the pencil on the legal pad. "Your Honor, unless she saw the shots fired, she can't say with certitude where the shots came from. If Mr. Matthews wants to put an opinion on the record, fine. I have witnesses that also have strong opinions about the origins of the shots. But let's call it what it is. Ask the witness where she thinks the shots came from. If she can say 'with certitude,' better still. It will make the jury's job easier."

The witness was rattled. "I believe they came from inside

the building, because the building vibrated from the explosion coming in."

"Thank you, Miss Hine. Your witness, Mr. Barnes."

Barnes didn't even stand. "Miss Hine, did you see the man
sitting next to me fire any shots?"

"No. I was alone on the second floor."

"Miss Hine, you just said, 'The building vibrated from the
explosion coming in.' Does that suggest to you the possibility
that the explosion could have occurred outside of the Depository building and what you heard, was, as you stated, 'Coming in'?"

"I'm not sure. I can't say."

"Thank you. Have a nice trip back to Dallas." Barnes and
Matthews knew that had been a useless exchange. They also
both knew that every useless exchange was a small victory
for the defense.

"Gentlemen, before we launch into anything further this
morning, I'm going to recess for lunch. Let's be back here at
1:30. The jury is reminded not to discuss the case amongst
one another. That is all."

After lunch, the debate was again heated at the prosecution table. This time, however, Earl Vincent was arguing
heatedly that the only person they could put on the stand
next was Howard Brennan, who had had the best view of the
sixth floor shooter, however fleeting. Matthews was not buying it, however, as he knew that if Brennan didn't make it
through cross-examination, the people who saw even less
would be meaningless.

When the judge had the jury brought in, Matthews closed
the question, telling both Graves and Vincent, "It has to be
done this way. Think back as far as yesterday and realize
how many witnesses have so far done nothing of substance
to help this case. Also bear in mind that each such witness
either helps the prosecution or the defense. Before yesterday,
we thought Dallas and Washington had given us the whole
case; they gave us what they found—another matter entirely.
We've still got to prove our case, and we're going to do it one
witness at a time. We'll get to Brennan; what scares me is
one, that he is now almost blind, and two, Barnes will probably get to him also. He wasn't kidding when he said we've got

nobody that saw Oswald with a gun. Brennan's as close as we get, and he's a maybe. So we have to go with circumstances. Eaton, I want you to call Couch and you handle the direct. Let the jury know this is a team."

Graves was almost surprised to hear himself say, "The state calls Malcolm Couch."

The witness, a young radio executive, was called and sworn, and settled comfortably in the witness box. After establishing where he was and why on November twenty-second, Graves got to the point: "At any time, did you see anyone, besides police officers, of course, with a weapon or weapons in Dealey Plaza?"

"Well, I saw, it was only a brief glance, but I saw eight to ten inches of the barrel of a rifle being pulled inside an upper floor window of the Book Depository."

"Could you be more specific when you say 'upper floor'?"

"Either the top or next to top floor—probably not the top, but, well, high up."

"Thank you, Mr. Couch. No further questions."

Despite the presence of such legal expertise as that possessed by Robert Dean, Barnes was going to handle this one himself, although he was tempted to toss this meaningless biscuit to Miss Jeffries to let Matthews know that the defense gopher was better than the prosecution gopher. Barnes kept it to himself, and was brief: "Mr. Couch, could you describe the individual holding the rifle you saw for a fleeting glance?"

"Absolutely not. I did not see any person in the window. Just part of a barrel, and then only briefly."

"From what you saw, could you make a positive identification of this weapon?" Barnes asked, showing Couch the Mannlicher-Carcano.

"Again, absolutely not. You could show me a hundred or a thousand guns, and I couldn't help you. I just saw a few inches of some kind of rifle."

"You said you saw 'eight to ten inches of barrel,'" Barnes continued, picking up the gun. "How long is the barrel of this weapon?"

"About four inches."

"In point of fact, Mr. Couch, you've helped me immensely. No more questions."

Matthews, unperturbed by Barnes's nonchalance, pressed ahead: "The state calls Pauline Sanders."

Barnes explained to Oswald that this was still sparring, because it's too much of a gamble to put your best witness on first. Their exchange, and Oswald's growing sense of confidence now that the trial was going, occupied the time while Miss Sanders was sworn.

Matthews got right to the point, establishing that the witness worked at the Book Depository, and had gone outside to watch the motorcade. "And was there anything out of the ordinary that you heard?" Matthews asked.

"Well, I heard three loud blasts."

Matthews, leaning on the jury rail, looked over at Barnes and continued, "Since it seems we'll be asking for some opinions, were you able to form a strong opinion as to where those three loud blasts originated?"

"I feel very strongly that the shots or whatever it was came from the building above me."

"What building is that, Miss Sanders?"

"Oh, forgive me. The Book Depository."

"And nowhere else?" Matthews asked almost cynically.

"Just right up above me there, is what I heard."

"Thank you, Miss Sanders. No further questions."

Barnes remained seated and asked his usual obvious opener: "Miss Sanders, did you see the gun that fired the shots, or the person firing it?"

"No."

Barnes then got up and walked over to the witness stand, almost to punctuate for the jury the seriousness of his next question. "Miss Sanders, from your vantage point in front of the Book Depository, your observations are of great value to this court. The defense, in speaking to witnesses before you, has made mention of the probability that shots were fired from that building. Maybe you can still help us somehow. Did you see anyone exit or enter the building in haste immediately after the shooting?"

A bell should have rung in Matthews's head when the phrase "or enter" was mentioned, but he missed it. The witness then made him regret his omission. "Well, I would say that within a matter of ten seconds, a uniform police officer in a white helmet ran into the building."

"That quickly? Sounds like good police work." Barnes then repeated the point: "Ten seconds?"

"Yes, sir. Right quick, he was."

"Thank you, miss. I have nothing further, Your Honor."

"Time to wake up the jury," Matthews told Graves and Vincent. "Your Honor, the state calls Phillip L. Willis."

A robust, ruddy-complected man approaching fifty entered the courtroom, brushed back a strand of thinning hair and spoke forcefully in promising to tell the truth.

"Mr. Willis," Matthews began, playing to the jury all the way, "I must tell you that it is indeed a pleasure to meet the U.S. serviceman who captured the first Japanese prisoner in World War II." Barnes considered an objection, but knew he would carry the day with the witness, so allowed Matthews's grandstanding. "Now, sir," Matthews droned on, "we're going to show some photographs on these screens, and when they're done, I'll ask you about them individually." The jury then saw twelve slides, taken a few seconds or minutes apart, and then Matthews returned to the questioning. "Now, if we could have slide number five again, please. Good. Mr. Willis, would you please tell us the circumstances surrounding this particular slide? Where you were, when you took it— your best recollection."

"Certainly. I was across from the Book Depository, and having taken slide number 4, shown as the presidential car was making the turn, I refocused, and as I was about to take slide number five, the sound of a shot caused me to squeeze the camera shudder."

"Can you tell us anything else of what you saw or heard?"

"I believe I can. I saw what transpired in the presidential car, I heard three shots, about two seconds apart, and I then tried to get the attention of the police because I felt quite strongly that the shots I heard had come from the Book Depository."

"So there is no doubt in your mind that the shots you heard came from the Book Depository?"

"None whatsoever."

"Thank you, Mr. Willis. Your Honor, I would like to enter Willis slide number 5 into evidence at this time."

Barnes was immediately up. "Your Honor, if it please the court, I believe all of Mr. Willis's slides should be entered as exhibits at this time."

"Since you showed them all to the jury, I would assume you have no objection to that, Mr. Prosecutor."

"None, Your Honor, but I don't see where the remainder have any evidentiary value," Matthews replied, and then was frozen in his tracks by a sideways glance from Barnes that said, "I know something you don't know."

Barnes would have use for the pictures in the coming weeks, but for now, he proceeded on towards the witness stand. "It would seem, Mr. Willis, that you not only captured a famous prisoner, but some interesting pictures as well. Now let's see if your skills at recollection are as good as your skills at photography. You said in your testimony that you saw what transpired in the presidential car, but you weren't asked to tell the jury what you saw. Could you tell us now?"

"Yes. Immediately after I took slide number five, the President began to move forward and to his left, at least for a period of a few seconds. Then, and I greatly regret that I saw it happen, as well as my wife and daughter, but he was hit in the head and was slammed into the backseat of the car and towards Mrs. Kennedy."

"So you are telling us that three shots were fired from the Book Depository, behind the presidential car, and one of them drove the President backwards and to the left?" Barnes asked, disbelieving.

"Oh, no. Let's sort this out. I know I heard three shots from the Book Depository. No doubt about that. But as I told the men of the President's Commission, I'm involved in the deer-hunting lobbying activity, and I've shot a lot of deer, and never had one fall toward me, so I know that head shot came from somewhere else. No doubt about that either."

Matthews was instantly up and vocal: "Your Honor, move to strike. Conclusion on the part of the witness."

The judge leaned back in his seat and looked out into the empty spectator gallery, over the heads of both sets of lawyers. "We can't have it both ways, Mr. Matthews. You called the witness. You asked him about the shots. You accepted his opinion, and we've come to an unwritten agreement about that, and now the defense gets nothing more than further clarification of that opinion, and you have a problem with it." Judge Davis then looked quickly from one table to the other. "Let's discuss this in chambers, gentlemen."

Barnes stood casually against a bookcase of neatly matched legal tomes, while Matthews sat. The judge, to the surprise of both attorneys, offered them a drink, and when they declined, the bottle was replaced, unused, in the desk drawer. "Gentlemen, in here, for all I care, it's Frank, Ray, and Eddie; out there's different, because out there is the biggest legal question this country is going to deal with for a while to come. So here's how it plays. Ray, are you interviewing these witnesses before you put them on?" Matthews indicated he was. "Eddie, it's obvious you've done your homework, and I commend your 'let's find the truth' attitude as demonstrated in your opening statement—and let's hope you were serious and we are able. But all three of us better leave this room with an understanding of something, and that is that there are strange forces at work here—I've got a very strange feeling about this case."

Barnes cut in, "I apologize for interrupting you, Judge, but I have to agree. There's times when the scope of this—not what we know, but what we don't know . . ."

"I hear you," Davis agreed.

". . . makes my skin crawl," Barnes concluded.

"Ray?" the judge asked.

"Frank, I've read every report and shred of paper I've been given, and so have my assistants. But I know there's a lot missing, and it's impossible to try a case properly when you know there are gaps, when the jury realizes there are gaps, and when the defense counsel, doing his job, drives a tank through those gaps. But what's worse, well, take Willis out there. Combat veteran. Personal friend of LBJ. I read his affidavit, his testimony before the commission, and I spoke with him on the phone. Now he comes in here and tells a somewhat different story. And I think he's the last person on my discovery list—or on Mr. Barnes's list that I'd accuse of perjury. I don't get it. I just don't get it."

Judge Davis looked to Barnes. "Eddie, I'm sure you and Ray are not tremendously well acquainted. I'll say it in here because this is off the record, but this case is already the best legal battle I've been involved in, and I've presided in over two dozen murder cases, and some were extremely brutal to the point of sadistic. You're good, Eddie, and that's your job. I've known Ray over there for almost as long as you've been alive, son, and he's very good—which is his job. So both sides are clearly well represented, which will make the resolution of this case permanent when it is resolved. Nobody will claim one side bullied the other. For what it's worth, neither of you have the reputation as the 'hired gun' who can't lose, but you two are very competent attorneys, facing a strange case which, I suspect, still has many bumps in the road, and somebody has to hit them. Okay, we've spoken our minds. Now, let's walk back out there and do our jobs. And let's have the understanding that from this point forward, there's a lot more than the eyes of Texas upon us. Whatever happens, the whole world is watching." Barnes translated the last sentence, to himself of course, to mean the case given to the prosecution was having the air let out of it.

Back on the bench, Davis overruled Matthews's objection, and Barnes thanked the witness for clarifying the confusion. Judge Davis then instructed Carson to take the jury out and indicated there would be a ten minute recess.

Barnes walked to the front of the defense table, so he could huddle with Dean and Jeffries and the defendant would hear the muted conversation also. He told them what had transpired in chambers, and allowed Dean to reassure Oswald that he was getting the fair trial he deserved, and that the defense was doing its job.

Things were not as rosy on the prosecution side. Graves and Vincent assumed things had gone poorly in chambers, but Matthews assured them that was not so. "But we've got to recontact every future witness," he told them, "and make damn sure we know everything they could say. We may also have to take a serious look at our witness list."

Earl Vincent challenged that. "I don't see how we can make it any smaller and hope to win," he commented sourly.

"I wasn't thinking of shortening it," Matthews said, surprisingly calmly. "I don't think Barnes was kidding when he said he'd call everybody we don't, so we may pick up some points on sheer volume of witnesses, and limit the scope of what can be said on cross-examination. For now, we've got Worrell, the high school truant, and Bob Jackson, the photographer. Then we'll probably start tomorrow with Brennan. After that, we've got some so-called experts, the Secret Service, and let's face it, they're not going to win a case after they've *lost* a President, and then, God help us, we've got some of the Dallas police 'finest.' We've got work to do."

As the ten minutes had ended, the judge reclaimed his seat on the bench and nodded to Carson to bring the jury back in. They did so, but with a perceptible slowness in their collective gait that suggested, at the very least, ennui. Both Barnes and Matthews were well attuned to little signals like that.

"Mr. Matthews?"

"Your Honor, the state calls James R. Worrell."

Barnes couldn't help but think to himself that the prosecution was desperate, for after the pep-talk in chambers, Matthews trots out a high school dropout who might as well have been wearing a sign saying "loser" and Matthews was probably unaware that this was another time bomb.

"Mr. Worrell," Matthews began, attempting to give dignity to a witness seriously lacking in that department, "would you please tell the court where you were when you observed the presidential motorcade?"

"I was in front of the Book Depository."

"Would you tell us your actions when the car passed?"

"Sure." Worrell shifted in his seat as if he were about to reveal the secrets of the universe. "I saw the car go by, then I heard a noise like a firecracker or a gunshot. I looked above me, five or six stories, and saw, oh, maybe six inches of a rifle. I then saw the rifle fire, and I ran, as fast as I could, to get away. While I was running, I heard two more shots. Then, when I was, oh, a hundred yards away, I stopped to get my breath, and I saw this man come running out of the Book Depository."

"Could you describe this individual to us?"

"As I remember, he was white, with black hair; about five-seven to five-ten, early thirties, wearing a dark shirt or dark sports jacket."

"Mr. Worrell, I ask you to look at the man in the dark coat in the second seat at the defense table. Do you recognize him?"

"Yes. The FBI showed me pictures of him." At that instant, Matthews figured that he, Matthews, might be the next person on trial for murder in Texas. He nevertheless tried again.

"Do you recognize him as the person you saw either fire the rifle or leave the Book Depository?"

"No."

"But you are certain about what you heard with respect to the shots?" Matthews wanted to get something out of this witness.

"Yes."

"Thank you. Your witness, Mr. Barnes." Matthews was thinking "make what you can with this idiot; he's not going to help anybody's case."

Barnes, however, had listened more carefully. "Mr. Worrell, with reference to the shots. You said you heard one, then you looked up and saw one fired, and then, while running, heard two more. How many shots did you hear?"

"Four."

"When you ran, where did you run?"

"Towards the back of the Book Depository, uh, away, from where the shooting was going on."

"So you ran, you told us, a hundred yards, stopped to get your breath, and saw an individual leaving the Book Depository in a hurry. In terms of time, and remember that you heard shots while you were running, how long was it from the time of the last shot—when you told us you were running, until you stopped running and saw someone?"

"Maybe three or four minutes." Now Barnes knew what a trap felt like, but he at least had a way out.

"Three or four minutes to run a hundred yards to escape gunfire," he repeated calmly. "And how long do you estimate all the gunfire took?"

"Five or six seconds."

"Okay. You're watching the parade. You hear a shot, you look up and claim you see a shot, then, while running, you

hear two more, and then three minutes and fifty-four seconds later, you complete your life-saving sprint of one hundred yards and see an individual leave the scene of the crime
in haste. Have I got it right?"

"Yeah."

Barnes walked from the jury rail to the prosecution table to
get document reference numbers, and while there, with his
back to the witness, he told Matthews, as a professional
courtesy, "This is going to get ugly, Ray. If I were you, I'd stay
out of it."

Barnes walked no further than the end of the defense table
nearest the witness, temporarily blocking out Carolyn Jeffries's view of Worrell. "Mr. Worrell, you're a fraud, and I'm
not going to let a case as important as this, or the reputa-
tions of this court, or its officers, or a very fine prosecutor
named Ray Matthews be colored by someone like you that
shuffles in off the street to spin an interesting yarn." The
judge looked to the prosecutor for objection but got none.

"How old are you, Mr. Worrell?"

"Twenty-one."

"So you were nineteen or twenty the day of the assassination?"

"Yeah."

"Where were you supposed to be that day?"

"In school, but I stopped attending in October."

"Could you tell the court the name of the college, just for
the record?"

"I was in high school, all right?"

"In point of fact, you were skipping high school. But let's
get past that. What time did you arrive at the Book Depository to watch the parade?"

"Between 10 and 10:45. I went directly there from Love
Field, because I didn't get a good look at President Kennedy
there."

"Okay," Barnes agreed, adding bait to the trap. "Now tell
us about the rifle firing."

"What can I say? It went off. I saw the smoke and a little
flame."

"Mr. Worrell, I can put an FBI report on these monitors.
That report will say that this gun on the evidence table pro-

duced *no* flame when fired in daylight, and that the only way flame was visible would have been if it had been fired in total darkness. Also, you couldn't have gotten a good look at President Kennedy at Love Field and been in front of the Depository at 10 or 10:45, because the President didn't arrive at Love Field until 11:37." Barnes let his words sink in, and then approached the witness so as to go face to face. "Young man, I'd love to have a twenty-one year old such as yourself tell the jury that the man you saw run was in his thirties, because on that day, the defendant was twenty-four. I'd love them to believe you heard four shots. I'd be happy if they believed you saw flame from the barrel of a rifle, because that would mean the defendant's rifle was *not* the one you saw. But my joy in your testimony is seriously weakened by the fact that you, sir, are a twenty-four carat *fraud.* The prosecutor, Mr. Matthews, has far too many legal scruples to send you up here to sing this fairy tale, so why don't you tell the court who did?"

"I don't know what you're talking about."

"Oh, yes you do, young man. You didn't get a good view of the President at Love Field, so you arrive, hours early, at the exact spot from which shots are fired? It was many miles from Love Field to the corner of Elm and Houston, the very last place on the motorcade route where people would be at the curb. You could have been anywhere in between, but you were right where a good eyewitness would be. Except you saw too much—nobody told you *not* to say anything about flames." Barnes paused to let the witness stew. "Notice, Mr. Worrell, neither the prosecutor nor the judge has objected to my tone nor to my questions. They want the same answers I want. What's behind this charade?"

"I don't know what you're talking about."

Barnes was almost done: "No, kid. You don't know what you're talking about. Next time, learn your lines better. Nothing further, Your Honor, and I apologize to the court for my volume."

"That won't be necessary, Mr. Barnes." The judge then squarely faced the witness: "Mr. James Worrell, I'm citing you with contempt of court. You will be escorted from this room by an officer of the Vermont state police. We'll provide you with lodging—you may not care for it, but the choice is not yours, and we'll give you some time to think about your statement, and then tomorrow, you will dictate a statement to a court-appointed stenographer." It was now the judge's turn to raise the volume: "And that statement will contain the truth. Remove the witness, please. The jury is instructed to do their best to disregard the testimony just given." Matthews appreciated what Barnes did, but he also knew Barnes had scored some big points.

Matthews looked at his watch. He could have gotten away with trying to call it a day, but he wanted to lead off with Howard Brennan first thing, and he knew that his next witness was at least reliable and professional, and would finish creating the crime scene from the outside, and hope Brennan could flesh it out a bit. "The state calls Robert Hill Jackson, Your Honor."

Barnes was writing a note on a nondoodled yellow pad reminding himself to "see revised Worrell statement," and he punctuated the memo by underlining the word "revised." In the meantime, the thirty-year-old witness had been sworn, and Matthews had raced through the preliminaries, letting the jury hear that Jackson was a photographer for the *Dallas Morning News* and was riding in a car approximately eight cars behind the President's limousine.

"Tell us what happened when your press car was on Houston Street," Matthews continued.

"Okay. I heard the first noise. There was confusion in our car, as somebody said it was a firecracker. Before that comment was over, there were two more noises, and they were shots. I looked straight ahead of me, where I thought the sounds were coming from, and noticed two Negro men in a window straining to see directly above them, and my eyes followed right on up to the window above them and I saw the rifle or what looked like a rifle—approximately half the weapon, I guess I saw, and just as I looked at it, it was drawn fairly slowly back into the building."

"I show you CE 347, a photo of the Texas School Book Depository. Could we have that on the screen, please?"

The monitors showed a picture of Houston Street as it approached the Book Depository. Matthews then asked the witness if he recognized the scene. Barnes interrupted to remind the prosecutor that he had introduced the photo as "CE 347, a photo of the Texas School Book Depository."

"So I did," Matthews said contritely, realizing that in his enthusiasm, he *had* said something he'd wished had come from the witness's mouth. "So, Mr. Jackson, now that we all know what building we're talking about, is that the building you saw the rifle in?"

"Yes, sir."

"And what floor would the rifleman have been on?"

"Counting the ground floor as one, he would have been on the sixth."

"Objection to the word 'he', Your Honor. Assumes facts not in evidence."

Matthews rose to suggest that such nitpicking was not in the best interests of justice.

"I have to sustain the objection this time, Mr. Prosecutor, but in the future, Mr. Barnes, unless you can put evidence into the record that it was a 'she,' I think we all had better get comfortable with the basic words of the English language. Okay?"

"Yes, Your Honor," Barnes answered, having gotten the message.

"No further questions. Thank you."

Barnes walked over to the jury rail and looked at the view the jurors had of the screen. Then he approached the witness. "Mr. Jackson, when you saw the part of the rifle that you testified about, were you as close, closer, or farther away from this building than this photo shows?"

"I would say I was slightly farther away. Perhaps a little bit back on Houston Street."

"And you said you thought you saw approximately half the weapon. Would you describe as precisely as possible what you saw?"

"Well, I saw about a foot of the barrel, and maybe eight to ten inches of the stock."

"Making a total of twenty inches?" Barnes was a master of the obvious.

"About that."

Barnes then walked slowly and got the Mannlicher-Carcano, and handed it to the witness. "Recognize this?"

"Only from photos in the papers. From that distance, I'd be lying if I said I identified any specific gun."

"I appreciate your honesty, Mr. Jackson. But maybe you can aid in the identification. You said you saw a foot of the barrel." Barnes produced a six-inch ruler from his coat pocket, slapped it against his palm so the jury would take note, then instructed the witness to measure the barrel of the weapon in his hands.

"Just over four inches," Jackson replied.

"Quite a ways from twelve inches, don't you think?"

"Objection. Leading."

"Sustained."

"Let me rephrase that, then. You told the court you saw a foot of barrel and eight inches of stock. Do you still stand by that statement?"

"Yes. That's what I saw."

"Good. Did you see a telescopic sight?"

"No."

"You also testified that you heard a first noise, and there was talk of a firecracker, then two noises that were shots. For the record, how many shots?"

"Three."

"Okay. And to the best of your recollection, if you can, how were they spaced, and what was the time elapsed?"

"That I remember well. It was between five and eight seconds, total, and there was a much greater interval between the first well, shot, than between the second and the third. They were real close together."

"Mr. Jackson, I'm going to ask you to point that weapon high up on the back wall of the courtroom. Sight in some object. Then pull the trigger, work the bolt, and sight and fire again. Now before you do that, work the bolt a few times." Barnes made serious eye contact with several jurors while Jackson struggled with the bolt. Matthews gave serious thought to objecting, but it was his witness, and he knew he had experts that supported the prosecution case. When Barnes reached the far end of the jury, he asked, "Ready?"

"Ready," Jackson answered, and did as Barnes had instructed him. When done, Barnes asked the obvious: "Did those close-together second and third shots that you heard seem to have as much time between them as your 'shots' just there?"

"The real shots were closer together than that."

"One more question about timing. You testified that you heard a noise, then shots, then your eyes noticed the two Negro men in a nearby window, and their expressions directed you one floor higher, where you had time to note the dimensions of a rifle, obviously not that one that you are holding, *slowly* being withdrawn. Did I hear you correctly?"

"That's just about it, yes."

"You also said the shot sequence was five to eight seconds, so how long would it have been from the shots to your eyes finding the Negro men, then looking up, seeing enough of a rifle to give dimensions, and see it slowly withdrawn? Include the five to eight seconds in your answer, please."

"Twenty seconds, altogether. Maybe a little more."

"Thank you. No furth—excuse me, one more question. Earlier I asked you about that picture, and you indicated you were probably farther away. Where were you when the rifle was slowly withdrawn?"

"Almost to the Book Depository. We were starting to make the turn there."

"And you saw no human forms in the window?"

"None."

"Thank you, Mr. Jackson."

Matthews rose for one question on redirect. "When you estimated 'Twenty seconds, maybe a little more,' is it possible that it could have been less?"

"Well, given the circumstances, ordinarily I'd have to say I could have been off by a few seconds. But that last question about the positions of the car, I mean, we were traveling slowly, and we were a hundred yards away when it started, and almost there when it ended. That's a lot of time. I'm afraid I can't honestly shorten my estimate."

"Thank you," Matthews muttered. "Recross?"

Barnes remained seated. "Given the timing you just seemed to realize, Mr. Jackson, does the possibility exist in your mind that someone in that window was intentionally trying to let witnesses see a rifle?"

"Objection. Calls for a conclusion."

"I withdraw the question, Your Honor." Try to get it out of the jury's mind, Barnes thought to himself, pleased with a very good first day of witnesses.

# Five

Thursday, January 7, 1965. A bright sun was shining well before nine o'clock when the prosecution team arrived together, looking and feeling tired. The best they could hope for on a few hours of sleep was that the weather was an omen.

They had spoken at great length the previous evening with Howard Brennan, a steamfitter who had been working at a construction site near the Book Depository and had taken his lunch break to view the motorcade. Facts and observations were carefully reviewed, with Matthews asking the questions and both Graves and Vincent playing devil's advocates. To himself, Matthews regrettably admitted that the two of them did not add up to one Barnes.

Now, in the bright sunlight, they knew they were making a major roll of the dice, as Brennan was as close as they were going to get to an eyewitness. The only trouble was, an accident, well after the assassination, had left Brennan with extremely poor eyesight, not the best character trait for a key eyewitness.

Their strategy rehearsed, they appeared upbeat when the

members of the defense team arrived separately, a few minutes apart, near ten. The defense had also worked the night before, but more in the area of photo-optics than in moot-court playacting. They had a pretty good idea of what Brennan was going to say. They just had to make sure the jury heard what they wanted it to hear. Barnes also insisted that everyone be well rested. "Remember the Nixon-Kennedy debates," he reminded his team. "JFK looked good; Nixon spoke well, but he looked like hell. People buy image," he concluded, "and we're going to look *and sound* good tomorrow."

Judge Davis entered with little fanfare, and Oswald was escorted in and allowed to feel comfortable before the jury was brought in. During that minute, Oswald asked Barnes if there was any news about the incident with the boy the day before. Barnes told him it would be days before there was anything more said or done about that, and that it might just be kicked back to Dallas.

Preliminaries completed, Matthews indicated that the state would call Howard Brennan, who was then led into court by a Vermont trooper and guided to the witness stand. Barnes and Dean exchanged looks; he might make a lousy witness, but on the other hand, he was worth a bundle in sympathy. Matthews then asked the virtually rehearsed questions, and it was established that he had left his construction site, still wearing his "hardhat" and gone to the concrete structure directly opposite the Book Depository to view the motorcade.

"Mr. Brennan, before we go any farther," Matthews went on, "perhaps you should explain the condition of your eyesight to the jury."

"I will do that as best I can. As a steamfitter, it was always my job to deal with hot piping, frequently live steam. In an accident almost a year ago, last January to be exact, an error was made and I received a serious blast of steam into my eyes, and into the forehead region. Since that time, my vision has been impaired, and although I do not know the precise medical terms, it is not likely that my eyesight will ever improve."

Barnes was ready to ask for handkerchiefs to be issued to the jurors, but he knew he'd get his chance before sunset.

Matthews pressed on with his advantage: "Now, Mr. Brennan, going back to November twenty-second, 1963, when your vision was sound . . ."

"Objection, Your Honor. Assumes facts not in evidence."

"Sustained."

"Fine. Mr. Brennan, for the record, how would you characterize your eyesight on November twenty-second?" Barnes had hoped for this question.

"Rather poor." Matthews was stunned. Before he could disengage without a total calamity, Barnes again objected. "Best evidence, Your Honor. The defense has a statement from Mr. Brennan's eye doctor, as well as the specialists who treated him following his 'accident.' I would like to admit them as Defense Exhibits 1 and 2, respectively, and let them speak for themselves."

"Mr. Matthews?"

"I'd like to see the documents, if that is possible," he answered, with more than a trace of hostility in his voice. Barnes passed over Xerox copies, delivering the originals to the bench. Matthews perused them and asked his witness if the names affixed were, in fact, his eye doctors. Learning that they were, he then questioned why they would be Defense 1 and 2, since Barnes had used the paper bag with Buell Wesley Frazier the morning before.

" 'Used' is the correct term, Mr. Prosecutor. I had no intentions then or now to introduce that worthless bag into evidence. That's not my job." Matthews was ready to scream: his best witness was on the stand and the jury would be so confused his impact would be lost totally.

Matthews walked to the prosecution table, selected a couple of documents, wrote the numbers on a pad, then returned to the wreckage of the witness stand. On the way, he decided to borrow a page from Barnes's book. "Mr. Brennan, let's try to sort this out. Mr. Barnes, the defense attorney has said to witnesses before you, and I'm sure he'll say it again, that he's interested in the truth in this case. Well, so am I. What I need to know from you is this: in the events you are about to testify to, was your eyesight good enough that you can honestly tell us what you saw on November twenty-second, or were you seeing blurs and coming here looking for a headline? I don't mean to be blunt with you, sir, but that's the bottom line. Are you able to truthfully tell what you actually saw?"

"Yes, I am."

"Then let's proceed," Matthews said quickly. "If we could have exhibit 477 on the screens please. Mr. Brennan, ah, there it is. Can you tell us what this picture shows?"

"Actually, I can't. But I can tell you that there were two pictures taken of me, after the accident, with me demonstrating to the FBI fellas where I was sitting on November twenty-second. One was taken from the steps of the Book Depository, which would be looking south, and the other was taken from behind me, looking north. That picture would include the Book Depository in it. Which one is on the screen now?"

"Mr. Brennan, the picture on the screen shows your back, the Book Depository, and you are wearing your construction helmet."

"Oh, yes, my hardhat. Just like November twenty-second. Do you have the other picture?"

"That would be exhibit 478 please, for the jury's benefit." The picture changed to show the witness from the front, sitting right in the middle of a concrete retaining wall approximately sixty feet long made of semihollow, design masonry blocks.

"Mr. Brennan, did you have any difficulty locating where you sat on November twenty-second?"

"No, sir, I knew I was right in the middle of that wall, just like in them pictures. I looked at them with a magnifying glass, and that's the spot, okay."

"Please tell the court what happened when the presidential motorcade passed your location."

"Well, it was a crazy day. I seen one fella have a seizure of some kind right over there, but nobody took much notice, what with the President coming. Then I heard what I thought was a backfire. It ran in my mind that it might be someone throwing firecrackers out the window of the red brick building and I looked up at the building. I then saw this man in the window and he was taking aim with a high-powered rifle. I could see all of the barrel of the gun. I do not know if it had a scope or not. As it appeared to me, he was standing up and resting against the left side of the windowsill, with the gun up against his right shoulder and he was holding it with his left hand and taking positive aim, and he fired his last shot. As I calculate a couple seconds passed, then he drew the gun back from the window as though he was drawing it back to his side and maybe paused for another second to assure himself that he hit his mark and then he disappeared. And, at that same moment, I was diving off that fire wall and to the right for bullet protection of this stone wall."

"That's quite a story, Mr. Brennan. Why don't you have a drink, catch your breath, and we'll continue."

"Thank you."

"Did you see enough of the person firing the rifle to be able to give this court a description?"

"The man I saw in the window was a white male, oh, early thirties, slender, nice looking, would weigh about one hundred sixty-five to one hundred seventy-five, and was wearing light-colored clothing."

Matthews knew he had to choose his words carefully. "Mr. Brennan, I realize, given your optical impairment, that it would be unreasonable to ask you to identify anyone today, but let me ask you this: were you taken to any police lineups on November twenty-second?"

"Yes."

"And did you recognize anyone in those lineups?"

"Well, I had seen pictures of that Oswald fella on television before I went down to headquarters, so it wasn't hard to recognize him, and I told the officers that he looked like the man . . ."

" 'He' being Oswald?" Matthews coaxed.

"Yes. Oswald. But I told them I could not make a positive identification of any of the men in that lineup."

"Okay. Let's go back a little bit. What did you do when you saw this individual fire?"

"Well, he disappeared. And, at the same moment, I was diving off that fire wall and to the right for bullet protection of this stone wall. Then, I would say from the time the last shot was fired, and me diving off the wall there, and getting around on the solid side, and then running across to the officer, the time element is hard to figure, but it would still be *in seconds.* Then I gave my report to the officer, a policeman, I told him the window under the top row, and then he had taken me to Mr. Sorrels, and put me in an auto sitting in front of the Texas Book Store. Uh, could I add one detail about the lineup?"

Matthews knew he couldn't refuse the question. "Of course, please do," he insisted, grinding his teeth.

"The man in the lineup that resembled the man with the rifle looked much younger on television than he did from my picture of him in the window—not much younger—but a few years younger—say five years younger."

"I'm sure your eyesight and circumstances would account for that, Mr. Brennan. Thank you for sharing your many observations with us today. Your witness."

Barnes and Dean, in a preplanned bit of theatrics, were deep in whispered conference when the judge interrupted to remind Barnes that it was his turn to question the witness. "Your Honor," Barnes began, rising slowly, "may we approach?"

The judge waved them ahead, and Barnes gave way to Matthews, only to ambush Matthews by having Dean and Jeffries follow both attorneys of record to the bench. While Matthews was looking at Graves and Vincent and trying to make sense of it, Barnes, carrying his briefcase, addressed the issue: "We need to meet in chambers, Your Honor, and it might be helpful if the court reporter were present with Mr. Brennan's testimony."

Judge Davis announced a ten minute recess, suggesting that a court officer stay with the witness while another keep the defendant company. The jury would stay in place.

Judge Davis's chambers were quiet, almost eerie, as eight people filled the smallish office. Matthews was visibly beside himself, as the testimony of his best witness was being made a mockery by what seemed theatrics. The judge cut through the confusion: "Eddie, what's on your mind?"

"Judge, I'd like the court to offer the witness an unconditional amnesty so we can go back out there and find out what really happened."

Matthews interrupted loudly: "He already told us, under

oath, what happened. What's wrong? Somebody suggests your boy did it and you panic?"

Judge Davis interrupted to remind Matthews not to raise his voice in chambers. Then he asked Barnes what his point was.

"It's very simple, judge. The witness has already perjured himself several times. Those two exhibits, 477 and 478—they're fraudulent, and then there's—"

"We're going to need more than your word for that, young Edward," Matthews insisted.

Barnes had more than his word: "Look at the flip side. Exhibit 479, which is but one frame of the movie taken by Mr. Zapruder. Between that photo, taken with the presidential car passing, and a photo taken months later to recreate the scene, there's no question in a 'best evidence' sense. Four hundred seventy-nine clearly shows Mr. Brennan, in construction fatigues and hardhat, on the east end of that retaining wall, looking back over his shoulder, as the car went by. He just sat out there and lied to all of us. Beyond that, nobody read those doctors' reports carefully. When he said his vision was poor on November twenty-second, he was being coyly honest. He could see distance fine; he needed glasses *to read.* Since his 'accident' his vision hasn't deteriorated nearly as much as he'd like us to think. I can put three rebuttal witnesses out there that will testify that they've spent time with him and, when out of the public eye, no pun intended, he sees fine. The point is, he doesn't want to. And that should tell us something.

"Of equal importance, I have," he slowed down, removing a file from his briefcase, "an affidavit from one Sandy Speaker, Mr. Brennan's employer at the time of his so-called accident. In this deposition he tells that the government, or government agents, called on Mr. Brennan, and he was away from the site for almost three weeks before returning to work. From that time onward, Brennan spoke not another word of the assassination—it was like it never happened—and soon after, through his own negligence—probably because his mind was elsewhere, the accident—no big deal, happened."

"Your Honor," Matthews interrupted, "I had no idea of this."

"Nobody has said you did, Ray," the judge answered.

"Is that all, Eddie?"

"Not quite. Look at what we have in testimony. He can describe the guy down to 'nice looking'—was that the phrase, Mrs. Martinez?"

"Here: yes, 'nice looking.'"

"Okay. So he i.d.'s somebody that closely, then can't make the guy after he's seen him on TV, and even claims he was much younger on TV than in the window. There's a major confusion there. Then, he tells us about the last shot and seeing the shooter disappear, then he dives for cover! After the last shot! And if he was right in the middle of that wall, he couldn't have fallen to the right for bullet protection of the stone wall. That could only have been afforded if, as shown in the Zapruder film, he was on the east end of the wall, not dead center as someone staged him to be. There are other contradictions as well, as I'm going to bring out in cross, but there's also the Zapruder film. He's in a lot of frames of that movie, and he *never* looks up. We could run it right now, it's only twelve seconds."

"I don't think that will be necessary now," the judge said, sternly. "Ray, I don't think your witness is telling the whole truth, yet I don't see a motive for perjury, with the possible exception of fear. Which leads to the next question: fear of what? If he saw the defendant do it, he should have said so—on November twenty-second, or today. Hell, we can protect him. No, I think he's afraid of something much more serious than our young Mr. Oswald, and I'm not convinced that even an amnesty is going to unlock the whole story. But we have to start there. Does everyone agree?"

Silence provided an unanimous consensus.

The group trooped back silently into the courtroom and Judge Davis was not even back on the bench when he ordered Carson, with a trace of bitterness in his tone, to take the jury out. Once that was done, he confronted the witness: "Mr. Brennan, evidence has come to light in my chambers that suggests that you have not been completely honest in your testimony today, nor for that matter in the restaging of the photos taken for the President's Commission. Now, what I am saying to you amounts to serious charges, crimes—and ones that carry heavy penalties. I'm going to ask you a few questions, we're going to make decisions, and then I'm either going to bring the jury back in and continue this trial, or get a grand jury going down the street and consider you for perjury and obstruction of justice. So, let's have a look at exhibit four hundred seventy-seven. Mr. Brennan, and I want the truth now, can you see what that picture shows?"

"Yes, Your Honor. But not very well."

"Is it accurate?"

"No. I was much farther around the curve, almost on Houston Street. The President's Commission showed me a *negative* of a photo and told me to identify myself," he continued, approaching a point of panic, "and I did. Then they took me out and photographed me as in four hundred seventy-seven and four hundred seventy-eight."

"Relax, Mr. Brennan. Did government agents spend much time with you after November twenty-second?"

"Yes. Look. I'll tell the truth. I swear. What I said was true before, except the location. I can't tell the President's Commission one thing and this court another, can I?"

"No. But you can, and will, tell this court the exact truth. The witness is given an amnesty for his testimony. Mr. Brennan, that means you will not face any criminal charges. We know you were a witness to the crime—that's all we want you to be, understood? Carson, get the jury back."

When that was done, the judge resumed. "Mr. Barnes?"

"Thank you, Your Honor. Now, Mr. Brennan, when the jury was absent, we cleared up some confusion about your position during the motorcade. Perhaps if we could have exhibit 479, please. Now, Mr. Brennan, would you point yourself out for the jury, please."

"I'm sitting there, at the east end of the wall, looking over my shoulder as the presidential car passed."

"If you had been looking straight ahead, which street would you have been facing?"

"Houston."

"Okay. Then you said you heard a backfire or firecrackers, and you looked up at the building, and you saw someone aiming for their last shot. Did you see the shot? You know, smoke, recoil—anything that would suggest that the rifle you were looking at actually fired?"

"No."

"You gave a most detailed description of the individual, down to the detail that he was 'nice looking.' Yet you could not positively identify him, although in a sheriff's department affidavit that day you said, 'I believe that I could identify this man if I ever saw him again.' "

"I thought I could identify him. Maybe if he had been in the lineup, I would have."

"So you did *not* positively identify the defendant?"

"No."

"Could you do so now—is Lee Oswald the man you saw?"

"I could not say that."

"Do you recognize this weapon?" Barnes asked, holding the now familiar Mannlicher-Carcano.

"I can't say whether I saw a scope or not, and that clearly has one, so I can't identify it."

"You told us, Mr. Brennan," Barnes spoke casually, circling around as if deep in thought, "that your dive and recovery, which lead you immediately to report your sighting to a police officer, took a matter of seconds. Is that correct?"

"Yes."

"And you dove off the wall for protection after the last shot was fired and the shooter casually disappeared?"

"Yes."

"This is critical, Mr. Brennan. After the so-called last shot which you did not actually see, how much time elapsed before the shooter was out of your sight?"

"A couple of seconds to bring the gun in, and then he must have stood there while I recovered from my dive, because I got up in time to see him disappear. He wasn't gone when I got up. So I'd say, fifteen or so seconds."

"Then you quickly found a policeman, who put you in Mr. Sorrels's car?"

"Yes."

"Who is Mr. Sorrels?"

"Secret Service."

"Crucial again, Mr. Brennan. How long, from the time you dove off the wall, until you were in Mr. Sorrels's car?"

"No more than three to five minutes, I'm sure of that."

"Mr. Brennan, Mr. Sorrels was in the lead car with Chief Curry, Sheriff Decker, and Secret Service Agent Winston Lawson. They accompanied the presidential car to Parkland Hospital, secured the area there, and then returned to the Book Depository, by Mr. Sorrels's account, about twenty-seven minutes later. Yet you were talking to him in no more than three to five minutes?"

"That's the way it seemed."

"Okay, Mr. Brennan, you've had a rough day." Barnes walked over and got the Mannlicher. "Stand up, please, sir. I want you to sight in that weapon, using my outstretched arm as the windowsill, and do exactly what you saw happen in that corner window, and as you're doing it, tell the jury what you are describing. Do you understand what I want you to do?"

"I think so."

Brennan rested the gun on Barnes's forearm, telling the jury that he's watching the parade and he hears a backfire or firecracker, and he's seeing it approximately from fifty feet below where the policeman is running the tape machine, off to his left across the courtroom. "Then I looked up, and 'Bang,' I guess I heard, another shot. The gun came in slowly," as the witness removed it from Barnes's arm, holding it in his right hand and bringing it down to his side. Then he stood there, explaining that's what the shooter did, then he backed away, with the rifle.

"So the gun was on his right shoulder?" Barnes had the gun on his own right shoulder as he returned it to the evidence table.

"Yes."

"And after the shot you heard, the shooter simply stepped back—he didn't stand up first?"

"Stand up? He was up, he stayed up. I don't understand."

"Indeed you don't," Barnes told him. "The window you saw is thirteen inches from the floor at its bottom and twenty-six inches from the floor at the top of its opening. So either the shooter was kneeling, and stood up, or shot through the glass, or was one of the seven dwarves." Barnes walked back toward the defense table as if he had gotten every last mile out of this witness, then stopped dramatically and asked, "Mr. Brennan, in your little recreation a minute ago, you said, 'Bang.' Correct?"

"Yes, I did. I heard the shot."

"So you did. But you didn't eject the shell that went 'Bang' from the rifle did you? No further questions, Mr. Brennan." Barnes looked at Matthews and dared him to ask his star witness another question. He didn't.

Barnes then moved to admit CE 477, CE 478, and CE 479, and it was done without objection.

Matthews was relieved to get Howard Brennan, who he had thought would have been his star witness, off the stand without a perjury indictment, but as he weighed the pluses and the minuses of the situation, it had not been a total loss. Brennan *had* put a shooter in the sixth floor window, albeit with some difficulty, but that would be long forgotten by final summation.

Matthews's thoughts turned briefly away from his witnesses and focused on his adversary. He began to understand why Barnes had wanted to do *pro bono* work, as indigent clients, like Oswald, could never afford Barnes's legal expertise. He was beginning to find a grudging admiration for Barnes; he hoped Barnes did not confuse the prosecutor with the prosecution's case, which Matthews had been handed, with guarantees. He was now becoming convinced that if it had been his case from November twenty-second, things might be different. Alas, he did not have time to ruminate further on those possibilities. In the meantime, he still had to put a weapon in Oswald's hands, and he had to deal with this recent eyewitness testimony that suggested that the final shot had never been ejected from the rifle, a fact totally at odds with the Dallas claims that when they found the gun—whatever gun it was, it had a live round in the chamber.

Matthews couldn't think about it too long, however. "The state calls Adrian T. Alba, Your Honor." Let's see Barnes twist one of his words, Matthews thought.

While Barnes knelt at the far end of the defense table and was quietly discussing something with Carolyn Jeffries, the witness, a vigorous man in his early thirties, was sworn and gave testimony that he was the part owner of the Crescent City Garage, 618 Magazine Street, New Orleans, Louisiana, and that the defendant, a man he knew only as "Lee," had visited the garage regularly to use its soda machine, its coffee pot, and to look through the outdoor life and gun magazines available in the small waiting room.

"Now, Mr. Alba," Matthews went on, "did you and the defendant, that man sitting at that table over there, ever discuss guns?"

"All the time. Matter of fact, that was about all we talked about." The jury seemed to take an interest in the crispness of that answer and Barnes made notes accordingly.

"I don't want to put words into your mouth, Mr. Alba, so . . ."

"And I don't want you to, either," Barnes quipped, getting a laugh from everybody but Matthews.

"So," Matthews continued, "why don't you tell us about these discussions."

"Well, I recall discussing some of the guns I owned, and how I was in the process of sporterizing a couple of them at that time. Lee told me on one occasion that he owned 'a couple of guns' and later told me he owned, I think he said 'several rifles and several pistols' but he didn't go into detail as to what they were—no specifics at all, really. The thing I remember the most about our little talks was he was always asking how to go about ordering guns through the mail—how many had I ordered, how long did it take, where did I get them, that kind of thing. That's about the best of my recall on gun talks. Oh, there was one other thing. A few times I'd talk about this gun or some other one I owned, and Lee, well, he'd always get interested, and ask me if I'd sell whatever we were talking about. But once he heard the price on any of them, that was that—no further discussion."

"Did the defendant ever borrow any of the gun magazines that you kept in your lobby?"

"Yes. I'd say about five times. He would ask if he could borrow a certain magazine, then take it, and later, make a point of telling me he was returning it."

"So he talked about guns. No further questions. Thank

you, Mr. Alba. Your witness," Matthews concluded, almost defiantly.

Barnes got up slowly, walked behind the defense table, and stopped at the far end of the jury box so that the jury, as well as some distance, separated him from the witness. "Mr. Alba, I know for a fact that you've never been arrested, and the New Orleans Credit Bureau gives your business, the Crescent City Garage, an excellent credit rating. Would I be correct in saying those things in front of the jury?"

"I believe you would, yes."

"Now, Mr. Alba, since the prosecutor called you to testify, what do you suppose my job is?"

"Objection, Your Honor. Irrelevant, and besides, defense counsel shouldn't have to be told what his job is."

"With a little latitude, Your Honor," Barnes replied very calmly, "I can show relevance."

"A little latitude, Mr. Barnes. Overruled."

"So what's my job, Mr. Alba?"

"I suppose you want to weaken what I said about Lee," Alba replied with a great deal of sincerity in his voice.

"Ordinarily, you'd be right. But not this time. In fact, I haven't come to bury Caesar, but to praise him. Have you ever heard that expression?"

"Once or twice," Alba replied, somewhat surprised.

"You testified that you and 'Lee' talked about guns—what he owned, or at least that he owned a bunch of guns, plus what you owned or were sporterizing at the time, how to order them, where, what was in the magazines. That about right?"

Alba, still off guard from this approach, answered, "Yes, that's about right."

"Well, you know something, Mr. Alba, I'm going to say this for all the court—the judge, the attorneys, and especially the jury—to hear: I believe you one hundred percent." Barnes then made a slight turn to face the jury head on. "I mean what I just said, gentlemen, this man is not lying. He's telling the God's honest truth. He and the defendant discussed guns. Does that satisfy the promised relevance, Your Honor?"

"To my satisfaction; how 'bout you, Mr. Matthews?"

"First witness he's left alone. Objection withdrawn."

"I'm glad we got that out of the way, but here's the tough part, Mr. Alba, and I'm going to say it again, because I really *do* believe you—you talked, as you said, almost exclusively, with the defendant about guns. You're an honest business-man with a spotless police record. But why you? That's my problem, and when all this is done, it's going to be the jury's problem. You see, Mr. Alba, we're going to hear from many witnesses. Dozens, maybe hundreds, I can't say exactly and neither can anybody else here. And you, Adrian Alba, to the best of my understanding, are the only person that the de-fendant ever talked with about guns.

"He avoided the subject when he was surrounded by guns in the Marine Corps, even to the point of regularly getting in trouble with his superiors for not cleaning his unused ser-vice weapon. Mr. Frazier, who has already testified, and owns at least one quality weapon, did not testify about Lee ever discussing guns. And because you have a coffee ma-chine in your garage, you become a mutual gun-admiration society, and the defendant goes out of his way to point out that he's taking your *gun* magazines, and returning your *gun* magazines. So again, why you? It just seems too neat, too slick, too orchestrated. One person, out of hundreds, testi-fies to this. I believe you, as I said. But the whole notion, that the defendant was a gun nut or a gun fanatic would have a whole lot more believability if we had someone besides you— maybe ten others, to say the same thing. See what I'm say-ing?"

"Yes. But he did—"

"I said I believed you. It just got me curious. Let's move on. You *do* own several guns—rifles, correct?"

"Many."

"More than ten?" Barnes asked, putting a lilt of incredulity into his voice.

"Sure."

Barnes fetched the Mannlicher. "Ever see one of these be-fore?"

"Yes. As a matter of fact, I helped Lee put a sling on a gun similar to that one."

"Can you positively identify it as this weapon?"

"No."

"But it was similar?"

"Very. The same cheap junk."

Matthews was up. "Objection. Argumentative."

"Sustained."

Barnes tried a different approach: "Mr. Alba, do you own a gun of this type?"

"No."

"Is there a specific reason why not?"

"Well, I know I'm not allowed to speak for anybody but myself, but as a gun collector, I would not pollute my collection, which I take great pride in, with that cheap war-surplus junk."

"Mr. Alba, do you hunt or go target shooting?"

"Do both."

"With your expensive collection of weapons?"

"Yes. Might use them all in a season."

Matthews again objected on the grounds of relevancy and was overruled.

"What do you do with your guns before deer season starts, Mr. Alba?"

"I have them sighted in if they've been sitting any length of time."

"Exactly." Barnes walked to the defense table, got the screwdriver and went to the evidence table, talking all the while about the need for a rifle to be sighted in. "Now, I've taken this Mannlicher apart, put it in this bag, and I plan to shoot something with it. Naturally, I reassemble it," which Barnes did quickly (from lots of practice), "then what do I do, Mr. Alba? I'm on the sixth floor of a building, I've just reassembled this war surplus junk as you called it, and I've got a target in mind. What do I do?"

"You'd have to sight it in to hit anything."

"How do I do that?"

"Pick a target, oh, couple hundred yards away, fire about twelve rounds, and adjust the sights as you go along."

"Actually fire the bullets, not just pull the trigger?"

"Fire a dozen rounds. Maybe two or four dozen. Till you get it right. Then you go after your target."

"Thank you, Mr. Alba. Now, your Crescent City Garage. Good business, as we said. Have any major contracts there?"

"Yes, sir. We service, and sometimes store, all the government vehicles—FBI, Secret Service, Navy Intelligence, all of those agencies are within a block or two of the garage, and we have an exclusive contract with them."

"The agents, the men who drive these cars," Barnes continued, "do you know them well enough on sight to guarantee that you don't ever give the keys to one of the cars to a potential criminal?"

"Of course. I have to be careful."

"Did you ever see the defendant engaged in conversation with any of these known law enforcement agents?"

Matthews was insistent this time. "Objection, Your Honor, he's fishing."

"Let's see what comes out of the water. Overruled."

"Mr. Alba?" Barnes prompted.

"Well, two times I can remember, I had just turned a car over to FBI men. I knew who and what they were, but they showed me their credentials anyhow, out of routine, I suppose, and on these two occasions, the car drove a little ways —maybe six car lengths away from me, but then they stopped alongside the defendant there, held a brief conversation, then handed Lee a good-sized white envelope which he put under his shirt. Happened once, then again the next day. Seemed strange to me."

"Objection to the conclusion about 'strange.' "

"Sustained."

"Mr. Alba, you testified earlier that the defendant always asked to borrow magazines and then told you he was returning them. Was it your practice to treat your materials as if they were library property?"

"Heck, no. I don't even know why he went to all that fuss and bother to tell me he was takin' 'em, then bringing them back."

"Neither do I, Mr. Alba, neither do I. One last thought: Do you talk about guns much with other people you know, or was it just with Lee?"

"Close friends of mine are gun collectors. We're always

talking to each other about what we've bought, or seen, or heard about, test-fired, you know."

"Are you able to state that the conversations about guns that you had with the defendant were similar to the ones you had with your friends?"

"Well, with Lee, I sometimes got the very strong impression that he was trying to impress me when he didn't have the slightest idea of what he was talking about. He'd say that a gun had, oh, a real good operating bore, which is like saying a car has good operating hubcaps. Made no sense."

"No further questions, Mr. Alba. Thank you."

Matthews had a redirect for the witness: "Are you certain this is not the exact weapon and sling you worked with?"

"Could be. But like I said, I wouldn't give that junk a second look—and I didn't."

"Redirect, Mr. Barnes?"

"Mr. Alba, I'm going to show you a page that the President's Commission suggested was torn from a magazine of yours by the defendant. Could we have Holmes Exhibit 2, please?"

Everyone looked at the screens as Barnes went on. "Please examine this ad, everyone. In the upper right, a seventy-one dollar rifle with scope. To its left, thirty point oh six, with the designation 'NRA very good or better'; then two U.S. surplus pieces, both seventy-eight dollars seventy-eight cents each. Then the Mannlicher, without comment, for less than thirteen dollars. Does this ad tend to reinforce what you said earlier about the quality of the Mannlicher?"

"War surplus junk," Alba replied. "Nothing more."

"Nothing more, indeed. Move to enter Holmes Exhibit Number 2, Your Honor," Barnes concluded. The prosecution was upset that Barnes was able to finish up the morning's business with such a rhetorical flourish. And they would fume for another ninety minutes, as the judge consulted his pocket watch and announced the lunch recess.

Robert Dean stayed behind until Oswald was removed for the lunch recess. Barnes and Jeffries had left together, with a certain optimistic bounce in their respective steps.

Matthews and his staff sat in silence, as yet another witness had been methodically picked to the bone. There was no discussion, none of the usual caustic remarks about Barnes or the lousy case they had been handed by Dallas incompetents. There was just nothing. Finally, in frustration, Matthews leaned over to Dean, and asked in quiet tones, "Bob, you got a minute?"

"Always got a minute for you, Ray. We've known each other too long," Dean answered with sincerity. Dean watched as Matthews searched for words that wouldn't come, then spoke what he thought his old friend was leading up to: "It's not going well for you, Ray."

"That may be an understatement," Matthews answered.

"While we're being honest, I'll level with you, for what it's worth, Ray. It may get a lot worse. I came into this after 'Fast Eddie' got into the hunt, but he's got witnesses from here to Dallas, and even when you sell your case to the jury . . ."

"Which I haven't yet," Matthews interrupted.

"Oh, you'll get their attention with what you've got, Ray. But I can tell you, Ray, I was in Dallas representing a client back when this was happening. People were scared. They wouldn't come forward then—some still won't. But I owe you the respect and the professional courtesy—hell, it sounds like I'm talking down to you, and we've been friends too long —I owe it to you as a friend to tell you that the defense case is *solid.* Believe me when I say that. When this is over, Ray, you'll be able to say you did your job, because that's what's happening, even if you're not rejoicing over the results right now. But heads—big names—are going to roll when this comes unglued.

"I'm saying this to you as a friend, Ray. You're a good—a very good trial attorney. Always have been. You're looking at your case, but you've no idea of the magnitude of what's going to hit you when the Minnesota kid comes at you. And you know you've got to rebut, then prepare closing arguments. If I were you, Ray, I'd also spend a few hours carefully preparing a statement for the press so you don't find yourself with microphones under your nose and nothing to say." Dean got up, shook hands, gave Matthews a "keep your chin up" look, then drove his point home: "And don't wait too long to put that statement together—you may need it sooner than you think." Dean turned and left, briefcase tucked up under his arm.

"What the hell does that mean?" Eaton Graves asked.

"I have no idea," Matthews answered slowly, fear creeping into his voice, "but if Bob Dean tells you that, you better stay close to a typewriter. He's no ambulance chaser, and he's straight as an arrow. If he says we're standing in front of a fan, we'd better hope for a power failure. Well, I don't know about you two, but I'm going to go pretend I have an appetite, then get back here and get ready to hammer it to the jury that Oswald at least bought those two friggin' guns. For now, let's get out of here. Wait, one more thing—if you get the chance one of these days, brace Barnes. If he opens up, ask him what he would be doing if this had been a 'conspiracy' case. If he doesn't open up, shoot the breeze and drop it."

A short eighty minutes later, the judge and jury were back in place and Matthews, his appetite about the same as it was before he skipped lunch, announced, "The state calls Heinz Michaelis."

Barnes, briefed by Dean about the earlier conversation with Matthews, decided for a change of tack this afternoon. Matthews was down, Barnes knew, from talking with Bob Dean. He also knew he couldn't let down in any way. But Matthews might be getting used to his fastball, so he was about to get a look at Barnes's curve.

Matthews approached the witness, confidence in his stride. Barnes anticipated the testimony: "Your Honor, if it please the court, in an attempt to save time, the defense will stipulate, based on Michaelis Exhibit #7, that Mr. Michaelis, an employee of Merchanteers, Inc., of Los Angeles, California, received and processed an order, invoice number A-5371, in the handwriting of the defendant, Lee Oswald, for a pistol, numbered 510210 on the butt end and 65248 on the crane, and that such order as stipulated was shipped on March twentieth, 1963, to A. J. Hidell, P.O. Box 2915, Dallas, Texas. The defense will further stipulate that this gun is, in fact, the pistol found on the defendant's person, or, as it were, taken from the defendant at the time of his arrest in the Texas Theater on November twenty-second, 1963." Barnes sat down, went back to his pad and studiously avoided eye contact with Matthews. Oswald, as he had with the police, quietly denied the allegation to Barnes, who brushed it aside, saying, "Save that story for your memoirs."

Matthews hadn't recovered from the shock when Judge Davis asked him if the stipulation covered the testimony that he was about to elicit.

"Yes," he responded haltingly, and walked to his seat. The judge then explained what had transpired to the jury. "Do you wish to cross-exam the witness, Mr. Barnes?"

"Just one question, Your Honor." Then, to the witness, "Mr. Michaelis, does your firm, or do the documents you brought under prosecution subpoena, have any record whatsoever concerning who received the weapon shipped on March twentieth, or who paid either the ten dollars down payment or the remaining nineteen dollars ninety-five cents c.o.d?"

"No idea whatsoever," came the answer.

"Nothing further from the defense, Your Honor."

"The prosecution would like to have the documents marked as evidence and admitted, Your Honor."

"So moved."

Dean walked behind Barnes. "Eddie, that was very clever, throwing him off stride like that. But why?"

"Two reasons. I didn't want that gun handled. It could remind the jury of the second crime, and that one is the one they might make; secondly, if you just noticed, Matthews did not have the gun admitted. He may regret that."

"May?" Dean asked.

At the defense table, Vincent asked Matthews, "Since when is Barnes on our side?"

"Since never, junior. That was a clever stunt, and perfectly timed. You think all the jurors understand what happened? Those aren't fourteen lawyers over there. For some of them, *Green Acres* is an intellectual challenge. Barnes totally confused them, and juries don't convict on confusion. They want evidence, and we've got to give them some. Your Honor, the state calls Mitchell J. Scibor."

As the middle-aged man entered the courtroom and was sworn, Matthews stared defiantly at Barnes, almost daring him to pull the same kind of stunt. Barnes appeared sheepish and hurt, unlikely ever to repeat such a performance.

"Now, Mr. Scibor," Matthews began.

"Your Honor, again in the interest of time, the defense will stipulate that Mr. Scibor, in his position as general manager of Klein's Sporting Goods in Chicago, Illinois, did furnish information to the FBI on the evening of November twenty-second that Klein's had purchased a consignment of Italian rifles from the Crescent Firearms Company, and that one of those rifles bore the serial number C2766, identical to the serial number of the Mannlicher-Carcano rifle on the evidence table."

"Does such stipulation create any problems for the prosecution?" the judge asked.

It makes the prosecution very upset, Matthews wanted to answer, but he had no choice, as Barnes was cleverly staying well within the bounds of courtroom ethics. "Just for clarification, Your Honor, could the court reporter reread the stipulation for the jury's benefit?"

"So ordered." In ninety seconds, Matthews's chance to get anything out of the witness was over.

"Cross-examination, Mr. Barnes?"

"Mr. Scibor, it is now a matter of record that you received a six point five Italian carbine, serial number C2766 from Crescent Firearms. Do you understand that?"

"Yes."

"Do you know where they obtained that particular gun?"

"I'm sorry, I have no idea."

"Don't be sorry. Now, to your personal knowledge, were there any legal problems concerning the shipment of carbines you received, which included the one discussed today?"

"Yes, but that was after we sold it."

"Would you tell us about it?"

"Well, we were notified that those guns were the subject of a lawsuit, claiming they were defective."

"When you use the term 'defective,' what do you mean?"

"Objection. Calls for a conclusion," Matthews added.

"If I may," Barnes asked the judge. Davis nodded in the affirmative.

"Mr. Scibor, how long have you worked selling rifles at Klein's?"

"Almost nineteen years."

Barnes looked at the judge. "Objection overruled. Please tell the court what you meant by 'defective,' or better still, to clarify this, what you interpreted 'defective' to mean."

"Well, either they were exploding when someone pulled the trigger, or they were of such poor accuracy that there was some inherent manufacturing defect. A rifle is a simple machine, and nobody's going to buy one of those for its beauty."

"No further questions, Mr. Scibor. Enjoy your trip back to Chicago." Barnes looked at Matthews as much as to say, "I respect your years and convictions, but I went to law school, too."

Matthews told his assistants to breathe easy, as Barnes couldn't pull yet another stipulation on the next witness, and they'd make up lost ground and then some. "Your Honor, the state calls William J. Waldman."

A fiftyish, executive-looking mid-sized man was brought into the courtroom and he seemed to be surprised at its relative emptiness. Once sworn, Matthews almost seemed to charge the witness to ward off the unthinkable possibility that Barnes would preempt him again.

Halfway there, Barnes, still seated, interrupted: "Your Honor, if it please the court." Matthews stopped dead in his tracks and launched into a protest which Barnes calmly weathered.

"Carson," the judge began, "I think the jury needs a few minutes of fresh air." He then sat back, hands clasped behind his neck to wait for the jury to leave and let the two lawyers claw at each other. "Now, Mr. Matthews, what seems to be the problem?"

"These gentlemen, Your Honor, have been brought here at great expense to testify for the prosecution. They sit down and turn into defense witnesses. If this continues, I'll have no choice but to withdraw from this case."

The judge calmly beckoned both attorneys of record to the bench with a quick wave of both hands. Both stood awaiting a decision that would affect strategy down the road and would possibly determine the outcome of subsequent motions. "First of all, you spoke of great expense, Ray, and you're not going to spend Texas's money and then walk away. Make no mistake about that. Now, about these stipulations. They're legal, and you have the same right, counselor. In the interest of time, they're appreciated. Kindly think about what was said in chambers about this case being bigger than all of us, and let's get on with it. As for you, Mr. Barnes, I would have done what you're doing when I was younger—but I made mistakes then, too. Hear?"

The jury trudged back in, almost as if nothing had happened. The judge then announced, "Mr. Barnes, you were about to say something before the slight adjournment."

"Thank you, Your Honor. The defense will stipulate that the records, to be discussed subsequently, in the possession of Mr. William J. Waldman, Vice-President and Supervisor of Klein's Sporting Goods in Chicago, Illinois, are honest and accurate, and that they reflect the following information: that a coupon, clipped from an advertisement, to wit, the February 1963 issue of *American Rifleman* magazine, plus a postal money order in the amount of twenty-one dollars forty-five cents, in the handwriting of the defendant but purporting to be from A. Hidell, in an envelope bearing a U.S. airmail stamp, constituted a legitimate purchase order for a Mannlicher-Carcano six point five mm Italian Carbine, model C20-T750. The defense will then further stipulate that Klein's filled this order for a rifle and a scope, under Klein's invoice #270502, and shipped the stipulated weapon to A. Hidell, P.O. Box 2915, Dallas, Texas, on March twentieth, 1963."

"Mr. Matthews?" Judge Davis asked.

"Acceptable as far as it goes, Your Honor, but there's more to this story," Matthews said the word "more" right at the jury. In his haste to spar with Barnes and squeeze an extra sentence or two out of the witness, Matthews's desire had gotten a slight lead on his good sense.

Addressing the witness, he continued, "Now that the preliminaries are out of the way, Mr. Waldman, I wonder if you can identify this weapon that I hand you, a six point five mm Mannlicher-Carcano, serial number C2766, as the weapon that Klein's shipped to this 'Hidell' in Dallas?" Matthews looked to the jury to savor the witness's response.

"No, I can't."

Matthews took Barnes's bait. "Why not?"

"First of all, I didn't ship it. I never saw that gun. And second, it's an Italian World War II standard issue weapon. They made thousands upon thousands of them, as you might expect. But they were made, or the metal parts were made, in several foundries, just as the stocks were made on many, many different lathes. Because of that, each factory, however many there were, could have produced a gun with C2766 on it. Maybe that's the one we sold, and it may be, but maybe it isn't. We don't stamp our company name on such products."

Matthews saw an opening, which Barnes hoped he'd take. "When this gun was shipped, was it shipped with a scope?"

"Yes. That's reflected in the price. The gun was just under thirteen dollars, and then almost twenty dollars with the scope."

"Would the scope have been mounted when it was shipped?"

"Without doubt."

"Now, Mr. Waldman, look again at this weapon, serial number C2766. It has a relatively inexpensive Japanese scope. Did every Italian factory in World War II install such devices, or does that help your identification?"

"No doubt that it points towards an identification, but that's all it does. It is the cheap kind of scope you'd expect with an inexpensive weapon of this sort. But I'm still not the person to positively identify it."

"No further questions." Matthews knew he should have stopped at the stipulation. He was growing weary of being outmaneuvered by Barnes, but it struck him that it was the nature of the evidence, not the adversary, that was at the heart of the problem. While Barnes gave the jury a minute by fiddling with some papers, Earl Vincent made the suggestion that perhaps the prosecution's phones were being tapped. Matthews rejected the notion out of hand with a "by whom?" and a stare that would have killed.

"Mr. Waldman," Barnes began, "I must extend to you my admiration for the records-keeping system you have at Klein's; but it almost seems like overkill at times."

"How so?" Waldman asked, seemingly animated by a detailed question about his business practices.

"Try to follow me," Barnes instructed. "You brought

records, the ones I stipulated a few minutes ago, and in addition, there is a document that shows you deposited Hidell's money order on March thirteenth, 1963, as part of an overall deposit of thirteen thousand eight hundred twenty-seven dollars ninety-eight cents. Am I correct on that?"

While Waldman looked through his papers, as yet unopened because of Barnes's stipulation, Matthews asked Graves, "Where is he getting this stuff?"

"Here it is, yes. That figure is correct."

"Okay. So the Hidell money order amounts to a small fraction of one per cent of the total. Put another way, thirteen thousand eight hundred twenty-seven dollars ninety-eight cents would have bought 644 Mannlicher-Carcano rifles with scopes, or over 1,000 such guns without scopes. Would you keep the coupons, and the envelopes with the airmail stamps for all of those orders?"

"Not usually."

"Then why now? Why does every *atom* of paper dealing with this one transaction still exist?"

"I have no answer for you, sir."

"No answer is a form of answer, Mr. Waldman. Let's change the subject. You told Mr. Matthews that the gun was sent with the scope mounted. Are you certain of that?"

"Yes. We do that as a matter of policy unless the customer orders us otherwise. Sometimes they fancy them up themselves."

"Do you have personal knowledge as to who mounted that scope before it left Chicago?"

"William Sharp mounted that scope."

"When—*or if*—Hidell unpacked the weapon, with the scope, would it have been 'sighted in' in such a way that a rifleman could accurately use the weapon?"

"Objection. Calls for a conclusion, and assumes facts not in evidence about the rifleman."

"Let me rephrase the question. If an expert rifleman unpacked that weapon after it was shipped one thousand miles, would Klein's guarantee its accuracy to the purchaser?"

"Of course not. The scope is just mounted—screwed in place. For that price, you're not getting accuracy."

"Mr. Waldman, if someone sat in that chair you're sitting in now and testified that your product, a weapon like the one over on that table—maybe even that one—was a high quality, accurate, rapid-fire weapon, how would you as the vice-president of Klein's deal with such praise?"

"Rubbish."

"The praise or the weapon? Strike the question, please, the answer probably applies to both. Thank you, Mr. Waldman. No further questions."

"Redirect, Mr. Matthews?"

"No, Your Honor, but I'd like the court to catch its breath and make sure that the necessary exhibits have been introduced. I offer the court Waldman Exhibits 1 through 10, Michaelis Exhibits 1 through 7, Commission Exhibits 785 and 788, the envelope and the order for the rifle, and the money order to Klein's. Any objection to that, Mr. Barnes?"

"No, but I'd like to clarify one more issue with the witness before he's excused."

"Quickly, I hope," the judge suggested.

"Very quickly." Barnes grabbed the Mannlicher. "Mr. Waldman, the order in question was for a C20-T750. That weapon is thirty-six inches long. This gun is forty point two inches long. Any comment?"

Waldman was weary of traps, and in his weariness, he fell into another. "It sounds like a difference of four point two inches," he responded simply.

"It does indeed, it does indeed," Barnes echoed, trying to make the whole tempest in a teapot sound sinister. "Thank you again, Mr. Waldman."

After seeing the latest in a long string of witnesses weakened by the defense, Matthews leaned back, let out a sigh, and calmly concluded that bad luck was better than no luck at all, for whatever sense that made. He then requested a brief recess, since the defense's stipulations had thrown off his witness timetable, and some checking needed to be done.

In point of fact, it was the occasion for a calm, reasoned debate as to how to proceed for the prosecution. It had been expected that at this point, the FBI documents expert, James Cadigan, would be called, and would, with his expertise and FBI i.d. on his lapel, impress the jury by showing that Oswald had signed his name or "Hidell" to a variety of questionable documents. But Barnes's stipulations had removed the most damaging testimony, and there were very few remaining documents. Eventually, it was decided to put him on the stand, and try to get to the Moscow Embassy personnel that Oswald had run afoul of in his Soviet travels. Having shown what Oswald was capable of in 1959 at the embassy, the plan was then to lead off, on Friday morning, with Dr. Hartogs, who had examined a truant thirteen-year-old Oswald in 1953 and could provide the jury with the tale of a life gone bad for many years.

"Your Honor, the state calls Special Agent James C. Cadigan of the Federal Bureau of Investigation." Matthews announcement was still professional and upbeat with no reflection of earlier events. Barnes was inwardly pleased, as Cardigan was one of the most vulnerable of the FBI's "experts."

Matthews was able to begin his examination of the witness safe in the knowledge that there would be no stipulations here, so after a few questions to establish Special Agent Cadigan's bona fides, Matthews requested that he be designated an "expert witness."

"Any problems with that, Mr. Barnes?" the judge asked.

"None whatsoever," Barnes answered, in a tone that Matthews had heard before.

"Mr. Cadigan, the defense attorney, in the course of testimony given this afternoon, has made stipulations about some of the items we were planning to discuss. Covered under those stipulations was CE 785, the purchase order to Klein's Sporting Goods, and the money order sent to Klein's. So it will no longer be our job to verify them. It has been admitted that the defendant was responsible for them. Nevertheless, we still have business. I show you CE 791, an application for P.O. Box 2915 in Dallas, the address to which both the pistol and the rifle were shipped. Would you tell the court who wrote this application?"

"The defendant, Lee Harvey Oswald."

"And this Selective Service card, found on the defendant at the time of his arrest . . ."

"Objection," Barnes said in a clipped tone. "No foundation.

We don't know about that card at the time of the defendant's arrest."

"Sustained. Perhaps you could rephrase your question, Mr. Matthews."

"Mr. Cadigan, I show you a Selective Service card, bearing a photo of the defendant and the name Alek James Hidell. What can you tell us about that?"

"Without going into detail that the jury might not understand, it is a photo forgery. The document was once a valid Selective Service card, was altered, photographed, and made to look like an original. It's a simple process."

"I now show you CE 818, a 'Fair Play for Cuba Committee' membership card, bearing the signatures of Lee Harvey Oswald and Alek J. Hidell. What does your expert scrutiny of this document reveal?"

"It was signed by Lee Harvey Oswald."

"Now, Special Agent Cadigan, let me ask you about the brown paper bag that was found on the sixth floor. I believe the FBI reference number for that was Q-10?"

"Yes, Q-10."

"Did you perform comparison tests on the bag found on the sixth floor of the Book Depository with materials available for daily use in the Depository?"

"We did, and they were found to be identical." This statement got the jury's attention. Sensing that, and knowing that about all he had left was a fake Hidell vaccination certificate, Matthews concluded he had no further questions for the witness and returned to the defense table to his two uncharacteristically smiling assistants.

Barnes remained seated and turned to a new, clean page on a yellow tablet. "Mr. Cadigan, for the record, are there any plain, old FBI 'agents,' or is everyone so employed a 'Special Agent'?"

"The usual title accorded to accredited bureau personnel is 'Special Agent.'"

"Good. They're all special. Even I was special when I was employed by 'the bureau', as you say. But you're extra special, Mr. Cadigan, because you learned your lines with Mr. Matthews very well."

"Your Honor," Matthews interrupted, "counsel is clearly badgering the witness."

Barnes apologized before he could be reprimanded in front of the jury, then told the court he would prove his point. "Mr. Cadigan, when you testified about the Selective Service card a few minutes ago, you wrapped it up in a neat little package. Answer this: Did the defendant sign the name Alek J. Hidell on that card?"

"That was not able to be determined either way."

"So you cannot say, 'The defendant did.' "

"No, I can't."

"And when you testified about the Cuban Committee membership card, you said it bore two names, and Lee Harvey Oswald signed it. Were you saying he signed both names, or just his own?"

"Just his own. We were not able to reach a conclusion as to who signed 'Alek J. Hidell.' "

"Then you testified about the bag, Q-10, I believe it was. Did your study of this bag develop any evidence that the bag had ever contained a Mannlicher-Carcano six point five mm Italian rifle?"

"No."

"You also testified, and I rudely suggested your lines were well rehearsed for which I apologized, that Q-10, the bag, was identical in composition to a bag, designated K-52, that was made from materials found in the Book Depository. Did you so testify?"

"Yes."

"Was the tape on Q-10 the *identical* width of the tape available in the Depository?"

"No. It was not identical."

"Could we have CE 2444 on the screens please?" Barnes waited while the material was brought up and had time to cast a quick smile in the direction of Ray Matthews, who sank down in his chair as if he were looking for a hurricane shelter.

When the document came up, Barnes walked back to Cadigan and began, "Now, Special Agent Cadigan, let's see if the bureau's lab can verify your testimony. As I read it, the document on the screen says, 'Specimens received

12/10/63; (paragraph) K52 A replica sack made at the Texas School Book Depository from paper and tape available in the shipping room of the Texas School Book Depository. (paragraph) Result of examination: It was determined that the paper and tape used for specimen K52 is *different* from the paper and tape used for the Q10 paper bag that was previously submitted in this case.' End of statement. Well, Mr. Cadigan, that FBI laboratory report does not exactly support your testimony, does it?"

The witness was silent and avoided Barnes, who requested the court to get an answer for his question. "That's only one test," Cadigan testily replied.

"And there is only one truth, sir. I again apologize for suggesting you had rehearsed your lines. Obviously, you had not. Two final questions, Mr. Cadigan. You testified about the defendant's rental of a post office box and ownership of a membership card in the Fair Play for Cuba Committee. Are either of those actions a violation of any local, state, or federal law?"

"Not in and of themselves, but . . ."

"Thank you. Secondly, Mr. Cadigan, did you develop any evidence as to who performed the simple photographic forgery of the Selective Service card about which you testified?"

"I have no idea about that."

"Mr. Matthews?"

"Your Honor, at this time, I would like CE 785, 791, and 818, as well as the original bag, Q-10 admitted as evidence."

"Mr. Barnes?"

"No objection to the first three, since they are meaningless, but until and unless there is better testimony than what we just heard regarding the paper bag, I would move that it be ruled inadmissable. While we are admitting evidence, I would like CE 2444 admitted."

"Please approach, gentlemen." Judge Davis waited while Matthews handed a file to Graves. When all were present, he continued: "Now, I have no problems with the first three either, but I can't rule either way on the bag until we've heard more; but know this, Ray, we can't have any more—I don't want to say the word 'perjury,' but I can't think of a synonym, regarding that bag or anything else. Resume your places.

Seven hundred seventy-three, 791, 2444, and 818 are admitted. Q-10 will be reviewed further. And Special Agent Cadigan, your testimony, I must warn you, may result in legal action being brought against you. You're dismissed."

Matthews just barely gave Cadigan time to clear the witness stand before calling Richard E. Snyder, who had been the senior consular officer in the Moscow Embassy on the day when Lee Oswald had shown up at the embassy, slammed his U.S. passport down, and announced that he intended to become a Russian citizen and share all that he knew about American military secrets and technology with his newfound comrades.

The prosecutor established all that, with minor difficulties and no objections from Barnes, in direct examination, with the highlight being the statement that the defendant, whom he identified, but with the understanding that he had not seen him in a few years, "threatened that he would make available to the Soviet authorities or to the Soviet Union what he had learned concerning his specialty—he was an electronics expert of some sort, a radar technician—at any rate, he would make available to the Soviet Union such knowledge as he had acquired while in the Marine Corps concerning his specialty."

Matthews also asked if Oswald had submitted a written request that his U.S. citizenship be revoked, and Snyder answered in the affirmative.

Barnes, in cross-examination, picked up on that theme, eliciting a distinction from the witness that although Oswald did submit a request in writing, it was not in the proper format and was therefore ignored. "Then, Mr. Snyder," Barnes asked loudly, "did the defendant in fact renounce his citizenship—was he at any time anything other than a U.S. citizen?"

"No. He was always a U.S. citizen."

"Mr. Snyder, in the diplomacy business, would you say that a prerequisite is an understanding of people?"

"Absolutely."

"Such being the case, how would you characterize Mr. Oswald's behavior?"

"Objection," Matthews interposed. "Calls for a conclusion on the part of the witness."

"I'll allow it. Overruled."

Snyder spoke clearly: "He was extremely sure of himself. He seemed to know what his mission was."

"That's a very interesting characterization, Mr. Snyder, and very astute. And what was your mission?"

"I don't understand."

"How much of the time were you working for the State Department and how much of it were you working for the CIA?"

"I'm not going to answer that," Snyder replied angrily.

"Oh, yes you are," Judge Davis singsonged in a calm voice.

"All embassy personnel routinely route traffic and messages to the attention of intelligence agencies. It goes with the job."

"Agreed," answered Barnes, "and that would be acceptable if you were a clerk. You weren't. Does the judge have to remind you that you swore to tell the truth?"

Snyder looked to Matthews for help, who tried an end run: "Your Honor, we are dealing with sensitive matters here."

"Indeed we are, so they should be addressed."

"I report certain sensitive information directly to the CIA; I was posted to Moscow to do that. Does that satisfy you?" Snyder was still upset.

"Completely," Barnes answered calmly. "Just two more questions. First, when the defendant angrily arrived on that October day in 1959, was his anger directed against people, places, or ideologies?"

"Well," Snyder said, calming down and focusing on the question, "he was mad about some things in the U.S., but just what I don't recall. He certainly had, as you phrased it in your question, some ideological differences, but there were no statements that I can recall about any individuals."

"Finally, Mr. Snyder, it was something of a scandal, when, a few months after this particular incident, almost three dozen Soviet recording devices were discovered in the U.S. Embassy where you were employed by your, uh, various bosses. Is it possible for you to think back to that day and allow for the possibility that the defendant, in making the statements that he made that day, *wanted* the Russians to believe he was attempting to defect?"

"Conclusionary again, Your Honor," Matthews griped.

"Sustained."

"Nothing further, Your Honor."

Matthews called for CE 910 for the screens for redirect. "Mr. Snyder, I call your attention to this document, which is labeled 'Department of State, CONFIDENTIAL,' and which concludes, about the defendant, 'Says has offered Soviets any information he has acquired as enlisted radar operator.' Not 'will offer': *'has offered.'* Does that sound like someone talking to Russian microphones?"

This time it was Barnes's turn to say, "Conclusionary."

"Sustained."

"No further redirect. I would like CE 910 submitted into evidence at this time."

Judge Davis so ordered.

Barnes had strength in his tread as he approached the witness for recross. "Mr. Snyder, I need a simple 'yes' or 'no' from you on one question that is swirling all around your testimony and this case. Here's an individual that sneaks off to big bad Russia, offers secrets—important ones at that, makes a scene at the embassy, suggests renunciation of his U.S. citizenship to become a Russian, drops from sight for quite a while, then shows up with a Russian wife and wants to go home. His behavior, taken at face value, sounds treasonous. But the State Department, one of your employers, hands him a check to get him home, and returns his passport. Yes or no—is this standard procedure to hand over American taxpayers' money to send such a person back to America with no questions asked?"

"No. It certainly is not standard procedure."

"Thank you, sir. I regret the need to explore the depths of your career. I hope you understand."

Prosecutor Matthews then bolstered Richard Snyder's testimony with that of John A. McVickar, a consular officer who had been present on several of the occasions when the defendant had presented himself at the embassy. He told essentially the same story as Snyder, including, in cross-examination, the notion, as he put it, that "It seemed to me there was a possibility that he had been in contact with others before or during his Marine Corps tour who had provoked him and encouraged him in his actions," and suggested that in all the moves he had made in his so-called "defection," he had been well coached.

McVickar was not able to make a conclusion, due to Matthews's objections, as to whether it had been Americans or others who had encouraged the defection. Barnes scored a few points when he reminded McVickar that he had testified that perhaps Oswald had been influenced "before" his Marine Corps days. Barnes concluded with what seemed to be a throwaway question: "Mr. McVickar, did you testify before the presidential commission?"

"Yes, in a rather run-down building in Washington."

"And where were you serving in the diplomatic corps when you were summoned to Washington to tell, essentially, of conversations you overheard?"

"Bolivia."

"Your Honor," Matthews objected, "I see no relevance to this line of questioning. None at all."

Barnes walked to the bench and was going to speak to the judge in hushed tones whether Matthews accompanied him or not. Not wanting to be left out, Matthews made haste to be included. "Your Honor, and you too, Ray, the question is relevant simply because the U.S. government flew McVickar to Washington *from Bolivia* to report hearsay, when there were dozens of eyewitnesses to the crime who wanted to testify, or others, like Jack Ruby, who requested eleven times to be taken to Washington to tell his story. They were all denied. This witness was flown in from Bolivia for vintage 1959 hearsay. There's something rotten in the state of Denmark, gentlemen."

"I'm glad you didn't say 'Texas,' Mr. Barnes. Back to your benches." The judge then addressed the court. "The court will allow the statement with respect to Bolivia, but sees no purpose served in exploring that any further."

Barnes indicated he was done with the witness.

Matthews assessed the day as a poor one, but was open with his assistants when he said that Barnes had handed them a gift on a silver platter by introducing the pre-Marine

Corps days, as the next day's leadoff witness would paint a very negative picture of the defendant during those days. Given that, something of great value had been salvaged from the day.

As defense counsel packed up after assuring the defendant that everything was fine, Dean was very pleased that the first FBI expert had virtually been caught in perjury. "But," he cautioned, "you and I both know, Eddie, that such a situation is very unlike the FBI. They don't lie to win their cases. What's the bottom line?"

Barnes didn't know and didn't pretend to know, but he offered Dean the theory that they would probably get the answer to that question at roughly the same time that they got the answer to two other questions: who was Oswald, and who was in the window on November twenty-second? Dean accepted the wisdom of that hypothesis.

# Six

Friday, January 8, 1965. Barnes was in court early, having spoken with his wife the night before only to learn that their eight-year-old boy had chipped a tooth in school. Having been absent for so long from home, the news hit Barnes hard, and knowing he would not sleep, he reviewed the case, aware the weekend was coming and hoping that somehow, by working all night, the case could be brought to an end sooner. Of course, that gambit had failed, so now Barnes was at Bailiff Carson's coffee machine, counting on Maxwell House to keep him awake. He was beginning to doubt if Matthews's witnesses could.

Earl Vincent shared a joke with the Vermont state trooper at the door, then joined Barnes at the coffee station. "Won't need much coffee today, Eddie," he began. "Could be a short day; maybe the judge will shut this down early for the weekend." Sure, Barnes thought, and maybe the real killer will come in and confess.

"Part of me loves the idea of a long weekend," Barnes replied, upbeat, "but the rest of me says, 'Let's get this over and get back home.' My kid chipped a tooth yesterday. No big deal, except when daddy is a thousand miles away."

"Sorry to hear that," Vincent replied with sincerity. "I'm sure it won't distract you during testimony."

"Depends. Who you got today?"

Vincent could have played ignorant, but if he was going to get anything from Barnes, he had to meet him halfway. "I think Ray's going to start with Dr. Hartogs."

"Then we'll have a long weekend, 'cause he won't even make it to the stand. I don't care what the case is, the testimony of someone who examined a thirteen year old over a decade ago—and for truancy, no less, is worthless. That, of course, is my opinion; there's also the old matter of doctor-patient privilege, which will guarantee that no doctor that ever treated Oswald will testify unless called by the defense."

Vincent knew when to play the good guy. "You might just be right, Eddie. God knows you've been right more times than Ray so far this week. Uh, I'm a little curious. Could I ask you something, off the record?"

"As long as the steno isn't here," Barnes answered, "it is off the record. Shoot."

"Well," Vincent began, seeming to be lost for words, "I've been trying to figure this case out, and either something's wrong, or my inexperience is showing." Consider the possibility that you're right on both ideas, Barnes thought. "Anyhow, Eddie, I was wondering, would this thing have shaken down differently if the prosecution had gone for a conspiracy charge?"

Barnes was surprised and somewhat unprepared for the question. "Off the record, you said. Well, it would depend on a couple of things—the wording for one, and I don't even know the possible sentences, and that would certainly be a factor. Secondly, if the crime had happened here in Lubbock, and Ray, Eaton, and you had been in charge, I would have bet that you would have filed conspiracy, and made a whole lot better—probably winnable—case than the one you inherited. But let's just say hypothetically, if it was a pure conspiracy charge, I probably would have been to your office in haste to see what kind of a deal we could cut so our boy Lee would tell us all he knew about the others. If it was an 'accessory' charge, depending on the sentence, either cut a deal or plead him guilty."

"How many 'others' are you talking about?" Vincent asked, almost forgetting the remainder of Barnes's answer.

"Before I answer that," Barnes told him, "let me ask you something. With what you know already, do you think the patsy did it alone?"

"It doesn't seem that way," Vincent answered.

"That's because it wasn't," Barnes said with finality. "You've got multiple—two, maybe three—shooters, and they were pros, so you may have an accomplice right there with a shooter to catch the cartridges. Then you've got people on the knoll being ordered around by Secret Service before and after 12:30, and those Secret Service are counterfeit. There just were no Secret Service there. Then you've got fake witnesses. How many people gave reports to the police about this or that, and the police have no record of who the witnesses were? Once, maybe twice, in the confusion, that might make sense. But as a regular occurrence, it doesn't wash."

"So you're talking about a dozen or so people?"

"Yeah. And the minnow is on trial." Barnes looked at Vincent to reinforce his point.

"Patsy for whom?" Vincent asked.

"Not my job, Earl, and to tell you the truth, except to help 'the minnow,' I don't want to know. They're well financed, they're powerful, and they're deadly. *And they're smart. . . .* How much of the work did you do on the discovery end of this?"

"Quite a bit of it, such as Dallas gave it to us."

"Here's a freebie for you, and for Ray, so you can appreciate the counterfeit nature of the case you're doing your best to win. Reread the testimony by Palmer McBride. When you digest what he's got to say, ask me again about this. Also remember I warned you Hartogs wouldn't make it to the witness stand." Barnes raised his refilled coffee cup and headed for the defense table. Vincent affected a bored look and headed out to share what he had learned with his boss, who was surprised by Barnes's plea bargain candor, but not thrilled that Barnes was assuming that Hartogs would not testify. Little did Matthews know that he was just reaching for the cheese.

Gradually, the remaining principals arrived, and Judge Davis took the bench promptly at ten. Before bringing in the jury, he told both attorneys that James Worrell had been deposed the previous day and had been such a case of nerves that he had neither added nor subtracted anything of substance. He continued by stating that Mr. Worrell would be the guest of the state of Texas over the weekend, and another attempt would be made to get a coherent statement from him, but failing that, a grand jury would be summoned to begin hearing testimony where there was suspicion to warrant it. With that, the defendant preceded the jury by about two minutes, and everyone was settled in when Prosecutor Matthews announced, "The state calls Dr. Renatus Hartogs."

Barnes was immediately up, and cast an icy stare over his shoulder at the Vermont officer guarding the door. The officer did not move to summon the witness. "Your Honor," Barnes began, "the defense can see no possible relevance whatsoever in the testimony of this witness. He had contact with the defendant in 1953 over the issue of school truancy, hardly a capital crime, and has undoubtedly had thousands of teenagers pass before him since then—and the memory is a fragile thing to begin with. Beyond that personal objection, there is the question of doctor-client privilege, which has been held sacrosanct by American courts since time immemorial. Testimony twelve years old could be almost automatic grounds for appeal down the road."

Matthews rose confidently to address the challenge: "Your Honor, on the first point, need I remind the court that it has been the defense which has constantly requested a bit of latitude in order to show relevance? The prosecution asks for only the same latitude. On the question of privilege, the young Oswald was ordered to be treated, if that is the correct word, by Dr. Hartogs; he did not seek the constitutional protection of the doctor-client privilege. I assure you, the prosecution would not call witnesses subject to the privilege rule, and we can furnish legal citations—many of them—in which doctors in situations like Dr. Hartogs finds himself in are regularly called to the stand. Defendants are *ordered* to undergo testing. Mr. Oswald, admittedly a teenager then, and hardly more now, was *ordered* to undergo testing for infractions of standard codes."

"I'm going to allow the witness, Mr. Barnes. Naturally, you retain the right to object or cross-examine, as always."

"I would then request, Your Honor, that the defendant *not* be present in the courtroom initially." Barnes had a strategy in mind with that ploy, and he needed to recoup from what had been an excellent rebuttal by Matthews.

"I see nothing oddly irregular in that." Oswald, who knew of Barnes's plans, was escorted back to the tank.

The witness was then brought in, and while Matthews established his bona fides of having been chief psychiatrist at the Youth House in New York City since 1951 and having overseen a staff of three hundred, Dean told Barnes, "Good job, Eddie. I was afraid you were going to overact."

Matthews requested that Dr. Hartogs be designated an expert witness.

"Mr. Barnes?"

"As you recall, Your Honor, I had difficulty with this gentleman as a witness, much less an expert . . . and forgive my nativism as well, but I have immediate difficulty with these doctors who do not hold any medical degrees whatsoever from colleges or universities in the United States."

"Your concerns are noted, Mr. Barnes, but it is difficult, as you imply, to have this witness without him being an expert, wouldn't you agree?"

"Exactly," Barnes said. "And what this court really doesn't need is an amateur psychiatrist. I withdraw my objection." As he sat down, he gave Matthews a wink and the prosecutor had the sudden urge to thank the witness for coming and dismiss him.

After a few preliminary questions as to the date of contact between the witness and defendant, and the reason, school truancy, Matthews asked what the findings had been.

"I found him to have definite traits of dangerousness," Dr. Hartogs replied.

Barnes was again up quickly. "Just what I warned the court about, Your Honor. I would suggest that if we consult any leading textbook on psychiatry, we will not find the term 'dangerousness.' Could we get a clarification? Was he a threat to pigeons in the park, was he a threat to break into song when the sun came out? Dangerousness—really."

"Could you put your diagnosis in other words?" the judge asked.

"Well, in other words, this child had a potential for explosive, aggressive, assaultive acting out which was rather unusual to find in a child who was sent to Youth House on such a mild charge as truancy from school."

Matthews thanked his witness for clarification, and asked if there were any other traits he remembered.

"Yes. He was polite. He was in full contact with reality." But you may not be, Matthews thought.

"And what was your recommendation, doctor?"

"Objection, Your Honor, best evidence. Surely such a bureaucratic processing of a truant child as this would generate paperwork. This court should see the documents, not be asked to rely on the witness's twelve-year-old recollection."

"Mr. Matthews?" the judge asked.

"Your Honor, the witness was subpoenaed to bring records, but was unable to produce any whatsoever, perhaps, as Mr. Barnes suggests, because it was a long time ago. The best we can offer, therefore, is his recollection."

"I'll reserve judgment on the objection until the witness has completed his testimony, but the defense does have a valid point here. Continue, Doctor. What was your recommendation?"

"I recommended that this youngster should be committed to an institution." This was the kind of testimony that Matthews had wanted the jury to hear all week—no wonder Barnes objected. And that sly wink.

"No further questions. Mr. Barnes?"

Barnes remained seated, leaning back almost casually in his chair. For now, he wanted to be the jury's focus, not the witness. "Dr. Hartogs, you stated your facility had a staff of three hundred or more. How many of them were psychiatrists?"

"Two or three."

"That many," Barnes thought out loud. "And what did that

mean to you, in terms of case loads? How many different children would you deal with in a week?"

"A dozen, sometimes more."

"Which would make about six hundred or more per year, for fourteen years, that's over eight thousand children, doctor. It's amazing that without any documents you can remember this individual truant."

"We are trained to do that, sir."

"Let's test your training," Barnes challenged, while Matthews began to hear a disquieting tone. "Do you recall the first time you were interviewed by the FBI regarding the defendant?"

"One does not quickly forget a visit from the FBI, though we have been visited about other patients."

"On that first occasion, Doctor, did you indicate a recollection that you had occasion to treat Lee Oswald?"

"I could not recall the boy, no."

"But obviously you have since, because you made us aware of his dangerousness, and how you recommended he be institutionalized."

"That is correct."

"Can you describe this boy you treated?"

Matthews was desperate for an objection, but he knew it was he who had asked for the latitude and he couldn't very well take it back.

"Yes. He was medium sized, slender, curly haired, not very talkative."

"Medium sized *and* slender? You can't have it both ways, Doctor. And when did he sprout curls?" Barnes nodded to the Vermont trooper at the far entrance, and Oswald was brought in, thinning, wispy hair and all, for the jury to see, while the witness sat contemplating a question for which nobody had an answer.

"Is this the medium-sized, slender, curly haired person you treated twelve years ago?"

"I believe it to be, yes."

"And he was polite?"

"He was not emotional at all; he was in control of his emotions. He showed a cold, detached outer attitude. He talked about his situation, about himself in a, what should I say, nonparticipating fashion. I mean there was nothing emotional, affective about him, and this impressed me. That was the only thing which I remember."

"This testimony strongly contradicts what you said a few moments ago, Doctor," Barnes said with belligerence as he picked up a note pad, "when you spoke of explosive, aggressive, assaultive acting out . . ." One minute you say he's polite, then explosive, then 'not emotional at all.' Which is it?"

"It's what I said."

"I could ask the court to hold you accountable to be more responsive, Doctor, but your evasiveness is helping me. Now, you said you recommended that the defendant be put in an institution. What kind? The institute for better table tennis? The institute for the prevention of dancing mailmen? You can't dodge this one, Doctor."

"I don't recall specifically, but it would have been either a mental hospital, a training school, or residential treatment center."

"Because he was polite and nonemotional?"

"That was my finding, sir."

"Without documentation to support it?"

"It was a long time ago."

"Indeed it was, Doctor. Do you remember a man named John Carro?"

"I believe he was the case worker who brought this case to us."

"Indeed he was. Could we please have Carro Exhibit Number one on the screens?" Barnes said, volume increasing, as he rose from his chair. Approaching the witness as the screens came to life, Barnes pounded away. "This, Doctor, is the report you failed to bring although ordered to do so by subpoena from Mr. Matthews. It is available through the New York City Board of Education, and the original is still, in fact, on file there, surprisingly enough, under the name 'Oswald, Lee Harvey.' Would you like to read it all, or shall we skip to your recommendation, Doctor?"

"I would like a minute to review it."

"Take all the time you want, sir." Barnes returned to the defense table, leaning against the front of it with his legs crossed. Matthews told Eaton Graves that if the prosecution had any other expert witnesses planned for the day to send them home.

"When you want to see the next page, just announce that, Doctor, and it will appear on the screen. In the meantime, Your Honor, I withdraw my earlier 'best evidence' objection." The jury was scrutinizing the witness's dilemma. Dr. Hartogs reviewed a couple of pages, then announced that he recalled the report.

"And what does the report say about recommendations, Doctor?"

"There doesn't seem to be anything about an institution, I must confess," Hartogs answered.

"Confess is a perfect choice of words, Doctor. As I read it, and please stop me if I misspeak, it says, 'we' and I'm intensely curious who '*we*' are, but 'We arrive therefore at the recommendation that he should be placed on probation under the condition that he seek help and guidance through contact with a child guidance clinic, where he should be treated preferably by a male psychiatrist who could substitute, to a certain degree at least, for the lack of a father figure'; there's more, but did I miss the part about the institution, *Doctor?*"

"No."

"One last question, Doctor. Did you state the belief before the President's Commission that you felt presidential assassins were mentally disturbed persons?"

"Yes, I did."

"And what of other murderers? Are they just normal people who have a weapon handy and make a slight mistake? Don't bother with the answer, Doctor, it probably would be polite, nonemotional, yet explosive, and I fear your dangerousness. Your Honor, I'd like Carro Exhibit Number 1 entered as a defense document, and I am totally through with this . . . witness. Mr. Matthews, to make up for the witness's refusal, I'll furnish you with a copy of the report. In the meantime, it's in volume 8 and 19 of the records of the presidential commission."

Matthews had to choke back his emotions and look good before the jury. "No further questions at this time." Earl Vincent had told Graves and Matthews that Hartogs would never get to the stand, and now they understood why Barnes wanted him there.

Matthews didn't have time to reflect on this most recent ambush, but as he announced, "The state calls Officer Marrion L. Baker," he was consoled by the note written by Graves on the pad in front of him: "It's Friday."

A well-conditioned police officer entered, wearing his uniform. Nice touch, Barnes thought. After being sworn, he told of the position of his motorcycle, approximately half a block behind the presidential car, at the time of the shooting.

"And what was your impression of the source of the shots?"

"My immediate reaction was that they sounded high, so I looked up. It also occurred to me at the same time that they were coming either from the building right in front of me, which would be the Texas School Book Depository, or the one across to the right of it."

"How many shots did you hear, Officer Baker?"

"Three evenly spaced shots."

"What actions did you take?"

"I steered right for the Book Depository, got off the motorcycle fast, dashed through the people, and got inside as quickly as I could. I then encountered Mr. Truly, who identified himself as, well, he was somebody important there, and I wanted him to get me upstairs fast. The elevators were already upstairs, so I had him lead me to the stairs. When we got to the second floor, and I can't be more specific about it, but somehow my eye caught the movement of someone in the lunchroom there, so I went in there, and there was that man sitting over there, and I went up to him, and asked Mr. Truly if this guy worked there, and he said that he did, so then I left and went upstairs, eventually getting out onto the roof and watching the commotion develop."

"Did the defendant appear to be hurrying, when he somehow caught your eye?"

"Conclusionary," Barnes gambled.

"Overruled."

"I have to think that I stopped him because he was hurrying—why else would I, if I thought the shots came from high up? But when I got to him, he gave no indication of being out of breath or anything."

"Officer Baker, did you reconstruct these movements for the President's Commission, as well as for my office?"

"Yes, sir. I think I now know the route by heart."

"I'm sure you do. Would you tell us how long, it was determined, it took you to encounter the defendant?"

"Well, with the Washington people, it was ninety seconds, but it was faster than that, 'cause they didn't have me in any hurry, and I know I was moving. When we did it again, I went at a trot, and that was seventy-five seconds."

"Thank you, Officer. No further questions."

Barnes began his cross-examination by commending Baker for his quick reflexes and told Baker that unknown to the witness, he, too, believed that something happened "up high" in the Texas School Book Depository. He also told Baker that he must indeed have been in a hurry, because one witness testified that a white-helmeted officer entered the building within ten seconds of the final shot.

"That could only have been me," Baker said proudly.

Barnes changed gears: "Where were you originally assigned to ride your motorcycle that day, Officer?"

"Right alongside the President's car, but our orders were changed about five, ten minutes before the parade started."

"I see. Now, when you heard the first shot, you said you thought it sounded high, so you looked up. Did you see either of the other two shots you heard actually fired?"

"No. I glanced over those building windows, but I couldn't see anything."

"You said the shots were evenly spaced. How long between, to the best you can remember, given the fact that you were already reacting to the event?"

"Three seconds. About, I'd say, as fast as you could bolt one of those bolt-action rifles. I don't believe it would be over three seconds."

"So, if I understand, you're saying, 'shot,' three seconds, 'shot,' three seconds, 'shot,' for a total of about six seconds?"

"That's right."

"Officer, in your training, do you use rifles?"

"Certainly."

Barnes walked over and retrieved the Mannlicher-Carcano. "Officer, I'd like you to perform another reconstruction for the jury. I'll walk back here, about ten feet away. What I want you to do is shoulder that rifle, pull the trigger with the gun facing me, then work the bolt, pull the trigger again, then work the bolt and trigger action a third time. You follow me?"

"Sure." Baker did as instructed, "shooting" Barnes three times.

Barnes then took the gun away, and looked back over his shoulder to ask, "Is that about the way you remember the spacing of the shots?"

"Yes. Like I said, about as fast as you could work the bolt."

"I remember what you said, officer; it just struck me that you might have taken a bit longer *if you had had to aim the weapon at a target a few hundred feet away.* But you didn't," Barnes said, more calmly. "Now, did the defendant have anything in his hands when you saw him?"

"If he had anything, it was a soda bottle, but I just can't be positive."

"But he had no gun?"

"No gun."

"Is your lack of certainty about the soda bottle the reason your original report to the FBI first said 'drinking a coke' and subsequently that phrase is scratched out?"

"I wasn't aware it was scratched out."

Barnes let the jury ponder that thought for a moment, then pressed on: "When you saw the defendant, were you suspicious of him?"

"No. He was calm and collected."

"Officer, I show you CE 673, which is said to be the shirt that was worn by the defendant when he was arrested. I would like you to take a good look at it and tell us if you can identify it as the shirt that was worn by the defendant in the time frame immediately after the shooting when you encountered him."

"This is not the shirt he was wearing. The shirt he had on was more of a greenish brown, and had a peculiar sort of pattern to it. This is not it."

"Officer, were you on the upper floors of the Book Depository when a rifle was found?"

"Yes."

"Did you see the weapon before it was removed from where
it was hidden?"

"Yes."

"Were you present when it was established that there were
not latent prints visible on the stock or trigger housing?"

"Yes."

"Those reconstructions, ninety seconds and seventy-five
seconds. When did the timing start?"

"With the first shot," Baker stated.

"Officer, we've had some interesting testimony this week.
As I told you, one witness complimented your speed in getting into the building. Another witness told us of seeing the
last shot fired, diving for cover, and seeing the assassin casually leave the scene. Now we know that the gun was hidden,
not just dropped, clean of fingerprints, *and* that the elevators
were stuck on an upper floor. You've told us that you were a
man with a mission that afternoon, Officer. Now, Officer, you
were there when the event happened, and for the reconstructions. Can you tell this court to a certainty that a defendant,
in seventy-five seconds after the first shot, seen by a witness
who said he was *not* acting in haste, who may have lost precious time wiping clean a stock and trigger housing, as well
as placing, not throwing the weapon in hiding, and unable to
ride the cumbersome elevators, could have been encountered by you on the second floor and give the appearance of
being calm and collected?"

"That question has been asked before, and I won't pretend
to have an answer. I'll tell you this, though. If what you say is
accurate, there's no way *anybody* from the sixth floor got to
that second floor lunchroom ahead of me."

"Thank you, Officer. Nothing further."

Matthews leaned over to Barnes, now back at the defense
table, and asked for another reconstruction, but this time
using bullets. Barnes played the part of the gracious winner:
"Only if Oswald is firing them, Ray."

The prosecutor had the briefest of intervals to digest
Barnes's attempt at humor before calling Roy Truly as his

next witness. An older yet reasonably spry man entered the court, was sworn, and indicated in preliminaries that he was the superintendent of the Texas School Book Depository. Further questioning elicited that he had furnished the police with an address and a description of a missing employee named Lee Oswald, and that earlier, he had quickly reentered the building after the shooting and encountered a police officer, whose name he did not know until March of 1964, and was in his presence when the defendant was approached, and subsequently led the policeman to the roof. From there, he testified, he returned to a "regular madhouse" on the first floor.

"Was a reconstruction done in order to 'time' the events as you described them?"

"Yes. Between ninety seconds and two minutes."

Matthews wanted to reinforce a point: "And the defendant was the only one missing?"

"His absence was the only one I noticed at the time. I saw a couple of the other boys outside, walking away, after the shooting, so I considered them accounted for."

"Thank you, Mr. Truly. Your witness, Mr. Barnes."

Barnes walked slowly toward the witness stand, hands in his trouser pockets, trying to create a deep-in-thought look. "Mr. Truly, when you told the officers that Mr. Oswald was missing, had you made a complete check of your employees?"

"No. We just lined up as many of the order-fillers, and I tried to remember who had been there that day, and who wasn't in that group. Plus the fellas I had already seen walking up the street a few minutes after the shooting."

"When you hired the defendant, was it more or less understood that it was temporary, just for the fall rush?"

"Yes."

"So the defendant, when hired on October fifteenth, had no way of knowing that he would still be employed on Novemeber twenty-second?"

"It was most unlikely that he would have been. Except that we took some of the boys to replace flooring, the orders would have been done sooner, and Oswald and possibly others would have been out of work."

"How was Mr. Oswald's work?"

"I would say a bit above average," Truly answered.

"Could we have CE 1949, please? Mr. Truly, will you please, if you can, identify the document that comes up on the screen?"

"Uh, oh, yes. That is the W-4 form for Mr. Oswald's employment at the Texas School Book Depository."

"Does the presence of that form suggest to you that monies were withheld from Mr. Oswald's salary?"

"Absolutely."

"I asked you that, because there is some question about Mr. Oswald paying his taxes. Could we have CE 1311, please?"

The photo on the screen showed an individual with a crew cut measuring the heights of the openings of the sixth floor window from which an assassin had allegedly fired. "Mr. Truly, do you recognize what this exhibit depicts?"

"Yes."

"I call your attention to the window, which appears, to be kind about the characterization, to be lacking in regular maintenance. Were the windows in the Depository cleaned regularly?"

"In the offices, yes. In the stock areas, obviously not."

"Sir, did you have any dust or cement complaints?"

"I don't understand your question . . ."

"Mr. Truly, we've had witnesses testify that when the ejected shells, from the rifle, hit the floor up there in the corner, that cement fell on the heads of the people on the floor down below. Now if a less-than-one-ounce hull can cause cement to fall, I am asking you if there were dust or cement complaints as the book cartons were moved, or as large men walked around up there. Were there complaints?"

"That's absurd. It is an old building. But it's strong—there were hundreds of tons of books up there, back then." Truly's voice trailed off as he said "back then," as Depository business had decreased since the assassination and the building's future was in serious doubt.

"Could we please have CE 1144?" Barnes paused. "Mr. Truly, you and the jurors are about to see a Secret Service report, ah, there it is, signed by Arthur W. Blake. In that report, there is a statement from you that Mr. Oswald never missed a day of work from October fifteenth to November twenty-second. This is a very important question, Mr. Truly. Is that an accurate statement?"

"Yes. He did not miss a day."

"Your Honor, I'll be finished shortly. In the meantime, I would like CE 1949, CE 1311, and CE 1144 entered."

The judge looked to Matthews, who had no objections. "So moved."

"Mr. Truly, would you tell us what you observed before encountering the motorcycle officer who you subsequently learned was Officer Baker."

"Well, I was in front of the Depository, with Mr. Campbell, vice-president of the Depository, and Mrs. Reid, clerical supervisor, and I saw the car approaching. The driver swung the car out too far to the right, and he came almost within an inch of running into an abutment there, between Elm, the street in front of the Depository, and Parkway, the street that the presidential car turned onto. He had to slow the car down to a crawl to get back in the right position. A few seconds later, I heard an explosion, which I thought was a toy cannon or a loud firecracker from west of the building. . . . And immediately after two more explosions, which I realized that I thought was a gun, a rifle of some kind. Then I saw JFK's car stop, the crowd surged back, and then I saw the motorcycle officer coming fast on foot."

"To the best of your recollection, where did the shots originate?"

"To the west of the building, down by the railroad yards, or the WPA project there."

"By 'WPA project,' do you mean the concrete pergola?"

"Yes."

"Officer Baker testified that the elevators were unavailable. Can you tell us about that?"

"Yes, they were up on the fifth floor."

"In the time between the last shot, Mr. Truly, and when you and Officer Baker reached the elevators, could an assassin from the sixth floor have come down in either of those elevators and sent them back to the sixth floor?"

"Absolutely not. They're very slow, and we were there very quickly after the final shot."

"During the ninety- to one hundred twenty-second reconstruction, *what exactly* were you reenacting?"

"The first shot to us reaching the seventh floor, but we were doing it at a slower pace than it happened."

"Uh-huh. Were you a witness to the encounter between Officer Baker and the defendant?"

"Yes. He wasn't panting or out of breath, like he'd been running. Maybe a little startled, but I would have been startled also if someone put a gun in my stomach."

"Mr. Truly, during Mr. Oswald's tenure of perfect attendance, did you ever see him in conversation with any strangers?"

"No."

"Mr. Truly, were any security measures taken at any time with respect to the Texas School Book Depository, inasmuch as it was a tall building with windows opening onto the presidential motorcade route?"

"No."

"Mr. Truly, at any time in the three days prior to the assassination of President Kennedy, did you observe any rifles in the Book Depository?"

"As a matter of fact, yes. On Wednesday, that would have been November twentieth, Mr. Warren Caster, an employee in one of the offices, brought in two rifles that he had just obtained for the hunting season for himself and his son."

"Do you know what kinds of guns they were?"

"Objection," Matthews piped up. "Irrelevant."

"Overruled," Judge Davis replied in a strident tone.

"Well, one was a high powered Mauser. That was for Warren. I think he had something less, a twenty-two maybe, for his son, but I didn't see it."

"So the second gun, the non-Mauser, could have been any . . . kind . . . of . . . gun?"

"Well, yes. But he took them home that afternoon."

"Did you personally see the guns leave the Texas School Book Depository?"

"No."

"So it was not a major event, or a security breach when two

guns were routinely brought into the Texas School Book Depository, which was on the presidential motorcade route, a mere two days before that motorcade was due to pass the building?"

"No."

"And there were no safeguards taken to guarantee that the weapons left the building?"

"No. Nobody—well, I wasn't even thinking about the motorcade."

"No further questions, Mr. Truly. Thank you."

Judge Davis cast a sideways glance at the pocket watch he kept on the bench and wearily instructed Prosecutor Matthews to call his next witness.

"The people call Cecil J. McWatters, Your Honor." A slightly stooped, middle-aged man with the onset of a receding hairline was sworn and settled into the witness chair as if he were testing it in a furniture showroom for possible purchase.

Matthews established that McWatters had been employed by the Dallas Transit Company since 1945, and asked if his route took him within a few blocks, as well as a few minutes, of the presidential parade on November twenty-second.

McWatters hedged: "More or less, yes. I was driving down Elm Street, which is parallel to Main street. As I neared the Book Depository . . ."

"By that," Matthews interrupted, "do you mean the Texas School Book Depository, located at the corner of Elm Street and Houston Street?"

"Yes. The traffic began to slow up a little, I'd say about ten or twelve blocks east of that building, as I was heading west, toward it."

"Please go on."

"But I was on schedule. I should have been at Elm and St. Paul Street at 12:36 P.M. and I was, and one lady got off there and that left me with five passengers. Then I picked up two or three more. I can't remember exactly which stops, and then this man came up and knocked on the door of the bus, just like that, about even with the corner of Griffin Street—that's not a regular stop, but with traffic slowing and a practically empty bus, I figured it was somebody seen the parade, and it's a few pennies for the company . . ."

"Would you describe this man for us?"

"Well, nothing unusual, just a fare off the street. He was, oh, I'd say, five feet seven, five eight, maybe, and about one hundred thirty-five–one hundred forty pounds, something in there."

"Is there anyone in this courtroom that resembles the man you picked up because he was pounding on your door between bus stops?"

Barnes, still seated, interrupted, "Objection to the word 'pounding', Your Honor. The witness testified, I believe, to 'knocked.' Also, 'resembles' falls far short of an identification."

"Sustained."

"Mr. McWatters, let's simplify this. Does anyone in this court look like the man who knocked on your door on November twenty-second?"

"Yes, the man seated between the lawyers at the other table."

"Are you in fact indicating the defendant?"

"Yes, but . . ."

Matthews quickly changed tempo: "Now Mr. McWatters, I show you Exhibit 381A, a bus transfer number 004459. Do you recognize it?"

"Yes. That is the kind of transfer issued by the Dallas Transit Company, and that one was issued by me."

"How can you say that to a certainty?"

"Because each driver has a different—a unique, sort of individual punch—and that one is mine."

"Your Honor, I would like CE 381A admitted for the record as the transfer found on the person of the defendant on November twenty-second."

Judge Davis leaned back in his chair and put both hands behind his head as he asked Barnes if there were any problems with the admission of the evidence.

Barnes stood and addressed the judge squarely: "No objections to its admission, Your Honor; in fact, I'm grateful to Mr. Matthews for putting it into evidence. I would respectfully ask, however, that the admitting record be amended to reflect that it was found on the person of the defendant at 4:05 P.M., well over two hours after he was first taken into custody by the Dallas Police."

Matthews seemed confused. "I can't see what difference it makes one way or the other, Your Honor. We are in agreement that it was found on the defendant's person. What does the time matter?"

"Mr. Barnes?"

"Taken purely in and of itself, Your Honor, the time factor is not that critical. But it is, in the totality of the events of the day, just one more example of how this entire situation was mishandled. We have come to a reasonable understanding that the alleged crime for which the defendant was apprehended is not at issue and will remain a nonissue in these proceedings; nevertheless, it cannot be overlooked nor can we pretend to overlook the fact that the Dallas police have arrested a felony suspect, and they have no clear record of what was found on him at the time of his arrest, just prior to 2 P.M. Yet they discover in a subsequent search—and let's face it, you can only really claim legitimacy to one search unless the article in question is secreted in a body cavity—a bus transfer and five *live* bullets. I again state that I have no problem with the admission of this exhibit, nor will I have any objection to the admission of the five live revolver rounds, as long as it is understood by the jury that these items were discovered at 4:05 P.M. in a 'subsequent search' of the defendant."

Davis faced Matthews and then the court reporter before speaking. "Let the record be amended to show that the transfer, CE 381A, was found on the defendant's person subsequent to the initial search of the suspect, and that it was found, in fact, at 4:05 P.M. Mr. Matthews?"

"Let's finish up, if we can, Mr. McWatters. How long did this particular passenger, who knocked on your door and later received a transfer, travel with you?"

"Oh, I'd say four, maybe five minutes tops, in time, but see, we only went two blocks. Traffic by that time was slowing considerably, so the passenger asked for a transfer, which I punched and dated, kind of randomly, at one o'clock, and he got off."

"Mr. McWatters, was there discussion on your bus about the shooting of the President, and if so, would you tell us about it?"

"Well, after the man knocked and got on the bus, another man, uh, well, white male, came up to the bus and told us that the President had been shot. Well, at least he told us he heard that on his car radio."

"What happened then?"

"By that time, we're sitting there stalled—just going no-where. That's why the fella was able to tell us—he just got out of his car, which was also going nowhere, and I guess he had the urge to, or the need to tell someone about what he had heard."

Barnes rose and flipped a pencil onto the pad in front of him. "Your Honor, the last remark clearly called for a conclusion on the part of the witness. However, I think if we're going to get a full understanding of just what did occur, and what human emotions were at work on that Friday, occasionally we—Mr. Matthews and I—may both have occasion to listen to people like Mr. McWatters who deal with the public and occasionally share conclusionary comments."

Judge Davis seemed unsure. "Are you objecting or not, Mr. Barnes?"

"No objection, Your Honor, although I feel the jury should be made aware that the witness drew a not-necessarily-correct conclusion."

"Noted for the jury. Mr. Matthews?"

"You were stuck in traffic, Mr. McWatters?"

"Yes, sir, and one lady, and this man that I gave the transfer to, exited the bus there. Only then, after they left, was there any discussion of—or any speculation about what had happened to the President."

"Thank you, Mr. McWatters. Your witness, Mr. Barnes."

Barnes rose and purposefully approached the witness. "I've listened to your testimony with some fascination, Mr. McWatters, because I've always been amazed at how people who deal with the general public every day—and you certainly fit into that category—how they can keep track of all the details that they remember. So let's take a look at what you said. You were on time at St. Paul and Elm, correct?"

"Yes. There's a dispatcher there, and they don't want you to reach stops early or late, if you can help it. Now, that day, with the parade, I don't think there would have been any great problems, a few minutes either way. But I was on time."

"And you had five passengers?"

"Yes."

"How many did you have on your bus one hour later, at 1:36 P.M., Central Standard Time?"

"I don't know. Haven't given it much thought," McWatters's voice trailed off.

"Is it possible that your 12:36 estimate could have been four or six, and not five?"

"Sure. I can say with certainty that it was a small number —no more than a handful."

"That's okay, Mr. McWatters. I was just testing the powers of your recollection. Let's get to the bottom line, now. You testified that the defendant 'looked like' the man who knocked on your door, rode two blocks, and got off after hearing a car driver tell you about the President's car being fired upon when you found yourself stuck in traffic."

"That's correct."

"At any time subsequent to the time period we are talking about—at any time after, oh, say, one o'clock, were you given an opportunity to identify the defendant?"

"Yes."

"And what happened?"

"The Dallas police came and got me at the garage at 6:15, maybe 6:20, and they took me down and had me look at suspects in a lineup."

"Were the suspects similar in age, height, weight, that kind of thing, so you had to be careful in any identification you might make?"

"No. They were different ages, different sizes, and different heights. And they asked me if I could identify any man in particular there, and I told them that I couldn't identify any man in particular, but there was one man there that was about the size of the man."

"From what you told us a minute ago, were you saying that it would have been virtually impossible that there would have been two to choose from because of the difference in sizes?"

"Yes. It was this one fella, and the other three, well, they weren't close."

"So what did you do?"

"Well, then they showed me the transfer."

Barnes acted shocked: "While you were still in the lineup room?"

"Yes, sir."

"This is fascinating. Go on."

"So they showed me the transfer and refreshed my recollection about it being issued that day, and so forth, and then asked me again if I could identify anyone, and I told them I could say that there was one man in the lineup that was about the size and height and complexion of a man that got on my bus, but as far as positively identifying the man, I could not do it."

"Mr. McWatters, I must admit to a little confusion. When you went to the lineup, and one of the men resembled one of your passengers, was it the defendant he resembled?"

"No."

"Now I ask you, Mr. McWatters, can you positively identify the defendant, sitting over there next to my empty chair, as the man that got on your bus, rode two blocks, and asked for a transfer? Wait—let's make it easier. Can you identify the defendant as positively having been on your bus on November twenty-second?"

"No, I can't."

"Mr. McWatters, was that the last time, before your court appearance, that you were asked to identify the defendant?"

"No. Later on, I can't say exactly when—sometime early last year, I was shown photos that were supposed to be of Oswald—Mr. Oswald, over there, and the police asked me if that made my recollection any easier."

"Did it?"

"I couldn't identify him on November twenty-second, I couldn't be positive a year ago, and I can't identify him today."

"I think we can finish with a couple more questions. Were

you a party to a conversation about the President being shot after the man got out of his car in traffic to tell you?"

"Yes. The passengers and I all reacted about the same way —and anyhow, I repeated what he had said. One lady tried to say that it just couldn't be, you know, that anyone would do that, but I believed the man when he told me. And then this young boy—well, a teenager, he announced to those of us up front that the President, because he was riding in a convertible, must have been shot in the head or temple."

"You absolutely recall those words?"

"Yes. And he kind of smirked about it."

"Is there any chance that the person who made this statement, about the temple, and then 'smirked about it' I believe you said—could *that* person be the defendant?"

"Absolutely not. The boy that said that only got on the bus at Elm and Houston—come to think of it, that's where the shooting took place, and he has ridden with me subsequently and I identified *him* to the police, and I was able to positively pick him out of a lineup."

"No further questions. Thank you, Mr. McWatters."

"Those 'shot in the temple' statements would have been nice," Matthews told Graves, somewhat ghoulishly, "but I think we put the fleeing suspect on the bus, don't you?" Graves agreed wholeheartedly, at least to Matthews.

Matthews rose to call William Whaley, who identified Oswald (a bit thinner now) as a passenger in his cab between 12:45 and 12:55 P.M. on November twenty-second, the fare originating not too far from where Oswald had left a bus and concluding in the five hundred block of North Beckley, despite Oswald's original request to be driven to the seven hundred block. The witness, not in response to a question, groused about the five cent tip he received.

"Were you subsequently able to pick the defendant out in a lineup?"

"Yes."

"Was there any doubt whatsoever?"

"No. He was up there with teenagers, yelling at the police for putting him up there with teenagers. Anybody could have identified him."

"Nothing further."

Barnes remained seated, as Matthews sensed this was his habit before springing a trap. "Mr. Whaley, I imagine you've driven many, many people in your taxi. Am I correct in that assumption?"

"I never counted them up, but yes, quite a few."

"And you are sure the defendant was that one, out of the many that you have driven, to the five hundred block of North Beckley in Irving on November twenty-second?"

"Absolutely."

"Good. I was hoping you would say that. Now, could we please have CE 2146, page 1 followed by page 7? Mr. Whaley, page one of this document indicates that it is a press conference with Mr. Jesse Curry, Dallas police chief, held on the evening of Saturday, November twenty-third. Page 7 now, please. Now, here, we see, about a third of the way down, the statement about the defendant, 'We have heard that he was picked up by a Negro in a car.' Mr. Whaley, I hate to have to ask you a personal question, but are you now, or have you ever been, a Negro?"

Matthews objected strenuously, protesting to one and all that Barnes was making a mockery of the issue. Judge Davis didn't seem particularly thrilled, either, but he told Barnes to make his point.

"Just this, Your Honor, and with no disrespect intended for the court, but *with* disrespect intended for those who manufactured this charade fourteen months ago, Mr. Whaley testified that he picked up the defendant, and drove him in his taxi to within a few blocks of the defendant's rooming house. He further identified him in a lineup, and I believe him. But a witness who has not yet testified said that he saw Oswald get into a vehicle driven by a dark-complected man, which gave rise to this ridiculous statement by the Dallas police chief *after* Mr. Whaley's identification, which should have cleared up the matter entirely. Now, we are faced with a serious issue. Either Mr. Whaley is mistaken, which I don't believe, or the other witness, Deputy Sheriff Roger Craig, is mistaken, which I also don't believe, or we have two Oswalds, which is a frightening image to conjure up, but which is supported by a great wealth of other testimony. The only other answer is that Mr. Whaley was the Negro seen picking up Oswald, and that question had to be asked."

"Thank you for pointing out the possibilities, Mr. Barnes. You needn't answer, Mr. Whaley. The court will stipulate that Mr. Whaley is not now, and has never been, a Negro."

"Could we have CE 370, please?" Barnes waited, then asked Mr. Whaley if he could identify the exhibit.

"Yes, that's my time sheet for November twenty-second, 1963."

"Mr. Whaley, you told us you identified the defendant as the person you drove to the five hundred block of North Beckley that day. Here on your time sheet, line 14, the point of origin is listed as 'Greyhound,' which I take to be a bus depot, and the terminus is five hundred No. Beckley. And the fare was ninety-five cents, as you testified earlier. But the times give me problems. 'Time out' indicates 12:30, and the defendant could not have been in your cab *and* upstairs at the Book Depository at the same time. Or could he?"

"I only can tell you that the man sitting over there rode from the bus depot to North Beckley and tipped me a nickel."

"Thank you. No further questions for the witness. Move to admit CE 370 and CE 2146."

"So moved. Your next witness going to take a while, Mr. Matthews?"

"Quite possibly, Your Honor."

"Such being the case, we will adjourn for lunch now and return at one P.M."

Graves and Vincent left the defense table almost immediately, but Matthews stayed behind long enough so his assistants would not hear him ask Barnes, "Have you ever been a Negro, indeed. Is that what they taught you in law school?"

"Ray, you could cut the tension in this room with a cake knife. I was waiting for you to break it. I just got there ahead of you. Enjoy your lunch."

Matthews began lunch by cursing that "carpetbagging" Barnes, but gradually came to the conclusion that humor was just Barnes's way of doing business, a clear alternative to the stress that Matthews was currently feeling. Matthews also realized that Barnes's occasional ventures into levity might be having an impact on the jury, to the point where a serious—deadly serious—Barnes, in final summation, could carry the day. It was interesting to consider, but Matthews knew he could no more make a courtroom laugh than a pig fly.

All were present in court for the afternoon session at the appointed hour, when Matthews called Dallas Deputy Sheriff Luke Mooney, who, like Officer Baker, entered in uniform, and was sworn. Rather than let Barnes steal his thunder, Matthews established that Mooney had had no police responsibilities relative to the President's visit, and had been watching the parade when he heard "the echoes of shots" which he believed came from the area of the embankment above Elm Street. Finding no evidence there, he was quickly ordered to the Texas School Book Depository, where he closed the rear entrance and left a civilian there with the responsibility to keep it closed. Matthews winced at the second half of that bit of testimony.

"Now, Deputy Sheriff Mooney, what did you find in the southeast corner on the sixth floor of the Book Depository?"

"I found three empty cartridges, right there under the window. Not bunched together, but within a foot or two of each other."

"What did you do then?"

"I notified Captain Fritz and Sheriff Decker."

"Your witness, counselor."

"Mr. Mooney, let's examine your statements one at a time. You told Mr. Matthews you heard three shots. How were they spaced?"

"Well, there was a lapse between the first and second. The second and third shots were pretty close together."

"And you spoke of hearing 'echoes.' Could you explain that?"

"Well, a bullet travels faster than sound in some cases. So I call the sound 'the echo' because the bullet is far gone and far away by the time you hear it."

"And you proceeded to the embankment, because that's where you heard the shots come from, although the Book Depository was between yourself and the embankment, correct?"

"Yes."

"How thorough was your search up in the knoll area?"

"We were only there a few seconds until we had orders from Decker to cover the Texas Depository Building."

"Are you certain the orders were from Sheriff Decker?"

"No. But I don't know who else would give them. They just wanted us out of that railroad area, and in the Book Depository."

"*They* wanted you out of the railroad area . . . interesting. Then you left a civilian to guard the back door, went upstairs and found three cartridges by the window?"

"And some cartons arranged . . . like a firing rest for a gun."

"You said you notified Captain Fritz and Sheriff Decker. How did you do this?"

"Well, the captain was right up there on the floor, so I went a few feet away and yelled over to him. Then I think I yelled out the window to Sheriff Decker."

"Then what happened?"

"Then Captain Fritz came over and picked up the shells."

Barnes was incredulous at this and Matthews wasn't exactly thrilled by it. Barnes pressed the witness: "You saw Captain Fritz pick up the shells?"

"Sure."

"Mr. Mooney, since you lay claim to having found the hulls, that would seem to make you the first person to enter that particular area. Did you smell any gunpowder?"

"No, sir."

Barnes made a point of speaking into the exhibit-link microphone: "Could we have the Alyea Affidavit, please?"

"Mr. Mooney, crazy as it seems that a police captain would pick up evidence before it has been photographed and checked for prints, there is corroboration for your story. There, on the screen, is an affidavit by news cameraman Tom Alyea, employed by WFAA-TV in Dallas. After the 'I do hereby depose' part, Mr. Alyea says, 'I entered the TSBD before it was sealed, and filmed the Dallas police searching for evidence. Although federal officials wanted me to leave, local, "friendly" contacts permitted me to stay. I saw, on the sixth floor, behind some boxes, the shells on the floor, but could not get the large camera in a position to photograph them because of book boxes in the way. Noting the problem, Captain Fritz picked them up, held them in his hand for photos, then threw them down on the floor again. All this occurred before the crime scene search unit arrived.' Deputy Mooney, do you know a Detective Richard Sims?"

"Yes, sir. Dallas police force. Good man."

"Could we have page three of Sims Exhibit A, please?" Barnes remained intentionally silent and pensive as the screens initially went blank, then finally emitted another document. "Deputy Mooney, would you please read from the end of line eight?"

"Lieutenant Day or Detective Studebaker took another picture of the hulls and said they had already taken pictures of the scene. Sims picked up the empty hulls, and Lieutenant Day held an envelope open while Sims dropped them in the envelope."

"Fritz picked them up," Barnes recounted. "Fritz threw them down, Sims picked them up, and they were put in an open envelope. No more questions, sir. Your Honor, I would like the Alyea Affidavit and Sims Exhibit A entered at this time."

Barnes returned to his seat feeling reasonably happy. Matthews couldn't wait for happy hour.

Mr. Matthews then stood, weary after a week of setbacks, but yet with the confidence of someone willing to fight one more: "The prosecution calls Lieutenant J.C. Day."

Barnes cast a sideways glance at Dean, who immediately searched through a stack of folders and handed a thick one to Barnes. As he did so, a balding man of about fifty entered the courtroom. He was wearing a suit, but with a bow tie instead of the traditional four-in-hand. He made his way slowly to the witness stand, where he made eye contact with Prosecutor Matthews after being sworn.

Still behind the prosecution table, Matthews directed the witness to state his name, occupation, and rank, which was done routinely. In the course of the preliminaries, it was learned that Day had been a police officer for twenty-three years on the day of the assassination, and had been working with fingerprints and crime scenes for the past fifteen.

Thinking that Day's answer was complete, Barnes rose. "May it please the Court, Your Honor, the defense would like to have Lieutenant Day designated as an expert witness." Expecting comment from the judge on this surprising request, Barnes remained standing.

He wasn't disappointed. Judge Davis turned from looking at the witness to face Barnes, and the change in focal distance caused him to squint slightly, giving Barnes the feeling he was going to get a tongue lashing, not comment. "Mr. Barnes, the counsel who calls the witness usually makes such a request—or am I mistaken?"

"No, sir," Barnes answered, with an air of confidence that was not yet justified. He knew, however, that it had to be played that way, as Day was one of the witnesses that he was convinced would make or break the case in the jury's eyes, and he knew he had to appear to remain in command. "But given Lieutenant Day's unique position, I felt that the interests of justice would be served if his expertise were requested by both counsels. I had no hesitation that Mr. Matthews was going to request such a designation. If I am incorrect in that, then we must treat the lieutenant's testimony accordingly."

Judge Davis turned to the prosecution table. "Well, Mr. Matthews?"

"I was going to make such a request, Your Honor. I am, however, troubled that defense counsel took it as his own prerogative to take such liberties with my witness," he concluded, looking down at Barnes and dragging out both letters in the word "my."

"It's yet to be proven whose witness he is, Mr. Matthews," Barnes quipped. "All we have so far is his name and pedigree. I propose we let the court decide and proceed." Barnes looked at the jury, this time letting his glance linger at the jurors and the far end of the jury box, as if to send a message to three of four of them that he was going to make a decisive stand very shortly.

"Lieutenant Day is designated an expert witness. You may proceed, Mr. Matthews." Judge Davis was looking at Barnes when he made his statement.

"Thank you, Your Honor. Now, Lieutenant, would you please tell us what your duties involved from 12:30 P.M. onward on Friday, November twenty-second, 1963, which was the day the President was killed in Dallas, Texas."

Day fidgeted in the witness chair and seemed to be speaking to a nonfixed point rather than to any particular individual. "Sometime after the shots were fired, which I had no knowledge of, a rumor swept through headquarters that an incident had been reported with respect to the President's parade. Then, at one o'clock, I was told to report to 411 Elm Street, the location of the Texas Book Depository. My notes indicate I arrived there at 1:12."

"And what did you do then?"

"I was directed by Inspector Sawyer to report to the sixth floor, where some evidence had been found."

Matthews, hoping Day would say something of value before he lost the jury, was a little miffed that he had to continue to prompt the witness and began to question his wisdom of having Day classified as an expert. He nevertheless plowed ahead. "Please tell the court what happened."

"Well, I was directed to the sniper's nest that had been found, and . . ."

Barnes was not even fully out of his seat when he loudly stated his strenuous objection to the term "sniper's nest." Barnes also, however, was thinking ahead, and did not want the term totally squashed. "If it please the court, the witness, the expert witness," looking at Matthews, "can call the scene whatever he wants, but only after he has viewed it."

Judge Davis squarely faced the witness. "Lieutenant, do you know what it means to be designated an 'expert witness'? It means you may give opinions when asked, but only then. Now I have to tell the jury to disregard totally that last remark you made, and hope that they will. In the future, please confine yourself to your own personal observations. The jury will disregard the conclusion drawn by the witness. Mr. Matthews . . ."

Matthews faced Day squarely as if to command his attention. "Where were you directed, Lieutenant, and what did you find?"

"I was directed to the area in the southeast corner of the sixth floor of the Texas Book Building. This would be the area which included the last large window at the end, as well as a few feet around it in each direction. When I arrived there, I was shown three spent rifle hulls on the floor, up against the wall under the window. Uh, slightly spaced apart. I don't want anyone to think they were jammed together. We then photographed the hulls before they were moved, and once they were photographed, I carefully lifted each one and examined each for latent fingerprints. We then photographed the cartons as they were arranged, you know, to rest a gun on, so—"

Barnes was on his feet again. "I must again object, Your Honor. Neither this witness nor any other yet produced has demonstrated any personal knowledge that any gun was ever rested on any carton on the sixth floor of the Texas School Book Depository."

"Sustained for the time being. Lieutenant Day, I would remind you again, please confine your remarks to that which you have observed. If, however, the prosecution asks you your opinion of the configuration of the boxes, the court will be happy to hear from you then."

"Since the question has been raised, Lieutenant, when you observed these boxes, did you photograph them?"

"No. Mr. Studebaker, who works under my supervision, photographed them."

"Lieutenant, these photographs, labeled Studebaker Exhibits A, B, C, and D, are they the photographs exposed at that time?"

"Yes, those are the photos taken at the time."

"And, in your opinion as a crime scene expert, what do they show?"

"I believe they show an area where a gunman would have sat, in the easternmost portion of the window, and cartons which would have served as a gun rest—one of which had a noticeable crease in the middle of it—a couple feet away in the center of the window."

"Lieutenant, if you were going to shoot out of that window, what logistical arrangements would you have made?" Matthews asked the question as if he were approaching a moment of triumph.

"I probably would have constructed a seat and a gun rest

configuration something very similar to what you see in those photos."

"Thank you, Lieutenant. Your Honor, I would move that these four photos be submitted as Studebaker Exhibits A, B, C, and D."

"Mr. Barnes?"

"No objection, Your Honor."

Matthews passed the photos to the court clerk and returned to Lieutenant Day. "Now tell the court what occurred next."

"Well, having taken the photos and retrieved the shells and checked them for prints, they were secured as evidence, and virtually at the same time, someone yelled, 'Here it is!' "

"Here what is?"

"Some of the officers, at least a couple, all of a sudden seen the—well, a rifle hidden under some cartons at the other end of the floor. Captain Fritz, that's Will Fritz, called me over, and I examined the rifle before it was moved, so that when I moved it, I only touched it where I knew no fingerprints existed on the wooden stock. After I did that, Captain Fritz worked the bolt and ejected a live round, which I marked with my initials and checked for latent prints."

"Did you find any?"

"No. I then scratched my initials onto the stock of the weapon, noting the serial number, C2566."

"Are you sure of that number, Lieutenant?" Matthews asked, masking his displeasure.

"What did I say?" Day answered, with uncertainty in his voice.

Judge Davis asked the court reporter to read, which she did, verbatim, as ". . . noting the serial number, C2566."

Day flushed slightly. "Excuse me, it was C2766."

"Thank you. Please continue."

"Okay. Sorry for the confusion. We next examined the gun for prints, and there were none apparent at the time."

"Did you subsequently develop any prints?"

"Yes, at headquarters we were able to—"

"Fine, Lieutenant, I just wanted that noted for the record. Before we discuss that, could you tell us the remainder of what happened at the Book Depository?"

"Yes. The rifle was briefly examined by the boys there—visually only, of course, and I went back to the—uh, the area where the hulls had been found, and there we found a paper bag, a long paper sack, long enough and wide enough in my opinion that it might have evidence value as the means by which the rifle had been brought into the building. That was found at the east wall, laying parallel to the south wall. At the same time, we conducted a thorough search of the boxes that I testified about previously, and lifted several prints from those cartons."

"Was there anything else there?"

"Yes. There was the remnants of a lunch. A paper sack, some chicken bones, and a pop bottle."

"Were they duly processed along with the other evidence?"

"The bottle was fingerprinted. We never really got to the other stuff, and when Oswald was shot and it looked like the case was done, well, one day, one of the boys just decided that the lunch bag and the bones was too much to have sitting around and they just tossed them out." Day paused for a moment, and realizing that Matthews was not getting the responses as expected, he continued on his own. "I then proceeded down to the first floor, where they have the shipping end of the building, and examined the tape and paper used there, and I found that it resembled the long, thick bag we had discovered upstairs."

"That's good police work, Lieutenant. Now, could you tell us what you found back at headquarters? At least with respect to the evidence you had directed there?"

"Yes, sir. As to the rifle, we noted all identifying marks, and it was then carefully taken apart. In that condition, on the bottom side of the barrel, which was covered by the wood when assembled, I found traces of a palm print. I dusted these, and tried lifting it, the print, with scotch tape, in the usual manner. A faint palm print came off . . . even then, though, I could still see traces of the print under the barrel. We also were able to lift some palm prints off the cartons. As to the bag, we found no legible prints . . ."

"This is the large bag, not the lunch bag?"

"That is correct. We found no legible prints on that, although there is one there now. It was on it when it was returned by the FBI on November twenty-fourth. We were unable to develop any fingerprints on the soda bottle."

"All right, Lieutenant. It sounds like you were thrown into a hectic, unforeseen situation over there that day. Now, when things calmed down, and you were back at headquarters, what did the palm prints show? Did they resemble those of the defendant?"

"Resemble, yes. In certain points, they were very similar. But as far as the rifle, I could not make a positive identification of those prints."

"Didn't you just testify that they resembled the prints of the defendant?"

"Yes. But in fingerprinting it either is or is not the man. So I wouldn't say they were his prints. I could not make a positive identification as being his prints."

"And the cardboard boxes?"

"Same thing. Similar, but not sufficient to make a positive identification. Not enough to fully satisfy myself that it was his palm."

Exasperated, Matthews asks, "Was there anything else on that particular day, Lieutenant?"

"I can't think of much. Well, there was—later on, oh, nine or ten that night, I think, somebody brought the hulls back up and I marked the two that were there for identification."

"Thank you, Lieutenant. I have no further questions of the witness at this time, although he is subject to recall."

"Mr. Barnes?"

"Thank you, Your Honor, but if it please the Court, I would first like to submit an affidavit executed by the architectural firm of Corcoran, Poole, and Hubbard, who, incidentally, have received most of the public contracts let by the city of Dallas from January first, 1960, through January first, 1964. The affidavit sets out the exact measurements of the area described by Lieutenant Day, as well as providing blueprint drawings of the area. The above-cited firm then recreated, for use by the defense, a mock-up, a portable wall, if you will, containing an identical window to the one described in the specifications in the affidavit and designated as being the southeast window on the sixth floor of the Texas School

Book Depository. I would like both the affidavit and the mock-up admitted as evidence."

Judge Davis tried to conceal his surprise at this turn of events. "This will take me a minute or so to review." At the prosecution table, the three lawyers were deep in conference. The judge spoke again: "This seems in order, Mr. Barnes, subject to any objection by the prosecution. When do you propose to produce this mock-up?"

"Today, Your Honor. It's in the hall."

The judge faced the prosecutor. "Mr. Matthews . . . ?"

"My initial reaction, Your Honor, is that it's just cheap theater, but I will withhold any specific objections at this time."

"Please proceed, Mr. Barnes."

Barnes took his time approaching Lieutenant Day, saying nothing until he was resting an arm at the end of the witness box. "Lieutenant, you said the first thing you did after arriving at the southeast corner area was to photograph the hulls or cartridges, is that correct?"

"Yes."

"How do you know they had not been moved before you photographed them—or before Detective Studebaker photographed them?"

"I was told they hadn't been moved."

"By whom?"

"Detective Sims told me. I believe it was Detective Sims."

"Did Detective Sims find the shells?"

It was Matthews's turn to object. "Your Honor, if Lieutenant Day was called to the scene because hulls had been found, obviously he would not have personal knowledge of who found them."

Barnes spoke quickly: "I withdraw the question, Your Honor. Now, Lieutenant, did any officer, upon your arrival, tell you that he had been the first to locate the hulls and had remained with them, without them being moved, until you arrived?"

"No."

"Then you are assuming that they were not moved?"

"Yes. That's a basic police assumption."

"But an assumption, nevertheless," Barnes reminded him.

"Well, let's move on. Lieutenant, in this photograph, CE 715, would you circle the hulls, please?"

The witness did so, hesitatingly. Barnes then asked, "Now, Lieutenant, how many hulls have you circled?"

"Two."

"Is it standard police procedure, Lieutenant, that when three hulls are found and photographed, that only two show up in the picture?"

"All three are visible in the other picture. I guess Detective Studebaker just didn't catch the whole angle in that first photo."

"Thank you for clearing that up, Lieutenant. Speaking of Detective Studebaker, I show you Studebaker Exhibits A, B, C, and D, and ask you if, upon your examination, they depict the identical scene in the sixth floor window of the Book Depository?"

Day examined the four photographs carefully, taking time occasionally to compare one to another and finally spreading out all four on the ledge of the witness stand. "They do not depict the identical arrangement of the boxes."

"How do you account for that?"

"A couple of ways. First, I believe people were going to the window to yell out to the officers down below, and the boxes could have been moved in that way. Secondly, when we moved boxes to check for fingerprints, they were not always replaced exactly."

"Lieutenant, that suggests that these photos were taken over a period of time . . ."

Lieutenant Day looked over to Ray Matthews, then down at the floor. "It is possible that not all of those pictures were taken the same day. I know one, similar to this, Exhibit 726, that was taken on Monday the twenty-fifth, but it was to re-create our recollection after we moved boxes for prints, which we considered urgent at the time."

"I understand that, Lieutenant, and I appreciate you being so forthcoming. Now, maybe you could help me here. I show you CE 482, taken at 12:31 from a car in the motorcade. Can you tell me what it shows?"

"I'm familiar with this picture," Day answered, regaining

some of the initiative. "It's of the exterior of the book building, showing the fifth and sixth floor, southeast corner."

"Does it, in your opinion, show the window where you concentrated your search?"

"Yes, it does."

"I asked that, because there seems to be a discrepancy between the position of the boxes here at 12:31 and your photos, beginning, I believe you said, at 1:12 or after. Any thoughts?"

"Only that the cartons, as originally positioned, could have been bumped or moved slightly by officers yelling out the window."

"But you do agree there is a discrepancy?"

"Oh, yes."

"Is it possible, then, that those same officers, could have slightly moved the hulls?"

"It's possible, but I don't see what difference—"

"Thank you, Lieutenant. Let's change the subject a bit. I assume you have been at crime scenes before. Is that a correct assumption?"

"Yes. A great many."

"Besides looking into the corner and seeing boxes arranged in a certain way, and a bag, and a smaller bag and lunch, and, of course, the hulls, did you make any other observations at 1:12?" The witness was allowed to ponder the question as Barnes moved to the end of the jury box most distant from the witness.

"I'm not sure, sir. I believe I've testified to everything I saw."

"The question was not limited to your powers of sight, sir."

"Well, the noise level was a factor to be reckoned with . . ."

Barnes, feigning exasperation, continued, "You've missed my point, Lieutenant." His voice then gradually rose to the point at which he was afraid his point would be lost to an objection: "Did you, by any chance, in this tight enclosure that you have spoken of, smell *gunpowder?*"

"No, I didn't. But again, there must have been so many officers in and out of that area that—"

"You did not smell gunpowder. Fine. Now, you testified about this large bag, which, you said, in your opinion, could have once contained the rifle. Could we talk about that for a moment?"

"You're asking the questions."

"I'm glad you noticed. You'll like this one. You testified that you found the bag '. . . at the east wall, laying parallel to the south wall.' Are you aware that east-west and north-south are not parallel?"

"Well, the bag was on the Houston Street side, but its length ran along Elm Street."

"That clears up some of the confusion, Lieutenant. Did you find any oil in or on the bag?"

"Oil?" Day asked, not understanding the question.

"Oil, sir, as in gun oil. Rifles don't operate unless they are oiled."

"I never looked inside the bag," Day answered.

"Please answer the question as asked. Did you find any oil in or on this long bag?"

"No."

"None, whatsoever?" Barnes asked slowly.

"None, whatsoever," Day answered quickly.

Barnes pressed his advantage: "Would you please read, for want of a better term, the 'evidence label' on the bag, Mr. Day?"

"It says, 'Found next to the sixth floor window gun fired from. May have been used to carry gun. Lt. J.C.Day.' "

"You never looked inside it, you found no oil, you testified that you found no prints, yet you labeled it in that manner?"

Prosecutor Matthews rose and objected that counsel for the defense was badgering the witness. Barnes withdrew the question, knowing the jury had heard it.

"I apologize, Lieutenant. I suppose it must be remembered that you were just trying to do your job on that Friday and I'm just trying to do mine today. Now, a couple last questions about the bag. Did you take it from the Book Depository to police headquarters?"

"No."

"I show you the bag again. Is there any indication who did deliver it?"

"No."

"Lieutenant, do you know what the phrase 'chain of possession' means?"

"Certainly. But that is my label on it, and I marked it at the scene. It's not a matter of life or death who brought it to headquarters, because my mark is still on it."

"I'd like to remind you of two things, sir," Barnes said in stern tones. "First, it may well be a matter of life or death to the defendant, and second, without the knowledge of who transported it, the jury is allowed to conjure up the possibility of tampering with the evidence. You testified earlier that you found no fingerprints on the bag, yet there were prints, possibly the defendant's, when you got it back from the FBI. Do you see my point, sir?"

Day's silence was answer enough and Barnes did not demand any verbal response. "Mr. Day, you testified earlier, and were commended for your efforts, that having seen this bag, you went to where paper and tape were kept in the Book Depository . . ."

"In the shipping department."

"Exactly so, and that you noticed that the paper and tape there resembled that from which the bag was made. Did it shock you that brown paper and sealing tape resembled brown paper and sealing tape?"

"No, I just—"

Barnes pressed on, "Did you take any samples from the Book Depository for comparison?"

"No."

"Okay. Now about this rifle, this 'C2766,' did you warn the other officers about the handling of it at the time it was discovered?"

"Certainly."

"And during the course of your immediate inspection of it, there at the other end of the sixth floor, did you make further conversation with respect to the handling and identification of the rifle?"

"I certainly did."

"Did anyone at that time suggest that the gun found was a *'Mauser'*?"

Matthews was instantly on his feet, as were, almost as if by similar instinct, his two assistants. "Objection, Your Honor. Hearsay."

Judge Davis looked over to Barnes, who was approaching the bench, but who spoke loud enough to be heard. "Your Honor, it sounds to me like Mr. Day was part of the conversation, making it admissible under Texas law."

"Objection overruled."

"Lieutenant, you were asked if the trade name *'Mauser'* arose in connection with your identification of the weapon."

"I recall that it did, but I could not tell you who said it."

"Do you recall how it was phrased?"

"There were a couple of things said, like, oh, 'Looks like a Mauser,' or 'German Mauser action,' that type of thing."

"Thank you. Now I show you CE 139, a six point five mm Italian made Mannlicher-Carcano rifle. Can you tell me if this is the gun you checked for prints on the sixth floor of the Book Depository on November twenty-second?"

"That appears to be it. And that seems to be my mark down there on the stock," Day answered with some sarcasm in his voice.

"Appears to be, thank you. Your Honor, could we have a ten minute recess to allow the mock-up to be brought into the courtroom so that Lieutenant Day can continue his testimony?"

Matthews saw his opportunity and was not about to miss it. "If it please the court," he drawled, "I have to object to this mock-up being used. Mock-ery is more like it. It was not alluded to in direct examination, so therefore I would consider it inadmissible now."

Barnes needed no prompting. "If it does please the Court, Your Honor, the 'crime scene' was at the heart of the direct examination by the prosecution, and given the fact that the model, subject to anyone's inspection, is satisfactory, the only alternative is to request that we adjourn these proceedings for the sake of the entire court sitting in that window in Dallas. That would entail great expense, time, and I think those factors would work against justice being served in these proceedings."

Judge Davis reached for his gavel. "The court will take a ten minute recess during which time the jury will not be in the court room. The court will inspect the model and if found in accordance with the architectural affidavit, will be deemed a suitable equivalent of the crime scene itself. Court is in recess."

Matthews leaned over to Graves and whispered, "This pompous clown Barnes will never work in Texas again."

Graves, much to his employer's chagrin, replied, "At the rate he's going this week, he'll never have to."

When the court reconvened, absent the jury, the judge announced that he was satisfied with both the affidavit and the model, and asked if the counsel for the people had any problems with it. Grudgingly, the answer was no, but they reserved the right to object at any time they felt the exhibit was being misused. Judge Davis agreed that they had that right. The jury was then returned to their seats. Lieutenant Day was reminded that he was still under oath.

"Now, Lieutenant," Barnes intoned louder than necessary to bring the jury back mentally, "suppose you step over here," gesturing to the mock-up, which was lined up perpendicular to the bench, and the inside of which was parallel to the jury benches. "Does this reasonably resemble the southeast corner window on the sixth floor of the Texas School Book Depository?"

Day surveyed the model and replied that it was a remarkable replica, including detail he had forgotten. Matthews wrote "Idiot" on a yellow pad for Graves to see.

Barnes then pointed to several boxes. "Lieutenant, do you recognize these?"

"Yes. They are similar, if not identical, to the two styles of book boxes found in the corner by the window."

"Would you tell the court what you meant by the two styles?"

"Well, this one here, was the basic textbook box we saw there. They were all over. Then this smaller one, there was less of them—well, they contained kids' books, I think. These were the two kinds of boxes in the corner."

"Lieutenant, you told us earlier that you would position them much as they were found if you were making the shot. Would you take a moment and position them the way you found them on November twenty-second of 1963?" Barnes got out of his way as the officer did so, but Barnes remembered to remind him, "Just don't sit on anything, Mr. Day—those boxes are empty."

After a couple of minutes, Day looked at Barnes, standing in front of the jury. "That looks like it."

"Now, in your scenario, Lieutenant, the shooter would sit where?"

"Here, on this pile, on the left, farthest into the corner, but somewhat out from the wall."

"And the gun rest?" Barnes asked with a hint of skepticism in his voice.

"This pile here, next to the window, in front of, well, the seat, I guess I'd call it."

"Thank you, Lieutenant. Now let's orient the jury a little. If you sit here," and Barnes quickly obtained his chair and placed it so Day could sit where the boxes were, "and aimed from that stack of cartons," handing Day the weapon in evidence, "what street are you aiming at?"

"Elm Street. I stood right there in that window, looked out over the tree to where it happened. That would be Elm Street."

Barnes then took the gun from Day's hands, quickly repositioned the boxes and chair and reseated Day so he was aiming the weapon in what would have been a southerly direction on November twenty-second. "And what street are you aiming at now, sir?"

"Houston Street. This would be Houston Street, but I can't testify that I've tried this before, because the boxes were always aligned toward Elm. Even though this would have been . . ." At that point Day fell silent.

"Please continue your thought."

"Your Honor, this has gone far enough," Matthews complained somewhat bitterly. "The witness has testified to what he saw—boxes, bags, rifle, hulls. Now they've got him aiming in the wrong direction."

"I'm going to allow the witness to continue. Lieutenant Day, the court is curious about what you were going to say."

"I was going to say that doing it this way is a much easier, and no doubt a more accurate shot. It's a blind alley; traffic was stopped coming down Elm and going south on Houston. This shot was the one to take, in my opinion."

"Thank you for your opinion, Lieutenant. Now, if you'll just return to the witness stand, I have just a few more questions." Barnes spoke softly to calm the witness.

As Day reclaimed his seat on the witness stand, the display was removed. Barnes put some energy back into his voice: "Sir, you testified earlier that when you lifted the palm print from the disassembled rifle, you could still see a trace of the print on the weapon. What does your expertise tell you with regard to that?"

"If it was a new print, it would all be lifted. If it was an old print, many times you can still see it after the lift. In this case, as I testified, I could still see traces of it on that barrel."

"Indicating new or old—I think I grasp your meaning, I just want it clear for the jurors who may be unfamiliar with your scientific methods."

"It would appear to have been an old print."

"Thank you. Now, you testified about a variety of objects this morning—a large bag, some boxes, three hulls, one rifle, a soda bottle—in all of those items, did you, Lieutenant Day, find one fingerprint or palm print that you could positively identify as belonging to the defendant, Mr. Oswald?"

"No."

"Given the fact that Mr. Oswald was employed at that location, and given the fact that there has been testimony that he purchased a rifle with the serial number of C2766, would it have come as a great shock to you if you *had found* his prints on some of those items? It is strongly asserted that he owned the gun, and he worked around those boxes and that paper for over five weeks, and it's no crime to eat lunch. What I'm suggesting, sir, is that the crime scene in question, given all the circumstances, looks *too* clean."

"That may well be."

"Now, Lieutenant, with this amazing absence of prints, it would seem that either the evidence was not touched or it was wiped clean. In your expert opinion, could the weapon have been fired three times and found without any fingerprints on its exterior surface?"

"Not unless it was handled and fired with some type of glove that left no deposit or fibers."

"Do you have an opinion as to the probability of that?"

"I would consider it unlikely."

"How long, in your opinion, would it take to wipe that rifle as clean as it was found, assuming it had just been fired three times after it had been taken from that paper bag and assembled in that corner window?"

"The rifle itself—not long; but the trigger and the trigger housing were also clean, so I would have to say, and this is the best estimate I can give you—anywhere from, oh, say thirty to forty-five seconds."

"Thirty to forty-five seconds . . . that's a virtual eternity for someone who no doubt had escape on his or her mind, wouldn't you think?"

"I reckon."

"Now, Lieutenant," Barnes spoke in upbeat tones as he turned from the witness stand to procure an item from the evidence table, "I just have a couple more questions about the gun and those hulls."

Matthews crossed out "Idiot" on his legal pad and scribbled "dp. sht."

"Lieutenant, I show you CE 543, a hull allegedly found on November twenty-second under the southeasternmost window on the sixth floor of the Texas School Book Depository. Do you recognize it?"

"Yes."

Barnes rolled the shell around in his hand and walked to the jury box to display the shell, holding both ends. "How do you recognize it, sir?"

"By the dent in the open end."

"Yes, by the dent in the open end. Does your mark appear on this hull, Lieutenant Day?"

"No."

"Lieutenant, I can put five firearms experts on the witness stand that will testify that this hull, with this dent, could not have been fired from a weapon on the day it was found. Would you like to examine it and give us your opinion?"

"I can't say either way. There's no denying the dent."

"Fair enough. Now, why isn't your mark on the hull?"

"Because I marked the envelope the hulls went in, and only marked the hulls hours later, and that one didn't come up with the others."

"You marked the envelope, not the hulls?"

"That is correct."

"Which was used in the commission of the crime, Lieutenant Day, the envelope or the hulls?" Barnes asked with a belligerent tone.

"Objection. Badgering."

"I apologize, Your Honor. I regret my frustration."

"Objection overruled. Please read—"

"I know the question, Judge. The answer is the hulls."

"Was the envelope sealed?" Barnes asked.

"Not by me," Day answered. "I expected at the time to add more evidence to it. It should have been sealed."

"To whom did you give it?"

"To Detective Sims."

"When—what was the time of the transfer?"

"Somewhere around 1:25; right around the time the gun was found. Suddenly I had more jobs than arms."

"I understand the position you were in," Barnes sympathized. "Now, when did you get them back?"

"Objection, Your Honor, asked and answered already. The witness testified earlier that he got the hulls back between nine and ten o'clock."

"Objection sustained."

Barnes was moving in for the kill: "Who gave the two hulls that you did mark, *between nine and ten o'clock at night,* back to you?"

"I have no recollection of that."

"Did that envelope contain anyone's identifying marks and was it sealed?"

"No to both questions."

"Lieutenant, when you first saw the gun, the one spoken of as a Mauser and what not, where was it, let's say, with respect to the floor?"

"It was on the floor, under cartons, with the scope on top."

"Do you believe, that the weapon was 'placed' there, or was it hastily abandoned? How, in your best judgment, Mr. Day, did that weapon wind up where it was found?"

"It had to have been placed, and somewhat carefully, because it was, well, almost in a boxlike enclosure which covered it. It was well hid, I can tell you that. It wasn't just thrown there."

"Did anyone perform any kind of test to determine if the weapon found in that little enclosure there had, in fact, been fired recently?"

"No. It might have been tough, after an hour or so . . ."

"Indeed, Lieutenant, but we have to try, don't we? Thank you, Lieutenant. No further questions."

Judge Davis looked at Matthews. "Redirect?"

"Only one. Lieutenant Day, do you recall being told by Detective C.N. Dhority that it was he who returned the hulls to you?"

Barnes was immediately up. "Objection, Your Honor, leading the witness, and blatantly so. Lieutenant Day has already given his best recollection of his reception of the hulls on the evening of the twenty-second."

The judge turned to Day and asked, "Lieutenant, have you, in fact, given us your best recollection that you do not recall who gave the hulls back to you?"

"Yes, Your Honor, although I do recall Detective Dhority coming and saying that to me."

"I'm going to have to sustain that objection, Mr. Matthews. Do you plan to call Detective Dhority?"

"Yes."

"That would be the time to put such testimony in the record. Any recross, Mr. Barnes?"

"I'll be brief, Your Honor. Mr. Day, do you recall making a statement to *The Dallas Times Herald* on November twenty-third or twenty-fourth that it was, in your opinion, about one hundred yards from the sniper's window to, quote, where a bullet was discovered in the grass?"

"Vaguely. But I cannot now remember what I based it on."

"Uh-huh. The area where you found the hulls—was the flooring such that plaster or debris could have gone down to the fifth floor?"

"I don't believe so. I think it was tight there."

"Now, sir, after all this fuss and bother today, do you still firmly believe to be true, as you apparently did on November twenty-second, 1963, what you wrote on the label on one carton lid, which I quote, 'From top of box Oswald apparently sat on to fire gun. Lt. J. C. Day.' Do you believe that the testimony of J. C. Day, head of the crime scene search, justifies such a label based on the totality of your testimony today?"

"No."

"Lastly, sir, when you began your testimony earlier, you used, and I objected to, the phrase 'sniper's nest.' Do you remember that?"

"Quite well."

"Good. Now, sir, do you still believe that the area you searched, the southeast corner of the sixth floor of the Texas School Book Depository, was a 'sniper's nest'?"

Day saw the chance to redeem himself. "Yes, sir, I do," he told Barnes in strident tones.

"You know something, Lieutenant," Barnes spoke softly, "so do I. So here's the bottom line—did you, as the head of the Crime Scene Search Section of the Identification Bureau of the Dallas Police Department, develop any evidence—real evidence, not circumstantial suspicion—that it was, in fact, Lee Harvey Oswald's sniper's nest?"

"No." Day was clearly deflated and defeated.

"You are excused, Lieutenant." Barnes allowed the shaken witness a moment, thereby giving the jury equal time to digest the damage done to his testimony. Barnes then reached the defense table and addressed the court: "Your Honor, I would like CE 482, Sims Exhibit A, the affidavit of Tom Alyea admitted; and, based on the testimony of Deputy Sheriff Mooney, the statements contained in Sims Exhibit A, the sworn affidavit of newsman Tom Alyea, plus the testimony of Lieutenant Day, I would petition the court to rule exhibits 543, 544, and 545, that is, the three spent cartridges, as inadmissible due to repeated violations of the necessary chain of possession demanded of evidence."

Judge Davis turned to the prosecution table as Matthews was struggling to rise. "Mr. Matthews, I believe I can anticipate just about anything you could say now, and it won't mean much, believe me. But I'll give you the benefit of the doubt because of the gravity of these proceedings. But understand—the defense is on very solid ground here, and the burden is clearly going to be on *you* to demonstrate clearcut, absolute chain of possession. The open envelope or envelopes, and the time factor, in and of themselves, will get evidence kicked in most courts. And whatever you've got in this regard, sir, I'm going to want it soon. This court stands adjourned until Monday morning, and I again advise the jurors *not* to discuss the case amongst themselves."

Barnes leaned over and whispered to the defendant, "Whoever or whatever you are, pal, you're halfway home."

# Seven

The weekend had an eerie, almost surrealistic quality to it. It seemed, for both sides in the case, to go on forever.

For Barnes, it was an occasion to spend extra time on the phone to Minnesota, although both Saturday and Sunday afternoon were spent at Bob Dean's house to review the first week. Barnes was cautiously optimistic, Dean clearly more so. "What did they prove, Eddie? Carolyn, can you suggest anything that hurt us in week one? Hell, after the first two days, they were desperate to put somebody up there that could kick start their case, and it didn't happen. They've still got their 'experts,' but if they're anything like Mr. Cadigan . . ."

"I can tell you now that some of them are," Barnes cut in. "But I get concerned when the FBI tries too hard, and that's what they're doing here. They've got a ton—and I mean that literally—of evidence that I'd love to see, and it is as if the stuff never existed. We could win this case first thing Monday morning if we could get Oswald's 1962 tax return, but we'll all be quite old before the FBI suddenly unearths that relic."

"You don't need it, Eddie. You're right on track," Dean reminded him.

"I'm counting on you to be right, Bob, because I'd be the first to admit that I don't know anything about Texas juries. If this case was in Minnesota, I'd be just as concerned, but I'd feel a whole lot better. But I just can't get an idea of what that jury over there is thinking. They're just too quiet—almost like they made up their minds when they read the papers in sixty-three, and we're just tearing pages out of the dictionary and throwing them at each other for no purpose."

"Just let me assure you on that one," Dean told Barnes. "They take murder, especially this one, very seriously in Texas. But that's our advantage. For them to believe a murderer is guilty, they've got to see the evidence. Sure, everybody in Texas carries a gun, and that's the point—there is violence—and it's taken for granted. But for it to be the cause of a jail term or an execution, then it's got to be proven. And the prosecution hasn't done that yet."

Barnes, still deep in thought, spoke up, "Okay. On the one hand, we had a good week in that we didn't get our brains beat in except for Matthews's excellent opener. The prosecution only has the stipulations on the guns that we gave them, and that's better than if the witnesses had given that to the jury. We took their best shots and didn't get hurt. But it's what we don't know that still worries me . . . like who our client is. Maybe it's better we don't know."

A general concensus was formed and documents were reviewed for the coming week.

While the defense was guardedly positive, the prosecution team redoubled their efforts, as Matthews was as good a motivator as he was a trial attorney. They had very little on the positive side to work from, but there were more witnesses to be heard, and many legal traps yet unsprung. They also maintained the confident feeling that the truth of Matthews's opening statement would still carry the day, a feeling generated by the hope that Oswald's media conviction and odd political habits were already a part of the jury's psyche.

Matthews, hosting Graves and Vincent at his ranch, nevertheless had to ask the obvious: "What did we prove this week? That Oswald talked about guns with Adrian Alba?

That he took a bus and cab ride? We didn't put the gun in his hand, and all the king's experts aren't going to help us this week if we didn't succeed in week one. Sure, the FBI found prints, and will swear to them, but the jury has already heard the Dallas people say otherwise. Worse still, we have to hear from those three so-called pathologists who did the autopsy, and the defense will have a field day with them. Worst of all, the jury is going to wonder why we're not calling the Secret Service, or Curry, Fritz, and Decker, who should go on the road under the names Moe, Larry, and Curly."

"It's not that bad, Ray," Graves told him.

"It's far from won," Matthews countered. "We've been stalemated by an out-of-state p.d. But Barnes is only the executioner. The people that failed to make this case in the first place are the ones that are killing us. I can still see it on TV, back then when it happened. 'Open and shut,' they said. 'A cinch,' 'can't lose.' And you know something, I bought it. I can remember sitting right here watching Oswald get shot, and thinking to myself if only I had been able to prosecute that case."

Earl Vincent immediately responded that if it had happened that way originally, things would be a lot easier, because it would have been their case all the way, not somebody else's mistakes. He then refocused the issue: "We're definitely not going to win this thing by reliving it. Let's figure out where we are, and get ready for Monday."

"That kind of wisdom will make you a good lawyer some day, Earl," Matthews said, "and we do have to get ready. But make no mistake about where we are. Bob Dean wasn't kidding when he said I ought to have a press statement ready on short notice. Let's start with the question of how we keep those cartridges in evidence. I don't have the vaguest notion. Three people claim they picked them up, nobody marks them for hours, and in the meantime, they're God knows where." Matthews stopped in the middle of the thought. "The evidence is bungled by the Dallas police department. The defendant is shot in their basement, by someone known to virtually their whole force. They turn what they've got over to the Feebs, who bury it. The state of Texas wants to investigate, as do the House and Senate, but the new President steps in

and appoints the seven dwarves to gather all the evidence.
Not being trial lawyers, they botch everything they touch
. . . or did they?"

Silence as Matthews stared out the window at the expanse
of his ranch. "Gentlemen, this is no ordinary case."

Monday, January 11. The local radio that morning spoke
of a possible heavy snowstorm later in the week, a lack of
verdict yet in the assassination trial, and a reminder that it
was one year since the release of the Surgeon General's report on the dangers of smoking.

Graves and Vincent had argued to put the experts on first,
but Matthews convinced them you can't put the FBI specialists on and then call the people who found the gun. The pathologists were vetoed unanimously.

The courtroom session began with comments from the
judge to the jury about the weekend, with hints that he
would like to know if the case had been discussed. There
being none, he turned the proceedings over to Matthews.

"Your Honor, the state calls Dallas Deputy Sheriff Eugene
Boone."

A young, stocky man was ushered into the courtroom, ex-
uding a quiet confidence. After being sworn, he gave background information relative to his position with the sheriff's
office.

"Mr. Boone, were you part of the group that searched the
sixth floor of the Texas School Book Depository?"

"Yes, I was."

"Would you tell the jurors, please, what, if anything, you
found?"

"Well, I don't know who can claim to have found the rifle,
because Constable Weitzman, that's Seymour Weitzman for
the record, well, he and I spotted the rifle hidden under some
cartons at what seemed like the same exact second. I looked
at my watch, and it was 1:22 P.M. I'll never forget that moment."

"What happened then?"

"Some of the Dallas people—local officers, not sheriff's department—were called over to take pictures before the gun
was moved, and then it was observed for prints, and finally,

they dragged it out of that little cubby hole area there, and Captain Fritz worked the bolt and one round came out of the chamber."

"So the weapon was loaded?"

"Objection," Barnes cut in. "Asked and answered."

"Sustained."

"What did you do then, Mr. Boone?"

"Looked at the gun—I did not touch the weapon at all."

"Mr. Boone, I show you CE 139, an Italian Mannlicher-Carcano six point five mm carbine. Do you recognize it as the weapon you saw at, and after, 1:22 that afternoon?"

"It looks like the same rifle. But I have no way of being positive." Matthews hadn't expected the disclaimer, so he repeated his question about the similarity and Barnes got another "asked and answered" sustained. Matthews passed the witness to Barnes.

"Mr. Boone, from your testimony to the prosecution, it sounds like you were born up there on the sixth floor of the Book Depository. Was that the first stop on your agenda after the shots were fired?"

"No. I went first to the area behind the fence."

"Good enough. Now, Mr. Boone, you are the first witness for the prosecution who has demonstrated precision with respect to evidence, in that you noted a rifle was discovered at 1:22 P.M. Let's test your precision. Who picked up the rifle?"

"Captain Fritz picked it up by the sling when he removed it."

"Good observation. Now, do you recall anybody referring to the rifle that was found as being a 'Mauser'?"

"Well, I referred to it that way, because I thought it was a Mauser, and I believe Captain Fritz referred to it the same way."

Barnes excused himself from the witness and asked for the two Decker exhibits that involved affidavits signed by E.L. Boone. "Mr. Boone, do you recognize this document?"

"Yes, sir."

"Is it a valid document that you executed?"

"Yes."

"Please read your identification of the gun."

". . . Rifle appeared to be a seven point sixty-five Mauser with a telescopic site. I first saw the rifle at 1:22 P.M."

"Thank you. Could we have the next exhibit, please?"

"Detective Boone, same questions. Do you recognize this document and is it valid?"

"Yes."

"Your description again reads 'a seven point sixty-five Mauser with a telescopic site,' correct?"

"Correct."

"Your Honor, while I'm preparing the next exhibit, I'd like to have those two particular parts of Decker 5323 admitted."

"Mr. Matthews."

"I have serious reservations, Your Honor. The language is wishy washy. 'Appeared to be . . .' That kind of thing. There's no positive i.d. there."

"Certainly not of a Mannlicher," Barnes noted for the record, while plugging in a tape recorder on the defense table.

"Mr. Barnes, do you wish to add to the record?"

"Your Honor, the deputy executed two affidavits in precise police fashion. Would he be a deputy sheriff if he wrote affidavits saying 'The car appeared to be a Rambler' when, in fact, it was a Cadillac?"

"The exhibits are admitted."

Barnes returned to the witness stand. "Now, Mr. Boone, we are going to listen to CE 3048, labeled K-BOX, a Dallas Radio Station, Audio Reel #1, Item 33, Friday afternoon, November twenty-second, 1963. It's reasonably clear, so we should have no trouble hearing it."

Robert Dean then activated the tape recorder. "A rifle was found in a staircase on the fifth floor of the building in which the assassin is believed to have shot the President of the United States. Sheriff's deputies identify the weapon as a seven point sixty-five Mauser, a German-made army rifle with a telescopic sight. It had one shell in the chamber. Three spent shells were found nearby."

"Objection to that recording, Your Honor. Hearsay."

"Mr. Barnes?"

"I strongly disagree, Your Honor, based on what we did hear. The news report wrongly tells that the rifle had been found in a staircase on the fifth floor. That totally excludes the concept of hearsay, or that it was something overheard at the scene. The fact that no such event occurred indicates that this information had to have been furnished to the reporter, since he could not possibly have witnessed it. From there," Barnes went on rapidly, hoping the jury was hearing every word, "the details are accurate, again, as reported to the reporter, not overheard or seen and misunderstood. 'Sheriff's deputies . . . Boone, Weitzman. A telescopic site. One shell in the chamber. Three spent shells nearby.' I don't see hearsay in this, Your Honor."

"Neither do I. Overruled."

"Mr. Boone, do you recall making that statement?"

"No. But I can't say I didn't, either."

"Mr. Boone, the prosecutor tried to have your affidavits excluded, and I don't blame him, because you did, after all, make an identification of sorts. And you've told us that others also used the trade name 'Mauser'; now, let's examine the weapon. Would you tell the court what it says here," as Barnes pointed to part of the barrel.

"Made in Italy."

"And here?"

"Cal. six point five."

"Mr. Boone, is a six point five caliber weapon made in Italy a Mauser?"

"No."

"Thank you, Deputy. No further questions. Your Honor, I'd like CE 3048 admitted."

"Since we've already had an objection on that overruled, it shall be admitted."

Matthews consulted with Graves and Vincent about calling anyone further with respect to the rifle. Both maintained that Weitzman had to be called if they were to avoid being embarrassed by Fritz, and they also argued that Barnes would call Weitzman, so they might as well. "Don't sweat the semantics, Ray," Graves told him. "The gun up there is the one you'll have to sell to the jury. Don't lose any sleep over what it looked like in a moment of great confusion." Matthews accepted the logic and called Constable Seymour Weitzman, a man older than Boone, but with a youngish spring in his step and a seemingly pleasing disposition. Once sworn, he re-

peated how he and Deputy Sheriff Boone found the gun virtually at the same second, well hidden: "It was covered with
boxes. It was well protected as far as the naked eye because I
would venture to say eight or nine of us stumbled over that
gun a couple of times." You stumbled through two days, Matthews thought, while waiting for a follow-up question to
refocus the witness.

"Constable Weitzman, there's been some talk about the
gun being something other than a Mannlicher-Carcano. In
fact, the word 'Mauser' has been mentioned. Could you help
us clear that up?"

"Well, in a glance, that's what it looked like. I said that it
looked like one."

"In the confusion of the events of that early afternoon, I
can understand how that happened, sir. Thank you. No further questions."

Barnes walked to his now familiar place at the end of the
jury benches. "Constable, you had a very busy day from the
time of the shots until you found the rifle, is that not correct?"

"Objection, Your Honor," Matthews said strenuously. "The
only subject of direct examination was the discovery of the
rifle. Cross-examination must be limited to questions with
respect to that."

"Mr. Barnes?"

"Your Honor, the prosecutor dismissed what *he* considered
to be an erroneous identification of the weapon based on 'the
confusion of events of that early afternoon.' I think that
makes a discussion of them relevant."

"So do I. Overruled." Matthews took the objection personally, a condition the jury should not have seen.

"Now then, Constable, tell us what happened before you
searched the Book Depository."

"Okay. I was on the Main Street steps of the sheriff's office
when I heard the shots. The first one was not clear in my
mind as definitely a shot—maybe a firecracker, maybe a rifle
shot. But there was a report, then the second two seemed to
be simultaneously. I ran to the scene, and somebody said the
shots, or firecrackers, came from behind the wall, so I immediately scaled the wall. Back there, we noted numerous

kinds of footprints that did not make sense because they were going in different directions. I pointed this out to other officers, including Secret Service men—"

Barnes interrupted. "Constable, it's premature, and I may have to recall you on this point, but we have heard no testimony that there were any Secret Service men at the scene, and the first one to arrive there, from the motorcade, was Special Agent in Charge Forrest V. Sorrels. By the way, do you know Mr. Sorrels."

"Yes. Very well."

"Constable, if I told you that there were no Secret Service men in the area of Dealey Plaza from the time the motorcade sped away until 12:58, some twenty-seven minutes later, what would you say—you just told us about Secret Service."

"I'd say either you were wrong, which I have no way of knowing, or someone was impersonating the Secret Service —because I saw them twice. After I was behind the wall, someone told me there was something red in the street, and I went down there expecting to find a fragment of a firecracker, and what I found, well, I believe it was a piece of the President's skull. And I turned that over to a Secret Service man, and that was less than . . . what did you say, twenty-seven minutes? after the shooting."

"For what it's worth, Constable, I believe what you're saying. When this is all done, I hope you'll accept the fact that there were no Secret Service there. Now, where was this 'fragment' found?"

"Down there on Elm Street."

"Could you be precise as to the location—middle of road— where?"

"Oh, it was way over on the left side of the street, no more than eight to twelve inches from the curb."

"Then what happened?" Barnes asked, knowing he had the jury's full attention.

"I proceeded to the Book Depository, where they were going through floor by floor, with special attention to the sixth floor —they wanted that floor torn apart. They wanted that gun and they knew it was there somewhere."

"Who knew—and how?"

"I have no idea."

"Okay, then you and Deputy Boone found the rifle."

"Right."

"And the prosecution would like the jury to believe that you merely glanced at it and identified it incorrectly. But that's not entirely true, is it?"

"No. I even put it in a report to the FBI that it was a Mauser."

"Did that report give any other details about the gun?"

"Yes. I believe I said it was a two point five scope on it and I believe I said it was a Weaver scope, but it wasn't."

"Did you indicate the color of the weapon you saw?"

"Gunmetal."

Barnes got the Mannlicher, brought it back to the jury box for the jurors to see, then resumed his questions: "Mr. Weitzman, is this a Mauser?"

"No. And before you ask, that's not a two point five scope, it's not a Weaver scope, and the color is not gunmetal. Okay?"

"Okay. But you didn't change your mind about the weapon very quickly, now did you, Mr. Weitzman? Could we have Mr. Weitzman's affidavit in CE 2003, please?"

Barnes made a show of replacing the weapon until the document came up on the screen. "Mr. Weitzman, this affidavit is dated November twenty-third, 1963, which means you had a full day to think about your earlier observations from the sixth floor, and it bears your signature. The date and signature are correct?"

"Yes."

"It says, 'Deputy Boone and myself spotted the rifle about the same time. This rifle was a seven point sixty-five Mauser bolt action equipped with a four slash eighteen scope.' Now you've changed the scope, but it's still a Mauser, correct?"

"Correct."

"Two more questions, sir. What was your occupation prior to becoming a law enforcement official?"

"Your Honor, this clearly has no relevance," Matthews said offhandedly, although he knew, and feared, the answer.

"If it doesn't, Mr. Matthews, I'll sustain, and Mr. Barnes will look foolish for having asked."

"Your prior occupation?" Barnes reminded.

"I worked retail in sporting goods."

"And what did you sell?"

Weitzman looked Matthews squarely in the eyes, but with the eyes of an old dog. "Rifles," he answered.

"Your Honor, I'd like Mr. Weitzman's affidavit in CE 2003 admitted, and the former rifle salesman is excused."

"You two legal eagles have any other bright ideas?" Matthews asked his assistants. "We've got a handful of Dallas blue suits out there and one or two of them have to be able to put something into evidence." Graves suggested the arresting officer, and Vincent chipped in with a suggestion that they put Oswald's shirt into evidence, since the FBI report, they knew, spoke of fibers from the shirt found on the butt plate of the Mannlicher-Carcano. Matthews liked both ideas.

"Your Honor, the state calls Officer M. N. McDonald."

Barnes conferred briefly with Bob Dean while the young but robust officer virtually stormed through the courtroom on his way to the stand where it was established that he had completed an eleventh grade education in Arkansas in 1948 and had joined the Dallas police force in 1955. It was also established, despite some confusion, that he was known to everyone as "M.N."

"Were you on duty on November twenty-second?" Matthews began.

"Yes. Radio patrol outside of town."

"Please tell the court what happened at 12:30."

"Several units got called about that time to get to the Texas School Book Depository, Code Three. That means come running."

"And you did?"

"Yes. I got there in about ten minutes, and just then heard that the President had died. I then worked crowd control for a few minutes until we heard a civilian come over the police radio and indicate an officer had been shot." At this point, Judge Davis gave Matthews a look which indicated he could pursue this line of questioning as needed, but not to overdo it.

"What did you do when you learned of that news?" Matthews asked, as if he understood the tacit admonishment.

"We left the Depository in search of the suspect."

"And where did your search finally take you?"

"To the Texas Theater, located at 231 West Jefferson."

"Tell the court what happened."

"Well, we had the place surrounded, and several other officers and myself entered through the back door, onto, well, the stage area. Then they gradually brought up the lights, and you could see that there were perhaps fifteen or so people spread out throughout the theater. The shoe store salesman had pointed out a suspect, and we gradually closed in on him. I was the first to actually reach him, and he took a swing at me, hit me pretty good, and then the other officers subdued him."

"Do you see that suspect in this courtroom?"

"Yes, sir. That younger man right over there." Barnes wanted, for personal reasons, to object to the characterization "younger."

"Did you, at that time, seize a weapon from the defendant?"

"Yes. A thirty-eight pistol, fully loaded."

"Officer McDonald, I show you CE 143, a thirty-eight caliber revolver. Do you recognize this weapon?"

"That is the gun taken from the suspect in the theater. It has my mark on it—that 'M.' "

"Thank you, Officer. No further questions."

Barnes approached the witness slowly yet purposefully. "Officer, you were asked about what happened at 12:30, and you just told us that you heard a Code Three, got to the Book Depository in about ten minutes, and learned that the President had died. Do I understand your testimony correctly?"

"Yes."

"Officer, the President was not pronounced dead until 1 P.M. Were you present for that?"

"No."

"Then if you arrived at the Depository to learn of his death, and it took you ten minutes—in haste—to get there, then you haven't really told us what you were doing at 12:30. In fact, there's the possibility that the jury may have heard a suggestion that you were ordered to the Book Depository at 12:30. Now was that the case?"

"I can't be positive about the exact times."

"Fair enough. Now, Officer, can you tell the court what 'probable cause' means?"

"Well, it more or less means you have to have a reason for arresting someone. Or searching them. You can't just trample somebody's rights."

"That's pretty close, Officer. And I'm sure it helped the jury, which, after all, is what we're trying to do. Now, I have a little confusion, and you can help me. Before we're all through here in Lubbock, I'll put a good number of people on the witness stand who will testify that shots came from the area down there on Elm Street known as 'the grassy knoll.' As I understand your testimony, and the other officers before you, policemen were being taken out of the area where many witnesses will say one or more shots originated, and many of those officers wind up at the Texas Theater to surround and arrest a man for . . . well, you tell me. What was the probable cause here?"

"The shoe store man thought this individual was acting suspiciously and had entered the theater without buying a ticket."

"So within minutes of the announced death of the President of the United States," Barnes announced loudly, "a veritable cadre of policemen go to a theater to arrest someone who hadn't bought a ticket?"

"Well, we had a description."

"Which was?" Barnes asked, suspiciously.

"The first description was 'white male, approximately twenty-seven, twenty-nine years old, and he had a white shirt on, weighed about one hundred sixty pounds.' "

"Since you said 'First description,' there was obviously another?"

"Well, it was five foot ten, white male, twenty-seven years old, wearing a white shirt."

"So what the two descriptions have in common are white male, twenty-seven years old, wearing a white shirt?"

"Yes."

"And what color shirt was the defendant wearing when you arrested him?

"Dark brown."

"So where is your probable cause, Officer? You told us that

it meant you couldn't just deprive people of their rights. Now you tell us that this manhunt for an individual who had the audacity in broad daylight to enter a theater without a ticket was for a white male in a white shirt, and even in a less-than-ideally lit theater, you arrest someone in a dark brown shirt."

"Objection, argumentative."

"Sustained for the moment. Perhaps you could restate your question, Mr. Barnes."

"It's tempting to request having this whole thing thrown out for lack of probable cause, Your Honor, but I'll withhold that. In the meantime, I withdraw the last question. Officer McDonald, did you write an account of your contact with the defendant in the Texas Theater for the Associated Press on November twenty-third?"

"Yes, they were very interested in my story, because my face had been scratched and puffed in the scuffle."

"Did you write the story?"

"Well, I wrote a brief description of events. I don't know if I'd call it 'a story' or 'an exclusive.' "

"I show you this clipping from the wire services dated November twenty-four, 1963. Would you take a moment to read it and tell the jury if you recognize it?"

"It's been a while, but that's it, okay."

"Your statement says, 'I noted about ten to fifteen people sitting in the theater and they were spread out good. A man sitting near the front, and I still don't know who it was, tipped me the man I wanted was sitting in the third row from the rear of the ground floor and not in the balcony.' Am I reading this correctly? A theater patron, sitting in a seat watching the feature, tells you that an individual sought for two capital crimes, is sitting directly behind him?"

"That's the way it happened."

"Doesn't that strike you as odd?"

"Objection. Calls for a conclusion."

"Sustained."

"Does a total stranger telling you this information come within the bounds of probable cause, Officer?"

"No."

"Do there exist *any* records of who those other nine to fifteen people were in the theater?"

"No."

"Marvelous police work. Did it take six squads to escort one prisoner out?"

"Argumentative."

"Sustained."

"Could we please have C 11, please, on the screens? Is that the shirt, Officer?"

"Appears to be."

"Officer McDonald, if you say it is, it must be. You were the arresting officer, correct?"

"In a manner of speaking."

"I don't understand, Officer. Did *you* arrest Lee Harvey Oswald, the 'young' man you identified sitting between us senior citizens, or if you didn't, who did? Whose name appears on the arrest report?"

"I have no idea."

"This may sound foolish, Officer, but *was there* an *arrest report?*"

"I have no idea."

"Well, if that's the case, I have no idea what you're doing up here except to prove beyond a reasonable doubt that the defendant probably did assault you, but we didn't need to move to Lubbock to prove that. Now about this pistol, here, Officer, the one with the 'M' on the steel plate. You testified that was your mark."

"Yes, sir."

"Where were you when you marked this pistol?"

"Police Headquarters."

"Did you personally have complete custody of the weapon from the moment it was taken from the defendant until it was marked for identification?"

"No. Some of the other officers had it, then it was given back to me when we got to headquarters."

"Thank you, Officer McDonald. Move to strike the weapon as inadmissible."

Matthews was instantly on his feet. "This is a travesty, Your Honor. There was only one pistol, the one in evidence. The serial number matches with the purchase order which defense counsel, in his wisdom, stipulated was ordered by the defendant. Now, he's in effect excluding his own evidence."

The judge looked at Barnes with absolutely no telltale signs of emotion. "Mr. Barnes?"

"Your Honor, my stipulation was that the defendant *placed an order* for the gun with that serial number. Subsequent testimony from that witness, Mr. Michaelis, failed to elicit any proof whatsoever that it was ever received by the defendant. The prosecution, to date, has offered no such evidence. Now I'm certain that they can put several policemen on the stand to indicate that the defendant brandished a weapon in the Texas Theater, but all of that is irrelevant. What is relevant, as in my move to exclude the hulls, is chain of possession. Mr. McDonald is claiming that this was *the pistol*, but he can only claim, not prove, that allegation. Your Honor, I think a couple of more questions can focus the issue."

"Proceed."

"Officer McDonald, you testified that the pistol you seized was a thirty-eight caliber, fully loaded. How many of the shells did you mark for identification, and where were you when you did it?"

"I recall marking one, at Police Headquarters."

"That's all I have," Barnes concluded.

"Mr. Matthews, although it's premature for the lunch break, I'll allow you free use of the telephones in my chambers. But by the afternoon session, you better burn up the wires between here, Dallas, and wherever else you need to call, and you had better convince me both on the hulls and the pistol with respect to chain of possession. Court is in recess."

The prosecutors followed the judge into his chambers, while Bob Dean assured Barnes that there would be no "Texas collusion" between the judge and the prosecution. "Davis is not that kind of guy, and he can't be bought, so rest easy. Do you really think you can get the pistol kicked?" Dean concluded.

"Not a chance. But I think it's enough to get the hulls thrown out, and that's the damaging evidence. The pistol isn't at issue in the assassination, and I think I convinced the jury it became a necessary prop after the patsy realized the fix was in. Besides, we may win them both, and if we can do that, that evidence table will be thinning out in the next few days. In the meantime, we can have a nice leisurely lunch, not like the one Matthews is going to have to digest."

Dean left Barnes and Jeffries with the promise that he would "work the phones" during lunch, and asked Barnes to bring him back a sandwich. When he started to reach for his wallet, Barnes froze him with a half-friendly, half "how dare you?" look.

"What does work the phones mean, Eddie?" Jeffries asked.

"Boiled down, Carolyn, it means Bob Dean will find out everything Matthews does, and just about as fast."

*"How?"*

"Simple, really. You don't get to be as famous in Texas as he is without contacts, and he's on the phone to them right now. He'll know who in Dallas is suddenly getting urgent calls from Lubbock, and then by putting labels on the various people, we know the level of whom we are dealing with. Another tactic, if he has the time, is to get inside Matthews's head, figure who he'd call, and call them. If they're 'on another line,' he knows he's on the right track. If they're out on a case, day off, sick leave, or vacation, or testifying, he knows Matthews can't reach the people he wants to, and that just makes the prosecution's problem that much stickier."

"Sounds challenging," Jeffries commented, hoping maybe she'd get a chance to be more than a spectator.

Barnes, hearing that tone, diverted the issue with a war story. "It can be challenging, or incredibly boring. Matter of fact, it was nonstop boredom like that which caused me to leave the FBI. Work the phones. You might make three *days* of phone calls and come up with nothing more than ear wax. One time I got lucky, though. Perp name of Horace. We had an arrest and search warrant, on a thin beef, believe me. So we roust the guy in the middle of the night, toss the place, and come up empty. And you know what? The guy's wife cooked *us* breakfast. So about two weeks later, I decide to be Mr. Nice Guy, and call to thank the lady, and ask about Horace. Well, damned if she doesn't say something like 'Thanks for calling, but Horace isn't here right now. He said he was going out to buy hats.' We got a warrant, tossed him again, and he's still in the joint."

"I don't follow you."

" 'Hats' is the street term for the capsules that diluted heroin is put into. The wife, dear lady, had no idea Horace was out buying drug paraphernalia. We had probable cause, got another warrant, caught Horace on the way in, and he took four to seven for p.i.c., and another five to ten for the horse, uncut mind you, inside. All for a thank you call for a breakfast."

Barnes and Jeffries spent the remainder of lunch trying not to focus on the case, which was not easy to do. Matthews had about as much success in his endeavors, which he reasoned would not be enough.

When court resumed, the judge summoned all six attorneys into his chambers, leaving the defendant in court with his captors, a bored steno, and a state trooper who had nothing to record.

Judge Davis came right to the point: "How does it play, Ray?"

"Well, on the pistol, Your Honor, we were able to trace the chain of who held it from the time it was taken from the defendant's hand until Officer McDonald belatedly marked it. It might take a couple days to get all the parties here . . ."

"Are there that many?" Davis asked incredulously.

"No. But one is 'on hold' to testify, and one had the day off . . ." as Matthews's voice trailed off.

"So you're saying that in a few days, we could meet with a few individuals and straighten out the pistol?"

"Yes."

"Then I'll hold that motion to exclude in abeyance. What about the hulls?"

"I'm afraid you know as much of that story as we do, Your Honor. I'm almost afraid to try to piece it together, because the memos, dated in July, are . . . forgive me, Miss Jeffries . . . well, they're 'cover your ass memos.' And with that in mind, I can't imagine how testimony is going to resolve one, who picked up the hulls, two, were they ever checked for prints, three, where they went, and four, why Carl Day didn't get them back to mark them until nine o'clock. And finally, I have nobody's testimony that the envelope was sealed. So there it is, Your Honor."

"You realize you leave me no choice, Ray."

"I understand fully, Your Honor, but I wouldn't feel any more comfortable than you if I got a conviction based on sloppy or worse, irregular police ethics." Don't worry, Barnes thought, you won't.

The courtroom was filled with its normal complement—lawyers, staff, defendant, and jury, when the judge explained that a subsequent hearing would be held regarding the admissability of the pistol, but that the hulls were henceforth and forever being excluded from evidence. "Now, you must understand as jurors," he continued, "that this is not an empty technicality. You must literally forget that those hulls ever existed. When you consider the crime scene in the future, they are not part of it, because they have no legal entitlement to be part of it. Before we continue, do any members of the jury have a question about this? If so, please stand and be heard."

The jurors seemed to understand.

"Mr. Matthews, please call your next witness."

"The state calls Paul Bentley."

Barnes was totally unaware of the boring preliminaries, as this was his first chance to find out what Bob Dean had learned, which was essentially that the July memos had been FBI-inspired, and that Carl Day and everyone above him in the Dallas police hierarchy were concerned about still having jobs when all this was over, and they certainly weren't going to add anything even resembling perjury to their dossiers. In fact, they were scared. Barnes and Dean agreed that was a very good sign indeed. Barnes came back to the present when he heard Matthews ask, "And is this the shirt that the defendant was wearing at the time of his arrest?"

"Yes, it was. When it was removed, a little later in the afternoon, I marked it for evidence with my initials on the tag down there."

"When you say 'a little later,' could you be a little more specific?"

"Sometime around dinner—no, excuse me, I misspoke. It

would have had to have been at the end of the day. I recall having more or less to wait, just to i.d. the items of clothing, and that was a long day to just wait. It would have been after the 'midnight' press conference, but prior to the second arraignment."

"But the defendant did not change clothes from his arrest until you marked this shirt?"

"What would he have had to change into?"

"Objection. Nonresponsive."

"Sustained."

"No, he didn't change clothes."

"Your witness, Mr. Barnes."

"With it fully understood that this witness is subject to recall, I have no questions at this time."

Matthews was piqued. "Your Honor, these witnesses, many from Dallas, others from the nation's capital, cannot cool their heels until Mr. Barnes gets around to them. If he has a question in mind, it should be asked now."

"Mr. Barnes does have the right to request recall, counselor, but I also understand your point. Mr. Barnes, is it that urgent?"

Barnes made it look tedious. "Mr. Bentley, I gather you followed the defendant around all day, in order to label his clothes, is that correct?"

"Basically."

"And that shirt we just saw was the shirt, to the exclusion of all others, that he was wearing when taken into custody by your fellow officers?"

"Absolutely."

"And did the shirt leave the custody of the Dallas authorities?"

"Yes. It was turned over to Special Agent Vincent Drain of the FBI."

"Could we please have CE 2011, heading 'Brownish shirt, C11'?"

A document came up on the screen. "Mr. Bentley, you testified, and dozens of pictures corroborate you, that Mr. Oswald was indeed wearing the shirt at the 'midnight' press conference. The document on the screen, however, indicates that, quote, 'The brownish shirt, C11, was delivered to Special Agent Vincent E. Drain on November twenty-two, 1963, for transmittal to the laboratory of the FBI, Washington, D.C., for examination.' I don't see how a shirt could have been worn at a midnight press conference and delivered to an FBI agent, in a sense, yesterday."

"I can only surmise that we thought of November 22, 1963, as a continuous event—that it was that awful Friday until we went to sleep, if we did, or until breakfast reminded us that it was Saturday."

"That sounds very reasonable, Mr. Bentley. Just one more question. Do you, Paul Bentley, have any personal knowledge or evidence, that the defendant was wearing that shirt, C11, at 12:30 P.M. when the President was killed?"

"No."

"To your knowledge, what Dallas or other local jurisdictional officer accompanied the shirt when FBI agent Drain took it to Washington?"

"To the best of my knowledge, no local officer went with it."

"Thank you for now. Move to admit the relevant parts of CE 2011." Then, as a reminder to the prosecution, "Subject to recall."

Earl Vincent quickly got Matthews's ear to point out that Barnes had missed a chance to get the shirt excluded as evidence, based on the fact that it had been out of Dallas jurisdiction.

"I doubt the word 'missed' is accurate, Earl," Matthews told him. "I'd wager my prime steer he's going to ask Agent Drain the same question about the rifle, and then we are totally out of the frying pan."

Barnes figured that sooner or later that day, Matthews would put somebody on the stand with something to say, so while one juror, clearly in the early stages of a good cold, sneezed repeatedly, Barnes leaned over, affecting a serious attitude, towards Matthews, and good-naturedly asked: "What's next, Ray? Going to have the trousers admitted? Then win the case with his socks?"

Matthews would not take the bait. "The people call Detective Richard S. Stovall." A mid-thirtyish, well-conditioned police veteran entered, in street clothes, and was sworn.

Matthews decided to one-up Barnes and be very thorough.

"Detective, what were you doing at approximately 12:30 P.M. on November twenty-two, 1963?"

"I was home watching television. That's how I learned the President had been shot." Matthews realized that in his dual with Barnes he had forgotten that his witness had been off duty, but scheduled to go on at four, and had come in early when he heard of the day's events.

"Directing your attention to the time when you came on duty, Detective Stovall, what was your first major responsibility that afternoon?"

"I was assigned, along with Detectives Rose and Adamcik, to proceed to 2515 West Fifth Street in Irving, Texas, to search a residence there."

"Would you tell the court who lived there?"

"A Mrs. Ruth Paine and her young children, and a Mrs. Oswald, with two young children."

"Please tell the court what happened."

"Well, first off, we had to wait down the block when we got there, because we were supposed to be joined by county officers. See, Irving is out of our jurisdiction. So when they, the county officers, Harry Weatherford, J.L. Oxford, and Buddy Walthers arrived, we knocked on the door, and Mrs. Paine said something like we should come in, she was expecting us based on what she'd seen on the TV."

"And then?" Matthews hated prompting.

"At that time we told her that we wanted to search the house. We explained to her that we did not have a search warrant, but if she wanted us to get one we would, and she said, 'That won't be necessary.' So then we searched the place—there's a list of what was confiscated, and then our search was directed to the garage when Mrs. Paine told us that Mrs. Oswald . . ."

"Objection, Your Honor. Privilege."

"Nonsense," Matthews replied.

"Please approach, gentlemen," the judge instructed in a soft, kindly voice. When the two lawyers were shoulder to shoulder, he continued, "You first, Mr. Barnes."

"Your Honor, it's as simple as this—Mrs. Oswald cannot be brought into this case in a way that is injurious to the defendant."

"Mr. Matthews?"

"The law is clear, Your Honor. A wife cannot be required to testify against her husband. There's no *testimony* by her at this time."

"On the contrary," Barnes interrupted. "The law states that a wife cannot 'give evidence' against her husband, and that's what's at stake here. I know you're getting at the blanket, Ray, and you're welcome to it. If you want to have the prosecution evidence table looking like a rummage sale, go right ahead, but you're not able to have Mrs. Oswald so clutter it."

"Step back, gentlemen. Detective Stovall," Judge Davis continued, "please exclude the defendant's wife from any comments you make with respect to evidence."

"If I may restate the question," Matthews said, "Detective, was your attention directed to the garage?"

"Yes. Mrs. Paine suggested—well, told us, that we should look into the contents of a particular blanket, partially wrapped with white twine, that was on the floor of the garage."

"And what did you find?"

"An old blanket, wrapped, just like I said, with white twine, which was empty."

"So the blanket was empty," Matthews intoned, trying to give it a sinister connotation for the jury.

"Yes. Rose carried it into the house, empty."

"Could we have Stovall Exhibit A, please?" Matthews would have asked for almost anything at this point to convince the jury that the monitors were not only for Barnes's use.

Two typewritten pages appeared, side by side, and the jurors were allowed to peruse the items. Matthews then asked that it be admitted as evidence.

"Mr. Barnes?"

"No objection to that typed piece of paper being admitted, *at this time,*" Barnes said, with a hint of foreboding.

"So moved. Please continue."

"What happened then, Detective?"

"The two ladies, as well as their children, were taken down to police headquarters, and I think the husband, Mr. Paine—

the Paines were separated . . ." Matthews winced at the reference and wondered if the Dallas police were hiring off the street, ". . . he came down there too. Wanted them to have a look at the rifle. Later on, we had to round up Buell W. Frazier, and his sister, Linnie Mae Randle. Put the Frazier fella on the box."

"Could you clarify that for the jury?"

"He had to take a lie detector test. Then, of course, we went back the next day between noon and one P.M., with a warrant, but there was nobody there."

"Did you find any additional evidence in this second search?"

"Objection to the word 'evidence', Your Honor. I hardly think that the seizure of Mrs. Paine's collection of phonograph records, an electric bill from New Orleans, and the birth certificate of a baby is going to crack the case wide open."

"While agreeing in principle, Mr. Barnes, what was taken, was in fact brought in for whatever evidentiary value the jury ultimately puts on it. Overruled."

"The *evidence,* Detective, on Saturday?"

"We found snapshots of a white male holding a rifle and wearing a pistol on his right hip, along with the negatives from those photos, as well as negatives for the Alek Hidell Selective Service identification card."

"Do you see the person shown in those photographs in this courtroom?"

"Yes, sir. Right over there," pointing a strong accusatory finger at the defendant.

Matthews should have known when to quit. "Detective, I show you a 6.5 Mannlicher-Carcano carbine. Do you recognize it as being depicted in any of the photographs?"

"There is no way I could say that positively. There are certainly similarities, but there is certainly no distinguishing feature about that gun that would allow me to say that it is the same one as in the picture."

"Fair enough, Detective. Excuse me, could we please have Shaneyfelt Exhibits 1 and 13, side by side, please?" Detective, are these pictures you seized pursuant to your search of the Paine residence on Saturday?"

With the jury looking intently at what was clearly incriminating evidence, the witness soberly intoned, "Yes."

"Thank you very much, Detective. Nothing further. Move to admit Stovall Exhibit A, and Shaneyfelt 1 and 13." As Matthews walked to Barnes, he commented, "Trousers, eh?"

Barnes knew it might be a little difficult, but he had a gut feeling that this was going to be a textbook cross-examination, and that Ray Matthews would never, ever, buy, or read, that text. Matthews got his first clue when he saw Barnes take up his familiar spot all the way at the end of the jury box. "Detective Stovall, you testified that you waited for county officers to arrive, because Irving, Texas, is not in your jurisdiction."

"That's correct."

"Did you, or Detectives Rose, Adamcik, or county Officers Weatherford, Oxford, or Walthers, at any time prior to or during the search—the Friday search, advise either Mrs. Paine or Mrs. Oswald of any rights they might have under a document called the United States Constitution? Before you answer, I want you to understand my question—you're searching a residence *visited* by an individual suddenly faced with the two most serious capital crimes that could have been committed in the state of Texas. With the possibility that you could have found ammunition, other weapons—after all, you did seize a weapon from Mr. Frazier, did you not?"

"Yes."

"So for all you knew, you could have walked through the door and found the evidence to cinch the case—and in the process, certainly charge the two females as accessories to murder; were they appraised of any rights?"

"Mrs. Oswald did not understand English."

"Don't give me that, Detective," Barnes fired back. "Mrs. Paine certainly did, and she was employed to tutor people in Russian. She certainly could have translated. Did you make the two ladies aware of their constitutional rights?"

"No. They weren't suspects."

"It's nice to know who the suspects are and who they are not in advance," Barnes editorialized.

"Objection, Your Honor. He's playing to the jury."

"As long as it's not *Othello,* I'll allow it, Mr. Matthews. The comment was relevant to the answer."

"Thank you, Your Honor," Barnes said humbly, but in a way that let the witness know that he was now on the spot. "Now, Detective, you told us you searched the residence at 2515 West Fifth Street in Irving, Texas. Who owns that residence?"

"It's the Paine residence."

"I didn't ask who lived there; who owns it?"

"Mr. Paine."

"Thank you. To your knowledge, sir, were either Mrs. Paine or Mrs. Oswald, or any of the children, paying rent to Mr. Paine to occupy that residence in the fall of 1963?"

"Mrs. Oswald was not, to the best of my knowledge. I have no idea why Mrs. Paine would be paying rent to her husband."

"Neither do I," Barnes stressed. "But let's get past that. Did you, or Detectives Rose or Adamcik, search the residence?"

"Yes. I testified to that."

"For how long?"

"Two, two and a half hours."

"Was the garage searched on Friday? Strike the question; to your knowledge, Detective, was the garage searched on Friday?"

"Yes. Detective Rose searched it, during and after the time spent with the blanket."

"Ah, yes, the blanket—what was that all about?

"Well, we were told a rifle was kept in it. But as I said before, it was empty."

"Do you want the jury to get the idea that an empty blanket somehow conveys the sense that the owner of the blanket killed the President?"

"No. But with the gun missing—"

"Detective—listen to me. There were probably one million blankets in Dallas on that day that *did not* contain rifles. I would also suggest to you that there were many rifles that should have been somewhere on that day, and for one reason or another, they weren't. Now are we talking evidence, or an empty blanket?"

"An empty blanket."

"All right. Now, if we could have Stovall Exhibit A on the screens again, please. Detective, let's take a closer look here. The first time one reads this inventory, the reader is struck by the large amount of camera equipment and film. Did you see these cameras?"

"Yes."

"Characterize them for us."

"Well, some of them, you know, like everybody has—take a picture of the new car, what have you. Others, though were kind of small and fancy looking."

"Detective, if I told you that a leading camera firm in Dallas, Texas, when shown photos of the cameras in this and subsequent property inventories, put a value on those cameras in excess of all the money earned by the defendant in the year and a half since his return to the U.S., would that fact surprise you?"

"Objection. Conclusionary."

"Sustained."

"Detective, the crime at stake here is murder; to wit, homicide with a rifle; not photography. Given that fact, did you find one piece of evidence to support the charge of murder with a rifle?"

"No."

"Did you find any gun-cleaning tools, any gun oil, any ammunition?"

"No."

"Anything whatsoever gun related?"

"Only those photographs."

"Have you ever handled a case where the victim was killed by a photograph?"

"Objection. Argumentative."

"The question follows logically from the witness's previous response," Barnes argued.

"Overruled."

"No. We've never had a killing with a photo."

"Could we have Decker 5323, reference J. L. Oxford, please? Detective, ah, here we are. This document also mentions cameras with film. To your knowledge, was any of that film *ever* developed?"

"Not to my knowledge."

"Do you have any knowledge of where it is now?"

"If it exists, the Feebs have it."

"Feebs?" Barnes asked, knowing the answer.

"FBI. They grabbed everything we got our hands on."

"I see. Okay. Now, you testified that the ladies, along with Mr. Paine, who had arrived late, and the children, were taken to police headquarters. Were they not, in fact, subjected to threats to get them there?"

"I don't know if I'd use the word 'threat,' but I guess we were a little rough on them. Overeager on our part, and I'm sorry for that."

"Be that as it may, Detective. One person's definition of 'overeager' may be another's definition of 'threat.' Now, what happened to the marvelous evidence you seized on Friday— the phonograph records, the cameras, the movie projector, the baby's birth certificate . . . what became of all of that?"

"It was all put in boxes and loaded into the trunk of the car and put back in one of our interrogation rooms there." Matthews wrote "Motion to Exclude" and slid it across the table for Graves and Vincent.

"And when did you see it again for the purpose of preparing the inventory, Stovall Exhibit A?"

"The next day, Saturday."

"And with hundreds of reporters and photographers literally everywhere in that headquarters, and security so lax that a strip-joint operator could shoot the defendant the following morning, are you prepared to tell me that in your absence, that evidence was secure? Not that it has any value whatsoever, just that it was secure?"

"It was awful crazy in there."

"Okay. So the adults go down to headquarters while the phonograph records collect dust. What happened?"

"Well, we wanted to see if anybody could i.d. the rifle."

" 'Anybody,' of course, being the defendant's wife, since Mrs. Paine is a Quaker and a pacifist."

"We didn't know that."

"Did you ask the Paines to identify the rifle?"

"No."

"In violation of legal ethics, did you ask the defendant's

wife to identify evidence that, *if identified,* would be used against him?"

"Yes."

"How was she asked?"

"Through an interpreter."

"Just as a curiosity, can you name the interpreter?"

"No."

"Okay, then, would you tell the jury the results of those efforts to get an identification of the rifle?"

"She said she could not identify the rifle, having only seen an inch or so of the butt plate of the gun that was supposed to have been in the blanket. She also pointed to the sight and the translator, speaking rapidly, said she was saying, 'What is this? I don't know of this,' that kind of thing."

"Then if, in this incredible moment of stress when only the God's honest truth could save her, she indicated that she had no familiarity at all with a telescopic sight, who, then, took the photos of the defendant with the rifle with the telescopic sight? Never mind—strike the question. Detective, were the three county officers with you when you returned on Saturday?"

"I don't believe so. But we had a warrant."

"Did Irving, Texas, become part of your jurisdiction overnight?"

"No."

"And to whom did you give the warrant?"

"Nobody was home."

"Indeed they weren't, Detective. Yet you found evidence, possibly to the crime of the century, on Saturday, that you had 'overlooked,' shall we say, the day before. You've been an officer for ten years, and a detective for three. Have you ever before searched a residence in a double felony, capital crime, and left the scene before the search was completed?"

"No."

"Is it police procedure to do so?"

"No." Stovall knew he was sinking.

"Since the residence was vacated at the time of the Saturday search, and inasmuch as there had been massive media coverage, what would have prevented someone from planting the evidence that you did not find on Friday, but was suddenly available on Saturday?"

Stovall mistakenly tried to outlawyer a lawyer. "Well, it sure wasn't the defendant who did it. He was in jail."

"You've got that right, Detective. No more questions." Barnes moved slowly to his seat, and sat down in silence.

"Redirect, Mr. Matthews?"

"No, Your Honor. The state calls . . ."

"Forgive the interruption, Your Honor, but if there's no redirect, I think we should keep Detective Stovall on the witness stand in case any questions arise with respect to defense's motion to exclude all evidence found at the Paine residence."

"On what possible grounds?"

Barnes and Matthews reached the aisle simultaneously, and Barnes said quietly, "You know 'why,' Ray." Both attorneys then approached the judge and asked that the jury be removed. Barnes took a list of items from Bob Dean while the jury was walking out, and Matthews's mind raced and braced for what was coming.

"What is the nature of your objection, Mr. Barnes?"

"Actually, Your Honor, there are six parts to it." Matthews was thunderstruck, seeing Bob Dean behind this, and even the judge had a knee-jerk reaction when he heard "six parts" calmly recited.

"First, is the search legal in its inception? The residence is owned by Mr. Michael Paine, who, though absent, retains all custodial rights thereto. Since neither adult resident paid him rent or any other binding contractual fees, they have no entitlement to allow a search of someone else's property. There are three citations in Texas law which will be passed to the bench with respect to this first objection, and in each case, the court found the search illegal, since the legal owner of the residence did not give consent for the search." Dean then walked to the bench and put a brief to the judge's right, so it would not distract him from Barnes's narrative.

"Secondly, there was no thought of legal rights to the two females present."

Matthews interrupted. "They were never charged."

"Which tends to point up the irrelevancy of the evidence we

are now debating, and which brings me to the third point. Detective Stovall testified that county officers were needed at the scene because Dallas officers had no jurisdiction. What Detective Stovall did not tell the jury is that in such cases, the individuals *with* jurisdiction must perform the entire search and make the legal seizure of the evidence. A process must then be undertaken to transfer that evidence, assuming proper chain of possession to that point, to the authorities that need the evidence for subsequent prosecution. There's not a shred of that in the testimony. Those county officers were simply hood ornaments on Friday, and were not even present on Saturday.

"The evidence was put in interrogation rooms in the back of police headquarters and left there in that hectic atmosphere where it required a cordon of officers to get the Chief of Police across the hall. That alone disqualifies the evidence.

"The delay, the deliberate leaving of the scene on Friday, to return at a time unknown, to see if there happened to be anything else lying around, again in a charged media atmosphere and with the tenants—and owner—all absent, is a factor militating—along with the absence of jurisdictional officers, to disqualify the evidence.

"Lastly, the warrant—finally, a warrant—existed, but was not served on Saturday. In many jurisdictions, that by itself is an illegal search. There are precedents on both sides of the issue. If the constituted authorities—in this case, county officers, had reason to believe that the dwelling was unoccupied and had been permanently vacated, or if there were extenuating circumstances, such as evidence relating to an ongoing kidnapping where the victim's life hung in the balance, then such a search is usually held valid by courts. But the Paines go grocery shopping and their house can be torn apart?"

"Your last point *has* been seen both ways in Texas precedents, Mr. Barnes, so it will not help you. Given the nature of the offense at stake, I would have to rule against your sixth point. But I'm aware of the legal precedents regarding ownership, you are on strong ground with respect to failure to warn, the jurisdictional question again makes me wonder *what* was going on in the minds of the law enforcement community that day, and the chain of possession question reinforces my concerns in that area. Delay is a gray area. Mr. Matthews, there is nothing you can say at this point. The defense could not possibly be on better grounds. The motion to exclude is granted. I will explain the result, but not the causes, to the jury. Detective, you're excused, and I will make the suggestion, off the record, Mrs. Martinez, that you and your fellow officers back in Dallas read up on procedures involving evidence. Mr. Matthews, I imagine you might be desirous of a bit of a recess here. Court is adjourned until three."

During the adjournment, Barnes, Dean, and Jeffries stood by the coffee area, giving the prosecution team the privacy to huddle and regroup after the most recent setback. Carolyn Jeffries was absolutely in awe of what she had just seen, despite having worked with Barnes before.

"It's important, Carolyn," Barnes told her, with a sense of caution in his voice.

"But it's far from over," Bob Dean cut in.

"Far from over," Barnes echoed. "They know their case has been hurt, and sooner or later it's going to be hurt worse. The question now is whether or not they realize it or to what extent they do. I have to think we're going to see a change in strategy."

At the defense table, Matthews came immediately to the point: "Who is left out there from the Dallas p.d.?"

"R.L. Studebaker—took the pictures for Day, Hicks and Barnes . . ." Matthews bristled slightly at the name, ". . . with reference to the paraffin test and fingerprinting, and J.H. Sawyer," Graves answered.

"Okay. Eaton, you take a look at everything we've got on Studebaker and Sawyer. Earl, same thing for Hicks and Barnes. At 2:55, I need to know if there's anything—any reason why we can't put them on the stand. In the meantime, I'm going to telephone good old Dr. Humes and give him directions to the ranch. He's going to be our dinner guest tonight—and he may wind up being the one roasted."

Dean was noticing what the prosecution was doing, and

casually commented, "I think they're measuring their assets, Eddie."

"Wouldn't you?" Barnes asked.

"Don't blame Ray, Eddie—just be glad he didn't make this case," Dean insisted. "He was here in Texas fourteen months ago. Hell, I remember seeing all of them—Dallas District Attorney Henry Wade, Curry, Fritz, even Texas Attorney General Waggoner Carr, on TV after Oswald was shot, and every one of them told what a cinchy case it was. 'No doubt in our mind,' 'the case was cinched,' even that worn-out cliché, 'beyond a reasonable doubt.' And Ray bought the story, just like I did—at the time. But Dallas thought they wouldn't have to try it, so they handed Ray a bill of goods. You can bet he's going to have some interesting comments when this is all done."

"Where do we fit into *that* scenario?" Barnes asked his Texas colleague.

"Not to worry, Eddie. Ray's a professional. Hell, he and I go a long way back, and I know you've earned his respect. You don't have any personal loathing for him—this is business—so why should he dislike any of us? Circumstances brought us together. When this is done, I'll get everybody over to my place . . ."

"When this is done," Barnes interrupted, "I'm on a fast plane north to a family that misses me and concerns me." With that, they noticed Matthews walking doggedly back into the courtroom and returning to the prosecution table.

Graves was sitting back, with a pencil lying on a legal pad in front of him and a few pages of documents to his right. It appeared that Vincent had one more page of a report to read, and when he finished it, he put it down and turned to realize that Matthews and Graves had been waiting for him.

"Eaton, what about Studebaker and Sawyer?"

"Weak. Studebaker only began work in the crime lab on October one, 1963, so he's going to look wet behind the ears. On top of that, we have the confusion, testified to by Carl Day, about the location of the boxes and when the pictures were taken. His testimony before the President's Commission is very compelling. Boxes here, hulls photographed in this way—a tidy package. But he wasn't cross-examined by them.

As for Sawyer, he's a grizzled veteran and he'd make a good visual witness. The jury would see a tough cop. But they would hear a very confused one. The description he called in was for someone about thirty, five foot ten, and slender, which makes it useless."

"How so?" Matthews asked.

"About thirty, five foot ten, and slender is all he said; a minute later, the dispatcher, on his own, added 'white male.' Also, he's got a couple different rifles mentioned, none correctly, and he spoke of the hulls being found on the fifth floor."

"And now they don't exist on any floor," Matthews reminded both. "Yes or no to those two?"

"I'd have to say 'no,' unless we want to add a few facts and take another pounding."

Matthews turned to Vincent. "Earl, what about Hicks and Barnes?"

"All they can tell us is that they fingerprinted and gave the paraffin test to Oswald. The problem is that they're both liabilities in cross-examination, because it has been alleged that Oswald was fingerprinted by the FBI while he was comatose, and if Hicks testifies that the prints he took were satisfactory, the jury may well believe that the FBI was collecting prints to plant here and there, like on the rifle. Officer Barnes is a liability because there's the question of consent in something like a paraffin test. And Oswald asked him flat out, 'Are you doing this to determine if I fired a gun?' and Barnes dodged the issue. I think the safest course is just to insert a fingerprint record in there somewhere and avoid the paraffin test altogether, which the jury will understand about as well as they will neutron activation analysis."

"All right, then. At least we know where we're going today. If anybody thinks there's anything to be gained by putting any of those four on the stand today, or ever, say so now." Matthews listened to footsteps returning to the defense table, but from the far end, out of courtesy. "So those four are out— then we've got nobody for today. We have to go for a continuance. Tomorrow is Humes. We've still got some experts who can impress a jury with their titles and the fact that their office is only two floors away from Hoover's, but the last thing we want is for the autopsy people to be our last witnesses. If we put them on next, then the experts, we've got a chance. If we put them on last, Barnes wouldn't need to call one witness, and the jury would take a half hour to vote not guilty. We have to have an autopsy, fellas, and soon."

"What about getting the bullet into evidence before Humes testifies?"

"Good question, Earl. When you figure out who can do that, call them tonight and tell them they're leading off tomorrow. Well, gentlemen, here comes the judge."

Judge Davis entered the courtroom and nodded to Carson, heading off any chance that Matthews could request a continuance in the absence of the jury. It couldn't be helped, however, for as soon as they were seated, the judge explained that once again, for legal reasons having no bearing on either the prosecution's or the defense's contentions, the evidence gathered from the Paine residence, on both Friday and Saturday, had been ruled inadmissible. "Mr. Matthews, you may now . . ."

"Your Honor, due to circumstances beyond our control, we must ask for a slightly premature adjournment today. Our next witness may take quite some time . . ." Quite some time to get here and learn his lines, Barnes thought.

"That is acceptable to the court. It is late, and we have had a busy day. Adjourned." Matthews hated, as any attorney would, to have a session adjourned immediately after some good evidence, in this case the Oswald-rifle photos, was excluded, but it couldn't be helped. Barnes told his team to have a good evening, and then quietly told Oswald that he had better start thinking about an attorney for his trial "concerning the other matter." Oswald looked shocked and started to say, "You mean . . ." but Barnes finished the thought: "I mean, they won't convict you on this one. You'll walk, or get a hung jury. And the state is not going to pay for another trial like this, when they can go after you for something else a lot cheaper for the state of Texas. And before you ask, Lee, I'm going home—or at least back north. I don't even know if I'm safe for having defended you once. But understand, once is my limit."

\* \* \*

As soon as the prosecution team arrived at Matthews's ranch, he had a fire going in the fireplace and Barbara Matthews kept the bourbon bottle, glasses, and ice handy. Knowing that Humes would not be arriving for almost two hours, the case was once again hashed out, but this time in a venue where voices could be raised and thoughts expressed openly.

"It's not as bad as you seem to think, Ray," Earl Vincent offered. "The FBI experts will undo a lot of damage that the Dallas cops did, and you know how juries love FBI specialists flown all the way from the fancy crime lab in Washington."

"Earl, Eaton," Matthews began, putting his glass down and his feet up on a planked coffee table, "make no mistake about it. We are not where we should be. We're a football team that's thirty points behind in the second quarter and we're trying to win the game on one play. It just can't be done. Sure, we've got experts. But let's assume they're twice as good as what we've seen so far. How good does that make them? Two times nothing is still nothing. What can an expert testify to, in the absence of evidence? His bona fides, and that's about it. It's all form and no substance. So," he took another small sip of bourbon, "we're going with Humes tomorrow, and he's going to have to be brilliant, as well as untouchable in cross-examination. Look what they've done to Carl Day, Dr. Hartogs, Seymour Weitzman, and Bob Dean hasn't even gotten into it yet. Whatever you think of Eddie Barnes, legally speaking, he's a street-wise punk. Bob Dean is the chairman of the board. I had a case, oh, maybe seven years ago—long before you two were on board the D.A.'s office—couldn't lose. I even had a confession. And Bob Dean kicked my butt all over that courtroom."

Matthews let that sink in, then dropped the other shoe: "So, Humes is brilliant tomorrow, or we change course and hope somehow, to focus on two or three jurors—right now, I'd say the second from the left in the front, and the two in the back row, center, are our best chance, and go for a hung jury . . ."

"How does that help us?" Graves asked. "The weaknesses of the case will be obvious for whoever retries it."

"That's the beauty of the hung jury option. If we can avoid

a rout, Oswald will be tried for whacking the cop, and I don't care who his lawyer is, or how lousy the evidence may be, they'll get him. A Texas jury might not convict somebody for shooting a Massachusetts lover boy, but you kill—or be suspected of killing—a Texas cop, and you are in deep problems. So somebody else, another prosecution team, another jury, and another judge, will convict and fry the little Red creep, no doubt . . ."

"Agreed . . ."

"And in the meantime, they'll say, 'Well, another trial for the murder of the President would be expensive, and we can't execute him twice,' so that will be that. And somehow, history will put the stamp of presidential assassin on him, even if we couldn't."

"Do you really think it will come to that?" Vincent asked.

"What have we accomplished? Very little—unless the jury made up their mind on opening day. We've gotten more evidence thrown out than we've gotten admitted. And Barnes hasn't even called one witness yet. Just be prepared to circle the wagons immediately after you hear me say, 'The people rest, Your Honor.' There are a lot of people who know more than they are telling, as we're finding out from our own witnesses, and Barnes will parade them through that courthouse. They can't all prove that Oswald is innocent, but they can raise a whole lot more questions than that jury is prepared to deal with. A whole lot more." Matthews sat back and stared at the fire. After another sip of bourbon, he asked Vincent if he'd followed up on that tip Barnes had given him.

"Which . . . oh, yeah, Palmer McBride. Another Barnes stunt. He gave us that name, so he wanted us to think, out of sympathy, so we wouldn't call him. But I reread the affidavit, and I don't see any weaknesses."

"Enlighten me," Matthews said calmly, still relaxed.

"Well, he claimed that he and Oswald were working in a dental clinic, New Orleans, I think, in December of 1957. Somehow, the subject got around to politics, and McBride distinctly recalled Oswald saying something about Eisenhower doing a lousy job and how somebody should take a rifle and shoot him. McBride even identified Oswald in the 1963 photographs, although he had to be confused somehow, because he said something like, 'I recognize him all right, even the big ears and the mustache.' "

Matthews sat up slowly as a cold chill ran down his spine. Saying nothing, he stared at Vincent as if he were looking through him. After only a few seconds of that, Vincent asked, "What? That's his story."

"And you think Barnes was setting us up? He *was* doing us a favor." Both Graves and Vincent noticed that Matthews was frozen in the rabbit-caught-in-the-headlights look.

"Ray, what is it?"

"You're Barnes, right now. What's the weakness?"

"The mustache? No big deal. Oswald wasn't allowed near a razor while in Dallas custody."

"The mustache is nickel-dime, Eaton. December, 1957. *Lee Oswald was a marine in Japan.*" Matthews sat back, but continued, "Or should I say, 'The Lee Oswald that we have on trial was a marine in Japan in December, 1957?' Do you realize what this means?"

"Suddenly, I don't think I want to," Vincent said.

"I don't think we've got much choice but to face the very real possibility that a fake identity, going back as far as six years, was established, with some future sinister purpose in mind. Now, obviously nobody knew in December of 1957 that in five or six years a Catholic President would upset the apple cart and actually do things that the average citizen would appreciate, but somebody—or some lunatic fringe group— was grooming the image of Lee Oswald for future trouble."

"Should we be getting ready for Humes's arrival?" Graves asked.

Matthews finished his drink. "Good idea. Sure beats the hell out of that other chat we just had." Matthews put another log on the fire and went to the kitchen to see how his wife was faring with expanded dinner responsibilities.

Humes arrived, briefcase in hand, announcing that he was cold, hungry, and thirsty. The bourbon and the fireplace answered two of those needs, and he soon found himself seated at a table with three lawyers, one busy wife, and a tableful of Texas hospitality. It was agreed that the case would not be discussed at dinner, so the weather and geography of Texas and the Washington suburbs, as well as the meal, were the main topics of discussion.

The men adjourned from the dinner table back to the family room, where Matthews had to reinvigorate the fireplace. Matthews, Graves, and Vincent alternated asking questions, and each quickly got the sense that the navy doctor was unsure of himself. Matthews then tried to teach a quick confidence course, reasking the same questions to Graves, who gave the answers that Humes had given, but with confidence and in a very credible tone.

There was particular concern regarding Humes's burning of "certain preliminary draft notes," which Humes dismissed by telling them how he had once visited a museum which contained the chair in which Lincoln was sitting when shot in Ford's Theater. In Humes's memory, the chair showed bloodstains from Lincoln, and this horrified him, so when it came to JFK's papers, right from the autopsy room with blood on them, he destroyed them.

"I think a court will accept that," Vincent offered.

"Absolutely," Matthews chimed in, to keep Humes confident.

The discussion continued, but what was lacking was a sense of medico-legal expertise on the part of anybody. Humes knew there were holes in his story, but he was reticent to bring them up. He did, however, show concern as the evening wore on, about the schematic diagrams, which he took from a folder, and spread out on the coffee table. "They were prepared from memory, but I believe them to be accurate," he insisted.

Matthews, giving Vincent a nod, again spoke confidently: "You probably won't have to worry too much about those. The defense will demand the 'best evidence,' which is comprised of these, the autopsy photos, and X rays."

"Oh, I should probably see them before I testify," Humes said, all too matter-of-factly.

"What?" Matthews erupted, destroying whatever confidence may have been programmed into the witness. "Are you telling us you've never seen these?"

"Not any of the photos and only a few glances at the Roentgenograms."

The three lawyers sat there, drained, silent, each no doubt devising a lottery system to choose which one of them would get to tattoo Humes with a hot cattle iron. Finally, Matthews broke the silence, telling Vincent to spread them out.

Humes took a few moments to view them, saying nothing. Then he went back to the left side of the table, and began a commentary on what he saw. "This one, showing the face from the subject's right. The tracheostomy is accurate, but there's been some reconstruction of the forehead. That becomes obvious if you compare it with this one here," pointing to an anterior-posterior X ray. "See how much bone is missing there? It just doesn't compare with the photo. This one is interesting," Humes continued, pointing to the photo showing Kennedy's back wound. "We only found that later on. I didn't know they were still taking pictures." We only found a bullet wound later on? Matthews thought.

"These two are good shots, well, good photos of the damage done to the top of the skull . . ."

Graves interrupted. "Where was there damage besides the top?"

"On the right side, in front of the ear, and in the back, above the entry wound. See that's the problem I have with this picture, here, showing the back of Kennedy's head. It didn't look like that, and our report certainly made no mention of an entrance wound up here. The entrance was down here," Humes went on, demonstrating, "and the exit, well, presumably the exit, began up here in the back. There's something very wrong with this picture, which, unfortunately corresponds to the posterior part of that X ray, uh, this one here. It's correct as to frontal bone damage, but you can see that the entrance in the back does correspond to this entrance, but they're both too high."

Sensing the situation could be saved with a correct answer here, Matthews very quietly asked, "How much too high are they?"

"I'd say about four inches. If I'm asked about that tomorrow, what should I say?"

Matthews was more shocked by that statement than any he had heard. "You will have already sworn to tell the truth. I strongly suggest you do."

"Fine. Where are the rest of the pictures?"

"This is it, Doctor. You were there, don't you remember?"

"I remember very well. We directed the photographer to take photos of the open chest, showing the undamaged pleura. There were also pictures taken of the brain, or what was left of it."

"That will about bring us to our final question, Doctor. You just said, 'What was left of it.' How much was missing?"

"There was incredible disruption. A good bit was gone, most of the upper right hemisphere. Which makes me wonder—look at this X ray. See this trail of metal—that's a few dozen dustlike fragments from a bullet."

"So?"

"So there was no brain there. What was holding up the metal?"

"If you don't know, Doctor, how are we supposed to? In the meantime, what is the weight of a normal brain at autopsy?"

"Thirteen fifty to fifteen hundred grams—roughly three pounds."

"And some of Kennedy's was gone?"

"More than just some," Humes reported. "I spoke to the Dallas doctors after the autopsy, and they said there was brain matter all over the floor in the emergency room. I know that I read somewhere that one of the motorcycle policeman was splattered with brain, and that Governor Connally had some on his clothing. So there was a lot missing. That man died on impact."

Just as your testimony will kill this case, Matthews wanted to say. "Doctor, in the supplemental autopsy report it indicates, and I quote, 'Following formalin fixation, the brain weighs fifteen hundred grams.' How? The rest of it goes on, as you said, to describe the loss of brain, yet the weight is normal. We're going to have problems with this. You'd better get a good night's sleep, Doctor, and be confident tomorrow. The jury has heard from several witnesses who told of working under adverse conditions that day, so they're getting used to it. You just tell the truth. Eaton, did you call for a cab?"

With Humes gone, the fire appropriately died, as the atmosphere of the room took on that of a wake. "If Barnes knows his stuff medically, we'll have to go for a hung jury," Matthews lamented.

"But they'll still fry the little weasel for killing the cop," Vincent reminded him.

"That's right," Matthews said confidently, "but with one difference. Oswald will be sitting on our laps when they throw the switch. But, believe it or not, that's not the scary part."

"What is?" Graves asked, quietly.

"Did you just hear our star witness? He all but asked us if we wanted him to perjure himself tomorrow. He's career government. The government has all the evidence. It's their case. He knows that today he's Director of Labs at Bethesda. If he blows it tomorrow, he could find himself head lighthouse keeper at Penguin Point in Antarctica—and he knows it. That means we have to reread all his stuff tonight to make sure our own witness is telling *us* the truth. What movie are we missing on TV, *It's a Wonderful Life?*"

# Eight

Tuesday, January twelve, 1965. The four vehicles carrying the six attorneys of record almost formed a parade as they pulled into the courthouse square virtually simultaneously, at just a few minutes before ten, the time court would convene.

Matthews was quickly joined by Graves and Vincent, who had carpooled, and they quickly restated their concerns regarding Humes, the most serious being his credibility. "If one word does not smack of the truth, I have to know it," Matthews told the other two. "This guy may not give us much, but we can't afford to lose any points whatsoever. If he misstates a fact, and thinks he's doing us a favor, I'll ask for a minute with the witness and set him straight and then go back on the record. By the way, did anybody notice that Barnes and the young babe arrived together?"

"Concern" was also the operative word for the defense team that morning, though they still retained the sense of optimism that had begun Friday and built over the weekend and through the previous day.

Papers were barely spread out on both legal tables when

Judge Davis was announced, promptly at ten, and, once seated, noted that a great deal of work had been accomplished in the first week and thanked the attorneys for their diligence. He then nodded to Carson, who had not traveled three feet before Barnes stood up.

"Your Honor, there is one matter of business that I feel should be attended to before the jury is brought in." Matthews, Graves, and Vincent each assumed another impending cataclysm.

"Go ahead, Mr. Barnes," the judge ordered.

"Your Honor, Miss Jeffries has a statement to make to the court. Carolyn . . ."

"Judge Davis," Jeffries began haltingly, "I received a telephone call last night at approximately 9:35 P.M. at my hotel room. Assuming the call to be from either Mr. Barnes or Mr. Dean, I answered by saying 'Hello.' The caller then asked for me, by name. Without indicating whether or not I was, in fact, Carolyn Jeffries, I asked who was calling. The caller identified herself as Dorothy Kilgallen, adding a phrase about being a nationally syndicated columnist, although by the time the recognition of who it was hit me, it blurred a little bit and for a second I thought she said 'Nationally syndicated Communist.' I asked why she was trying to reach Carolyn Jeffries, which I guess confirmed my identity to her, and she said that she had material that would, to use her phrase, 'crack this case wide open.' I asked what case she was talking about, and she knew which case it was. I then told her she had the wrong party, but she quickly told me, no, she had the right party, and she was talking to Carolyn Jeffries, and she had incredible information that she was 'willing to trade' for information about the trial. I then told her that if I was Carolyn Jeffries that she must understand that my only recourse would be to report this conversation to the court first thing in the morning. I then hung up the phone, left it off the hook until ten, and then called Mr. Barnes and repeated the essentials of the conversation to him."

"I find this very troubling, Miss Jeffries. Please do not misunderstand—I find nothing wrong with your behavior. Is there anything else?"

"Mr. Barnes told me not to answer any more calls, and that he and Mr. Dean would be there to get me quickly, and that I should be packed and ready to go. In the next few minutes, the phone rang twice more, for approximately one minute each time."

The judge shook his head. "This is very troubling, but I suppose something like this had to happen. Were you relocated, Miss Jeffries?"

"Yes, Your Honor."

Barnes interrupted to add, "We relocated Miss Jeffries eventually, Your Honor, but not until after I had made a few creases, so to speak, in the local highway speed ordinances. I had the distinct feeling we were being followed."

Without being told to do so, both lawyers instinctively approached the bench. "Anybody have any ideas?" Davis asked.

"Your Honor, I can assure you," Matthews began.

"Ray—I trust you implicitly—understand that," Barnes stressed. "Your Honor, I can assure you," Barnes continued, "that I have the fullest confidence in *every* person in this room—the attorneys, the court staff, the out-of-state 'wardens'—these people have not leaked anything."

"I would agree," Matthews added.

Barnes then showed a piece of paper to Matthews, who read it silently and then gestured questioningly to Barnes if he should hand it to the bench. Barnes nodded back.

Judge Davis, seeing this exchange, already had his glasses on. The note read: "Business as usual in A.M. Make a statement that the phone call last night was just a hoax, and pretend to forget it. Lunchtime: have the entire courtroom, and your chambers, swept for electronic listening devices, and if you make a call to have the place swept, do it from at least three blocks away, pay phone."

"Well, Mr. Matthews, Mr. Barnes, I don't think we have to concern ourselves too greatly with this one isolated phone contact. Naturally, you are all reminded to report any such subsequent contacts, but I really feel this was just an isolated event and won't be repeated. Thank you both. Back to your places." The judge then gave a fatherly nod and paternal smile to Carolyn Jeffries, as if to say, "Sorry."

While the jury was being brought in, Dean asked if Barnes had noticed who was in the hall. "How could I not? The short, dumpy one with the jowls and the rumpled suit is Humes. The other one, younger and better dressed, is a stranger, but make no mistake about it, he's federal."

"How do you know that?" Dean asked.

"Cuff links. Part of the FBI, Secret Service, FBN, you name it, dress code. There was also a bulge under his left arm, and it wasn't this morning's paper."

Oswald spoke, to Barnes's surprise: "Are you sure you won't reconsider what you said yesterday?"

"Lee," Barnes said, looking the defendant straight in the eye, "I would reconsider—only reconsider, mind you, if you and I could have a little sit down back there in the lockup and you come 100 percent clean. To this point, you haven't. Time to go to work. Think about it."

"Your Honor, the State calls Special Agent Elmer Lee Todd." Dean looked over to Barnes to acknowledge that his "guess" had been right on the money. "Get the file," Barnes told him.

A sleepy-looking man, hardly displaying "Special Agent" quickness, trudged through the courtroom, was sworn, and it was established that he was a Special Agent of the FBI. Barnes, hearing his former agency, decided to shake Matthews's chain immediately. Before the preliminaries were completed, Barnes interrupted: "Your Honor, it offends the dignity of this court to have an armed witness on the stand." Matthews turned to look at Barnes, then decided to draw the line. Before he could do that, the judge asked the witness if he was armed, and if so, to surrender his weapon immediately to the bailiff. Matthews was stubborn: "Your Honor, this man's agency requires him to carry his service revolver whenever on duty."

Judge Davis pointed to the six-inch-barrel Magnum that Carson was now carrying, cylinder open. "Is that your idea of a service revolver, Mr. Matthews?" Matthews finally realized this was not the time to argue, but the judge was upset by the witness's arrogance in this act. "Is he in the performance of his duties now, counselor? If so, tell me what active investigation he is pursuing. If not, tell me you would not have

had a problem if any of your earlier witnesses—Junior
Jarman? Dr. Hartogs? had been carrying that cannon. . . .
Now, let's examine the witness."

"Thank you, Your Honor, and I apologize to the court for
this procedural confusion. Now, Special Agent Todd, I show
you perhaps the single most important piece of evidence in
this case, a copper-jacketed bullet, labeled CE 399. Do you
recognize it?"

"Yes. I marked it for identification after it had been given to
me by Mr. Rowley, the Chief of the Secret Service."

"When did you receive it?"

"On the evening of Friday, November twenty-two, 1963."

"So you did not discover it?"

"No. I was told . . ."

"Hearsay."

"Sustained."

"But you did receive it from James Rowley, and mark it for
identification?"

"Objection. Asked and answered."

"Sustained."

"No further questions. Thank you, Special Agent Todd."

"Your Honor, may I have a moment, please?"

"A moment, Mr. Barnes." Matthews and his assistants believed the delay was caused by Barnes's sudden confrontation with a real piece of evidence that he couldn't just dismiss on some technicality.

In the meantime, Barnes had walked down to Bob Dean
and put it on the line, "Now or later, Bob?"

"So far, it's always been later. You've milked the evidence
for its defense purposes, weakened the witness, then gotten
it excluded. There's a lot of good we can get out of that bullet
before we have it excluded. On the other hand, I could see
why you'd want to do it now. 'The single most important
piece of evidence,' if excluded, would kill their case dead in
the water. It's your call, Eddie."

Barnes made no decision as he approached the witness,
going right to the witness stand, which Matthews took as a
good sign, assuming that Barnes knew he had to confront
the witness somehow. Actually, Barnes just wanted to satisfy
his own curiosity about whether or not FBI agents were still

required to wear cuff links. In making the casual observation, he noted that the witness's watch read 4:20, which meant he was six hours off.

"Special Agent Todd, when you received this bullet, this 'single most important piece of evidence,' did it contain any human material—blood, tissue, anything like that, to indicate that it had wounded, or passed through, a human being?"

"No."

"Mr. Todd, as a former FBI agent, I know that much of your investigative work involves drawing conclusions. So I'm going to ask you a question which calls for a conclusion. If Mr. Matthews had done that, I would have no doubt objected, and he has that right now. Can you tell the court why, in your opinion, there was no blood or tissue on that bullet when you received it?"

"Well, as I said, I took custody of it several hours after it had been fired, and I was told," the witness looked to Matthews for a hearsay objection but heard none, "I was told that at least four people had handled it before I received it. Given those circumstances, I was not shocked that it bore no blood or tissue samples."

"That makes sense," Barnes agreed. "Would the same factors account for the lack of fiber striations?"

"The lack of what?" the witness asked.

"Fiber striations. Surely, Mr. Todd, you are aware that when high powered rifles fire bullets through clothing, particularly several layers of clothing, the fibers of the garment leave telltale striations on the bullet. Do you see any such fiber marks on this bullet?" Barnes handed the witness the bullet.

"No."

"Now, I repeat the original question. Would the handling by four people, which could theoretically remove bloodstains and so forth . . . would that handling remove fiber striations?"

"No."

"Then how do you account for the absence of them?"

"Well, they would be barely visible to the eye at best, and

that piece of evidence has no doubt been handled a lot just for its curiosity value, and a lot of time has passed."

Barnes saw his chance. "Speaking of time, Special Agent, what time do you have on your watch? Be precise, please."

Matthews didn't know what was going on, but he didn't like the smell of it if Barnes had anything to do with it. "Objection, Your Honor, the time of day has no relevancy."

"Mr. Barnes?"

"Latitude, Your Honor?"

"Overruled. The witness will answer the question."

"It is 4:28," Todd answered.

"How do you explain that?" Barnes asked. "Court just convened for the morning session."

"I was investigating the murder of an American diplomat in Paris when I was notified yesterday of the need for me to testify today. I flew straight in from Paris, having to change planes in Atlanta, Georgia. I just simply never reset my watch."

"I again object, Your Honor. The answer demonstrates lack of relevancy."

"On the contrary, Your Honor," Barnes countered. "The answer demonstrates the length that the prosecution will go to in order to dupe this court and the jury. They fly in someone from Paris to identify what they call 'the single most important piece of evidence,' when it is acknowledged by the witness that *four* people—for the record, O.P. Wright and Darrell Tomlinson of Parkland Hospital, here in Texas, and Special Agent Richard Johnsen . . . that's spelled with an 'e' at the end, Mrs. Martinez, and Secret Service Chief Rowley —all of whom were available in the United States, had previously handled it. Given those circumstances, I would move to exclude the testimony of Special Agent Todd on the grounds of best evidence."

Matthews's frazzled nerves, no doubt edgy from the knowledge that Dr. Humes was the next witness, finally boiled over. *"Your Honor, the prosecution will simply no longer allow the defense to . . ."*

The movement of the judge's gavel was imperceptible to the human eye, but its reverberations broke Matthews's statement. "This court, counselor, will not allow itself to be dictated to. Now, take your seat, catch a breath, and talk nicely to the court."

Matthews sat down, chided. "The witness testified that he received the bullet, admittedly without blood or fiber marks, from the head of the United States Secret Service. What better evidence can there be?"

"Mr. Barnes?"

"May we approach, Your Honor?"

"Come ahead." The judge's command gave Barnes the chance to get Matthews on his feet again, and hopefully, his blood boiling.

Matthews stood, rocking slightly. Barnes spoke quietly. "Your Honor, the defense finds itself in a serious dilemma that perhaps the court can lend its guidance to. That bullet, CE 399, may well be the single most important piece of evidence . . ." Barnes walked quickly, for the jury's purpose, to the defense table and retrieved a file, "but if you read this document, a series of FBI reports, you'll see there is the very strong likelihood that CE 399, like so much earlier evidence, will be excluded. That is why I object to this witness putting it into evidence." Barnes handed the judge and Matthews a copy of the FBI report, which indicated that neither O.P. Wright nor Darrell Tomlinson, of Parkland Hospital, could identify CE 399 as the bullet they saw on November twenty-second. Neither could Special Agent Richard Johnsen nor Secret Service Chief Rowley, when shown the bullet by FBI Agent Elmer Lee Todd.

"This is incredible," Davis whispered, peering over his glasses.

"I was not aware of this," Matthews offered apologetically.

"So what is the defense dilemma, Mr. Barnes?"

"The only way we're going to get at the truth here, Your Honor, is to let witnesses, like Dr. Humes out in the hall, testify. If that bullet is excluded now, then all subsequent testimony becomes hypotheses. 'There might have been a bullet,' and so forth. I propose we compromise by thanking Agent Todd for his jet lag, but I think we have no choice but to dismiss his testimony. Then we let subsequent witnesses testify, and if what they know about CE 399 gets us closer to the truth—guilt or innocence of the defendant, that's what we're here for. Ultimately, that report will have to go in the record, and I can't imagine that bullet staying in evidence."

"Neither can I," Davis agreed, looking questioningly at Matthews. "Okay, gentlemen, take your places."

Matthews was back at the defense table before Barnes took his seat. "Read this," Matthews told his assistants, "then choose which one of you is going to tell me 'We've still got a case.' "

Judge Davis used his gavel again. "The jury will disregard the statements made by Special Agent Todd. The witness is dismissed and the court regrets the lengthy travel involved in his coming here to testify. We will take a five minute recess." As Davis looked up, Barnes was pantomiming someone making a phone call. Davis understood not to use the phone in his chambers.

During the recess, Barnes explained the legal tap dancing he had done with respect to CE 399, which he felt sure would be excluded at the proper time. On the prosecution side, Graves and Vincent could not believe what they were reading, commenting either that wholesale perjury was taking place on the part of witnesses, or wholesale obstruction of justice on the part of somebody else.

"I just don't want us to look like the 'somebody else,' " Matthews reminded both assistants. "We've got to get through Humes before we can deal with the fact that nobody can, or wants to," he added, "identify a simple rifle bullet."

With the recess over, Matthews called "Commander James J. Humes" but was immediately disappointed when the familiar Humes entered the courtroom, not in his impressive military whites, but, worse still, in the same rumpled suit he had worn the evening before.

The prosecution then went through a litany of questions, medical and pathological clubs and associations, certificates of merit, honorariums, and other minutiae, which, on Barnes's watch, consumed seventeen minutes and proved nothing more than that Humes probably had a well-decorated office somewhere in his home. Barnes was brought back from such boring ruminations when he heard the phrase "expert witness" introduced.

"Any objection, Mr. Barnes?" the judge asked.

"Yes, Your Honor, the defense does object to this witness being accorded the status of 'expert,' and will, when our objections are completed and ruled upon by the court, ask that the witness be treated as a hostile witness during cross-examination."

Matthews suspected that Barnes's hostile witness ploy was nothing more than a way to have the witness's expertise diminished, but he wasn't going to have the jury watch the exercise, either. So the panel had heard nothing more than Humes's pedigree when they were temporarily excused.

The judge then asked Barnes to state his objections.

"If it please the Court, Your Honor, since the jury is not present, perhaps a few questions from the defense could help the Court in determining this witness's expertise, and therefore his fitness to give opinions—without which, I'll admit, he probably isn't going to have much to say."

"Proceed, Mr. Barnes."

Barnes returned to his place behind the defense table, but remained standing. "Commander Humes, how many autopsies have you performed in which the victim died as a result of one or more gunshots inflicted by someone else?"

"None."

"And how many times have you testified in nonmilitary courts regarding findings you have made at autopsies?"

"None."

"Commander Humes, let's understand something here. Last week, in something called an opening statement, I referred to you, Dr. Boswell, and Colonel Finck as 'classroom clowns' that were given the assignment to perform the autopsy on the President. I made that reference because in my business, I've had to read many—hundreds—of autopsy reports, and I must tell you, I found your report, as well as the Supplemental Report, on President Kennedy to be unique, and I don't intend that as a compliment, Commander." Barnes, speaking in even tones, gave his listener a moment to grasp what he was saying. "Commander, were you the highest ranking naval officer in that autopsy room on the night of November twenty-two, 1963?"

"Certainly not. Virtually the whole chain of the Bethesda

command was there, and there were army personnel who outranked me."

"Commander Humes, what would high-ranking army officers be doing at a Naval autopsy?"

"I have no idea."

"Okay. You were not the ranking officer. At any time during that procedure, were you given orders from a superior officer as to what you should or should not do, at that moment in time, with respect to the President's body?"

"Yes. We were given orders."

"Commander, did you section—I assume you know what that means—did you section the track of the wound which you described as being in the border of the upper scapula?"

"No, we did not."

"Is it not customary to do so if the work you are performing is to be considered an autopsy?"

"I agree that the wound track should have been sectioned."

"Was the President's brain similarly sectioned before you reached your conclusions regarding the path of the bullet or bullets?"

"No."

"Commander, did you make all the conclusions stated in your report, number A63-272, while the President's body was still in front of you, or were they made after telephone calls had been made to the medical authorities in Dallas?"

"I spoke to the people in Dallas to confirm my conclusions," Humes answered forcefully.

"Did you have any idea, when you dialed the phone to Dallas, that the gash in the President's anterior neck, had anything whatsoever to do with a bullet wound?"

"No."

"Conclusions, indeed. Last question, Doctor: prior to your signature on the undated report, number A63-272, did you view the autopsy photographs, the X rays, or the President's clothing?"

"I saw some of the X rays."

Barnes looked up from his list of questions, stood full, and faced the judge. "Your Honor, inasmuch as the witness was forthcoming with respect to difficult questions, I withdraw my 'hostile witness' request. However, with respect to the doctor being called an 'expert witness,' I believe the testimony he just gave indicates that he was following orders on November twenty-two, and also that, by not sectioning the two clearly defined wounds, there was in point of fact, no autopsy, in the legal sense, ever performed on the President. What occurred on the evening and night of November twenty-second was a pathological examination of a cadaver whose cause of death would have been obvious to anyone. That could have been ascertained by opening the casket, looking in, and closing it. But for this man to tell us where the shots came from, given what he just told us, gives the defense great difficulties."

"Mr. Matthews?"

"Once again, Your Honor, we're dealing with a sudden, tragic event . . . a series of circumstances that Commander Humes and his staff found themselves thrust into, and one which they tried to make the best of."

Now it was Barnes's turn to speak up: "Your Honor, we've really and truly heard enough of the 'tragedy' story. Yes, it was a sad day for Americans. Many people, including the defendant, left their place of employment and went home. Others, like the Dallas police, the medical staff at Bethesda, and the nearby morticians did not have that luxury. Some of those mentioned above stayed at their posts and did what they do best. I don't hear anyone bemoaning the fact that the President had a lousy funeral because the people in charge of the arrangements were struck numb with grief. No, they did their job. And a pathologist's job is to examine remains and make determinations. And then to testify on those determinations. In point of fact, any navy personnel, even those who scrubbed the President's blood off the floor at Bethesda, were required to sign a statement saying they would never speak of what they saw there, and any violation of that agreement would lead to court-martial."

Judge Davis looked at Humes. "Is that true, sir?"

"I signed such an order, but I cannot speak for the others."

"I see. All right, gentlemen, here's how we're going to leave it for now. There will be no expert witness designation, and unless the testimony I hear bespeaks a thorough professionalism, the word 'autopsy' will be used sparingly. Now, Mr.

Matthews, if opinions are called for, as I'm sure they will be, given the nature of the witness and his purpose, they may be requested—with caution, and with the understanding that each is subject to defense objections. Carson . . ."

"Thank you, Your Honor," Matthews said, as the jury was being brought in, in an attempt to create the image of victory in the battle they had missed. The judge then told them that Commander Humes would neither be an expert nor a hostile witness.

"Commander Humes, before we discuss what you saw that evening, there has been a controversy in the press regarding certain documents you destroyed. Would you explain that to the court, please?"

Humes then told the Lincoln-Kennedy parallel and the jury seemed to buy it. Barnes was impressed by Matthews's grasp on an issue he, Barnes, had hoped to make some points with.

"Commander, what other doctors assisted you in the, uh, procedure that took place on the evening of November twenty-second?"

"I was assisted by Doctor Thornton Boswell, of the United States Navy, and by Colonel Pierre Finck, of the United States Army."

"Were photographic and X ray records made of your proceedings that evening?"

"Yes. There were pictures taken at the outset, and as we proceeded, and the same would be true with respect to the X rays."

"Turning now to the wounds, Doctor. Would you tell us about the wound in the upper thoracic region—the one commonly referred to as the 'neck wound'?"

"Objection, Your Honor. Best evidence. The prosecution has a photograph of that wound and the jury has every right to see it. In point of fact, it's a back wound, not a neck wound."

Judge Davis agreed: "Mr. Matthews, the defense's point is well taken. Those of us who deal with these cases come to get a sense of what a medical specialist, such as this pathologist, is saying. But a juror may not have that clear awareness. So when X ray or photographic evidence is available, I think it fair to the jury, as well as to both sides in this case, to let the jury see it." Then, turning to the jury: "I caution you, gentlemen, the pictures you will see may shock you severely. They are not very pretty—in fact, they are rather graphic and may give you a sleepless night or two. For that, I apologize. However, I must also caution you that the severity of these pictures is no reflection on the defendant in this case. We are here viewing these pictures *to determine* if he was the cause of them, not immediately to decide how to punish him for them. Mr. Matthews?"

"We'll need autopsy photograph number 4, please. Doctor, when that picture comes up on the screen there, give the jury a moment to view it and then tell us what it shows, please."

"Well, as you can see, the wound is on the upper border of the scapula. It measured seven by four millimeters, with the long axis roughly parallel to the long axis of the vertical column."

"And what does that suggest to you, Doctor?"

"He was shot in the back."

Matthews had been expecting incompetence, so he wasn't disappointed.

"Did the wound depicted in the photograph bear the characteristic markings of a wound of entrance?"

"Yes, very much so. It was a clean, neat puncture, with no jagged edges."

"Thank you, Doctor. Now, if we could have photograph number 1, the posterior scalp, please . . . and when that comes up, if you would tell us what is depicted there."

"This shows the back of the late President's head. The entrance wound was measured to be two point five centimeters to the right and slightly above the external occipital protuberance."

"Could you explain that to the jury, please?"

"Forgive me. The external occipital protuberance is the bump one feels on the back of the head, hence the name."

"Thank you. And can you give us your thoughts," Matthews was careful not to abuse the word "opinion," "with reference to that shot?"

"Well, it came from behind, and above. That wound measured 15 by 6 millimeters, so it was clearly from an angle.

Exactly where, I could not say, unless I knew the precise position of the victim as he received the wound."

Matthews took a gamble. "We can arrange that, Doctor. Could we have Zapruder frame 312, please?"

Humes seemed more taken with the exhibit than the jurors, and his fascination with it became obvious. "From this, I could conclude that the shot came from behind and above."

"Could the shot have come from the right, as well as high and above?"

"I could not say that. The fragment pattern went, as we viewed it, from the point of entry, toward the right side, which would be difficult if fired from the right. Would that young man at your table please come forward?" Humes asked Matthews.

Eaton Graves approached the witness stand knowing the witness was talking too much. Commander Humes stepped down, and had Graves stand facing directly away from the jury. "If the inshoot were here,"—pointing to a spot on the back of Graves's head—"and metal was present in this general direction"—pointing forward, through Graves's hair to the right side of his head—"it would be difficult to say a shot came from over here," indicating the right side of Graves. Humes then drew a line from the right, to the entrance, then to the right, a line which created an elongated "v."

"Could the shot have come from the right and impacted in such a way that the fragments went to the right, Doctor Humes?" Matthews asked, while Graves seated himself and ran a hand through his hair.

"Anything is possible, sir," Humes answered.

"Before I request the next exhibit, I apologize to the jury for having to introduce such material. Could we have picture number three please, the superior head pose?"

The jury leaned forward and then let out a collective gasp when they saw the massive hole in the top of the President's head, with an area where brain matter should have been was simply a crater.

"Now, Doctor, your thoughts on what the jury is viewing now . . ."

"This defect was over the right side of the skull," Humes began, telling the jurors nothing they already didn't know.

"This defect involved both the scalp and the underlying skull, and from it, brain substance was protruding. It measured thirteen centimeters at its greatest point, and there were a series of complex, radiating fractures accompanying it."

"And what does this wound represent?"

"As best we were able to determine, this represented the exit of the bullet which had entered in the rear of the head."

"So when your work was concluded on that evening, Doctor, how many bullet wounds would you say you had dealt with?"

"Two."

"And what was their origin?"

"From behind. Behind and above."

"Thank you, Doctor. No further questions at this time. Move to admit the exhibits used during this questioning."

"Mr. Barnes?"

"No problem with the exhibits; however, Your Honor, I'm afraid the defense's questions for this witness are going to consume a great deal of time. Perhaps if we recessed now, we could resume at one P.M. . . ."

"Agreed. Court is adjourned until one P.M."

The entire prosecution team agreed that they were in for a very rough afternoon with the cross-examination of Humes, for they knew that they had gotten what little good he had to say, and that the rest of his thoughts were pure poison in the hands of someone like Barnes. The best they could hope for would be for something to come of the electronic sweep of the courtroom, either to distract the issue temporarily, or in the best of all possible worlds, to create a mistrial and let them off the hook.

Immediately after lunch, the judge took one step out of his chambers, still in his business suit, pointed to both attorneys, and gave a hand signal that they were to join him in chambers. When the principals, plus Carson, were standing around his desk, Judge Davis held up a pad printed with large letters from a dark felt pen. The first page read, "Bugged." All parties in the room exchanged sincere, concerned looks.

The judge's next page said, "Make some motion—then keep up the 'game.'" Barnes got the hint quickly, "Your Honor, it has come to our attention that one of the witnesses, in the discovery process, may have misspoken." The judge's next page, read while Barnes spoke, said, "Four devices found . . . so far." Matthews then spoke up, "With respect to that witness, Your Honor, the prosecution had no idea, and it does not seem that the error, unintentional as it was, was significant." The judge then pointed to his telephone, then spread his hands apart, as if to be saying, "I don't know about that, yet." Barnes, taking his turn to talk, suggested, "Your Honor, if we reinterview the witness, and explain to him in a friendly way, even extend another amnesty, I'm sure the matter can be cleared up." Barnes then looked to Matthews to chatter, and while he did, Barnes whispered to Carson to go outside, call the judge's number, and claim to be a law student looking to clerk in the summer. Barnes told Carson to be persistent and keep talking until the judge hung up on him.

The fake banter continued until the phone rang. It was Carson, as expected, and as soon as Barnes heard his voice, he motioned to the judge for the receiver. He quickly dismantled the lower end, discovering a cheap, thinly disguised listening device in the process. He then replaced it, just as found, handed the phone back to the judge, and indicated he could cut Carson off. "Son, we're trying a major case right now. Perhaps if you'd call back in the spring . . ." Then he hung up.

Concerned looks were again exchanged, and the silence was deafening. Matthews took the pad from Davis and quickly wrote, "My ranch, after adjournment. Have the troopers make sure we're not followed. I'll lead the way." Barnes nodded his head in agreement, and, to Matthews's surprise, extended a handshake. Matthews returned it firmly, then both lawyers shook hands with the judge. A common purpose, beyond the scope of the trial itself, had been formed.

Within two minutes, the judge had his robe on, Carson had the jury in place, and the defense was told to proceed.

To Matthews's utter shock, Dean rose and announced, "Robert Dean for the Defense, Your Honor." Only the jurors murmuring amongst themselves could have drowned out the four-letter comment that Matthews had intended only for his own ears. "If we thought we were in trouble with Barnes, we're in the bottom of the cesspool now, boys. Watch carefully, this will be stuff they don't teach in law school."

Dean fastidiously buttoned his suit coat, which was a tailored pinstripe which fit a man approaching sixty better than most suits usually do. Dean stood initially so he could look at both the witness and the jury, a tactic only used by Barnes during his opening argument.

"Commander, for the record, how many autopsies have you performed where the victim was killed by gunshot and the cause of death was not suicide?"

"None, as I said this morning."

"Indeed, sir, but the jury was not here this morning. I thought perhaps they might be curious." Matthews wanted to object, but the judge's decision in the morning had virtually ratified this line of questioning, so he kept quiet while Dean rehashed all the questions, in finer detail, more articulate English, and with amazing inflections in his voice, that had caused Humes to be excluded as an expert witness.

"Commander, this morning you testified that you were assisted by Drs. Boswell and Finck. Is the jury to understand that they, and they alone, are the only other individuals who have knowledge with respect to this pathological procedure that occurred on November twenty-second?"

"Well, no. There was a photographer—he took the pictures . . ."

"That is what photographers do," Dean reminded Humes.

". . . and two X-ray technicians, as well as two lab technicians."

"So eight people—three doctors, a photographer, who, for the record, took pictures, and four technicians—took part in this procedure?"

"That's correct."

"Would you identify these people for the record?"

"I'm not sure if I can."

Dean pounced: "Are you saying you don't know who they are?"

"No, no. It's just that we signed documents . . ."

"May I remind you, Doctor, that this morning you testified

that you signed a document to keep silent on what you saw, but you could not speak for the others. Are you now saying that they signed similar documents?"

"I assume they were forced to."

"Why didn't you tell us that this morning? You submitted an undated report, A63-272, as noted, and a supplemental report, CE 391, which purport to be the truth, sir. If they are the truth, why the secrecy? The Americans know that the President was shot in the head—that's no secret. It's no secret *he died.* Why the cloak and dagger?"

"I have no idea."

"In that case, why don't you give us the names, for the record. We have them. The defense is curious *if you have them.*"

"Reibe, oh, and Stringer—took photos. Custer and Reed were the X-ray techs, and Curtis and O'Connor assisted the pathologists—handing instruments, recording observations, that sort of thing."

"Thank you, Doctor. Your Honor, if it please the court, perhaps it would serve justice better if we exhibited the remaining photos and X rays from the collection, so that the jury has the opportunity to view them dispassionately, and then we'll go back to them as the testimony progresses."

"Any objection, Mr. Matthews?"

"No, Your Honor." Only to anything Humes is going to say, when pressed, Matthews thought.

For the next five minutes, the jury saw all the pictures and X rays available, and even though they had seen the worst in the morning, it was still a difficult procedure. Finally, the screens went blank.

"Now, Commander, what we just saw—is that all of the photographs and X rays that you requested or recall?"

"No."

"What is missing?"

"Well, I know we photographed the chest cavity, when it was open, to try somehow to find where the shot in the back went. And there were some pictures—when I say pictures, the photographer usually took two of each, just to be sure—there were pictures taken of the brain."

"And why aren't these pictures here?" Dean said, with an intentionally accusatory tone in his voice.

"I have no idea."

"You must have some idea, if you let them out of your jurisdiction." Bob Dean was a master at baiting witnesses.

"My jurisdiction?" Humes was almost shouting. "The guys in the suits—civilians—grabbed those pictures literally as the film came out of the camera. One roll was exposed to light and destroyed right there."

"Why?"

Humes realized he had said too much. "They weren't important."

"Why not?"

Humes said nothing until prodded to answer the question by the judge. "They showed who was in the audience."

"So you're telling us that pictures of the President's brain and chest cavity are just not available, and that other pictures, showing who was present at Bethesda that evening, were intentionally destroyed?"

"That's what I'm telling you."

"During the course of performing your duties on November twenty-second, did you have the opportunity to see the photographs, including those now missing, and the X rays?"

"Some of the X rays. Our primary purpose was to search for bullets."

"Of the pictures, when and where did you first see them, Doctor, or is this the first time you are seeing them?"

Matthews wanted to slide off his chair and suck his thumb under the prosecution table. Failing that, he had to listen to Humes's candid answer: "I saw them last night at Mr. Matthews's lovely ranch."

Dean was still looking at the jury and allowing that revelation to sink in, when he reminded the witness that he had testified earlier that he had requested, and been denied, access to the President's clothing. "Have you subsequently seen them, because we know that those materials are here, not at Mr. Matthews's lovely ranch?"

"Yes, I was shown the President's coat and shirt when I testified before the President's Commission."

"Let me ask you this, Doctor, before we get to those exhibits. What did your examination of the President's coat and shirt reveal?"

"Both garments had holes, in the back, approximately six inches down from the collar line. The jacket had no defects in the front, but the shirt had two overlapping holes in the front."

"Did these holes correspond to the wound you observed on the upper border of the President's scapula?"

"Roughly. But we didn't have the clothing that night, and when we did view it, it had been, well, cut this way and that, for testing I guess, by the FBI."

"Is it your belief that the holes in the clothing—the holes in the back of the President's coat and shirt, which you stated were approximately six inches down from the collar—and for the record, they are five and five-eighths inches down, were made by a bullet or bullets?"

"By a bullet."

"Commander, I'd like you to look at something. Could we please have CE 385, please. Commander, do you recognize this?"

"Yes."

"Would you please tell the jury about it?" Dean retreated slightly to lean against the far end of the spectator railing behind the prosecution table, creating the illusion that the witness was on his own, which Humes was.

"This is a drawing supervised by me and the other two pathologists to depict the wound received by the President. It was done from memory, and without recourse to the photos, X rays, or clothing."

"Is that wound depicted five and five-eighths inches down from the top of the collar line?"

"No."

"As shown, does it depict a wound on the upper border of the scapula?"

"No."

"Does it depict a wound in the President's neck or back?"

"Neck."

Dean's voice rose slightly with each question. He was approaching a crescendo: "And where was the wound, in the neck, or in the back—easy question, Commander. You've seen the pictures and so has the jury."

"The wound was in the back."

The crescendo passed, and Dean delivered the first coup de grace with considerably diminished volume: "Then which is it, Commander? When you testified before the President's Commission, did you commit perjury or was it obstruction of justice?"

Matthews was up immediately. "Your Honor, this witness is not on trial here."

Dean had expected that, replying: "With all due respect, Mr. Prosecutor, some of the people you have paraded through here *will* eventually be on trial here, for charges as just specified. I'm trying to discover if this is just one more of them."

The judge had heard enough: "Gentlemen, let's confine ourselves to the facts. If they don't sort out properly, the court has a pretty good idea what to do."

"Forgive me for that outburst, Commander," Dean said, diplomatically, "but I have difficulty—serious difficulty," he continued, walking toward a package on the evidence table, "when an exhibit such as that one on the screen is admitted into evidence, *under oath,* as you are now, depicting a wound in the neck, and I study this piece of evidence," holding up a once blood-smeared suitcoat with one hand and allowing a finger to loom through the "defect" for the jury to see.

Folding the coat over his arm for the moment, he approached the witness stand, while Matthews was lamenting to his two assistants that Dean even moved like he had been scripted. "Now, Commander, let's talk about this back wound. What has been your prior testimony with regard to that back wound with respect to the angle of it?"

"It entered at about a forty-five-degree-down angle."

"Commander, would you be curious as to the angle shown in that drawing on the screen which you had prepared for the President's Commission, which was obviously not composed of mathematicians?"

"It should show forty-five degrees."

Dean made the jury aware of his impatience: "It shows, sir, a down angle of *ELEVEN DEGREES.*"

Humes had to sit silently, since Dean had been careful not to ask him a question. Then Dean summoned Barnes to the jury rail, where Barnes took off his own coat and carefully slid into the President's coat, which, despite its blood-related rigidity, was a reasonable fit. Dean put his finger into the hole in the jacket, put pressure on Barnes with the finger so he slowly turned for the jury and then Humes to see the *back wound,* then asked the obvious: "In layman's terms, Doctor, where is my finger touching this man?"

"His back."

"Is it close enough to the neck for it possibly to be confused with a neck wound?"

"No."

Matthews tried a gambit. "Your Honor, best evidence. There's no way to say that the suit coat in question was not bunched up on November twenty-second, but we do have Commander Humes's precise measurements of the location of the wound at autopsy."

"Mr. Dean?" the judge asked. In the meantime, Barnes took off the coat, returned it to the evidence table, plainly visible, and returned with the President's shirt, then put his own coat back on and headed back to his place.

"Your Honor, best evidence indeed. The coat could have bunched perhaps, but the shirt as well?" Dean displayed the hole in the shirt, in virtually the identical place as the coat "defect"; he then continued: "And let's have no talk, Mr. Prosecutor, of 'precise measurements,' because they are anything but. In fact, this is the only autopsy I have ever read of where locations were measured from nonfixed points." Then, to the bench, "May I, Your Honor?"

"Should the jury see this?" Davis asked.

"I believe so. If Mr. Barnes will again assist." Barnes had been primed to wear a dark blue suit coat, and arrived at the witness stand with a ruler in his hand, and masking tape and chalk in his pocket. "Commander Humes, you wrote on page 3 of your report, A63-272, that the wound in question was 'measured to be fourteen centimeters from the tip of the right acromion process and fourteen centimeters below the tip of the right mastoid process.' Now, the acromion process presents no difficulty. But before we get to that, would you please, using this ruler, measure down five and five-eighths inches from the top of this man's shirt collar, and mark it with this chalk, please?"

Humes adjusted his glasses, placed the ruler, measured and made the mark. "Very good," Dean commented, stroking the witness for the ugly task ahead. "Now, please measure down fourteen centimeters from the tip of the right mastoid process." As Dean spoke, Barnes craned his head far back, so that his neck was hunched up. Humes wanted to object, but being the good soldier, did as he was told. The mark was below the existing chalk mark. Dean then asked him to do it again, just to be sure, and Barnes now moved his head all the way forward, so his chin was virtually resting on his chest. This mark was almost on the collar of the coat. Barnes then turned for the jury as well as the judge to see the three marks.

"As I said, Your Honor, the tip of the mastoid process is not a fixed point, so best evidence is invalid here."

"Mr. Matthews, your objection is overruled." The jury didn't really hear that; they were almost hypnotized by the marks on the *back* of the coat.

"Commander, let's change directions here. Let me refresh everyone's memory. You testified earlier about this wound of entry, I believe 'rather round, and there were no jagged edges'?"

"That's absolutely correct."

Dean let the jury digest the response, then went back to the defense table and shuffled papers. "Please forgive me, Doctor, but the description I just read to you was a description of the wound in the *front* of the President's throat made by a Doctor Carrico at Parkland Hospital."

Prosecutor Matthews was again up and vocal, but he was not perfectly sure what his specific objection was. Dean asked that the question and answer be stricken. Matthews sat down and read the handwriting on the wall—Barnes, an out of towner, could *never* have gotten away with that stunt. So here's Bob Dean, a good old Texas boy, getting away with it. He could only suspect the worst was yet to come.

"Commander, we've seen the defects in the jacket and the

shirt. This is critical. Did you find any fibers in the accompanying wound?"

"Come to think of it, no. And you're the first person to ever ask me that."

"Is there any way that the absence of fibers can be accounted for?" Dean said, with sincerity, because he wanted a cogent, sincere answer to his question.

"It may be a long answer . . ." Humes offered.

"I'm all ears, Doctor."

"Well, we probed that wound and got nowhere. No lanes for exit. Didn't even have any luck with a metal probe. As a matter of fact, I asked that those chest-cavity pictures be taken, because we could see, physically *see*, the metal probe hitting the inside of the pleura, which indicated a dead end—the missile went in, and didn't come out. We then hypothesized that it could have come out during the pounding involved in closed chest rescusitation attempted at Parkland Hospital. If that happened, the fibers would have been on the tip of the bullet, or possible at the terminus of the wound, but I consider that unlikely."

"But you agree that there should have been fibers?"

"Oh, yes. Absolutely. When they leave the garment, they have to go somewhere."

"And you found absolutely none?"

"Not one thread."

"Did you subsequently change your thinking about that wound?"

"In a manner of speaking, yes. When I spoke with Dr. Perry the following day, after the President's body was gone and unavailable for verification, only then did I learn of what they thought was an entrance wound in the anterior—that's the front—of the throat. Now we're in a quandry. There's a wound in back with no bullet, and a wound in front, possibly in some alignment, also with no bullet. See, the wound in front had been, well, obliterated by a tracheostomy, so we never saw it as a wound. So we're stuck with two wounds, no bullets, and a damaged trachea, suggesting that at least one of the bullets penetrated deeply, so we considered the possibility that it passed through."

"Doctor, let's take another look at that particular autopsy

picture please. Could we have the anterior neck pose, please?"

"A true representation, Doctor?"

"I believe so."

"Mr. Barnes, please rejoin Commander Humes and me." As Barnes did so, Matthews noted to Graves and Vincent how Dean was playing the witness like a well-tuned fiddle.

"Commander," Dean instructed while Barnes removed his tie and opened his collar, "please put a piece of this tape where the tracheostomy was performed." Humes did so. He was then directed to measure, with a six-foot ruler, the height, from the floor, of that wound. "Sixty-one and one half inches," Humes replied.

"Now, please measure the mark you made which was five and five-eighths inches down from the coat collar." Humes did as directed and announced, "Fifty-eight and one half inches."

"For the record, Doctor, which mark was higher?"

"The front."

"And you testified that the back wound entered at a down angle of forty-five degrees."

"Yes, and I would still so testify."

"I would hope you would. Thank you, Mr. Barnes, for the cleaning bill that demonstration will involve. Doctor, do you believe that missile entering the back struck any bone?"

"No. We found no such evidence."

"Now—you didn't section the wound, so you didn't see all of it. Could it have struck just an eighth of an inch of the vertebral column, and if so, would that account, if such an account is needed, for its upward path?"

"If it had struck bone, that would—or could, account for the discrepancies raised here," Humes concluded.

"Doctor, based on your term—'the discrepancies raised here'—would you conclude that one bullet passed through the President and then went on to wound Governor Connally?"

"I can't say positively either way on that. But I will tell you one thing—not from gunshot experience but from understanding wounds and ballistics. That bullet that I was shown in Washington . . ."

"Excuse me, Commander, are you referring to this one?" exhibiting CE 399.

"Yes. I told them, and I'll tell you. *That* bullet did not pass through both men. There was simply too much metal taken out of, and some still left in, the governor, for that bullet to have done the damage. I may not have done a perfect job on every aspect of this, because we were told not to track the wounds . . ."

"You were told not to? By whom?"

"By people with more gold braid on than I did, and that's all I know. But as I was saying, I will tell you that for a bullet to have shattered two bony areas—a rib and a wrist, and to pass through seven layers of tough, elastic skin and wind up in the femur, it is going to be disfigured. And that bullet is not."

At this point, Dean requested the witness be given a five-minute recess, and then he resumed. "Turning now to the head wound, Commander, does the picture on the screen, which I requested during the recess, reflect your measurements as stated, two point five centimeters to the right and slightly above the external occipital protuberance?"

"No. The wound depicted there is much higher."

"Could we have the next exhibit, please, CE 386? Doctor, before the brief recess, we looked at CE 385 and found fault with it. Now, does this exhibit adequately reflect the wound which penetrated the President's coat?"

"Definitely not."

"Then how did the President's Commission take it to be the truth—they had the coat longer than you did!"

"People will sometimes believe what they want to."

"Indeed they will, Doctor. But let's look at the rest of this picture. That small wound in the back of the head, not that irrelevant hole in the neck, but the small hole in the head, is that accurate?"

"Yes. That was an entry as we saw it."

"As we saw it?"

"In my conversations with the Dallas people, I got the impression they saw rather different damage to the back of the head than I did."

"Did that fact trouble you at all?"

"Sure. But I reported about what was on the table at Bethesda—nothing more."

"And the wound shown above the small wound, the massive defect in the upper right scalp—that accurate also?"

"Just as I saw it."

"Could we have CE 386 and the previous autopsy photo side by side? Doctor, you've said that except for the neck hole, CE 386 is an accurate, if artistic, interpretation of what you saw that night. Now, is that photo also an accurate interpretation of what you saw?"

*"No."* Humes was emphatic.

"You are not responsible for the photos, Doctor. Be assured of that. Could we have the anterior-posterior X ray please? Doctor, in your testimony to the President's Commission, you described the head wound as an entrance and an exit, naturally, and also an incredible series of radiating fractures. Am I correct?"

"Yes. Those fractures so badly shattered the skull that pieces came apart as we moved the subject during the examination."

"Doctor, look at that X ray on the screen, please. Are the entrance wound and the corresponding fractures in accord with where you believed the entry wound to be, or where it is shown on the photo we just saw?"

"It matches up with the photo."

"In spite of that, Doctor, do you still maintain the entry was lower?"

"Yes. And that X ray also depicts frontal bone damage we did not see. There was damage, to be sure, but there's an absence of frontal bone in that X ray."

"With respect to the frontal bone damage, doctor, what could have caused it? Did you not remove fragments?"

"There were two types of fragments. Some, perhaps as many as forty, were little more than dust particles. The other two, found behind the right eye, were roughly the size of pencil points."

"Could they have done the frontal bone damage, Doctor? Either the damage you saw or what is shown in this X ray?"

"No. Certainly not."

"Do I hear a suspicion that this X ray and your recollection of the damage do *not* overlap?"

"You hear correctly, sir."

"Doctor, I've read your testimony with regard to the head wound very carefully, and I'll go through it slowly, and in lay terms for the jury's benefit. If I misspeak, please stop me. First, there was a laceration through the brain from the entry, veering somewhat to the right, which you believe exited from the top right of the skull."

"Correct."

"You also stated that there was a laceration of the corpus callosum, which is a body of fibers which connects the two hemispheres of the brain to each other."

"Correct."

"You further described, from the underside of the brain, a longitudinal laceration of the mid-brain through the floor of the third ventricle . . . this laceration partially communicates with an oblique one point five centimeter tear through the left cerebral peduncle. Doctor, for the jury's benefit, where are the cerebral peduncles located?"

"Just above the roof of the mouth."

"And for all this damage, smashed skull, numerous radiating fractures, several bullet paths through the brain, including one as low as the roof of the mouth, the only metal found amounted to some dust and two pencil points?"

"That's all that was there."

"Doctor, how could a bullet tear the cerebral peduncle and not be found?"

"There are only two ways. One, if the bullet did not do it directly, but caused the brain literally to explode, with such force and magnitude that in erupting it totally disrupted such underlying structures as the cerebral peduncle—in effect, the explosive force brought everything up and out . . ."

"Which would virtually leave no brain whatsoever," Dean suggested.

"Correct. And there was part of a brain there."

"So what's the other explanation?"

"Somebody got that bullet fragment out before I saw the body. When I called Dallas, I asked them specifically if they had done any cutting on the President's head."

"And?" Dean prompted, with an economy of words.

"They told me they were trying to save him, not kill him."

"Doctor, you testified to two wounds, one measuring seven by four millimeters, and one measuring fifteen by six millimeters. The alleged assassination weapon, and, by inference, bullets, are six point five millimeters. Could such bullets inflict wounds smaller than their stated size?"

"In skin, yes, but not from six point five down to four; in skull, not even six point five down to six. If you tell me it's a six point five bullet, I'm looking for holes that measure fully seven or more."

Dean believed the jury had heard enough for one day, so he asked for an early adjournment, based on "prior considerations," which he meant the adjournment to Matthews's ranch, and he also knew that he could get double the mileage out of the witness if he had him on the stand again the following day. Matthews, numbed by what he was hearing, did not object.

The principals left the courtroom after the "night shift," the Oregon state troopers, had been roused, some from sleep, to provide security. The prosecution went in Matthews's car, the defense in two cars, and Judge Davis rode in Carson's car. He insisted the bailiff accompany him for the purpose of witnessing any statements should an issue be made of such a meeting down the road.

An unmarked car, driven by one of the six security officers, led the group, with a security car after each car involving principals. Once on the main road to Matthews's ranch, the last two cars simply formed a barricade across the road and stopped all traffic for ten minutes. In later years, no doubt, people would tell their children of the great Lubbock traffic jam caused by Oregon state police.

Once at the ranch, Matthews provided a couple of fifths of good sipping whiskey, somewhat needed by the group which was huddling outside the house for fear of electronic surveillance within. Matthews noted this was the "damnedest legal proceeding I've ever been involved in," while Bob Dean, always gracious, viewed the situation as highly irregular.

Judge Davis focused the issue: "Understand that Carson is

here as my witness, and that there is no discussion of any aspect of the case as already heard. It is our concern as to what we do about this . . . invasion . . . that has occurred. I don't for one second harbor any suspicion whatsoever that anyone here, anyone related to the court, or any of the state officers has anything to do with this. But that does nothing to lessen my rage, I must tell you. Eddie, let's start with you. What's your take?"

"Well, Judge, that phone bug we saw while Carson was job hunting was most likely FBI, and if they did the phone or phones, they did the courthouse as well. The best way to verify it is to have one of the state officers check the phone booths for a block in every direction. When the Feds want a place wired, they're thorough."

Matthews, showing no hostility to Barnes but still prone to being adversarial, asked, "Why the FBI, and not the CIA, the Secret Service, or the Dallas police?"

Barnes spoke calmly, alternating his glance between Matthews and the judge. "Ray, you know I was FBI, and that phone bug was déjà vu, believe me. It might as well have said, 'Property of. . . .' " Second, the Secret Service doesn't have the resources—or the motive for this. If the CIA was in this, either we would have known it on day one, because they can be incredibly sloppy at times, or we'd have never known, because they would have installed a disguised parabolic system a mile away, with microwave technology that could detect a hiccough in that courtroom. And you can forget the Dallas p.d. They're already taking a beating on this, so they can't afford any more bad ink. Besides, what would they be hearing that they don't already know? No, for my money, this is J. Edgar and Company at their finest."

"But why them? What have they got to gain?" Graves seemed to ask what his boss was thinking.

"Everything to gain and nothing to lose. Your Honor, if I overstep the ground rules, stop me," Barnes warned. "So far, everything out of the Dallas p.d. has come up short. When they needed help, they got expert help from Washington, at a price, of course. See, what most people don't know, and it should be obvious to us—the FBI flat out has no jurisdiction in this case. You can talk about certain civil rights cases, but there's no federal statute about assaulting the President. So what's their angle? Simple. Publicity and power. They've had their nose in this case virtually from the time of the last shot echoing. Hoover was telling people on the afternoon of the twenty-second that it was a lone-nut Communist, at a time when the defendant was still on the spot for only the other crime. He knew before the Dallas cops, which should send a shiver up and down all our spines. Their game is publicity. If John Q. Citizen needs the FBI and there's no publicity in it for them, to hell with John Q. Citizen. I saw it happen every day. But if there's a headline to be grabbed, three hundred agents will be assigned to the most meaningless nonsense imaginable.

"In this case, and this hasn't been brought out yet in direct or cross, FBI agents combed every rifle range for *miles* around Dallas—I mean they got down on their knees, got good and dirty, and picked through literally millions of expended cartridges to find anything that looked like Mannlicher shells. They found over thirteen thousand possibles. Now, imagine the man hours and cost—but imagine the headline if they struck paydirt with a match for C2766. Out of the million they went through, thirteen thousand possible, only eighty were from Mannlichers, and none from C2766. What if they had found five? Would that have proven the defendant left them there? No. But the FBI would have gone up to Capitol Hill, talked about man hours, and gotten more money in next year's budget. The other thing is, and I'm sure we've all heard the rumors, Hoover has a set of files on anybody who is anybody. And if he could get something on us— you, Judge Davis, myself, Ray, Bob, any of us—no matter how this turns out, we would then have to make statements to the press that it was the FBI who did the work and either got the conviction, no offense, Ray, or it was the FBI who almost was able to save a crumbling local case that collapsed in Dallas."

"So it's publicity, power, and blackmail, Eddie?"

"Maybe more, Your Honor, because here's this defector to Russia who returns to the U.S. and is virtually ignored by the FBI. Then he's thrust into center stage, and all the agents that ever had anything to do with it all parrot the official line.

It's too pat. I don't know exactly, but my money says they know they missed something—either something sinister for which the defendant should be convicted, or something conspiratorial that says he's the patsy he claimed to be, and they're very scared the world will somehow learn of it. So they have to know everything we know and do."

"So where do we go from here?"

Matthews spoke up. "Well, we certainly can't walk into a bugged courtroom every day." Most seemed to agree with that. Most, that is, except Barnes: "We could sanitize that building and the phones in a couple of hours and prevent a recurrence, but what does that prove? They know we're wise to them, and they'll come at us another way. No, we've got to get them out into the open, and I think I know how. Let me kick it around overnight, and we'll go through our paces tomorrow. In the meantime, Judge, do you have a radio in your chambers?"

"Not much of one, but yes."

"Okay, tomorrow morning, turn it on in chambers—news, classical music, whatever—something that whoever is listening in will believe. We'll be able to talk in your office and find a way to focus this problem—problem, hell, this felony."

"If we're agreed on that, Carson and I will depart," the judge announced. "See you all tomorrow." Then, after a look at the horizon, "By the way, for you folks from Minnesota, it will snow tonight."

Barnes was about to say his good-byes when Matthews invited the defense team in, to the surprise of both the defense and the prosecution. In what was probably the most amazing bull session in Texas legal history, for the next couple of hours, over snacks and beer, Minnesota and Texas swapped war stories in a very cathartic session. Finally, Barnes reminded Carolyn Jeffries she had homework, which was false, but Matthews didn't have to know that. Everyone then drove back to the courthouse and reclaimed their vehicles as the snow was beginning to fall.

# Nine

The judge's weather forecast had been accurate, so on that Wednesday, January thirteen, the participants had to leave a little earlier to make it to court on time. Precisely at ten, Judge Davis's door opened, suddenly providing the courtroom with talk-radio. "Forgive me," he told the two sets of attorneys. "My wife hates to have to drive in snow, so I have to monitor road conditions at times like this." Davis disappeared into his chambers, and then reopened the door with no noise coming out. Barnes knew the judge would give his plan a try.

Carson quickly had the jury in place and Commander Humes was recalled to the stand to complete his cross-examination by Bob Dean. Humes was politely reminded that he was still under oath.

Matthews had predicted to Graves and Vincent that Dean would use the second day to remind the jury of what they had heard, from the defense, of course, in the first day. He was quickly proven correct.

Dean moved right to the attack. "Commander, we had a very busy and informative day yesterday, and I'm glad to see you look well-rested. I believe we established that the photos and X rays available to us do not comprise the complete set, and that you only saw many of them for the first time on Monday evening."

"That's correct."

"We also determined yesterday that the President sustained a back wound, at a forty-five-degree down angle, for which you never did find either a lengthy 'track,' or an exit."

"Correct again."

"And to the best of your recollection, that wound more or less corresponded to the defects in the President's clothing, the fibers from which were never discovered?"

"Correct on both counts."

"We further developed the fact that your measurements with respect to the distance between the entry wound and the external occipital protuberance was at serious variance with the photographs and the X rays, is that correct?"

"Yes."

"Could we then say, Commander, that either your findings, the measurements you performed on the body of the President, were incorrect, or the pictures are inaccurate representations of the President's body."

"One of those circumstances must be the case. The wound I saw, and the wound depicted in that autopsy photo, not any of the drawings we saw yesterday, but the photo," Humes insisted, "were at odds by four inches. It's not a matter of, well, a half-inch, explainable by a clot of blood or matted hair. No. Four inches different. And I stand by my measurements of that wound."

"Since you did not see the photos before Monday, Commander, is it possible that your recollection has become clouded by time?"

"No, sir," Humes answered adamantly. "I don't mean to insult the sensitivities of anyone in this court, but I will say to you that if the President's body was lying face down on that table behind you, with his head covered by a towel, if that towel had the external occipital protuberance marked with a spot, from that location, I could put my finger right on the entry wound, so that when you moved the towel, my finger would be pointing right into it."

"Based on such conviction, Commander, I can only surmise that you place no faith in the veracity of the photo in question."

"Anything is possible, sir."

"Yes, you said that yesterday."

"Finally, Commander, we established yesterday that there was incredible damage both to the President's skull and to the cortical substance—brain matter—and that you hypothesized that either the brain was torn out by the force of the bullet or someone other than yourself removed the missile responsible for the damage."

"That is correct."

"And since you removed a brain, or part of one, then we must give somewhat less credence to the exploded brain theory, wouldn't you say?"

"That would be dangerous speculation," Humes replied.

"It probably would," Dean responded, letting his glance pass across the jury as he said it.

"Now, Commander, I was about to ask you about the beginning of report A63-272 when we adjourned yesterday. Could we have page 2 of that clinical summary, please? Commander, the first paragraph of your report deals with the fact —there it is on the screen, that the President was in a certain vehicle, with other individuals, traveling down a street. Isn't that material essentially irrelevant at an autopsy?"

"It is sometimes helpful to establish conditions as they existed."

"I understand that. But shouldn't something with the ominous weight of an autopsy—the pathological, scientific, precise determination of the exact cause or causes of an individual's death—shouldn't that be as objective as possible and as minimally subjective as possible?"

"Well, I can see what you're saying."

"Commander, let's try an analogy for the jury's benefit. Suppose your report began, 'At the time of his death, John Doe was seen swimming in shark-infested waters.' "

Matthews objected on grounds of relevance.

"I'm glad you did, Mr. Matthews, as relevance is what I'm trying to get at in this autopsy's clinical summary."

"Objection overruled. Please conclude the analogy quickly, Mr. Dean."

"Commander, if we know that Doe was in shark-infested waters and we see horrible abrasions and gouges in the flesh, our tendency might be to assume—to add one and one and get three and conclude shark attack, when it could have been barracuda, or for that matter, a fatal encounter with a coral reef, after which the sharks did damage to the cadaver."

"That's a fair analogy."

"Thank you. I made it up when I realized I was in shark-infested waters. Now, in your second paragraph, and we can all read it there, you state, 'Three shots were heard and the President fell forward bleeding from the head.' Then it goes on to quote a newspaper source as saying he had seen a gun withdrawn into the Book Depository. Now, sir, doesn't that paragraph, in and of itself, disqualify objectivity from this examination? You've said three shots—of which you had no personal knowledge whatsoever. You found a hole in the back; another near the bump on the back of the head; another large one in the head; torn brain tissue above the roof of the mouth; and there was a hole in the front throat that was obscured by a tracheostomy. Now that's more than three holes, and there may be a perfectly good pathological explanation how that could be done with only three shots. But if you are stating as a fact, which you are, sir, that there were only three shots, not two, nor four or five, then you are limiting your options—*to the sharks*."

Dean didn't give Humes a chance to reply. "Before you answer, Commander, there's another exhibit to view. Something I doubt you've seen, and something I know the jury hasn't seen." Dean then walked to the defense table, looked down for a moment with his back to the witness, then turned to face the jury. "Members of the jury, you are about to see a motion picture film taken by Abraham Zapruder on November twenty-second. It shows, in about fourteen seconds of living color, the entire sequence from the President's car coming down Elm Street, to when the first shots were fired, to the fatal shot, to the reaction, or lack of it, by those within and without the automobile. You will see it once, just as taken, then again, for detail, and finally a third time, showing a slow motion close-up of the President. I must tell you that it is more graphic and more horrible than the photos of the late President in death, because it shows that split second when he passed from life to death. I must also tell you that it may be shown to several other witnesses, so if you are weak of stomach, please view it carefully this time and etch it into your mind, if you need to turn away in the future.

"Before we see that, Commander, I return to the statement in the second paragraph shown in your clinical summary: 'and the President fell forward bleeding from the head.' I don't know what your source was for that statement, sir, and you may choose not to tell me, but we're going to watch this film for about one minute, and then I'm going to ask you, very simply, 'Did the President fall forward, bleeding from the head?' Could we have the Zapruder film sequence, please?"

Silence was pervasive and all eyes were riveted on the screen. When the head shot occurred, the jury, almost as one organism, recoiled as did the victim. The second and third showings did not make the viewing any easier.

Humes intertwined his fingers and looked at the floor, silently hoping that somehow, with some divine miraculous intervention, he would not be asked the question that the defense attorney had promised to ask him. Knowing it was inevitable, he spoke quietly: "I was told the President fell forward."

"Did he?" Dean asked calmly.

"No."

"Commander, the defense commissioned photographic experts to study the key frames in the film we just viewed. They will testify that from frame 313 to frame 321, a total of nine frames exposed in just less than one-half second, the president's body traveled not forward, but *backward,* at a rate of just over one hundred feet per second, or the rate of sixty-eight point two *miles per hour.* Doctor Humes, you testified yesterday afternoon that your findings were that the President was struck twice, from above and behind. Is that finding consistent with what you just saw?"

"No."

Dean moved in close enough to lean on the witness stand, and told Humes that there were just a few more points that needed clarification and then they would be done. He also regretted that the doctor had been put through this wrenching ordeal for two straight days.

"He would have had him up there a week, if he could have," Matthews told Graves and Vincent.

"Doctor," Dean continued, "when you viewed the tracheostomy, which was then unknown to you as a bullet wound, what do you recall about it?"

"Well, it did not appear to us as a wound. It was seven or eight centimeters long, with irregular, gaping edges."

"Could we have the anterior neck autopsy pose again? Doctor, is this an accurate depiction of what someone's neck should look like following a tracheostomy procedure?"

"No. As I have testified, I asked the Dallas doctors if they did any cutting." Humes was on a roll, and was going to somehow prove he was the medical expert. "See, a tracheostomy, which most people call a tracheotomy, is perhaps the most routine surgical procedure. A scalpel—an instrument with a very narrow blade, makes a two to three centimeter incision . . ."

"Commander, you testified to seven or eight centimeters . . ."

"That's what we found."

Dean walked to the defense table and returned with a piece of paper and a standard as well as metric ruler. "Commander, I'd like you to measure a line, seven or eight centimeters, then tell the jury how long a line that is in inches."

Humes took about thirty seconds, checked his work, and announced "eight centimeters is three and one-eighths inches," his voice trailing off somewhat.

"Doctor, you testified that the Dallas people told you they were trying to save the President, not kill him. Look at that picture on the screen. That looks like someone slashed that victim and he would have died from that wound depicted. Have you ever seen a tracheostomy that looked like that?"

"No."

"And there was no idea in your mind that there was a wound. Should there have been?"

"Quite possibly. A bullet wound in elastic skin is five to seven millimeters; a scalpel blade is literally micro-thin. It would go through a five to seven-millimeter wound without disturbing it. Yet we found no evidence of even the margins of a wound."

"Doctor, maybe we can make sense of this in another way. Could you tell the jury what a cut-down is?"

"Generally speaking, a cut-down is a procedure done to insert a tube into a patient, either to provide drainage out of the patient, or to introduce emergency fluids—blood, or Ringer's lactate, into the patient."

"How is such a procedure done?"

"Scalpel incision, tube inserted."

"Similar, then, to a tracheostomy?"

"Yes, except that which is inserted is smaller."

"Were cut-downs performed on President Kennedy in Dallas?"

"Objection. The witness was not in Dallas."

"Sustained."

"Doctor, when you examined the President's body in Bethesda, Maryland, did your examination reveal any marks which you would have attributed to life-saving measures, done by a scalpel, usually referred to as cut-downs?"

"Yes, there were four, I believe. Two in the upper chest— one on each side, possibly for drainage. One in the left arm, and one in the left leg."

"Doctor, did *these* scalpel incisions look the way you would have expected them to?"

"Yes. Routine."

"But the tracheostomy clearly did not?"

"Clearly."

"Doctor, let's take a look at CE 391—if we could have that exhibit please. Doctor, this exhibit is a supplementary autopsy report, dated December six, 1963, which discusses the President's brain. Take a minute and tell the court if you recognize this document."

"Yes I do."

"And that is your signature?"

"Yes."

"Doctor, I'm very troubled. We've already discussed, to use your phrase, 'discrepancies'—photos that don't agree with your measurements, artistic renderings which don't match the President's clothing, and statements in the initial report which, in the absence of any personal knowledge, tell of the number of shots and the President's reaction—stated incorrectly. Now we come to the report about the President's brain. This report mentions 'the right cerebral hemisphere is found to be markedly disrupted.' Also: 'There is considerable loss of cortical substance above the base of the laceration, particularly in the parietal lobe.' Doctor, was a good portion, twenty or more percent of the President's brain, missing?"

"Yes."

"Was the cerebellum intact?"

"Yes."

"Doctor, have you weighed brains at autopsy before?"

"It's standard procedure," Humes answered, while some jurors seemed to be considering skipping lunch that day.

"And what is the weight of a brain, or the range of the weight, of a brain that is undamaged?"

"Thirteen fifty to fifteen hundred grams, give or take a little."

"And what is the weight you recorded for the late President in this document, having just admitted that a good portion of the brain was missing?"

"Fifteen hundred grams."

"Do you see my dilemma, Doctor? The most it should weigh is fifteen hundred grams. You saw the movie, in which we witnessed 'considerable loss of cortical substance' and you want the jury to believe that no weight was lost? How are we to explain this, Doctor?"

"I have no explanation," Humes mumbled.

"Doctor, you took two oaths. One was directed at the dignity of human life, and somehow reflects the philosophy that human life is sacred and that you would never violate a human body except to repair damage. The other oath you took was administered to you yesterday afternoon, and that epitomized the notion that you would tell the truth in these proceedings, and you have certainly done that. Now, Doctor, let's go back to November twenty-second. You are shown that graphic movie that we viewed together. You are given a chance to see the President's clothing. You are shown the bullet which allegedly did all this damage. And no superior officer, no person 'with more gold braid than you,' gives you orders. You simply perform a valid autopsy. Would your results be the same as this document you submitted?"

"The cause of death would not change . . ."

"Agreed," Dean interrupted. "Beyond that, is this document valid? Can you accept future generations seeing that film and the President's clothing and wondering about the competency of a Commander James J. Humes who said both shots came from the back, and one, which went through the back of the President's clothing, hit him in the neck, but ranged downward at forty-five degrees and emerged higher than it entered?"

"The cause of death was a gunshot to the head. Your film proves that—you didn't need me or anyone else to tell you that. The rest of the report rested on what we were told about the shooting, and what we were told not to explore. In that context, you have shown it to be invalid."

"Thank you, Doctor. No further questions at this time. Your Honor, based on the witness's last statement, and the discrepancies noted, the defense moves to exclude the autopsy report and the supplementary autopsy protocol."

"Mr. Matthews?"

Matthews walked to where Humes was now fidgeting. "Doctor, do you still feel that, regardless of what else might have happened, the President received a bullet wound in the back of his head?"

"Yes. But it would now seem obvious that it was not the only head wound."

"But there was a rear head wound?"

"Yes."

Matthews then insisted to Judge Davis that the witness's statement was enough to maintain the validity of the report. Dean walked over, but before he could say anything, Matthews wanted to know why. Dean was concise: "You just had redirect. I'm entitled to recross."

Matthews had been hoisted on his own petard, and he knew it. "Doctor, much of this difficulty could be resolved if you, Dr. Boswell, and Colonel Finck would simply reexamine the brain, based on what has been discussed the past two days. Your report based on that examination would certainly be acceptable to the defense."

"That would be extremely difficult," Humes said, in low tones.

"Why?" Dean asked incredulously, although he knew.

"There is no brain. Don't ask. It's gone, and I don't know who, how, where, when, or why. It was taken from us when we finished. Prior to our testimony, we *had* every intention of verifying our work. We were told 'It's gone, and don't look,' or words to that effect."

"Your Honor," Dean addressed the bench, "the witness's testimony is clearly more valid than his earlier, misguided report. If the prosecution can convince the court that the testimony should be excluded, then I would withdraw my move to exclude the two reports. Otherwise, the defense will continue to contend that the witness's testimony has seriously undercut the credibility of those reports, and they therefore be excluded."

"Approach the bench, gentlemen. Mr. Humes, you are excused with the thanks of this court."

As Humes left, the judge spoke squarely to Matthews: "Bob's right, Ray. You can't have it both ways. And the jury has now seen all the exhibits and film that Humes never saw that night. I have no choice." Davis paused, expecting some kind of argument from Matthews, who remained silent. "Okay, back to your places.

"Members of the jury, you are to base your deliberations of this case on the evidence you heard from the witness; however, the initial reports, from 1963, are excluded as evidence. The court will conduct hearings, in your absence, to pass judgment on the validity of some of those autopsy pictures and X rays. We will take a brief recess during which I will see the attorneys in my chambers. Court is in recess."

Barnes, seemingly a spectator to the last hour's events, closed the file he had been using, alternately, to make marginal notations, or doodle, but which, in fact, contained a brief script he had lined out the night before.

Once everyone had gathered inside the judge's chambers, under cover of the radio playing, Barnes gave Graves and the judge one sheet of paper and suggested they ad-lib or follow the dialogue, and make sure they play to the still-present microphones.

Graves spoke first, ad-libbing, "Your Honor, I understand your concern for your wife driving in snow, but the matters at hand are such that we could deal with them more effectively without the radio." The old Motorola was then silenced, and Graves came to the point: "Judge, as an officer of the court, I am bound to come forward if I have information bearing on the case that has not been addressed. Inasmuch as it had no direct bearing on the witness just completed, I thought it could wait until now. I have known about it, for the record, for about four hours. On the way in this morning, it dawned on me that January thirteenth is the birthday of my best friend, now a very successful person in the nation's capital. I called him from a phone booth, and he told me he knew things about this trial, which, if they came out afterwards, would seriously undercut the judicial proceedings in progress here. I apologize for the handwriting, Your Honor, but here are the allegations." Barnes nodded his head to Graves for a job well done—so far.

The judge looked around at everyone present, allowing for thirty or so seconds to pass, then announced, "These allegations are incredible. Unbelievable. Mr. Barnes, I think you should see this. Here, I'm done with that page. How?" the judge asked. "How could this be? If even part of this is true . . . I'll need the identity of your friend, Counselor." The judge wanted to avoid naming his source.

"I can do better than that, Your Honor. Here are three names. One of them was the source of the information, the other confirmed it. Which ones exactly, I was told I would not learn over an open phone line."

"Let me see the names. I only recognize one. Barnes, you know these people?"

"Oh God," Barnes said in feigned agony. "Those are three of the four most senior and powerful officers of the FBI. The only name missing from the upper echelon is that of the Director, Mr. Hoover."

"Gentlemen, find seats," the judge ordered. Although it was crowded, and Barnes sat on the corner of a table containing briefs and files, everyone managed. The judge then spoke, intentionally in nonspecifics: "I don't know what to do with this, but for at least today and tomorrow, I shall do nothing. Copies of this will be made and placed in secure places, just in case. As to how this affects the case we are trying, we go on. If any of this is true, and I have to say I hope it's just a cruel hoax, we still have to arrive fairly at a verdict of guilty or not guilty. In the meantime, Counselor, you burn up the wires to see if you can get anything else. Beyond that, well, let's leave it for now. Let's finish this morning, although I have to tell you my concentration will be diminished." The judge then motioned for everyone to remain, but concluded, "Okay, give me five minutes with the weather and I'll bring the jury back."

With the radio going, Barnes explained to a closely huddled Davis and Matthews that if it was the FBI, this would force their hand, but they must all be careful—very careful, in the meantime. He told them the delay in court action would give their "listeners" time to react, and on either Friday or Monday, the next step would be to let the microphones know that the available information would have to go to a hastily convened, special grand jury to look into obstruction of justice at the highest levels. Matthews was little more than a curious observer, although it galled him privately that the court was being bugged while his case was being dismantled, piecemeal. The judge thought Barnes's plan was a good one, and offered the thanks of the court. Everyone but the judge then left, one at a time, quietly.

As soon as the court recess concluded, Matthews called Dr. J. Thornton Boswell, the second of the three autopsy doctors present at Bethesda, in hopes of recovering some of what Humes had lost, and reinforcing, if that was the correct term, what little positive there was from Humes's testimony.

Matthews established Boswell's education and medical certificates, wondering in the process if he was repeating the mistake he had made with Humes, then got quickly to the point: "Doctor, what was the cause of President Kennedy's death?"

"Massive head injuries caused by gunshot wounds."

"And what can you tell the court about the source of the wounds?"

"Well, we were told the shots were fired from a window behind the President, and he fell forward, so—"

"Doctor, forget what you were told," Matthews interrupted, wisely preferring Boswell's thoughts to someone else's. "What did you learn from your observations?"

"The President was struck twice, from behind. The lower wound was probed by each of us, up to the knuckle, where the wound track stopped. We also probed the wound with a metal probe, but found no track. The upper, or head wound, caused far more damage than was apparent to the eye at autopsy, as the President's brain was quite easily removed without recourse to surgery."

"Doctor, was there general agreement among the three of you as to the conclusions that were reached?"

"Absolutely. The report, which was signed by Commander Humes, was in complete accord with our unanimous conclusions."

"Thank you, Doctor Boswell. Nothing further. Move to admit CE 397, Dr. Boswell's preliminary notes and sketches from the autopsy." Matthews had hoped the witness would just say he agreed, without mentioning a report that had been discredited earlier in the day.

Dean again rose for the defense. "Doctor, you said you were all in agreement. Did your agreement extend to all of you sharing a belief that one single bullet, which, for identification purposes is CE 399, could not have done all the damage that the President's Commission suggested?"

"Yes. You must understand that we adjourned Friday night in the belief that the lower wound—"

"Which," Dean interrupted, "we learned this morning was a back wound."

"Yes, that wound. We left Friday night thinking that it had penetrated a short distance and had worked its way out of the shoulder during cardiac massage in Dallas. It was never our contention, nor could it ever be our contention, that one bullet—an undeformed one at that, ever wounded both men."

"Doctor, we need to look at one last exhibit. Could we have

CE 397, please? Doctor Boswell, did you prepare this document?"

"Yes, I did."

"It is titled, 'Autopsy.' How is such a document referred to in practice?"

"It's an autopsy face sheet."

"Would you tell the court its purpose?"

"Only so many of a pathologist's observations can be recorded verbally. At some point, there has to be a visual record created—for reference, to fix points, but mostly to allow the pathologist to visualize the damage—the wounds, not just read about them, in formulating conclusions."

"Is this face sheet accurate? And before you answer, Doctor, by my count, there are ten observations on this document—three wounds, actually two plus the tracheostomy procedure, four cut-downs, two notations regarding the President's eyes, and one old scar. Again, are they accurate?"

"Not perfectly."

"Doctor, you testified that this drawing is used to visualize your final conclusions. The court and the jury can see the very specific measurements made, and even the fact that the head wound has an arrow for some reference purpose. Is there anything grossly inaccurate there?"

"Certainly not."

"Could we have CE 385 and this document side by side please?" Dean looked like he was waiting to pounce as the exhibits changed. "There, Doctor. On the left, you and the other doctors told the President's Commission of a neck wound. On the right, you clearly showed a back wound, identical to the holes in the President's clothing. Can you explain the discrepancy in these two exhibits? One is clearly wrong."

"One is clearly wrong," Boswell replied.

Judge Davis was clearly dissatisfied with the answer. "Dr. Boswell," he addressed the witness, while calmly reclining in his chair, "this morning, your colleague, Dr. Humes gave his testimony, and it was so contrary to the subsequent exhibits —the holes in the President's clothing, the autopsy photographs and X rays, some of which he questioned the validity of—as well as his own sudden recollections, that the autopsy report of the President of the United States had to be excluded from evidence. Now let me tell you, sir," the judge grew loud and came forward in his chair, "that answers like 'one is clearly wrong' just will not be acceptable. You are going to tell this court the truth and help it arrive at a verdict in a capital crime or you will find yourself facing a grand jury for obstruction of justice. Do you understand me, Doctor?" Davis had intentionally used the words "obstruction of justice" for the hidden microphones.

"The dot on the autopsy face sheet is accurate, if slightly low in terms of its accurate location. The President's lower wound was in his upper back, not his neck. In defense of our actions before the President's Commission, Your Honor, we were under tremendous pressure. There was talk—"

"Hearsay, Your Honor," Matthews interrupted.

"Agreed," Davis said, looking right at Matthews. "Carson, take the jury out. The court is going to hear the end of this answer."

Ninety seconds later, Boswell concluded: "There was, or there had been talk to the effect that what we saw at autopsy —the hole in the back that went downward and terminated— if that was true, then there was conspiracy. Now I don't know the facts in this case, but I can tell you that the President's Commission practically wrote our script. They wanted a scenario that said that the back wound passed through the President and hit the governor. We gave it to them. But when it came to us saying that one undeformed bullet did all that damage, enough was enough, and we said 'no'! It's in the record."

The judge had one more question: "How do you know you all said that one bullet didn't do the damage suggested?"

"We were all in the same room together. They asked all the questions to Commander Humes, and he gave the answers. Then they basically asked us, 'do you agree?' I've seen my testimony there. It's less than a page."

"Carson, the jury." Then after a pause, "Mr. Dean, do you have any further questions for this witness?"

"No, Your Honor. I would like to thank the court for that clarification."

"Mr. Matthews?"

"The state calls Colonel Pierre Finck." A middle-aged army officer, in uniform, then strode through the courtroom, directly to the witness stand. Bona fides were again ascertained, and it was shown in this process that Lt. Col. Finck had been added to the autopsy team because of his expertise in gunshot wounds. Matthews then asked that Finck be accorded expert witness status, and Dean had "no objection whatsoever." Matthews then asked, "But Commander Humes was in charge?"

"He supervised," Finck answered, "but an army general made it clear that he was in charge and gave directions." Matthews was hoping the witnesses would just answer the questions. That they were going well beyond suggested to him that they had been heretofore gagged and were now speaking out. He didn't enjoy being their suddenly newfound audience.

"What was the cause of death, Colonel?"

"Massive injury to the head, caused by gunshot wounds."

"And where, in your opinion, did that wound originate?"

"From above and behind."

"Is it correct to say, Colonel, that it was your work on fragments that arrived during the course of the autopsy that proved that a bullet exited from the front right side of the skull?"

"That is correct. There was a massive hole in the President's head, the greatest dimension of which was thirteen centimeters—that's over five inches. These bone fragments, while not totally completing the process, did fit in such a way that inside and outside of the fragments could be determined, and, based on that, beveling of the wound showed the exit as it passed through the bone from the inside to the outside."

"Thank you, Doctor. No further questions."

Dean rose, and, purely to put the prosecution on its guard, walked slowly to the spot at the end of the jury box that Barnes usually frequented when he was about to destroy someone's credibility.

"Doctor, since you are the expert, will you give us your definition of forensic pathology?"

"Forensic pathology is the study with the naked eye and

with the microscope of injuries, including missile wounds, trauma in general."

"For the record, Doctor, your definition did *not* include the gathering of data from telephone calls the next day to Dallas, Texas, the introduction of data such as the spot from which the shots were fired *before* it was ascertained at autopsy, and it also does not include being handed bones of clearly dubious pedigree. Did you have any way of identifying those skull fragments as belonging to the defendant?"

"No."

"Did you have access to the President's clothing, which could be observed by the naked eye and the microscope?"

"No. We requested those materials and were refused."

"Who is this mystery person running the autopsy, and how, how indeed, would the Bethesda Naval Hospital allow an army general to give the orders on an autopsy at its facility?"

"I have no answers for your question, sir," Finck said.

"I believe you, Colonel. Are you in agreement with the testimony of the other two doctors that the back wound only penetrated an inch or two, and at a severe downward angle?"

"Yes, but I don't know if forty-five degrees constitutes a severe angle."

"But you agree that the angle of the back wound was about forty-five degrees?"

"Yes."

"Colonel, testimony will show that the angle to the sixth floor window was twenty degrees at the time of the first shot, and slightly less for the head shot. How do we reconcile a forty-five degree angle?"

"I can't help you answer that, sir," Finck answered in clipped tones.

"As the expert testifying here, Colonel, would you tell the court why the back wound was not dissected?"

"We were told not to."

"Uh, huh. Colonel, did you find any evidence of a wound in the front of the throat?"

"A gunshot wound, no. Clearly, there was a wound there, created by the scalpel. But I examined every millimeter of the borders of that incision, and I have no idea why that wound was not visible. Trach or no, it should have been there."

"Colonel, Dr. Boswell just testified that he, Dr. Humes, and you virtually testified together before the President's commission. Is that correct?"

"Yes."

"The previous pathologists have testified that they would *not* accept the theory that one bullet passed through the President and then inflicted a number of grievous injuries to the governor and emerged from his femur bone unscathed. As the expert here, what do you say about that?"

"It could not have performed as described and emerged pristine. We were supplied the reports relative to the governor, and there are too many fragments described in that wrist."

"Doctor, when you were asked a few minutes ago about the cause of death, and you talked of the massive—five-inch—hole in the top of the President's head, what would have precluded a shot from the rear, causing the damage you described, and a subsequent, almost immediate shot, then entering 'the hole'? Would that be possible, and would it explain the massive brain damage *in various places* throughout the head?"

"It's possible, but certainly not from the same gun. Beyond that, I cannot give you a reason for the massive damage. The entry we saw, and the exit I recreated from fragments, would indicate a path well away from much serious damage."

"Colonel, when asked about cause of death, are you aware that your answer was, 'Massive injury to the head, caused by gunshot wounds'—*plural?*"

"Did I say that?"

"Nothing further, Your Honor."

"Redirect, Mr. Matthews?"

"No, Your Honor."

"The court will recess for lunch, although appetites may be slightly suppressed after the morning's viewing."

Matthews rose to take exception to the judge's comments as prejudicial to the case. Davis noted the exception. Dean told Barnes, "Go easy, Eddie. He's hurting. I've never seen him take this kind of pounding, and I gave him a good one a few years ago."

Matthews, Graves, and Vincent seemed unusually friendly to Barnes after lunch, almost as if the shared knowledge of the bugged courtroom, coupled with the previous day's bull session, had given all parties a great deal in common. Barnes, however, knew his job and Matthews's were totally dissimilar, although he went along with Matthews's back-slapping and chitchat. Matthews was curious, however, as to why Barnes had changed clothes since the morning session. "You're putting the FBI on this afternoon, Ray, and you know they always dress well. I saved my best for this."

Once all participants were settled, the prosecution called Special Agent Alwyn Cole, an FBI document and handwriting specialist. On hearing the name, Barnes and Dean knew the time had not yet come.

Matthews established the witness's experience with documents, and requested that he be designated an expert. The defense had no objections.

"Agent Cole, naturally the prosecution regrets having you come all this way and be unable to testify about the defendant's handwriting on the records from Klein's with respect to the purchase of the assassination weapon, so . . ."

"Your Honor, the defense would request a cautionary note at this time. The stipulation regarding the Klein's order was made. To repeat it now, with this so-called expert up there, is to invalidate the stipulation and make a final argument."

"Mr. Matthews, limit your questioning to facts which have not been heretofore stipulated to."

"Mr. Cole, did you have the opportunity to study, at length, the Selective Service card in the name of Alek J. Hidell found on the defendant's person at the time of his arrest?"

"Yes."

"And what did your examination reveal?"

Barnes figured he had nothing to lose, so he offered an objection based on relevancy, stating that Oswald, not Hidell was on trial, so there was nothing pertinent in this line of questioning.

Judge Davis indicated he was inclined to agree, but would

allow some latitude. Cole then indicated that the Selective Service card in question was a photographic forgery, "phonied up" from Oswald's own Selective Service card, "a relatively easy job to do."

"Thank you," concluded a smug Matthews. "No further questions."

Barnes opened up a folder and was perusing it as Matthews returned to the prosecution table. Then, throwing Matthews and the prosecution off completely, Carolyn Jeffries spoke up, "Mr. Cole, prior to your designation as an expert witness, there was some explanation of your duties at bureau headquarters in the Capital. Would you mind telling the court how many questionable Selective Service cards you have examined?"

"Oh, many . . . many."

"Mr. Cole, 'many' is hardly an answer from an expert; if I had many unpaid bills, it might be twenty; if I claimed to have read 'many' books, it could be hundreds. Could you be a little more specific?"

"Hundreds, maybe thousands."

"Thank you. So, since you've studied thousands of these documents, and since there is only one defendant in this case, is there any correlation whatsoever between having a false Selective Service card and assassinating the President?"

"No."

"Thank you. Nothing further." Barnes gave Matthews a disinterested look, with his glasses perched on the end of his nose, that indicated that from here on in, it was going to be a team effort for the defense.

"Your Honor," Matthews said, keeping an eye on the defense table, "the state calls Special Agent Cortlandt Cunningham." For Matthews's benefit, Barnes and Dean shook their heads "no." Matthews was miffed, but pressed on, establishing the witness's pedigree, and asking that he be accorded expert witness status. Barnes rose for the defense: "Your Honor, defense has no objection, if, in fact, Agent Cunningham is to be the FBI's expert with respect to the weapon. If there is someone else, then we're faced with two experts, two sets of opinions, and confusion."

"Point well taken, Counselor. Mr. Matthews, is this man your weapons expert?"

"We do have someone who has studied the weapon further, Your Honor."

"Then we'll consider his expertise, and possibly hear his opinions. Agent Cunningham is denied expert witness status."

"Special Agent Cunningham, did your duties at FBI headquarters involve testing this rifle, serial number C2766?"

"Yes. There was a concern about the time it would take to assemble the rifle if a sniper was acting in haste. I was able to put that specific rifle together in six minutes, using a ten-cent piece, and in only two minutes with a screwdriver. I also believe I could have done it faster with practice."

"Objection, Your Honor, assumes facts not in evidence. There has been no testimony that the defendant had either a dime or a screwdriver in his possession prior to 12:30 P.M. on November twenty-second."

The judge had to suppress a grin at Barnes's constant, yet legally allowable, objections. "If Mr. Cunningham wants to conduct such tests, Mr. Barnes, he's allowed. You are correct, however, that the burden is on the prosecution to show that the defendant was in possession of such items as stated. So I'll allow it."

"Agent Cunningham, we've heard some admittedly limited testimony about the use of paraffin testing on suspects. Could you share with us your FBI expertise on that test?"

"Certainly. I think the test has no validity whatsoever. I've given it over a hundred times, and there are so many outside factors which can enter into a test such as that, that it loses all meaning."

"Thank you, sir. Nothing further. Your witness, Mr., uh, Miss . . . the defense may question the witness."

Barnes walked to his familar place at the end of the jury box, scanned the jury with a look that said, "Why are we listening to this clown in the first place?" Then, with his left hand sliding along the railing to the jury box, Barnes approached the witness. "Special Agent Cunningham," he addressed the witness in stern tones before turning much lighter, "do the taxpayers know about you? Really, working yourself into a lather putting the gun together with a dime. Proving what? That a poor man can kill a President? One wonders how many stop watches you burned out doing this fascinating bit of Sherlock Holmes detective work." Barnes then completely turned his back on the witness, leaned on the rail and looked at the jury: "Agent Cunningham, do any of your tests give any indication whatsoever that the man next to the empty chair at the defense table assembled that weapon on November twenty-second?"

"No."

Barnes then faced the witness. "No, indeed. Now, let's talk paraffin. Considering that the test was done on the defendant in this particular case sometime after nine in the evening and that whatever nitrates he would have accumulated in discharging a weapon would have been at least eight hours old, I can see where there is a lack of validity in this case. But your testimony intrigues me. You totally trashed the test—basically worthless, am I correct?"

"Yes."

Barnes now got right in the witness's face: "Yet you gave it over one hundred times? Agent Cunningham, if you, or I, or any member of this jury tried to start an automobile that had no engine, when they got unsatisfactory results, as you suggest are common with such tests, and they knew any future results would be unsatisfactory with an auto with no engine, do you think they would try another one hundred times? I don't . . . and by the way, you never answered my question."

"Which one?"

"Do the taxpayers know about you?" Cunningham looked to the judge, then to Matthews, but Barnes had already walked away. "I have no further questions for this dime-wielding witness," he said over his shoulder.

Matthews looked down at his ever-dwindling list of witnesses, and mentally reviewed their statements, hoping to put somebody on that could say something after the first two FBI men. The only solace he found was that if Barnes was right about the FBI bugging the courtroom, the last two witnesses would soon be pounding a beat in a newly opened Alaskan field office. "The state calls Special Agent Sebastian

F. Latona." A third well-dressed bureaucrat was sworn, gave his background, and Matthews again asked for expert witness designation. Barnes said he had no objections as long as this was *the* fingerprint expert. The designation was agreed to.

"Mr. Latona, I show you this . . . paper bag, which witnesses have testified was found . . ."

Barnes could not resist, and it was a good legal point, besides: "Your Honor, one witness, Lt. Carl Day, testified as to where that bag was found. Best evidence would, of course, be Studebaker Exhibits A, B, C, or D, but the exhibit in question oddly does not appear in any of them. Nor, for that matter, does it appear in any photos of the crime scene."

"Your photographic objections are best held to closing arguments, where they may or may not find a receptive audience. As to the testimony, perhaps Mr. Matthews could rephrase his question . . ."

"Agent Latona, a Dallas crime scene expert testified that he found this bag in the southeast corner of the sixth floor of the Book Depository. The Dallas police were able to find no fingerprints on it. Could you tell us what transpired after you received it at FBI headquarters?"

"Yes. Our first concern was to remove the fingerprint powder which the Dallas officer or officers had used; this was done using the iodine-fuming process. We had hoped, also, to develop prints in that process, but we were not successful. We then used silver nitrate and found one palm print and one fingerprint."

"Can you state who those prints belonged to?"

"Definitively, no. But we did find points of comparison with the three fingerprint cards given to us, of the defendant."

"So the prints on the bag matched the prints on the fingerprint card of the defendant?"

"Yes."

"And you do enough of this work to state that with a certainty?"

"We process between twenty-three thousand and twenty-five thousand fingerprints every three days."

"Objection to the last answer, Your Honor. Irrelevant whether they process one print a month or forty million a day. An identification is an identification. Beyond that, the prosecution is muddying up the waters with statistical trivia. And the answer was nonresponsive to the question as phrased; the witness does not process that many."

"Sustained."

"Could we have CE 3131, please?"

The screens came to life for the first time that afternoon with blowups of palm prints. "Special Agent Latona, will you tell us what you found with respect to the boxes, which were found in the southeast corner of the sixth floor of the Book Depository and configured in such a way that they may have been a seat and rifle rest for a sniper?" Matthews looked to Barnes for an objection, but hearing none, knew he was either on solid ground, or deep trouble.

"In order for me to answer, I would need to show the configuration of the boxes." Matthews asked for Studebaker Exhibits C and D. Latona then spoke, pointing to boxes and describing them as he went along. "In the report I submitted, I designated this box,"—pointing to the one which would logically have been the gun rest—"as Box A. On that box, we found nine fingerprints and four palm prints. One of the fingerprints belonged to the defendant, as did one of the palm prints. Let me rephrase that. One palm print and one fingerprint matched the fingerprint card represented to us as having come from the defendant, and matched in a certain number of points. Here,"—pointing to the box on which the sniper would have sat—"I call this Box D, and that contained two fingerprints, subject unknown, and one palm print which coincided with the palm print allegedly taken from the defendant. Now in this last one, Box C,"—pointing to the box under the gun rest—"there were several prints, but none of the defendant's."

Matthews walked back to the prosecution table, as he had forgotten the exhibit number he wanted introduced, and as he got there, Barnes made a point of telling Oswald, "He hasn't proven anything," hoping Matthews would take the bait. "Your Honor, the prosecution would like CE 3131 admitted."

"Mr. Barnes?"

"Fine with the defense, Your Honor, if it survives cross-examination."

Matthews should have known when to quit, and probably would have, if the fatigue, shock, and disappointment from recent days were not forefront in his mind. "Can you therefore give us your expert opinion, Mr. Latona," he said, across the courtroom, "that the prints you processed without doubt place the defendant at the scene of the crime?" Matthews looked at Barnes.

"No, I cannot. Palm prints are just not as good evidence as fingerprints, and there weren't enough of them, and the suspect did, in fact, work there. Also, since I did not print the suspect, I have to rely on the work of others, and I have a concern there, because the FBI found absolutely nothing—I have to say that again for your understanding—absolutely nothing on the weapon, the shell cases, the unfired shell, or the clip, and that's unusual. Then, a week after the murder, and only then, did we learn that the Dallas people had a palm print from the gun. And I have to tell you, it was very similar—suspiciously so—to the one we developed on Box D."

"Thank you for that clarification, Special Agent. No further questions."

Barnes remained seated but leaned back, as if he were holding back. "Mr. Latona, how many identifiable 'points' are there in a print?"

"Between eighty-five and one hundred twenty-five."

"I thank you for that, inasmuch as I'm sure the jury was unaware of that. Now, sir, when you first spoke with the prosecutor, you spoke of your extensive experience with fingerprints, which I must say is obvious and you are very professional in your presentation. You also indicated that you had testified in court many times with respect to fingerprint evidence. In testimony, sir, how many points are required to be considered a match?"

"Courts usually require twelve."

"Is it not true that in recent years, certain nations of Europe have petitioned the FBI to raise the minimum number of points to sixteen, because with the standard twelve, there is still the possibility of error?"

"That is correct, and the situation is under study."

"Then I ask you, sir, what is the highest number of points you found on any print that you have testified may have come from the defendant?"

"Nine."

Matthews asked Graves, "Do we ever get a break?"

"Would you go to court, ordinarily, with nine?"

"No. The testimony I have given is from the expert standpoint. On sheer interpretation, if nine is all I have, then there's no i.d. That is why I hedged everything said earlier—I'm giving my opinion."

"You testified that three sets of fingerprint cards were submitted. From where?"

"Well, the Dallas police certainly took one . . ."

"And the other two?"

"I have no knowledge relevant to the other two."

"For what it is worth, sir, the defense does . . . and FBI agents took the prints. As defense witnesses will demonstrate, sir," Barnes told the witness. "You may have to be recalled to give expert testimony with regard to that, Mr. Latona. As a matter of policy, does the FBI have a right to fingerprint a suspect while comatose in a hospital?"

"Only persons taken into custody for federal violations as such."

"What federal law had the defendant been charged with breaking?"

"None that I know of."

"You testified that you checked the weapon and found no prints, whatsoever?"

"That is correct. I even had a technician take that cheap old weapon apart . . ."

Matthews interrupted. "Objection to the 'cheap old weapon' characterization."

Barnes regained the initiative. "The man is a prosecution witness, and an expert, Your Honor. He even dazzled us with the number of thousands of prints per day the FBI handles. I suspect that in his work he's dealt more with guns than with any other tangible objects, and I would ask that the characterization stand."

"Overruled, Mr. Matthews."

"The cheap old weapon was taken apart?" Barnes let the jury hear the comment as part of his question.

"Having studied the entire weapon, no latent prints were developed."

"Mr. Latona, is it odd—or does it strike you as odd, that the weapon you checked was, by your own testimony, free of prints, yet the person who allegedly fired it was found, by a police officer, several floors below the alleged assassination window, within seventy-five seconds?"

"Objection, Your Honor; conclusionary in an area in which the witness is not an expert."

"Mr. Barnes?"

"Your Honor, we have had testimony—expert testimony, from Lieutenant Day, that suggested it was time consuming to wipe a gun totally clean of fingerprints, thus making the seventy-five second figure difficult to match up to known facts about the defendant's whereabouts in the Book Depository. We now have a fingerprint expert to testify, and an expert at that."

"I would allow fingerprint testimony, but Mr. Matthews is on solid ground with respect to this witness giving expert characterizations about escape times."

"Mr. Latona, we have heard testimony that it would take roughly twenty to thirty seconds to wipe a rifle—the stock, the trigger housing, all those little parts, clean. Would you agree with that assessment?"

"Yes. If you asked me 'Could it happen?' To wipe a gun that clean—spotless, takes time. But on the other hand, Lord knows what went on with the Dallas authorities. For all I know, in their haste to find prints, they cleaned the gun. So I can't give you a precise answer there, I'm sorry to say."

"That's okay. It's obvious that you are working to arrive at the truth, and that's why we're here. Now, you spoke of a total of thirteen prints, possibly two from the defendant, on Box A, the box the weapon might have rested on. Were you able to discover who owned the other eleven prints?"

"No."

"Was no effort made to fingerprint the other Depository stockboys?"

"Oh, no. They were printed. The prints on the box did not match up to any of them."

"Now *that* is interesting. One last question, sir. If there was no evidence other than your expert testimony on these prints, is that enough, in your mind, to convict an individual?"

"Not with the limited number of identifiable points and the presence of other, nonidentifiable prints. Plus a spotless gun."

"Correction . . . a spotless cheap old weapon. No further questions at this time, but subject to recall, Mr. Latona."

Matthews asked the judge for a moment to confer, then spoke briefly to Vincent and Graves. "Look, it's getting late in the afternoon, and we're going nowhere today. Who's available that is not gun related?"

Vincent and Graves looked through their witness lists and Vincent was the first to speak up: "Harry Holmes, the postal inspector, and Paul Stombaugh, the FBI lab expert on hair and fiber."

"Not counting gun experts, that's it?"

"That's exactly it," Graves volunteered, seemingly willing to share the heat with Vincent.

"A Hobson's choice, really," Matthews thought out loud. "If we go with Holmes, he'll tell the court about Oswald's little peculiarities of having post office boxes wherever he went, and knowing how cheap Oswald was—or had to be, Barnes will have the jury convinced that the postal boxes were of a surreptitious nature . . . and I'd believe him. So Holmes is out. Which leaves us with another FBI expert, God help us. Can he add anything?"

"He'll win as much as he'll lose, Ray, but at this point, we need whatever we can put in the record. I think it's going to take all those gun people, all at once tomorrow, to convince one juror of anything. So I would say accumulate here and there—but not Holmes—and make quantity sound like quality in final summation."

"I like the logic," Matthews told Graves, "but I don't like to play odds that long. On the other hand, it's the only game in town." Matthews paused, told his assistants to put on confident faces, then called Special Agent Paul M. Stombaugh.

Following the by now familiar preliminaries, Matthews requested an expert designation, and Dean answered that the defense had no objection. The confusion of spokespersons by the defense was beginning to get under Matthews's skin, but he sensed that was its purpose.

"Agent Stombaugh, did the crime laboratory of the Federal Bureau of Investigation, under your direction, conduct tests on the blanket found in the Paine garage?"

"We did."

Barnes wrote a note on his pad and let everyone at the table see it: "All Paine materials have been excluded. This will be fun when it's our turn."

Matthews, intent on the case and somehow seeing the famous blanket as an entity unto itself and not just more of the "Paine evidence," pushed ahead. "Please tell the court what you found."

"Obvious wear, some creases, and some human hairs."

"Were you able to match the human hairs?"

"Well, I found limb, pubic, and head hairs. Of the limb and pubic hairs I removed from the blanket, several matched Oswald's in all observable microscopic characteristics and could have originated from Oswald."

"Turning now to this exhibit, CE 673. Do you recognize this, Agent Stombaugh?"

"Yes, that is the shirt we received from Dallas on November twenty-third, 1963. It was missing the top two buttons and contained a hole in the elbow."

"Could we have CE 674, 675, and 676, one at a time, please?" As each appeared, the witness told how they were microphotographs showing the "match" of the fibers taken from the shirt, CE 673, with a tuft of fibers found in the butt plate of the weapon, the Mannlicher-Carcano, serial number C2766.

"Turning now to the paper bag found in the southeast corner window of the sixth floor of the Book Depository, what did you find with respect to that?"

"There was nothing on the exterior of the bag except fingerprint powder," the witness answered matter-of-factly. "Fibers inside the bag, however, matched the Paine blanket, although there were only a small number of such fibers. The number was so small as to make any identification tentative."

"But you are able to say that the bag contained blanket fibers, the rifle showed fibers from the defendant's shirt, and the defendant's hair was found in the blanket?"

"Well, yes, those were stated conclusions."

"No further questions, Agent Stombaugh. Thank you for your expert testimony."

Barnes walked slowly to the witness stand and began his questioning very softly, almost as if he was sharing a secret with the witness: "You had no way of knowing, did you, Agent Stombaugh, that the blanket found at the Paine residence had already been excluded from evidence?"

"I had no idea."

"The prosecutor did," Barnes reminded him.

Matthews was up again. "Need I remind defense counsel, you had the right to object. You allowed that testimony into evidence."

"I wanted the testimony, Mr. Matthews. We'll all deal with the evidence soon." Then, back to the witness, "So, the hair samples that you found. How do you know they match up to the defendant?"

"Hair samples were taken from him."

"Including, I assume, CE 672, which I do *not* want on the screens, please, an exhibit entitled 'Lee Oswald's pubic hairs'?"

"That is correct."

"Do you have any personal knowledge, or were documents forwarded with these hair samples to indicate that the defendant gave his consent to having various parts of his anatomy shaved in this manner?"

"No. I assumed—"

"We're not here to discuss your assumptions about evidence, Agent Stombaugh, but rather your deductions and opinions. Now, you told us that the hair found in the blanket was the defendant's. Could it have been anybody else's?"

"Absolutely. They could have come from the defendant, or from other Caucasians of similar hair classifications."

"Which narrows down the hunt to everyone in this courtroom, except Mrs. Martinez." Barnes paced down in front of the jurors. "Agent Stombaugh, did you find any oil, or any-thing similar—expended cordite powder—anything to indi-cate that the blanket we are discussing ever contained a rifle?"

"No."

"But it did contain human hairs, indicating that, crazy as it may sound, somebody perhaps slept in it?"

"It contained hairs, some possibly belonging to the defen-dant, and others which clearly did not belong to him."

"And the butt of the rifle contained fibers from the shirt, CE 673, which was the shirt seen in every newspaper *after* the defendant was arrested?"

"I can't say about the newspapers, but the rifle contained fibers from CE 673."

"It's a shame that the defendant didn't wear that shirt to work that morning. Do you find that odd, Agent Stombaugh, because I do. The FBI gets a gun and a shirt and announces a match. But the shirt was only put on at one o'clock."

"Your Honor," Matthews interrupted, "that has only been suggested in testimony."

"If it please the court, Your Honor, Officer Baker has testi-fied that the shirt worn by the defendant when encountered by Officer Baker was *not* the one he was wearing when ar-rested. We have had no 'suggestions of testimony' to the con-trary."

Judge Davis indicated the record spoke for itself and coun-sel could move on.

"Thank you, Your Honor," Barnes said, to convey to the jury the idea that he had just won something.

"Agent Stombaugh, did you examine the shirt, particularly in the upper, shoulder areas, to determine where the tuft of fibers could have come from?"

"No."

"Did you find any debris, gunpowder residue, or oil on the shirt?"

"No."

"Did you look?"

"Yes. Thoroughly."

"Did you find hair samples or blanket fibers on the rifle?"

"No."

"Could we have CE 2404, please?" This time, the screen took a while to come to life, but Barnes didn't mind as long as a prosecution witness was sitting there nervously. "Do you recognize this, Agent Stombaugh?"

"No."

"As you, and the jury, can see, it lists hair samples, fingernail scrapings, and such conclusions as you told us, including the fact that the hairs came from Oswald, 'or from another Caucasian person whose limb and pubic hairs exhibit the same individual microscopic characteristics.' Your Honor, I'd like CE 2404, as well as CE 673, 674, 675, and 676 admitted at this time, and I have no further questions for the witness, but subject to recall."

"The items are admitted. Mr. Matthews?"

"Your Honor, inasmuch as the hour is becoming late, and conditions may still be hazardous, I would like to petition the court to end our labors a little early today."

"Any problems with that, Mr. Barnes?"

"No, Your Honor."

"Court is then adjourned for the day. Safe trip home, everyone," the judge concluded, maintaining the radio charade started earlier in the day.

Oswald was lead away, the prosecutors had left, and Barnes, Dean, and Jeffries were left at the defense table. Aware of the microphones, they spoke softly, with Dean stating the obvious: "It's rifles tomorrow, Eddie."

"Which will make the whole day worth getting up for," Barnes answered.

# Ten

Thursday, January 14, 1965. A warm front had softened the snow, which was about the way Matthews had viewed his case: once a solid snowman, it was now oozing slush and quickly losing recognizable form. He knew, as he trudged into court, however, that a good day today could regain some lost ground, particularly if he was being honest with himself when he shifted priorities and began talking about a hung jury. The worst that could happen was that he could possibly finish up today and announce those blessed words, "The prosecution rests." His eight days of watching witnesses get chopped would be over. Barnes could no doubt run through what little he had in a few days, and Matthews might even get a little payback.

Matthews was the last of the attorneys to arrive, and in his absence, Barnes had orchestrated a faceoff with Eaton Graves. While Carolyn Jeffries made small talk to Earl Vincent, Barnes tried to get coffee grounds out of his cup and complained to the waiting Graves that the coffee machine was worse than the prosecution's case. "Be kind, Eddie," Graves had answered. "We really thought Dallas was handing us a neat little package with a ribbon on it. It just didn't turn out to be that tidy, that's all. The jury's still got to decide, and we've still got witnesses."

"Bupkis is what you've got, Eaton. Witnesses? More FBI stooges? Where are the Secret Service, Fritz, Curry, Wade? Don't you think the jury is going to find it odd that none of them were ever heard from?"

"What can they contribute?" Graves asked, sincerely curious.

"At this point, Eaton, nothing. I'll give you that. But they were at least *there*. Seeing a few of the S.S. say that the shots came from right rear is more significant than somebody you're going to put on the stand to testify that he fired bullets through goat carcasses to test ballistics. I'm telling you, Eaton, up front, today is going to be a rout. Make no mistake about it. Your experts are going to kill you. And if you put Drain on the stand—and I actually liked him when we worked together—your case goes down the drain. I won't even need a defense. Remember I warned you, and good luck with the coffee machine." Carolyn Jeffries rejoined Barnes at the defense table and quietly asked if Graves bought the strategy. Barnes answered that they didn't have much choice, but the decision would be up to the "big fish" then trudging his way into the courtroom.

Graves immediately went to speak with Matthews, repeating Barnes's warning about FBI Agent Vince Drain. Matthews didn't like the smell of it, but Graves reminded him that Barnes had warned them about Dr. Hartogs, and that had been a disaster. "That's what troubles me, Eaton. He warned us about Hartogs, true enough. But did you ever think that there might be one witness he really does not want up there, and a similar warning might throw us off?"

"That slick s.o.b. He almost had me fooled. That's why you call the shots, Ray." Graves privately remained unconvinced.

Once everyone was settled in, Matthews began the day by announcing, "The state calls Special Agent Lyndal Shaneyfelt," and then quickly looked at the defense table where Barnes and Dean were once again shaking their heads "no." Matthews was almost hoping for a "yes" to take the mystery out of this situation.

Matthews began establishing the background with this older, but typically well-groomed FBI specialist, who claimed that he had been doing FBI document and photograph work since 1937, and when asked how many such examinations he had made, he initially said, "one hundred," but then amended it to "between one hundred and three hundred." Matthews then routinely asked that Shaneyfelt be designated an expert witness.

"Any objections, Mr. Barnes?"

Barnes caught Matthews off guard. "Every objection, Your Honor. The witness has already provided affidavits and testimony to both the local officials in the original venue, and to the President's Commission, but much of the material he testified with reference to has already been excluded. Secondly, he told us of one hundred cases—that was his first, nonamended answer—one hundred cases in twenty-eight years. That boils down to just over three and a half cases *per year;* now I get my teeth cleaned four times a year, but that doesn't make me a dentist." Barnes knew the joke would hurt the witness with the jury, but the judge wouldn't buy it, so he came very quickly back to the point: "And finally, we have absurdly contradictory testimony that makes me question his validity as a witness, much less an expert. Before the President's Commission, he gave Shaneyfelt Exhibit number 26, with reference to the curbstone allegedly hit by a stray bullet on November twenty-second. In that exhibit, he claimed that the curbstone in question could not be located because rain or street cleaning had washed away the evidence of a bullet hitting a curbstone. Then, in Shaneyfelt 27, the very next exhibit, he has found the curbstone, *assumed* that the shot which hit it came from the so-called sniper's nest rather than doing some real investigative work and finding out where the path pointed, and told the composition of the bullet stain. This is not an expert, Your Honor. It's a three hundred dollar suit with a cute story to tell the jury."

Matthews could hear Graves telling him that Barnes had predicted a rout today. The judge asked the witness if Barnes's statement was correct, and he puffed out his chest and said it was, and that he was prepared to stand on it.

"And so you shall, but not as an expert. Proceed, Mr. Matthews."

Matthews, chastened more by the witness's obstinacy than by Barnes or Judge Davis, quickly lead the witness through the re-creation of the assassination, in which each frame of the Zapruder film was re-created, with stand-ins for the President and the governor. It was learned that Kennedy's back was exposed during one frame, frame 185, but otherwise was not a target until frame 210, at a distance of one hundred seventy-four point nine feet from the rifle, assumed to be in the sixth floor window of the Depository, and that the angle of the rifle to the President would have been twenty-one degrees, fifty minutes at frame 210. It was further ascertained that in frame 313, the one showing the President struck in the head, the distance was two hundred sixty-five point three feet from the rifle, at a slightly lesser angle. He further testified that the curb would have been hit at frame 410, and added in passing that the car was traveling at an average of eleven point two miles per hour.

"And when you did find the curb, sir, what did your analysis of it show?" Matthews asked.

"It was spectrographically determined to be essentially lead with a trace of antimony," he answered precisely.

"And in your judgment, it was the last shot fired from the window?"

"Objection, conclusionary *and* without proper foundation."

"Sustained on both counts. We've got to do a little better than that, Counselor," Judge Davis told Matthews. Matthews didn't mind the complaint; the jury had heard the word "window."

"I apologize for my choice of words in the heat of the moment, Your Honor. No further questions."

Barnes was tempted just to say "No questions," but he didn't care for the witness's arrogance, and he'd seen enough of that in his own FBI career. "Mr. Shaneyfelt, I show you CE 399, which, by the prosecutor's own words is the single most important piece of evidence. Getting past the fact that it is six point five caliber, would you describe this missile to the jury?"

"Standard military issue copper-jacketed round."

"Copper-jacketed?" Barnes asked rhetorically. "Mrs. Martinez, would you please read back the witness's answer to the question regarding the chemical composition of the curb?"

". . . spectrographically determined to be essentially lead with a trace of antimony."

"Thank you, Mrs. Martinez. No copper whatsoever found on that curb—yes or no?"

"No."

"Thank you. Now about this simulation of the positions. Why the fake car?"

"I don't understand your question."

"I think you do, and very well so, Mr. Shaneyfelt. The President was riding in a new-model deep blue Lincoln convertible when he was killed. All your simulation photos are of two actors—and the governor's stand-in must have been a contortionist—sitting in a 1956 *Cadillac* convertible."

"I still don't see your point."

"My point is apparently obvious to everyone in this room except you, sir. A 1956 Cadillac and a 1961 Lincoln are not identical automobiles. I can submit supporting specifications to the court. And don't tell me you didn't know they were *not* the same. I also don't want to hear that the simulation approaches perfection, because the cars are different—in size, height, location of seats to fixed points, and in other areas as well."

Matthews objected to Barnes's tone: "Your Honor, he's badgering the witness."

"The witness's responses invite such questions, Counselor. In the meantime, Mr. Barnes, can we turn the volume down slightly?"

"Sorry, sir. Mr. Shaneyfelt, why wasn't the Lincoln used?"

"It was not available."

Judge Davis leaned over the bench and told the witness to answer the question posed by Mr. Barnes.

"The Lincoln had been sent, shortly after November twenty-second, back to Detroit. It was virtually rebuilt from the ground up."

"Before it was sent out, was any person representing the defendant's rights in this matter allowed to examine that automobile?"

"I have no way of knowing that."

"One last thought. How long, in real time, is the difference between frame 313, about which you testified, and frame 410, about which you hypothesized?"

"About five and one quarter seconds."

"And you want this jury—these fourteen men who have heard evidence that I know you are totally ignorant of—you want them to believe that someone, in your view a shooter in the sixth floor window, fired a shot five seconds after the President's head exploded? The President was prone on the back seat—he was no longer a target. So who was? Mrs. Kennedy? Clint Hill?"

"I have no idea."

"Indeed. Excused. Your Honor, I would like Shaneyfelt number 27, both the photograph and the accompanying report, admitted at this time."

"Mr. Matthews, do you have any objection to having *your* witness's documents admitted?"

"Certainly not, Your Honor." After a brief pause, he called Dr. Vincent Guinn to the stand. At the defense table, Carolyn Jeffries put her coat on and left, and this time, Barnes and Dean nodded their heads, "Yes."

Barnes rose. "Your Honor, while we are waiting for this next witness, inasmuch as the pathology testimony seems to be concluded, the defense at this time would like to admit the document, CE 2011, presented earlier at the conclusion of the testimony of FBI Agent Todd, Reference Rifle Bullet C1, which indicated that, when interviewed by FBI Agents Bardwell Odum or Elmer Lee Todd, Darrell C. Tomlinson and O.P. Wright of Parkland Hospital, Special Agent Richard C. Johnsen of the Secret Service, and James Rowley, Chief of the United States Secret Service, were all unable to identify the pristine bullet which we have been discussing, CE 399. Based on the clear and obvious lack of chain of possession found in that report, I would move that CE 399, the pristine bullet allegedly discovered at Parkland Hospital, be excluded from evidence at this time."

"Mr. Matthews?"

"Your Honor, the prosecution is clearly at a loss here. There is only one bullet under consideration, CE 399. Mr.

Tomlinson found a bullet, passed it to his supervisor, Mr. O.P. Wright, who then turned it over to Secret Service Agent Johnsen at the hospital. Agent Johnsen returned with the group that departed Love Field, reported to his headquarters, gave the bullet to his ultimate superior, Mr. Rowley, who then passed it to Special Agent Todd, who then initialed it. Agent Todd identified it."

"Four generations of identification too late. If the others don't identify it—all of them, Agent Todd might as well have initialed a cannonball," Barnes added.

"The defense is on solid ground here, Mr. Matthews. The exhibit is excluded. Carson, let's swear in this obviously bewildered Dr. Guinn." Guinn, slightly shaken by the dramatic exchange that took place during his entrance, was sworn, and established as an expert witness.

Matthews moved right to the attack with the witness: "Dr. Guinn, can you briefly tell us about your scientific specialty, neutron activation analysis?"

The witness began to speak in highly technical language, and had to be reminded by Matthews that it was urgent that everyone in the courtroom be able to understand the process. In essence, he was telling the witness to speak English and calling the jury stupid, but he got away with it. The witness then explained that if a given substance is bombarded with neutrons, it will yield a given, observable chemical result. If a similar substance is tested, similar results should follow. Different substance, different results. In all, a very precise science which was emerging in many ways, one of which was in the area of police work. "Though I am not, I confess, a policeman," Guinn concluded.

"I show you CE 843, fragments of bullets found in the presidential limousine, Dr. Guinn—"

"Your Honor," Barnes began slowly, "let the record show that we are all accepting in good faith that those fragments came from the presidential limousine. There has been no testimony, and no documentation, and given the handling we've seen consistently with regard to evidence in this case, those pieces in CE 843 could be most any bullet fragments, though my sense of skepticism inclines me to believe that they originated sometime as Mannlicher-Carcano ammunition."

"Do you wish to make an objection, Mr. Barnes?" the judge asked.

"No, Your Honor, as I said, I just want the record to show that this evidence was introduced without foundation."

"Proceed, Mr. Matthews."

"What did your tests show with respect to the CE 843 fragments?"

"It is my conclusion that it is highly probable that they came from two bullets, and that they were of Mannlicher-Carcano origin."

"Doctor, are those tests reflected in this FBI report which shows that there were no significant differences found in the various fragments?"

"Yes," the witness answered quickly, as if it were an answer the prosecution did not want to hear.

"Thank you very much, Doctor," said a confused Matthews. "No further questions."

Barnes asked for, and was granted, a moment with Bob Dean, to stall until Carolyn Jeffries returned. After stalling as long as possible with small talk, Barnes was told to proceed. He then rehashed the essence of neutron activation analysis with the witness, drawing out its precision as a testing vehicle. Playing the part of the doubting nonscientist, Barnes asked questions to make sure the jury understood exactly how the procedure worked, including the margin for error. The witness assured him that there was none—that was the beauty of this new endeavor. In all, it was a time-consuming but worthwhile process, as Barnes knew jurors were impressed by phrases like "scientifically proven." Matthews let Barnes drone on, as he was confident with Guinn's bona fides and testimony.

"So," Barnes concluded, "you test a sample of an item, and you get a very exacting, precise readout?"

"That's correct."

"Then, Doctor, if you tested something else, and the readout was not identical, that would indicate that the substance was not identical to the earlier substance tested?"

"Also correct," Guinn answered. "See, it's really easy to understand."

"Indeed it is," Barnes answered him. "Because a while ago,

to refresh the jury's recollection since I took you on that scientific detour, you testified that the fragments you tested exhibited 'no significant differences.' That statement hints that
there were, in fact, *differences,* which, although they may not
be significant, are differences nevertheless and your testimony just a few moments ago told how exact and precise this
work is."

"There were differences in the samples. The FBI chose the
wording of their report. 'No significant differences' is an interesting wordplay, as you discovered, Counselor." Barnes
was satisfied. Matthews now understood why Guinn had answered "yes" the way he had. At that moment Jeffries came
back into the courtroom carrying a moderate-sized grocery
bag.

"Dr. Guinn, did you encounter any difficulties or any unusual circumstances in conducting these tests on which the
prosecution is basing their case?"

"Well, I was told to make a comparison of some small fragments—the ones described in CE 843 are sizable portions of
bullets. But I was asked to make comparisons of smaller
fragments, and when the materials were delivered to me, I
found myself opening empty boxes."

"Empty boxes?"

"Just that. Two, perhaps three containers holding nothing
but air. I even used a tiny magnet like a vacuum cleaner, and
there was literally no metal in any of those containers. I don't
have any idea what they wanted me to test."

"I see. . . . Well, with the fragments you did test, those
which showed 'no significant differences,' could you tell the
gun which fired them?"

"No. Ballistics is not part of this. This is to determine similarity."

"And the FBI, in reporting 'no significant differences,' was
essentially, then, reporting differences?"

"That's the way it works."

Barnes went and got the grocery bag at the end of the defense table. "Let's test out your science, Doctor, in a way that
everyone in this courtroom can understand. You've spoken of
matching samples and similarities, so . . ."—Barnes
reached into the bag and withdrew a quart of milk, in a stan-

dard red and white container. "As an expert witness, Doctor, can you identify this?"

Guinn knew he was being put on, but not why, so he played along: "My expertise suggests that's a quart of milk." Matthews wanted to object, but he'd been burned too many times, and he was still mentally sprinting to the point where he could say "The prosecution rests."

Barnes then walked back to the defense table with the quart of milk in his hand, put the bag down, and removed from it a second, similarly packaged quart of milk. He then returned to the witness stand. "Doctor, in my left hand here is milk you identified. Would you care to hazard your professional opinion again as to what is in my right hand?"

"Again my expertise suggests it's a quart of milk."

"I'll only trouble you with one more question," Barnes said, walking to the end of the jury box with both quarts of milk very available for the jury to see. Then he turned to the witness and said quietly but sternly, "Identified as similar; certainly look similar. Doctor, did they come from the same cow?"

Matthews objected now, but it was all lost on Barnes, who had returned the cartons to the grocery bag and had indicated that he had no further questions. The judge instructed the jury, several of whom were laughing, to pay no attention to the defense's theatrics. Matthews had no redirect.

Matthews then called "FBI Ballistics expert Robert A. Frazier." As the Vermont trooper headed for the door, a stare from Barnes told him that fireworks were coming, and Barnes rose to light the fuse. "Your Honor, the defense will object to every question asked of this witness, unless it is established that the ballistics tests conducted were done in Dallas, with the assistance of the local authorities there."

"I don't see the difficulty, Mr. Barnes," the judge answered.

"I allowed the last witness to testify without foundation, Your Honor. Fragments allegedly found in a car that the defense never saw—not even the Dallas police ever saw that presidential limousine for the sake of evidence gathering. Now here's a Washington, D.C., lab expert who is going to testify, and the prosecution has not shown that the weapon in question ever got to Washington. It was seized as evidence on the sixth floor of a building in Dallas, Texas. If someone is going to testify about that gun based on their experience in Washington, there has to be foundation."

"Mr. Matthews, I'm inclined to agree."

Matthews turned to Graves and Vincent: "Now we know why he tried to con us into sending Vince Drain home. He took the gun to the FBI lab. This, gentleman, is the moment we get some payback." Turning to face the court, Matthews announced that Special Agent Frazier would be called *subsequent to* the testimony of *Special Agent Vincent Drain.* Barnes knew he had sprung the trap.

Special Agent Drain was sworn, relieved of his service revolver, and there were no questions of bona fides or expertise. Matthews came right to the point: "Agent Drain, do you recognize this weapon, a Mannlicher-Carcano six point five mm Italian carbine?"

"Yes, sir."

"Agent Drain, did you transport this weapon, by government aircraft, sometime after midnight on November twenty-third, 1963, from Dallas, Texas, to the FBI lab in Washington, D.C., and return it sometime after midnight on November twenty-fourth, 1963, to Dallas?"

"Yes, I did." Matthews was satisfied. "I would now like once again, to call Special Agent Robert A. Frazier, FBI ballistics expert."

"Do you recall anything in law school about something called cross-examination, Mr. Matthews?" Barnes asked.

Matthews turned red and apologized, insisting, however that the facts were clear as presented by the witness.

Barnes put both hands in his pants pockets and approached the witness with his head down, as if lost for words but needing to say something, not just let the witness go unchallenged. Matthews figured Barnes was trapped. Barnes appeared to start to say something, halted, started again, halted again, then finally spoke softly into the microphone connected to the room where the television screens were activated, "Could you please prepare, but *not* show, the two pages of Decker 5323 on form 127, please." Barnes then slowly ambled to the evidence table to make sure that enough time was taken that the exhibit would be ready when needed. He returned to the witness stand holding the rifle. "Agent Drain, just a few moments ago, the jury saw the prosecutor, Mr. Matthews, tell you exactly what this rifle was, and in response, you nodded your head and said, 'Yes, sir.' I'm not going to repeat that charade, but I am going to ask you to tell us what this weapon is."

Drain seemed bored by the question. "It's an Italian made, Mannlicher-Carcano carbine, caliber six point five."

Barnes, holding the weapon at the end of the witness stand, wanted one more bit of cheese in the trap. "I'm sorry, Special Agent," he began, patronizingly, "your voice trailed off at the end there, 'Mannlicher Carcano carbine . . .'?"

"Caliber six point five," Drain repeated, loudly.

"Caliber six point five," Barnes echoed. "Could we please have those exhibits now?" Barnes walked to the defense table, still holding the rifle, and, after a glance at Matthews, and one at Dean which asked "Go for it?" he addressed the judge: "Your Honor, the defense moves to quash the indictment in this case. As you can see on the screens, the reports indicate that the main charge, the murder of the President, as well as the collateral charge, the attempted murder of the governor of Texas, are both predicated on a weapon described in those respective documents as, quote six point two five Italian rifle. There's no indication of the type of rifle, nor the serial number, so we are not even availed the presumption of a clerical error. Clearly, the witness has indicated that this is not the gun. I see no point in going forward with this case."

Matthews stared dumbfounded at the screen nearest him, as two documents, charging the defendant with the two crimes committed on Elm Street, clearly indicated that the weapon was a six point two five Italian rifle. The judge, as did Barnes, knew it was a clerical error, but that wasn't Barnes's problem. Davis knew it was his. "I'll see the attorneys of record in my chambers immediately," he announced, with the word "immediately" being intoned while he was already in motion.

Matthews knew he couldn't let Barnes say any more, but he couldn't know that Barnes set this trap to lose, knowing he would win the next round, which was more important.

"Judge Davis," Matthews began, searching for the perfect phrase which just didn't seem to come, "we all have to see this for what it was: a clerical error made in haste. We've seen enough examples of how business was done that day in Dallas to know that they were far from perfectionists."

"It's obvious you've suffered through your share of other people's mistakes in the last few days, Ray, but the simple fact is that the charge is murder and attempted murder with a six point two five rifle. And if it had to come down to a textbook ruling right here and now, I'd quash the indictment, release a scathing report of incompetence—present company excluded, and I'd convene a grand jury which would have the choice of examining all the evidence all over again, and go from there. So understand, Ray, I take this most seriously." Then to Barnes: "Obviously you didn't just discover that document last evening, did you, Mr. Barnes? And you don't really expect it to work, do you?"

"Worth a shot," Barnes answered, tongue in cheek.

"Here's the bottom line, boys. Mr. Barnes, as you may already suspect, Texans know a little about guns. As it happens, there is no such thing, to my knowledge, as a six point two five caliber rifle. Now if you can show the court that there is, Mr. Barnes, I'll rule favorably on your motion. But I don't think that's your intention. You're trying to cloud the water for those fourteen good old boys on the jury out there so they do my job of ending this trial, once and for all."

"Just doing my job," Barnes said quietly.

"I wouldn't expect less," the judge complimented him. "I only wish those Dallas clowns had been as thorough. So, we're going to assume it's a typo, because there's no such gun, but I will instruct the jury, in my charge, that they are to consider that six point two five allegation in their deliberations. In the meantime, I have to rule against the motion to quash."

"I fully understand," Barnes said, evenly.

"Thank you, Your Honor," Matthews said, wondering why Barnes was taking it so well.

"Don't thank me, Ray. Thank all the taxpayers that would have your butt if this trial, after this expense, got kicked today. I'm here for their interests, too. And remember—etch it into your mind—this trial would be over right now if such a gun existed." The last sentence was music to Barnes's ears.

Once back in court, the judge explained his decision to the remaining attorneys and the jury, commenting openly on the sloppiness of the presentation made by the Dallas authorities. Both Barnes and Matthews thought the remarks helped their case. "You may continue with the witness, Mr. Barnes."

"Oh, yes. Agent Drain, I'd almost forgotten." Barnes was about to ask a question when Drain answered, "Yes, Drain. I'm not going to be your whipping boy on that last stunt." The judge then chided the witness, but Barnes asked that the comment be kept in the record.

"As you wish."

"Now, Agent Drain, you testified that this was the gun that you transported to and from Dallas, Texas, to the FBI lab in November, 1963. On what basis do you make that statement?"

"I recognize it."

"That's great—what detective work. 'I recognize it.' Thousands—hundreds of thousands of these were produced, Agent Drain, yet you can recognize this one from all the rest. Did you mark the weapon with your initials for identification?"

"No."

"Please tell the court, if there were no federal laws violated by someone allegedly using this weapon on November twenty-second, what business of yours it was to snatch this gun away from the legally constituted authorities—bad enough the body was taken—where's your justification?"

"The FBI, through the director, had—"

"The director would be who?"

Drain was becoming hostile, as Barnes hoped. "Mr. J. Edgar Hoover is the director, and you know that as a former agent." Drain said "former agent" as one might say "leper."

"Oh, yes. Mr. Hoover. So he had . . . you were saying?"

Drain continued, "The director had made available all the resources of the bureau to help in this investigation."

"Did the FBI have jurisdiction?"

"No," Drain replied, calming down a bit.

"Then please tell the court," Barnes instructed, voice rising, "which officers of the Dallas police or the Dallas county sheriff's office, who *did have jurisdiction,* accompanied you *and the weapon* for those twenty-plus hours when it made its first trip out of Dallas, Texas."

"Nobody. I took it, I delivered it."

"Thank you, Agent Drain. You are excused. I don't mean to presume, but I doubt the prosecution will have any redirect. Your Honor, the defense moves to exclude this rifle from evidence, as its time spent in the sole possession of this agent, without proper marking or accompanying officers with jurisdiction, clearly taints it."

Matthews's thoughts raced back to his prediction about the pedigree of Oswald's shirt when it went to Washington with Special Agent Drain. Drain, meanwhile, rose in the witness stand and lashed out at Barnes, only to be told by Judge Davis to apologize or face a contempt citation. Drain apologized, and concluded with calm, sincere remarks that he was only trying to do his job. Barnes accepted the apology and told Drain that everyone in the room felt the same way about doing a job.

"Mr. Barnes, that motion presents this court with a very deep concern. There is certainly a basis for it. If accepted, there might be recourse for the discussion just held in chambers to go the other way. And given the law, I don't know of a way to reject this. The earlier situation we could find as clerical. But this is chain of possession, and clear cut. Mr. Matthews, I need to think this through. We will meet in my chambers—all attorneys, at nine tomorrow morning, and a decision will be reached on the motion at that time. The jury will be excused for the day. Court is adjourned until ten A.M. tomorrow." The gavel sounded—for the first time at the end of a session.

Matthews looked at Barnes with contempt. "I warned your boy about Drain, Ray," Barnes told him.

"Who listens?" Matthews answered, brushing past.

# Eleven

Friday, January fifteenth, 1965. For Barnes, it began unusually early: 12:01 A.M., to be exact, because for the first time since he had heard of Lee Harvey Oswald, Barnes had difficulty sleeping. Initially, he tried to pass it off as a combination of things: the letdown that comes when you know the end of a trial is in sight, but the adrenaline continues to flow even then, sending the body confusing signals; a gnawing uncertainty that Davis would rule against the exclusion of the rifle, something that Barnes had counted on; the bugging of the courthouse, no doubt.

Suddenly, Barnes's nervous system felt like it had been sandpapered. He knew of Vince Drain before this trial, and knew the man had a reputation as a good agent and decent person. So why would he, of all people, explode in front of a jury? Barnes could feel the hair on his arms bristling.

He gave up all pretense of sleeping, got dressed, drove to a phone booth a couple of miles away, and called home collect, instantly upsetting his wife, who was immediately concerned at being awakened. Barnes first calmed her, then told her to get a pad and pencil.

"I don't want you to panic, but I'm concerned, so listen carefully, write it down, and implement the plan first thing in the morning. Drop the boys at school, like always. Go into the school and speak to the person who lives up the block from us (who was the guidance counselor) and explain to him that under no circumstances are those kids to leave at 3:10 with anyone but you. Then get home and pack a few things for the boys and yourself. Go where we spent Easter Sunday . . . do you remember whose house that was? Don't answer, just remember . . . cigar smoke and a cat that sheds? I'll call you there after court later today, or I'll be there later today if my schedule will let me. Also, assume that the home phone, the one you're on now, is bugged. I can't answer all the questions I know you have. Don't worry. I miss you and the kids and I'll try to see you in a few hours. And stop crying. It will be okay . . . maybe it's just my usual paranoia, but please do as I asked until I talk to you again. Now get some sleep . . . oh, I'm sorry I forgot . . . I love you, kid."

Barnes was the one weeping when he hung up his end, but he drove back to the hotel, convinced himself that nobody had been in his room in his absence, and eventually got to sleep. Daylight nevertheless came quickly.

Although Barnes and Matthews, except for legal degrees, were essentially opposites, the evening hours were just as difficult for Ray Matthews. Unable to sleep, he paced his den and wondered about many things: the unfairness of it all, the loss of face he, and more importantly, his well-connected wife and corporate lawyer sons might have to endure, and how it could have been avoided. His ruminations stopped there. Was Barnes a genius, or was he just an actor, amidst the stage props that he spoke of in the defense's opening statement? No group of cops, detectives, and police authorities could bungle something so badly. Unless they knew there would not be a trial.

That concept got Matthews on the phone. He first called Graves and Vincent and told them to wake up anybody they could possibly think of who had not testified and see if anything was still available. His final marching orders had been "not to sound out of breath or at the end of your rope." Then Matthews personally called the leading Dallas names, beginning with Henry Wade, who couldn't understand why Oswald hadn't been fried yet. Matthews, however, could and did cut the chatter short. Sheriff Bill Decker was forthcoming when he told Matthews that his department forwarded all reports, but beyond that, he didn't seem to think he could help. Will Fritz hung up on Matthews. The last call, just after midnight, went to Dallas Police Chief Jesse Curry, whose line was busy. It was busy all night, similar, Matthews thought, to the night of November twenty-third–twenty-fourth, when Dallas officers, having received a threat against Oswald, tried to call the chief without success, and finally dispatched a squad car and learned that the phone was off the hook. It meant, to Matthews, that one of his previous callers had already gotten to Curry, and Curry had cut his anchor adrift. Matthews saw the sun rise feeling very tired, not an altogether new sensation, and very alone, a feeling he had never encountered before.

The door was open to the judge's chambers when the group of lawyers arrived between 8:45 and 8:55, stopped to deposit jackets and briefcases, grab a cup of coffee, and walk through the door, perhaps to the end of the case. Judge Davis, present since 7:30 that morning, had not yet donned his robes and alternately made small talk or was a good listener until all the attorneys and Carson were present, then, surprisingly, he launched into a discussion of a 1937 homicide case in Texas that clearly had no relevance to the matters at hand. While doing so, he unfolded the morning's paper, which had two items circled. The first, entitled, "Major Shakeup Underway Among FBI Brass," indicated that two of the three names mentioned very recently were already in trouble.

The second article, buried on page 11 under the fold, announced "Congressman Sheffield Appointed as Deputy Ambassador to Saigon." Davis had written the word "source?" over the article, and showed it to Graves and Vincent. They confirmed that the information had come from him. The judge then went back to the "FBI Brass" story, and quickly wrote on a yellow tablet, "implicate the third one!" Vincent then spoke up, saying that although it had nothing to do with the 1937 precedent under review, and he realized everyone was deep in thought, he felt obligated to report that his source, and a second one as well, he said with a wink, had indicated that the real problem had come from the deputy director, not the other two individuals he had suggested earlier.

Davis, who took it very seriously, minimized its impact for the microphones, commenting instead that he wondered if Vince Drain would be transferred when the FBI learned that he had embarrassed the bureau in yesterday's session. "It won't be anywhere he'll need a bathing suit," Barnes commented. Given the gravity of what they knew the situation to be, there was forced laughter all around. Barnes then wrote, "The paper proves we were right. Now the bugs can go . . . let's clean this place out this weekend—*and* get some more security." Matthews and Davis both nodded their understanding.

"Now, as to the matter of the continued admittance of the rifle as evidence, or its possible exclusion," Davis began, searching for words. "It would be an understatement to say I have given it a lot of thought. In any other case, with any other victim—and I know what you're going to say, Mr. Barnes, but we can't forget the victim, and anyway, I'm still thinking out loud—any other case or victim, that gun would probably have been packed away yesterday without deliberation. And if the gun goes, with the bullet, the cartridges, and what would appear to be key prosecution testimony already excluded, what is left? Some cardboard boxes, a defendant without an alibi, no eyewitnesses, and a jigsaw puzzle with three times as many pieces as are needed. Again, thinking out loud, gentleman, and Miss Jeffries, if the gun stays— either permanently or temporarily—then we can hear from the gun experts which I'm sure you both are prepared to present, and although I doubt they are going to tell us that the defendant did it, they may get us closer to the truth. I guess what I'm getting at is this: if the gun goes, school's out. I assume you understand that, Ray, and why it could happen."

"It had my complete attention for the last eighteen hours, Frank," Matthews told the judge.

Davis changed tack slightly. "For the record, did anybody here sleep last night?"

Carson indicated that he had.

"Let's get back to it then. If the gun goes, so goes the case, period. Dismissal of lack of prima facie case, or directed verdict of not-guilty. But what happens then?"

"Judge Davis," Barnes interrupted, "I've been talking about getting to the bottom of this all along, and I'm still prepared to do that. If keeping the gun will do that, fine. But we—as officers of the court, can't simply keep it to keep egg off the faces of those who saw to it that it should have been excluded . . ."

"I agree one hundred percent, Eddie," Davis said. "But there's no more truth to get to after the gun goes, and *what will* the papers say? Make no mistake about it: it has been obvious since November twenty-second of 1963 that Texas is going to come out of this looking very shabby. And this trial is only going to make that worse, through no fault of anyone in this room. But we may be doing a disservice to the defendant out there if he goes free in this way—personally and judicially. There will be too many unanswered questions. There will be too few people who will take the time to read the transcript of this trial, which no doubt will be serialized in newspapers for days. And . . . don't look so upset, Ray, you are doing your job. What concerns me is that the defendant in this case is *not* going to have a snowball's chance in hell in the other case—the policeman—if he walks out of here on technicalities—legitimate as they may be. Does everyone understand my concern?"

The judge's final concern—the next case, was something that had not occurred to anyone, and it made sense to all concerned. "Your Honor," Barnes spoke up, while looking at Matthews, "without handing the prosecution my working papers, I will tell everyone here that we will have additional information with respect to the exclusion of the weapon at a later time, although I admit I was prepared to come in here and argue, if necessary, the 'Mauser' confusion again if it would have helped get the rifle kicked. But as I said, I do have more factors for the weapon's exclusion, so perhaps the better course of wisdom, from the jury's perspective, would be for me to withdraw my motion in front of the jury and reintroduce it down the road."

"So I get clobbered then and not now?" Matthews asked.

Davis spoke up: "How many cases have you lost before you even finished with your own witnesses, Ray?"

"None," Matthews answered dogmatically.

"Wouldn't you like to keep it that way?" the judge asked.

"I see your point. But I hope that doesn't mean we're just going through the motions the rest of the way."

Again, it was Davis who answered: "Certainly not. Juries are strange things, and I don't have to elaborate that point to anyone here. In addition, we still have the fact that no official finger has been pointed at anybody else, so the public still believes that the defendant is the person who did it, prejudicial as that may be. So we still have a prosecution to complete—roughly how many witnesses, Ray?"

"Half a dozen, give or take."

"Eddie?"

"Somewhere between a dozen and three hundred, Judge. I intentionally made my discovery list a lengthy one, in case the prosecution didn't put some of their people up there."

"Okay. We can't get into those details now, for obvious reasons. But there is one thing we can do. Carson?"

Carson took out what looked like a walkie-talkie and began sweeping the judge's chambers for listening devices. Barnes, needing no cue, began dismantling the phone receiver and looking in other places his experience had taught him were obvious. Barnes found three devices with his bloodhound's nose; Carson came up with two. The five small objects sat on the judge's desk, the phone bugs still active. "You bastards haven't heard the last of this, though you've heard the last of this case," he concluded, as he thanked the attorneys for coming in early.

At ten, the jury was brought in, and Barnes rose to state that he would like to withdraw, for the time being, his motion to exclude CE 139, the rifle, from evidence. He was glad that he emphasized "for the time being," as the jury looked genuinely disappointed. Unbeknownst to any of the attorneys, seven of the fourteen had packed the night before.

"Mr. Matthews?"

"Your Honor, the state calls Robert A. Frazier."

An older, nattily dressed individual, still rankled from sitting on a hallway bench for the entire previous morning, walked to his place on the witness stand with thinly veiled contempt for the entire process. On the other hand, considering what he had to say, few witnesses would look forward to the experience.

Beginning with his experience on the University of Idaho rifle team in 1937, the witness provided his credentials, and Prosecutor Matthews asked that he be accorded expert witness status.

"Mr. Barnes?"

"Your Honor, I would ask the court at this time for the right to question the witness briefly to determine just what exactly he is an expert on."

"Firearms," Matthews insisted.

"Your Honor?" Barnes asked.

"Quickly, Mr. Barnes."

Barnes remained seated. "Mr. Frazier, how many different types of weapons have you fired in your career as an FBI ballistics expert?"

"Hundreds, no . . . thousands would be more accurate."

"Thousands of weapons. Would handguns, derringers, shotguns, and machine guns be included in that figure?"

"Certainly. All types."

"So the number of rifles you have fired is much less than the total you just testified to?"

"Well, yes."

"Mr. Frazier, when you testified before the President's Commission, how many rounds did you tell them you had fired on your way to being an authority?"

"Fifty to sixty thousand."

"Did you tell them you were widely read on the subject of firearms and ballistics?"

"Yes."

"Did you cite any standard textbooks on the subject?"

"Yes. *Firearms Investigation, Identification, and Evidence,* by Major Julian S. Hatcher."

"What is the copyright date on that, sir?"

"1936."

"Yes, 1936. Four years before the weapon in question went into production. We must update our reading, Mr. Frazier. Now, you've fired a lot of bullets out of a lot of guns. How many times, roughly, had you fired a Mannlicher-Carcano carbine *prior to* November twenty-second of 1963?"

"I have no idea."

"Try to give us a rough idea. A thousand times? A hundred? None?"

"I have no idea."

"Your Honor, I submit that the witness clearly possesses a good working knowledge of weapons in general. However, given that he has no available recollection regarding the Mannlicher-Carcano weapon, the defense must request that he be denied expert status. If he wants to give opinions regarding random weapons, the defense will object only on an item-by-item basis and will attempt to respect his expertise. But the defense would have to object to his rendering of any opinions, at least any favorable to the prosecution, with respect to a weapon he has *not* sworn to knowledge of."

"The witness may testify about weapons and ballistics. Please reserve opinions with respect to the weapon in question. Mr. Matthews?"

The prosecutor then lead the witness through testimony regarding the refitting of the weapon in question, from a seven point three five mm carbine originally, to an eventual six point five mm carbine, to the severely worn condition of the lands and grooves in the barrel, through a discussion of the sling, the clip, the speed of the projectile, a precise two thousand one hundred sixty-five feet per second. There was also discussion that the shells would normally eject a distance of eighty-six inches, and then there was discussion about test firings made with the weapon.

"Based on those test firings, Mr. Frazier, would you say that this weapon was adequate—"

"Objection, Your Honor. This is exactly the kind of speculation that was specifically ruled out during the discussion of whether or not this witness was an expert."

"Sustained." Then, to Matthews: "You were here for that discussion, were you not?" the judge asked rhetorically.

Matthews then turned the discussion to the tests performed by the witness on the clothing "allegedly" worn by the President on November twenty-second. The witness confirmed that the holes in both the President's coat and shirt were between five and six inches down from the top of the collar, and slightly to the right of the midline. Frazier told of having spectrographic analyses performed on portions of the holes, and that traces of copper were found. He then testified regarding tiny fragments found in the presidential limousine in the early hours of November twenty-third, each fragment weighing less than one grain. Further testimony revealed that in tests run by J. F. Gallagher, the fragments were found to be similar.

Barnes objected, and strenuously. "Your Honor, first of all, we have a best evidence situation here. If J. F. Gallagher ran the tests, it's his testimony or hearsay. Secondly, we are asked to take Mr. Frazier's word, without documentation. Third, we have learned from Mr. Guinn's very sophisticated testimony that the word 'similar,' as just used by Mr. Frazier, has as much evidentiary value as two similar quarts of milk."

"Sustained. The jury will disregard."

Matthews, clearly playing to the jury, then led the witness through a series of very candid admissions, which included testimony that the governor's clothes were useless as evidence because they had been laundered before they were examined, the inability to match the varying fragments from the limousine or the governor to any specific bullet, and the concept that if a bullet passed through the President, it would have to strike something in front of it, which meant either a part of the automobile, which was ruled out, or Governor Connally. Matthews then asked for Zapruder frames 207 through 210 to be shown, and Frazier suggested that the governor could have been struck during that time.

Barnes objected again, citing no expertise on the part of the witness in either photographic interpretation or forensic pathology, and adding "for the jury's benefit" that it should be noted that Governor Connally is not visible in the frames in question. The objection was sustained, with the additional comment from the judge that testimony from this witness should be limited to weapons and ballistics.

"Based on what you know of weapons and ballistics, then,

Mr. Frazier, could you tell us if all the damage done to the occupants in the presidential limousine could have been inflicted by three bullets?"

"Three shells were found, so I would have to agree that all the damage was done by three bullets."

"Your witness, Mr. Barnes."

Barnes marched defiantly to the witness stand, as if he'd been waiting to ask the one question that would unravel the whole case, looked the witness in the eye and asked, again, "Do the taxpayers know about you?"

Matthews objected on the grounds of badgering, as Barnes had hoped, giving him a chance to put a couple of items immediately into the record. When chided by the judge for his repeated use of the taxpayer remark, Barnes replied, "If it please the Court, he's just testified that three shells were found, so therefore that is the extent of the damage. That unfortunately overlooks the wounding of Mr. James Tague, a bystander, and it also begs the question that if the individual or individuals in the sixth floor window had picked up the three cartridges, central to the witness's theory, then we could presume the President was unhurt. I further based my comment on his earlier testimony about what he found when he examined, quote, 'the hole.' I don't care what hole anybody examines, you will find the same thing: nothing. If a geological expert digs a hole five feet long, five feet wide, and five feet deep, and examines the hole, he will find air, and nothing more. What would be interesting is what would be discovered at the margins or borders of the hole; but a hole, by definition, is the absence of anything."

"Your points are well taken, Mr. Barnes. In the future, however, the court would appreciate if you just made them without the editorial."

Barnes, unfazed, then retreated gradually to his position at the far end of the jury benches. "Mr. Frazier, there are certain, shall we say, 'gaps' in your testimony that I would like to explore. You testified that the Mannlicher-Carcano was once a seven point three five weapon, but is now a six point five. Is that true of this gun only, or of thousands of these weapons?"

"Probably most of them."

"Probably. Then you testified about the lands and grooves being badly worn. Would this not tend to limit the weapon's potential for ballistic matches with bullets?"

"Not necessarily. I had tested one bullet and was prepared to testify that it had come from that rifle to the exclusion of all others, so the ballistic potential is still there. It's just that the bullet shows similar, worn markings."

"Are you surprised that I haven't yet objected to that testimony you just snuck into the record, about the only possible bullet that you could have matched, and one which you know has been excluded from evidence?"

"Frankly, yes."

"Lawyers work that way sometimes, Mr. Frazier. Sure, you said something that might have hurt the defense's case. But balance that against the credibility of your entire statement if and when you're indicted for perjury."

Matthews was quickly on his feet to complain of further badgering, "to the point of slandering the witness in front of the jury with that lame perjury threat."

"Your Honor, if I may?" Barnes asked.

"Please."

"Mr. Frazier, do you know, as a weapons and ballistics expert, what a sabot . . . that's s-a-b-o-t, Mrs. Martinez, is?"

"Yes."

"I doubt the jury does," Barnes continued. "Tell them."

"Well, a sabot is a kind of clip that holds the slug, or the bullet part, and that clip, holding the bullet, can be refitted into a cartridge casing larger than the caliber of the bullet held within a sabot."

"Thank you for that explanation, Mr. Frazier. Now, if a sabot were used, could a bullet already fired from a Mannlicher-Carcano, caliber six point five, be fired a second time, from a Mauser, caliber seven point six five?"

"Yes, it could."

"And if that bullet were recovered, and tested ballistically, would the ballistics expert conclude that it was fired from a Mauser, or a Mannlicher?"

"They would not conclude Mauser. They would conclude Mannlicher, if it had previously been fired from one. If the bullet had never been fired, it would be inconclusive."

"So, a Mannlicher bullet, once fired, is fitted into a sabot, fired from a Mauser, then recovered, and you might testify as you did, that it came from the original Mannlicher, not the Mauser that fired it at the crime scene, to the exclusion of all other weapons?"

"Yes I would."

"But would your testimony be accurate and honest?"

"Honest, yes, because I have no way of knowing that a sabot was employed, which in this case I don't. Accurate, no."

"So the phrase, 'To the exclusion of all other weapons' really means, 'To the exclusion of all smaller caliber weapons.' "

"Yes."

"Thank you. When you examined the rifle over there on the evidence table, did you encounter any problems with it?"

"Well, for one, the sling was too short. It . . . well, actually, all you could do really was put your arm through it."

"As given to you, would that sling have proved an aid or a nuisance to someone trying to squeeze off three shots in less than six seconds?"

"It would probably be a nuisance to anybody."

"Any other problems?"

"Well, of course, the sights were not accurate."

"Ah!" Barnes exclaimed. "There's a concept that might somehow have a bearing on whether or not someone could hit a moving target, going downhill, at a distance of two hundred sixty-six feet. Tell the jury about the sights, please."

"When we got the weapon, it was necessary to adjust the sights, then fire several shots to adjust the crosshair ring . . . even with that, it could not be sighted properly. What was really needed, in order to make it work, was for shims, little metal pieces, to be added to bring the sight into adjustment."

"Were those shims present when the FBI received this weapon?"

"No."

"Was anything else unusual noted with respect to the telescopic sight?"

"I don't know what you mean."

"Could we please have CE 2560?" Barnes then waited, and

when the document came up, Frazier read it silently and concluded, "It was installed as if for a left-handed man?"

"Left-handed, Mr. Frazier. I thought you had prepared that particular FBI report, but I guess you hadn't seen it. To continue, what did your initial tests on the weapon show?"

"Our first test firings," Frazier said, beginning to fidget in his seat, a reaction not unnoticed by all attorneys present, "took nine, eight, and six seconds, respectively, and all shot patterns were high and to the right."

"At what distance were these firings conducted?"

Frazier looked to Matthews, who was silent. He then answered softly, "Fifteen yards."

Barnes asked for CE 548 and 549, but did not pause in his cross-examination: "This gun, which I've been calling junk for ten days now, was not even accurate from fifteen yards?"

"No."

"And these exhibits, CE 548 and 549, clearly reflect that inaccuracy?"

"Yes."

"And it took your experts nine, and eight seconds in their first two firings? How many chances did the assassin get—?"

"Well, we repeated the procedure several times, and were able to reduce the speed, with secondary purpose accuracy."

"Say that in English, please."

"We could work the bolt and trigger fast enough, eventually, to do what the film showed, but the faster we fired, the less accurate we became."

"How very interesting," Barnes commented, letting the jury think about it for a few minutes as he got a document from a folder on the defense table, then stood there and read it. "With all that you've just told us—inability to sight the weapon, the need for shims, the uselessness of the sling, the length of time your experts took and their diminished accuracy—with all of that, would you still stand on the testimony that you gave to the President's Commission, which I can read to you from page 413 of Volume III?"

"Well, I'm not sure—"

"Shall we read what you said and then reconsider the word 'perjury' that the prosecutor objected to earlier?"

"I hope that won't be necessary."

"For your sake, so do I," Barnes told him, putting down the folder and returning directly to the witness stand. "You also testified that you found traces of copper on the back of the President's shirt and jacket. Did you find traces of copper on the margins—not the hole itself—of the hole in the *front* of the President's shirt?"

"No. And to anticipate your next question, in point of fact, the hole in the President's shirt front is of unknown origin. I could not determine whether that hole was made by a bullet or not."

"Was there, in fact, any—copper or otherwise—any metallic residue on the President's tie?"

"No."

"Regarding what was found in the presidential car in the early hours of November twenty-three, 1963. How can we accept at face value that those fragments are legitimate?"

"The car was under guard every minute it was in the White House garage, I can assure you of that."

"I'm sure you can. It seems only logical that after one man has his brains shot out in Dallas, a reasonable security network would be established for the White House in Washington, D.C. But my concern is different—your testimony implies the sanctity of that evidence, yet there is no guarantee that the car was fully secured while at Parkland Hospital, where reporters and other curiosity seekers edged close to get a peek at history. It was, after all, a period of over twelve hours before the evidence was found inside that car."

"I can only vouch for the security of the automobile in the White House garage."

"Was lead found in the windshield of the limousine?"

"Yes. In the middle, approximately—"

"The dimensions aren't vital, Mr. Frazier. If the prosecution wants them in the record, they can get them during redirect. But there was lead there?"

"Yes."

"Was lead found in the chrome around the windshield?"

"Yes."

"With respect to your earlier testimony, then, it is possible that the bullet that struck the President did not exit the car and could be accounted for in either of the locations just

suggested and did not, as you suggest, virtually guarantee
that the missile struck the governor?"

"It could have gone almost anywhere. As you suggested
before, I am not a pathologist."

"Speaking of pathologists, we have had testimony that the
angle to a hypothetical rifle in the sixth floor window during
the shooting sequence was between twenty and twenty-one
degrees. As a ballistics expert, how would you account for a
medical report that showed an entrance, in the case of the
President, of forty-five degrees, and in the case of the governor, thirty-nine degrees?"

"The governor's wound, at your thirty-nine degree figure—"

"For the record," Barnes interrupted, "it was the attending
physician's figure."

"Could be accounted for if it hit something else first, or
from a higher building. The forty-five-degree figure on the
President, well, either there's an answer in wound ballistics
that I'm not familiar with, or he was in some very convoluted
position with respect to the horizontal axis when struck, or
we're dealing with something sinister."

"I appreciate your honesty, Mr. Frazier. I have no more
. . . I have only a couple more thoughts here. Mr. Frazier,
you testified about being on the University of Idaho rifle
team. Would you be confident of winning a rifle competition if
you were using the weapon on the evidence table?"

"No. If it can't hit a target at fifteen yards . . ." Frazier let
the thought trail off, and Barnes was satisfied with it.

"Last question: Did you, Robert Frazier, FBI ballistics expert, at any time, duplicate the feats attributed to that rifle
we just spoke of . . . three hits, less than six seconds, moving target, one hundred seventy-four to two hundred sixty-
six feet?"

"No."

"Nothing further." Barnes felt he had silenced the most
dangerous of the rifle experts, and the word perjury would
prevent the possibility of redirect. "Move to admit CE 2560,
FBI statement of left-handed sight on weapon, and CE 548
and 549, showing the rifle fired high and right when tested."

Matthews didn't blink an eye. "The state calls Ronald Simmons." Having quickly established that the witness was the "Chief of Infantry Weapons Branch for the Department of the Army," Matthews quickly pressed for expert witness designation.

"Mr. Barnes?"

"Your Honor, I would be derelict in my duties if I didn't object. This jury has seen a passing parade of government employees—FBI so-called experts, and military personnel. I'd really like to hear from a civilian—an NRA consultant, just to get an objective view. Those are personal objections. More to the point, the defense took a deposition from this witness, and reviewed his testimony before the President's Commission, and there just is not expertise there. He has been working at the job he does—testing weapons for the U.S. Army at Aberdeen, since 1953. The weapon in question in this case became obsolete with the surrender of Italy twenty years ago in 1945. Are we to be asked to believe that the Mannlicher-Carcano, which has so far received very negative reviews from witnesses, would come under his purview—that an obsolete Italian rifle would be considered to replace the modern weaponry of the U.S. Army? There would be a revolt in every infantry barracks in America if troops leaving for Vietnam were issued Mannlicher-Carcano carbines. And finally, the reconstruction staged by Mr. Simmons borders on the fraudulent. Naturally, that will be for the court and the jury to decide, but based on what I have read, it cannot be taken seriously."

"The court will reserve judgment, Mr. Matthews; in the meantime, the defense will retain the right to object. If you reach a point in your testimony where you want to ask an opinion, please indicate so to the court, and a decision will be made then as to the witness's expertise. Proceed."

The witness then explained how a simulation was held at Aberdeen Proving Grounds, with expert riflemen taking turns firing at stationary targets placed, based on figures supplied, at one hundred seventy-five, two hundred forty, and two hundred sixty-five feet away. The riflemen were given all the time they wanted to fire their first shot, and were then timed. The only conclusion supplied was that the shooter would have to have "sufficient practice" in working

the bolt in order to achieve success. Matthews knew this testimony was of little evidentiary value, but it *sounded* impressive, so he was pleased with it. Barnes would be another
matter.

"Mr. Simmons, are you an expert rifle shot?" Barnes
asked, beginning his cross-examination.

"No, sir. I rarely fire the weapons. I'm the project coordina-
tor at Aberdeen."

"Have you fired a weapon at any time in the last four
years?"

"Oh, sure, yes. But I'm not an expert."

"Nobody has yet said that the defendant was either,"
Barnes added, only to have the comment stricken on objection.

"Mr. Simmons, before you ran these tests, did you have
any difficulty sighting the weapon?"

"Well, they could not sight the weapon in using the telescope, and no attempt was made to sight it in using the iron
sights. We did adjust the telescopic sight by the addition of
two shims, one which tended to adjust the azimuth and one
which adjusted an elevation."

"Were these adjustments necessary in order for the rifle to
fire as accurately as it could be fired for the purposes of these
tests?"

"Absolutely. The weapon couldn't be sighted in without
them."

"So the gun as you received it," Barnes said, picking up the
Mannlicher, "this gun, in fact, could not be accurately fired
when you received it for testing?"

"It could not."

"Mr. Simmons, how long were the streets of downtown Dallas closed off in order for you to conduct this simulation?"

"You must not have heard me, sir. We did the testing at
Aberdeen." As if Barnes didn't know, Matthews fumed.

"Is there a large brick building identical to the Texas
School Book Depository there?"

"Of course not. We built a platform, approaching thirty feet
high."

"Which is how many stories high?"

"Three."

"And your expert riflemen were allowed all the time they wanted to sight in and aim at the first target?"

"That's correct."

"And the targets were all stationary?"

"Correct."

"Was there a tree blocking the view of the first target?"

"No, they were all out in the open."

"Did the elevation of the targets slope down twenty-four feet?"

"Uh, no. I believe the ground was level."

"Did the riflemen practice with the weapon before you actually timed their performances?"

"Yes."

"Were any difficulties encountered?"

"There were several comments made, particularly with respect to the amount of effort required to open the bolt. As a matter of fact, Mr. Staley had difficulty in opening the bolt in his first firing exercise. And, of course, any gun with awkward bolt movement would pull the gun off target."

"This Mr. Staley. Is he an expert with a rifle?"

"Yes. All the shooters were."

"Says who?"

"They are certified by either the Department of the Army, or some qualified rifle group, as to their expertise."

"How often?"

"At least yearly. They have to be certified in order for our day-to-day work at Aberdeen to have any precise value."

"When these simulations were conducted, Mr. Simmons, were any of the shooters in danger of being killed?"

"I don't understand your question, sir."

Barnes had him now. "Try to follow me, Mr. Simmons. You ran a simulation, for the purpose of providing the state with evidence. Now, *if,* and I emphasize that we're only discussing a possibility here, but *if* a gunman was in the sixth floor of the Book Depository, your test is inadequate because the sixth floor is sixty point seven feet high, where your platform was, in fact, thirty feet at its apex, not from where the shooter fired; your targets were stationary, not moving. Your shooters, recently certified as experts, had all the time in the world, where an alleged sixth floor assassin had to sight-in

the limousine as it suddenly emerged from foliage and fire
with scant warning. Your shooters also had the benefit of dry
runs before doing their labors. A sixth floor assassin had
only one attempt—no practice. As to the last question, that
alleged assassin had no way of knowing that he would not be
wounded or killed in a hail of bullets, known in the business
as 'return fire.' I'm asking you if your shooters were operating under that pressure."

"Of course not."

"Thank you. Now, tell the jury the results that your experts
compiled in their various tries—accuracy as well as time,
please."

"Well, they all hit the first target . . ."

"That shouldn't surprise anyone," Barnes added.

"The second target was missed on at least the first four
attempts, but they had better luck on the third target. The
average time for the first run was eight point two five seconds, and seven seconds for the second trial."

"Mr. Simmons, let's get to the bottom line. That man, sitting at the table over there, is accused of firing three shots in
under six seconds, and with no practice, over a tree, at a
target moving downhill, with an unadjusted sight, at a live
human being, with his own life at least theoretically in jeop-
ardy. Did or could any of your experts perch themselves in
the sixth floor and with no practice, hit three targets as precisely and in as little time as the defendant allegedly did?"

"They didn't with repeated practice, so I don't see how it
would be possible the first time out—especially with the
sights so far off."

"Could you do it, Mr. Simmons?"

"Certainly not. I'm a technician. I've only fired infre-
quently."

"And the defendant is only a stock boy and there's been no
testimony that he has fired a weapon since his discharge
from the Marines in 1959. Thank you, Mr. Simmons."

Matthews wanted to reconsider his remaining civilian experts, so he and Barnes approached the bench and Matthews asked for a slightly early lunch break, and, with gestures, indicated that the time could also be used to sweep the
courtroom.

The jury was excused for the morning. Matthews was wondering what, if anything, his next move was. Barnes was wondering how things were going in Minnesota.

The lunch break had been premature, Matthews concluded. He could have gotten one, or maybe two more of his witnesses on the stand, then taken lunch, concluded with the final witness in the afternoon, and rested his case, with Barnes left holding the bag with no one to call and egg on his face until Monday morning. But that was water under the bridge now.

Barnes was not even focused on the trial throughout lunch. He called Minnesota repeatedly, both at the number he told his wife to stay at, and at home as well, with no luck. His final call, in desperation, was to the airlines, such as it was in Lubbock, which could get him to Minnesota in six and a half hours, counting the three hour layover in St. Louis. Once his reservation was confirmed, he was back on the case.

The prosecution team arrived back in the courtroom in time to receive an indication from bailiff Carson that the place was "clean," which provided some comfort. There was serious concern about the direction that the afternoon should take. The three planned witnesses each had obvious flaws, but it was quickly agreed that they could not rest their case after the testimony of a firearms whiz kid whose most expert riflemen were unable to do what the likes of Oswald was charged with. So when it came to sorting out the flawed experts, the consensus was to go with all of them, to blunt further the loss absorbed by the prelunch witnesses.

When Judge Davis entered the courtroom, he mounted the bench, and deliberately looked around the courtroom taking deep breaths, as one might do on that first spring day when the smell of new-mown lawn is in the air. It was his way of telling the attorneys that they had regained their privacy. The defendant and the jury were then brought in, with Oswald curious as to how much longer this might go on. "As far as Matthews is concerned, not much longer," Barnes told him. "But if it gets to be our turn, it could take a while.

You've just given me an idea, Lee. Thanks." Oswald had no idea what Barnes was talking about.

"Mr. Matthews?" the judge intoned.

"Your Honor, the state calls Dr. Alfred G. Olivier, wounds ballistics supervisor for the Department of the Army at Edgewood Arsenal, Maryland."

A robust, middle-aged man in an expensive suit entered the courtroom with a military bearing and was sworn in a procedure now familiar to everyone. In his introductory questions, Matthews homed in on the witness's length of experience in working with wounds and testing the effects of bullets on gelatin samples, skin, and on occasion, cadavers.

Barnes stood to ask that the witness clarify for the jury what a cadaver was.

"A corpse. A deceased individual."

Matthews completed his questions, then petitioned the judge, "Your Honor, I would like *Doctor* Olivier designated an expert witness, subject, of course, to the bickerings of the defense attorneys."

"Your Honor," Barnes began in soft, measured tones, "I would like, in a nonbickering manner, to petition the court as to just exactly what it is that this so-called doctor is being presented as an expert in."

"In wound ballistics," Matthews answered, facing Barnes and not the court.

"Your Honor, I'd like to question the witness, but I think there are far too many ears for this discussion . . ."

"Carson, take the jury back for dessert," the judge ordered. Barnes then walked around in front of the bench, deep in thought, hands in his pockets, until told to proceed. "Now then, Doctor Olivier, just so the court knows what side of the fence you are sitting on, we're going to have a little reading from your testimony before the President's Commission. Your Honor, I hand you a copy of Volume V, open to page 74 and 75—you can follow along with your copy if you like, Mr. Matthews, and review the data supplied on Wednesday, May thirteenth, 1964, by Dr. Alfred G. Olivier. Judge, if you look at page 75, about three fourths of the way down, where Mr. Specter asks, 'Was the Mannlicher-Carcano rifle . . .' Do you find that?"

"Yes, I have it," the judge answered.

"Before I read, Dr. Olivier, as a so-called wounds ballistic expert, do you recall what you told the President's Commission when asked about your tests with the Mannlicher-Carcano?"

"It was used to test the penetrating power of bullets, as there was some thought that the nonfatal presidential wounds as well as the wounds sustained by the governor might have been caused by the same bullet."

"Good answer, Doctor, and I'm sure it's one the jury would like to hear. And I wouldn't mind one bit if they did. However, that was *not* your answer. So I'll rehash the truth that you have forgotten: 'Question: Was the Mannlicher-Carcano rifle then fired for comparison purposes with the other bullets where you already had your experience? Dr. Olivier: No; it was fired for the purposes for which—to try to shed some light on say the factors leading to the assassination and all, not for comparison with the other bullets.' End of quote. Your Honor, did I read that as written?"

"Word for word."

"So, Mr. Ballistics expert, you were firing the weapon to find out what caused the assassination, and not for comparison with bullets? Who pulled the trigger, Dr. Olivier—Sigmund Freud?"

"I don't know what you're talking about."

"Excuse me, Doctor, but the problem seems to be that you don't know what you are talking about. That rifle can't talk. It can't tell you about causation, and firing it once or ten million times is not going to shed one ray of light on the factors leading up to the assassination. I submit to this court that this is the biggest bushel of rubbish yet to pass through this bar of justice."

"Your Honor," Matthews insisted, "Mr. Barnes is being a little rough with the witness." The judge however, seemed to be enjoying the show, absent the jury, and said nothing, allowing Barnes to continue.

"Let's probe a little deeper. These tests—not the ones to determine why the rifle decided to go off on November twenty-two, but the ones that were intended to have serious evidentiary value—how were they done?"

"Bullets were fired into cadavers—which, by the way are corpses, deceased humans, as well as into gelatin-filled skulls and anesthetized goats."

"Let's set the record straight—Doctor. I know what a cadaver is, and my vocabulary also includes words like ghoul and charlatan, so if you want to play that game, fine. But are you saying that these goats were alive, anesthetized, and then killed to prove that a bullet could have done a certain type of damage to the governor?"

"That's correct. That's done routinely at Edgewood."

"Doctor, I know the answer to this next question, and so does Mr. Matthews, but I'm not sure that Judge Davis does. So for the record, please tell us exactly what kind of doctor you are."

"I am a Doctor of Veterinary Medicine."

Judge Davis was no longer amused. "You will testify to questions as asked, Doctor, but not as an expert. I will tell you further that I am now requesting Mrs. Martinez, our court stenographer, to prepare a copy, in toto, of your testimony, for forwarding to such authorities as would render a verdict on whether or not you should continue to be licensed to practice veterinary medicine. You will win the day, of course. No doubt Edgewood Arsenal has an abiding need for someone with your talents. But the testimony elicited by Mr. Barnes has convinced this court that you are in a very gray ethics area when you testify to shooting animals to prove virtually nothing, and then claim to be a doctor of veterinary medicine. Carson, let's get the jury back while I still have an interest in this man's testimony."

"Carson, Your Honor, I have one more point," Barnes interrupted.

"Hang on, Carson, Barnes isn't out of rope yet."

Matthews objected both to Barnes's continuance and to the judge's reference. The judge replied that it was Barnes who had been fair in suggesting the jury not hear the exchange, which Matthews should be extremely thankful for, and second, this was still his courtroom. "If I say something the jury should not hear, that's different. Continue, please."

"Your Honor, my final point is a fine point of law, and it falls somewhere in the gray area between proper foundation and best evidence. Having read the witness's deposition, he is going to testify about the simulated recreation of the governor's wounds, and we have not heard expert, or for that matter, *any* testimony about those wounds. None of his attending surgeons have testified, and although they may, for the defense, but without the facts regarding the wounds, anything that this witness can say for purpose of comparison has very little, if any, probative value for the jury."

"I strongly agree, Mr. Barnes. But Mr. Matthews wouldn't want to lose his witness, so I shall issue a caution to the jury and we shall hear what the good veterinarian has to say." Davis may have hoped Barnes would continue to skewer the witness, but he could give no indication of that. When the jury returned, the judge gave a fair and impartial rendering of his version of the witness's credibility, while at the prosecution table, Graves argued to "keep it short and then rest," while Vincent said "keep it short and sweet, but go with the trio." At the defense table, Barnes walked down to Carolyn Jeffries and asked her to see who was waiting outside.

Matthews, in keeping it short, elicited testimony that an anesthetized goat had been shot in a simulation of the governor's wounds, proving that one Mannlicher-Carcano bullet was capable of doing serious damage, even in an anatomical structure considerably larger than a human. The bullet, he continued, did shatter bone, but went through with great velocity. A human cadaver was used to simulate the wrist wound sustained by the governor, and again, the bullet had the power to do the indicated damage. Finally, a series of gelatin filled skulls were impacted with Mannlicher ammunition, and the simulation produced fragments similar to those found in the car. Matthews, having had the jury's complete attention, and believing he had accomplished quite a bit with this testimony, turned the witness over to Barnes.

Barnes walked to the jury box and put his hand gently on the shoulder of the second juror from the left in the first row. "Doctor Olivier . . . excuse me, Doctor of Veterinary Medicine Olivier . . . that was for the jury to understand your testimony of murdering goats, Doctor, the shirt this juror is wearing, is it similar to this one, over here, indicating the fifth juror (one counted on for a hung jury by Matthews) in the back row?"

"Yes, it seems similar. So what?"

"Just what I was going to say. Could you cut those two shirts in half and restitch them to each other and have two usable garments?"

"I wouldn't wear them," the witness answered.

"Exactly. Because they're only similar, which is the best you, or anybody else so far, can tell us about the wounds. By the way, I wouldn't wear them either. They're too nice to ruin with goat blood.

"The bullets that performed these specific tests," Barnes went on, "did they come out of the goats or the human wrists undeformed?"

"No. They were badly deformed."

"Could we have Exhibit 853 please? Like this one, Doctor?"

"That looks like one of them."

"As a ballistics expert—not as a veterinarian, would you describe the condition of the bullet?"

"It is obviously quite flattened."

"And the wrist bullet had a similar appearance?"

"The wrist bullet actually was more damaged, but we must recall it was only fired into the wrist, so it had a greater penetrating velocity. Incidentally, it did more damage to the cadaver wrist than was indicated in the governor's X ray."

"Which the court hasn't seen," Barnes reminded the witness. "Doctor, you said your gelatin skulls were similar to that which was found in the car. What knowledge do you have as to what was found in the car?"

"I was made aware in a general way of what was found."

"Who made you aware?"

"Agents of the Secret Service."

"And your tests on the goat, Doctor," Barnes said with a tinge of sarcasm, "were they, in your estimation, reasonable simulations?"

"Yes. They were even dressed in garments—a shirt, an undershirt, and suit coat for the purpose of simulating the governor's clothing."

Barnes had made plenty of points, especially with two jurors, ones he wasn't sure of from reading faces. Having learned from Carolyn Jeffries that there were "two military uniforms" sitting outside, he knew what was coming, so he wanted to conclude this witness with a nice touch, but he knew it would take timing. "Just one more question, Doctor, with respect to the goat . . ."

"Yes?"

"Did it get reelected?" Barnes then gave Matthews one second to object before he withdrew the question. "You're excused, *Doctor.* Your Honor, I would like CE 853 admitted."

"So moved."

Eaton Graves asked for a moment to confer, and Barnes used the interval to retrieve the copy of Volume V he had loaned the judge, who told him quietly, "I'll never figure that one out."

Matthews then calmly called Major Eugene D. Anderson. Barnes rose to announce that he would accept the witness as an expert. Matthews, still at the defense table as the smartly dressed marine officer strode through the courtroom, got advice from both Graves and Vincent: "If Barnes made it that easy, watch it, Ray."

Major Anderson then testified that the defendant had received intensive rifle training, as well as training with other types of weapons as a marine recruit, and on December twenty-first, 1956, under ideal firing conditions, he had achieved a score of 212 on the "A" Course, indicating a rank of sharpshooter. Subsequently, on May sixth, 1959, Oswald had scored a 191, one point above the lowest qualification, marksman, and the witness hedged that score to try to explain why it was so low.

"Major, have you been shown photos taken from the sixth floor window looking down toward Elm Street where the shots were fired at the President's car?"

"Yes, sir, I have."

"Could an ex-marine sharpshooter make those shots?"

"The shots were not difficult."

"No further questions. Thank you, Major."

Barnes decided to try a friendly approach before crucifying this counterfeit marksmanship expert: "*Semper Fi,* Major."

"*Semper Fi,*" he replied.

"Major, for the record, you translated all those numbers,

hedging a bit on the 191, but are you an expert at training or at marksmanship?"

"Both."

"Good for you. And when did you earn this expert rating with a rifle?"

"Many years ago. And I've kept that rating every year."

"Do I understand you, Major, that you are testifying that to be considered an expert, you have to requalify on at least a yearly basis?"

"That is correct, sir."

"Well, then if the defendant's scores dropped twenty-one points in two and a half years, from December 1956 to May 1959, how many points would they have dropped if there is no proof at this point that he fired a rifle after May 1959. What would he have qualified as in the summer of 1963?"

"I can't answer that."

"I realize the question was difficult, Major. Let's put it this way, is it common for someone to cease using a rifle for a lengthy period of time—a few years—and have their firing scores vastly improve the first time they subsequently handle a weapon?"

Matthews was burning to object, but the witness was, after all, an expert. "It is not very likely that someone is going to be away from firearms for a lengthy period of time and have their ability improve. It could only deteriorate."

"Okay. 'Deteriorate,' you said. Let's look at the document you furnished. Could we have Anderson Exhibit 1, please?" Barnes turned to give Matthews a "circle the wagons" look while the exhibit was being brought up. "Now, Major, do you recognize this exhibit?"

"Yes, sir. It is the documentation that was requested from the Marine Corps regarding the weapons capability of the marine Lee Oswald."

"Looking at the second page, there, Major, at the top it states 21Dec56, Course A, Weapon M-1, score, 212mm. What does mm stand for?"

"It stands for Marksman, but . . ."

"You testified that Oswald was a sharpshooter—that's a big difference."

"If you look at page 1, at the bottom, that is explained as a typographical error."

"Major, if you got a promotion for every typographical or clerical error we have seen in ten days of this trial, you'd be the commanding officer of the U.S. military for the next five centuries. But let's get to the bottom of the document, on page 3, if we could have that brought up please. Major, I'm going to read the conclusion supplied by Lt. Col. A. G. Folsom in this document, and the jury can follow along on their screens. He says, 'Consequently, a low marksman qualification'—would you say 191, one point above the minimum 190 was a 'low marksman qualification'?"

"Virtually the lowest."

"Again, 'Consequently, a low marksman qualification indicates a rather poor "shot" and a sharpshooter qualification indicates a fairly good "shot." ' Now, based on these documents and your testimony, can we conclude that the defendant was a fairly good shot on twenty-one December 1956?"

"The record so indicates."

"Can we conclude that he was a rather poor shot on May 6, 1959?"

"The record so indicates."

"And based on your word, 'deteriorate,' what category below 'poor' would the defendant be placed in after years in which there is no proof in our record that he handled a rifle?"

"Poor is poor. How much worse can you get?"

"Indeed. How much worse can you get and then have a distinguished marine expert come in here and say it was an easy shot to make for someone who was a poor shot in the marines?"

There was no answer and Barnes did not prod for one. But he wasn't through, either. He picked up the Mannlicher and brought it to the witness stand, making a great deal of contact with it with his free hand to focus the jury's attention on it. "Major, have you ever fired one of these?"

"Not that I recall."

"Please examine the weapon, and take your time." Major Anderson did so, showing, by his inspection of it that he knew what to look for in a gun. When done, he handed the weapon back to Barnes and waited for the inevitable question. "Major, let's assume that Colonel Folsom, who signed that report on the screens a few minutes ago, relieves you of your duties on the range and puts you in charge of a regiment of marines in Vietnam. Every soldier you command, every marine life that is entrusted into your hands—each man—is issued a weapon identical to the one you just examined, not the M-1 indicated in Mr. Oswald's marine record. React, Major."

Barnes waited patiently. "Your men's lives, Major. Is that weapon superior to the weapon provided to Marine trainees way back in 1956? Yes or no?"

"No."

"Is it superior to the weapons issued to our brave men going to Vietnam right now as we sit here in Lubbock?"

"No."

"Have you done any simulations which were comparable to the shots allegedly fired by the defendant?"

"I don't get you, there."

"Major, we've had one expert after another—and I don't mean to impugn your expertise. I recognized it when I granted you expert witness status. But we've had one expert after another come in here and say words to the effect that the shots from the sixth floor window were easy. Yet no one has recreated them—three shots, two killer hits, maybe three, in approximately five point seven nine seconds using war surplus junk and twenty-year-old ammunition on a gun that couldn't even be sighted in by experts. Now I'm asking you: have you done it or are you just saying it's easy?"

"I haven't done it."

"I tell you what, Major. On my way here from Minnesota, I stopped at one of the major automobile producing plants. They've got a car there that is remote controlled. No driver. It steers straight down the road on a radio signal, turns left, turns right . . ."

Matthews knew what was coming and didn't like it. "Your Honor, I'm sure Mr. Barnes had a wonderful trip, and we'd love to see his slides, but he's wandering and it is not relevant."

"He's been relevant so far, Mr. Matthews. Overruled."

"So they have this car, Major, and for some free publicity,

they told me they would ship it to Dallas, Texas, actually to Dealey Plaza in Dallas, and let an expert take three shots at a mannequin in the backseat with the convertible top down. Now, Major, you look to me like that expert. We can adjourn this court to Dallas, put you in that window, and duplicate the event exactly. You'll have no practice, since there's no indication the defendant did. The car will come up Houston at fifteen miles per hour, make the big turn onto Elm, lose itself in the foliage, then emerge . . . and you go to work with this Mannlicher-Carcano, three bullets and five point seven nine seconds. And here's the sweet part. If you can score three kill shots on the dummy, I'll plead the defendant guilty. . . . But if you can't, then you're not the expert marksman you claim to be, and, of course, you'll resign from the Marine Corps and waive any rights to your pension. The test will be supervised by these court officers from Vermont, you won't be allowed to test fire the Mannlicher, and the shims will be removed from the scope. Have we got a deal, Major?"

Every juror, the judge, even Mrs. Martinez—every attorney —was riveted with Barnes's sudden unexpected challenge, and taken at no less than face value. The witness leaned back, looked at the ceiling as people sometimes do when in search of an answer, then looked at Barnes and said, "Son, I've been in the corps almost twenty-eight years, and as much as I'd like to see justice done, you're asking too much."

"I thought it was an impossible shot, too, Major. No further questions." For the first time since the trial began, jurors were talking to one another and the judge had to use his gavel for silence. "The court will come to order and we will take a five minute recess."

When court reconvened, Barnes excused his interruption of the prosecutor and asked that Anderson Exhibit Number 1, referred to by the previous witness but lost in the confusion following the testimony, be admitted into evidence, with the understanding that it contained one error which occurred during its preparation. Matthews agreed to the amended exhibit and it was admitted.

Matthews then announced, in a tone not heard before by

anyone at the defense table, "The state now calls Sergeant James A. Zahm."

As the witness entered, Barnes leaned behind Oswald and told Bob Dean, "I think this is it. The closet's empty. Has he made a case?" Dean held up an index finger to indicate "give me a minute," and then began writing.

The witness was sworn and Matthews began eliciting testimony that indicated that Sergeant Zahm was a marine weapons expert whose specialty was telescopic rifle sights. Matthews asked that he be accorded expert witness status.

"I fail to see the point of that, Your Honor," Barnes began, reaching into a paper bag at his feet. "These, uh, reference materials are price guides issued in 1963 by the leading firearms dealers in the United States, and the scope on the weapon on the evidence table, CE 139, cost seven dollars. There is not one telescopic rifle sight in any of these catalogues that costs anywhere near that little. So what can this expert testify to? That it's the cheapest available? We already know that."

"I'm not sure, either, Mr. Barnes, but let's hear him out. The witness is designated an expert on telescopic sights."

Matthews strutted as if he had won the case. While he approached the witness, Barnes read the note from Dean: "He's playing for a hung jury, Eddie. He figures at least two of the Texas—not Minnesota, Eddie—jurors, will have our boy pegged, if nothing else, as either a psycho or a commie, or both, and that will be enough to prevent an acquittal stampede. But know this: he can't win. He knows you've kicked his ——. Dean."

Barnes didn't know whether to laugh or cry, but in the meantime, he had to focus in on the witness, who was being asked if the scope was of high enough quality to enable a shooter to perform accurately.

"It is."

"Could the defendant have made the shots as you understand them to have been made, using this rifle, with the telescopic sight that is mounted on it?" Matthews was handling the Mannlicher for one of the rare times, and he realized that Barnes had shown it to the jury far more often than he had.

"With the equipment he had, and his ability . . ."

"Objection," Barnes bellowed, to drown out the remainder of the witness's testimony. "I apologize to the court for my volume, Your Honor, but the jury, in my opinion, should not have heard the rest of that sentence because this witness cannot testify to the defendant's ability. The last witness did that and did so quite clearly. If I'm wrong, you'll tell me, but I believe he needs to be reminded that he is here as an expert on scopes."

"Agreed. The witness will confine the 'scope' of his expertise to exactly that, scopes. Perhaps the process will be aided if your questions are couched in that area, Mr. Prosecutor."

"Sergeant Zahm, let me restate the question asked earlier to clarify your answer. Is this telescopic sight, which has been maligned by the defense as a cheap piece of junk, sophisticated enough to fire accurate shots at a target moving at eleven miles an hour at a distance between one hundred seventy-five and two hundred sixty-five feet?"

"Yes."

"Thank you, Sergeant. No further questions."

Barnes knew he was walking a tightrope. Strongly suspecting that this was the final witness, he did not want Matthews to win even this witness, but at the same time he didn't want to lose the many points he felt he had already made with the jury.

"Sergeant, given the facts as presented by the prosecutor, it is easy to see how you could answer in the affirmative. But let's examine the whole story of that rifle and the attached scope. Naturally, you are looking at the scope and saying 'a scope is a scope,' and in your business, I have to understand that. But some of us have been here for a couple of weeks, and we've heard hundreds of thousands of words of testimony, Sergeant, which, if you had heard, might color your perceptions of events. So let's try to arrive at some truth, okay?"

"Fine. I'm listening."

"Good. Now, we've heard testimony from the individual responsible for selling that rifle that it was sold with the scope mounted, but that translates to 'attached,' as it was not sighted in by the seller. From that date, roughly March 1963, we have heard no evidence or seen no documents that the weapon was sighted in. It has been suggested, but not proven, in testimony, that the weapon was dismantled sometime prior to November twenty-two, and reassembled in the Texas School Book Depository, from which we are asked to believe, since no witness identified the rifle or its shooter, it was fired. Then it is discovered by local authorities in Dallas, the FBI grabs it up, but every test by every expert indicates that the weapon could not be sighted in accurately, that it was aligned for a left-handed shooter, and that shims had to be added to cause it to fire accurately. Now, Sergeant, are you still with me?"

"Yes, sir, I heard you."

"Is it still your opinion, given all that negative input, and lack of evidence to the contrary, that the shots you described as possible, were, in fact, that easy?"

"Sir, I can't testify as to what the FBI did or didn't do, and as for shims, well, if they were needed, that scope could have been whacked out of alignment in any of several different ways unrelated to the shooting ability of the weapon. But the answer is fundamental: if that weapon was disassembled, then reassembled, regardless of what you told me, it would be capable of being sighted in by firing ten rounds and using sight manipulation."

Barnes had him: "Sergeant, do you, or perhaps you'd prefer to confer with Mr. Matthews, have any knowledge—or, for that matter, has there ever been a suggestion—that the defendant fired ten rounds after the weapon was assembled in the Book Depository and before it was aimed at the President? You may be an expert on scopes, Sergeant, but your testimony tells me you know nothing of the event in question."

"The scope would have been reliable after ten rounds."

"What about the first of those rounds? . . . The second? . . . The third?"

"Ten rounds is the best I can do, sir."

"Your lawyer wants that jury to believe that the defendant, or some assassin still walking around free did a whole lot better. What material is the scope on this rifle, CE 139, made from?"

"Plastic."

"Nothing further, Sergeant."

"Given that exchange, Mr. Matthews," Judge Davis began, "do you want any redirect?"

Matthews rose slowly and with as much majesty as he could muster. "No, Your Honor. The state rests its case."

Barnes knew it was coming, but still couldn't believe it. The jurors buzzed amongst themselves for the second time in two witnesses and this time, the judge did not stop them, as he, too, was registering a sense of surprise, although he knew he had to conceal it from the jury. Once composed, he asked the obvious: "Mr. Barnes, when will the defense be prepared to present its case?"

Barnes rose slowly, attempting to establish eye contact with as many jurors as possible before speaking. "If it please the Court, Your Honor, based on the initial discovery proceedings, in which the prosecution presented a far lengthier list of witnesses than what they actually called, the defense certainly cannot be expected to be prepared to proceed now, midway through a Friday afternoon. However, I would promise the court that we will be prepared to begin Monday, and we will keep the promise made at the outset of the trial that the defense will call the witnesses to this event not called by the prosecution. I would also like to offer two considerations to the court at this time." Barnes waited for the judge to grant him the go-ahead, which was done.

"First, I would like to suggest that out of fairness to the members of the jury, who have made many personal sacrifices and are continuing to do so on a daily basis, that beginning on Monday, we work from 9 A.M. to 5 P.M., and use Saturdays for testimony as well, in order to speed things up."

"Any problems with that, Mr. Matthews?" the judge asked.

"None, Your Honor, except that if we start at 9 A.M. on Monday, I can't see how we'll still be here Saturday," Matthews answered in a feeble attempt to upstage Barnes's obviously successful play to the jury.

"We'll be here next Saturday, Mr. Matthews. Mr. Barnes, I believe you said you had two considerations to put before the court. Is that both of them—the nine to five and Saturday?"

"No, Your Honor, that was the first. The second is that the defense moves to have the charges against the defendant dismissed inasmuch as the prosecution has failed to establish a *primae facie* case." Coming like an afterthought following a scheduling suggestion, the motion hit everyone in the courtroom like a fragmentation grenade.

"You can't be serious," was the first comment heard, and was made by Prosecutor Matthews.

"I never joke around making motions to dismiss in capital crimes. The only thing more serious than my motion is the harm done to this defendant by this absurd witch-hunt and the greater damage done to America's judicial system in the eyes of the world when the case, if that's what you call it, against this defendant is made public."

Judge Davis cut short any further debate, suggesting yet another meeting in his chambers. But Barnes objected to that, saying that although the jury should hear no more, any further legal wrangling or discussion of relevant evidence and testimony before the bench should be part of the record.

The judge agreed, allowed a few moments for the jury to be escorted out for perhaps the last time, but said he wanted time to think over the issues and that oral arguments on the motion would be heard at 8 A.M. on Monday morning. Looking directly at Matthews and then at Barnes, he concluded, "And make no mistake, gentlemen. I will take this motion most seriously. It has much to be said for it."

Matthews knew he needed trial transcripts to date and had a lot of work to do. Barnes knew he had reservations to cancel. He also knew he had to make a decision about Oswald's other trial, because he knew it was going to be held.

The relief that Matthews had hoped for when he was able to rest the prosecution's case was simply not forthcoming. Such relief only occurred, he rationalized to himself, when an attorney rests a case he is going to win, or one he may lose that will never make the papers. This case fit in neither category.

The weekend was a nightmare for almost everyone involved. Barnes was unable to head north, and had to settle for a couple of cryptic phone calls and a promise to steal some time and write. Carolyn Jeffries's problem was just the opposite, as she realized that letters from her boyfriend were coming less frequently and that the content was now more news and weather and less heavy breathing.

The defense team's problems, however, personal as they might be, were nothing compared to the hellish two and one half days spent by the prosecutors. Upon the adjournment of the court, Matthews told Graves and Vincent to get home, pack a bag, and plan to spend the weekend at his ranch reading trial transcripts, which Vincent would have to collect from Mrs. Martinez "sometime after six o'clock" that Friday.

Although they knew the transcripts would not paint a rosy picture, at least they had them, and Ray Matthews tried to explain to his junior assistants how tough this would have been only a few years before, prior to the advent of the Xerox machine. In those days, he recalled, the court stenographer might type a couple of carbon copies, which lose readability, but there would never be enough carbons for this trial, so they would have to be farmed out to other typists, something that clearly was not going to happen in *The People* v. *Oswald*. Eaton Graves then told Matthews not to wax too emotional about Xerox machines.

"Why not?" Matthews asked. "There's got to be a silver lining here somewhere."

"Ray, you asked me to find out about Eddie Barnes when the defendant picked him. Well, I had a private eye in Minnesota check him out—perfectly legit, good record, clean—all the stuff I told you back last summer. What I didn't tell you, as it seemed of no significance then, was that Barnes got a sizable inheritance—upwards of fifty grand, roughly a year before November twenty-two, 1963. As you just showed, a lawyer has an appreciation for Xerox machines, and Barnes took the whole inheritance, bought Xerox stock—and bought it cheaply. Since then, it has gone through the ceiling, and has split five for one, twice. So the hundreds of shares he bought, on an inheritance, yet, is now thousands of shares, which means he's sitting on upwards of a cool mil in stock paper. Still like Xerox machines, Ray?"

"We've got work to do." Five hours, one dinner, and a couple of bourbons later, the three prosecutors sat in silent disbelief, like mourners at a wake, numb in the knowledge that they had proven virtually nothing in seven and one half days of testimony. Each day, they knew events had gone poorly. But when the record, the written word, of witnesses' testimony, overruled objections, and excluded evidence was digested in one sitting, it was overwhelming.

"Where do we go from here?" Vincent asked.

"Probably to another case," Matthews answered, "because if I were presiding over this trial, I'd fold it up on Monday morning. After reading these transcripts, we have no chance, except on the thin possibility that Davis, and even Barnes, will want to put the defense on, to destroy forever any lingering doubts the public might have entertained if only allowed to read what, for the sake of humor, will be referred to historically as 'the prosecution's case.' It's a disgrace, and even though no one has said it to us, we didn't do the best we could have done . . ." Graves and Vincent allowed Matthews the liberty to think out loud, hoping it would create a kind of catharsis, rather than a paralysis, and get all three of them to the end of the trial, whenever that might be. "Well, at least Bob Dean was up front with us when he said I should have a statement ready for the press, and that statement, in addition to everything else we have to do, will be prepared this weekend. Which reminds me," Matthews said, with more animation in his voice than in his earlier dirgelike soliloquy, "Earl, do you still keep in touch with that reporter, uh . . . Kingston—John Kingston?"

"Sure. But not in the last couple months, because of this trial."

"Okay. Call him tomorrow, chitchat. Say nothing about the trial—we'll have no violation of legal ethics. See if he can say anything about it. Better yet, call Sunday afternoon. The judge may alert the media for what is coming Monday, if a dismissal is in the air, and I would assume he'd tell you that something is up."

"Will do," Vincent replied, trying to keep Matthews's, and his own, spirits up.

"In the meantime, let's get some sleep, and maybe tomorrow we can find a few cogent facts that demand we keep this trial going."

As the weekend progressed, a second and third reading of the evidence, for want of a better term, did nothing to improve the spirits of any individual on the prosecution team. The low point of the weekend, however, was clearly discernible. On about his third time through, Eaton Graves interrupted the reading of the other two to ask, "What are we going to say Monday if Barnes makes the point that there is no weapon in evidence?"

"What are you talking about?" Matthews asked, clearly not in a mood to banter.

"A gun, Ray. A weapon. I've read this three times now, and although we rested our case, we never asked that either the pistol or the rifle be admitted as evidence. Little wonder Barnes was so coy in his motions to exclude them—we never moved to include them."

"Are you sure?" Vincent asked, saving further egg from Matthews's face.

"Until somebody shows me in one of those glorious Xerox pages that Barnes is making a profit from, I don't see it. And this time through, I was looking specifically for it."

"We can only blame Dallas for just so much," Matthews was thinking out loud. "This is our screwup, and when somebody takes a careful look at that transcript after it hits the papers, we're going to look like fools."

A few miles away, the defense had its own dilemma, albeit a more pleasant and strenuous one. On one hand, Barnes and Dean were huddling about the specific content of what should be included in the oral arguments regarding the motion to dismiss. Barnes felt that they should simply review the record and cite the wreckage of strewn prosecution witnesses and evidence.

Dean, however, shared some experience with Barnes, suggesting that Barnes make three essential approaches: first, review Matthews's opening statement, and demonstrate to the court that certain parts of it had been fulfilled, but a great deal had not, much as he would normally do in final arguments; phase two would be a breakdown of the evidence admitted, showing that much of it came, in fact, from the defense, highly unusual at mid-point in a trial, and citing that which had been excluded. Finally, Dean argued, Barnes should measure each of the forty-seven prosecution witnesses, and because the defense had clearly won, show the judge what facts the witnesses had made for the prosecution, and what facts the defense had added to the case from the same forty-seven people. In Barnes's style, he would have just been measuring what the defense did, admittedly a lot, but it would leave open the possibility that the prosecution had also done a lot. In Dean's reasoning, they could easily afford to rehash the prosecution's case, because the defense had effectively neutralized it. Barnes accepted the logic and the two men worked from that standpoint.

Carolyn Jeffries, beginning early Saturday, worked the phones. On Friday night, all three had gone through their witness list, and had added some names based on prosecution omissions, bringing their list of possibles to a staggering three hundred. They then broke the witnesses down into categories, which were followed by numbers in parentheses: those who thought they heard firecrackers, which to Barnes meant one shot from the Mannlicher with weak, war surplus ammo, (11); gun-related witnesses, (12); knoll witnesses, (30); "oddities," for want of a better catchall name, (31); those with testimony regarding more than three bullets, not shots, but bullets, (9); Secret Service—threats against JFK plus the agents on duty in Dallas, (19); witnesses who could suggest ties between Oswald and the intelligence community, (18); those with knowledge of threats against Oswald's safety, an iffy category, (3); those who had seen the President's wounds in Dallas, (25); those, besides the three autopsy pathologists that could testify from Bethesda, (13); theater patrons with interesting stories to tell, (6); stories of potentially "fake" Oswalds, (21); witnesses regarding the Harper Fragment, bone matter found on Saturday, (3); Dealey Plaza witnesses, (25); those who could provide an alibi for the defendant at one time or another, (9); those with photographic evidence not yet seen or evidence of importance that was never returned, (9); experts, (9); witnesses with stories to tell of Oswald's days in New Orleans, (6); witnesses who could challenge existing defense evidence, (20); those who thought, like John McVickar at the U.S. Embassy in Moscow, that Oswald was well coached in his answers to officialdom, (3); Jack Ruby oddities that would add spice to the record, (7); and, finally, "other," (12).

The total of over three hundred staggered the three attorneys, given that Matthews, seeming with a well-shuffled deck, had only forty-seven; as they worked through the weekend, Barnes and Dean added to the number. Carolyn Jeffries, given priorities by the two men, had to contact either the witnesses themselves and let them know when they would be asked to comply with previously issued subpoenas, or, in some cases, to contact process servers, just in case the trial did not end, to serve additional subpoenas to a few witnesses who would certainly not come voluntarily. It made for a hectic weekend, and Barnes looked forward to the moment when he could make his presentation on Monday morning, and hopefully it would end there.

# Twelve

egardless of what either the prosecution or the defense wanted, Monday, January eighteen arrived, and early, as the judge had set eight o'clock for arguments with respect to the defense motion to dismiss. Ironically, the prosecution would have been happy if it had been granted, and the defense subconsciously wanted to call the witnesses they had labored so hard to depose and prepare.

Judge Davis entered the courtroom at precisely eight o'clock on Barnes's watch, made sure everyone had their coffee, and then asked if both sides were ready to proceed with the motion to dismiss. Both answered in the affirmative.

"Before we get to that," Davis began, "I must tell you that Special Agent Drain apologized, in writing, for his comments to the attorney of record for the defense.

"I must also report to you that our other guest, Mr. Worrell, was found early Saturday morning very near death from a suicide attempt with the sheet off the cot. He is expected to survive and recover, yet this raises those same nagging questions that have been with us these past two weeks." The

judge seemed lost in thought for a few moments, then continued, "Now, as to the motion to dismiss . . . Mr. Barnes?"

Although not thrilled by what he had just heard, Barnes
rose, but remained behind the defense table to work from
notes. "Your Honor, the defense would like to approach the
motion to dismiss from three angles. First, we would like to
show the court the promises, contained in the prosecution's
one thousand nine hundred twenty-word opening statement,
that were kept, and those that went, well, let's say unful-
filled. Second, we would like to demonstrate that of the exhibits introduced so far at this trial, almost half were put in
evidence by the defense, six major exhibits were excluded,
and no weapon was entered in a homicide, forcing us to ask
the jury to believe, for lack of evidence to the contrary, that
the defendant beat the President to death in less than six
seconds . . ."

"Your Honor," Matthews tried to interrupt.

"Be assured you will get your opportunity, Mr. Matthews,"
the judge told the prosecutor, cutting him off.

"And finally, Your Honor, the defense will examine what
was entered into the record by the forty-seven defense witnesses who were sworn and testified. If we only viewed the
positive side, it is clearly the defense's contention that insufficient evidence was presented to continue these proceedings. But that exceedingly thin testimony, when coupled with
facts elicited during cross-examination, points to the certainty that there never should have even been a true bill returned in this case, much less a trial. Is it acceptable to the
court that we proceed along these lines?"

"Proceed."

Barnes spoke evenly and clearly, with a sense of deference
to a superior, not as he would to an intimidated witness or
for the jury's benefit. "The prosecution promised to produce
the assassination rifle, but they have not done so in any evidentiary sense save that it has been suggested, but not
proved, that the weapon we have been looking at was found
at the scene. I have no doubt the defendant purchased that
weapon, but that is almost irrelevant. There's no proof it was
fired that day, or, if so, by whom. And the overwhelming
sense one gets from the last group of prosecution witnesses

is that, despite what they might have wanted the jury to believe, this weapon was just what the defense has contended all along: cheap junk, unsuitable for anything more sophisticated than a carnival shooting gallery, where its blatant inaccuracy would be an economic blessing to the carnival operator, who would never have to award any prizes for marksmanship.

"Further, with respect to the rifle, it was on the advice of the bench that the defense withdrew the motion, which still has validity, to exclude the weapon from evidence for both chain of possession and for the Mauser-related discussions *and* paperwork.

"The prosecution's cartridges and whole bullet were excluded. Nothing could be determined ballistically about any other piece of metallic evidence. Fingerprints were promised and suggested at, but not positively identified. The paper bag remains just that: a paper bag, unproven to be anything but a stage prop. Also absent is definitive proof that the defendant entered the Book Depository with the bag in his possession. It has been shown that he took a bag—not necessarily the prosecution's bag, but a bag, with him when he left Mr. Frazier in the parking lot. But that proves nothing. Forgive my analogy, Mrs. Martinez, but he could have also left Mr. Frazier's car with a full bladder and entered the Depository without one. The black and white photos, which the defense's experts were looking forward to dealing with, were of necessity excluded because of an improper search, along with a collection of largely meaningless junk, amidst which there appeared a photo of the residence of General Edwin A. Walker, U.S. Army resigned. That photo depicts an auto with no license plate. At the time it was seized, the license was visible. It may be for the best that such evidence was excluded, as it raises far more questions than it answers.

"There has been no proof that the defendant and the weapon came together at any time between noon and 1 P.M. on Friday, November twenty-two, 1963. Despite some Joe McCarthy-like rhetoric in the prosecution's opening statement, we have heard no evidence that the defendant had any identifiable political beliefs other than a patchwork of statements which only raise more questions than they answer.

"The prosecution has not even hinted, except in an unful-filled opening promise, at a motive for this crime. There has not been a syllable of testimony that the defendant had any reason to want to harm the victim, or that the defendant had a history of violence or some neurosis which could have caused such behavior. What has been weakly demonstrated was that the defendant had a history of truancy and was not good at holding a job, the second factor, when tied together with his inability to operate a motor vehicle, suggests a cer-tain lack of coordination which would make the crime as suggested a virtual impossibility.

"In spite of the presence of military and law enforcement 'experts,' there has been no convincing testimony that the defendant possessed the marksmanship skills necessary to commit the crime as suggested. There has been an equal paucity of evidence that the defendant honestly and sincerely demonstrated at any time either a genuine anti-American at-titude, or a pro-Soviet or pro-Cuban attitude. What we have is posturing; what it means, we do not know, and frankly, that sphinx who is in your lockup has shed no light to any-one on the defense team as to his 'Red' leanings.

"Lastly, to conclude the unfilled promises category, we have an autopsy report and a supplemental autopsy report both excluded because the testimony of their author or au-thors, as the case may be, was so at odds with the report that we were forced to choose between what they freely told us and what they were ordered to do or not do into the late hours of November twenty-second. Beyond that, the autopsy photos and X rays raise serious questions of tampering with evidence that would approach literally the highest levels of the United States government.

"On the other hand, it has been shown, and we are asked to continue the case, based on the fact that the defendant did order two weapons, and was identified by a taxi driver. Fur-ther, there is compelling evidence, which I do not dispute for location purposes, that shots were fired from above and be-hind the President. A gun was clearly seen in the sixth floor window, but what gun, and more importantly, what gun-man? And fibers from the shirt the defendant was wearing *when arrested* matched fibers found on the butt plate of the weapon allegedly found on the sixth floor, which, if the defense did not withdraw its exclusion motion, would now be a moot tuft of fibers.

"This then, is the promise versus the reality of the prosecution's case." Hearing Barnes's accurate recitation made the case sound just slightly worse than reading all weekend, Matthews thought, but he knew Barnes was only warming to his task.

"With reference to the exhibits, Your Honor, it would perhaps be redundant to recite them all, but suffice to say that they go no further than what was cited in the 'promises kept' part of my last summation, except in cases where documents or exhibits merely suggest behavior—the ownership of a postal box, ownership of a Fair Play for Cuba Membership card, plus some fake identification. Oh, and a bus transfer. These do not measure up to the standards of hard, concrete evidence that our system of justice demands in order to obtain a conviction against a defendant. They do not, in fact, begin to measure up.

"Lastly, what did we learn from the prosecution's forty-seven witnesses, at least eight of whom committed perjury either in this courtroom or when sworn before the President's commission in 1964?"

"Buell Wesley Frazier, a likable and no doubt honest man, told us the defendant had a package and took it in the direction of the Depository. But he also told us the bag was too small to hold the rifle, that he could not identify the bag, and that he thought the shots came from west of the Book Depository."

"Harold Norman, James 'Junior' Jarman, and Bonnie Ray Williams, occupants of the fifth floor, southeast corner window, told varying accounts of hearing the rifle bolt and shots, or of hearing nothing, or of hearing shots from other locations, but their actions—in going to the far end of the building—clearly betray their words."

"Amos Lee Euins, clearly an honest young man, told us what he saw and how officialdom interpreted it. But he didn't see a scope, heard shots in too-rapid succession, and had his words come out that the defendant wasn't wearing a hat. Now we've all heard hundreds of descriptions of or by witnesses, and it's rare indeed to add the unnecessary. You don't tell what a suspect didn't have unless it matters. If he was missing an arm, or a hand, that narrows the field, but 'no hat'? That's just further tampering.

"Geneva L. Hine told us it was her impression shots came from the Depository. I believe her. And so might the jury, but the Book Depository is not on trial here. A person is, and Ms. Hine has no knowledge of that issue.

"Malcolm Couch also implicated the Depository but not the defendant, and saw more barrel than is visible on the alleged weapon.

"Pauline Sanders also implicated the Depository, as no doubt others could have, but to the same dead end. The most important thing Miss Sanders told us was that she saw an officer, most likely Marrion Baker, enter the Depository in greater haste than we had suspected, thereby making his encounter with the defendant all the more indicative of innocence.

"Mr. Phil Willis also spoke cogently and honestly, in my estimation, about shots from the Depository. But he also saw the President hit in the head and will not allow for the possibility that the shot that inflicted that wound came from the rear.

"Then we heard from James Worrell, who either can't tell time or should serve some.

"Photographer Robert H. Jackson, like Malcolm Couch, saw a weapon in an upper floor window, but again, saw no scope, too much barrel, and the timing of shots two and three was too close in time to have been fired from a bolt action relic.

"Howard Brennan, the Rosetta Stone of this case, became the sphinx. We may never know exactly what he did see, so we must rely on what he told us, and that took an amnesty to begin to get at the truth. Given his preamnesty testimony, even if he put the defendant in that window, which he did not, it would have to be given scant weight in the overall picture, based on seriously declining credibility.

"Adrian Alba has the unique distinction, if we believe the prosecution's witness list, of being the only person on this planet that the defendant ever talked about guns with. With everybody else, he was a silent loner or a sophomoric political theoretician, but hardly a gun nut. Makes me wonder, I'll tell you that.

"Messrs. Michaelis, Scibor, and Waldman, gave us indication that the defendant purchased two weapons: a cheap carbine with scope 'attached,' and a thirty dollar pistol. It would have been more believable if a would-be assassin had put his whole fifty dollar gun budget into one semidecent rifle. On the other hand, their records are just too good, the gun was under litigation for defects, and there is a discrepancy between the gun that was ordered and the one in this courtroom . . . yet another possible reason for its exclusion in the absence of a statement explaining the discrepancy, as yet unheard.

"Special Agent Cadigan was very cagey in allowing the belief that Oswald signed more documents than he in fact signed, and then told us that the gun bag and the materials in the Depository were a match, despite FBI lab reports to the contrary.

"Embassy employees Richard Snyder and John McVickar testified to some interesting, if pointless, theater enacted at the U.S. Embassy in Moscow, but both admitted that the defendant, for all his bombast, never renounced his U.S. citizenship, and both also felt he had been coached. The question then arises, 'By whom?' Of further interest, as demonstrated in cross-examination, Mr. McVickar was flown to Washington from Bolivia to provide hearsay testimony when hundreds of witnesses in Dallas were not even deposed. Why McVickar, at huge expense, when others were local and free?

"Then we have Dr. Renatus Hartogs, who put on the most clearly erratic and unprofessional performance I have ever encountered from a witness with knowledge of a patient's case history. Physician, heal thyself . . .

"Marrion Baker and Roy Truly, testifying, in effect, in tandem, gave no evidence against the defendant; on the contrary, they indicated he was calm and not out of breath when encountered within seconds of the final shot being fired.

"Cecil McWatters no doubt had the defendant on his bus, but he could not positively identify him. William Whaley, the cabbie, could, but a taxi ride is not against the law, and the defendant was hardly behaving as a fleeing felon when he offered an elderly woman the taxi. Further, the defense has a witness who will testify that the defendant entered a station wagon driven by a dark-complected individual. The vehicle is clearly not that of Whaley, nor is he the dark-complected individual. And the defense witness is a highly decorated sheriff's deputy.

"Officer Luke Mooney was part of the confusion involving who found, picked up, threw down, and did or did not maintain chain of possession of the cartridges which were excluded. He did not smell gunpowder in the so-called sniper's nest, and on the way in, he posted a civilian at the rear door of the Depository, clearly not optimal police procedure nor a clear indication that the Depository was either sealed or considered a primary crime scene.

"Lieutenant Day, an honest, well-intentioned man, was out of his league on November twenty-second, and his testimony showed it. But that does not excuse poor police work. He also told us that he smelled no gunpowder, that the print he did lift was an old one, that there was no proof that the gun had been fired except the cartridges—circumstantial at best— and he also told of a report he filed regarding a bullet discovered in the grass, which makes far too many bullets for three cartridges.

"Deputy Eugene Boone and Constable Weitzman, both likable men no doubt dedicated to their work, filed very competent reports, down to the minute—1:22 P.M.—of the discovery of the rifle. But both spoke of a Mauser, and Constable Weitzman, who should have known better if it was not a Mauser, made misidentifications of the scope and the color of the barrel. So we are left with professional but inexcusable, or professional and correct, meaning Mauser.

"Officer McDonald essentially told us that the defendant punched him. We could perhaps draw an inference that he was the arresting officer, but there's once again an alarming absence of clear documentation, and in that absence, he becomes just a policeman assaulted by a theater patron who, for reasons as yet unknown to this court, had a reason to fear police.

"Paul Bentley did his job in identifying and submitting as

evidence the shirt worn by the defendant at the time of, and subsequent to, his arrest. But there's no law against wearing a shirt, and neither Mr. Bentley nor anyone else has offered testimony that the shirt in question, which matched a tuft of fiber found on the rifle in question, was the shirt worn by the defendant *before* he returned to the boarding house, where, we have heard testimony, he changed shirts.

"Detective Stovall executed one of the poorest searches in the history of evidence, and when this record is made public, I have no doubt that, with names changed, his account will be a textbook model of how to destroy a case. Except that in this case, he did not find anything—repeat, anything of evidentiary value on November twenty-second, and only found interesting items on the following day, raising further doubts and suspicions.

"FBI Special Agent Elmer Lee Todd flew all the way from Paris, France, to attempt to enter into evidence a bullet that he knew, from interviews he had taken previously, could not be identified by anyone in the chain of possession hierarchy. And if one link, much less all, breaks, the chain is broken. He knew this, yet he came here to enter the exhibit," Barnes's voice turned sinister, "or to destroy the case a little further.

"Doctors Humes, Boswell, and Finck were clearly not the three best individuals to perform the autopsy on the late President. If this event had occurred differently, and let's suggest that no shots were fired at the presidential car, but rather that the vice-president had been killed, I believe it is a reasonable assumption that President Kennedy would have either insisted on following Texas law and have a thorough Texas autopsy, or, failing that, would have insisted, and I mean insisted, that a thorough evidentiary autopsy be held so that the truth could be found, regardless of whom it pointed at. The only credentials that those three doctors brought to that table were their military uniforms: they could be given orders, and as military personnel, they would take them. I cannot imagine Dr. Milton Helpern, Medical Examiner of the City of New York and the leading authority of autopsy pathology, letting someone with stars on his shoulders tell *him* how to determine the track of a wound. Beyond that, the three doctors raised the question of faked evidence in the photo exhibits, obstruction of justice in film missing or purposely destroyed, and little problems like no fibers in the President's wound and too much metal in the governor for the subsequently excluded bullet to have remained pristine.

"FBI Special Agent Alwyn Cole testified to the defendant's fake Selective Service card. To be brief, 'So what?' It's more an indication of a multiple identity, intelligence-related operation than a punk assassin on his own leaving a fake trail.

"Cortlandt Cunningham could assemble the weapon in six minutes with a dime, which is about what his testimony was worth. He also went out of his way to testify to the uselessness of paraffin testing, yet admitted that he had done it over one hundred times!

"Sebastian Latona, another FBI expert, told us that courts require twelve points of identification for fingerprints to matter, and that no such lift existed with reference to the defendant. No more than nine, in fact, which may mean something to a juror, but, in point of law, it means no identification.

"Paul Stombaugh, another FBI expert, told us that the hairs found in the excluded blanket came from the defendant —or one of a zillion other people. And really—pubic hairs?

"Lyndal Shaneyfelt, yet another faceless bureaucrat who has been taking money under false pretenses for all these years, first denied a curb marking, then admitted it, then showed there was no copper on the bullet which struck the curb. Then he fit the media conclusion—one assassin, three shots, to the evidence, so that the curb would have had to have been hit five and one-half seconds after the President's head exploded, clearly a time a successful assassin would have been using to escape. But not to Mr. Shaneyfelt—a government man telling the official, Washington, D.C., verdict— even if his story is *absurd.*

"Dr. Guinn honestly testified that he found differences in fragment composition, and though of little variation, any variation is significant—meaning samples are exactly identical, or school's out.

"Drain, Frazier, Simmons, Dr. Olivier, and the military boys—Anderson and Zahm, also parroted the government line, but with words only. The proof was lacking because all

the king's horses and all the king's men could not put that
cheap rifle in anyone's hands and have them duplicate a feat
of shooting that an unpracticed, uncoordinated, roustabout
useless human being is supposed to have accomplished despite being fazed out of the marines as a 'rather poor shot.'
Those people told us nothing except that the government
wants to convict Lee Oswald at any cost, or make such a
shambles of these proceedings that the truth will never
emerge from the wreckage. And to this point, they—the government witnesses, relying on the one-sided presidential
commission, are still succeeding in doing just that.

"Your Honor, I restate the defense's motion to have these
charges dismissed inasmuch as the prosecution has failed to
present a *primae facie* case."

"The court will duly note your repetition of your motion,
Mr. Barnes, as well as your most cogent presentation of it.
Mr. Matthews, rebuttal?"

Barnes sank down, almost adrenaline-drained. Although it
had been easy to say, it seemed like each word had carried
the threat of life or death to the defendant. He was glad his
oral argument was over. As for the case . . ."

Matthews stood, as did Barnes, behind his respective table. "If it please the Court, Your Honor, I would be less than
candid if I attempted to convince the court that whatever I
could say at this point would constitute a rebuttal." He
paused, still searching for the right word or phrase. "Yet,
somehow, and while admitting the weaknesses of the prosecution's case, the failure to come through with promises,
which I might add, were made in good faith when made, and
even added to the growing list of evidence that has been excluded through no fault of the prosecution, I still believe that
this is a case the jury should hear all of, and render a verdict.
You have it in your power, Judge, to rule for the defense, but
a fourteen-month-old trail of tainted or tucked away evidence is a cold trail indeed. If justice is to be served in this
process, one of three things must happen: the jury can convict the defendant, which, I admit, seems unlikely; the jury
can fail to arrive at a verdict, always a possibility regardless
of the way the evidence may look; or the jury may walk into
the jury room, chew the fat for two hours, and acquit.

"I know from Mr. Barnes's discovery documents that he has many witnesses. They may tell us nothing, or they may tell us a great deal more than the prosecution was able to tell the court. I can deal even with the worst of those eventualities. But those people need to be heard. Their words need to go in this record. Lee Oswald freed by the judge, halfway through, raises questions about the judicial system and not as much about the case. Lee Oswald convicted, acquitted, or no verdict rendered, does justice to the process and either answers all questions, in the case of conviction, or raises monumental ones in the case of the other two possibilities. Judge Davis, you are the law. But the jurors are justice. I obviously cannot stand before you and tell you that the prosecution has presented such an overwhelming case that this trial must continue—I wish I could, but we must all be honest. But we also know that there have been many bizarre and unusual forces at work here and those forces, in the final analysis, force all of us out of our traditional stereotypes and make us become seekers of the truth. Right now, the truth is more important to the prosecution than a conviction, and the truth—and a verdict that will compel continued search for the truth when our labors are done—can only come from the jury. Thank you, Your Honor."

"Would anyone like to add anything to what has been said by either the defense, in support of their motion, or in support of the prosecution, in their efforts to have the court deny the motion?"

Anxious looks were exchanged among all participants as silence enveloped a large room containing ten individuals: six attorneys, a judge, a bailiff, a stenographer, and a faceless state policeman operating a tape recorder. Each looked to another for an answer, but with none forthcoming, the judge focused the issue: "Mr. Barnes, certainly your presentation carried the day from the standpoint of legal rights of your client, and equally with respect to the fact that the prosecution has not presented a *primae facie* case. I could gavel this court closed, *sine die*, right now, and leave these grounds in perfect conscience, because the law is clearly, and overwhelmingly, on the side of the defense and the defendant. Or, Mr. Barnes, I could rule against you, and we could bring in the jury and the defendant, and you could stand and announce, 'The defense rests,' in which case I would either accept a motion to grant a directed verdict of not guilty, or else instruct the jury with respect to the evidence in such a way that they would understand that I was telling them to acquit. I'm certain that if I pointed out to them that the only person who truly identified the defendant was a taxi driver, that would not carry with it a conviction. But Mr. Matthews carried the day philosophically, arguing correctly that the truth will only be arrived at when all has been said and done here in Lubbock. We cannot undo Dallas—neither the tragedy, nor the police comedy. But we can fill the record with the truth, and let the chips fall where they may. Mr. Barnes, if I thought that your defense witnesses were going to convict your client, I would move favorably on your motion. Based on the extremely high quality of the work of Mr. Dean, Miss Jeffries, and you, Mr. Barnes, I can only assume that your defense will aid this court in getting at the truth in this matter.

"Therefore, it is the ruling of the court, and I want it in the record that Judge Franklin W. Davis, in spite of having every reason to dismiss the charges against the defendant, ruled against the motion by the defense.

"Gentlemen, Miss Jeffries, we are all no doubt drained by this morning's proceedings. We will reconvene at 12:30 P.M. and begin hearing defense witnesses, of which I understand there are quite a few. Perhaps if we could informally sort out some of the duplications, if there exist any, and use stipulations or depositions to put material into the record, that would expedite matters. And gentlemen—and ladies—let's dedicate ourselves to finding the truth in this matter. That is, ultimately what this system—and the offices of the court in this case—are all about. Recess until 12:30."

Following the judge's ruling, the prosecution team departed, with Matthews giving Barnes a friendly "see how you like it" look, letting Barnes know that it was his witnesses, not Matthews's, who would now be grilled and subject to intense scrutiny.

Not that Barnes cared. The judge had already said the defense was ahead; the question now was how best to win it. Barnes, remaining at the defense table and thinking out loud, tried the suggestion, hinted at by the judge, that they simply rest their case.

Bob Dean thought otherwise. "Step back from it for a minute and think about it, Eddie. This is no longer a personal thing between you and Ray; it is also more than a question of whether the prosecution can prove whether the defendant is guilty in a legal, technical sense, or whether the case will collapse from legal, technical reasons. We've already won that battle. Davis said so. But this is not just a Texas homicide. What are the citizens of California, Kansas, Pennsylvania, and Maine going to think? That the defendant did it, but a couple of slick shysters got him off? That's a small victory at best. No—what we have to do now is wave that legal victory in our left hand and put on the defense's case with our right hand—and pound it home. Let's get another opinion: Carolyn, if Oswald walked right now on this case, what would your innermost thoughts and legal expertise tell you about him if you were to write a memoir of this case?"

"Well, we've won, or so it seems, because, one, somebody wanted the defendant to take the fall all by himself—no conspiracy charged where there should have been, and there just wasn't any solid evidence that he did it. Circumstantial evidence in abundance—maybe too much of it, but it was there, and then excluded for horrible police work. If I had to speculate on Oswald's role, and you may not want to hear this . . ."

"I want to hear exactly what you're thinking," Dean told her.

"I don't think he's completely innocent. I strongly suspect he was manipulated, set up, whatever, but that he didn't pull any rifle trigger that day. And I think we've already put that thought in the jury's mind, and our defense will prove it. Having done that, however, we have created a situation in which a second jury, deciding whether or not he killed the policeman, will find self-preservation a very strong motive, and they'll get him for that one. Unless, of course, he suddenly becomes cooperative and tells what he knows. Personally, if given the choice between an interview and the electric chair, I'd have my vocal chords in top form."

Dean looked at Barnes: "I strongly agree with Carolyn. The question then becomes, 'Do we change our strategy? Do we do such a convincing job that we win this one in grand style and allow for our client to lose round two?' "

Barnes interrupted: "Yes. Round two be damned."

Dean tried to read Carolyn Jeffries's expression, and then repeated the process on Barnes. "Of course we do. As you pointed out, Carolyn, it may be the only way we ever hear anything from that enigma we've been calling a client."

Changing the subject briefly, Dean commented that he was getting hungry, and the afternoon session would go from 12:30 to 5, so they had better grab lunch while they could. Everyone agreed. "We still going for an afternoon of playing 'Shock the Jury,' Eddie?"

"Would we do it any other way?"

At promptly 12:30 P.M., Judge Davis entered the courtroom, had the defendant and jury brought in, and then instructed the jury that while he found much substance in the defense's motion to dismiss the charges, he was denying the motion, for the time being. Both Barnes and Matthews were surprised that Judge Davis had added the phrase "for the time being."

"Mr. Barnes, is the defense prepared to proceed?"

"Yes, Your Honor. The defense calls former Vice-President Richard M. Nixon." The jury was shocked, as Barnes had hoped, by the mere introduction of his first witness.

The former vice-president entered, was sworn, and took his place in the witness box looking fit, dignified, but yet a little bit uncomfortable about being cast in this role.

Barnes made a couple of gratuitous remarks about respecting the witness's coming to give testimony, knowing full well that the seasoned politicians of the world go most anywhere at most anytime to get some free ink. In response to further questions, Nixon indicated that his residence was New York City, mentioning that he had previously lived in California and Washington, D.C., feeble attempts at humor, and that his current occupation was attorney for a New York firm in which he was a partner.

"Mr. Nixon, calling your attention to the time period of November eighteenth, 1963, to November twenty-second, 1963, do you have a recollection of where you were during that week?"

"On Wednesday, which would have been November twenty, I visited Dallas, Texas, to speak at a soft drink bottlers' convention. One of the leading soft drink bottlers was a client of the firm in which, as I testified a moment ago, I am a partner."

"And when did you depart from Dallas?"

"I believe it was on the morning of Friday, the twenty-second."

"You believe?" Barnes asked, incredulously.

"Yes, it must have been, because I learned of the tragedy while riding in a taxi from the airport in New York to my apartment."

"I see. Now, before we arrive at your apartment . . ." Barnes said slowly, walking to the defense table and picking up a newspaper, "Mr. Nixon, would a newspaper article entitled 'Nixon suggests LBJ to be Dumped as VP' be a fair characterization of remarks you made to the press while you were in Dallas?"

"I don't recall my exact words, but I did make some remarks on that subject. As a former elected official, I felt that there was friction between the liberal and conservative wings of the Democratic party, and as a Republican, regardless of my feelings, it's not unusual behavior to stir up the other party when possible."

"Particularly when the other party is coming to town the next day," Barnes reminded him. "Now, could you tell us what happened when you learned of the events in Dallas?"

"I can only conjecture, from reconstructing times, that the assassination occurred about the time my plane was landing. My cab stopped for a light in Queens, and a guy ran over and said, 'Have you got a radio? The President's been wounded.' I thought, 'Oh, my God, it must have been one of the "nuts." ' "

"Which 'nuts'?" Barnes asked.

"One of the lunatic fringe-type element that had attacked U.N. Ambassador Stevenson roughly a month before."

"Okay. So what happened after the taxi ride?"

"It must have been, oh, a half hour later I got to my apartment and the doorman told me he was dead . . ."

"I'm not sure the court understands who was dead—was it your doorman or the President?"

Nixon was becoming flustered. "The doorman told me the President had died. I called Edgar Hoover and asked him, 'What happened? Was it one of the nuts?' Hoover said, 'No, it was a Communist.' "

"Do you have a recollection as to the time of that call?"

"It would have to have been around mid-afternoon, possibly as late as 3:30."

Barnes pressed on: "Mr. Vice-President, were you able to bring the telephone records that were subpoenaed?"

"No, I was not."

"No matter. Let's use your recollection. 3:30 in New York is 2:30 in Dallas. The Dallas Police had, at that time, only recently brought in a suspect for the killing of a police officer, and that suspect was not charged with the killing of the President until the following day. How could Edgar Hoover have known who the killer was?"

"Objection. Conclusionary."

"Sustained."

"Mr. Nixon, you testified you are an attorney, so I assume, and I believe the court can, that you can make certain legal judgments. Try to help us here. Since the prosecution offered no testimony whatsoever that Mr. Oswald had any Communist affiliations, do you have any idea of the identity of the Communist that Edgar Hoover was referring to?"

The witness sat silently, while Matthews tried another objection but was overruled.

"No further questions, sir. Thank you very much for taking time out of your busy schedule—attending soft drink conventions to talk politics and what not, to be here."

"Your welcome, Counselor," Nixon answered, ever the politician. "Would it be possible that I have that newspaper if you're not going to admit it into evidence?"

"Sure," Barnes told him, walking over and handing it to Nixon.

"This is today's paper," Nixon noted. Barnes asked that the irrelevant comment be stricken from the record.

Matthews would have liked nothing better than to be able to pounce on one of Barnes's witnesses, but that would have to wait, as it was not good form to pounce on a former vice-president who had carried Dallas County in 1960. "Mr. Nixon, could that 3:30 call have been made later in the day, perhaps?"

"I don't think so. As I told that young fellow, who was so kind as to give me today's paper, it might have been as late as 3:30. People my age remember very clearly where they were when they heard the news of Pearl Harbor, the death of President Roosevelt, and the killing of President Kennedy. As of a half hour before my arrival at home, the news had him wounded. When I got home, the doorman told me the news, which strongly suggests to me that it was very recent news, or he would have attempted to console me, assuming that I had heard of an event that was fifteen minutes or so old. No, 3:30 would be an outside estimate."

"And you immediately called the head of the FBI, just like that, with all he had to deal with that afternoon?"

"Oh, sure. Edgar and I go back a long way. I once wanted very strongly to be an FBI agent. I called him and he told me where the case stood at that time."

"No further questions." Matthews's dream of dicing up Barnes's witnesses would have to wait. The former vice-president was excused and the jury had heard evidence that the FBI had convicted the defendant before the Dallas police had charged him.

"The defense calls the Honorable Waggoner Carr," Barnes announced. Matthews looked across the aisle with a deeply pained expression. Barnes leaned across the aisle, after the witness passed through, and told Matthews, "He was on your list, Ray. No sense wasting his expertise."

Although the jurors had a pretty good idea who the witness was, Barnes had him state his occupation for the record.

"Attorney General for the state of Texas," he replied.

"Mr. Attorney General, drawing your attention to November twenty-second, 1963, would you please tell the jury about the care that was taken with respect to the wording of the indictment that was to be drawn up against the defendant?"

"Oh, it was no big deal. Probably just something that happened because of the existing tensions."

"Nevertheless, Mr. Carr, would you please tell the jury about it?"

Carr had no place to turn. He wasn't going to get any help from the prosecutor, who knew nothing of the event, as it had never been a topic of conversation between them. The judge, no doubt, wanted an answer to Barnes's question.

"Well, somewhere between eight and nine P.M., Texas time, of course, I received a long-distance call from Washington from someone in the White House. I can't remember for the life of me who it was. But a rumor had been heard here that there was going to be an allegation in the indictment against Oswald connecting the assassination with an international conspiracy. There was concern reflected that someone might thoughtlessly place in the indictment such an allegation without having the proof of a conspiracy. See, if we say it was a Communist conspiracy, including the defendant, we have to prove every word there—one, that it was a Communist conspiracy, and two, that the defendant did it. So I consulted with Mr. Wade, and . . ."

"For the record, who is Mr. Wade?" Barnes interrupted.

"Henry Wade, District Attorney for Dallas."

"Thank you. Please continue."

"I spoke with Mr. Wade, and he said there would be no such allegation, and then I called back—as I recall I did—and informed the White House participant in the conversation of what Mr. Wade had said, and that was all of it."

"Thank you, Mr. Attorney General," Barnes quipped. "Let's now analyze what you just said from a couple of perspectives. First, you're the Attorney General for the state of Texas. You receive a phone call from the White House on the day its occupant has been killed *in Texas*, and *they* tell you that *they* have been hearing rumors and *they* try to tell the state of Texas how to write an indictment?"

"That is what I testified to."

"I heard what you testified to, sir. I want to know if it's

normal procedure for the White House to call you and dictate terms of indictments."

"Of course it isn't," the witness replied.

"So then, Mr. Carr, I take it from your last statement that it doesn't happen often?"

"I can never recall it happening before."

Barnes moved in close and stared his witness down: "And you can't recall who was on the other end of the telephone in this one isolated time that it happened? On the day the President was killed, in your jurisdiction, you get a phone call from someone in the White House and you want the jury to believe you treated it like a wrong number?"

Carr looked at the floor. Barnes, sensing his dilemma, figured he could try a spinoff of his ploy with Nixon and the newspaper. "Mr. Carr, I'm going to put other witnesses on the stand. The name of your caller will be in the record. It would seem to be to your advantage if the information came from you. We wouldn't want the people of Texas to think their attorney general didn't know how to mind the shop, would we?"

"I believe it was Cliff Carter," Carr replied.

"For the jury's benefit, who is Cliff Carter?"

"He's a close staff aide to President Johnson."

"Thank you for plumbing the depths of your recollection and supplying the court with that information. Now, I'm curious about what you told us about indictments. Am I correct in interpreting your remarks to say that whatever is alleged in the indictment must be proved?"

"That's correct."

"Even details? Let's take an example. We know that the caliber of the rifle . . . this rifle, Mr. Carr," Barnes said, displaying the weapon again. "We know that the caliber of this rifle is six point five mm, because it says so right here, stamped into the barrel. Are you telling the court that if it was alleged that the defendant killed the President with a rifle, but the indictment said, oh, let's say a six point twenty-five mm rifle, then the indictment would be invalid?"

"That's correct. Under Texas law, whatever is stipulated in the charges must be proved. So you have to keep it simple."

"Mr. Carr, were you aware that the defendant had been

charged with shooting the President and the governor with a six point twenty-five mm rifle?"

"That's absurd."

Judge Davis interrupted: "For your benefit, Mr. Carr, the court has seen the documents, and those were the specified charges."

Carr had no answer. Barnes was hoping for silence anyhow. "Mr. Carr, as far as this squashing of the conspiracy rumor goes, what processes were at work in Texas that would have compelled a highly placed White House aide to telephone the attorney general of Texas? I realize you cannot testify to the caller's state of mind, but, at the Texas end, what was the conspiracy concern?"

"I wasn't close enough to the case to know the answer to that, but there were scattered bits of rumor and there were certainly a number of witnesses who had come in and told us of events or people they had seen which, if accurate, would have shed doubt on the allegation that one person did the crime alone."

Barnes let that sentence sit with the jury as he leisurely drank half a glass of water. "Mr. Attorney General, one last concern. Did you personally notify anyone either on the President's Commission, or on the staff of that Commission, that you had knowledge that the defendant, Lee Oswald, was a paid FBI informant?"

Matthews objected on the grounds of relevancy. He was overruled.

"I notified Mr. Lee Rankin, who I believe was general counsel to the President's Commission, on January twenty-second, 1964, that I had information to that effect, yes."

"Would you characterize your concern as something that was serious enough that you, as an officer of the court, felt bound to report, or were you just passing along gossip for the folks in Washington to kick around?"

Matthews objected again and got the same result.

"I took the allegations very seriously then. I received the information from a highly reputable source, who was, in fact, a former FBI man."

"Thank you, Mr. Attorney General. Your witness, Mr. Matthews." Barnes knew this was another witness that Matthews would have to handle very delicately.

"Mr. Carr, what proof can you offer—in effect, how can you be certain that the alleged call you received on the evening of the twenty-second was in fact from the White House and not from some little den of subversives trying to hoodwink you in a moment of extreme confusion?"

Carr stared Matthews down. He had expected to be grilled by Barnes, but not by a Texas prosecutor and his facial features betrayed that. "There was nothing alleged about the phone call, and you may recall that the man who became President that day was a Texan, as were many members of his staff, including the one who called me—a close acquaintance of mine. I'll admit that I was surprised by the call and it was a crazy day, but you can be sure that call came from 1600 Pennsylvania Avenue, because that is where I called to answer their concern."

Matthews tried another approach: "Are you aware that the President's Commission treated your information that the defendant was a paid informant as nothing more than, quote, 'a dirty little rumor'?"

"Yes. And I would too . . . if I wanted to bury it. But I stand by my statements."

"No further questions."

Barnes rose, casting a glance at Matthews that indicated the heavy guns were gone and he could soon make a run at a witness, and announced, "The defense calls Willie Somersett." Matthews's staff, as was their habit by now, turned to look for the witness coming through the rear doors, but he was escorted in by a Vermont officer through the entrance Oswald usually used. The middle-aged witness then took his place, was sworn, and scanned the courtroom as if looking for hostile faces.

"Mr. Somersett, the court may be curious regarding the way you entered the courtroom. Would it be a reasonable characterization to state that you are employed in the state of Florida in a law enforcement capacity?"

"Yes."

"Does that employment involve hazardous, potentially dangerous undercover assignments?"

"Yes."

"Thank you, Mr. Somersett. I hope that satisfies the court's curiosity as to why you were separated from the other witnesses. For further clarification, since you entered from the prisoner's entrance, are you now facing any criminal charges or serving a sentence for any convictions?"

"Absolutely not."

"Okay. Then let's go back to November 1963. Did you have an undercover assignment at that time that related to threats made against the life of the President of the United States?"

"Yes."

"Please tell the court about your assignment."

"Certainly. My, uh, law enforcement superiors . . ."

"Mr. Somersett, let's clarify that for the jurors. You are employed by . . . ?"

"By the state of Florida. Not a local department, nor anything federal. Is that satisfactory?"

"It is to me," Barnes answered, waiting for an objection from Matthews, or at least for additional clarification. "So your superiors . . ."

"My superiors were concerned about information they had been receiving about a suspect named Joseph Milteer, a leader, if you believed him at the time, of a right-wing group that did not particularly embrace the policies of President Kennedy."

"Were you able to carry out an undercover penetration of Mr. Milteer's organization?"

"I spoke with him on a couple of occasions. I did not, however, become directly acquainted with what you characterized as 'his organization.' "

"What did you learn from your conversations?"

"I spoke with him on November nine, 1963, a Saturday. He told me, without any hesitation, and with a sense of bragging, that the killing of President Kennedy was in the works, and that he would be killed with a high-powered rifle from an office building."

"Did he indicate the name or names of those involved?"

"No."

"Did he indicate that he would be the killer?"

"He did not."

"Was anything else said at that time?"

"He said, 'They will pick up somebody within hours afterward, just to throw the public off.' That was a direct quote, and that scared me as much as his revelation that a plot was in the works to kill the President."

"What did you do with this information?"

"I turned it over to my superiors."

"Do you have any personal knowledge that your contact with Mr. Milteer had any results?"

"I was told that my information caused President Kennedy's proposed motorcade in Florida, on Monday, November eighteenth, 1963, to be canceled. For a couple of days, that knowledge gave me great satisfaction."

"But as we know, the Dallas motorcade was not canceled. Of your own personal knowledge, do you know anything about that?"

"No. I was told that my conversations had led to concerns for the President's safety in Florida, but that was as far as it went."

"Did you have any additional conversations with Mr. Milteer?"

"Yes. He called me, from Dallas, he said, on November twenty-second, and told me 'JFK will never visit Miami again.' Of course, the news on the radio had already made that known. I also spoke with him the following day. He told me at that time that everything had run true to form, and he kidded me for my lack of belief in his preassassination predictions. He also told me not to worry about the arrest of Lee Oswald because 'he doesn't know anything.'"

Matthews was listening to this, and telling Graves that this was not the man's testimony when deposed before the trial. Barnes continued, "Could we have the photographs I sent down during lunch, photo one first please?"

A somewhat grainy picture came up on the screen, showing a row of people. Centered in the picture was a slightly heavyset man with glasses and tousled hair. "Mr. Somersett, please look carefully at this picture and tell me if you can identify anyone in it."

The witness studied the photo, and Barnes hastened to the

defense table to provide the witness with a magnifying glass
he had meant to have in his pocket. The witness took better
than a minute to make his examination. Then he asked
Barnes, "Do you know if it was windy when this was taken?"

Barnes answered, "I can tell you it was breezy, with occasional gusts, but as you can see from the clothes, the temperature was mild."

"If it was windy, then I would say that the man in the center, arms folded, with glasses and mussed-up hair, is the
same Joseph Milteer that I spoke with."

"That figure is the same man who told you that the President would be killed?"

"Yes."

"Could we have the whole photograph from which that one
was taken, please?" Twenty seconds later, the jury gasped,
as they saw Milteer, circled in the background, standing on
Houston Street, with the Presidential limousine and the
Secret Service backup car in the foreground. The jury could
not escape the conclusion that Milteer had been in Dealey
Plaza to witness the execution.

Barnes returned the magnifying glass to the defense table.
"I won't ask you to identify anyone in this picture, Mr.
Somersett, but I do have one more question. Except for the
reference that Mr. Milteer made regarding Lee Oswald on November twenty-third, that 'he doesn't know anything,' did the
subject at any other time mention Lee Oswald?"

"No."

"When you get back to Florida, Mr. Somersett, tell your
superiors they were overreacting to cancel that Florida motorcade. We have evidence that Mr. Oswald was in Dallas on
Monday, November eighteenth, and nobody is *that good a
shot*. No further questions for the witness, Your Honor, and I
would like Somersett Exhibits Numbers 1 and 2 admitted,
with the notation that these were *not* seen or entered by the
presidential commission."

"So moved."

Matthews, Graves, and Vincent conferred briefly as to the
best method for dissecting this obviously damaging testimony. Barnes, in the meantime, working behind the defense
table, took a bulky tape recorder out of a canvas bag, and

began to thread a tape onto the "play" spool. "It's a bluff," Matthews told his assistants. "Nixon and the newspaper all over again. If he had Milteer on tape, we'd have damn sure heard it already. We'll call his bluff right quick and win some points this afternoon. I just hope the jury can see the rope he's laying out to hang himself."

Matthews sat at the prosecution table, to minimize the significance he attached to this witness. "Mr. Somersett, how did you suddenly gain enough importance that someone who claims to represent such an organization is going to speak openly to a relative stranger about events of such incredible importance, and events fraught with such obvious implications for the participant—or participants?"

"I did not just meet the subject in November. I had been moving closer to him, and had been provided with a cover as a wealthy individual with conservative views, perhaps ultra-conservative would be a better characterization, and that I would like to see political action taken, and that I might finance such activities. Mr. Milteer seemed only too glad to consider accepting my generosity, but what he told me seemed to me to be saying that the assassination would greatly lessen the need for political activities."

"And you want the court to believe that these conversations occurred exactly as you testified? I find that very difficult, Mr. Somersett. This seems more like publicity than evidence."

Barnes looked at his witness and shook his head sideways, indicating "no" to further responses. Then he pushed the "play" button on the tape recorder and the court and the jury heard a less-than-perfect recording of the conversation as reported by the witness.

Matthews, in frustration, lashed out at the witness: "I took a deposition from you two months ago. You never told me the conversation was recorded."

"You didn't ask. You shrugged it off as if I was inventing it."

"I also asked you, sir, if your conversations, or the substance of them was offered to the President's Commission. Do you recall me asking you that?"

"Yes."

"And what was your statement at that time?"

"That it was not *given* to the commission."

"So what do you expect this jury to believe?" Matthews asked, thinking he had the witness.

"I expect them to believe the truth, which I have told. The President's Commission was offered the tape, reports from my superiors, and my deposition—but not an appearance, due to the nature of my work. The President's Commission wasn't interested in any of it."

"No further questions."

"Redirect, Mr. Barnes?"

"Not at this time, Your Honor, but I would like to enter the recording—Defense Recording Number 1—at this time."

"So moved." The witness then left using the same door he had entered through, and Matthews was beginning to experience a sense of *déjà vu.*

"The defense calls Richard Randolph Carr."

A ruddy-complected middle-aged man entered the courtroom through the usual door, and took the stand to be sworn. Barnes then asked, "For the record, Mr. Carr, we had a witness a little while back named Waggoner Carr, who is the attorney general for the state of Texas. Are you any relation to him?"

"No. I wish I was, but I'm not."

"Also for the record, did you have any criminal record—and by that I mean arrests or convictions, prior to the twenty-second of November, 1963?"

"No. None."

"Please tell the court where you were on the morning of November twenty-second, 1963."

"I am a steel worker. I was on an upper floor on a building under construction closely adjacent to the site of the presidential assassination that day."

"From your elevated perch, did you have the opportunity to see any individuals in upper-floor windows of the Texas School Book Depository?"

"Yes. I saw one man up there, but the event seemed of little significance prior to the shooting. After the shooting, I saw this man again, leaving the Depository, as I was coming down from my own upper-floor location. I followed the man for one block and he got into a Nash Rambler station wagon, driven by a dark-complected Spaniard or Cuban."

"Do you see that man in this courtroom today?"

Matthews interrupted: "Your Honor, I see no relevance in this at all. There's no description of 'this man,' nor is there any hint that he had done anything deserving the scrutiny of this court."

Barnes knew the rebuttal: "Your Honor, Mr. Truly has testified that all employees, except the defendant and certain others that he saw walk away from the front of the building at the time of the shooting were accounted for. So where did this individual, seen by Mr. Carr, come from? And if he's irrelevant, how can we account for the as yet unheard part of Mr. Carr's testimony?"

"Which is probably equally irrelevant," Matthews added.

"I'll decide, after I've heard it, Counselor. Overruled."

"Is the man you saw—in an upper floor of the Depository and running to enter a Nash Rambler driven by a dark-complected man, the same man who is sitting at the defense table?"

"No. I saw the defendant's picture on TV that day and I was certain then that it was not him."

"What did you do with the knowledge of the events you had seen?"

"I ruined my life."

"Objection. Nonresponsive."

"Sustained."

"Mr. Carr, put your bitterness aside and tell the court what happened when you took your knowledge to the authorities."

"At first, I was told, by someone who flashed a Federal i.d. under my nose and said 'FBI,' to keep my mouth shut. He didn't ask me what I saw, he *told* me what I saw. Later, I repeated what I had seen, and again, federal credentials, a bureaucrat in shirt and tie, made it even plainer: 'If you didn't see Lee Harvey Oswald in the School Book Depository with a rifle, you didn't witness it.' He didn't say it as a threat, but calmly, as a fact."

"Just like that?"

"Just like that. But then my house was ransacked by peo-

ple wearing Dallas police uniforms, while I was held at gun-
point, and . . ."

"What do you mean 'people wearing Dallas police uniforms'?"

"Well, that's what they were wearing. I don't want to believe
that they were, in fact, Dallas policemen."

"Tell the jury the end of your story."

"After that, I received a phone call telling me to get out of
town, and after all that had happened, and with there always
being steel jobs available, I moved to Montana, where I found
a dynamite charge in my car one day. I have been shot at,
and stabbed." Barnes had one more fact he wanted the jury
to hear, but he hoped Matthews would help him put it into
the record. "No further questions. I regret what you have
been through, Mr. Carr, and I know you did not want to appear here, as you made plain when my investigator contacted
you, so I thank you."

At the defense table, Graves and Vincent were imploring
Matthews to say, "No questions" and leave it at that. Matthews argued that Barnes had essentially put unassailable
witnesses on the stand, and it was the prosecution's job to
challenge them, even in some small way. He rose to address
the witness: "Mr. Carr, from your vantage point, could you
see *into* the corner of the sixth floor of the Depository—not
just into the window, but could you have seen an individual
behind the facade from where you were?"

"Objection, Your Honor, he's asking two questions."

"Sustained."

"Could you have seen an individual behind the facade of
the building?"

"I don't believe so."

"Could you identify the dark-complected man driving the
automobile?"

"I was more concerned in noticing the contrast—a white
male, in haste, leaving the scene of an unspeakable crime,
then gets in a car driven by a Latin or Hispanic—I could not
identify that person, no. I was seeing and registering the contrast."

"And you want the jury to believe that only one person has
ever been accused of this crime, and he's been in custody

since the crime, and people are following you all over?" Matthews said it; Barnes heard it.

Carr looked to Barnes. "All the allegations are in the record, sir, including the most recent assault on me, which took place in Atlanta, Georgia."

"We've heard most of this, uh, narrative, don't leave us hanging."

Carr now looked right at Matthews. "I was attacked. I killed the man who attacked me. It's a matter of police records in Atlanta. It was ruled self-defense. I was not charged nor indicted."

"No further questions. The prosecution, too, is sorry for your troubles." Matthews hoped for sympathy in lieu of a victory.

"The defense calls Detective Guy F. Rose."

A young, athletic-looking detective wearing a dapper suit entered the court to be sworn. Having stated that he was a detective on the Dallas police force and that he had seen the defendant in headquarters and had participated in the searches, Barnes moved in closer: "Detective, perhaps you are not aware of it yet, but the materials you helped to seize were excluded from evidence. So my questions to you with respect to any such items are procedural questions, not questions with respect to their value as evidence. Have I made myself clear on that?"

"Yes."

"Fine. In the hours subsequent to your searches of the Paine residence, did there come a time when you had a serious disagreement with an FBI agent over a piece of evidence?"

"Yes. One item we discovered was a small Minox spy camera—"

"Objection to the characterization of 'spy' as type of camera. This is a conclusion on the part of the witness."

"Sustained."

Barnes reminded the witness where he was in his testimony: "So you thought you had discovered a Minox camera . . . ?"

"We brought in a whole lot of photographic equipment. But this one piece, the FBI were calling it a light meter. But I know a camera when I see it. The thing we got at Irving out of Oswald's seabag was a Minox camera. No question about it. They tried to get me to change the records but it wasn't a light meter. I don't know why they wanted it changed but they must have had some motive for it."

"For the record," Barnes asked, facing the jury, "who are 'they'?"

"FBI agents."

"Thank you for your testimony, Detective. No further questions. Mr. Matthews?"

Matthews strolled over to the witness stand, hands in pockets, casually. "Detective, do you want this court to believe you are an expert regarding photographic equipment?"

"No."

"Please tell the nature of any courses of study you may have taken in the subject of photography."

"No courses of study. Anyone who goes through police training is taught how to take pictures, though."

"Would that police training make you an expert on the sophisticated pieces of equipment involved in various different kinds of photography—other than photography used at crime scenes?"

"It would not make that person an expert. And I have made no claim that I'm an expert."

"Then how can you sit there and tell this court that you were dealing with a camera? Have you ever considered that perhaps the FBI people were photographic experts?"

"Objection, Your Honor. Two questions again."

"Sustained. Rephrase it, please."

"Why should the jury believe you that this item was a camera, and not believe the FBI, who said it was a light meter?"

"I opened it. It had film in it. Have *you* ever seen a light meter loaded with film?"

While Matthews tried desperately to come up with something to say, Barnes went on the record to have the earlier exclusion of the word "spy" overruled. The judge considered the question briefly and addressed the witness: "Detective, have you come across such cameras before?"

"Yes, Your Honor."

"Are they somewhat miniaturized?"

"Yes."

"Was 'spy camera' a routine designation that you would put on such an item, if seized in a search?"

"Yes."

"The court overrules itself on the earlier objection. Spy camera is an acceptable designation for the piece of evidence that was excluded. Mr. Matthews?"

"No further questions, Your Honor," Matthews answered.

Barnes would have liked to share with the jury as many as possible of the almost fifty witnesses who felt very strongly that shots had originated from locations other than the sixth floor of the Depository, but those necessary to participate in this show of force had not yet arrived, so he had to fall back on his next resource, the United States Secret Service, who had arrived by government jet and were eager to appear co-operative. "The defense calls Robert I. Bouck."

After the witness was sworn but before Barnes could begin, Judge Davis called Carson in front of the bench and asked him to go into the witness waiting area and inform the government agents that there would be "no cannon" in court. Carson seemed to relish the assignment.

Barnes went to work, eliciting testimony that the witness was the head of the Protective Research Section of the Secret Service, that there had been thirty-two thousand items relative to the President's safety received in 1963, and although some were dismissed as cranks, one hundred sixty-seven people were arrested for genuine threats against the President. It was also learned that thirty-four individuals in the state of Texas were considered potential problems in the event of a presidential visit.

"Are these records kept on computers, microfilm . . . strike that, please. How are these records kept?"

"On cards—like index cards."

"And how many of these cards are in the files of the Protective Research Section of the United States Secret Service?"

"Just about one million."

"Was the name Lee Harvey Oswald known to the Secret Service at any time prior to the twenty-second of November, 1963?"

"No, sir; we had never heard of him in any context; his name doesn't appear at all."

"So on November twenty-second, 1963, you had about one million people that the Secret Service considered more dangerous to the safety of the President than the defendant?"

"I can't answer that except to say that we had a million identified concerns, and the defendant was not among them. In that sense, yes. On the other hand, some of those million people were in confinement on November twenty-second, so the million figure, well, it has to be placed in context."

"As does the defendant's absence from the list," Barnes reminded him.

"Yes."

"In the state of Texas, you said thirty-four individuals. Was that the starting figure, or the final tally when you sorted out the maybes from the probables?"

"We actually looked at a volume of cases approximating four hundred in connection with the President's trip to Dallas."

"And was anyone taken into custody as a protective measure?"

"No."

"Mr. Bouck, as the Head of the Protective Research Section of the Secret Service, can you tell us if any extra precautions were taken with respect to the President's visit to Dallas in light of the attack on Ambassador Stevenson in Dallas as well as the two documented threats against the President in the month of November 1963?"

The witness shifted uneasily in his chair. "There was certainly concern after the Stevenson incident. Special Agent Lawson—that's Winston Lawson, who was the advance agent for the Dallas part of the Texas trip—had gone to great lengths to gather intelligence from local officials who monitor radical groups. They assured Agent Lawson that there was no perceived threat." Matthews wanted a hearsay objection, but this material was favorable to the prosecution, so it was no time to be procedural.

"That answers the Stevenson concern, Mr. Bouck. What about Chicago and Miami?"

"What are you talking about?"

"I'm talking, Mr. Bouck," Barnes said, in strident voice, "about two American cities on President Kennedy's agenda in the month of November. Now you can tell the court what happened with respect to those trips, or you can say, 'I don't know,' in which case other witnesses, some who have already testified and some who will soon testify, will perhaps put you in a position you don't want to be in."

"Well, certain changes were made in those cities for security purposes."

"Please tell the court what those security purposes were."

Bouck tried to take the initiative, turning to the judge: "Your Honor, these are highly classified matters, and I don't see what relevance they have to events in Dallas, Texas."

Davis wasn't buying: "Mr. Bouck, they were matters regarding the security of President Kennedy, correct?"

"Yes," came a confident reply.

"Then you'll tell us about them. President Kennedy is dead and nobody can hurt him anymore. Someone in this room is on trial for his life for allegedly killing President Kennedy. So *anything* you can tell us about threats made in the month the President was killed would be, shall we say, helpful. And don't wave that secrecy banner again, please."

Bouck understood total defeat. "In Chicago, a man named Thomas Vallee, a former marine with a history of mental illness and a member of the John Birch Society, was taken into custody with an M-1 rifle and 3,000 rounds of ammunition. It was learned that he had already arranged to take off from his job the day of the President's visit, which was canceled."

"Does that complete the Chicago concern, Mr. Bouck?"

"No. We had another threat. This was a four-man team, with high-powered rifles. Two of the suspects, one with a Latin name, were detained, and two got away."

Barnes approached the bench, but so everyone in the court could hear: "Your Honor, would the Court issue a bench subpoena so that the documentation of these events in Chicago could be studied?"

Before Davis could answer, Bouck interrupted: "You would be wasting your time. There is no documentation of these events. And there was no mention at the time to any other Secret Service office. It was seen then as a local, Chicago concern, and we did not want to create panic, either within the service, or the nation."

"Was the Miami incident also shoved under the rug?"

"I don't know. All I know about that is that the proposed motorcade was changed to a helicopter ride because of a tape-recorded threat, the threat being made there in Miami, that the President would be killed by someone in a tall building with a high-powered rifle. We did not make any connection to the President's trip to Texas, hundreds of miles away, which would occur three days later."

"And end, tragically, four days later. No further questions, Mr. Bouck. Your witness, Mr. Matthews."

Matthews rose but remained behind the prosecution table. "Mr. Bouck, have there been serious concerns about presidential safety—not just the safety of Mr. Kennedy, but others as well—that have come from people not previously in your file?"

"Oh, yes."

"Would it be fair to say that people who send crank letters are for the most part venting a concern, and pose no real threat to the President, whereas the true killer will remain an unknown until his job is completed?"

"Objection. Calls for a conclusion. Argumentative as well."

"Sustained on both counts."

"Mr. Bouck, given the resources of the Secret Service, is it possible for your agency to guarantee—I mean absolutely guarantee the safety of the people it is assigned to protect?"

"We can only do what is within our ability."

"No further questions. Redirect, Mr. Barnes?" Matthews seemed to be issuing a challenge.

"Yes, I believe I have one or two questions on redirect. Mr. Bouck, we have heard testimony and seen documents that the defendant did not miss one day of employment from the time he was hired at the Book Depository until the twenty-second of November. You testified that he was unknown to the Secret Service before the twenty-second of November. Does that mean he was not, to the knowledge of the Secret Service, part of either the Chicago or the Miami events?"

"Not to our knowledge. We never heard of him."

"Thank you. A minute ago, you testified that 'we can only

do what we are able to,' or something like that. Have you seen the Zapruder film, Mr. Bouck?"

"Yes, I have."

"Did Special Agent Roy Kellerman, sitting in the front seat of the presidential limousine, do his best work by remaining in the front seat of that automobile and picking up the telephone, or would the President—the late President have been better served if Mr. Kellerman got out of that seat and went to his aid?"

Matthews objected as calling for a conclusion.

"I think we need to hear the witness on this one, Your Honor. He's the head of a department, and he's in the protection business—that gives him a unique expertise."

"Overruled. The witness will answer."

"Mr. Kellerman certainly did not accomplish much by picking up the phone. Agents are trained to jump, dive, rush, throw themselves in front of—the subject. Yet when it happens so suddenly, the decision to pick up the phone seems clearly wrong."

"Thank you, Mr. Bouck. Recross, Mr. Matthews?"

"Could Mr. Kellerman have arrived in time, Mr. Bouck?"

"I have no way of knowing, sir. We can only try, and measure the results. When we don't try . . ."

"Nothing further."

"The defense calls Special Agent Winston Lawson."

Once sworn, the witness indicated that as the advance agent for the Dallas portion of the trip, his job was to monitor concerns and coordinate all phases of the Dallas portion of the trip—including which site the luncheon would be held at, and once that decision was made, where the motorcade would then logically go. Barnes was able to learn from Lawson that the Protective Research Section had told him that there were no perceived threats in Dallas, and the witness volunteered that he had received some information about right-wing groups who planned to do some picketing.

"In planning a motorcade, is it standard procedure to run the entire route of the motorcade, Mr. Lawson?"

"Yes."

"Did you?"

"Not quite. Chief Curry took us from Love Field, through

the motorcade route, to the point where Main Street intersects Houston Street. He then indicated, to the effect, well, there's the highway right there and the Trade Mart is a couple miles down, and we'll have that closed off."

"So you had no knowledge, in the planning stages, that the motorcade would have to turn right on Houston Street and then left onto Elm, or Parkway, to reach the highway?"

"That's correct."

"Is there anything in Secret Service regulations that would prevent such a motorcade route from being chosen?"

"Yes, there is. The regulations are quite clear that a presidential automobile cannot make a turn of greater than ninety degrees, because it requires it to slow down too much. As I'm sure you're aware, the turn at Elm is much greater than ninety degrees."

"Indeed it is, Agent Lawson. The tragedy is that you were not aware. Were you disciplined in any way for not having such awareness?"

"No."

"Agent Lawson, how many agents actually were in the presidential detail in Dallas on November twenty-second, 1963?"

"Twenty-eight."

"Let's break that down," Barnes suggested. "Who was with Chief Curry in the lead car?"

"Two agents. Myself and Dallas Special Agent-in-Charge Forrest Sorrels."

"Agent Lawson, where were you seated in Chief Curry's car?"

"Front right passenger seat."

"And what was your responsibility?"

"To look out the back and make sure that the presidential car is not too far back or too close to us."

"And where was Mr. Sorrels?"

"Right rear seat."

"And, to your knowledge, what was his job?"

"To scan the motorcade route—check for open windows, any basic security concerns."

"Does it make any sense to you, Agent Lawson, that perhaps your job, and that of Agent Sorrels, could have both been accomplished far better if you had exchanged seats—so you could do your job and look out the back and he could do his and scan buildings without the car roof in his way?"

"Objection. Argumentative."

"Sustained."

"Okay, Mr. Lawson. Two agents in the lead car. Where were the rest?"

"There were two in the presidential car, eight in or on the running boards of the follow-up car, one in the vice-president's car, three in the vice-presidential follow-up, a few at the Trade Mart, and the remainder guarding the aircraft at Love Field."

"So there were none, freelancing, so to speak, looking for open windows or snipers?"

"No."

"Were agents—not in cars—in Dealey Plaza before or during the shooting?"

"No."

"Mr. Lawson, several people will testify they encountered Secret Service agents within two minutes of the assassination. Are you telling me there weren't any there?"

"There were none there. I've heard those stories. They're not true. There were no agents there."

"The stories would mean individuals were posing as Secret Service agents, Mr. Lawson . . . but you would have no way of knowing that, would you? Now, we will be hearing from a Mr. Kirkwood, the proprietor of an after-hours drinking establishment in Fort Worth, the city where the President spent the last night of his life. Mr. Kirkwood has deposed, and will testify, that seventeen Secret Service agents were in his establishment as late as 3:30 A.M. on November twenty-second. Is there anything in Secret Service regulations about that?"

"Absolutely. It's forbidden. And it is grounds for dismissal from the service, without question." Barnes didn't press the point. He had other witnesses for that.

"Tell us about the shots, Agent Lawson."

"The lead car was just about to the underpass when I heard the first noise, which, at first flashing through my mind did not say rifle shot to me. It sounded different than a rifle shot. My first impression was firecracker or bomb or something like that. The second and third shots were real close together."

"Thank you, Agent Lawson."

Matthews wanted one point in the record: "Mr. Lawson, when you heard these noises, where did you consider their origin to be?"

"They came from behind me."

"Thank you. No further cross-examination."

Barnes had redirect: "Agent Lawson, you testified that you were almost to the underpass when you heard what you described as the first noise. Correct?"

"Yes."

"Are you familiar with the area that has come to be known as the 'grassy knoll'?"

"Yes."

"When you heard that first noise, where was the grassy knoll in relation to the vehicle you were in?"

"Behind me."

"Thank you again, Agent Lawson. Recross?"

"None."

"The defense calls James J. Rowley."

A well dressed and clean-cut man entered the court, walking with a gait that suggested that he was going to make a profound speech, and then depart at his leisure. Both Matthews and Barnes noted the swagger. Once sworn, the witness told that he was the head of the Secret Service from 1961 through November twenty-second, 1963. Barnes then moved quickly to the allegations of after-hours drinking by Secret Service agents guarding the President, and the witness admitted that the men were required to give statements, and that appropriate notations were put in their service folders.

"So they got away with it?" Barnes asked.

"I did not say that. I testified that a report of their conduct was placed in their folder. Down the road, this will no doubt prevent them from ever holding my job, for instance."

"Secret Service regulations are clear, however, Mr. Rowley, regarding dismissal in cases of such behavior, is that not so?"

"It is. But it was felt that with the suddenness of the tragedy, it would be a lifetime stigma on the men involved—good men, by the way, who could have done very little if they had had a full night's rest."

"I understand that, Mr. Rowley, but in the case of Paul Landis, he admitted he was *out* until 5 A.M. and he came back on duty at 8 A.M. So how rested was he? And where was he in the motorcade? On the running board of the follow-up car— in a critical spot."

"It all happened so fast," Rowley tried again.

"I appreciate what you are saying, Mr. Rowley. One last question. You testified before the President's Commission, and your testimony covered thirty-eight pages. You did a lot of talking to those eminent folks. Yet there was no mention of the events of November 1963, with reference to presidential security in Chicago or Miami. Why not?"

"They never asked."

"That tells us quite a bit, Director Rowley. No further questions. Mr. Matthews?"

"I have no questions for the witness. Thank you for coming, Director Rowley."

Barnes glanced at his watch and realized he'd either have to hurry to complete the Secret Service today, or he'd have them to lead off tomorrow. The latter was normally good strategy, as it gave the defense two shots at the testimony. In this case, however, Barnes assumed they'd all go back to the same hotel and discuss what had been asked and of whom, and by tomorrow, he'd be hearing well-rehearsed narratives. He decided to go for broke today.

"The defense calls Forrest V. Sorrels," Barnes announced, and while the witness entered, he explained to Dean what he had decided. Dean agreed, if it could be done without losing something of value.

Barnes asked questions designed to have the jury hear that Sorrels was the Secret Service agent-in-charge of the Dallas office, that he had, as a "routine matter" helped plan the motorcade route, that he considered *all* buildings a potential threat, that there had been concern about some right-wing picketing, and that the Stevenson incident, which Sorrels thought had occurred some sixty or more days before, was a fact to be reckoned with.

"With respect to the motorcade, Agent Sorrels, we have heard testimony that you were in Chief Curry's car, in the right rear seat, and it was your job to observe the parade route for any possible concerns, while the person sitting in the front seat, Agent Lawson, spent his time looking out the back window at the President's car. Is that correct?"

"Yes, it is."

"Did your placement in the backseat obscure your ability to make observations?"

"Oh, yes."

"Do you recall observing the Texas School Book Depository?"

"Yes."

"Did you notice anything unusual or anything that was of concern to you?"

"Nothing unusual."

"Tell us what happened then," Barnes instructed, sensing he had a witness who would lay out the story as he recalled it.

"Well, we were well down Elm, and I heard a shot and turned to look up on this terrace part there, because the sound sounded like it came from the back and up in that direction."

"Agent Sorrels," Barnes interrupted, walking to the defense table to pick up some enlarged photos, "I show you some blown up photographs of Dealey Plaza. Will you point to the spot you thought the shot you heard came from?"

"In here."

"Would I be correct in calling that area the grassy knoll?"

"I have read of it being referred to that way, yes."

"Please continue."

"After the first shot, there was an interval, maybe three seconds, then two more similar reports, six seconds total, with a much greater lapse between one and two than between two and three. I then yelled, 'Let's get out of here!' "

"As a curiosity, why did you yell that? Isn't your job, essentially, to be there?"

"I see your point. Perhaps I was trying to project my thoughts, my escape urge, to the presidential vehicle, which did not accelerate until well after the last shot."

"Interesting. Go on."

"Well, then they hit the gas and outran us quickly, but we caught up with them at Parkland, where we stayed briefly, then returned to the Book Depository in twenty or twenty-five minutes."

"Why there?"

"That's where the focus seemed to be, although security was wretched. A black man, an employee, was watching the back door, and I was able to just walk into the building without identifying myself."

"How many agents accompanied you there?"

"None. They had responsibilities at the hospital. I was the only agent in Dealey Plaza for quite some time."

"Who were you protecting at the Depository?"

"Nobody. I, uh, well, it seemed like somebody from the Secret Service should be there, and since I was not on White House detail, I was the logical choice."

"Did you meet with any witnesses?"

"Yes. I spoke with Howard Brennan and a young boy, Amos Euins, and I escorted them to the sheriff's office where witnesses were giving statements to the FBI."

"Where do you figure they fit in?"

"How's that?" Sorrels asked.

"There has been no federal crime spoken of. Why do we have the FBI interviewing witnesses in the Dallas county sheriff's office?"

"I am afraid I don't have an answer for you, although I see your point—it was a Texas crime, and there are certain procedures to be followed."

"Indeed there are. They are called 'The Law.' And the absence of those procedures has caused grave problems with these proceedings," Barnes noted. "Did you interview Arnold Rowland?"

"Yes, I did. Can I ask you—will he be called as a witness?"

"Yes, he will," Barnes answered.

"Then I won't presume on his testimony, except to add that I believe the man was sincere in what he told me, but that I only wished he had spoken with someone in authority when he made his observations."

"Did you hear from any other witnesses?"

"Well, there was a lady, told me a story about being stuck in traffic there on Elm Street that morning, and seeing a gun case going up the knoll, but I didn't pursue that because by then we had reports of a gun and shells being found in the Depository—"

"Which, apparently to your mind precluded any possibility whatsoever that there could have been a second gun, or more than three shells."

"I guess it did. It's not easy to watch the President of the United States be executed in the town in which you are the Secret Service agent-in-charge, then ponder the future that you no longer have, and hear the whispers, 'There goes Sorrels . . . remember him? S.A.I.C. in Dallas back in sixty-three when Kennedy got it . . .' I know I wasn't thinking one hundred percent straight. But I'll tell you I worked that day. I met with the dressmaker who had taken the movie and we got that to a laboratory so it could be developed, then it was back to the sheriff's office, with the media and FBI agents all over the place, and—"

"FBI again," Barnes interrupted.

"Yes. They had to be, now that I think of it, because I know I talked to at least a couple of them that knew the FBI had a file on Oswald."

"Were you allowed to see any of that?"

"No."

"Mr. Sorrels, how did it wind up with Mr. Brennan?"

"Well, I was there when he was shown the defendant in the lineup, and he came right to me, because I talked to him earlier, at the Depository, and he said, 'I am sorry, but I cannot do it. I was afraid seeing the television might have messed me up. I just can't be positive. I am sorry.'"

"In other words, he could not identify the defendant in the lineup?"

"That is correct."

"So, Mr. Sorrels, three shots, six seconds?"

The witness was staring at the floor, talking to no one in particular. "Yes. I will hear them forever."

"So will I," Barnes told him. "I'm just curious who up there on that terrace fired them. No further questions, sir."

Matthews walked to the witness stand. "Mr. Sorrels, you

spoke of thinking the shots came from the rear, and toward the terrace, yet when you came back to Dealey Plaza, you went to the Book Depository. Did you ever visit the terrace as you call it?"

"No."

"That suggests to me, at least, that you had changed your mind about the origin of the shots."

"I can't say. By the time I got back, though, the focus was on the Depository."

"Understandably so," Matthews concluded. "Nothing further."

"Your Honor, I have one question on redirect. Mr. Sorrels, if you did not enter the general area of the grassy knoll, would it be correct to say that no agents of the United States Secret Service were located there between the hours of 10 A.M. and 2 P.M. on November twenty-second, 1963?"

"That would be accurate."

"Thank you." Barnes looked at Matthews, deep in discussion with Graves, and called Clint Hill as his next witness. Hill entered with a slow stride, and immediately was recognized by jurors as the well-built man who raced to the stricken occupants of the limousine, pushed Mrs. Kennedy back to safety, and risked his own life on a perilous four-mile-dash to Parkland Hospital. Subconsciously, they might have also been noticing the only person who realized what was going on that day.

Barnes was most gracious: "Mr. Hill, do you recall when we spoke on the phone late last summer?"

"Yes."

"I have to tell you, Mr. Hill, I have the deepest respect for both you and police officer Baker, who has already testified. Out of all the law enforcement people in Dealey Plaza that day, you two stand out as the two who best upheld the oaths they took prior to receiving badges."

"I still got there a couple of seconds late," Hill answered, somewhat morosely.

"Don't blame yourself. We're not in this courtroom to condemn your behavior, but to see justice done. Would you tell us what happened?"

"I'll try. When we reached the end of Main Street, the crowd thinned out. I think all of us, collectively, breathed a sigh of relief. I knew we would go another block and then accelerate —not from shots, but when we hit the parkway. I did not know of the terrible turn the car had to take. But it made it, though it almost brushed a restraining curb. Then, we went a little farther, and I heard a noise from my right rear, which to me seemed to be a firecracker. I turned in that direction, as I've seen in photos, then when I looked at Mr. Kennedy, I ran to the car, and just about as I reached it, there was another sound, which was different from the first sound—it seemed to have some type of echo."

"Could it have been two shots extremely close together?"

"They would have had to have been extremely close together. So, Mrs. Kennedy—I was on her detail, not the President's, well, she reached out, it looked like something was coming off the back of the car, but I cannot say that for sure. I pushed her in, and the car took off. Then I saw the President. The right rear portion of his head was missing. It was lying in the rear seat of the car. His brain was exposed. There was blood and bits of brain all over the entire rear portion of the car."

"Including the trunk?"

"Yes. All over. I secured Mrs. Kennedy, who was talking to Mr. Kennedy, and then I just pounded one fist in frustration. I was a couple of seconds late."

"Did you make further observations of the President when you arrived at Parkland?"

"Yes. I removed my suit coat to cover the horrible wounds so that no photographer would take pictures of that awful sight."

Barnes spoke into the screening room microphone: "Could we have the autopsy photo showing the rear of the President's head?"

When the picture came up, Hill just stared at it. Finally, sacrificing the dramatics to protect the witness's fragile recollection, Barnes asked, "Is that the way the President's head looked from the rear—understand, Mr. Hill you saw him longer than anyone except possibly Mrs. Kennedy, and nobody wants to put her on this witness stand."

"That photo bears no resemblance to what the President looked like when I reached his automobile."

"There's absolutely no doubt in your mind about that?"

"No. I could look at the back of his head and see brain matter. That picture looks somewhat like the way the President appeared at Bethesda at about 2:45 A.M., when I was asked to go to the autopsy room to view the wounds. They— the morticians or whoever did the work, had already begun preparing the President for the funeral, when I observed an opening in the back, about six inches below the neckline to the right-hand side of the spinal column."

Barnes asked for the autopsy photo depicting the back wound. "Would this be accurate, Mr. Hill?"

"Reasonably so, yes."

Barnes then asked for CE 385, the drawing prepared for and accepted by the President's Commission, showing an entrance in the neck, and a downward arrow to an exit in the front of the throat. "Would this be accurate, Mr. Hill?"

"No. The entrance in the back was well below what was depicted there."

"Special Agent Hill, earlier you testified that the two sounds you identified, presumably as shots, did not sound the same. Taking into account that you were not in the same spot when both were fired, did they appear to come from the same location?"

"I'm not sure. The first, the firecrackerlike sound, was right rear. That I know. The other, different sound, was right, but I cannot say for sure that it was rear."

"Agent Hill, there's perhaps one more thing you can help me with. We've seen still pictures of November 22nd, and you were dressed professionally—a suit and shoes. And unless you were an olympic track athlete, I am wondering how you could have jumped off that follow-up car, and dressed in a business suit and shoes—not an outfit designed for speed— how could you have caught up to the President's car?"

"Like I said, I didn't quite get there fast enough, but I saw it slow considerably, and it slewed in the road a bit, so it wasn't hard to catch."

"Your Honor, Mr. Prosecutor, inasmuch as this witness has had Secret Service protective training and was the one agent to react, I would like him accorded expert witness status to answer one or two questions."

Matthews looked at the jury and realized they were looking at the witness as someone who changed his clothes in a phone booth, so he could not deny the request. "No objection from the prosecution."

"Mr. Hill, the fact that you were able to catch the car so quickly suggests what reaction within the car?"

"Well, obviously, they slowed down. Several of us have seen movies of the event—I've seen myself more times than I frankly care to, and in one of the movies, you can see the brake lights come on at the rear of the President's car."

"Okay. They reacted by slowing down. Now you, Clint Hill, had arguably the best reactions of any Secret Service man that day. What would your reaction have been? You're driving the President, the governor, two wives, yourself, and another agent. You hear a report . . . react."

"I put my foot on that pedal as hard as it will humanly go and wait about one second till that big car builds up horsepower and burns up that pavement."

"That's exactly what I've always thought," Barnes told him, almost like two men were talking football at a tavern. "Yet it didn't happen that way. Mr. Hill, suppose you thought the shot came from the front?"

"Then I'm trapped. I panic. Stop. Look for quick ways out, but there weren't any, because you had an embankment on one side, and people, with children, in the plaza. So the driver's stuck then, but eventually he has to hit that gas."

"And Mr. Greer did—eventually. It sounds to me like you are describing a reaction to a shot from the front."

"It would be a subconscious opinion at best."

"I understand and respect that." Barnes then paused before concluding.

"Mr. Hill, I know this has been a wrenching experience for you, so I thank you for your appearance today and again commend your courage in going to the aid of the stricken President as bullets were still being fired at him. Mr. Matthews?"

Barnes had just gotten back to his seat when Matthews

began, "Mr. Hill, is it not true that you have undergone extensive psychiatric treatment since the events of Nov—"

Barnes wouldn't even allow the question to be finished. "Your Honor, this line of questioning offends the dignity of this entire proceeding. Of twenty-eight agents in Dallas, this witness and this witness alone risked his life on November twenty-second, and the events of that afternoon are still so vivid that he needs professional help in dealing with them. There's no distortion of reality, or anything like incipient insanity, so I would petition the court to direct counsel to get off this line and ask his questions."

"Mr. Matthews, please confine your questions to the witness's observations."

"Mr. Hill, do you know enough about medicine to state unequivocally that the piece of skull you saw in the automobile came from the place on the President's head where there was an absence of skull?"

"I'm not a doctor. But when I see a wound, a head wound, with skull and scalp missing, then see a piece of skull and scalp, it seemed a reasonable match. One area missing. One fragment noticed. I'm not sure you'd need medical expertise. But either way, I don't have it."

Matthews saw there was no point in browbeating a witness the jury obviously identified with, so he also thanked the witness for his attendance and courage and concluded his questioning.

"The defense calls Special Agent Paul Landis." Barnes knew he had already impugned this witness with testimony that he got very little sleep, and that in the early hours preceding the assassination, so he would have to tread carefully. He decided to handle that issue first, then try to get some points in the record.

"Agent Landis, it has been suggested that you kept rather strange hours between midnight and 8 A.M. on November twenty-second, 1963. Did this behavior affect your job performance in any way on that day?"

"No."

"Would it in any way weaken your ability to testify with accuracy as to what you saw—in other words, are your recollections of the assassination clear and cogent, or were they dimmed by your lack of sleep?"

"Let me say this for the record. You have no doubt heard Secret Service regulations. But the other side of the issue is that sometimes we work shifts, and sometimes we work, literally, until relieved. The average person, who aims for eight or so hours of sleep a night would not last thirty days as a Secret Service agent. In addition, my own chemistry is such that I never sleep very much, but when I do, I sleep soundly and wake up refreshed and ready to go to work. Answer your question?"

"Thoroughly," Barnes said in upbeat tones. "Now, with respect to the events of November twenty-second, would you give the court your recollections?"

"I had scanned buildings throughout the motorcade, and seen many open windows and many people in them. When we turned into that little plaza there, the last tall building before we would reach the Trade Mart, was the Book Depository, and I looked up there. None of the windows were open, and I did not see anyone standing by them. After we made the turn, I heard what sounded like the report of a high-powered rifle from behind me. I heard a second report and saw the President's head split open and pieces of flesh and blood flying through the air. My reaction at this time was that the shot came from somewhere toward the front . . . and looked along the right side of the road. When the first shot occurred, I turned to look behind me, and when I looked at the President, he seemed to be turning to look in the direction of the shot, somewhere towards the front, right hand side of the road."

"No further questions. Cross-examination? . . ."

Matthews asked if CE 1024, page 4 could be brought up, and then approached the witness. "Agent Landis, would you read over that document? It suggests not that you heard the report of a high-powered rifle, but that the first sound you heard created uncertainty in your mind, according to that report, because you were thinking flat tire or firecracker. Do I understand your report correctly?"

"No. That report says high-powered rifle, but seeing no smoke or immediate reaction, I considered that I had heard a firecracker, and I even checked the front tire of the President's car for a blowout. We were too close to observe the back tire of the car. I alternated my gaze from the President to the front right side, and I remember that the last thing I saw before going under the underpass was a motorcycle policeman abandoning his cycle near the spot where I had been looking. Then I was physically pulled into the car by other agents as it accelerated."

"I see. No further questions."

"The defense calls Special Agent Emory Roberts." Barnes knew time was running out on the afternoon session, having seen the judge reach for his pocket watch.

"Agent Roberts, do you have any recollection on which to base a determination as to where the shots came from on November twenty-second?"

"I could not make a positive determination, but I felt they had come from the right side. There was discussion, which I initiated, in the car, and no one was sure. In terms of data, I saw what appeared to be a small explosion on the right side of the President's head, saw blood, at which time the President fell farther to his left. To me, that meant the right side was the origin."

"Nothing further."

Matthews tried to weaken the witness's testimony: "So your recollection is a mosaic of educated guesses, and not based on any visual sightings?"

"That's correct."

"I have nothing further, either," Matthews concluded.

"Defense calls Special Agent Sam Kinney." A burly, rugged-looking, large man entered the court, quickly removing his sunglasses to adjust to the light in the courtroom. Barnes elicited testimony that Agent Kinney was the driver of the Secret Service back-up vehicle, and that it was policy to try to drive virtually bumper to bumper with the presidential vehicle.

"Were you able to maintain that policy—bumper to bumper —throughout the Dallas motorcade?"

"Virtually. We did have a little trouble on that last turn, though, as Bill Greer, the driver of the presidential car, took the turn a little wide, so we had to slow down, then catch up."

"Tell the court your observations from that point onward."

"I heard a shot; there was a second of pause, and then two more shots were heard. I saw one shot strike the President in the right side of the head. The President then fell to his left. At this time I stepped on the siren and gas pedal at the same time. Agent Greer driving the President's car did the same."

"So the shooting sequence, in your mind, was clearly concluded before the President's car accelerated?"

"Absolutely."

"Agent Kinney, what happened to the automobiles—the President's car and your follow-up after the occupants of those vehicles left them at the hospital?"

"There was, of course, immediate concern for the two wounded occupants of the President's car. There was also concern about the vice-president's safety, so, based on what we saw—the President's head, and Mr. Hill's signal to us that it was very bad, we had orders from Agent Roberts to protect Mr. Johnson. We left the cars briefly in the custody of Texas state officers, then returned, put the tops on the vehicles and we took them away from there before the morbidly curious could have a field day."

"Would it be fair to say that the cars were gone from the hospital even before the announcement was made that the President had died?"

"Oh, yes. We got them out of there quickly."

"Agent Kinney, your testimony regarding events on Elm Street convinces me that you knew your duties and responsibilities. But did it ever occur to you that the events on Elm Street might have been considered a homicide and that pertinent evidence might be contained in at least the President's vehicle?"

"No one considered that possibility."

"Do you see my concern?"

"Yes."

"Nothing further."

Matthews tried his hands-in-the-pockets approach. "Agent Kinney, you were driving the back-up car?"

"That's correct."

"That would place you on the left-hand side of the vehicle. How could you see a shot hit the President on the right side of his head?"

"The President was seated at the far right of the backseat as we began down . . . Elm Street. Then the first shot, in the back, sort of rose him up, and he gradually drifted to the left, to the point where he was much closer to his wife than to his original position. Also, the car in front of us slowed, and steered somewhat erratically. Then the shot hit, on the right side of his head, and there was an explosion of, well, tissue, right there in the front right of his head. And I hit the siren and the gas."

"As to the removal of the automobiles, with crowds gathering, was there also a security concern?"

"Yes."

"No more questions. Thank you, Agent Kinney."

"Redirect, Your Honor. Mr. Kinney, what would have prevented you, for security reasons, from driving the presidential automobile to the police garage in Dallas so local authorities, with jurisdiction, could examine the vehicle for evidence?"

"Nothing. But we had no orders and we behaved instinctively."

"Thank you. Defense calls Special Agent Andrew Berger.

"Agent Berger, would you tell the court the events you witnessed with respect to the FBI at Parkland Hospital?"

"We—the agents not guarding the vice-president, who we knew was technically President—but the rest of us, were posted in key places, the most important being, of course, the door to the emergency room where Mr. Kennedy was being given emergency measures. Then two strange things happened. FBI Agent Vincent Drain arrived, with a doctor friend of his—seemed hardly necessary at a hospital—and there was also an unnamed and unintroduced CIA man with him. Still later, a self-proclaimed FBI man, six-two, one hundred ninety pounds, gray hair, tried to get in and got physically knocked down. He was FBI, but he had no business acting that way."

"With the FBI arriving so quickly, and with a doctor, yet,

did it seem they were trying to, shall we say, 'contain' the investigation?"

"Objection. Obviously conclusionary."

"Sustained. You know better, Mr. Barnes."

"No more questions."

Matthews didn't even rise: "Agent Berger, does the job description of an FBI man say anything about the investigation of crime?"

"I don't know, I've never seen one."

Barnes had to bite his lip to prevent a laugh.

"Would it come as a surprise that an FBI agent arrived at a hospital where a federal official was believed to be a gunshot victim?"

"Objection," Barnes interrupted. "The court has no knowledge of that which, in the job description of Secret Service agents, constitutes surprise."

"The question does call for a conclusion. Sustained."

"No further questions."

"Defense calls Special Agent Roy Kellerman." A tall, distinguished-looking man, fiftyish, entered the courtroom, acquainted himself with his surroundings as if he were about to escort a v.i.p. through the premises, and was sworn. Barnes, fighting the clock, quickly elicited testimony that Kellerman had been Acting Special Agent-in-Charge of the White House detail on November twenty-second, 1963, and that he had been riding in the front seat of the presidential car when the shooting occurred. There were a few side questions regarding why Kellerman's superiors were not present in Dallas, but they were heard by the jury and cast no light beyond that. On questions regarding placement of vehicles in the motorcade, the number of motorcycles, and their location, the witness showed an almost appalling ignorance of events he was supposed to be aware of.

"Tell the court what happened when the car passed down Elm Street."

"Well, there was this report like a firecracker, pop. The shot came from the right, perhaps to the rear. I thought I heard the President say, 'My God, I am hit.' I then grabbed the microphone, and yelled, 'Let's get out of here, we are hit.' Now, in the seconds that I talked just now, a flurry of shells came into the car; the President was sideways down into the back-seat."

"A flurry of shots? The accusation at issue here is three shots."

"The car accelerated as the volley came in. One report sounded like a double bang . . . something breaking the sound barrier."

"But did you hear three shots?"

"At least, at the minimum. I saw the damage done—there were several wounds to the President and several to the governor, and I have no knowledge that every shot hit its target, so there had to be a bunch of shots."

"Could you determine if the shots were fired from an elevated position?"

"No. Only that the last volley had a different sound than the first report."

"Mr. Kellerman, the record has to be clear, and questions have to be asked. The motion pictures, and there are a couple of home movies of the event, show the car speed up a few seconds *after* the President was hit in the head. You said the car accelerated as the volley was coming in, which either means your recollection was inaccurate or there was, in fact, a volley that came in after the President's fatal head wound. What do you say?"

"It just seemed like we reacted quickly, and we literally jumped out of that God-damned road. It happened so quickly."

"The other question that has to be asked is why you stayed where you were. When we talked over the phone, you told me that nothing—neither the governor, nor the overhead car frame would have prevented you from getting to the President if you had sought to. Why didn't you?"

"My concern was to get out of there, and fast. I can only rationalize that if the President is hit, it's going to take at least a couple of seconds before something else happens, and if we're moving, that's the best protection he has. It would have taken me that much time to get back there—and I would have been scrambling, believe me."

"Fair enough. Did you see the President's wounds on the way to Parkland Hospital?"

"No. Agent Hill was spread-eagled over the people in the backseat, and covering part of the trunk, and the governor and Mrs. Connally were also obscuring what vision I might have had. In addition, I was virtually navigating for the driver, Agent Greer, who had to perform some difficult feats to get to that hospital through traffic as quickly as he did."

"Did you see the wounds at Parkland?"

The witness took a deep breath, coughed. "Yes. There was a horrible gaping wound, more or less circular, about five inches in diameter—the rear portion of the head, more to the right side—this was removed. The entry into the man's head was right below that wound."

"So you are describing a small entry wound, and above it, a larger wound?"

"Correct."

"Where was this entry wound?"

"In the hairline."

Barnes asked again for the autopsy photo showing the rear of the President's head. "Does this picture, taken at the autopsy at which you were present, represent the wounds you saw on the President?"

"Absolutely not."

"Did you see the nonhead wound incurred by the President?"

"Yes, but only at the autopsy. I was standing right next to one of the Doctors, a Colonel Finck, I believe, while he probed the hole in the shoulder. I asked him where the bullet went, and he told me, 'There are no lanes for an outlet in this man's shoulder.' "

"Would you characterize the wound that you were examining as a neck wound, a back wound, or a shoulder wound?"

"Shoulder would be the best characterization. It was in that large muscle between the shoulder and the neck."

"Agent Kellerman, it is my understanding that the films exposed at the autopsy were given to you, undeveloped. Is that correct?"

"Yes."

"Is there a reason that they were not made available for the pathologists to use in the course of their work?"

"We assumed they could reach their conclusions from the

body in front of them. There was a concern that the photos, and you've seen—well, I don't know what you've seen judging from that one you showed me, but what I saw of the President was awful—gruesome. If those pictures ever became public . . ."

"They are becoming public as we speak, sir, and they tell a tale of evidence at odds with verbal testimony, including yours. Agent Kellerman, there has been testimony that one roll of film was removed from a camera and exposed to the light. Did you do that?"

"No."

"Mr. Kellerman, were you responsible for the removal of the automobiles and the President's body from the hospital before they could be seen by Texas authorities for their evidence value?"

"Yes, I did do that. I wanted the cars secure, and fast, as much as we seemingly had no further need for them then or in the immediate future. And I couldn't put Mrs. Kennedy through one unnecessary minute of agony. She was adamant —I mean, she said it and she meant it—that she was going to stay with Mr. Kennedy. All I could hope to do was to get the process over with fast. And she stayed, in those bloodstained garments, until the morticians had finished their work at Bethesda, and we took the President back to the White House at about 4:30 A.M. the next morning."

"Did it occur to you then, or does it occur to you now, that in a technical sense, you were obstructing justice?"

Kellerman reacted as if hit in the face with a live eel. "What are you talking about?"

"Mr. Kellerman, you are a high-ranking agent of the United States Secret Service. As such, you know it is a federal offense to threaten the President. It is not, however, a federal offense to kill the President. What happened that Friday, the nightmare on Elm Street, was a violation of *Texas* law, and subject to Texas procedures, one of which is that there must be a local autopsy performed or there can be no homicide charged. You removed the body of the President, which was evidence, from its proper jurisdiction. Certainly I can understand your feelings for the President's bloodied widow. However, considering that you testified that the autopsy photo you viewed was at odds with the wounds you saw, that compounds the felony: it suggests that the autopsy, taken from the local, impartial authorities and given to military men who followed orders, was not everything it should be. Now do you understand my question about your thinking at the time of these events?"

"Yes."

"Going back to the autopsy. When was the shoulder wound discovered?"

"Some time after the procedure started. The wound went unnoticed until the President was turned over."

"Mr. Kellerman, you testified the wounds were in the back of the head. The shoulder wound was in the back. How could anybody see one and not both? And how was it photographed?"

"I have no idea."

"And I have no further questions. Thank you."

Matthews approached: "Mr. Kellerman, were you present for the entire autopsy?"

"No."

"If you were in the same situation again at that hospital, with Mrs. Kennedy running alongside the coffin, would you turn the body over to local authorities or take it back to Washington as you did?"

"Knowing now that it has caused so many problems, I would have left it for local authorities and found a way, with the help of the President's staff present, to convince Mrs. Kennedy to return to the White House. None of that occurred to me that day, however."

"Thank you. No further questions."

"One question on redirect, Mr. Kellerman. The entourage was just described as running with the coffin. Why was there such an urgency to depart . . . nobody was going to shoot the coffin. So why the haste?"

"We wanted to get the President's body out of there."

"I won't ask why, Agent Kellerman. But I suggest you collect all your thoughts, put them on paper, and entrust them to someone."

Matthews rose: "Move to strike the last comment."

"Sustained."

"The defense calls Special Agent William Greer."

The judge interrupted to ask Barnes how long this would take, and Barnes replied that this was the last Secret Service witness, which would allow a dozen or so men to return to the capital that evening, saving considerable time and government expense. Davis agreed to the wisdom of that while Agent Greer, an older man with thinning hair and a wry expression, was sworn.

Barnes did not want to begin with the easy questions, since this was the last witness. "Mr. Greer, there has been testimony that twenty-eight Secret Service agents took part in the Dallas portion of the Texas trip. Which of those twenty-eight was the oldest?"

"I was."

"And how old were you, on November twenty-second, 1963?"

"Fifty-four."

Barnes considered editorializing at that point, but a couple of jurors were well past their thirties, so he thought better of it. "Agent Greer, please tell the court your educational record."

"I completed two years of high school."

"Turning your attention back to November twenty-second, please tell the court what happened from Houston Street until you went under the underpass."

"We turned onto Houston, and then it was clear that we were virtually at the end of the parade, and before that thought had a chance to register, I had to make that one hundred twenty degree turn at the corner of Houston and Elm, which I was not prepared for, and . . ."

"You had not driven the route previously?"

"No, sir. And that's common. The advance man knows the route, and he's in front of us and we follow."

"Please go on."

"So I made the turn, straightened out, and was looking ahead to the underpass with some concern, because there are not supposed to be people up there—somebody could throw or drop something. I didn't like it. I scanned for an alternate route, but there was nothing there. Then I heard a noise that I thought was a backfire of one of the motorcycle policemen . . . it did not affect me."

Barnes interrupted, "To make it clear for the jury, are you saying that what you now believe was the first shot sounded like nothing more than a motorcycle backfire, in spite of all your training and the many years you have been in the Service?"

"That's correct. I didn't give it a second thought. Then Kellerman, Agent Roy Kellerman, began to react, and I turned around, looked at the governor, saw him slumped, and I stepped on the gas. At just about that time, two shots came into the car, in virtually the same instant—almost simultaneously, one behind the other."

"Films show the presidential car to have a slow reaction. Do you have any accounting for that?"

"Well, the car is armor plated, making it very heavy, so when you step on the gas, it's going to take a couple of seconds to feel the reaction, which you will feel, just not immediately. Also, we were in low gear."

"Satisfy my curiosity. Why?"

"Control, for want of an expert automotive answer. It's a better quick-power gear, handy if someone runs alongside. You don't expect suddenly to have to be doing eighty. But to get from fifteen to twenty-five in a short burst without jostling the occupants, low gear has worked well."

"Did the car accelerate rapidly?"

"No. Believe me, sitting there it seemed like forever."

"For Mr. Kennedy, it was," Barnes noted. "Agent Greer, at the moment you stepped on the gas, did you know how to get to the nearest hospital?"

"No. Kellerman must have. He was doing all the talking I wanted to hear. The women behind us were sobbing and talking to their husbands, which convinced me the President was still alive."

"Did you see any damage to the automobile—cracks in the windshield, chrome, bullet fragments, anything like that on November twenty-second?"

"No. But I was shown them the following day. They were even larger when I was shown the windshield by the President's Commission."

"The car was crushed but the windshield survived," Barnes editorialized. "Agent Greer, did you see the nonfatal wound sustained by the President, and if so, tell the court its location."

"There was a wound in the back, just in the soft part of the shoulder."

"Thank you, Agent Greer. Mr. Matthews?"

"Agent Greer," Matthews began, approaching, "do you have any idea of the source of the shots?"

"It seemed like they came from the rear."

"Thank you. Nothing further."

Davis looked at Barnes for redirect, and getting no response to his eye contact, indicated that court was in recess, and asked Agent Greer to thank the members of the Secret Service detail for their attendance at that day's session.

Matthews felt he got a couple of good points in the record, but he realized that Barnes's witnesses stood on far more solid ground than his had, and that Barnes had begun with people who couldn't be verbally assaulted.

The defense team felt they had had a good day, despite the loss, at least for now, of their motion to dismiss. "Keep putting good people on, Eddie. Tomorrow we've got the Parkland doctors, and they are untouchable," Dean told him. "From there, you can nibble at the remaining shreds of Matthews's case. Then rest, repeat your motion to dismiss, and stand on it. It'll go."

# Thirteen

Tuesday, January nineteenth, 1965. A bitter cold day exacerbated by a wind that blew the hard, frozen air right at and right through a person. Barnes, Dean, and Jeffries arrived in the courtroom a few minutes before nine, each with a briefcase and another package, the most obvious being an 18 by 36 inch rectangular arrangement barely tucked under Carolyn Jeffries's arm.

Matthews, Graves, and Vincent were already there, looking tired. Barnes told Dean that if there was a white flag in the house, Matthews would be waving it, to surrender. Dean had the perfect answer: "If not this morning, Eddie, then certainly late this afternoon."

Judge Davis gaveled the proceedings to order promptly at nine, had the defendant and the jury brought in, and told Barnes to proceed. "The defense calls Dr. Malcolm Perry." Jurors, aware that Dr. Perry had done the most to save President Kennedy, were surprised to see such a young, vigorous man enter the courtroom.

Barnes requested, and got, expert status for the witness.

He then elicited statements from Perry that he was preparing to eat lunch on November twenty-second, when he heard an emergency page to the trauma room. By the time he arrived, Dr. Charles "Jim" Carrico was already examining the President's wounds. It was also ascertained that Dr. Perry had treated hundreds of gunshot wounds since his graduation from medical school, eight years prior to the events of November twenty-second.

"Dr. Perry, when you arrived in the emergency room, what was the nature of the damage you observed with respect to the President?"

"There was a wound on the neck, an entrance wound, just below the Adam's Apple. This was a clean wound, with edges that were neither ragged, nor punched out. There was also a large, avulsive wound on the right posterior cranium, with lacerated brain tissue extruding. There was blood and brain tissue on the cart."

"Did the nature of the wounds, as you viewed them, give you any indication of the President's chances of survival?"

"The wound in the back of the head was severe, but as long as there was a pulse, however stringy, or a heartbeat, I would take rescusitative measures—on the President. If a John Doe had been brought in with that damage, a sheet would have been pulled over his face. I had no doubt about the outcome: I was just trying to keep the man alive as long as possible."

"And what procedures did you take?" Barnes asked.

"I ordered a trach tray and performed a tracheostomy through the existing circular wound in the throat. In so doing, I noticed signs of a right lung puncture. A deviated trachea is a sign of a collapsed lung, as well as bubbling in the chest. I noticed both free blood and air in the right superior mediastinum, so while the trach tube was being inserted, I ordered that chest tubes be placed."

"Could we have CE 385 please?" requesting the autopsy schematic drawing of the "neck" wound. "Doctor, is this artist's rendering of a rear entry, aligned through the anterior throat 'exit'—is this consistent with the problems you just discussed *in the chest?*"

"No."

"Doctor, you spoke of wounds in the right posterior cranium. For the jury's benefit, as well as for mine, I might add, are you testifying that you observed damage to the back or the top of the President's head?"

"The back."

"And this damage, how big was it?"

"The size of a fist."

Barnes gave a nod to Carolyn Jeffries, who began to unpack the rectangular package she had brought to court. Barnes spoke up to keep the jury's attention on the witness. "Dr. Perry, when you made the tracheostomy incision, how long was it?"

"Two to three centimeters, which is standard for such an incision. It has to be just wide enough to accommodate an endotracheal tube, with a cuff, which involves about one inch. To go beyond that, you are exposing tissue to germ-laden air for no reason."

"Doctor, how long was it after that incision that the President was pronounced dead?"

"A few minutes at the most. The incision was made, the tube inserted and connected to the machine, and cut-downs were made, tubes inserted, then the heart massage—actually pounding on the chest, which, after two minutes or so, was discontinued as it was not reviving heart activity."

"One more question before I show you some photographs, Doctor, and this one relates far more to your education than to your experience. What is the weight of the normal human brain?"

"Thirteen-fifty to fifteen hundred grams, give or take."

"Thank you, Dr. Perry. Now, would you please examine this photograph right here," Barnes said, pointing to a blowup of the autopsy photo of President Kennedy's head. "Does this correspond to what you saw on November twenty-second?"

"In no way. That depicts an intact occipito-parietal area, which was *not* intact."

"Doctor, this is a photograph of the top of the President's head, showing the kind of massive damage you testified to. Does this look familiar?"

"No. The top of the head did not exhibit that kind of damage. The back did."

"Doctor, this is a picture of the President's back. Did you see this wound?"

"No. We were concerned with the more obvious damage, and once the President was pronounced dead, we were removed from the room by Secret Service agents."

"Doctor, this last photo," Barnes said, turning the next picture around, "purports to be the tracheostomy incision you made. Is this an accurate representation of your work on November twenty-second?"

Perry reacted sharply: "Absolutely not. That photo is a very poor rendition of my abilities as a surgeon."

"The autopsy pathologist testified that the tracheostomy incision he measured was about three and a quarter inches. Any comment?"

"He may be telling the God's honest truth. But the incision I made was no more than two to three centimeters, which at most is one and one-half inches. There's no reason to do more. Bigger is not better in that kind of procedure; it's worse. The more you cut, the more blood vessels rupture. Some trach procedures are done vertically, to minimize the threat to the major blood vessels."

"Doctor, these photos—have you ever seen them before?"

"No."

"They were presented to both the prosecution and the defense in this case as being the photographs taken at the autopsy of John F. Kennedy. Is it your testimony that they are not accurate representations of what you saw?"

"That is correct. They do not reflect the damage I saw, and I don't know one doctor from Parkland that in his wildest dream would tell you otherwise."

"Objection. Hearsay and argumentative."

"Sustained. Please answer the questions as asked, Dr. Perry. The court realizes your work and its integrity are at stake here, but please . . ."

"I apologize, Your Honor, but those pictures . . ."

"Doctor, on November twenty-second, considering what you saw, and realizing that you did not see the wound in the President's back as shown in this picture here, what was your theory as to what happened?"

"I believed the President was shot in the throat, which

would be from the front, and that the shot hit something, deviated upward, and blasted out the back of the head as it exited."

"Doctor, after November twenty-second, were you ever asked to change your story?"

"Well, the following day, Dr. Humes called me, and asked me if anyone at Parkland Hospital had made any wounds in the President's back. I answered honestly and said no, but I must tell you, I totally did not understand his question. After that, I was interviewed twice by the Secret Service and they asked me to think back and consider if the wound I saw in the throat could have been an exit wound."

"And what did you conclude?"

"Well I told them it could have been, although it maintained entrance-wound characteristics. Once I made that statement, they stopped asking."

"Dr. Perry, was a reasonable portion of the President's brain missing as a result of his wounds?"

"Certainly there was brain tissue gone when he arrived. Subsequently, other brain tissue fell onto the cart, or the floor, especially when I was pounding on his chest."

"Excuse me there, Doctor. Did it fall out through the back of the head or the top?"

"The back—where the large opening was."

"Doctor, a supplementary autopsy report on the President indicated that the President's brain, when removed and fixed in formalin solution, weighed fifteen hundred grams. Based on what you observed, is that a reasonable possibility?"

"On the contrary, it's impossible. Just that, impossible. What was left of that brain would not have weighed fifteen hundred grams if it had been fixed in mercury. It's becoming obvious . . ." Perry did not complete that thought. "It couldn't have weighed fifteen hundred grams."

"Doctor Perry, I want to thank you for coming here today, and add my thanks, and that of everyone here, for your valiant attempts to save the President in those few precious moments in which you tried to use all your medical expertise. I realize my questions have raised difficulties in your mind, and it was not my intention to trouble you. I hope you realize I'm trying to get at the truth. No further questions."

Matthews knew that final group of Barnes's thoughts, playing up to the doctor that worked on the President, would make it tough to tear him apart, and his testimony was solid. "Dr. Perry, the back wound that you did not see . . ."

"Yes."

"We have seen the President's clothing, which has holes corresponding roughly to that wound, and we have heard testimony that the President was shot in that area. Would that have accounted for the medical situation you discovered when you performed the neck incision—the free, oxygenated blood, the deviated trachea?"

"Very possibly the blood; less so the trachea."

"Doctor, did you take a good amount of time to view the wound in the back of the head?"

"No. This was lifesaving, not autopsy. I took a quick glance at it and went to work."

"Did you see any smaller, entrance wounds on the rear surface of the President's head?"

"No."

"Is it possible that in your quick glance, you missed such a wound?"

"It is very possible. My attention was clearly drawn to the severe wound."

"Thank you. Nothing further."

"The defense calls Doris Nelson." Matthews wondered why Barnes would lead off with the chief physician and follow up with a nurse. Graves suggested that he was trying to string out the doctors' testimony with snippets in between.

Barnes proved him right. After establishing that the witness was an emergency room nurse that day, he simply asked her if the photographs she was viewing depicted the wounds she saw on the President on November twenty-second.

"The tracheostomy is clearly too big, and the rear of the head is wrong. There was a large wound there."

"Thank you. Mr. Matthews?"

"Miss Nelson, how much time did you spend observing the President's wounds?"

"I was right at the table handing instruments and tubes, so I saw the tracheostomy for several minutes. As to the other wound, I did not have time to study it in detail, except to note it was the size of a baseball, not a bullet hole. And I've seen hundreds—perhaps thousands of gunshot wounds, and even though I didn't see the rear of the President's head for a lengthy period, I will never forget what I saw."

"Thank you. Sorry to bring you all this way to answer two questions." Matthews had hoped with that conclusion to minimize whatever impact she had on the jury.

As Carolyn Jeffries scurried to turn the photos around so the next witness would not see them until needed, Barnes called Dr. Robert McClelland. After establishing the witness's bona fides, as well as the fact that he did not perform any essential functions on November twenty-second, Barnes asked him, since he seemed to have much time to observe, what he did, in fact, observe.

"I was in such a position that I could very closely examine the head wound, and I noted that the right posterior portion of the skull had been extremely blasted. The parietal bone was protruded up through the scalp and seemed to be fractured along its right posterior half, as well as some of the occipital bone being fractured in its lateral half, and this sprung open the bones. You could look down into the skull cavity and see that probably a third, or so, of the brain tissue, posterior cerebral tissue, and some of the cerebellar tissue had been blasted out."

"For the jury, Doctor, in plain English, where was this wound?"

"In the back of the head."

"Not the top?"

"No."

"Doctor, would you step down off the stand, please?" Barnes requested. He then lead Dr. McClelland to the jury box and asked the foreman to turn around and face the juror behind him. "Doctor, please point to this man's cerebellum."

The witness put a finger just above the juror's hairline, in the middle. "And the cerebellum was, I believe you said, 'Blasted out'?"

"Yes," he said, reseating himself.

"Doctor, the autopsy report indicated no damage whatsoever to the cerebellum, and indicated that the President's brain weighed fifteen hundred grams. That would tend to contradict your testimony."

"Those statements tend to be nonsense, period."

Before Matthews could object, Barnes interrupted to say that such was a matter for the jury to decide. He then asked the witness if he had seen the tracheostomy.

"I did not see it performed, but after the President had been pronounced dead, and the tube was removed, I could see that it had been done right through the wound."

This surprised Barnes. "You could see the wound—the wound in the front of the neck—after the endotracheal cuff tube had been removed?"

"Absolutely. We all saw it."

Barnes nodded to Carolyn Jeffries, who began turning the photos around for the witness to see. He leaned over the witness stand and studied each of the half dozen as they were exposed. "What are those?" he asked.

"These, Dr. McClelland, are the autopsy photographs of President Kennedy. Are they at odds with your recollection of the President's wounds?"

"At odds? I told you, the cerebellum was blasted out. That picture—over there—the back of the head is intact. And that —the picture of the neck is most certainly not anything remotely resembling a tracheostomy. I swore to tell the truth here today, but I must tell you, I don't know what is going on here, and I'm very uncomfortable."

"I appreciate your candor, Doctor. I will not ask you anything further." Matthews knew Barnes had sandbagged another witness, or at least tried to, and he was going to have his say.

"Doctor, I hope you don't mind if I ask a question or two. I am allowed. If you would like to take a moment to compose yourself," Matthews added, hoping the jury would think the witness was having a breakdown or some such.

"Ask away, sir."

"Fine. You said you were standing so you could look into the skull. Now, from such a cursory observation, how can you possibly ask us to believe that you could differentiate damage done to cerebral or cerebellar tissue?"

"It is very simple actually. The brain is composed of two

cerebral hemispheres, which rest, in a sense, at least in the back, on the cerebellum. I testified that damage was done to both the cerebral tissues and the cerebellar tissues because both were extruding from the wound, and they are by nature very different in texture. I hope that answers your question."

"Sorry to have troubled you, Doctor. Nothing further."

"Defense calls Patricia Hutton."

Graves noted to Matthews that it was the doctor/nurse/ doctor routine they predicted earlier. Matthews answered that it was also a disaster if every medical witness was as solid as the first three had been.

Barnes established that the witness was one of the first of the medical emergency team at the hospital to reach the presidential limousine.

"Please tell the court what your participation was, and anatomically orient any wounds you describe."

"Several people helped put the President on the cart, and we then proceeded to the Major Surgery Section of the Emergency Room to Trauma Room number one. Mr. Kennedy was bleeding profusely from a wound on the back of his head, and was lying there unresponsive. . . . Perhaps I should add at this point that I have no knowledge of what happened to the governor."

"I understand. Please complete your testimony with regard to the President."

"A doctor asked me to place a pressure dressing on the head wound. This was of no use, however, because of the massive opening on the back of the head."

"This opening on the back of the head, could you tell if it was larger than a bullet hole?"

"Absolutely. When the dressing was applied, I could feel that there was a large area that it was not touching, which is to say that there was a large area with no scalp or skull present any longer. And it was bleeding in such a way that an untrained person would have realized it was not from a small hole."

"Thank you for your testimony, Nurse Hutton. Cross?"

Matthews sat behind his table, weary. "Do you recall which doctor made the request to place this dressing?"

"Objection. Irrelevant."

"I'll allow it."

"I don't recall. I was looking at the President, and looking at what I was doing, so I didn't see the face that gave the order. And there were several doctors there, all trying desperately to save him."

"There has been testimony, Nurse Hutton, that doctors present had the opportunity to observe the wound you just testified that you obscured with a pressure dressing. How would that have been possible?"

"My efforts, as I said, were to no avail, so they were discontinued. The blood that was being given to the President was coming out about as fast as it went in. Doctors could have observed."

"Nothing further. Thank you, Nurse." Matthews turned to Graves and told him it was time for a doctor. Graves hoped he meant on the witness stand.

"The defense calls Dr. Ronald C. Jones."

Carolyn Jeffries again reversed the pictures prior to the preliminaries, which established that Dr. Jones was one of the first doctors to see the President. "I observed a neck wound no greater than a quarter of an inch in greatest diameter, and a large wound in the right posterior side of his head."

"Right or posterior?" Barnes asked, for clarification.

"It was in the back, but on the right side of the back."

"Thank you, Doctor. Can you add anything with respect to the wound in the back of the head?"

"Well, it was a large defect, with—"

"How large?" Barnes insisted.

"Oh, five, six centimeters across."

"Which is a couple of inches."

"Correct," the doctor replied. "There appeared to be brain hanging out of this wound."

"What about the neck wound?"

"It had relatively smooth edges around it. I would judge it was caused by a missile of very low velocity or a bone fragment exiting from the neck."

"Would a missile of very low velocity be able to strike another human, directly in front, and shatter a rib and wrist before coming to rest in the femur?"

"No. A very low velocity bullet sometimes just makes it through the skin layer."

"Doctor, the report you wrote indicated you thought it was an entrance wound."

"I thought it was. But everyone who has asked me about it since then, in an official capacity, has spoken of exit. If it was exit, it was traveling very slowly, or it was from a bone fragment."

"But your assessment when you saw it was what?"

"Clean, smooth wound of entrance."

"Doctor, do these pictures aid your recollection any?"

"I did not see that wound in the back. Over there, the back of the head is intact. That is erroneous. The rest I cannot comment on."

"Thank you. No further questions."

Matthews decided to try another approach. "Doctor, it's early in the day and we've already heard from several different members of the Parkland Hospital staff. Generally, everyone—yourself included, has said almost the same thing. Is it possible, Doctor, that in all that haste, and with the President of the United States lying on that emergency room table, that one or perhaps two people in attendance mistook what they saw, then everyone, later on, discussed the event from the mistaken perspective, and you have all, unintentionally of course, agreed on incorrect wounds?"

"I know we talked about it. It was something that just wouldn't go away, especially since we found general agreement on the idea that a shot struck the anterior—the front throat and deviated up and blew out the back. Then we read in the paper that the victim was shot from behind. It didn't make any sense, so of course we discussed it. But doctors usually make precise observations, and can go back quite a bit in time and place a scar, or remember an illness that the patient has forgotten. I doubt anyone mistook what they saw in that room that day, sir."

"Thank you, Doctor. Nothing further."

"Defense calls Diana H. Bowron." Matthews calmly slid his right hand off the prosecution table and put it behind his back, where he collected a five-dollar bill from Eaton Graves.

As he did so, the witness, being sworn, answered "I shall" in a cockney dialect.

"Nurse Bowron, I have only two questions for you, so forgive me for bringing you all this way, but they are important questions . . ."

"No trouble at all. I was told America was like this."

"Well, I hope you are learning there is more to America than the events of November twenty-second, but, to return to that date, please tell the court what you observed with respect to the back of the President's head."

"The back of his head . . . I just saw one large hole."

"Thank you. It is my understanding that you had not been in America very long when your job as an emergency nurse at Parkland put you in the position of attempting to aid the fatally wounded President. And this, of course, was big news to your family in England. I show you a newspaper clipping, which the President's Commission labeled Bowron Exhibit Number 4 . . ."

"Yes, I remember that. Something like 'Thirty Minutes Diana Will Never Forget.' Big doings back home."

"I'm sure it was, because here it is on page 170 of Volume 19 of the President's Commission papers, and it tells just as you did a few moments ago about a large hole in the back of the President's head."

"Why is that labeled 'Top Secret'?" the witness asked.

"That was going to be my second question to you," Barnes told her. "Move to admit Bowron Exhibit Number 4 and I have nothing further."

"No questions of the witness," Matthews said, with lack of enthusiasm in his voice.

"Defense calls Dr. Kemp Clark," Barnes announced. While Carolyn Jeffries checked the blowups once again, a stern, balding man, in a sport coat and bow tie entered, immediately giving the impression he had no desire to be part of these proceedings.

"Doctor," Barnes began, "please tell the court who pronounced the President dead."

"I did."

"Doctor, I've heard that Dr. Perry was continuing cardiac

massage, although to no avail, when you stopped him and pronounced the President dead. Is that essentially correct?"

"Yes."

"Doctor, will you tell the court the nature of the wounds you saw?"

"As I have testified and deposed previously, I saw two wounds, one in the lower third of the anterior neck, and the other in the occipital region of the skull."

"Doctor, please tell the jury where the occipital region is located."

"In the back of the head."

"Please continue your testimony about that wound."

"It was an extreme wound. There was considerable loss of scalp and bone tissue. Both cerebral and cerebellar tissues were extruding from the wound."

"Doctor, I have no expertise in medicine. But I know that the cerebral and cerebellar hemispheres are of differing textures. With the bleeding such as it was on the rear of the President's head, if I knew they were different textures, would I have been able to distinguish the two types of tissue present?"

"I believe so."

Barnes then gave Dr. Clark the guided tour of the photos, which the witness found at odds with his own recollection, and then asked the standard litany about brain weight of 1500 grams, as measured at the autopsy, which also clashed with the witness's recollection of events. Barnes then handed the witness over to Matthews.

"Doctor, your answers make it sound like this issue has been talked to death. Is that a fair statement of how you feel?"

"Objection. The witness's feelings about rehearing evidence is not material."

"Sustained, Mr. Matthews, unless you can demonstrate that this witness is telling us this story to expedite his exit or for some other reason of gain."

"No further questions."

Barnes, having seen the earlier transaction involving five dollars, gave Eaton Graves a big wink and said, "The defense calls Dr. Jackie Hunt." Matthews dug angrily into his pocket and pulled out a twenty, suspecting collusion between Graves and Barnes. Barnes found humor in the notion that the trial, for the prosecution, had come down to four-to-one bets on witnesses.

Once sworn, the witness was simply asked to view the photographs and comment. "They are not remotely similar to what was seen at Parkland. I can do a lot of funny things in the darkroom, too."

Matthews objected to the last comment and was sustained. Barnes had nothing more for the witness. Matthews wanted to know how every doctor or nurse who testified from Texas had such difficulties with official photographs taken at a United States Naval Installation under the tightest security possible.

"Do you always answer your own questions?" the witness asked Matthews. Matthews had no further questions.

Barnes was beginning to sense that Matthews's lack of intensity was intentionally geared to rub off on the jury, and his best hope was to make this testimony seem meaningless. For that reason, and because he had made his case, he quickly ran through the remaining medical witnesses, learning from registered nurse Margaret Henchcliffe, a twelve-year veteran who had sometimes seen several gunshot wounds a day, that the throat wound was, to her, clearly a wound of entrance and that she had never seen an exit wound that looked like that, although people had asked her to conclude that it could have been an exit. Matthews repeated the question and she repeated her disclaimer.

The testimony of Dr. Marion T. Jenkins, which repeated the essential massive wounding in the back of the head, including the presence of herniated brain and cerebellar tissue, allowed for the possibility, which Matthews pounced upon, for the throat wound being a wound of exit. The remainder of his testimony was anatomically confusing, as he spoke of the left temporal area as the source of the wound, and there was discussion as to whether it was the patient's or the viewer's left. Little was proved either way.

When Barnes realized how quickly the morning was passing, he gave both Jeffries and Dean the odious task of rounding up witnesses for the afternoon, explaining that he had expected the medical people to take at least a full day. He also added to Dean that he had expected Matthews to fight back.

"With what?" Dean asked. "They saw the body, alive and dead, and they are the only nongovernment people that did. The prosecution's stooges had their say. Now let a jury of ordinary citizens hear some well-educated and well-meaning ordinary citizens. Judge Davis has a job for life just hearing the perjury charges that are going to fly when this case goes in the dumper."

While Dean and Jeffries were working the phones, Barnes examined Dr. Paul Peters, a cheery face amidst an otherwise somewhat gloomy collection, who reinforced earlier testimony that the most serious damage was done to the back of the head, which was "blown out . . . the wound was more occipital than parietal, because we had to get up to his head, to look in through the back, to see the extent of the wound." Matthews challenged the assertion that the entire cerebellum had been blasted out, but Peters's medical expertise, which suggested that "the cerebral hemispheres may have been resting on the foramen magnum," completely lost Matthews.

Before Barnes could call his next witness, the judge asked if the testimony would be lengthy, and Barnes admitted that the final two medical witnesses might consume some time. "With that in mind, we'll recess now and return at one P.M. Court is adjourned until then."

Barnes, alone at the defense table with Oswald, assured his client that the remainder of the trial would be downhill and gentle, but to maintain his composure. "They may never find out who did it, until you tell what you know, Lee, because there will always be the fact that the gun you ordered was deemed the murder weapon. Technicalities and lack of eyewitnesses helped immensely, but you better give serious thought to getting what you know off your chest, or you'll stay in the presidential assassin category. Think about it. I'll see you after lunch."

Barnes had used the word "lunch" with caution, as he had no stomach for anything beyond soup and crackers after hearing about herniated brain tissue all morning. He wished he could talk to the Vermont police, who escorted the jury to lunch, to see how their appetites were. If they ate normally, Barnes thought, either the medical testimony did not hit them, or it didn't change their thinking. If they, too, felt like skipping lunch, the testimony hit them hard.

Dean and Jeffries rejoined Barnes well before the prosecution team returned, and they tried to map out future strategy. Barnes felt it imperative that they put testimony into the record to show that many witnesses saw and heard things not reflected in, or even noticed by, the President's commission, and he also wanted Oswald's alibis, as well as the Oswald imposture in the record.

When the prosecutors returned, Barnes was thinking about his two remaining medical witnesses, as well as whether or not Graves bought Matthews's lunch with his winnings.

When court reconvened, Barnes called Dr. Charles Carrico, while Carolyn Jeffries once again laid out the enlargements, but so that the witness could not see them until they were turned around.

"Dr. Carrico, before we get to the events of November twenty-second, there is an obvious question that needs to be asked. Were you board certified in surgery on that date?"

"No. I was still an emergency room resident."

"Did you subsequently become board certified in surgery according to the normal internship-residency scheduling that would have been expected?"

"Yes, I did."

"Now, Doctor, calling your attention to the events of November twenty-second, 1963, please tell us your recollections."

"I was the first doctor to see the President. He was alive in the medical sense because there was a heartbeat, however faint, present. For all practical purposes, though, the man died at the time of the impact to the head. There was still blood in the body, so the heart pumped it."

"Tell the court about the wounds, please."

"I examined the President while he was still clothed, much as a policeman might check a suspect for a weapon, and that search revealed no large holes in the body cavity. I then took notice of the head wound, a defect more or less circular, approximately five by seven centimeters—two and a half inches or so. There was an absence of the calvarium or skull in this area, with shredded tissue, brain tissue, and it was of both cerebral and cerebellar type."

"Where was the wound located, doctor?"

"In the posterior skull, the occipital region . . . the back of the head."

"And it was bigger than a bullet hole?"

"Bullet holes are measured in millimeters; this was a baseball-sized hole which would be measured in centimeters."

"Did you see any other wounds?"

"Again, before the President's clothes were cut off him, which is standard procedure in emergencies, I noticed a wound in the front neck, approximately four to seven millimeters, almost in the midline, maybe a little to the right of the midline, and below the thyroid cartilage. It was rather round and there were no jagged edges or stellate lacerations."

"You saw this wound when the President was *dressed?*"

"Yes."

"We must then account for the hole in the front of the shirt and the tie, but that's not your problem, Doctor. The front neck wound—entrance or exit?"

"Inasmuch as I could not say positively that it was one to the exclusion of the other, I would have to say it could have been either."

"Fair enough. Now, the measurements you gave—four to seven millimeters. Is that the hole, or the hole plus the bruised skin?"

"The wound would include the hole plus the bruising on the tangential skin."

"The prosecution would like us to believe, Doctor, that the four to seven millimeter hole you described came from a six point five mm bullet. Could it have?"

"Only if the wound was in fact in the seven millimeter range. And to the best of my knowledge, that answer can no longer be ascertained."

"You are correct—it can't. Doctor, did you see the tracheostomy incision?"

"Yes. I was right there."

"How big was it?"

"Two to three centimeters in length, and the width of a scalpel blade."

"Doctor, does it resemble what is shown in this photographic enlargement?"

"Certainly not."

"Did the back of the President's head look like this photo?"

"Again, certainly not."

"No further questions, Dr. Carrico."

"Doctor," Matthews began, walking toward the witness deep in thought, "try to recall the throat wound. Were the edges of the wound going inward or outward?"

"Well, there were no jagged edges, and it was a round wound."

"Suggesting exit?"

"On the contrary. Jagged would have meant the bullet was coming out. Round and not jagged suggests that the bullet was going in."

Matthews tried again. "Could the bullet have, in fact, gone through the clothing, and in the subsequent time, with the head shot, the body recoil, the dash to the hospital, the removal of the President from the car, your search of the body cavity—could that have exposed the wound in the throat which had previously been under the garments?"

"Certainly."

"Thank you, Doctor. Nothing further."

Jeffries again concealed the pictures, while Barnes called Dr. Charles R. Baxter. He began by eliciting testimony that Dr. Baxter had heard the emergency page and went to the trauma area, but was essentially an observer. His testimony indicated that, like the previous witness, his recollection of the hole in the front of the neck was of a small hole, perhaps 4 to 5 millimeters in size, a measurement challenged by Barnes based on the caliber of the "alleged" murder weapon.

The witness stuck to his story, maintaining it was a smaller wound than the caliber suggested, being 4 to 5 millimeters at its widest dimension, that it was spherical, and that "It did not appear to be a jagged wound such as one would expect with a very high velocity rifle bullet."

"Doctor, did this wound appear to be an entry or an exit?"

"This would more resemble a wound of entry. If that had been an ordinary person on the table, we certainly would have examined that wound carefully after the victim had been pronounced dead, because someone in that room would have had to sign a death certificate. But the Secret Service cleared out the room."

"Preventing the medical staff from making observations?"

"Objection. Leading."

"Sustained."

"Doctor, you testified you were basically observing. What did you observe with respect to any other wounds the President received?"

"What I saw indicated the damage was beyond hope. The right side of his head had been blown off. There was brain matter lying on the table, and absence of temporal and parietal bones."

"Did you see damage to the cerebellum?"

"It was extruding from the massive defect in the skull."

"A moment ago you said the right side was blown off. The cerebellum is where?"

"In the center of the occipital area—the back."

"Thank you, Doctor. Nothing further. Mr. Matthews?"

Matthews remained seated. "Doctor, did you actually measure the wound in the neck?"

"No."

"And just how much of the brain was shot away? Can you say with precision?"

"I would estimate about one third. Again, the concern was for treatment, and then we were asked to leave the room."

"I have no further questions for this witness."

By the time the medical testimony was completed, Dean and Jeffries had returned from their labors, but neither was able to report anything more than limited success in rounding up the following day's witnesses. Barnes considered the problem briefly, hoping to avoid any interruptions in what he viewed as a defense juggernaut of ever-increasing power. He then gave instructions to Dean and Jeffries, with Dean expressing reservations, but in the end, he agreed to go along with the idea.

Noting Judge Davis's impatience, Barnes called Ruth
Paine to the witness stand. A young but staid woman entered
the courtroom, oriented herself towards the witness stand
with the help of the Vermont officer who held the door for
her, and seemed genuinely surprised and happy that the
court was relatively devoid of people.

Barnes knew that Mrs. Paine was a key witness, not so
much for anything she could put into the record, which was
virtually nothing, but for what she could keep out, as she
was one of the defendant's two alibis.

"Mrs. Paine, did you testify before the President's Commission?"

"Yes. Several times, and frequently for more than a day.
They sure had a lot of questions."

"Yes, they did, Mrs. Paine. Are you aware that your testimony, not counting affidavits that you signed, covered 253
pages of their proceedings?"

"No, I wasn't, but I can't say the number surprises me."

"Mrs. Paine, calling your attention to a more recent series
of questions put to you, do you have a recollection of the
telephone conversation between yourself and Mr. Dean that
occurred shortly before Thanksgiving?"

"Yes."

"Do you recall the length of the call?"

Matthews stood to object, claiming that Barnes was wasting the court's time with nonessential trivia. Judge Davis
said that he would sustain the objection, but would not be
able to sustain further objections based on foundation unless the witness and defense attorney were allowed to establish one. Matthews withdrew his objection.

"The length of the call, Mrs. Paine?"

"Brief. Maybe fifteen minutes."

"Did you and Mr. Dean, in your fifteen-minute conversation, cover as much of substance as you dealt with in 253
pages of testimony?"

"Mr. Dean and I probably accomplished more."

"Very well. Now, let's start from the beginning. Mrs. Paine,
please tell the court your religious affiliation, if you feel comfortable doing that."

"I belong to the Society of Friends, sometimes called the Quakers."

"Is there, in the religious practice of the Quakers, any specific doctrines regarding violence, Mrs. Paine?"

"Quakers are nonviolent, peace-loving people, sir."

"Mrs. Paine, do you speak the Russian language?"

"I was very busy trying to learn it, as it interested me—there were a number of Russian-speaking people in the Dallas-Fort Worth area, and it seemed like an interesting challenge. I was working very hard to learn it at the time I met Mrs. Oswald, uh, Marina, and since she didn't know English —not very much, anyway—I thought I could help her with her English and she could help me with my Russian. I must conclude my answer by telling you that my desire to continue to learn Russian has been dealt a setback by the events of November twenty-second."

"In what way?"

"People have misunderstood. I've been accused of being a Communist, or harboring Communists—plural—at the house, and my husband, who has a security clearance at his job, has heard rumblings also—all because I wanted to increase my knowledge."

"Mrs. Paine, for the record, this question must be asked. Have you ever been involved with Communist activities— read any literature, gone to meetings, anything like that?"

"Certainly not. It would be totally in violation of my religious beliefs to do so."

"Did the defendant, Mr. Oswald, ever discuss *his* political beliefs with you?"

"I would have to say that I could answer your question from events, not philosophies. Something would be on the TV, and Lee would say something, or make some pronouncement about the event."

"Did he ever give you any reason to think he was a Communist?"

"Lee used the phrase Marxist, and he would then, well, digress to explain the difference between a Marxist and a Communist."

"So he would tell you, in conversation, that, in fact, he was a Marxist and he did not want to be confused with a Communist?"

"Objection, Your Honor, leading the witness."

"Sustained."

Barnes broke it down for Matthews's purposes. "Mrs. Paine, did the defendant tell you on more than one occasion that he believed in something called Marxism?"

"Yes."

"On those occasions, did he make a differentiation between Marxism and Communism?"

"Yes."

"And on those occasions, did he clearly indicate that he was not a Communist?"

"Yes."

"During your conversations with the defendant, did he have opportunities to discuss the quality of life, based on his own experience, in the Soviet Union?"

"Yes."

"What did he tell you?"

"He had become very disillusioned with Russia and was glad to be back in the United States."

"Mrs. Paine, during your acquaintance with the defendant, did he ever make any reference to President John Kennedy?"

"Yes. Not often, mind you, because he wasn't the kind of person who talked a lot, and when he talked to Marina, he spoke Russian, and his Russian was much better than mine, so I couldn't always follow. But when he spoke of President Kennedy, he usually had very positive things to say about the President and his family."

"Mrs. Paine, I must ask you a couple of additional unpleasant questions for the record. Please do not feel as if you are being accused. In all the time you knew the defendant and his wife, prior to the afternoon of November twenty-second, 1963, did you ever know, or even have any hint, that the defendant owned any weapons?"

"No. I would not have allowed them under my roof under those conditions."

"Mrs. Paine, when you drove to New Orleans, and helped Mrs. Oswald move her family's belongings to your home, did you notice any package that was so structured that it could have contained a rifle?"

"No. I saw no such thing."

"Mrs. Paine, were you visited by agents of the FBI prior to November twenty-second, 1963?"

"Twice. On November one, and again on November eight."

"Please tell the court about that."

"Well, the first time, they knocked, I answered the door, then they identified themselves, asked if they could come in, and they asked about Lee—if he was working, and I told them yes, he was."

"Did you tell them where?"

"Yes. I had helped him get that job, and I know that it gave him satisfaction that he was working."

"So on November one and November eight, virtually the exact dates when the President's motorcade route was being planned, you gave the FBI information that indicated that a former defector to Russia, in whom the FBI was expressing interest, had a job in a large building overlooking the parade route?"

"Yes. But, of course, I didn't say it that way."

"Of course you didn't, Mrs. Paine, but that would not prevent the FBI from hearing it that way. Mrs. Paine, tell us about the defendant's visits to your home. When did he visit?"

"He would come out on Friday afternoon, sometimes with a few bits of laundry to have washed, and he would stay until Monday morning."

"Of your own knowledge, Mrs. Paine, do you know how he got there?"

"I know that he frequently rode with Wesley Frazier. But once, at the beginning, he took a bus, and called me from the bus station, but I couldn't go get him, so he had to hike it a couple of miles."

"Mrs. Paine, when did Mr. Oswald begin these weekend visits?"

"I have testified to this so often, I know it without looking at a calendar. He came out on Friday, October four, and every Friday thereafter until November eight; on the weekend of October eleventh, twelfth, and thirteenth, he stayed an extra day and I took him down to the neighborhood of the Book Depository so he could apply for the job. On November eighth, he stayed on Saturday the ninth, Sunday the tenth, and Monday, the eleventh, which was a holiday."

"Mrs. Paine, this is a question around which much of this case will revolve, so please listen carefully. When Mr. Oswald visited your home, on these Friday afternoon to Monday morning visits, did he actually remain at your home to the point where you can account for his whereabouts?"

Mrs. Paine looked like she was trying to phrase a long answer. "Initially, he never went anywhere, so I can tell you that he was at my home. Now, of course, in the legal sense, I can't tell you that he did not awaken at, oh, say 2 A.M., tiptoe out somewhere and be back before I awoke. But during my waking hours, he was there—always. Watching television, playing with the children, speaking Russian to Marina. I must also tell you that I tried to give him driving lessons," she continued, with frustration evident in her voice, "but I was with him on those occasions. We would drive to an empty parking lot and he would get some practice behind the wheel. Not that it did much good. He just couldn't get the hang of it."

"Mrs. Paine, was it that he didn't understand how to drive, or was unable to perform the mechanical skills necessary?"

"Objection. Speculative."

"Your Honor, a person who is teaching someone else a skill usually gets a sense, in the case of failure, as to why the failure is happening. If Mrs. Paine doesn't know, she may so answer. I'm not asking her to speculate."

"Mrs. Paine," Judge Davis pronounced, "do you have a solid feeling for why Mr. Oswald could not operate your car well?"

"He understood the concepts, Judge. He just was awful at the mechanics of it—turns, coordinating the brake and the wheel. Too much gas, not enough gas. That kind of thing."

"Objection overruled."

"Mrs. Paine, calling your attention to the weekend of November eighth through eleven, which included the Monday holiday. Would you tell the court about that?"

"Well, when Lee got home on Friday, he learned from both

Marina and me that the FBI had been by that afternoon, but had chosen not to stay, even though I told them that Lee was due to arrive soon. He didn't like them bothering his wife, I know that. On Saturday, the ninth, I drove everybody—Lee, Marina, and all the kids, downtown so Lee could go to the office where driver's license applications were processed, but they were closed when I got there, so we went back home. Everyone was there the remainder of the weekend."

"Mrs. Paine, the defense will put at least three witnesses on the stand who will say they saw Lee Oswald, that man over there," Barnes indicated by pointing at the defendant in a nonaccusatory fashion, "on that weekend, test-driving a new car, firing a rifle at a rifle range, and visiting a furniture store with a non-English speaking wife and two small babies. In all these cases, the Lee Oswald identified drove himself to the destination. I'm going to ask you again, are you certain that Lee was in your home during that weekend?"

"Absolutely. He used my typewriter for the better part of two days that weekend. Besides, if whoever they saw drove, it could not have been Lee."

Matthews was on his feet: "Your Honor, move to strike—argumentative and nonresponsive."

"We'll ignore the answer past the word 'weekend.' "

"Mrs. Paine, in fact is there any time when you cannot place the whereabouts of the defendant when he was supposed to be at your home?"

"Once he was gone for about fifteen minutes, on a Saturday. And given his usual habit of always being around, I thought that strange. He was soon back, with ice cream for the kids. On one or two other occasions, he went out in the evening with my husband, Michael."

"Mrs. Paine, did the President's Commission ask you these same questions?"

"Not word for word, but yes, over and over."

"And did you answer as you did today?"

"I told the truth then, and I'm telling it again."

"I have no reason not to believe you, Mrs. Paine, but obviously your being able to be an alibi caused problems for the President's Commission, because they made you sign some affidavits last June twenty-fourth, 1964."

"I was told that was procedural and everyone would have to."

"Mrs. Paine, let's move ahead. Did the defendant visit you on the weekend before the assassination, which would be Friday the 15th to Sunday the 17th?"

"No. There was a party scheduled for one of my children and Lee, who was always in the way, felt that he would be in the way, so he did not come out."

"When did you see him next?"

"On Thursday, November twenty-first, 1963. I was driving down the street, and there he was, on the lawn, playing with his daughter."

"Was there any discussion of the President's visit?"

"I did not hear any."

"Mrs. Paine, do you have any knowledge that Lee Oswald spent time in your garage that night?"

"No."

"Were you in the garage that night?"

"Yes. I went out to paint blocks for the children, and when I got out there, the light was on in the garage."

"Was there any indication that Lee had been in the garage?"

"No."

"Was there any brown wrapping paper or sealing tape lying around that should not have been there?"

"No."

"Mrs. Paine, did you have curtain rods, wrapped in brown paper, in your garage, to your knowledge, as of November twenty-second?"

"Yes."

"Did you see them after that date?"

"They were discovered by the police there in December."

"But they were not found in the searches of your residence conducted on November twenty-second and twenty-third?"

"I have no way of knowing. They didn't give us a receipt for what they took, and they took some things—like my record collection and my movie projector—just for the sake of taking things. What kind of evidence did they expect to find on old seventy-eight r.p.m. records?"

"Perhaps when the authorities get their day in court, Mrs.

Paine, they can answer you. Now, let's get to November twenty-second. What happened in your house?"

"Nothing unusual early. Then we put the TV on to follow the progress of the President's parade . . ."

"We?"

"I'm sorry. Marina and I."

"Okay. Please go on."

"Then we heard the awful news and it hit both of us very hard. We stayed glued to the news, and eventually heard that the President had died, and that there was some concern about the Book Depository. I told Marina at that point that because Lee worked there, we might get a firsthand account."

"So even though Mr. Oswald had returned from Russia and was not in love with the American system of capitalism, when you heard of the events in Dealey Plaza, there were no ideas in your mind that allowed for Mr. Oswald to be a participant in them?"

"None whatsoever. I never thought of Lee as a violent man." Matthews wanted to object, but he knew Barnes could get the answer into the record some other way, so one hearing of it was preferable to two. "Later on, the police arrived and searched the house, and only then did I learn, from Marina, that she thought she had seen part of a rifle in a blanket that had been on the garage floor. The blanket was empty when the police examined it."

"So they took your records and film projector?"

"And God knows what else," she answered, "and they said they'd be back to look some more. In the meantime, they were determined that they were going to take all of us down to police headquarters, and fast, because I told them I would go, but that I would have to arrange for one of the neighborhood teenagers to watch the children, and the police told me I'd better hurry, or my children would be watched by police at a juvenile center. It was a cheap threat, nothing more."

"Did you then go to police headquarters?"

"Yes. And my most vivid memory of the entire sad episode is when the police kept trying to get Marina to say that she had seen the rifle in the blanket. But she insisted she had only seen the, uh, the—the shoulder end of it—not the barrel part, that she could not identify the gun they kept asking her about, and that she could not remember seeing the telescope on it."

"Was that the end of it?"

"Almost. The house was searched again the next day, in our absence, and the Secret Service took Marina away and gave me the impression that I should not attempt to contact Marina. And one other strange thing happened. Lee called me that Saturday afternoon, and gave me the name of a lawyer that he wanted to represent him. His voice was calm, matter-of-fact, as if he was calling to ask if he could bring his laundry out. No fear whatsoever."

"Thank you very much, Mrs. Paine. I'm sorry to have been an additional burden on your time."

Matthews, who had not bothered to have a pretrial interview with Ruth Paine, now regretted it. Having considered her an innocent bystander originally, he now saw how damaging her ability to alibi the defendant was. He knew he had to weaken her credibility before the jury.

"Mrs. Paine, besides the defendant, you seem to be at the very center of this controversy."

"It has certainly seemed that way for fourteen months."

"Let's consider what you've told us," Matthews went on, cynicism evident in his voice. "You were learning Russian— seemingly an odd skill or hobby in the state of Texas; you took in a boarder, Marina Oswald, so she could help you with your language aptitude, but, viewed another way, to bring the defendant's wife, and the defendant after her, to Dallas, Texas. Then you help him secure employment in the building strongly suspected of being the origin of the shots . . ."

Barnes had heard enough. "Your Honor, the prosecution is trying to make it sound like this young lady is on trial, or if she is not, she should be. If they've got something, let the court see it, but let's cut the hand shadows."

"Could you get to the point, Mr. Matthews?" the judge asked.

"The point is obvious, Your Honor."

"It isn't to me," Davis responded.

"Given the facts elicited in direct examination, it seems like the witness is a pivotal person in this investigation, and I

wanted the jury to be aware of that. I have the right to be
curious as to why someone in Texas would want to learn
Russian, and why they would drive to New Orleans to round
up the daughter of a Russian intelligence official, and her
husband, a former marine who defected to the Soviets, and
then arrange for him to find employment in a tall, downtown
building when it was known that the President was coming
to Dallas."

"Your Honor," Barnes interrupted, "Mr. Matthews has
talked for five minutes and not asked a question, except perhaps to himself. If he wants the jury to hear the questions
and the answers, he'll have to pose the questions to the witness. If he wants to think out loud, we have a corridor outside for that."

Matthews froze Barnes with a stare, but to little value.
"Mrs. Paine, you've heard my comments—"

"With obvious malice intended," Mrs. Paine said softly.

"Your Honor, the prosecution would ask that the witness
be designated a hostile witness."

"Please approach, gentlemen." When Barnes, who took his
time closing a folder, finally arrived at the bench, giving Matthews time to cool his heels, the judge came right to the
point: "If there is anything hostile in this room right now, it is
the prosecution. Ray, you damn near told the jury that this
woman, a Quaker, should be treated as an unindicted cocon-
spirator. I understand the nature of your questions, Ray, but
you've already been instructed. Now I suggest you apologize.
Take your places."

Barnes let Matthews go first, then chuckled once, for Matthews's benefit.

"The witness will not be considered a hostile witness. Mrs.
Paine, the court regrets certain comments that have been
made, but sometimes questions have to be asked."

"I would add an apology for my remarks, Mrs. Paine," Matthews added. Then: "For the record, why Russian?"

"As I said, there is a group of Russian émigrés—very wonderful people, and I thought I could join their group more
easily if I spoke the language. Also, I had hoped, and I still
hope, that the United States and Russia will talk to each
other, not make war. If my learning Russian meant anything,

it could be that I was desperately looking for a peaceful way out of what appears to be an inevitable nuclear situation."

"And where do the Oswalds fit into this?"

"I met Marina at a party involving the Russian-émigré community. By the way, they are people who were children, or whose parents were children, in tsarist Russia, and who have no use for the Soviet Union. Marina needed help. Her husband did not always have work, and had, as you pointed out, the stigma of having left the United States to go to Russia for whatever his purposes were. My husband had left me in 1962 and if I could find company—obviously not another man, help someone in need, and advance my language abilities, then I would have concluded I had found the perfect person. For the record, I had no knowledge that Marina was related to anyone in the intelligence community of the Soviet Union. If she mentioned it, which I doubt, my Russian might not have understood the technical words she was using."

"And you helped the defendant get a job at the Depository."

"I would have helped Lee Oswald get a job washing and waxing John Connally's automobile if it would have given him the dignity of work. I never saw him as a violent person, and presidential assassinations were not something that were a daily preoccupation to me until the afternoon of November twenty-second, 1963. If you saw the caring that man had for his children, then you would know, or at least form a judgment that he would never perform an act that would cause himself to be separated from them or to taint their names."

Matthews at least knew when to quit. "Nothing further."

Barnes rose. "Your Honor, I would like the affidavit signed by Mrs. Paine on June twenty-fourth, 1964, admitted into evidence at this time."

"So moved." Judge Davis had not even asked Matthews if he had an objection.

"The defense calls Mrs. Earlene Roberts." Barnes walked down to the end of the defense table and told Dean and Jeffries, "Let Matthews try to intimidate this lady and he's going to get bruised."

"Mrs. Roberts, would it be correct to consider you the landlady for the rooming house at 1026 North Beckley Street, in the Oak Cliff section of suburban Dallas, Texas?"

"Yes. I run the place for the owners."

Barnes was geared to politeness. "Thank you, Mrs. Roberts. Now, even though there are not very many people in this courtroom, do you see anyone here that you rented a room to at the address of 1026 North Beckley?"

"Yes, sir. That boy right there."

Barnes walked behind Oswald and put his hand on Oswald's shoulder. "This boy, Mrs. Roberts?"

"Yes."

"Thank you again. Now, when did you rent this room to the defendant?"

"October 14, 1963."

"And what name was the room rented under?"

"I got the impression—'course I could have been confused —but I thought he told me his name was 'O.H.Lee,' so that's what I wrote in the register."

"As your tenant, Mrs. Roberts, did the defendant keep regular hours?"

"Could have set the clock by them. Left between six-thirty and seven in the morning, and was back in the door by five."

"Every day?"

"Every single day," the witness answered, for emphasis. "'Course some weekends, he wasn't there. Left on Friday morning with a little bag of laundry, I presume, then was back on Monday evening by five."

"So he was regularly there, strike that, please. So he slept there Monday, Tuesday, Wednesday, and Thursday nights, is that correct?"

"Yes."

"To your knowledge, did this Mr. Lee go out after he arrived home at five?"

"To my knowledge, he most certainly did not. He was always there. Like the furniture. Never went anywhere."

"Mrs. Roberts, we have heard testimony that he did not go where he usually went on the weekend before the President was killed, which would have been Friday, November fifteenth through Sunday, November seventeenth. Are you able to recall his whereabouts that weekend?"

"Ordinarily, I'd have to say I couldn't. But I was asked about that so many times back then, that I know the answer, and the answer is that he didn't go nowhere. He was a fixture. Whatever was on TV, he watched. Then he'd go to his room, read books, maybe come back and watch TV."

"Would you tell us what you recall of Mr. Lee's, or the defendant's, for the record, presence in your boarding house on November twenty-second, which was the Friday on which the President was killed?"

"He didn't come home Thursday night. Next day, I'm watching TV, getting the news about the shooting of the President, and he walks through the door in an unusual hurry. I spoke to him, about the President, but he didn't answer, or if he did, he was walking away. He went into his room, came out zipping up a jacket, then went outside, where he waited at the bus stop for a little while. Then later, the police came, and I saw his photo on TV and I said, 'That's O.H.Lee on TV.' So after that, they put me through the third degree—FBI, Secret Service, Fritz's men, Decker's men."

"I appreciate your recollection of detail, Mrs. Roberts, but could we back up a little? Could you place the time that the defendant walked into your premises?"

"Just about one o'clock."

"And how long did he remain there?"

"Three or four minutes."

"No more and no less?" Barnes asked her with a polite smile.

"No more or no less," she answered, still gruff, but with the beginning of an understanding that she was not the defendant.

"Mrs. Roberts, did anything out of the ordinary occur during those three or four minutes when the defendant was in his room?"

"Police car came down the street, stopped in front of the house. Two uniformed officers in the car. They honked the horn, gently, twice. A minute or so later, they drove off."

"So the defendant arrived at about one P.M., stayed three to four minutes, and left. Was his haste in leaving as extreme as it seemed to you when he arrived?"

"Never been asked that. But I'd say it was."

"Then you observed him at the bus stop for how long?"

"A few minutes more. That's the best time I can put on that, because it didn't seem important then."

"I understand, Mrs. Roberts. One final question, so I am sure I understood you. On the days the defendant would have been sleeping at your residence, you testified that he was always there, and never deviated from his television or reading routine."

"He was always there."

"Thank you, Mrs. Roberts. I have no further questions to ask you."

Matthews stood behind the prosecution table. "Mrs. Roberts, did you ever see the defendant in possession of a weapon?"

"What do you think I run down there? 'Course I didn't see no weapon." Barnes knew the wrong question would get Matthews in trouble quickly.

"Mrs. Roberts, were you aware that the police confiscated a holster for a pistol—"

"Objection. Hearsay."

"Mrs. Roberts, did any policemen tell you what they found in the defendant's room?"

"Not the first day. They just asked me a bunch of stupid questions, like I'm supposed to know he lived in Russia. They did tell me about what they found the second day."

"And what was that?" Matthews asked, expectantly.

"They thought it was funny, 'cause they searched his little room there and all they found was a paper clip and a rubber band. They was wondering who would get to deal with all that important evidence."

"Mrs. Roberts, why would a Dallas police car stop in front of your house and honk its horn?"

"I have no idea. But that boy over there knows."

"No further questions. Thank you, Mrs. Roberts."

Barnes rose. "Your Honor, the defense has the rubber band and the paper clip if you want them submitted for evidence at this time."

"Mr. Matthews, do you need those items introduced?"

"Not at this time, Your Honor."

"Your Honor, given the late hour, the defense would ask for an adjournment now rather than be in the middle of testimony when adjournment time comes."

"Agreed. Court is in recess until nine A.M. tomorrow."

# Fourteen

Wednesday, January 20, 1965, the day Lyndon Johnson would begin the term he had been elected to. In Lubbock, the temperature was about the same, but the wind took the day off, so it felt like spring. Matthews had given the prosecution team the night off, since it appeared to him that Barnes's case was winding down and their cross-examinations would amount to nibbling at the edges, which did not require intense preparation.

Barnes, Dean, and Jeffries had adjourned their own strategy session early, as they arrived, as planned, at the courthouse at 7:30 A.M. and were available to greet the almost three dozen individuals who trooped in, individually or in twos, until about 8:45, when the prosecution team arrived to find the three defense attorneys in animated conversation with the throng that had gathered in the courthouse rotunda. Matthews took Barnes aside and told him that he should have been notified if the ban on speaking to the press had been lifted, or if there were going to be spectators in the gallery for the first time.

"Relax, Ray, it's nothing of the kind. These are the morning's witnesses—or the day's, I guess I should say. Seems like a lot of folks saw or heard shots from locations other than the good old Texas School Book Depository."

"Be that as it may," Matthews argued, allowing Barnes to walk him toward the courtroom, "it's not relevant. We are trying someone who was in the Depository; whatever else may or may not have occurred has no validity."

"After what Davis told you regarding defense's motion to dismiss, do you really think he'll rule in your favor if you try to say that witnesses who saw and heard shots from other locations are not relevant? Ray, Davis is keeping the shop open to hear the rest of the story. Your half, or really the Dallas p.d.'s half, didn't get it done."

"That mob could take a day or two—proving what?" Matthews was clearly upset at the prospect of listening to thirty-five or so people further weaken his case.

"Proving," Barnes told him, "that it belongs in the record. They're doing you a favor if you think about it, Ray. Did the Dallas p.d. pursue the leads these people gave them? Not really. So when this all shakes down, you can point at this group, as well as the phonied up autopsy photos, which the Dallas doctors destroyed on the stand yesterday, plus the Secret Service, and a few other people not yet heard from, and say, 'Where was my case'? All you can do is present your case, Ray. Some law enforcement group had to *make* it for you—and nobody did. I'm not trying to destroy your career—"

"That mob out front isn't going to get me named prosecutor of the year, either," Matthews shot back, as he was joined by Graves and Vincent, who were equally confused about the mob in the rotunda.

"Look, Ray, I've got them all deposed. I'm sure you spoke with most of them—they were all on my discovery list that you got months ago." Barnes was casting bait.

"I talked to some of them by phone. They had a couple of sentences to say, period. I met one or two in Dallas, but they certainly look different when you put them all together."

"Suppose we do this: I'll put the first one on the stand. You make your objection on relevancy. If the judge buys it, we get the day off. If not, you can save a lot of time—and face, by putting a sentence or two from each of them into the record by stipulation. It won't make the greatest reading, but it cuts down on the sheer volume of defense witnesses. Of course, you can't cross-examine a stipulation, but I'll warn you that your cross could be a risk with some of these people, because they've been told *not* to talk, and I know you don't want *that* in the record."

Barnes then called Dean and Jeffries, who broke off their conversations, and all six attorneys entered the courtroom in time to grab coffee and await the arrival of the judge.

Judge Davis gaveled the proceedings to order and indicated that Barnes could proceed. "The defense calls Billy Lovelady." Barnes immediately sat down so the jury, as well as the prosecutors could focus on the witness entering the courtroom, who bore an amazing resemblance to the defendant. Barnes noticed several jurors look at the witness, look over to Oswald, and then look back at the witness. Barnes knew Matthews would have a difficult time getting this witness ruled irrelevant.

"Mr. Lovelady, calling your attention to November twenty-second, 1963, please tell the court where you were standing at the time the shots were fired at the President."

"On the top steps of the Book Depository, where I was employed, just a little bit inside the door. It was sunny that day."

"Could we have CE 369, enlargement, please?" Barnes waited for the first exhibit of the day to come up on the screen, then asked, "For the record, Mr. Lovelady, are you able to identify yourself in the photo?"

"Yes, sir. That's me, on the left, leaning around there to see what's going on."

"And you specifically remember wearing that particular dark shirt, unbuttoned at the top, that day?"

"Actually, I've always said I thought I wore a red-and-white-stripe—wide stripes, by the way—shirt that day, but I know that's me, so I must be mistaken about the shirt."

"Could we have all of CE 369 now, please?" The screens soon displayed a wide-angle shot of Elm Street, with the presidential limousine in the foreground, showing the President and the governor in distress, while Secret Service guards in the follow-up car looked to the rear or to the right. Lovelady was a smaller, but less grainier, speck in the doorway of the Depository. "That's still you, right?"

"Yes sir."

"Could we have CE 369 enlarged and a photo of the defendant in custody, side by side please? Now, Mr. Lovelady, while we're waiting for those pictures to come up, will you tell the court, from where you were standing, which, as you testified, was on the steps of the Depository, where you heard the shots originate from?"

"Objection, Your Honor. Irrelevant."

Barnes had begun to spring his latest trap. "Your Honor, must I remind the prosecutor that he was given latitude, by agreement with defense counsel, to ask similar questions of his witnesses? Secondly, we have not heard the answer, and if the answer is 'Six floors directly above me,' it has relevance. If Mr. Lovelady's answer is otherwise, then it still has relevance, as we have heard from only a handful of people with reference to shots originating from the sixth floor. A question the jury will certainly need to grapple with in making their verdict is the fundamental question as to whether or not shots were fired from there, and if so, were all shots fired from that site?"

"Mr. Matthews, I have to agree fully with the defense on this one. Please approach." When both lawyers were present, Judge Davis continued, "Ray, you did not put one witness on the stand that said he or she saw the defendant in that window or that he fired a gun from that window. So it's an open question. If people are willing to be sworn and give contrary testimony, the court has to hear it. Now, if they say the shot came from a spaceship, well, that's for the jury to deal with. But we will hear from witnesses who are willing to be sworn. How many, Eddie?"

"Roughly three dozen." The judge winced at the time factor involved and then turned to look questioningly at the prosecutor as if it were in his power to speed things up.

The lawyers left the bench, the judge overruled the objection, and directed Lovelady to indicate where he thought the shots came from.

"Right there around that concrete little deal on that knoll."

"Thank you, Mr. Lovelady. By the way, do you see any similarities between the shirt you are wearing in the photo on the left and that which the defendant is wearing on the right?"

"They appear to be identical."

"No further questions. Move to admit CE 369."

Matthews realized that stipulations were his best option, as it was tough to cross-examine someone's opinion. Documents and data were easy, but opinions could get out of hand. "Mr. Lovelady, is it possible that it was an echo that you heard?"

"Yes. But I know enough about echoes to know that if they originate where you are, you hear the original sound before you hear the echo. So if they were echoes, they didn't start from where I was, but rather someplace else, and I heard them as echoes down towards the end of the small Elm Street extension that runs in front of the Depository."

"But they could have been echoes?"

"Yes."

"Thank you. Nothing further."

"Your Honor, before the defense calls its next witness, perhaps we could save time if we made reference to this architect's rendering of Dealey Plaza." Bob Dean was in the process of removing the drawing from its wraps. When unfolded, it covered an area about six feet by four feet, and Dean then unpacked a large easel, with cardboards, and mounted the layout. "If the prosecution would care to examine the geography depicted . . ."

I will beat you at your own game, Matthews thought, giving greater thought to the stipulation option, which seemed a whole lot brighter than having witness after witness walk right in front of the jury to point to the grassy knoll.

"The defense calls Bobby W. Hargis," Barnes announced. Matthews was trying to place the name when a uniformed police officer, carrying a bespeckled white motorcycle helmet, entered the courtroom. Matthews knew then who he was and what the helmet was about, and huddled with Graves and Vincent while Barnes elicited testimony that Hargis had been riding motorcycle escort slightly behind and to the left of the

President's car during the shooting. The head shot, he testified, had splattered him with "blood and brain, and a kind of bloody water." Barnes asked his opinion as to the shots, at which he testified, "At the time it sounded like the shots were right next to me." To answer the question of direction Hargis indicated to his right, using the layout map.

Barnes asked Hargis if he had ever placed himself with respect to the car.

"I couldn't say for sure, but I believe I was just about even with the rear bumper."

"Could we have the Zapruder film, please? Officer Hargis, have you ever seen the movie that shows your position in the motorcade?"

*"No,"* the witness answered, angry that he had not already been shown the footage. The movie was shown to the witness and the jury, confirming the witness's testimony. Barnes then asked to have it reshown, in slow motion, for as long as the officers were in the film. Barnes then asked Hargis to watch himself and notice where he was observing during the sequence. Once shown in slow motion, the effect was again visible on the jury, and the motorcycle officer answered, "I was looking to the right, in front of the car. But I remember seeing the President hit in the head, so that must have happened after the film closed in on the vehicle."

"Is that the helmet you were wearing that day?"

"Yes. It is. I've often thought of cleaning it up, but, well, it's like a piece of history."

"Evidence that blood and brain traveled to the left rear after the President was struck in the head is also an accurate description of that helmet, Officer. One more question—where did you go after the shots?"

"I pulled off to the left, parked, and saw the commotion on the knoll. I looked around, including at the Book Depository, and nobody seemed to be looking in any set way as if there was a unanimous feeling as to where the shots came from."

"No further questions, Officer. Thank you."

"Officer," Matthews began, "you wouldn't have kept that helmet like that all this time because someday it might be valuable, would you?"

"It never occurred to me—not in the sense of money, any-way."

"Officer, did you find any evidence on the knoll that any-thing suspicious had occurred there?"

"No."

"Thank you." Matthews walked back to the defense table prepared to ruin the rest of Barnes's morning.

As Barnes deliberately rose to speak, Matthews also stood and indicated, looking at the jury, that the process could be expedited if Mr. Barnes would indicate the name of the wit-ness, the nature of the testimony, and if it was "more of this same whodunit guesswork" the prosecution would make a stipulation that the evidence be admitted.

Barnes then took the initiative, before Matthews could re-think his decision. "Will the prosecution stipulate that Mrs. Avery Davis, an employee in the Book Depository, deposed in CE 1381, thought the shots were fired from the viaduct?"

"So stipulated," Matthews answered.

"Move to admit CE 1381."

"So moved."

"James N. Crawford, Dealey Plaza eyewitness, testified be-fore the President's Commission that what he heard, quote, 'at that time I thought it was a backfire of a car . . . from down the hill toward the underpass,' and that the second noise was followed very quickly by a third one," Barnes con-cluded.

"So stipulated," Matthews repeated.

Barnes continued, "We would like to enter the testimony of John Chism, standing on the North Curb of Elm Street . . . about here,"—Barnes was now using the architect's render-ing of Dealey Plaza—"looking south, in this direction, as the presidential car came almost even with him, and the witness states that he heard what he thought was a firecracker, but that further reports were clearly gunfire, and that the gunfire came from directly behind him."

"So stipulated."

"Mr. O.V. Campbell, another Book Depository employee, deposed also in CE 1381, quote 'I heard shots being fired from a point which I thought was near the railroad tracks located over the viaduct on Elm Street . . . I thought the shots came from the west.' "

"So stipulated."

"Dallas police officer Earle V. Brown, a thirteen-year-veteran of the force who was located on the triple overpass on November twenty-second, and who testified before the President's Commission as to three shots, 'from the grade of a railroad is what it is . . . and I smelled this gunpowder.' Gunpowder? Did I read that right?" Barnes asked rhetorically. "Gunpowder four hundred feet from the Depository. Well, that's what he says."

"So stipulated as to the testimony, which makes no reference to the distance from the overpass to the Depository."

"Noted for the record," the judge added.

"Mrs. Virginia Rachley Baker, bookkeeper employed in the Book Depository, testified under oath before the President's Commission that she heard what she thought were firecrackers, but saw 'a shot or something hit the pavement' to the left rear of the presidential automobile, and further that she heard three shots which she thought originated 'from the area between the plaza and the underpass.' "

"So stipulated."

"Cecil Ault testified under oath before the President's Commission that he was observing the parade from the Court House on Main Street, and that he heard three shots, definitely from a high-powered rifle, and that the first and second were so close together that they could have come from an automatic rifle."

"So stipulated."

"Thomas Atkins, official photographer to the late President, was in the motorcade, uncharacteristically six cars back, and has deposed, quote, 'Shots came from below and off to the right side from where I was. I never thought the shots came from above. They did not sound like shots coming from anything higher than street level.' "

"So stipulated," Matthews droned on, wondering about the expertise of someone who had never shot anything more powerful than a focal lens.

"Danny G. Arce, employed by the Texas School Book Depository as a stockboy, testified under oath before the President's Commission, quote, 'I thought they came from the railroad tracks to the west to the Texas School Book Depository.' This was in response to a question regarding the origin of the shots."

"Stipulated."

"Dolores Kounas, a typist for the McGraw-Hill Book Company, which had offices in the Book Depository, was deposed regarding her statements to the FBI immediately after the shooting. Her statement to them was, quote, 'Although I was across the street from the Depository Building and was looking in the direction of the building as the motorcade passed and following the shots, I did not look up at the building as I had thought the shots came from a westerly direction of the viaduct.'"

"So stipulated."

"Mary Woodward, a writer for *The Dallas Morning News*, was standing near the Stemmons Freeway sign, looking south across Elm Street, when she heard a horrible, earsplitting noise, coming from behind her and *to . . . her . . . right.*"

"So stipulated."

"Steve Wilson, another Depository employee, who watched the parade from the third floor of the Book Depository, has deposed that he told the FBI, 'The shots really did not sound like they came from above me . . . At that time it sounded like the shots came from the west end of the building or from the colonnade located on Elm Street across from the west end of our building.'"

"So stipulated."

"Officer E. L. Smith, Jr., of the Dallas police, who was directing traffic at the corner of Elm and Houston streets, who testified under oath to the President's Commission, 'I heard three shots, I guess they were shots. I thought that the first two were just firecrackers and kept my position, and after the third one, I ran down the street there.' He further deposed that he thought the shots came from behind the fence, although he found nothing by the time he arrived there." Barnes threw in that last crumb to keep Matthews in a stipulating mood.

"So stipulated."

"Marilyn Sitzman, who was an employee of Abraham Zapruder, who took the home movie we have seen on several occasions, and who was standing on a pedestal next to Mr. Zapruder, halfway between the underpass and the Depository, indicated that she saw the fatal shot strike the President in the right temporal area, between his right ear and right eye, and I would add, for the record, that this testimony is based on events. Mrs. Sitzman has not seen the movie made by Mr. Zapruder."

"So stipulated."

"James Simmons, a railroad employee who was watching the motorcade from the underpass, deposed, quote, 'The sound of shots came from the left in front of us, toward the wooden fence, and there was a puff of smoke that came from underneath the trees on the embankment.' "

"So stipulated."

"Raymond Roberts, a member of the United States House of Representatives from the state of Texas, deposed that he smelled gunpowder when his vehicle in the motorcade was well down Elm Street."

"So stipulated."

"Eyewitness Frank E. Reilly, who testified under oath before the President's Commission that quote, 'It seemed to me like they (the shots) come out of the trees.' "

"So stipulated."

"John Powell, who was an inmate for three days of custody on minor charges on the sixth floor of the county jail, which commanded a clear view of the Book Depository, deposed that he watched two men with a gun in the window in question, and could see them clearly enough to be able to recall them fooling around with the telescopic sight. He added that one of the two men seen had darker skin than the average Caucasian. The defense would like to add here, for the record, but not subject to the stipulation, that if there are any future investigations into this matter, Mr. Powell indicated that there were a wealth of individuals who witnessed the same events on the sixth floor of the Depository."

"Stipulate to the witness's testimony."

"Mr. William Newman, an eyewitness situated on the north curb of Elm Street, looking south, and visible in some of the footage as the gentleman with the crewcut who is covering his children after the shot sequence, deposed, quote, 'I thought the shots were coming from right off the tops of our heads . . . I thought the shot was fired from directly behind where we were standing. I thought the shot had come from the garden directly behind me.' "

"So stipulated." As Matthews made the familiar pronouncement, Carolyn Jeffries left the defense table, went into the hall, and sent a good number of the people home.

"Mrs. Jean Newman, with William Newman, deposed, 'The first impression I had was that the shots came from my right.' "

"So stipulated."

"Thomas J. Murphy, deposed under oath by the President's Commission in CE 1421, told that he heard what sounded like two shots. 'These shots came from a spot just west of the Texas School Book Depository Building.' "

"So stipulated." Matthews was now beginning to understand fully that it was the Dallas case, not his, that had been battered.

"Cheryl McKinnon, who was able to place herself near the Newmans in available photographs, deposed that she heard three shots, and that puffs of white smoke hung in the air in small patches. She added, quote, 'The only thing I am absolutely sure of today is that at least two of the shots fired that day in Dealey Plaza came from behind where I stood on the knoll.' "

"So stipulated."

"Emmett J. Hudson, groundskeeper of Dealey Plaza, and visible as one of the men on the steps leading up to the picket fence here on the knoll," Barnes indicated on the chart, "testified under oath before the President's Commission that he was aware of, quote, 'a bunch of people in there,' indicating the area behind the fence, and he also gave testimony that a number of fixed reference points in Dealey Plaza, such as trees, signs, that sort of thing, were moved very quickly after the shooting. He also signed an affidavit on November twenty-second indicating, quote, 'The shots that I heard definitely came from behind and above me.' "

"So stipulated."

"Mr. S. M. Holland, another railroad employee who saw the events from the triple overpass, testified under oath before the President's Commission, with very accurate description of the sequence of firing as shown in the Zapruder film, and that he counted four shots, the first two or three of which came from the upper part of Elm Street, and the remaining sound, quote, 'There was a shot . . . a report, I don't know whether it was a shot. I can't say that. And a puff of smoke came out about six or eight feet above the ground right out from under those trees . . . It wasn't as loud as the previous reports or shots.' Mr. Holland also indicated that the third and fourth reports were very close together. When Mr. Holland immediately went to the area behind the picket fence to investigate, he was quickly met by FBI and Secret Service agents."

"So stipulated."

"Ruby Henderson, an eyewitness on the south side of Elm Street close to the corner of Elm and Houston, deposed that she saw two men, one dark complected, standing slightly back from the alleged sniper's window. She did not see a gun."

"So stipulated."

"Mrs. Edna Hartman, a bystander on Elm Street, deposed that after the shooting, she quote 'ran like the devil' down to the slope in front of the knoll. She further deposed, quote, 'There were not many people in this area at the time, but a policeman was there. He pointed to some bushes near the railroad tracks on the north side of the street and said that's where the shots came from . . . Then I noticed these two parallel marks on the ground that looked like mounds made by a mole. I asked, "What are these, molehills?" and the policeman said, "Oh, no, ma'am, that's where the bullets struck the ground." ' Mrs. Hartman further deposed that she realized the marks made by the bullets were in a north to south trajectory, indicative that they had been fired from a point in the north to a point south, slightly by east, and thus could not have originated in the Depository. When she made her findings or thoughts, shall we say, available to the FBI, they showed no interest at first but later told her that the marks were made by bone fragments from the President."

"So stipulated as to observations, but not to FBI conclusions," Matthews added.

"Fair enough, Counselor," Barnes replied. "Dallas County Bailiff W. W. Mabra, who was at the corner of Main and Houston Streets, who deposed that he felt that 'the shot' had come from the knoll, and joined in the crowd which headed that way."

"So stipulated." Matthews leaned towards Graves and Vincent and whispered, "Watch carefully how this is done, boys, so you never get whipped this bad in the future."

"Charles Hester, who, along with his wife Beatrice, were sitting on the slope of Elm Street, deposed under oath as part of Decker 5323, that the two shots they heard as the car neared the underpass came from immediately behind them and over their heads."

"So stipulated."

"Move to admit the Hester deposition in Decker 5323."

"So moved."

"Finally, Your Honor, the defense offers into evidence the testimony of Ed Hoffman, a twenty-seven-year-old deaf mute. I should indicate before giving his statement, we are prepared to put him on the stand if necessary, and have retained an expert in sign language for the purpose of communicating with the witness. With that in mind, Mr. Hoffman deposed that he was approximately two hundred yards west of the picket fence which sits atop the grassy knoll, expecting to see the President when the car emerged from the underpass. He also pointed out the obvious, that he did not hear of the events of November twenty-second, as his disability prevented that. He did, however, become aware of a man, wearing a dark suit, running west along the back side of the fence, carrying a rifle in his hands. As this individual reached the terminus of the fence, he tossed the rifle to a second individual, standing on the west side of the pipe near the railroad tracks. This second man, wearing light coveralls and a railroad worker's hat, disassembled the rifle, placed the parts in a soft brown bag, then walked away. The man in the dark suit turned around and went back toward the fence. The witness then visited the Dallas FBI office, left his name and address and a brief statement, and was never contacted."

Graves was imploring Matthews to fight, since this was Barnes's last stipulation, and if the last one could be won, the others would seem meaningless. Matthews simply asked Graves what he thought the odds were of winning a confrontation in front of a jury with a deaf mute ignored by the vaunted FBI.

"So stipulated."

"Your Honor," Barnes announced, "I have nothing further this morning. Perhaps we could reconvene at 12:30, as the afternoon will be busy if the witnesses we've scheduled are available."

"Any objections, Mr. Matthews?"

"No, Your Honor. 12:30 will be fine," to continue kicking my ass into the appendix of every history book for the next five centuries, Matthews thought.

"Recess until 12:30, and my thanks to the attorneys for expediting matters this morning."

Matthews and Graves left in haste, while Barnes, Dean, and Jeffries were unanimously deciding on the wisdom of trying to have the Dealey Plaza display left up. Earl Vincent left amidst their deliberations, and Barnes then put the question to Dean and Jeffries: "How many of that crowd were genuine and how many did we 'fake'?"

"They were mostly legit, Eddie. We had about eighteen, and some of them brought husbands or wives, or in one case, two grown-up children. Bob had five of his in-laws out there. Nobody will tumble to it," Jefferies assured him.

"I hope not. From here on, we have to have the people in place. Matthews is *not* going to stipulate our whole case, you realize."

"No, but he might wish he had," Dean concluded.

During lunch, Barnes, Dean, and Jeffries debated the strategy for the afternoon. Their witnesses consisted of eighteen individuals who, if the defendant's alibis were accepted at face, would give very solid testimony suggesting that a serious "Oswald impostor" had been operating to create a trail of evidence that would lead to the defendant.

All three defense attorneys agreed that the jury had believed both Mrs. Paine and Mrs. Roberts, Oswald's two landladies from early October through November twenty-second, particularly with respect to their strong indications that once Oswald walked in their doors, he was there for the duration. Most of the afternoon's witnesses would put him somewhere else, often either with a weapon, a car, or both, or with a scenario that had him coming into money shortly, and all of these sightings occurred either when the defendant had an alibi from one of the landladies, or was at work at the Depository, a fact previously attested and deposed to by Depository Manager Roy Truly.

The question was, how much did it help the case, and could Matthews use it to his advantage? There was agreement that cross-examination of any of these people would be most difficult, but there was still some concern about Sylvia Odio, Oscar Contreras, and Eusebio Azcue, who had seen someone resembling Oswald either in Mexico City when he was allegedly there in late September, 1963, or saw him elsewhere at the same time. It was a shame, Dean suggested, that the prosecution, in a situation where they could have made some mileage, made no mention of Oswald's little Mexican adventure. Barnes thought they might be saving it for rebuttal, but Dean suggested they hint to Matthews about the quality of their rebuttal witnesses, just in case.

As they were walking in for the afternoon session, Carolyn Jeffries had a reminder for Barnes: "The dentist's son asked to be called near the end of the day, Eddie."

"For God's sake, why?"

"Eddie, were you ever a teenager? He's looking to go on at four today so he can't get back to Dallas in time for school tomorrow. He wants the extra day off."

"By all means then, let's give it to him. Anything to make him an agreeable witness."

After Oswald was returned to the courtroom, but before the jury could be brought in, Barnes stood to address the judge: "Your Honor, before the jurors are brought back, it might be more effective use of the court's time to consider the afternoon's agenda with respect to relevancy." Barnes knew it was dangerous for *him* to bring up the relevancy of his own witnesses, but better to lose them now than in front of the jury, and he was taking the chance that the fight had gone out of Matthews, and that evidence of an Oswald impostor might be a thread that Matthews, in a moment of self-preservation, might find attractive.

"What is the nature of the testimony, Mr. Barnes? You realize you can speak freely since the jury is not here."

Barnes then briefly outlined, in general, what people had sworn to in local and FBI reports as well as before the President's Commission, and, when coupled with the seemingly ironclad alibis provided by Mrs. Paine, Mrs. Roberts, and Mr. Truly, introduced yet another bizarre twist to an already bizarre case, but one that might ultimately be of great value in sorting things out if allowed into the record.

Matthews, who had been extremely intrigued by this aspect of the case, had interviewed several of the suggested witnesses himself, and admitted to the court that he saw no harm in the testimony, subject, of course, to cross-examination, and added that the jury should have these facts at their disposal to deliberate. Matthews's acceptance of the concept reminded Barnes he had better tread carefully.

The jury was brought in, but before Barnes called his first witness, he asked that the defendant be returned to a holding cell and be available as needed for identification. He explained that since his brush with death, the defendant did not look the same as he did on November 22nd, and that he would initially rely on the witnesses' identification from photos which appeared widely after November 22nd. Neither the court nor Matthews had any objection to that.

Dean got Barnes's attention and told him, "You're giving Ray some ammunition for his closing argument. They may not buy the impostor story."

"But if they do, Bob, there is a much diminished likelihood of closing arguments." Dean agreed.

"The defense calls Albert G. Bogard." Barnes quickly reviewed his notes while a haggard-looking man in badly fitting clothing took the stand. Barnes established that the witness had been working for a Lincoln Mercury dealership during November 1963, although he was no longer employed there or in the automobile business.

"Mr. Bogard, the defendant in this case is not in the room now, and there's a reason for that, which we'll get to. In the meantime, for the record, which I'm sure you know, the defendant's name is Lee Oswald, and the crime he is accused of occurred on November twenty-second, 1963, in Dallas, Texas. Mr. Bogard, prior to November twenty-second, did you have occasion to meet Lee Oswald?"

"Well, let me answer this way. I vividly recall an incident, and when you interviewed me, and when Mr. Matthews interviewed me, you both showed me the documents to refresh my memory. Even without that, I can tell you that on November ninth, which was a Saturday in 1963, a man came into the automobile showroom where I worked as a salesman and inquired about a sporty little model we had on the floor. He introduced himself as Lee Oswald, asked a little about the car, then asked to test drive it. And *he did!* He had that car going sixty to seventy miles an hour, then we brought it back in, and he told me he wasn't ready to buy it yet, but that he would be getting some money in a couple or three weeks. Well, I wrote his name on the back of a business card, and I even spoke to the boss to see if we could let the guy take the car without the usual three hundred dollars down, but the customer wasn't in that kind of hurry. He also mentioned something—I can't tell you what he said, but he said something about Russia—seemed strange at the time."

"What time of day did this occur, Mr. Bogard?"

"It was somewhere between three and four in the afternoon, and occupied, oh, maybe forty-five minutes altogether."

"Mr. Bogard, have you taken many prospective customers on test drives?"

"Lots. When I was selling cars. The shiny look gets them in the door, but the smell of a new car sells it."

"Have you had other experiences where the customer drove the way you described this event?"

"Never. Sometimes a kid will step on the gas to find out what's under the hood, but we usually tell them how fast it will go, and they decide to find out on their own time."

"When the customer was driving at high speed, did he give evidence of being in control of the car?"

"Objection. Calls for a conclusion."

"Your Honor, it is a conclusion that this witness is able to make, and either way, it will benefit the record."

"Agreed that there's an element of conclusion, Mr. Matthews, but overruled this time."

"He was in control of the car."

"Please tell the court what happened at your place of employment in the early hours of the afternoon on November twenty-second."

"We were listening to the awful news . . . about Kennedy, and they interrupted the radio to say Lee Oswald was arrested. Well, it was like a couple of other salesman knew I had a prospect by that name, so they said he wouldn't be buying a car for a while, and I took out that particular business card and tore it up."

"Did it contain any information as to how you could reach Mr. Oswald?"

"No."

"Isn't it standard procedure, to get an address, phone number, some way to reach the prospect to let him know, oh, you know—you've got a great deal, or that little beauty you drove is still here, something like that?"

"It is pretty standard, but I just had a name."

"Now, Mr. Bogard, when you heard the name Lee Oswald on that afternoon, could you remember what he looked like?"

"No, I really couldn't. Of course, it was tough to think clearly, because of what had happened in Dallas that day, plus the fact that I would not be getting the sale, but I could not recollect the client visually."

"Did you subsequently recollect the client visually?"

"Yes. I recognized him from pictures on the TV and in the papers."

"Solid identification?"

"I think so."

"Okay, Mr. Bogard. You came here, at my request, to testify, so I obviously believe you. Mr. Matthews may have some questions for you, which will indicate if he believes you. But here's the problem, and here's why we invited you here. One, we've had testimony from Mrs. Ruth Paine, as to where Mr. Oswald spent November eight, nine, ten, and eleven, that the defendant was in her home on the afternoon of the ninth. It has also been testified to, by Mrs. Paine, that he was virtually incompetent when it came to operating a motor vehicle. He was twenty-four years old when you supposedly met him, and had no license. We've created a situation where we are asked to consider three possibilities: one, that Mrs. Paine is lying, and I doubt that. She's a very devout religious woman who would probably have done herself a favor to say that the defendant was all over town when he wanted to be. Or, we can suppose that you aren't telling the truth—but what have you got to gain by this story, which, I know, is supported by your employer at the time, Mr. Frank Pizzo. The third possibility is the intriguing one: that the person you saw was not the same Lee Oswald that is in a holding cell on the other side of that door over there. Mr. Bogard, were you ever asked to identify the defendant in a lineup?"

"No."

"Did your customer absolutely resemble the defendant in every circumstance in which you saw him that weekend?"

"Not perfectly."

"Is it possible that hearing the name 'Lee Oswald' and seeing someone in the media by the same name would have allowed you to identify someone who only resembled the defendant?"

"It's possible."

Barnes turned to the Vermont Officer. "Could we have the defendant, please?" Oswald was then unhandcuffed, brought into the room, and stood near the witness stand next to Barnes. "Remember, Mr. Bogard, this man was shot and nearly died two weeks after the date you thought you saw him, so his appearance might not be exactly as you remembered. Does this appear to be the man?"

"There's a similarity, for sure, but I wouldn't, or couldn't say, 'That's him exactly, no doubt about it.'"

Oswald was returned to the holding cell. "One more question, Mr. Bogard. Were you requested to take a lie detector test?"

"Yes. The FBI wanted me to take one, and I did, on February twenty-fourth, I believe. They told me I passed."

"That statement docsn't help the jury in the tough job it

has to do, Mr. Bogard. Did they explain what that meant to you?"

"Well, they said it proved I believed I was telling the truth."

"Okay. Fair enough. No more questions."

Matthews remained seated, to create the "this witness isn't important" atmosphere. "Mr. Bogard, since you have driven with a number of people, is there a correlation, in your experience, between people having licenses and being able to operate a car at sixty miles per hour?" Matthews smiled over at Barnes, feeling as if he'd given him a taste of his own rhetoric.

"I have no idea. I've never asked a customer if he or she has a license. I assumed the defendant had one."

"No further questions."

"The defense calls Mr. Frank Pizzo." A witness with better muscle tone than the preceeding one entered, was sworn, and Barnes quickly established that Albert Bogard had just given testimony regarding a client, one "Lee Oswald," whom Pizzo claimed to remember, as well as the incident when the business card was torn up. It was also established that Pizzo saw Oswald on TV and thought he recognized him. Barnes then asked for thirty seconds each of Commission Exhibits 451, 453, 454, 455, 456. After looking at all five photos, pictures of Oswald taken shortly before November 22nd, Pizzo saw a possibility in CE 455, but refused to find any similarity in any of the others. "The man I saw did not have as much hair as these boys in these pictures, so if it's yes or no, I have to say he is not the one."

Oswald was then brought in and Pizzo repeated himself, saying the defendant still had more hair than the person he saw. Barnes had nothing further and Matthews dismissed it with a "no questions" without even looking up. Barnes moved to admit CE 451, 453, 454, 455, and 456.

"The defense calls Hubert Morrow." Barnes then established that the witness was the manager of the Allright Parking Systems, which operated the parking service at the Southland Hotel in Dallas, considerably uptown from the Book Depository.

"In the month prior to the assassination, Mr. Morrow,"

Barnes continued, "did you have occasion to have conversation with someone calling himself Lee Oswald?"

"Yes. He applied for a job as a parking attendant at the hotel."

"In the course of this job application, did the applicant ask you any questions, Mr. Morrow?"

"Yes, and strange ones at that. He asked how high the hotel was and if it commanded a good view of Dallas."

"Why is that strange?"

"Well, for one, most people can figure out how high a hotel is by counting the floors. And if a hotel is high, which the Southland is, of course it has a good view of the city."

"Do you recall when this event occurred?"

"About two weeks before the President came to town. Don't pin me down though, it was during a weekday, midday, sometime, and I took no notice of it, except for the questions."

"Exactly. 'Except for the questions.' Thank you, Mr. Morrow."

"Did you consider the applicant for the job, Mr. Morrow?" Matthews asked.

"Why? There were no openings. He just came in and asked."

"Did you ever subsequently identify the person who made this application as the defendant in this case?"

"Couldn't. Forgot him as fast as he came."

"Nothing further."

"One question on redirect, Your Honor. Mr. Morrow, is it company policy with Allright Parking Systems that if you hire someone as a parking attendant, you require that person to prove he has a valid motor vehicle operator's license?"

"Of course. And we have to check his driving record, for insurance purposes."

"Nothing further. Defense calls Leonard Hutchinson." While the Irving, Texas, supermarket manager was being sworn and mugged briefly for the jury, Dean told Barnes not to waste any time with "the nobodies." Barnes then had Hutchinson repeat the story he had told authorities, that Oswald had come into his market with a check for $189, but that he, Hutchinson, had refused to cash the check. The incident in question had occurred during the day on Friday, November 8, while Oswald was still miles away at the Book Depository.

"This person who represented himself as Lee Oswald, had you seen him before?"

"Yes. Several times. Sometimes with two women."

"Place the times—weekdays, weekends, morning, noon, night," Barnes instructed.

"Weekdays, during the day."

"Nothing further." Barnes fully expected no questions from Matthews, but the prosecutor had several questions about the $189 figure, which Hutchinson stuck to, and vehemently. "Are you aware that the defendant was earning $1.25 an hour as a stockboy and was paid weekly?"

"I didn't know and I didn't care."

Matthews pressed ahead, with Judge Davis looking for some kind of objection from Barnes, who looked at Dean, and then it hit both of them: Matthews was subtly running up the white flag and wanted it in the record that either Oswald, or someone impersonating him, had more money, by a lot, than Lee Oswald had a right to have, and that there was something fishy there. Barnes let Matthews finish. The witness stuck to his story.

"Defense calls Edith Whitworth," Barnes announced, and while the witness entered the court, was sworn, and took her place, Barnes came around to the front of the table and told Dean that it was moments like this, when Matthews was weakening, that it was a shame that the trial wasn't in Dallas so they could grab other valuable witnesses and hustle them onto the stand before Matthews returned to the attack. "What attack?" Dean asked. "He's looking for a way out, and we're giving it to him."

Barnes then established that the witness was the owner of a used furniture outlet, which had a "gun" sign, from the previous owner, on the outside of the store. She further testified that early in November 1963 Lee Oswald, whom she thought she recognized after the shooting, had driven up in a two-tone Ford or Plymouth, asked a gun-related question while holding a small wrapped package in his hands, and that he further stated he would be needing furniture in a couple of weeks. Further questions elicited that Oswald had been accompanied by a woman who did not speak, and two small children. The witness indicated she recognized both Lee and Marina Oswald on TV and subsequently was able to identify Lee Oswald in CE 453.

"When did this visit to your furniture store occur, in which the defendant drove up?"

"I can only narrow it down to one of three days, but I'm sure it was one of those. Gertrude Hunter, a dear friend, and football fan, was there when it happened, and we were in the process of making plans to hightail it out of town on Friday to see the Friday night football game. The game would have been played on November eighth, and it couldn't have been the day before, so it had to be November fourth, fifth, or sixth."

"Mrs. Whitworth, I have here a calendar for November 1963. For the sake of accuracy, please notice that the date you mentioned, November eighth, as well as November twenty-second, two weeks later, were both Fridays. Would you tell the court what days November fourth, fifth, and sixth were?"

"Monday, Tuesday, and Wednesday."

"And what time of day did this visit take place?"

"The best I can tell you is close to lunchtime."

"Thank you. Nothing further."

Matthews felt the need to weaken some of these witnesses. "Mrs. Whitworth, did you see the defendant in any police lineups?"

"No. Just on TV and in the papers."

"Could you have identified the defendant?"

"Objection to form, Your Honor."

"Please rephrase the question, Mr. Matthews."

"Did the person you saw in your store strongly resemble the person that you saw pictured in the paper and on the television?"

"The man, the woman, the little girl. I recognized them all." Matthews knew this was going nowhere. "No more questions."

"Defense calls Malcolm Price." Matthews motioned to Barnes, who, surprised by this, made haste to the defense table. Matthews was curious when all Barnes's witnesses would be done, and Barnes told him it would probably take a week. Matthews thanked Barnes for the information. Dean wrote a note on his legal pad to find out what that discussion had been about.

"Mr. Price, the defendant, Lee Oswald, is not in this court-room right now, but I may ask you to identify him later. In the meantime, please tell the court your occupation in the fall of 1963."

"I was then employed by the Sports Drome Rifle Range, just outside of Dallas, Texas. It went out of business since then, I guess 'cause folks believed what they read in the papers about the defendant being there with his guns, and all."

"Tell the court your encounters with the defendant, and 'his guns' as you recall them."

"Well, he was the last customer we had on Saturday, September twenty-eighth—I know it was the last Saturday of that month. He drove in alone in an old Ford, maybe nineteen forty, nineteen forty-one model. He had a foreign rifle, and he picked up his empty casings before leaving. The next time was October thirteen, a Sunday, and this time he had what I think was a different gun, a heavy-bore model. He was back again on a Sunday, and I don't know that date, with the same heavy bore, and told me he paid eighteen dollars for the scope, which I looked through and found to be clearer than most American scopes. I handled the gun on that occasion and it was a Mauser-type rifle which had been sporterized and still had a shiny finish. The last time he came in was the Sunday before Thanksgiving. That's about all I remember."

The witness was then shown the photos seen by the other recent witnesses, and he recognized the defendant in one of them. Barnes then showed him the Mannlicher-Carcano rifle and asked him if he recognized it.

"This is definitely not the gun I saw."

"Thank you, Mr. Price. For the record, you testified that the last time you saw the defendant at the range was on the Sunday before Thanksgiving. In 1963, that was November 24th, and it's unlikely he was at the Sports Drome Rifle Range that day for target practice, as he was in the basement of the

Dallas police department being shot that day. No further questions."

Matthews stood and asked to have the defendant brought in. "Is this the man you remember seeing?"

Price looked carefully, almost as if he were seeing someone from his distant past. "Could be, but it's been a while, and he looks different."

"Nothing further." Barnes decided to keep Oswald in the courtroom.

"The defense calls Garland Slack," Barnes announced, before turning to Dean and asking if they should continue to pursue this line of inquiry. Dean's answer was "In for a dime, in for a dollar."

"Mr. Slack, please tell the court the encounters you believe you had with someone named Lee Oswald."

"I saw Lee Oswald at the Sports Drome Rifle Range when I was there on November tenth and seventeenth for target practice. I remember it well, because he was shooting at my targets. After what happened to the President, I came forward, and told my story to the FBI, and Agent Charlie Brown —FBI man Charlie Brown, he told me they knew who mounted the scope on the guns, and they had got the guy."

Barnes hadn't expected this, and neither had Matthews. "You are testifying that an FBI agent told you that the FBI was in possession of the identity of the person who mounted the scope on the rifle?"

"That's what I said."

"Then it was mounted twice, because the company that sold it guaranteed this court that it was sold with the scope mounted. Sorry for the interruption. Please go on."

"Well, what you say is possible. I went to the police right away and told them what happened. This fellow was there with three guns, junk really, all the same type, one with a scope, and two without. Then I seen the newspapers, and they showed the gun being held up for everyone to see at police headquarters, but that was no gun that I had ever seen, and I know rifles and I know scopes."

"Is this the weapon you saw?" Barnes asked, showing the alleged assassination rifle.

"No. That's junk, too, but not the same."

"Was the defendant alone when you saw him?"

"No. He was with someone else. They got that boy too."

"Objection. Hearsay."

"Sustained."

"Mr. Slack, can you positively identify the defendant sitting over there as being the man you saw at the rifle range with three weapons and who fired at your target?"

"There's a good resemblance, but the hair is different. I only picked him out in one of the pictures the police showed me."

"Were you ever asked to attend a lineup?"

"No."

"Nothing further. Thanks, Mr. Slack. Your witness."

"Mr. Slack, when the defendant fired at your target—"

"Objection again as to form, Your Honor," Barnes interrupted. "The witness was not able to identify the defendant, or the weapon in question, as having fired at his target."

Matthews interceded. "Strike the question. Mr. Slack, when someone fired at your target on the dates you testified, did they demonstrate marksmanship proficiency?"

"I really couldn't say, except to say that they hit my target. Now if they were aiming for my target, well, then he was able to put a hole through a large piece of paper. If he was aiming for his target and hit mine, I'd have to say he was a lousy shot."

"Nothing further."

Barnes was just rising as Dean turned a legal pad sideways so he could read the wording, "Don't use the Cubans." Barnes then looked at the dwindling list of other witnesses. "The defense calls Dial Ryder." A casually dressed man in his mid-twenties then entered the courtroom. Barnes established that Ryder had been employed at the Irving Sports Shop as the resident gun mechanic for over six years, had been employed there in November 1963, and Barnes then requested that he be accorded expert witness status with respect to his testimony regarding guns.

"It was my understanding," Matthews interrupted, "that these witnesses we have been hearing all afternoon are related to an individual alleged to have been impersonating the defendant. Why does this person need expert status?"

"Your Honor, Mr. Ryder's testimony will revolve largely around weapons. Inasmuch as he has worked on them and handled them for years, I believe he can give us some *civilian* input regarding weapons capabilities."

"Expert status granted with respect to weapons testimony."

"Mr. Ryder, please tell the court in your own words how you and the company you work for became involved in this investigation."

"The President was killed on a Friday in November of 1963, and I worked the following day, Saturday. That is one of our busy seasons because so many people bring in their weapons to have them sighted in for deer season. On that Saturday, I found a tag on the workbench. It had the name Oswald on it —no first name, address, anything else, just Oswald, and it was noted that from the number on the tag the weapon that went with the tag had been brought in between November fourth and eighth, and that three holes had been drilled for the mounting of a scope. Because an Oswald had been arrested, my employer called all the Oswalds in the phone book to try to track down who owned the gun, and, of course, he contacted the local police, and they came to check it out."

"Mr. Ryder, I show you the alleged assassination weapon. Do you have any recollection of doing any work on this gun?"

"Absolutely not. First, the bill is for three holes, at one dollar fifty cents per hole, and this sight, poorly mounted, has only two holes. Second, if anyone brought this cheap, common, flimsy looking thing in, I know I would have spent some time with that customer trying to sell them a better scope. This one is such a crude-built gun that it would be very easily knocked out of adjustment. Finally, I have never, even to this day, worked on a rifle of this manufacture and type."

"You are certain of that?"

"Yes."

"Mr. Ryder, do you have any recollection of an Oswald requesting work in the time period you suggested?"

"None. But like I said, that's our busy season."

"Explain that, and try to make your explanation to the jury so they understand the capabilities of this weapon."

"I'll try. If they're Texans, they'll know. A gun has to be

sighted in, sometimes repeatedly, and something as simple as driving it around on the backseat can whack it out of adjustment. So before deer season, people bring in most, maybe all their guns, and we sight them in, check, recheck, and make sure they're accurate. Then it's up to them not to get them out of adjustment, so they have to be careful putting them on the racks of the truck or wherever, or they won't be accurate."

"Mr. Ryder, you've been critical of this weapon. We earlier heard from prosecution witnesses—military officers and career soldiers who were said to be very competent experts with firearms. They told the jury that this was a first-rate weapon capable of being assembled from its parts in a couple of minutes and then firing three accurate shots easily within a five- to six-second time frame. Do you agree with that assessment?"

"Not at all. The gun is junk and so is the scope. You put that thing together from pieces and it'll be so far out of line it would take a miracle shot to hit a deer at fifty yards, much less a smaller target. It just wouldn't be accurate. Accuracy is something you pay for, in a quality weapon, and you preserve by having it sighted in. That's my job and hunters— who miss as often as they hit—keep me in business trying to keep their expensive guns reasonably accurate. That thing . . . there's no comparison."

"So you have no recollection of the customer?"

"No."

"How about the defendant? Does he look familiar?"

"Sure. He looks like a lot of people. And the police showed me his picture over and over, and I told them I didn't remember him, but after seeing all those pictures, of course I'm going to recognize him."

"Mr. Ryder, if I had three automobiles placed one hundred seventy-five feet, two hundred twenty feet, and two hundred sixty-five feet away from you, and you were up high in a building, using *this rifle*, without sighting it in, could you hit the automobiles—not the occupant, but the automobiles, three times in less than six seconds?"

"May I try the bolt?" Barnes handed him the weapon. After examining it for a few seconds, working the bolt, sighting up at a spot on the back wall of the courtroom, the witness used the witness rail as a prop and gave it a try. "No. Not in that time. That bolt is just as bad as the overall character of the weapon. I couldn't hit three cars in that time."

"Thank you. No further questions. Your Honor, defense would like this tag, Ryder Exhibit #1, admitted."

"So moved."

Matthews remained seated. "Mr. Ryder, I find it odd that this work-order repair tag just suddenly seemed to appear on your bench on the Saturday after the President was shot . . ."

"My boss and I found it odd, too."

"That saves me an entire line of questioning. Nothing further."

"Defense calls Dr. Homer Wood." Barnes checked his watch to see if he was keeping Dr. Wood's son as late as he wanted to be kept, and he realized he was cutting it pretty close. He had one witness, however, that he had to save for last.

It was then established that Dr. Wood was a dentist and a patron at the Sports Drome Rifle Range on Saturday, November 16, and that he thought he saw someone that day, with a gun that made noise like a "one hundred five howitzer," and because of the flame visible every time the weapon was fired as well as the noise, he gave his son and his son's friends cotton for their ears. He further testified that he did not believe he would recognize the gun. He volunteered that he had been shown photographs by the President's Commission and that the man in those photos looked like the man at the range. Barnes finally got to the bottom line: "Can you positively say that it was the defendant you saw?"

"I put it in the category that I couldn't be absolutely positive, but in my mind I was positive that it was Oswald that I saw out at the rifle range."

"I'm not sure I understand, or the jury understands what you are saying, Doctor," Barnes prodded him.

"In my mind, I identified him. But when it comes to swearing on a Bible and identifying him, I couldn't. So I guess that means it's not a positive i.d."

"Dr. Wood, with no disrespect meant for your testimony,

let's try to understand what it involves, and then try to come to grips with it. November sixteen was, as you said, a Saturday. It has been established by earlier witnesses that the defendant did not, as was his habit, visit his wife in Irving that weekend. It has also been learned that he stayed in the rooming house in Oak Cliff all of the day that you testified about. The problem is also complicated by the fact that if he owned or had secreted the gun, it was in Irving, not the rooming house. So not only does he literally have to sneak out of a populated rooming house, where the landlady swears he was virtually camped all that day, but he somehow has to get the weapon out of, and back into, another distant residence, without the boardinghouse landlady, any of the tenants, or the owner of the other residence, where his wife was staying, noticing. Now do you understand why you were called as a witness?"

"Yes. I see the confusion. But I also know what I saw at the Sports Drome that day."

"And I appreciate that, Doctor. And I also will say that I believe every word of your testimony. Which leaves us to conclude that either you have fooled us, or that the defendant completely tricked a landlady and other tenants at a time when the rifle was believed to be miles away, or else we must consider the possibility that the defendant was being impersonated. I won't ask you for your opinion on that, Doctor, as it forces you to draw a conclusion, and all I asked you for was the facts. Nothing further."

Matthews thought he saw some mileage in the witness, so he approached the witness stand for the first time that afternoon. "Doctor, would it be correct to say that looking at faces is an essential part of your occupation, which, I hasten to add, is a highly respected profession?"

"That's a fair statement."

"Then when you say that the identification was solid in your mind, there's a certain degree of assuredness in what you say?"

"Up to a point, yes. I just could not say back then, nor can I now, that it was absolutely and unequivocally him."

"Doctor, could a patient make an appointment for your

dental services, and send an impostor to keep the appointment that could fool you?"

"Objection, Your Honor, and again to form. The question
suggests that the doctor had seen the man at the rifle range
on a prior occasion and was trying to reestablish an identity."

"Sustained."

"Doctor, let's try this. Suppose for a minute that you
treated the defendant, and a week later—"

"Objection again, Your Honor. Speculative. The dentist saw
the man in question for a few moments and did not, to my
knowledge, make any dental inventory."

"Sustained." Matthews figured he'd made his point with
the jury, so he returned to his seat after thanking the witness.

"Defense calls Sterling C. Wood." A teenager, bearing a
slight resemblance to the earlier witness, entered the courtroom, and Barnes welcomed the boy, tried to make him feel
at ease, apologized for keeping him waiting all day, a gentle
reminder that he owed Barnes for the day of school he'd
miss, and then got down to business. The boy had been to
the Sports Drome with his father, Dr. Homer Wood, and he
had seen what he thought was an Italian carbine which,
when fired, "a spit of fire would come out and I could feel the
heat when he shot every time." He asked the shooter if the
gun was an Italian 6.5, and the shooter had replied, "Yes,
sir."

"Son, were you shown any photos of this man, for the purpose of identification?"

"I was shown a group of five photographs initially, and I
didn't recognize the man from the range in any of them. Then
the President's Commission showed me another one, and
this one had an 'X' over the man's head, so I identified him in
that photo."

"Young man, is the man you saw the same man as the one
sitting over there?"

"I can't say. What I remembered then, at the range, and
later, when we saw the pictures on TV, was a mean, stern
face, and I don't see that now."

"Was the man you saw alone?"

"No. He was with someone, but they didn't shoot together. They left together in a newer model Ford. I do remember that."

"You seem to have a good working knowledge of guns, young man. Please look at this Italian rifle and tell me if it is the one you saw."

Wood studied the gun for a moment before handing it back. "The scope looks a little funny to me."

"Let me give you some facts and then you tell me how that fits with your recollection as well as what you know about guns. The FBI tested that gun you just handled. They tested it a great deal. And they concluded that this Italian carbine did not emit visible fire except in conditions of total darkness. Now, both you and your dad testified that this gun was spitting fire—"

"It was."

"Easy, son. I'm on your side. I believe you. I don't think it was either the defendant or the rifle that you saw, but someone posing. What I want you to tell me, is there anything in your experience that would explain why the gun you saw was spitting fire?"

"Nothing that I can think of."

"Was the barrel of the gun you saw a standard barrel?"

"No. It was sawed off."

Barnes got the Mannlicher. "Is this barrel sawed off?"

"No."

"Thank you, young Mr. Wood. Good luck in your studies."

Matthews had to ask something, so he tried to rattle the witness gently. "Son, you said the man shot alone, but yet you saw him leave with someone. Do you make a study of all the people around you everywhere you go?"

"I'm not aware of doing that. I just noticed."

"Did you notice if the man you saw was a good shot?"

"Objection again, as to form."

"Rephrase your question, Mr. Matthews."

"Was the man you saw hitting his target?"

"Yes, he shot a high percentage of bull's-eyes."

"Thank you. Nothing further."

Judge Davis asked Barnes if his remaining agenda was a lengthy one, and Barnes replied that he had one more witness, and he would like to have this segment of testimony completed today. He was told to proceed.

"The defense calls Dallas Deputy Sheriff Roger Craig." A boyish, cleancut and well-dressed man entered the court, and, following Barnes's suggestion, opened his coat, removed his service revolver, opened the chamber, and surrendered it to Carson. He was then sworn.

Barnes immediately got testimony into the record that Craig had joined the sheriff's department in 1959, and had received four promotions, and was named "Officer of the Year" for 1960. Barnes then asked Craig about his duties on November 22nd.

"Nothing unusual. We knew that the President was coming by our building at lunchtime, but we had no security responsibilities or anything like that."

"Sheriff Craig, the defense will put witnesses on the stand who will testify that many police officers had their regular days off on that day, and that much of the parade route was guarded by police reserves. Now you tell us that a decorated officer, Deputy Sheriff Craig, had no duties that day. Is that standard procedure for a presidential visit?"

"No. It was odd. But Sheriff Bill Decker told us to take no part in the parade or security. It might have been a jurisdictional squabble between the local p.d. and the sheriff's office."

"Either way, security was lax," Barnes pointed out. "Now, please tell the court what happened from 12:30 onward that day."

"Okay. I watched the parade from Main Street, just around the corner from Dealey Plaza. Then I heard three shots. I would say there was perhaps three to four seconds between the first and second shots, and not more than two seconds between the second and third shots. It was real rapid. I then made my way into Dealey Plaza, got into the area where all the cars were parked, behind that picket fence there, and I arrested a woman who was driving around in there, because she had no business in there. I turned her over to Deputy Sheriff C. L. Lewis—everybody calls him 'Lummie.' "

"Tell the court what happened with this suspect you arrested."

"There's nothing to tell. She was released and there is not a shred of paper to indicate who she was or what she was doing back there."

"What happened then?"

"I went down into the plaza, where some people were looking for a curbstone where a bullet was thought to have struck before nicking a pedestrian, a Mr. James Tague. While I was at that spot, at one end of the plaza, I heard a shrill whistle, looked up, and saw a man run from the southwest end of the Book Depository, in a southwesterly direction, toward Elm Street, and he got into a Rambler station wagon, driven by a dark-complected man—I can't be more specific about the driver, I was concentrating on the passenger. I tried to make my way to the vehicle, as the passenger just struck me as being in an awful big hurry, but the car got away."

"Do you recall your description of the 'passenger'?"

"Five-eight, five-nine, one hundred thirty-five to one hundred forty pounds, twenties, medium brown sandy hair, blue pants, tan shirt."

"So you lost him. Then what?"

"I made my way up to the sixth floor of the Depository, making mental notes of the evidence, some little stuff—a lunch bag, some boxes, but I also got a good look at the gun."

"Go on."

"German Mauser. Had 'Mauser' stamped on the barrel. I know they've said other stuff in the papers, but I know what I saw."

"Did you see this gun?" Barnes asked, showing him the Mannlicher.

"No," Craig answered quickly. "That's not the gun."

"Tell the court what happened when you visited police headquarters that afternoon."

"Well, I heard they had a suspect, and I wanted to tell them about the person I had seen, and when I went in there, they were asking Lee Oswald questions, and I turned around, and went outside and told the people at the p.d. that he was the man I had seen running to the station wagon."

"You're certain of this?"

"I'm certain that the man I saw was Lee Oswald, or someone who bore a striking resemblance to him."

"You just raised two possibilities, Deputy."

"I know that. The President's Commission had real problems with my testimony, and I'm sorry for that, but I was doing my job that day, and I know what I saw. But they told me Oswald took a bus and a cab, and I told them I saw him get in that station wagon."

"Well, Oswald or someone who bore a striking resemblance," Barnes reminded him.

"Yes. If those other people—the cab driver—identified him positively, and he got a better look and had a lot more time than I did, then I at least have to consider the striking resemblance possibility."

"The man you saw in custody is sitting right there, Mr. Craig. Does he still look like the man you saw run from the Depository?"

"Not the way he looks now. I have to rely on my observations of that day only."

"One last idea, Mr. Craig. Since you gave your testimony to the President's Commission, have you had a chance to read it?"

"Yes. I reread it when you phoned me, to make sure I had put everything in the record, so you could work from it."

"Did it refresh your memory?"

"There's nothing wrong with my memory. But there's something wrong with something—maybe the stenographer didn't hear well, but they changed my testimony in at least fourteen places. Makes me very curious."

"Me too, Deputy, me too. Thank you for coming, and if you are able in the next few days to unearth anything about that individual you arrested, you will bring it to the attention of the court, won't you?"

"Absolutely."

Matthews remained seated. "Time has passed, Mr. Craig. Are you sure you saw the word 'Mauser,' or just heard it, and having seen the gun, thought, oh, it's a Mauser."

"I saw it, sir."

"Then how, Mr. Craig, does a whole police department suddenly produce another gun entirely? Surely one of the many people involved in such doings could come forward and sell their story for a lot of money. How could it happen?"

"I don't know. But if they can make my suspect vanish and get the defendant shot in police headquarters, I'm sure they can phoney up the pedigree of a rifle."

"Nothing further."

"Court stands adjourned until 9 A.M. tomorrow," Judge Davis announced.

# Fifteen

Thursday, January 21, 1965. Neither Matthews nor Barnes, miles apart, got a good night's sleep. Matthews's problem was simple: he had been guaranteed a "can't lose" case, and it had come apart like a cardboard suitcase. Gone were Matthews's hopes of glory, financial rewards equal to the money he had married into, and prestige for himself, Barbara, and his sons. In their place, there suddenly burned a desire in Raymond Matthews for the truth—and Dallas *and* the vaunted President's Commission be damned. With those thoughts in mind, coupled with memories of the previous afternoon's witnesses, which strongly suggested an Oswald impostor, Matthews took all the advice he'd been getting and sat down and composed a very honest and direct statement he would make to the press if and when *The People* v. *Lee Oswald* came crashing down around him. It was more "when" than "if" in his mind as he wrote, but he was honest, and the totality of what had been presented in court had given him a rough night.

In Barnes's case, he slept lightly, and the high winds that usually announce the advent of a storm—in this case, a snowstorm, woke him early and got him thinking about the events at hand. Like Matthews, he was more and more aware that the facts, as they were emerging, were so different from the "official" version, that his personal concerns grew, though he did not yet articulate them in his daily conversations with Amy in Minnesota, for fear of scaring her, and because he never knew he had a secure line. It made for a lot of long distance local news and weather, some promised passion—and he didn't care who was listening—and a promise that he would make up to the family for time lost.

Barnes also had an immediate dilemma. He was considering calling one of the witnesses to Oswald's arrest in the theater. If the policeman in question testified as he spoke at his deposition, Barnes would be able to get the pistol excluded as evidence, which would virtually guarantee that it could be excluded at the defendant's "other trial," but Barnes feared a backlash from the jury. If it became obvious to them, with the exclusion of the pistol, that Oswald might not be convicted in either trial, it might lean them towards conviction in this one. That couldn't be allowed; Barnes could not have his strategy backfire.

The courthouse rotunda was again crowded shortly before nine A.M., but this time, each of the six lawyers stopped to say a quick "hello" to a witness they recalled. Too bad, thought Barnes, this trial is getting downright businesslike.

With the defendant and the jury in place, Barnes rose to call the first witness of the day, Abraham Zapruder. A spry man entered the courtroom, seemed relieved that it was not packed with spectators, and was sworn. Barnes remained seated at first. "Mr. Zapruder, I recall meeting you a few months ago, and I know that events since November twenty-second, 1963, have not been easy for you, so I will try to make my questions as easy and as brief as possible."

"I appreciate that."

"For the record then, are you the same Abraham Zapruder who photographed the President's motorcade with an eight millimeter camera on November twenty-second, 1963?"

"Yes. I had just purchased the camera and was planning to take some film that day, but it seemed the weather would interfere. When the sun broke through, I went home, got the camera, then took up the position on the pedestal at the west end of the concrete arcade, which I thought would allow me to get a decent fifteen seconds or so of the President without a crowd in the way. I asked my secretary, Marilyn Sitzman, to accompany me. I'm an amateur photographer, but if my subject is interesting, I pursue it, and I was afraid I might lean the wrong way on that little pedestal and fall, so she was along for my safety."

"Mr. Zapruder, the court has seen a copy of your film on several occasions, so there is no need to reshow it unless you so request . . ."

"I have seen it in many nightmares, so I know what it shows."

"Okay, then, that will allow us to be done with just a couple of questions. There are a few places where the film is extremely crisp and clear, and other places where it is blurry. Do you have any explanation for that?"

"Yes." The witness then paused, trying to compose himself, and Barnes was wise enough not to hurry him. "The camera is an autofocus, and with a subject such as an approaching automobile, the camera will stay in focus. I think the blurs were caused when I reacted, involuntarily, I believe, to the sounds of . . . the . . . shots."

"Take your time to answer, if necessary. Where was the source of the sounds—the shots—you were reacting to?"

"I thought it came from back of me, although when I saw the last, uh, the shot in the head, I saw it hit the man in the side of the head, and I thought that one had to be fired from alongside of where I was."

"Mr. Zapruder, would you join me at the easel over here, and show the court where you were, and then where you believe the shots came from?"

Zapruder approached the easel unsteadily, pointed out his specific position, and then spread his hand over a general area where he believed the shots came from. The area was labeled "grassy knoll" and "parking area" on the map.

Barnes walked the witness back to the witness stand, and asked about payment received for the film at the time it was processed. Zapruder replied that Time-Life paid him $25,000 at that time, and that it had been donated to the Fireman's and Policeman's Benevolence. Barnes told the witness that he had done a noble service by that and thanked him for his appearance.

Matthews asked about the total payments, not just the sum paid on receipt.

"One hundred fifty thousand dollars," Zapruder answered.

"Did all of it go to charity?"

Barnes objected on relevancy and was sustained. Matthews had no further questions, which was just as well, since his monetary assault on the rather timid witness was not reaping any dividends with the jury.

"Defense calls Carolyn Walther." In the meantime, Barnes helped Mr. Zapruder down from the witness stand, and he was beginning to sob as Barnes did so. The emotion was not lost on the jury, and Matthews wished he hadn't brought up the money, which, as Barnes pointed out, was irrelevant.

Barnes established that the witness was standing opposite the Book Depository on Elm Street, and that she had a clear recollection of the epileptic incident that occurred shortly before the presidential parade came by. "Please tell the court what happened between that time and the time the President's limousine passed you."

"I saw someone in the Book Depository, and it would have been the most easterly window, probably the fourth or fifth floor. The window was open. A man was leaning out of the window with both his hands extended outside the window, holding a gun, barrel pointed downward, as the man looked south on Houston Street. This man was wearing a white shirt and had blond or light brown hair. The weapon had a short barrel and seemed large around the stock end. I thought it was a machine gun. I didn't notice anything like a telescopic sight that would have suggested it was a rifle. In the same window, the glass of which was very dirty, I must add, was a second man, to the left of the first. I could only see a portion of the second man, as he was standing up, where the first man was kneeling down to rest his elbows on the windowsill. For a few seconds, this caused me concern, but then I thought, well, I'm sure they have guards in all the buildings. Then the car came by, and I heard what I thought was a firecracker, then a second and third sound almost at the same time, then at least one more. I wish I had looked up, but I was watching the car, and seeing what happened, I guess I was kind of rooted to the spot."

"Did the reports you heard correspond, at the time, in your mind, to the location where you had seen the two men with the weapon?"

"I'm not sure. If they had, I'm sure I would have directed my attention there."

"Is it possible that the two men you observed were on the sixth floor of the Depository, if you count the ground floor as the first floor?"

"I'm sure it's possible. I didn't count."

"Miss Walther, you gave this testimony in CE 2086, which I will request be put into evidence. Did you encounter any difficulties in telling what you believed to be the truth?"

"Well, I'm not sure anybody wants to hear this, but the FBI tried real hard to get me to say that the second man I saw was a stack of boxes. There may have been boxes, but I saw two men."

"Do you recognize this, a Mannlicher-Carcano Italian rifle, as the weapon you saw that day?"

"No. I saw no sight, and though I'm no expert on guns, I know what a rifle looks like. The gun I saw looked different from the average rifle."

"Did the individual you saw with the gun look like either the man whose picture was in the newspapers, charged with killing the President, or did he look like that same man, who is sitting over there?"

"No. Facially, an average person looks like a lot of other average people, but not identical. But the hair was very different from any pictures I saw of Oswald back then, and that made me very curious."

"Thank you Miss Walther. No further questions at this time. Move to admit CE 2086 at this time."

"CE 2086, Carolyn Walther, is admitted. Mr. Matthews?"

"How much familiarity *do* you have with rifles, Miss Walther? Could you tell the difference between a Mannlicher, an Enfield three oh three, and a Mauser?"

"Objection, Your Honor," Barnes said, with sarcasm evident. "The witness has testified that she is *not* an expert with weapons, but knows enough about rifles to distinguish them from other types of weapons. She might not know a Buick from a Pontiac, but she knows a sedan from a jeep, and that is what she has testified to. If the prosecutor wants to find out who knows the difference between a Mannlicher and a Mauser, he needn't bother recalling any of *his* witnesses."

"The objection is sustained; the editorial noted."

"Miss Walther, you said the window was very dirty, yet you could still see two men?"

"As I said, the one with the gun was completely exposed—there was no glass in front of his upper body, face, hairline, or the gun. The other man, further back, I believe was standing up, or standing on something, so I could see from his knees to his chest, but nothing facially."

"And you heard more than three shots?"

"Yes."

"Nothing further."

"The defense calls James Tague." Barnes moved down to the end of the table to confer with Carolyn Jeffries as a mild-mannered, thirtyish man entered the courtroom and was sworn. Verbally, and using the easel, it was established that Tague, an auto salesman, was standing to the left of the center concrete piling of the triple underpass, a position 260 feet *away* from the President's car. "About this time I heard what sounded like a firecracker. Well, a very loud firecracker. It certainly didn't sound like a rifle shot." Barnes elicited testimony that the witness heard two more shots, which he thought came "from up by the monument" to his left, when he felt a stinging sensation on his face. The witness continued, telling that he related this to an officer, who noticed blood on the witness's face, and that he and the officer, Clyde Haygood, then searched until they found the curb. "There was a mark quite obviously that was a bullet, and it was very fresh." Matthews objected to Tague's conclusion, but Barnes reminded the court that prosecution witnesses had already established that a curb was nicked, and that the curbstone piece was flown to Washington for spectrographic analysis, which showed no copper.

Judge Davis overruled the objection. Barnes thanked the

witness for coming to testify, having intentionally left some questions unasked.

Matthews rose and came forward to confront the witness. "Mr. Tague, I've read the police reports of November twenty-second, and there's no mention of you or your alleged wound. You were wounded, is that what you're telling us?"

"I felt something sting me in the face. I never had the sensation of being shot, if that's what you mean, but when the officer said I had blood on my face, and I realized that shots had been fired, and there were no cars throwing gravel where I was, I thought I'd been hit by a ricochet. I did not require medical attention, and I wanted to help the officers in any way I could. I contacted the Dallas FBI office later that day in order to make them aware that something related to the shooting of the President had come in my direction, but I will tell you, sir, they were not in the least bit interested in my story."

"Mr. Tague, this is the FBI that you are talking about. It's hard to believe that they would ignore evidence of any kind relating to what took place in Dealey Plaza that day."

"And I'm telling you that they couldn't care less."

"Regarding your opinion that the shots came from your left, did you see anything that would lead you to that conclusion?"

"No."

"Neither has anyone else who has testified. That's all, Mr. Tague."

"Defense calls Roy Stamps." While the Fort Worth radio newsman was summoned from the hall, the last bit of testimony reminded Barnes that he was still in a standoff: Matthews hadn't put anybody on the stand to say they saw Oswald in the window. He hadn't rounded up anybody that saw a shot *fired* from the knoll. But he wasn't done, either.

"Mr. Stamps, in the course of your news coverage on November twenty-second, were you at Parkland Hospital?"

"Yes. We were a few cars behind the President in the parade, and we took off at high speed like everybody else. I arrived there before the President was taken out of his car. I rushed up and saw Mr. Kennedy lying in the car. His foot was hanging over the side of the car. The back of his head was gone. I knew he had to be dead."

"Please place your hand on the part of your head that you believe was missing from the President." Stamps did so, proving, if nothing else, that he knew where the back of his head was. Barnes then asked for the rear head autopsy photo on the screen and the witness looked mystified as he stared at it and shook his head from side to side.

"Mr. Stamps, are you acquainted with Jack Ruby, the former operator of a Dallas nightclub who attempted to kill the defendant in this case?"

"Sure. I've seen Jack Ruby on many occasions when I was covering things in Dallas."

"Did you see Ruby on November twenty-second?"

"Yes. At Parkland also. About 1:30. He was coming in the door, helping some network people move some equipment for a TV hookup."

"No doubt in your mind it was Jack Ruby?"

"It was Jack, okay."

"Nothing further."

Matthews remained seated. "For how long, sir, were you, a civilian newsperson, allowed by the protective Secret Service, to linger at the side of the President's car and view the President's wounds?"

"I wasn't there very long. But I wasn't chased away, either. One group of Secret Service was concerned with Johnson, and they were gone in a flash. The other group was looking around for the stretchers that should have already been there for Kennedy. Wasn't like they formed a shield around the car or anything. Other people saw the same things I did."

"Do you have any medical training, Mr. Stamps?"

"No, sir."

"Nothing further."

"Defense calls Dallas Police Deputy L. C. Smith." Barnes had seen a few uniformed officers when he entered the rotunda that morning, and was trying to create a mix of civilians and uniforms that would establish a rhythm for the jury. Smith, in dress uniform, testified that he had been in front of the sheriff's office on Main Street when the President went by, then he heard what he thought was a backfire.

When he heard a second and third report, he ran across the plaza toward the knoll, and was told by a woman "unknown to me" that the shots had come from the fence on the north side of Elm Street.

"Who was the woman?" Barnes asked casually.

"I have no idea," came an equally casual answer.

"Did it ever occur to you, Deputy, that you just might have confronted the single most important witness to the single most important crime of the twentieth century, and you allowed her to make her report and then vanish?"

"I know I didn't go by the book, but it was a crazy moment, you have to understand that."

"I'm trying to understand that," Barnes told him. "But if you had apprehended someone, that person you caught would stand a greatly enhanced chance of being convicted if you had someone to identify him or her. And you let a witness, who may remain forever unknown to this court, get away."

Smith was silent. "Why did you head across the plaza toward the knoll in the first place?"

"That should be obvious," Smith answered. "That's where I thought the shots came from."

"No more questions. Mr. Matthews?"

"No questions at this time."

"Defense calls Arnold Rowland." A well-groomed young man was then summoned and sworn. Matthews told Graves and Vincent to tune in carefully, as this testimony might have to be weakened somehow.

"Mr. Rowland, calling your attention to November twenty-second, 1963, would I be correct in saying that you missed part of your high school day that morning to witness the parade with your newly wed bride?"

"Yes. We had recently gotten married and were going to school and working, but we wanted to see the President."

"Please tell the court what happened."

"Well, we got to the corner of Houston and Main, which is about a block from the Book Depository, but there was still a crowd there, so we moved up Houston a little. There was an officer nearby, and we were able to monitor where the parade was by listening to his radio, or by asking him. At about

12:15, I started taking more interest—it was something that might only happen once—seeing the President, so I was taking in the whole scene. I saw a policeman on the underpass, and then I looked up at the Book Depository and saw two people on the sixth floor in open windows. One man, who I believe was a colored man, was in the window at the east end of the building, where Elm meets Houston. At the other end, the west end of the building, was a man with a high-power rifle with a big telescopic sight. I remember saying to my wife, 'You want to see a Secret Service man?' but as I said that, there was a distraction across the street from us—somebody suffered a seizure—and my wife's attention was drawn to that, and when I mentioned it again, I looked up and both the people I had seen were no longer in view. Wouldn't have mattered much, 'cause my wife's eyesight is not the best."

"Could you see the man with the rifle well enough to describe him?"

"He was slender, about one hundred forty to one hundred fifty pounds, light complected, with dark hair, probably black, and close cut. He could have been Caucasian or a very light Latin. He was wearing a light shirt, either a very light blue or a white shirt, open at the collar, unbuttoned. Agewise, he was in his early thirties."

"Is that the man you saw, sitting over there?"

"No. I couldn't identify him then or now."

"Did you give a statement to the authorities on November twenty-second?"

"After the car went by, we heard what we thought was a backfire, or a firecracker, and because nobody could see the car, at ground level, some people laughed like it was a joke. Then a few seconds later, it was more like gunfire, coming from the railroad yards, and that's where everyone converged. There must have been fifty cops there. I was in there also, and when the officers gave up looking, I told them what I had seen, and they took me to the police department, where I gave a statement. I was later shown that statement, and it was reworded."

"Could we have CE 357, please?" A moment passed, and the exhibit came up. "Is this the statement?"

"Yes. And it was a little scary. They came to my place of

work several times, and I only had one story to tell. They changed my words in that statement, and the FBI flat-out told me to forget that I had seen a colored man in the window that the shots supposedly came from."

"I guess that would be scary. Nothing further. Move to admit CE 357, please."

"So moved. Mr. Matthews?"

"Mr. Rowland, you must have the most incredible eyesight in the whole state of Texas, because you want us to believe that from Houston Street, you could see enough of a person inside the Book Depository to tell us that his shirt was unbuttoned?"

"That's what I saw."

"But the person you told to look up there, well, it would not have mattered, as her eyesight is not as good, am I correct?"

"Yes."

"And did you see any security people in or on any of the other buildings that were within the scope of your incredible eyesight in the plaza?"

"No."

"And the FBI essentially encouraged you to commit perjury?"

"Yes. And they tried to help by changing my statement."

"Nothing further."

"Defense calls former presidential assistant Kenneth P. O'Donnell." The jury, after seeing people they were unaware of, sat up at the introduction of this witness who typified the New Frontier that Kennedy had been creating. Barnes established that O'Donnell, along with Dave Powers, another aide, was riding in the Secret Service follow-up car which was directly behind the presidential limousine. O'Donnell told that the original plan had been to visit Dallas in the evening, but that Governor Connally suggested the Austin stop for the evening so they "could hit Dallas around noontime."

"Was it apparent that there would be a motorcade through Dallas?" Barnes asked.

"Certainly. We had a motorcade everywhere we went."

"Oh?" Barnes asked, feigning surprise. "In the month of November 1963, were there motorcades as parts of the President's visits to Chicago and Florida?"

O'Donnell clearly did not like the tone of the question, but he understood its intent. "They had to be canceled for security reasons. We had reason to believe there was danger to the President. Chicago was canceled outright; Florida was changed to a helicopter ride at the last minute."

"I see. So you're right behind the President's car. Tell us what you can about the shooting sequence."

"Well, I didn't know it was shots at first. My first impression was it was a firecracker. And then somebody said, 'He has been hit.' I heard three sounds altogether, and they took five to six seconds. As I recall, the first two sounds I heard were almost simultaneous, then a pause, and then the third one. The movement I saw on the part of the President, when he sort of slumped slowly to the left corresponds in my mind to the second noise I heard."

"Mr. O'Donnell, you sat in the highest councils of political power in this nation, and you participated, for a thousand days, in the decisions of this nation, so you know how the system works. You're here today because a man is on trial for his life. Please tell the court where you thought the shots came from."

"I thought the shots came from behind the fence, that is, from the front right of the car."

"You know, of course, why I asked you that."

O'Donnell merely nodded.

"You gave sworn testimony before the President's Commission last May eighteen that the shots came from the right *rear*. I'm sure Mr. Matthews will ask you about that, so we might as well discuss it now."

"I told my account of events to the FBI just as I did under oath a few minutes ago—the shots came from the right front, in the direction of the fence. But they told me it couldn't have happened that way, and that I must have been imagining things. So I testified before the President's Commission the way they wanted me to. I told them exactly what they wanted to hear. I would also add that it was in my mind, and I regret this, but when that testimony was given, I did not think there would be a trial, and I did not want to cause the Kennedy family any pain."

"So now, for the record, which is it—front right, or right rear—or unsure?"

"Right front."

"Thank you, Mr. O'Donnell. I don't mean to cause any problems for a family that means so much to you, but you must understand, I have a responsibility to a client, and to every family in this nation. No further questions."

Matthews stood almost behind the defense table to address the witness. "Mr. O'Donnell, you aren't the first, and I suspect you won't be the last, witness who has come in here and told stories that raise serious questions about the integrity of either the FBI or the witness. If these allegations are true, they have to be investigated, and thoroughly. With the permission of the court, I'd like to ask you to explain to us how your version of events went from right front to right rear." Matthews looked to Barnes for his silence and Barnes understood.

"Well, they took my statement, all with deference to the position I had held in the White House, and they let me say what I testified to here, right front. Now, of course, I didn't say I saw that, but rather that it was my clear impression, being about fifteen to twenty feet from the President at the time of the shots, that I heard something like a firecracker, then two other sounds, and what I could identify sounded right front. And they seemed to accept it. Then gradually, they kind of hemmed and hawed, and said, well, you know, Mr. O'Donnell, you're kind of sticking your neck out with reckless statements like that, because we have all the evidence, and it's clear that the shots came from the back. And it's certainly okay to say, 'right front,' but you're on your own, really, and it'll open up a whole can of worms that will cause problems for the family, because some nut somewhere will be screaming Communist conspiracy and whatnot. So I played the good soldier. But I didn't buy their con job."

"Can you make available to this court the names of the agents who deposed you in this manner?"

"Not at this moment, but I do have the names in my records, and I will supply them if asked."

Judge Davis interrupted: "Consider it an official request, please, Mr. O'Donnell."

"Certainly, Your Honor."

Matthews had saved a good bit of his own hide with this witness, and he saw one further opportunity. "You are also not the first witness to testify to hearing a first noise that sounded like a firecracker. Can you shed any light on that?"

"Well, as you might imagine, I am not a gun expert. But I have heard gunfire . . . besides those awful noises in Dallas, and I have, I guess, a layman's working knowledge of what gunfire sounds like. Most Washington staffers visit the FBI headquarters with civic groups, and they put on a little firearms display, that kind of thing. And a high-powered rifle, or a serious handgun—not a twenty-two that a woman might carry in her purse, but a real gun—makes a distinct sound, I know that much. And what I heard just didn't register that way. I don't mean to digress, but the night before the President died, he imitated how a sniper might crouch to shoot him from ambush . . . it's an image of Jack that I will never get out of my mind. One day kidding about it, the next day he's killed. So when I heard the sound, given the President's concern for a sniper, I really believe I would have immediately thought, and said, 'Gunshot!' But it was just a little bit of a 'pop'—a firecracker—nothing threatening. Then there were other noises—shots, which sounded like shots, but not like the first noise."

"Thank you, Mr. O'Donnell, nothing further." Barnes looked to Matthews, gave him a well-earned nod of respect, and felt slightly guilty for dumping on him in the early stages of the trial. Then he reminded himself it was not over and called Gordon Arnold as his next witness.

The witness, wearing an army uniform, testified that on November 22nd, he was in Dallas on leave from the service, having just completed basic training, and was due to leave for Alaska at the end of November, when he decided to watch the President's parade and take movies of it.

"Please tell the court what happened."

"Initially I went to the area behind the stockade fence, so I could rest the camera on the fence for clear pictures, but I was told by a civilian, a man in a suit, wearing a sidearm, that no one was allowed in that area. I decided to challenge his authority and go anyhow, but then he waved a badge in my face, told me he was a Secret Service agent, and that for security reasons I could not go behind the fence. So I moved down into an area a few feet in front of the fence, actually towards the end of the fence closest to the concrete monument there, and when the President's car made its turn, I started filming. Well suddenly, I felt a bullet pass my left ear. That's the only way to describe it. You feel it, you don't see or hear it. You feel something go by and you hear a report just behind it. I hit the deck and dug in. Then there was another shot, over me. It was a crack, just like I was right between the gun and the target, except I was grabbing for all the earth I could. And I stayed down. When I got up, there were people scrambling all over that knoll, and a policeman, who was waving his gun and sobbing, saw the camera and demanded my film. I gave it to him, and two days later I reported to my duty station in Alaska. Never did get my film, or even a copy back."

"And there's no doubt in your mind that shots originated behind you?"

"Some absolutely did. I can't and won't say they all did, because some reports sounded like a blend of more than one shot in a tiny space of time. But I felt one go by, and one go over, and I heard the sound right behind them, and they were right behind me."

"Mr. Arnold, suppose I told you there were no Secret Service in that area before, during, or for at least thirty minutes after the shooting. What would you say?"

"I'd say this fella was a good actor then, because he convinced me. Not the first time. Then he just said to get lost. But when I persisted, he took out the badge, real official like, stated his business, and said it was a security matter. I believed him. There was no reason not to."

"Of course there wasn't. Your Honor, I have no further questions for the witness, but I would like, for the record, to introduce corroborative evidence at this time. Senator Yarborough, riding in the motorcade, deposed on October nineteen, 1964, stated that he recalled seeing a soldier, on the side of the hill known as the grassy knoll, in a defensive posture that indicated the man understood evasive combat techniques, and that he had his wits about him in so protecting himself. At least that's the gist of his remarks as contained in this brief deposition. I saw no reason to bring Mr. Yarborough to these proceedings to testify that he saw a soldier."

"Defense has no objections, Your Honor," Matthews intoned, before he was asked. Then he approached the witness. "Did the policeman take your name, address, anything like that?"

"No. Nothing. Just, 'Hand over the film, it's evidence.' And he didn't hang around long enough for me to get his name, though it was probably on a little name tag."

"Did you try to report your observations to anyone at the time, or are you coming forward for the first time now?"

"I told the policeman, but he wanted the film. If he had stayed there to listen to me, I also would have asked him how such a thing could have happened if there was Secret Service right there in that spot."

"Thank you. Nothing further."

"One question on redirect, Your Honor. Mr. Arnold, were you called to give testimony to the President's Commission?"

"No, sir."

"That's all; thank you, Mr. Arnold.

"Defense calls Dean Morgan." Barnes noticed consternation at the defense table as they were trying to figure out who the witness was and what his testimony would be. Barnes established that Mr. Morgan was a resident of a Dallas suburb, had not seen the President killed, but had nosed around on rooftops of buildings in the Dealey Plaza area, and had found, and displayed, a bullet casing which he found under the parapet of the Dallas County Records Building, a tall structure on Houston Street with a clear view of the motorcade when it was in the position it was in when stricken. For the record, Barnes noted the casing was dated 1953, manufactured by the Twin Cities Arsenal, and that it had an odd crimp around the neck, suggesting that it had held a sabot, a device previously discussed in testimony which disguises the true caliber of the projectile fired.

"Mr. Morgan, how can you be sure that this slightly rusted casing is in fact the one you found just less than a year ago?"

"I put this mark on it, like police do on the television. And it's the only bullet I've ever marked, so this is the one I found."

"Nothing further. Thank you. Move to enter Morgan Exhibit Number 1, the shell casing, for future testing as events dictate."

"So moved."

Matthews objected on grounds of relevancy, but the judge let him know he clearly considered it relevant. The prosecutor then objected on grounds of foundation, and although the judge saw more of a point to that, he told Matthews that unless he could produce well-documented police evidence that every square inch of every roof overlooking Dealey Plaza had been thoroughly searched, he would have to allow the exhibit to be entered and it would be the jury's job to pass on its value and validity.

"Mr. Morgan, what is your purpose in bringing this matter to the court?"

"To get to the bottom of what happened. It occurred to me that anyone in that sixth floor window had an easy shot as the car came up Houston and made that big turn. It was a kill shot—you could have thrown the bullet and hurt someone. But to shoot at the target down the block said to me that there were others involved, so I beat around on a few rooftops and found that casing. That's it. I haven't sold the story to anyone, so there's no motive for me to be here other than to go on record."

"Did you go to the police with your discovery?"

"If I had, I would not be sitting here now. I'd be sitting home saying to myself, 'I wonder what happened to that casing I handed over . . .' Know what I mean?"

"I'm beginning to. Do you feel that casing should have any bearing on the guilt or innocence of the defendant?"

"That's why they have juries, sir. I only know he couldn't have fired that casing." Matthews mentally agreed. "Nothing further."

Dean quickly got Barnes's attention. "Have we got the other guy with the slug out there?" Barnes nodded to Dean, announcing, "The defense calls Richard Lester." More confusion at the defense table with another unknown, until they got to Lester's name in the fine print and realized he was a clone of the previous witness.

Once the witness was sworn, Barnes established that Mr. Lester, an eyewitness to the crime, later used a metal detector and combed Dealey Plaza, finding a bullet fragment at the end of the grassy lawn in the center near the triple underpass. Barnes had an affidavit from the Minnesota sheriff's Department indicating that the bullet was a 6.5 millimeter slug, but it was not in any way ballistically comparable to the test bullets fired from the Mannlicher by the President's Commission.

"Mr. Lester, did you offer your information to the authorities?"

"Not directly. I figured that because I was a bystander, I would be contacted to give evidence. I was never contacted. They didn't want to hear from me, I guess."

"Thank you. Nothing further. Move to admit Lester Exhibit Number 1."

Matthews knew a no-win situation when he saw one: "No questions."

Barnes realized he was having a good morning and wasn't going to waste a minute of it, so he decide to pour it on: "Defense calls Officer Joe Marshall Smith." Matthews and his staff were again put off that Smith, appearing for the defense, was wearing his Dallas police uniform, which, of course, Barnes had told him would look very dignified on the witness stand.

Barnes's first questions elicited responses that Smith had been on the west side of Houston Street between Elm and Main Street, and that he had witnessed the "epileptic seizure" that happened just before the arrival of the motorcade.

"Officer, have you had enough medical training to know a genuine epileptic seizure?"

"No. But this fellow was just thrashing around like a mad dog . . ."

"Who was 'this fellow'?"

"I have no idea."

"Did you check his identification?"

"Not that I recall."

"Was he wearing one of those bracelets that some people wear to identify diseases they have so that measures can be taken?"

"I did not see one."

"Did you look?"

"No."

Matthews rose slowly to savor an objection: "Your Honor, fascinating as this episode is, it has no relevance. The man was removed from the scene in an ambulance a few minutes before the motorcade arrived."

"Your Honor," Barnes answered, "that is the very point of this issue. There was such an event, and we know many crimes are able to happen because someone creates a diversion. This may have just kept the crowd on one side of the street while unknown events occurred within one hundred yards. Of equal relevance is the disposition of the case, as Aubrey Rike, driver for the O'Neal Ambulance Service, a private medical concern, has deposed, and will testify, if needed, that when he arrived at Parkland Hospital with the subject in question, the man jumped from his ambulance and ran away. None of this behavior sounds typical, and I believe it has relevance. Beyond that, I don't plan to pursue this line of questioning any further."

"Objection overruled, but let's move on."

"Tell the court what happened then, Officer."

"Well, I went on up to Elm and Houston to direct traffic—"

"For the record, what is located on that corner?"

"The Texas Book Depository."

"Then?"

"Well, then I heard shots, but I don't know where the shots came from, I just had no idea, because it was such a ricochet."

"So you were right there at the Depository, and you cannot say that shots came from there. Is that correct?"

"Yes."

"By ricochet, what do you want the court to understand?"

"It just sounded like the sounds were coming from all around. Couldn't pin it to one place."

"Who said they came from one place, Officer Smith?"

Barnes let the witness think about that while he rummaged through a meaningless file. "Okay, let's move on. Tell us what happened next."

"Woman came up to me and she was just in hysterics. She told me, 'They are shooting the President from the bushes.' So I immediately proceeded up into that area down by the overpass."

"Who was the woman?"

"I don't know."

"By your actions, obviously you believed what she was telling you. And if you believed her, it would make some sense to detain her as a material witness. She obviously didn't get the information she provided you from a newspaper or the radio. Do you see my point?"

"All I wanted to do was catch the guy."

"Officer, you're talking about 'the guy,' after a woman in hysterics tells you *'they're* shooting the President'; who did you think she was talking about when she said 'they'?"

"That didn't occur to me until you just said it."

"For the record, Officer, to your knowledge were any bushes found on the sixth floor of the Depository?"

"Objection, Your Honor. This is ridiculous. This is a repeat of the question to the cab driver regarding if he was now, or ever had been, a Negro."

"Your Honor, it may sound ridiculous on face, but when a woman in hysterics, who is believed by a police officer, tells that people, plural, are shooting the President from the bushes, it's well to know where they are to narrow the search. If there are none in the Depository, and there was such a female witness, what are we, especially the defendant, doing here?"

"Objection overruled. Please get on with it."

"Then what, Officer?"

"I went into that area, with my gun drawn, and a deputy sheriff—I don't know which one, but he and I ran into an unknown man, who showed me that he was a Secret Service Agent, and after that I checked the cars there."

"Officer, we have had testimony from the head of the Dallas Secret Service office, Mr. Sorrels, that there was never even one Secret Service man in the location you describe. Are you mistaken or was someone impersonating a Secret Service agent?"

"I was not mistaken about that. This fellow showed me his credentials."

"Did he help you search the cars?"

"I didn't see him for long."

"When you searched the cars, what did you do, exactly?"

"Looked in the windows. See if anybody was hiding in there. That kind of thing."

"Did you check every car there?"

"No."

"Did you open the trunks of any cars?"

"No. How could I do that?"

"Did you find any indication in that parking lot that anything related to the shooting could have happened there?"

"I smelled gunpowder there."

"No further questions."

Matthews remained seated. "What did this Secret Service man look like?"

"That's something I've asked myself, but I could not describe him, at least facially, as I was taking a real good look at the credentials. Beyond that, he, well, he didn't much look like what you expect in a Secret Service man. His fingernails looked like an auto mechanic, and he wasn't dressed in a suit. But like I said, we were searching for a shooter, and every second mattered, and I just didn't make that connection at that time."

"Thank you, Officer Smith. Nothing further."

"Defense calls former presidential assistant Dave Powers." Barnes was still mixing the witnesses well—a bystander here, then a cop, then a big name politician. Powers, one of JFK's Irish mafia, was balding and lacked the vigor of O'Donnell, who had testified earlier. Barnes then produced an affidavit dated May 18, 1964, and asked the witness to read it.

"The first shot went off and it sounded to me as if it were a firecracker. I noticed then that the President moved quite far to his left after the shot from the extreme right-hand side where he had been sitting. There was a second shot and Governor Connally disappeared from sight and then there was a third shot which took off the top of the President's head and had the sickening sound of a grapefruit splattering against the side of a wall. The total time between the first and third shots was about five or six seconds. My first impression was that the shots came from the right and overhead, but I also had a fleeting impression that the noise appeared to have come from the front in the area of the triple underpass."

"Thank you, Mr. Powers," Barnes said, walking to the defense table. "When this was happening, how far were you from President Kennedy?"

"About as far away as you are from me now," Powers answered, with emotion in his voice.

"So you had a good view of the tragedy?" Barnes was choosing his words carefully.

"Yes. Too good."

"Mr. Powers, in listening to what you just read, and I don't mean to put you through any personal agony, but is it possible that you were hearing noises from both places?"

"I have relived that event more times than I can count, and inasmuch as I am still unable to pinpoint exactly, I would have to say that your hypothesis is certainly possible."

"What was Mr. Kennedy's posture, if you recall, just before he was struck in the head?"

"He had moved from the right side of the car to either the center of the backseat, or a few inches either way off center. He had sort of gone upright at one point, then gradually leaned forward."

"Mr. Powers, at the time of the fatal impact, were you able to see the top of his head, this part?" Barnes indicated with gestures.

"No, because he was leaning forward."

"So what did you see?"

"The back of his head, and his shoulders."

"So when the fatal bullet struck, if you couldn't see the top of his head, how could you see the shot take off the top of his head?"

"Well, it took off the highest point which I could see."

"Which was what?"

"Well, the top of the back."

"No more questions, Mr. Powers. Again, I'm sorry to have

had to dredge out these painful memories of an agonizing event. I hope you understand."

Matthews stood. "Mr. Powers, is there any way that the last shot you described could have caused the wound as you originally described it, the top . . . ?"

"Well, if that wound was caused by a gunshot from the front, it would have driven him back, and I would then have had a clear view of the top. But that was a very sudden five seconds . . . a blur, a nauseating instant that you pray a thousand times every day you could undo, but—"

"I understand, sir. No further questions."

"The defense calls Ilya A. Mamantov." Again, Barnes was keeping the jury awake with the variety of his witnesses. Barnes quickly had the witness inform the jury that he had known of Lee and Marina Oswald, but had never met them prior to November 22, 1963.

"Under what circumstances did you meet them on November twenty-second?"

"I only met Mrs. Oswald. I was called by Jack Crichton, a petroleum operator who is connected with the army reserve, intelligence section, to translate for Mrs. Oswald when she was brought to police headquarters. I was then called a few minutes later by Chief Lumpkin, who repeated the request."

"Let's see if we've got this straight. You received a phone call, out of the blue, to translate for the Dallas police, and the call came from someone in army intelligence?"

"Yes. Jack Crichton."

"Then the Dallas police called and made it official?"

"Yes. And they sent a car."

"Tell us what transpired at police headquarters."

"I was to translate questions asked by Dallas men, or FBI men, to Marina, and then translate her answers to them. Most of it revolved around the gun they showed her."

This was one time Barnes wanted to prompt a witness: "Tell the jury and the court what happened, Mr. Mamantov. The truth is what we are after."

"Well, they wanted her to identify a rifle."

"You translated these comments to her?"

"Yes."

"Was there, at any time, any statements made to Mrs. Oswald that she did not, in fact, have to give evidence against her husband, or, for that matter, against herself?"

"No. Not at all."

"Okay, tell the court what you translated about the gun."

"Well, as I said, they asked her to identify this one gun they showed her. She told them she knew her husband had a gun in a blanket, but she only remembered seeing the end of the stock, which was dark brown, possibly black, she said. She also told them she believed the blanket contained the gun he had brought from the Soviet Union, and that it was her impression that Lee had always owned a weapon. An FBI man was taking down my translation, by the way."

"We'll get back to the gun in a minute. What happened to the words the FBI were taking down? First, were they verbatim?"

"I don't know."

"What happened to them?"

"Mrs. Oswald signed it."

"Did you translate it for her?"

"No. I wasn't asked to."

"So she signed a document in English?"

"Yes."

"Incredible. Anything else about the gun?"

Mamantov shifted uneasily in the witness chair, more from discomfort than anything he had to testify to. "She told them, through me, that she could not identify the rifle they were showing her. She said that all guns looked alike to her, but she did make a point of saying that she had never seen a gun with a scope—she didn't know what to call it—in her husband's possession."

"Mr. Mamantov, I show you CE 1778, which will come up on these screens in a moment. As you can see, it suggests that she presumed, since her husband was under arrest, that she was being shown the gun her husband owned, but even then she could not identify it. It further states that she had no recollection of the sight. Is that the way you recall the session went?"

"There was no presumption. That lady had fear in her eyes, of what, I do not know, but as a translator, I could hear her making sure every word was as precise as she could make it

—that's why she had difficulty with the scope. She had no idea what it was, or the word for it—it was foreign to her. And she would only say that she knew he had a gun, but she had only seen the back end of it. The folks asking the questions weren't crazy about her responses."

Matthews was up: "Move to strike the last response."

Barnes didn't argue it, and the objection was sustained. The witness was then turned over to Matthews, who wanted to know if the witness was called upon to do any further translating.

"Not with respect to the events of November twenty-second."

"Nothing further."

"Defense calls Lee Bowers." Barnes looked at his watch and realized he had time for a couple more witnesses before lunch, so he had to keep the pace moving. Bowers testified that he had been at work in the railroad tower, which had a commanding view of the parking area as well as the picket fence, the concrete monument, and the Depository. Further testimony indicated that he had seen three unusual cars enter the area between noon and the time of the shooting, and he was emphatic that such activity was, in fact, unusual: "I've worked there ten years, and I know who goes in and out of there."

Bowers further testified that he heard three shots: "One, a slight pause, then two very close together. The sounds came either from up against the School Book Depository or near the mouth of the triple underpass."

"Given your position, were you able to see anything occurring behind the picket fence?"

"At the time of the last shot, I noticed a commotion, some movement or flash of light that drew my attention to that spot, but I can't identify it any further. I did notice two men at that location when my attention was drawn to it. One was middle aged, heavyset, wearing a white shirt and dark trousers. The younger man was in his mid-twenties, and was wearing a plaid shirt or jacket."

"Did you testify to that before the President's Commission?"

"Yes."

"Did you also testify about some transients being taken off a train?"

"Yes. But when I received my sworn statement in order that I sign it, I think what I told them had been watered down."

"Tell us about the transients exactly as you remember the event."

"Shortly after the shooting, I saw three men sneak onto one of the trains. I notified the police of what I had seen, and as the person responsible for trains coming in and out of the yard, I just held up that train until the police took the three of them off of it."

"Nothing further, Mr. Bowers. Thank you."

Matthews approached the witness. "Mr. Bowers, it seemed like you allowed a large area in which the shots could have originated from. Is it possible that from your location, you were catching an echo, which could have originated almost anywhere?"

"I don't think so. What I heard was the original reports, from the area I suggested. Now they may have created an echo, but it would have seemed like the same report. No, I'm confident that what I heard was in the area I suggested. It's the same with the trains. I have to be able, in my job, to identify the exact location of train sounds, to prevent serious accidents."

"And the 'commotion' you saw—that's as close as you can pin it?"

"Yes. Something happened over there at the fence at the time of the last shot which caught my eye, but I cannot be more specific. I wish I could."

"Nothing further."

"Defense calls Malcolm Summers." An ordinary-looking civilian entered the court, looked around at the faces of those present, and had a look on his own countenance indicating that he wondered what he was doing in this situation.

Barnes elicited testimony that Summers was an eyewitness to the assassination, and had been down Elm Street beyond the end of the crowd, which allowed him to be one of the first to rush up the grassy knoll when the crowd surged in that direction.

"Tell the court what happened when you headed up to the knoll."

"I wasn't alone, but I don't know who the other people were. Bystanders, I guess. We got just so far and we were stopped by a white male, dressed in a suit, and he had an overcoat over one arm. Clearly visible under the overcoat was a gun. He told us not to come up any further or we could get shot or killed."

"Did this individual identify himself?"

"He did say something about the Secret Service, but I could not quote that part exactly. I was noticing the gun when he said that. Then he told us we were in danger, and I heard that part clearly."

"Nothing further."

Matthews leaned back in his chair as if to make light of the testimony. "Mr. Summers, can we take a moment to exam your testimony logically?"

"Sure. Go ahead."

Matthews then approached the witness. "Mr. Summers, if I had witnessed the damage done to the President, as you did, and I thought I knew where the shots came from, and I headed in that direction, and I was stopped in the manner you described, I think I would have turned to someone nearby and asked, 'Did you see that?' or something like that, and if someone else saw my version of events, I would have gotten their name and address, because I'm not sure people would have believed me that a Secret Service man suggested I might get killed. Does what I'm saying sound logical?"

"Yes. But it happened as I told it, and I wasn't thinking back to exercises in logic as that fellow was standing there with that gun saying what he was saying."

"Okay, I see. Thank you."

"Defense calls Carolyn Arnold." Barnes then told Oswald to sit up a little and try to establish eye contact with this witness, as it was someone who knew him.

The witness was sworn, and the jury heard testimony that she was the secretary to the vice-president of the Book Depository, and that on the day of the assassination, she was standing in front of the Depository waiting for the motorcade.

"What happened then?"

"I turned around, to see how many of the employees had come out, and I thought I caught a glimpse of Lee Oswald standing in the doorway."

"Did you know Mr. Oswald well enough that you could have made such an identification?"

"Oh, yes. He used to come in to the office for change for the vending machines often. I didn't know him in the personal sense, anything like that, but I knew him on sight."

"Is the man sitting over there the man we are talking about?"

"Absolutely. He doesn't look quite the same, but still recognizable."

"Okay. Now, did you see him at any other time in close proximity to the arrival of the motorcade?"

"I definitely saw him in the second floor lunchroom at 12:15 when I stopped what I was doing to go outside and view the motorcade."

"Was Mr. Oswald in the process of leaving when you saw him at 12:15?"

"No. He was just sitting there, alone, as he would usually do."

"No further questions. Mr. Matthews?"

"Is the 12:15 time absolutely accurate?"

"It is as accurate as I can be. We were expecting the parade at 12:25, and I looked at my watch every few minutes until finally, at 12:15, I thought, 'Go outside, you're not going to get anything else done sitting here looking at your watch.' And I got up from the office, stacked a few papers, and went through the lunchroom and then outside."

"And your observation of Mr. Oswald in the doorway. Can you say with positive certainty that it was Mr. Oswald?"

"No. It looked like him, but I just spanned the crowd for faces and I thought I saw him."

"Thank you."

"A moment on redirect, Your Honor," Barnes noted. "In the time sequence you just described, you talked of seeing 12:15 on your watch, then packing up, then going through the lunchroom. Does that allow for the possibility that you were in the lunchroom a minute or two *after* 12:15?"

"Most likely."

"Also, you said 12:25 was the time you expected the parade to come by. Do you have any knowledge that such time was the time that most of the workers expected the parade?"

"Several people spoke of it, and everyone said 12:25."

"Thank you again."

"Recross, Your Honor," Matthews stated for the first time. "Do you have any knowledge that the defendant, Mr. Oswald, was projecting the parade to come by at 12:25?"

"No."

"That's all I have on recross," Matthews concluded.

"Defense calls Officer Clyde Haygood," Barnes announced, and to Matthews's repeated chagrin, yet another Dallas officer appeared, in uniform, to testify. Barnes's first round of questions were beginning to get repetitive, and he knew it, but he also knew it would take quantities of such answers to carry the day, so he established that Haygood had been riding several cars behind the President on his motorcycle, had heard three shots, "It was the first, then a pause, and then the other two were real close." It was also established that people were pointing up to the railroad yard, so Haygood parked, or abandoned, his motorcycle and headed up there.

"Tell the court what happened then."

"Well, that area got crowded quickly, so I moved out into the plaza and I found a person who had been nicked in the face by something, and we started looking along the curbing for a ricochet mark, which we found quickly. Then this other man came up to me and said the shots came from the Book Depository. I reported this information to the dispatcher, who told me to get all the pertinent information, which I thought I had, but I did not get any information about the individual who made the report."

"Nothing further. Thank you, Officer."

Matthews didn't want to waste time with this witness, but at the same time, he did not want him to testify unopposed, either. "Officer Haygood, what expertise do you have that would instinctively convince you that some mark you saw on a curb had been the spot a bullet struck?"

"None, but—"

"Thank you. No further questions." The judge indicated that much time had passed, and the jury had a great deal to digest, but Barnes asked to be allowed to conclude the morning's presentation with one final witness.

"Defense calls James Altgens." As the witness entered the courtroom, Barnes asked to have CE 203 on the screens, noting that it was essentially the same photo as earlier seen as CE 369, and it came up as the witness was sworn. "You recognize this, I suppose?"

"Yes. I took that photo from the curb of Elm Street."

"How far away do you believe the President was when this was taken?"

"About ten yards . . . thirty feet."

"Mr. Altgens, are you aware of what frame this photo corresponds to on the Zapruder film?"

"I was asked that, to see if I knew, by the President's Commission, and I really had no way of knowing. They told me it was frame 255."

"Actually, their photo people did some studies, and 255 is correct. How far away from you was the President when he was fatally shot in the head?"

"About fifteen feet."

"Try to help the court make sense of what happened, Mr. Altgens. Here's what we know. The car traveled about sixteen point four feet per second, based on an estimated speed of eleven point two miles per hour. Your photo, at frame 255, is fifty-eight frames before the shot to the President's head, or about three point two seconds. In other words, the President traveled between fifty-two and fifty-three feet between your photo and Mr. Zapruder's frame 313, in which the fatal shot is obvious. Now you've said the President was thirty feet away in your picture, and fifteen feet away when the fatal shot struck. See the problem?"

"Yes. So did the President's Commission. I could be off with the distances, easily. Also, remember that I took that photo on the screen just as I heard a gunshot. Actually, it sounded like a firecracker."

"Mr. Altgens, if you took a photo at Zapruder 255 and there was a gunshot at that precise moment, we have very interesting questions raised by that testimony. In the meantime, please tell the court anything else you think might be of evidentiary value in this matter."

"Well, I'm sorry, first of all, if my testimony threw things off. But that was a strange day, I'll tell you. I tried to set up my equipment at 11:15 on the triple underpass down there, thinking I could get one or two, even three, perhaps, excellent photos—the motorcade, the Dallas skyline in the back—but I got run out of there, even though I displayed both my Associated Press credentials and my Department of Public Safety Identification. So I moved on up to Main and Houston, took pictures from there, and then raced down to the curb on Elm while the parade went up Houston and slowed to make that awkward turn. While I was there, I noticed some people behind the fence up on the knoll, including police, and I considered that unusual, as I wasn't allowed in such an area, and why would somebody watch from up there with so much curb space available?"

"Why indeed," Barnes echoed. "Since you were so close to the President, what observations, if any, were you able to make with respect to the fatal wound?"

"I saw it. There was no blood on his face or forehead, but . . . do you want me to be precise—it's gory."

"We all know that, Mr. Altgens. Please be precise."

"Well, so much flesh and particles flew out of the side of his head toward where I was, which was to the left, that I was sure the bullet had come out of the left side of his head. I didn't even bother to look on the triple underpass. I thought from what I saw the shot had to come from beside the car, on the right, or somewhere to the rear. I discounted the theory that it was on the right side of the car, because many of us went over there, and there were Secret Service there."

"For the record, sir, there were not. Getting back to that photo on the screen, your testimony to the President's commission was that this photo was exposed at a time when 'the shot was just a fraction ahead of my picture.' Is that the shot, or the sound? I ask you this because Governor Connally is in obvious distress in your photo, and the defense will try to show that he was wounded at approximately frame 236 of Mr. Zapruder's film, or one second before your photo. So could you have pressed the shutter, released it, just a fraction of a second after you heard the report of a shot that had already impacted?"

"That is certainly possible."

"Nothing further. Thank you."

"Mr. Altgens," Matthews began, "is it possible that your photo was two seconds earlier than you suggest?"

"I don't think it could be that long. In my mind, I heard a report. So it is possible that I opened the shutter at or just after, that sound, but this is what the camera saw. The camera doesn't record two seconds later. Part of a second, a second, depending on the steadiness of pressure on the shutter, and, of course, the distance to the focal source."

"Did you think to photograph the faces on the knoll, to complain that you weren't allowed in such areas?"

"I was getting paid to photograph the President. Nobody knew that faces on the knoll would be the big story."

"I have no further questions."

"If there is no redirect, we will adjourn for lunch and return at one P.M." Judge Davis looked to both attorneys, and hearing no problems with that plan, announced the lunch recess.

Having just orchestrated the largest one-session blitz of witnesses, Barnes sat back and took a few deep breaths once the lunch recess was declared. Oswald was led away, and the judge and jury disappeared. Ray Matthews, looking troubled, left his materials on the prosecution table and strolled over.

"This is getting ugly, Eddie," he said for openers.

"It gets worse, Ray, believe me. This afternoon, for instance."

"Can you say 'who?' "

"Sure. I got the whole Bethesda crew lined up. Not Humes or that ilk, but the gophers, plus some gold braid."

"You are aware that they wouldn't talk to the prosecution in the discovery process, I assume?"

"They wouldn't talk to us, either, so we're both going to be feeling our way in the dark. I can tell you, though, that if they had to sign secrecy oaths, and since virtually none of them testified before the presidential charade, they are *not* going to help the prosecution's case."

"Not in the traditional sense," Matthews answered, "but I've got to tell you, I'm thrilled that your motion to quash did *not* go through. You should probably have won it there, but thank God you didn't, because we would have looked like idiots. Now, your witnesses are making the people who handed us this case look bad, and I'd prefer that to having this stain on my reputation." Matthews paused, and Barnes could sense he was reaching for something.

"Whatever's on your mind, Ray, say it. The jury's not here, the tape recorder's off, and I'm not about to write my memoirs tonight. Sit down. This isn't easy for either of us."

"All right. Twenty-some witnesses from Parkland Hospital all say massive damage to the back of the head. A couple dozen stipulations that shots came from someplace other than the sixth floor window. At least half a dozen witnesses who were braced by phoney Secret Service agents on the knoll. Two presidential assistants riding in the follow-up car who say shots from behind the fence. Eddie, if *one* of those witnesses is telling the truth, then it's conspiracy."

"Do you think one of them is, Ray, or are they all committing perjury?"

"If I was on the jury, I would have bought the testimony of the vast majority. But how do you get fake Secret Service identification?"

Barnes's eyes bored into Matthews's: "I'm sure it's rather easy in MacLean, Virginia."

That gave Matthews much food for thought. "How about what seem to be obviously faked autopsy photos?"

"They were taken at a government hospital, and turned over to the Secret Service undeveloped. The people that took them never verified them, and the doctors, until Humes went to your ranch, never saw them. You know the phrase 'Time heals all wounds'? It could be easily modified to say 'Time can create strange wounds.' "

"It sounds so simple, yet so bizarre," Matthews said with an air of resignation. "I still have to run this case, even if it does suggest conspiracy."

"Suggest?" Barnes asked.

Matthews was lost for words again, so Barnes tried to pick up the thought. "This does a lot more than *suggest* conspiracy, Ray. It shouts it. You've prosecuted enough cases, and I've defended enough to know that even though witnesses may differ slightly in what they saw or heard, sooner or later, a pattern emerges. If it's a bank heist, you get a clear picture of how many robbers were in the bank, which tellers' windows they hit, the doors they went through, and at least the gist of conversation, or what a robbery note said. That's not the case here. Every witness has a different angle. Shot or firecracker? That question alone is fascinating. Some witnesses have said shots, others say firecrackers. To me, they're both right. The firecracker witnesses heard a different weapon fired out in the open. The 'shot' witnesses heard a gun fired in that sixth floor echo chamber. Some say shots one and two were real close; others say two and three. There's more confusion, and both are impossible, at least with the Mannlicher. By the way, Ray, since we're venting here, have you ever worked or fired that relic?"

"I did some tests with a replica. I'm no gun expert, but you don't have to be one when dealing with that thing. I damn near broke my jaw trying to work the bolt quickly."

"So did I," Barnes told him, "and you'll recall that I was a crack shot with the FBI. If they ever handed me that gun on a dangerous manhunt where it was kill or be killed, I'd have given them that gun back along with my badge. I wouldn't put my life on the line with that thing. On the subject of risking your life, let's consider the conspiracy angle."

"You mean who did it?" Matthews asked.

"No, no," Barnes said quickly. "I don't know and I don't want to. But let's suppose that those witnesses you mentioned before were telling the truth, and you've got a conspiracy—something powerful enough to get evidence altered, witnesses scared—you heard those people. What does it tell you about Oswald?"

"I haven't figured him out," Matthews said, with some disgust in his voice.

"Neither have I," said Barnes, "and I don't suspect I'm going to. But just as you wanted to talk logic with Malcolm Summers this morning, consider the concepts of conspiracy, and Lee Oswald, from the standpoint of logic. Somebody—I don't know who—but somebody is powerful enough to create a situation where massive damage to the occipital region of the President's skull comes out as a photo of an untouched occipital region. Would such a group of people leave the key job—that of creating the massive damage with a rifle and bullets—to an insignificant nonentity like Oswald?"

"It hardly seems likely."

"Next question: What is he doing on trial?"

"He was the 'patsy' he claimed to be—"

"Let's go have lunch, Ray. It'll be on me, since you just figured this case out."

An hour later, court reconvened, and before the defendant and jury were brought back, Barnes rose to address the court on the fact that his witnesses for the afternoon, a group of naval personnel from Bethesda Hospital, were subpoenaed but were uncooperative in the discovery process, not from any innate hostility, but because they had been forced to sign documents indicating they could be court-martialed if they discussed any aspects of the knowledge they possessed regarding events at Bethesda on the night of November 22–23, 1963. Barnes also pointed out that there was an irony in the fact that the people who should have known the most, Humes, Boswell, and Finck, were called before the President's Commission and before the current court, and felt able to speak freely, yet the people who scrubbed the President's blood off the floor hours later were required to sign a threatening order of silence.

"Please approach, gentlemen," the judge instructed. "This court will have no trouble getting around any documents these individuals may have signed, but are you both willing to put these witnesses on the stand without prior review of their testimony?"

"The defense will take its chances, Your Honor."

"The prosecution will listen to the testimony and object if necessary, Your Honor, but I think it's necessary to keep this trial moving."

"I agree, and I thank you both for your willingness to proceed, as well as for your absence of attitudes which frequently appear in this courtroom which are best described as childish. You call your witnesses, Mr. Barnes, and I will give each an amnesty for their testimony, such amnesty to cover any contingency except perjury. Understood?"

Both attorneys nodded. Davis ordered the defendant and jury brought in, and Barnes spoke into the microphone to ask to have the *Air Force One* footage prepared.

"With the court's permission, Your Honor, and Mr. Matthews, the witnesses to be heard this afternoon saw the President well after dark on the evening of November twenty-second, 1963, at Bethesda Naval Hospital. In order to understand their perceptions, I would like to introduce depositions given by Doris Nelson, supervisory nurse at Parkland Hospital, and Aubrey Rike, employed by O'Neill's, a company which supplied hearses as well as performed funeral operations in the greater Dallas area. Mrs. Nelson deposed that when the medical work to save the President was stopped, the Secret Service cleared the room of most of the personnel, and she and an orderly were left to tidy up, for want of a better phrase. She cleaned the President's body of some congealed blood, removed his wristwatch and gave it to a superior for forwarding, and then aided Mr. Rike, whose deposition corroborates Mrs. Nelson in this regard, in that the President's body, when cleaned, was placed inside a very expensive coffin. A piece of plastic was placed over the satin lining of the coffin to protect it from being bloodstained in shipment, and the President's body, naked, but with a sheet wrapped around his head to collect blood that was still seeping out, was put into that coffin."

"From there," Barnes continued, "there is a consensus that the Secret Service removed the body, despite the legal protestations of Dr. Earl Rose, coroner for Dallas county, and put the body in the hearse that Rike had delivered the coffin in, drove it, with Mrs. Kennedy and Secret Service agents, to Love Field, where it was immediately put aboard *Air Force One*. Following the swearing in of President Johnson, the presidential jet flew directly to Andrews Air Force Base, just outside of Washington, where the following scene occurred. Could we have that newsreel film clip now, please?"

Everyone in the court watched as *Air Force One* taxied to a halt, a ramp was brought up, and the coffin was removed under the supervision of Kennedy loyalists and Secret Service under the watchful eye of the President's widow and his brother, who had entered the front of the aircraft virtually as it halted. The coffin was then put in a gray navy ambulance, similar to a hearse, and became part of yet another motorcade which wound, for about 50 minutes, to Bethesda Naval Hospital. The clip ended with scenes of that motorcade.

"Defense calls Captain John Stover, Commander of the United States Navy Medical School at Bethesda, Maryland." Matthews, seeing a high ranking naval officer with a lot of gold braid and decorations enter the courtroom, remembered Barnes's warning that the afternoon session was going to get rough.

"Rough," as Matthews thought back three hours later, after Judge Davis had recessed the trial for the day, might have been too harsh a characterization, but "interesting" or "curious" were certainly applicable terms.

During the two-hundred-minute blitz, which was interrupted once when one juror became briefly ill and had to be escorted to the restroom, Barnes put nine witnesses on the stand, from Captain John Stover, Humes's immediate superior at Bethesda, to John Stringer, Floyd A. Reibe, Dennis David, Dr. John Ebersole, Jerrol Custer, Edward Reed, Paul O'Connor, and James Jenkins. These men comprised the lab technicians, the X-ray technicians and radiologist, and the photographers who had been present at the autopsy.

Collectively, the group told a story that added a dimension to the trial record, but did not do much, in the long run, to prove overwhelmingly the defendant's innocence. At the same time, they did nothing whatsoever to prove his guilt, prompting Barnes to think out loud at one point that their inability to add to the evidence against the defendant must have been the reason why they were ordered to silence. Still upset by the government's interference in the prosecution's case, Matthews did not object to the remark.

The nine witnesses were not unanimous in their testimony, and Barnes used the dissimilarities to demonstrate to the jury how perceptions of an event can differ. There was contradictory testimony with respect to the time when the President's body arrived, as some suggested that Mr. Kennedy's remains were in the Bethesda morgue well before the gray navy ambulance, supposedly containing those remains, arrived, while others would have had the court believe that the body was received at the morgue an hour after the funeral motorcade pulled into Bethesda. There was equally contradictory testimony about the kind of vehicle the coffin arrived in, and there was a suggestion that "decoys" had been considered, or used, as there was concern that the large, silent crowd that had gathered at Bethesda would become unruly when they actually saw for themselves the visual evidence of the tragedy that had occurred that day.

There was also confusion, which Barnes knew would not hurt the case, about the coffin itself and the way the President appeared within the coffin, as well as the question of who carried the coffin in and who lifted the President out. Barnes noted for the jury's benefit that, as in the case of famous historical events or extraordinary sporting events, after time has passed, many more people claim to have been present than actually were.

What the witnesses *agreed to* was significant. All who had seen the President were in agreement that there was massive damage to his head, and it was *not* accurately depicted in the photographs and X rays, some of which were being seen for the first time by the personnel involved. There also existed a consensus that there should have been more photos in the collection, that brain photos should have been included, and that the brain was so damaged that it could never have weighed the fifteen hundred grams suggested in the Supplemental Autopsy Report of Autopsy Protocol A63-272.

In separate testimony, there were also several additional damaging suggestions: that the track of the head wound, as seen on the table, strongly suggested a frontal entry and an exit from the rear of the skull, which Barnes noted editorially matched up with the Dallas doctors' testimony; that more lead, considerably more, was removed from the President than the "dustlike particles and two pencil points" that the pathologists had suggested; and lastly, there was a consensus from those who had been present throughout the autopsy, that there was a large group of civilians present, in the spectators' gallery, who, along with both army and navy "brass," were interfering with the process, occasionally suggesting conclusions to the pathologists, and that tempers occasionally flared.

One witness flatly stated there was "White House" interference.

Barnes made a point of asking each witness if they had been deposed by the President's Commission. Each answered a clear "No," although Captain Stover knew he had been mentioned by Commander Humes.

Barnes had wanted to ask if any of the witnesses had been contacted by Dallas authorities, but he decided to save that question for the Dallas authorities.

Matthews, in his cross-examination, made the most of the inconsistencies, suggesting strongly that if the witnesses disagreed so widely on coffins, hearses, and who lifted the President out, how could the jury believe them with respect to wounds, photos, or documents? He knew, when he finished up with the last witness, that he had prevented a rout, and had had a good afternoon—maybe that was Barnes's intention—but he also knew there was a lot more damaging information in the record, and not one syllable of it pointed toward the defendant.

Matthews could also hear himself, in his thought processes, paraphrasing Barnes's lunchtime words: "If one of these people suggest conspiracy . . ."

# Sixteen

Friday, January 22, 1965. The end of the third full week of testimony, and the end of the fifth week of the trial, the first two weeks of which had been occupied with jury selection and procedural matters.

Both attorneys of record were aware of the momentum of the past four days, and where the case was going. Notwithstanding, it was far from over, and there were thousands of words yet to be heard.

Despite Barnes's friendly warning to Matthews that things would take an ugly turn on Thursday afternoon, Matthews, and to a greater extent, his assistants, were struck by the enormity of the testimony from the plain folk at Bethesda who had been sworn to secrecy. Matthews had told his team that they would adjourn to his ranch to discuss it away from the courtroom.

It didn't get any easier once they had a bourbon in one hand, some hot Texas chip and dip in the other, and a fire going in Matthews's fireplace.

The most commonly asked question was best paraphrased as, "Two coffins . . ." a concept that would have seemed ghoulish days before. Another agenda item was whether or not the Bethesda staff could have been lying or confused. Matthews brushed both suggestions aside, saying that nobody is going to confuse the finest coffin money can buy with a tin shipping box, and almost ridiculed the suggestion that as many people as testified to it would be lying. "It's quite possible that our boys, Humes, et al, were on the wrong side of the fence when it came to their testimony," he concluded.

Eventually the testimony sank in, and then they began to grapple with the reality of it, beginning with the obvious postulate that the totality of the bad news they had heard—what the Dallas doctors testified to, what the Dealey Plaza witnesses saw and said, the testimony of solid citizens who saw Oswald where he could not have been, the accumulation of fake Secret Service presence in Dealey Plaza, the Bethesda revelations—none of it, sadly, could be even remotely hung on the defendant. None of it. And they could see no possible way to link the defendant, at this late date, to anyone who had the means to bring about any of those scenarios.

Legally, it was a dead end. If it was not the case of the century, and all three members of the prosecution team wished it wasn't, they were of a mind to go to chambers, vent their collective spleens, and move to dismiss. But they couldn't.

In desparation, Matthews telephoned Barnes, who was surprised by the call. "You said it was going to be ugly, Eddie, but you didn't say how ugly."

"Is this line secure, Ray?" was Barnes's first thought.

"I have no way of knowing," Matthews told him, "and to be honest, I don't give a damn."

"Then neither do I," Barnes assured him. "But as far as this afternoon went, I didn't know exactly what they were going to say. We picked up little bits and pieces of what happened at Bethesda almost by accident. Bob Dean, who has handled more murders than I have, knew there had to be others in the autopsy room. Finding the first was the hard part. Once we found him, he gave us the rest. And the secrecy angle told us *something* was amiss, actually, everything you heard this afternoon, and a whole lot more."

"There's more?" Matthews asked, astounded, and causing

Graves and Vincent to become intently curious, since they could only hear half the conversation.

"There's actually a lot more, but it's not at all relevant in *People* v. *Oswald*."

"This is just unbelievable. How do you figure the public is going to react to this kind of sordid stuff?"

"Well, if the case goes the way it's headed—hell, either way —there will be serialized transcripts in the papers beginning a day or two after the verdict, and it will probably be out in paperback within a fortnight, and when that happens, Ray, I would not want to be any of the following people: LBJ, for one. Earl Warren, or any of his commissioners, J. Edgar Hoover, or Jesse Curry. That lot will take some serious heat, but it will pass, although a grand jury may just be upset at the amount of Texas money spent to prosecute that stooge we're dealing with, and there may just be some obstruction of justice indictments and/or a couple of perjury capers. But don't you worry, Ray. You've done your job, and you'll do it to the end. Nobody will accuse you of anything but giving it your best shot."

"Thanks—but what about your client?"

"He's got another case to deal with, which has some interesting turns to it, but they'll probably get him. But that will be on page five. In the meantime, page one is going to ask the obvious: if it wasn't Oswald in the window, and if somebody was on the knoll, who were they? And who is powerful enough to phony up autopsy records and cover evidentiary tracks the way they've been covered? Did it ever occur to you, Ray, that if Jack Ruby's aim had been a little better . . ."

Matthews finished the thought: "The public would have accepted the official verdict—that Oswald did it alone. And no questions would have been asked."

"Oh, they would have been asked, but down the road a piece. There have already been books written in Europe about this, and some are now in progress here. But every day, the trail gets a little colder. When do you think the American people would have seen the autopsy photos if Jack Ruby had been a better shot?"

"You and I would both be quite old," Matthews answered.

"And so would Oswald's kids," Barnes reminded him.

"You're probably right, Eddie. Meantime, I don't know what you've got for Friday, and I've got no right to ask, but this week has been a nightmare. Any way we can work some stipulations and give everybody's minds, including the jurors, a break tomorrow?"

"That sounds like very good law, Ray. But you're going to have to cut me some slack, because my calendar for tomorrow is not stipulation oriented. I can hunt the stuff up tonight, but the witnesses aren't going to be packed tight in the hall. If we agree to go the stipulation route, then we both have to be of a mind to put some serious material into the record without any shenanigans on either side. I won't go beyond the discovery depositions, and I'll stay within procedural boundaries, if you can keep the objections to a minimum."

"Hang on, Eddie." Matthews quickly pitched Graves and Vincent, and they just as quickly bought in. "Done. See you in the morning."

Twelve hours later, with brisk sunshine making an attempt to melt some lingering snow, Matthews entered the courtroom to find Barnes stirring coffee. "We still have a deal for the day's agenda?"

"We may not go the whole day," Barnes told him, "but this approach may save us a couple of days when all is said and done."

"I like it already," Matthews told him.

The courtroom was quickly populated with the players in the drama, and the judge welcomed and thanked the jury for their "diligent patience" and continued willingness to make sacrifices for the cause of justice.

When Judge Davis nodded to Barnes to begin, Matthews rose, as if on cue, to indicate that certain preliminary witnesses' testimony would be taken by stipulation that day, and that the defense and the prosecution had agreed to stay within the limits of the discovery process as it applied to those stipulations. Matthews asked if it would be possible to have a brief explanation by the judge of the discovery process, to aid the jury in their understanding of events.

"That may be a wise suggestion, Mr. Matthews," the judge commented. "Members of the jury, let me try to explain what

Mr. Matthews just referred to as the discovery process. Recently, oh, as recently as ten years ago, there was virtually no such thing. Lawyers on both sides of the argument would do everything they could do to find witnesses and then keep them all to themselves. This led to some situations in which many, many hours were spent selecting a jury and hearing testimony, only to have the last witness called to testify, and truthfully so, that he and the defendant were five hundred miles from the scene of the crime at the time it occurred. Now that got expensive, and seemed unfair, so we are in the process now of finding our way through the discovery process. In cases over the last few years, each lawyer, such as Mr. Matthews or Mr. Barnes, was required, as they were specifically in this case, to provide the other attorney with a list of names of all the witnesses they intended to call. The idea would be that there would be no surprises, and if there was a witness, for instance, that could prove he was in Hawaii with the defendant, Mr. Oswald, on November twenty-second, that information would save the state of Texas a lot of money."

Davis paused for a breath before concluding. "So you have seen the discovery process at work here. Every witness called by Mr. Matthews before the prosecution rested its case was subject to questioning by Mr. Barnes, and all of Mr. Barnes's witnesses were subject to questions by Mr. Matthews. Now, that does not guarantee that the process works perfectly and perhaps it is not supposed to. If the crime at issue is bank robbery, it is possible that one attorney will ask every witness many questions regarding events *within* the bank, while overlooking the fact that there might have been a getaway car parked right out front, with a driver who could be easily identified. If the other lawyer just happens to ask all the right questions, he has a serious advantage over his opponent in court." Matthews swallowed hard at that part of the explanation.

"If anyone on the jury has any questions about this, please feel free to ask them at this time."

One juror in the back row stood, was recognized, and asked, "Does this mean that the prosecution has asked the defendant all the questions it wants to?"

"Only if the defendant is going to take the witness stand, sir," Davis replied. "And as you know, a defendant in a court in America has every right *not* to be forced to take the witness stand. Are there any other questions?"

There were no further questions from jurors, but the one question asked caused Bob Dean to whisper to Barnes a reminder to "go for a directed verdict." Barnes knew Dean was reading the juror's question as at least one vote for conviction, which was one vote too many, as it could guarantee a hung jury, clearly not a good prospect. Dean and Barnes had communicated, however, without the defendant being aware of their concerns.

"Mr. Barnes?" the judge asked.

"If it please the court, we would like to introduce the testimony of Special Agent Charles Taylor, of the White House detail of the Secret Service, who aided in the inspection of the presidential limousine at the White House garage on the evening of November twenty-second. He noted at the time a small hole just left of center in the windshield."

"So stipulated." Tedious as that line would sound to Matthews by the end of the stipulations, it beat trying to cross-examine witnesses who stuck to their stories, unlike most of the people he had called.

"Towards the same purpose," Barnes continued, we would like to introduce the testimony of Sergeant Stavis Ellis, a Dallas motorcycle officer who was riding flank on the lead car in the motorcade. In addition to deposing that he turned and saw a bullet hit the pavement, Sergeant Ellis told of seeing a bullet hole in the windshield of the limousine at Parkland hospital. He stated that he had no doubts of what it was, and that he could have introduced a pencil into it from the exterior surface and it would have pierced the entire glass into the interior surface. He added, for what it's worth, that while he was making that determination, he was told by a Secret Service agent, identity unknown, that the hole he was observing was not a hole."

"So stipulated."

"Defense offers the testimony of motorcycle officer H. R. Freeman to corroborate the testimony of Sergeant Ellis. Officer Freeman stood right beside the limousine and could have put his finger into the hole, concluding it was obvious to anyone who wanted to see that it was, in fact, a bullet hole."

"So stipulated." Graves, rethinking the decision to go the stipulation route, asked Matthews rhetorically why they were making it so easy. Matthews told him that none of what had been heard hurt their case: "So there's a hole. Who said Oswald didn't make it? On the other hand, do you want a parade of police blue coming in here to testify for the defense?" Graves contented himself with being a spectator.

"On a more sinister and serious note," Barnes said with some gravity, "the defense would like to offer the statement of Edward Partin, a minor functionary in the leadership of the Teamster labor organization who was recruited by the Justice Department, well before November 1963, as an informant. Mr. Partin has deposed that he listened to many outbursts of temper aimed at both John and Robert Kennedy by Mr. James Hoffa, and when he sensed that Hoffa was past the talking stage in his threats, he made his information known to the government, who paid him to report. His reports spoke of Hoffa's discussions of the merits of the use of plastic explosives, as well as the use of high-powered rifles with telescopic sights, adding that the attempt on the President's or the attorney general's life should be made somewhere in the South, where some hate group could take the blame."

"So stipulated."

"In a similar vein, the defense offers the testimony of Jose Aleman, a resident of Miami, and a wealthy Cuban exile, who, like Mr. Partin, offered his services as a government informant, in this case to the FBI. He has told of a meeting held in the Scott-Bryant Hotel in Miami in September 1962, with one Santo Trafficante, reputed mob boss of the Tampa, Florida, area. When the subject of politics arose, Mr. Aleman suggested that John Kennedy had a great popularity and would be reelected. Mr. Trafficante's response was to the effect that Kennedy was not going to make it to the 1964 election because he was, quote 'Going to be hit.' Mr. Aleman reported this conversation, which prompted authorities to question Mr. Trafficante, who claimed that he had meant Kennedy was going to be hit by an earthquake of ballots.

Thereafter, Mr. Aleman had to fear for his own safety, and I would have been concerned for his safety had I been required to produce him. One final note, Mr. Aleman reported that James Hoffa was also a principal in this effort."

"So stipulated."

"Outside of the stipulation, but for the record, Mr. Aleman also deposed that the FBI took no interest in the Hoffa connection when it was brought to their attention."

Barnes didn't know what that would prove, and Matthews knew it couldn't hurt his case, so it stayed in the record.

Barnes then shifted gears: "We would like to introduce at this time a verbatim transcript of a message from *Air Force One*, en route from Dallas to Washington on November twenty-second, 1963. The speaker, who identifies himself, was General Chester Clifton, a presidential military aide. The part of the transmission which bears a relevance on yesterday afternoon's witnesses included the passage, 'This is General Clifton. We do *not* want a helicopter to Bethesda Medical Center. We do want an ambulance and a ground return from Andrews to Walter Reed, and we want the regular postmortem that has to be done *by law* . . .' and here it is obvious that the general was ignorant of both Texas and Federal law, concluding, '. . . under guard performed at Walter Reed. Is that clear?' It is also to be noted that in the history of the 1001st Air Base Wing, which includes *Air Force One*, the comment reads, 'the body of the slain President was removed to Walter Reed General Hospital . . .'"

"So stipulated."

"In yet another area of concern, the defense introduces the testimony of Philip B. Hathaway, who was walking north on Main Street, near Akard Street, a few blocks from the Book Depository at approximately noon on November twenty-second, 1963. He deposed that he clearly saw a very large man, Hathaway himself being six-foot five and two hundred pounds, roughly six-six or six-seven, two hundred fifty pounds, in his thirties, with dirty blond hair worn in a crewcut. This individual was wearing a gray business suit and a white dress shirt, and was carrying a soft, combination leather and cloth gun case which had such substance to it that it convinced Mr. Hathaway it contained a rifle. Mr. Hathaway assumed, based on the size and dress of the individual, that he was a Secret Service agent. For the record, his deposition is also part of Decker 5323, which has been referred to earlier."

"So stipulated."

"The defense would like to add, possibly as corroborative evidence of Mr. Hathaway's observations, the testimony of Ernest Jay Owens, who observed, after the shooting, a heavily built white male, wearing a dark-colored suit, with what he described as a 'foreign made' rifle being carried out of one of the parking areas adjacent to the Book Depository. For the record, there are photographs of the police removing weapons from the Depository, and these were shown to Mr. Owens, and he indicated that what he saw was clearly a clandestine effort to remove evidence by a participant to a crime. In other words, he did not believe he saw police or detectives."

"So stipulated."

"The defense would like to offer the testimony of Dallas Police Captain W. R. Westbrook, who was the officer in charge of the crime scene at the Texas Theater, a location on Jefferson Street, in Dallas, where the defendant was taken into custody. He deposed that he gave orders to his command to take everyone's name, and was subsequently given the name of one individual. For the record, I would like it indicated that Captain Westbrook went on to depose that it is possible he only got one name because everyone else present at the time, some twenty-odd people, were all theater employees. His exact phrase was, 'I'm sure at that time of day you would have more employees than patrons,' clearly no way to run a business, and verifiable by asking the ticket seller how many employees there were and how many tickets had been sold, neither of which was asked. When asked how many names of patrons he had personally taken, the Captain indicated none."

"So stipulated."

"Continuing with events which transpired at the Texas Theater, we offer the testimony of Julia Postal, the ticket seller. She deposed that she saw the defendant pass her location, but not enter the theater. When told by shoe salesman Johnny Brewer that someone suspicious had entered the theater, she called police. She deposed that the police told her he fit the description, but found that odd since she did not recall giving a description. She also deposed that a uniformed officer asked to use the phone in the box office, and though she has no idea who was called, the officer told the party, 'I think we have got our man on both counts.' "

"So stipulated."

"The defense was able to locate four other witnesses to events in the Texas Theater and introduces their testimony at this time. John Gibson, deposed by the President's Commission, indicated that he witnessed the arrest of the defendant from relatively close range, yet no one asked him, or anyone else he saw, for their names or addresses."

"So stipulated."

"The defense would like to add the testimony of Mr. Jack Davis, a theater patron who was eighteen on the day in question. Mr. Davis deposed that he was seated in the right rear section of the nine hundred-seat theater, saw the opening credits of the feature, which were played at one o'clock as near as can be determined, and was 'startled' a few minutes later by a man who squeezed past him and took the seat next to him, behavior he considered unusual in that there were only twenty seats occupied, and hence eight hundred eighty empty. He indicated that this unknown person then repeated the process of moving and sitting directly next to someone else twice, and some twenty minutes later, at approximately 1:35, the house lights went on, and the person who had sat next to him was placed under arrest after a scuffle with police."

"So stipulated."

"The defense would like to offer the testimony of W. H. 'Butch' Burroughs, the concession stand operator of the Texas Theater. Mr. Burroughs deposed that he had heard the doors open at approximately 1:35, but had seen no one enter. He also testified that he saw *the defendant* in the theater shortly after 1 P.M., and was able to place the time because it was 'shortly after the feature started, at 1 P.M.,' and that a few minutes later, approximately 1:15, the man later arrested came to the concession stand and bought popcorn."

"So stipulated."

"Outside the parameters of the stipulation, but for the record, it should be noted that the defendant's landlady on North Beckley was firm in her insistence that the defendant was in her premises slightly before and slightly after 1 P.M. that afternoon, and I am inclined to accept her testimony, which, essentially says that the defendant could not have been near that theater at the times suggested by both Mr. Davis and Mr. Burroughs. Nevertheless, since there have been suggestions of impostiture, it was more for that reason that the testimony was put into the record. This is not to suggest that perhaps the landlady could not have been mistaken by a few minutes, but given that the defendant was seen by police in the Depository, on the second floor at 12:32, it would have been difficult, in the ensuing chaos, to have traveled the distance to North Beckley Street in less time, changed clothes, and so forth."

Barnes looked at his notes and continued, "We would also like to add the testimony of George Applin, theater patron, who volunteered his name and later went to the police department to make a statement. The odd part of his testimony revolves around the defendant's arrest. Mr. Applin, seeing both the defendant and several police armed, was quite frightened, while another patron, quite nearby the arrest scene, watched all of it, totally unfazed, a situation which struck Mr. Applin as extremely unusual, given the tumult of the moment."

"So stipulated."

"The defense offers the deposition of Lieutenant Francis Fruge of the Louisiana state police, who deposed that on November twenty, 1963, he was ordered to Eunice, Louisiana, to interview an individual, Melba Christine Marcades, also known as Rose Cheramie, who, although somewhat confused, gave indications that she had been tossed from an automobile carrying two individuals who were heading for Dallas with the intent of killing the President on November twenty-second. Lt. Fruge took the woman into custody after the shooting, and she repeated the story with a far-more lucid mind-set. Lt. Fruge contacted Captain Will Fritz in Dallas with this information, only to be told Captain Fritz was 'not interested.' "

"So stipulated."

"We would also like to offer the deposition of William Walter, an FBI security clerk in New Orleans, who swore in the deposition that he saw documents, prior to November twenty-second, 1963, indicating that when the defendant was interviewed by Special Agent Quigley subsequent to the altercation in New Orleans, a file check indicated that there was both a security and an informant file on Lee Oswald. Mr. Walter further deposed that the New Orleans office received a teletype labelled 'urgent' and signed 'Director' on November eighteen, 1963, indicating that there was a perceived threat against the President as part of his trip to Dallas, that the threat was posed by a militant revolutionary group, and that all special agents were to seek pertinent information from their informants. The original of this document was destroyed, but Mr. Walter retained a copy if the court is interested."

"Stipulated as to the contents. Waive best evidence."

"We would like to add at this time the deposition of Mrs. Delphine Roberts, secretary to former FBI Chicago Special Agent-in-Charge Guy Banister, now deceased. Mrs. Roberts deposed that she saw the defendant with both Mr. Banister *and* Mr. David Ferrie on numerous occasions in Mr. Banister's rented office space in New Orleans, an area of anti-Castro activity and weapons storage. When Mrs. Roberts expressed a concern about Mr. Oswald's now-famous pro-Cuban leaflets, she deposed, she was told by Banister that the defendant was basically doing what he was told. This deposition, I might add, was corroborated by eyewitness and earwitness testimony of Mrs. Roberts's daughter."

"So stipulated."

"The defense would also like to enter the deposition of Frances G. Knight, head of the Passport Office, who testified before the President's Commission, that there had been no concern regarding the defendant's 1963 application for a passport, which he received in one day, 'Because FBI reports which had come to the Passport Office during his sojourn in the Soviet Union and after, did not indicate that he was a Communist.' "

"So stipulated."

"I would like to offer the testimony of Dennis H. Ofstein, employed at Jaggers-Chiles Stovall at the same time that Mr. Oswald was. Mr. Ofstein deposed before the President's Commission that he met the defendant because they both spoke Russian, a valuable skill at that firm, and although Mr. Ofstein had been trained in Russian at the U.S. Army School at Monterey for one year, the defendant's skills were vastly better. He also gave information that indicated that the defendant had skills in microdot processing, which Mr. Ofstein lacked, but which is an essential skill in the espionage business."

"So stipulated as to the testimony, but not on conclusionary thoughts on skills."

"Analagously, although we have already had reference to the defendant's military record regarding his rifle proficiency or lack of it, based on that record, Lt. Col. Allison G. Folsom testified before the President's Commission that the defendant had taken a Russian test on February twenty-fifth, 1959. Beyond the scope of the stipulation, it should be obvious to all concerned here that such a test is well outside of the perimeters of a private, first class, serving in California."

"Stipulated as to content only," Matthews commented.

"And finally, the defense would like to offer portions of two documents forwarded to the President's Commission by J. Edgar Hoover, Director of the FBI. In CE 2974, it was noted, 'No oil has been applied to the weapon by the FBI; numerous shots have been fired with the weapon in its present well-oiled condition.' In CE 3133, as indicated earlier, it was noted that the weapon in question, CE 139, serial number C2766, emitted no flame when fired, and only 'a small amount of white smoke.' I must add here, beyond the bounds of the stipulation, that Mr. Hoover was subpoenaed to attend these proceedings and has not to this date honored that subpoena, so the material had to be entered into the record in this way, with the particular concern for the statement regarding the oil, which was *not* found on the bag discovered in the Depository, nor on any garments worn by the defendant."

"Stipulated as to the contents of the exhibits."

"In Decker 5323, Deputy Sheriff John Wiseman deposed that he received a photo from Mrs. Mary Moorman, which had the whole of the Book Depository in the background. The photo, he continued, was turned over to the chief criminal deputy of the sheriff's office, Mr. Alan Sweatt."

"So stipulated."

"Also in Decker 5323, Mr. Sweatt confirmed the receipt of the picture, which he then said was turned over to Secret Service Agent Patterson. Beyond the bounds of the stipulation, I would move to admit Decker 5323, CE 2974, and CE 3133, and would add that the aforementioned photos have been subpoenaed but the defense's request has not been addressed."

Matthews accepted the stipulation, and a very curious Judge Davis said a bench warrant would be issued for the photo.

Barnes looked at his watch while Matthews spoke and grimaced that it was barely past ten o'clock, and he had promised to do his best to fill the day with stipulations. Rather than ambush Matthews, he requested a ten-minute recess, which was granted, and went across the aisle to confer with the prosecutor. "I hope I haven't violated the spirit of last night's agreement, Ray, but that's all I could put together with regard to what we discussed. Believe me, there were others, but in fairness, they may need some prodding to get the whole story, and some clearly need cross-examination."

"Who does that leave to fill the next few hours, if I may ask?"

Barnes spoke slowly but deliberately: "Does the name Jesse Curry ring any bells?"

Matthews uttered a one-word expletive, but on reflection, realized that both he and Barnes now had common purpose in discrediting the Dallas police investigation. Barnes, to continue the juggernaut that pointed to his client's lack of guilt as well as in some sinister directions, and for Matthews, to demonstrate that it was the Dallas police, and not he, who were responsible for this hideous miscarriage of justice.

"I don't imagine there's much of a choice, and he should be most entertaining," Matthews added.

"Ray, have you ever been fishing, and you're about to land something big, when a shark comes along and just rips into your catch, tears it all to shreds, and then there's a feeding frenzy?"

"Sure. Why?"

"Because on cross, you're going to be the feeding frenzy." Matthews understood perfectly.

When the jury was returned to the courtroom, Barnes rose and called Dallas Police Chief Jesse Curry to the witness stand. A look of deep concern was evident in the chief's face as he entered the courtroom, having been called by the defense rather than by the prosecution.

"Your Honor, before we begin, I would request the court to designate Mr. Curry a hostile witness."

Davis looked to Matthews, expecting some response, but Matthews had no objection. The judge then asked the attorneys of record to approach the bench. He then specifically asked Matthews if he had any objections to the designation, but Matthews again had none. "This is most peculiar," he commented, looking from Matthews to Barnes.

Barnes then said, "Most peculiar indeed, Your Honor, for the defense to call the chief law enforcement officer of the jurisdiction where the crime occurred. In most cases, the prosecution would call him, but Mr. Curry's performance, as you shall see, made that a difficult option, as his incompetence, as well as that of the department for which he was responsible, make him a vital defense witness. However, he may not be immediately forthcoming—who would be?—so we request the 'hostile witness' designation."

"Return to your places, gentlemen. Inasmuch as there are no objections, Mr. Curry is designated a hostile witness."

"For the record, Mr. Curry, would you please tell the court the nature of your employment on November twenty-second, 1963?"

Curry, nettled by the "hostile witness" tag, replied curtly, "I was then, and am still, chief of police in Dallas, Texas."

"Mr. Curry, *Air Force One* touched down at Love Field at 11:37 A.M. on November twenty-second, and President and

Mrs. Kennedy came down the ramp a few minutes later. Were you present then?"

"Yes."

"What was your job in the motorcade?"

"I drove the lead car. That's something of a confused name for it, because there's a pilot car, which is way ahead of the parade, and then the lead car, which is the first car in the parade."

"Who was in the lead car with you, and where were these passengers seated?"

"I drove, as I indicated. Sheriff Decker was sitting behind me, in the rear passenger seat. Secret Service Agent Lawson was sitting in the front passenger seat, and Agent Forrest Sorrels was seated in the rear passenger seat."

"Was it an open or closed car?"

"Closed."

"For the record, what are the responsibilities of Agents Lawson and Sorrels?"

Curry was slightly surprised that there was not yet a frontal assault by Barnes. "Well, Forrest, that's Agent Sorrels, is the Dallas Secret Service Agent-in-charge. Agent Lawson was the advance man for the President's trip."

"Chief Curry, when the Trade Mart was selected as the site at which the President would speak, and you and those Secret Service agents met and decided on a motorcade route, did you drive the route for Agent Lawson?"

"Yes."

"The entire route, Chief?" Barnes asked with obvious skepticism.

"Well, from the airport, through town, down to the end of Main Street, and from there, I pointed to the freeway and pointed out the road to the Trade Mart."

"So you did *not* take them past the Depository, where the left turn onto Elm Street violates Secret Service regulations?"

"I don't know about Secret Service regulations."

"Answer the question, then. Did you take Agent Lawson, the advance agent for the motorcade, onto Houston Street to where it makes the turn onto Elm in front of the Book Depository?"

"No."

"Where was your lead car when you, or anyone in the vehicle became aware of the gunfire?"

"Almost to the overpass. Not quite there, but very close to
it. The Secret Service—one of them, had just written in his
log, something like '12:35, arrived Trade Mart.' We were literally at the end of the parade."

"From your position, then, where was the area of the picket
fence known as the grassy knoll?"

"Behind us and to our right."

"And where did you think the shots came from?"

"Well, from behind us and to our right. But that doesn't
mean they came from the knoll, either."

"Why don't we let the jury draw the conclusions, Mr.
Curry. My job is to ask the questions, and your job is to
answer them. I realize that's a reversal for you, but we have
time, and you'll get used to it. Now, once the shooting
started, what happened?"

"Well, Sheriff Decker got on the radio and ordered people
into the railroad yards there, and a motorcycle policeman
came alongside us and indicated that there had been
wounds in the presidential car, and within a couple of seconds, that dark-blue limousine came roaring past us on the
right and kept going to the hospital."

"So you were not the lead car anymore?"

"No."

"Did you go to the hospital or remain at the scene of the
crime?"

"We went at high speed to the hospital. I remained there
until I was asked by the Secret Service men, about an hour
or so later, to arrange transport for Mr. Johnson, his wife,
and some of his staff, back to Love Field."

"Was there any police work to do at the hospital?"

"I don't understand."

"That's why you've been designated a 'hostile witness,' precisely because you don't understand. I'm asking you, first, if
there were any suspects or anything of a police nature, with
regard to the crime already done, that you could do at Parkland Hospital?"

"Not really."

"Then why did you go there?"

"Well, we were leading the President, and my concern was for him, the governor, Mr. Johnson . . ."

"I respect your concern, sir, but every minute that you, as Chief of Police, were away from the crime scene . . . were those not *lost* minutes that could never be recovered?"

"Well, I don't know. We had people there."

"Yes. You said Sheriff Decker ordered men into the railroad yards. What did you order?"

"I sent men to the building up at the end of the block."

"Why?"

"I can't say for sure."

"Think hard, Chief. You are the chief of police of a major American city the President is visiting. Shots are fired and it is confirmed that occupants of the car are wounded, possibly worse. Definitely worse, as it turned out. And out of the blue, for reasons you can't explain, you give orders that go counter to orders already issued by the sheriff, and then you leave the scene of the crime to put yourself where you are of no use whatsoever. Or did you think there were assassins lurking at Parkland Hospital?"

"No. I was with the Secret Service. They go with the President. I was driving them, we all went."

"While you were at the hospital, did you make any effort to help the coroner, Dr. Earl Rose, in his efforts to have the President's body autopsied in the proper jurisdiction, that is, in Texas?"

"No."

"Did it ever occur to you as the body was leaving the hospital and being taken back to Washington that you had no legal case of homicide without a Texas autopsy?"

"No. You have to understand. It was a sudden tragedy that no one was prepared for."

"What I understand, sir, is that as chief of police of a large American city, it is *your* job to be prepared for the unexpected. And it sounds like you were not. Could we please have the photo of the swearing in of President Johnson aboard *Air Force One*, please?" Barnes let the chief stew in a moment of silence. "Can you identify yourself in that photo, chief?"

"Yes. I am standing on the left side of the photo with my

face partially obscured by President Johnson's upraised right hand."

"So you are. The question is, what were you doing there?"

"I had driven the Johnsons there."

"That has been established. Once they climbed the ramp, your job as far as their security was at an end. They were on the plane, and so were Secret Service agents, as Agent Lem Johns is visible in the rear of that photo. Were there any suspected assassins on the plane?"

"That's ridiculous."

"I take that as a 'no,' Chief. Nevertheless, your presence is totally unexplained. The President of the United States has been brutally murdered in your city, and there you are, big as life, rubbing elbows with the politicians instead of doing your job, which was directing the investigation of the assassination, to the exclusion of all other duties."

"Captain Fritz's job is the homicide department. He was in charge."

"Chief Curry, understand something. You're on the witness stand in the most important trial to be held in the twentieth century. People are going to talk about this trial, and read about it, for decades. So save yourself a lot of grief and stop trying to make us think that this case was just another homicide, because it was not. For the record, did you fly to Washington aboard *Air Force One*?"

"No. I got off after that picture was made, and I stayed at the airport for an hour or so, then went back downtown to the office."

"The President was shot at 12:30 or 12:31," Barnes said, with obvious disgust in his tone, "and you went to the hospital, did nothing to help your case autopsywise, then performed valiantly as a chauffeur when there were others who could have done the same thing, then you posed for photos, and then you hung around at the airport. What time *did* you get back to your office?"

"About four." Curry was beginning to dislike the sound of his own answers.

"When did you learn of the arrest of the defendant, Mr. Oswald?"

"While I was at Parkland, and the best I recall, it was around one o'clock or maybe a little after one o'clock."

"I owe you an apology, Chief. Here I am, thinking you may well be the most incompetent person ever to be a big-city chief of police, and you knew of Oswald's arrest at one, when he was in fact arrested at nine minutes before two."

"I may have been confused as to the time."

"Which would allow me to think you may also have been confused as to the killer, but we'll let you discuss that shortly. When you finally did return to your office, how would you describe conditions there?"

"Well, City Hall was overrun with the news media."

"As police chief, and with possibly the most important defendant of the twentieth century being held in that 'overrun' building, what did you do about that situation?"

"I didn't do anything." Curry looked down at the floor, and Barnes took his time to phrase his next question, looking over at Matthews in the meantime and noticing that he seemed to be enjoying Curry's discomfort.

"Did you have anything to do with the interrogation of the defendant?"

"No, I did not. I was in the office once or twice while he was being interrogated, but I never asked him any question myself."

"Inasmuch as you chose not to say anything, is that an indicator that you were satisfied with the way the interrogation was being handled?"

"No. There were several people in the office. It seems to me, looking back, that we were violating every principle of interrogation."

"But you did nothing about it."

"Look, there are jurisdictional matters here. Captain Fritz runs the homicide and robbery bureau, and the fact is, it's his castle. There were many things done that I didn't like, and I told them so. They'd get some bit of evidence, and show it off, and Henry Wade—the D.A. would call me and tell me to tell Fritz not to go public with this stuff or the defendant could never get a fair trial. But he persisted."

"I appreciate your candor, Chief. Were any recordings, either electronic or stenographic, made of the questions and answers put to and given by, the defendant?"

"No."

"Why not?"

"We didn't have a tape recorder, and the room was too crowded to fit another person, such as a stenographer in there."

"You're going to make great reading, Chief. Let's change the subject just a bit, and maybe you'll be able to tell us something useful. It's my understanding that the Dallas Police force involves one thousand one hundred seventy-five men. Is that an accurate number?"

"Very accurate."

"Naturally, police work is a seven-day-a-week responsibility, although the men generally work a standard five-day week, is that correct?"

"Yes."

"So approximately two out of every seven of the men would ordinarily have the day off on a given day—a Friday, for instance?"

"That's a close estimate. Not exact, but close."

"So approximately three hundred twenty-nine men were due to have Friday, November twenty-second, off. That leaves eight hundred forty-six men on duty, but with three shifts. That means roughly two hundred eighty-two men on duty at any given time. Was that number augmented by calling in men who were scheduled to have that day off?"

"No. But we beefed up our force by calling in reserves. We were up over four hundred."

"Reserves to guard the President . . . are they armed?"

"Not always. But we tried to take additional precautions and the Secret Service turned us down."

"Tell the court about that," Barnes requested, moving to his favorite space at the far end of the jury box.

"For one thing, we had had many more motorcycles lined up to be with the President's car, but the Secret Service didn't want it that way. We also strongly urged that a Dallas police car be situated between the Presidential limousine and the follow-up car. And I can tell you, they would have been shooting back before the firing ended."

Hearing that response, Barnes looked at the jury and knew this was as good as it would get: the jury saw in one witness the fiasco that had been Dallas on that horrible day. Barnes had about a dozen things he wanted to say about Curry's last answer, but he left them unsaid.

"Chief, earlier you spoke of your frustration with Captain Fritz regarding his willingness to make facts about evidence available . . ."

"It's not against the law."

"Not unless you overlook the constitutional precept that a defendant has the right to a fair trial," Barnes reminded him before getting to his point. "But what I was about to ask you was whether or not you yourself had made statements to the press, which, we understand might have been made during a very difficult time, but, upon the reflection of fourteen months, might not seem as wise. Did you make any such statements?"

"Well, you realize you couldn't even go out in the hall without being bombarded by questions. On occasion or two, I told them I thought it was proceeding very well, that we were obtaining good evidence to substantiate our suspicions that this was the man that was guilty of the assassination."

"It sounds like you just made a statement that would convict a defendant in the press." Barnes intentionally did not phrase it as a question, and had another one ready in case Curry began to respond. Notwithstanding, he thought this would be a good time to request the lunch recess, which was requested and granted. Barnes gave Curry a look that suggested he was in for a long afternoon.

The defense team, as was their habit, ate lunch together, and all agreed that the chief of police of Dallas, Texas, had come as close as humanly possible to making a complete ass of himself, and that it would only get worse. Carolyn Jeffries, who had deposed Curry in Dallas (after having cooled her heels for four hours in his outer office) had told Barnes and Dean that he was a veritable Jekyll and Hyde as far as this case went, and the trick would be to catch him in an unguarded moment. Barnes expected that moment to come that afternoon.

When court reconvened, Oswald told Barnes quietly that he wasn't feeling well. It was nothing major, just that prison food wasn't staying down well when he knew that the case was winding down and his fate would soon be decided. "Your fate won't be decided for two years, junior, so go back to eating. They haven't a prayer of winning this case, and at best an outside shot at a hung jury. That's the worst that can happen, and if it does, believe me, they won't put you through this case again. They'll go for the cop case, and *that* will decide your future. If you win it, you're home free; if you lose, there are appeals, maneuvers, hell—you might even finally loosen up and tell everybody everything you know about that day. If I were you, I would give it some thought. I hope you feel better. Listen carefully to this clown on the stand—maybe that'll cheer you up."

Barnes then returned to the attack. "Chief, before the lunch recess, we discussed a statement that you agreed that you made to the press about having gotten evidence that made the case look solid. Do you remember that testimony?"

"Yes."

"Good." Barnes walked behind the defense table and picked up a newspaper from a stack of several in front of his chair. "Chief, do you recall making a statement about the defendant, quote 'We have heard that he was picked up by a Negro in a car'?"

"Yes. But that proved false."

"I am aware of that, Chief. The taxi driver testified here that he was not a Negro." Barnes put that paper down, picked up a second, turned a couple of pages, then asked, "Did you also make the statement, regarding the rifle in the window, 'I read in the paper where someone said it'?"

"I seem to recall that."

"Do you get all your important evidence from reading newspapers?"

"*You* seem to." Curry chuckled.

"Yes," Barnes agreed, "But I don't arrest people. I defend them because police chiefs read the papers instead of their subordinates' reports."

"I read the reports."

"Did every report you read speak of the gun being an Italian Mannlicher-Carcano?"

"Yes."

"Did you read the reports by officers of the sheriff's department, Deputy Boone and Constable Weitzman, which described the weapon as a seven point sixty-five Mauser, a weapon of German origin, which, according to Weitzman, had a two point five Weaver scope?"

"Those are sheriff department's reports—if Decker sent them over, I read them. But it's not important. There was so much confusion that day that anything could have happened with respect to the guns."

"Could you explain that a little more clearly?"

"I read the reports. I know what they said—Mauser, all that. I know we eventually got an Italian gun. If you are asking me if a German gun was found and we put an Italian gun into evidence, I am unable to say for certain *what* happened."

The court sat in silence. Barnes put the paper down that he had been reading from and removed his glasses for dramatic effect, tossing them on the newspaper pile. The jurors bolted upright, awakened from several days of occasional doldrums. Matthews and his staff wished they had any gun —German or Italian, to use on the witness. The judge looked at Barnes for a repeat of his motion to exclude the weapon, but Barnes, sensing the judge's purpose, gave an ever-so-slight sideways nod of the head, which the judge took to mean, "not yet."

"Chief, are you saying that you are not one hundred percent satisfied that the gun on the evidence table is the gun discovered by the officers at the scene?"

"It's not going to make me popular back home, but I am not satisfied. I never was."

"Were you nevertheless satisfied to charge the defendant with the murder of the President?"

"Again, no. Now understand, I'm not a lawyer. And Fritz was handling the case, and he had a gun, and shells, and the defendant was missing from the building, and the other shooting seemed incriminating, but my problem was, I've got, or rather Fritz has, the defendant, with the entire world watching, waiting for us to tie it up with a ribbon, and we didn't have any proof that the defendant fired the rifle. We never had such proof. We had no witness who was ever able to put the defendant in that building with a gun in his hand."

Barnes gave that statement time to sink in. He then dredged up yet another old newspaper. "Did you also state, to the best you can recall, on Sunday morning, when asked if there were *no* accomplices, 'I would not make that statement'?"

"I didn't rule out accomplices then or now. Hell, your questions about me being on the airplane made me look bad, I know that. But I know police work. And when they got that film developed, that afternoon, and we saw it . . ."

"Which film is that?"

"The dressmaker . . . Zapruder."

"What did the film indicate to you?"

"By the direction of the blood and brains from the President from one of the shots it would just seem that it would have to be fired from the front rather than behind."

Matthews rose and objected that the witness was not an expert on photographic interpretation, and, in fact, his testimony to this point had not demonstrated that he was an expert at anything except delegating important responsibilities to subordinates. Barnes did not contest the objection—the jury had heard it and Matthews had been otherwise very cooperative. It was sustained.

Barnes then removed a bulky, bound stack of typewriter paper from underneath the stack of newspapers. "Chief Curry, I show you what has been represented to the defense as a true and genuine copy of radio logs of Dallas police radio traffic from 12:30 onward, for Friday, November twenty-second, 1963. Would you like to take a few moments to review it so that you can certify that it is, to the best of your knowledge, accurate?"

"I would like a couple of moments."

"Take your time. I want you to be certain." Barnes also wanted the jury to have time to digest the totally shocking revelations of the past few minutes which, to use Carolyn Jeffries's idiom, had probably come from Hyde, not Curry.

"Yes, they seem to be in order," Curry told Barnes.

"If you will work from that copy, Chief, using the tabs on

the indicated pages, the first tab is a transmission that says officer 158 has a prisoner, time 1:12, and he is taking him to the downtown jail. Who would that prisoner be?"

"I have no idea. I assumed it was Oswald. He was arrested when?"

"To the best of my knowledge, and Mr. Matthews may contribute if he has any information, but my understanding is that Mr. Oswald was arrested, as I stated to you earlier, at 1:51—nine minutes before two. So this is a different prisoner, and I am sure the jury would like to hear the details of the arrest."

"I am not sure."

"Referring to the page with tab number 2, there is a transmission that an officer has a drunk wearing a loud colored jacket who matched the description. Chief, everyone in this court is aware of how easy it is to fake being drunk. Many people, in fact, are very good at faking sobriety when they are drunk. Any comments about this individual?"

"I have no knowledge of this individual."

"Tab number 3; there is a transmission, time 1:35—that's one hour and five minutes after the shooting, 'The building is being secured now.' Any comments about that?"

"That's been a constant mystery. There were officers who said they sealed off the building quickly, but there were reporters and God knows who else in and out of that building, just like they were at City Hall."

"Chief, in the confusion you just described, we know Mr. Oswald walked out of the building. Would you allow for the possibility, based on that transmission, that other person or persons involved in this crime could have made a getaway in the confusion?"

"It seems possible to me."

"Tabs 4 and 5 are of curiosity value. Number 4 tells that the governor's wife was being flown in to be by his side—a curiosity in that she was next to him when he was wounded in the limousine. Number 5 tells of a surgeon being flown in from Galveston, and there's not another scrap of paper on this planet that I've seen about that. And it certainly wasn't for the President."

"No, he was shot up pretty bad."

"Yes he was. Tab number 6, Chief, tells of three men in the Braniff area at Love Field—suspects being brought in. Know anything about them?"

"No. You might ask Fritz about them, though."

"Be assured I will. In the meantime, I thought I'd ask his boss. Tab number 7 is a transmission instructing an officer to hold the presidential cars for fingerprinting, but the reply came back that they were already gone. Now, in examining another witness, I questioned the haste of the departure of those vehicles, and I still do. But what, if you know, would have been learned by fingerprinting those cars? It's very clear who was in them. Was there any suspicion of an assassin being secreted in the cars?"

"I must tell you that transmission makes absolutely no sense to me either."

"Chief, since somebody thought they had value as evidence, did you ever demand, or even make an attempt to have someone from your office see those cars?"

"No."

"Tab number 8 is a call in to dispatch for a wrecker for, quote, 'The suspect's car.' That man seated over at the defense table never owned a vehicle in his life, and when given the chance to learn how to operate one, did a lousy job of it. So what is this about?"

"I don't know."

"Tab number 9, which suggests—strongly suggests—that at least one idiot was using the radio that day, time 12:51, asks if the President was still planning to go to the Trade Mart. Could anyone in police authority still be ignorant of events at 12:51, when the President was in his agonal moments and the best equipment available was barely detecting an electronic suggestion of a heartbeat?"

"I don't know what that's about, either."

"Tabs number 10 and 11 mention vehicles. Ten tells of a 1957 Chevy Sedan, license NA 4445; 11 speaks of a white and green 1957 Ford, Texas plate DT 4857. Does your department have any records on the drivers, or owners of those vehicles?"

"Not to my knowledge. Fritz or the highway patrol might know."

"Tab number 12 raises the problem of building security again, as it indicates that an officer was needed at the rear of the Texas School Book Depository."

"Like I said, confusion. That's all I know."

"Do you understand now, Mr. Curry, why I was so insistent in asking if you made a good judgment in choosing to go to the hospital instead of remaining at the scene?"

"Yes," Curry said quietly.

"Your Honor, I would like CE 705, the radio logs, admitted as evidence, and would request a fifteen minute recess to give the witness a moment."

"So moved on both requests."

Bob Dean was out of his seat as soon as the jury filed out, and was insistent that the defense team have a quick huddle, absent the defendant, somewhere where they could talk. They left the courtroom and went to the far end of the center hall, where Dean aired out his agenda: "This is it, Eddie. Curry just forfeited the whole prosecution case. What have you got left to ask him?"

"Well, we've got the names of a few people who were arrested that day, and I think I can show that he has no knowledge of them, and then I'm fairly sure we can get him to testify that the Feds wanted the evidence, even though they had no jurisdiction. Besides that, he'll probably trip over his own tongue a few times at random."

"Eddie," Dean started slowly, in very clipped tones, "Carolyn and I were whispering down at our end, and we're convinced that when you finish with Curry, you get the gun kicked, then you rest the case. I know we haven't gotten to the photo or acoustic experts, but they deal with evidence pointing to the Depository and elsewhere. Curry has just said the gun was a hoax, there was no real case based on the absence of witnesses, and he's proved that the Dallas police were totally incapable of making a provable case against anyone, including the defendant. The jury won't convict now under any circumstances, and if the gun is excluded, you go for a directed verdict from the judge. He might strenuously object to putting that onus on himself, but what choice does he have?"

"None, really," Barnes said, thinking out loud. "Look at it

this way. . . . If the gun is excluded, and for good measure we'll ask Curry which of his men went along with it with Vince Drain, the answer of course being nobody, but if the gun is excluded, what could the judge possibly say to the jury in his charge to them? In order to find the defendant guilty, since there is now no gun, no shells, no bullet, you must be convinced in your mind that the President was killed by the defendant secreted in another location, with a different weapon, and different bullets."

"It's a dead end, Eddie," Jeffries said. "He can give us the directed verdict, or he can charge the jury to bring such a verdict in, which is his only other choice, but more sensitive legally, or, he can let them go, and if they bring back any verdict besides innocent, he can overturn it. But that is also sensitive. The directed verdict is his out. It may not be popular, but when the public reads the transcripts, and believe me, *they will*, they will see the charade that this case was."

"You are both right, of course. It just seems a shame that there is so much more we could put into the record. If we go this route, it will end, possibly as soon as tomorrow. If we keep going, the jury will put Curry's devastating testimony somewhat aside, and it will be slightly more difficult. But anything we can add from here on out might help that poor slob of a defendant in the other case . . . assuming of course that's our purpose. He may just have to take the heat on the policeman, and that's not our problem."

Dean looked Barnes squarely in the eye. "Eddie, we may have to put together a closing argument tonight. Allow for the possibility that the defendant is not as guilty as the police made him out to be, and not as innocent as we'd like the jury to think. He didn't run out of that building, and go home for the pistol so he could avenge the President's murder. He's part of this, somehow."

"We've all known that from day one—but given what we've learned about the Dallas p.d., is it possible that he shot the cop in self-defense?"

Carolyn Jeffries seemed surprised by that theory, but not Dean. "It is very likely that it was self-defense. But that's not related to our case. We're on the one-yard line with two minutes to go. Why go back to midfield just to show how great our offense is? Go for the win now. Today."

"Let's go do it," Barnes agreed.

"Your worries will soon be over, kid," Barnes told Oswald when he returned to his seat. Oswald seemed surprised, but did not ask a lot of questions. Chief Curry and the jury returned to their places and the judge nodded to Barnes to continue his examination.

"Chief Curry, when you were subpoenaed to appear at this proceeding, you were also legally requested to bring with you certain documents. Did you bring them?"

"They were not available. I don't recall specifically what was called for in your evidence subpoena, but I had my staff look everywhere, and nothing was found."

"We'll get back to that in a moment. In the meantime, for the record, in whose jurisdiction did the murder of the President of the United States occur?"

"Dallas, and, of course, by extension, Texas."

"So it was *not* a federal crime?"

"Absolutely not. But that didn't stop the FBI and the Secret Service from climbing all over us and insisting that they get their hands on the evidence. And, of course, as you probably know, by about midnight, Friday night, we agreed to let the FBI have all the evidence. There was pressure, you see. Nobody was telling us who was behind the insistence that the government get the evidence, but it was obvious it was someone in high authority."

"Objection. Conclusionary."

"Your Honor," Barnes countered, "we've already heard testimony by the attorney general for the state of Texas, Mr. Waggoner Carr, who told the court that he received calls from the White House, on November twenty-second, directing his office as to how the indictment of the defendant should be worded. If this witness was privy to that series of events, his testimony is valid, or at worst, hearsay."

The judge swiveled to look at the witness. "Chief Curry, did you have personal knowledge that pressure was being brought to bear from official circles in Washington, D.C.?"

"I was constantly aware of the pressure. I do not know

which specific official circles it was, but Washington was putting the heat on us."

"The objection is overruled."

"Chief, when the Mannlicher-Carcano rifle was removed from your jurisdiction, taken to Washington, and returned twenty-four hours later, what members of your department accompanied that evidence?"

"Nobody. The FBI didn't want it that way, and given the way they wanted to dominate the case, the last thing on our minds was to insist that we get in their way."

"Chief, when you turned over evidence to the federal authorities, can you tell this court that you received all of it back?"

"I can tell you we did not."

"Getting back to my questions about the subpoena, do you know who Jack Lawrence is?"

"No."

"Donald Wayne House?"

"No," Curry said slowly.

"William Sharp?"

"No again. I'm sorry."

"Perhaps I can refresh your memory, Chief. Jack Lawrence was arrested in Dallas, Texas, in connection with the assassination of President Kennedy. Donald Wayne House was the driver of one of the vehicles I mentioned when we were talking about the radio logs. He was arrested in Fort Worth at approximately 2 P.M., and Secret Service agents Roger C. Warner and James H. Howard left their guard posts at Air Force One to question him. William Sharp was arrested by uniformed Dallas officers and turned over to Detective James Leavelle. Could we have Leavelle Exhibit A, please?"

The exhibit came up more quickly than some had, and Barnes gave Curry a minute to look at it.

"Let's examine this portion here, Chief. 'The uniform officers came up with a white man named William Sharp of 3439 Detonta, who the officers said had been up in the building across the street from the Book Depository without a good excuse. I took charge of this man and escorted him to the sheriff's office, where I placed him with other witnesses.' Chief, this individual clearly sounds like a suspect, yet he was placed with 'other witnesses.' What kind of police procedure is that?"

"Lousy. But he was taken to the sheriff's department, and I have no knowledge of that."

"Do your two departments communicate?"

"Not always, which I guess is obvious."

"Very obvious," Barnes echoed. "Do you know who Jim Braden is?"

"Yes. Now I know who he is. He was pointed out by employees in another building down in the plaza there, as not belonging there, and he was brought in, but he had no arrest record, so he wrote a statement saying he went into the building to use the phone, and he signed it and was released."

"How was it ascertained he had no arrest record?"

"To the best of my knowledge, the name Jim Braden was checked, and it came up clean."

"Was he fingerprinted?"

"I don't believe so."

"I don't believe so, either, Chief, as a fingerprinting of Jim Braden would have revealed that his real name was Eugene Hale Brading, that he had a record of thirty-plus arrests, and that he was visiting Dallas, on November twenty-first and twenty-second, oddly enough, with the permission of his California parole officer. So that's who Jim Braden is."

"That one got by us, I guess."

"Could we have the photos of the transients taken off the train, please?" For the next few minutes, several pictures, showing three men, very casually attired, being equally casually guarded by police, were exhibited. "Chief, have you seen these pictures before?"

"I think so."

"Do you know what they depict?"

"The three civilians, more or less in line, were seen getting into a boxcar back there in the freight yards off to the side of Dealey Plaza. The tower man for the railroads notified police, and we took them in."

"For what?"

"Questioning. See if they knew anything about the shooting, or if any of them had a record. That kind of thing."

"Look at the photos again, Chief. The individuals are not handcuffed, and the police—two of them, which would have allowed three defendants to run away, with guaranteed success for at least one, are carrying their scatter guns very casually."

"That is apparent."

"Who were the three men?"

"I have no idea."

"Who were the three suspects captured in the Braniff area of Love Field later in the day?"

"I have no idea."

"Mr. Curry, the defense has asked you about ten people—Lawrence, House, Sharp, Braden, the three transients, and the three people at the airport. We know from testimony that Wesley Frazier was briefly a suspect, and that Roger Craig apprehended a female individual who disappeared. That's a dozen people, chief. Now you've sat here and told us that the gun might well be a fake, and you had no witnesses to the shooting. Wasn't there any thought about finding out who those dozen people were? You sure covered the defendant's life in minute detail."

"The others told their stories and were released. The defendant, I have to tell you, made me think he had been trained in interrogation techniques and resisting interrogation techniques."

"Yes, but by whom? Well, you would have no way of knowing that, since you didn't ask him any questions that he could avoid. Could we please have CE 5, please?"

A grainy photograph of a large but ramshackle-looking residence came up on the screen. In the foreground was a 1957 Chevrolet with the license plate removed. "Chief, have you ever seen this photo before?"

"Yes. I saw that picture when it was brought in after the search of the residence where the defendant's wife was residing. We identified it as the residence of General Walker."

"Chief, is that picture that you see identical in every detail to the one you saw 'when it was brought in'?"

"Actually, no. In that picture there, the license plate is missing on the auto, like it's been cut out. When I first saw that picture, the license was there. Whether or not it was readable, I cannot say. But it was there. The rest of the details look all right."

"Chief, if I told you that at least three of your officers testified before the President's commission that the photo you see was missing the license plate when it was found, what would you say?"

"I'd ask you for their names and bring them up on charges. That plate was there."

"Chief, I have one final question for you, and it involves facts of which you cannot have knowledge because they occurred in this courtroom. The evidence seized at the Paine residence, which included that photo, was excluded from evidence. So were the bullet shells found in the southeast corner window on the sixth floor of the Book Depository. So too was the whole, pristine bullet which allegedly caused multiple wounds to both the President and the governor. Your testimony regarding the possible, well, let's be kind and say 'confusion' about the rifle, plus your testimony that none of your men accompanied it to Washington, may guarantee that it, too, is excluded as evidence. Now chief, if you had no gun, no bullet, no shells, and no evidence seized at the defendant's residence, would you have filed for an indictment against this defendant?"

"Objection. Calls for a conclusion."

"Save it, Mr. Barnes," the judge told the defense attorney. "I have to overrule that one, Mr. Matthews—this man's job is to make decisions as to who is charged and who is not. He will answer the question. Do you want it repeated, sir?"

"That won't be necessary. Without the items suggested, and as I indicated my own troubling concern for a lack of a witness earlier, there certainly would not have been any filing."

"Thank you, Chief. You have been most cooperative, and I regret the 'hostile witness' designation. I—excuse me. I said that was my last question, but I have one more for you, and then I'll let Mr. Matthews speak with you. A little while ago, we reviewed the radio logs. Conspicuously absent from those logs is any hint that there was ever any communication such as, oh, 'Post men at the bus depots,' 'Cover the airports,' 'Set up roadblocks on major roads leading out of town.' There just isn't a hint of that, Chief, and it almost sounds like the people who did not do that—your department—it almost sounds like they knew they were magically going to catch the one and only one assassin somewhere in town before he tried to get away."

Curry interrupted before Barnes asked about such a scenario. "If you're going to ask me if such ominous radio silence means what you are suggesting, I'll tell you now that I will not deny it as a possibility. It certainly should have been done. It is done in cases—well, hell, every other case is far more routine than this one—and it is done then. Answer your question?"

"Yes, it does. Thank you, Chief. Mr. Matthews?"

Matthews remained seated, as was his wont with a witness for whom he had nothing but contempt. He would have liked to skewer the man most responsible for handing him, as Barnes had said in his opening to the jury, "an outline of a case," but he still had a job to do. "Chief, is it possible that those twelve other people who were picked off the streets or grabbed out of boxcars were just bystanders and did not, in fact, have anything to do with the shooting?"

"It is possible—entirely possible," Curry said, looking across the court to Matthews. "But you must understand, I say that without full knowledge of those individuals, as some were already gone by the time I got back, and some were taken to the sheriff's department, and I have no control over what happened there."

"Chief, did you have any prior indication that there was going to be an attempt on the life of the President, the governor, or, later, the defendant?" Matthews knew Barnes could object to his three-part question, but he knew Barnes wanted to hear the answer.

"As to the President, we had some previsit nuisance reports, but no threats of violence. We also knew that one potential problem, General Walker, was out of the city. There was no information of any sort that there could have been a problem of a security threat posed against Governor Connally. As far as the defendant, well, we got some crank calls, but nothing that posed a serious threat." Barnes began making notes when he heard that last answer.

"Mr. Curry, did your department ever establish a link, or a tie, between the defendant and any of the other principals named in this case, or between Mr. Ruby, the defendant's convicted attacker, and any principals in this case?"

"No tie was established between the defendant and anyone except the Frazier fellow who drove him to work, and I truly believed my officers overreacted in that case. There was no connection between Ruby and anyone, either. I am quite sure he was not acquainted with Officer Tippitt."

"Chief, the defense attorney asked you whether or not you would file for indictment under given circumstances, and you said you would not. Yet you did file on this defendant, so you must have had cause. Am I correct?"

"Not completely. Like I said, I'm not a lawyer. It was the responsibility of the district attorney to make such decisions, and he did. And Fritz was the one that would have said that the evidence was there or it wasn't. I've already told you about my concerns, and they were genuine. But we were under immense pressure, and that's all I can say. We had to indict somebody."

"Absolutely nothing further." Matthews didn't even bother to thank the witness.

Curry started to rise, but Barnes was quicker. "Chief, you testified that there were no threats against the defendant. One of the officers has testified before the President's commission that there was a serious perceived threat received in the early hours of Sunday, November twenty-fourth, the day of the attack on the defendant, and that he tried for three hours to reach you, even to the point to getting the phone company to check your line, which, it turned out, was off the hook. Is that good police work in the middle of an investigation of the murder of the President?"

"No, I must confess it is not. I regret it."

Barnes then approached the witness with four sheets of lined yellow paper, each of which had a name at the top. "Chief, do you know who Clyde Haygood, D.V. Harkness, Marrion Baker, and Joe Marshall Smith are?"

"Of course I do, so no tricks, young man. They are officers —or should I say that men with those names are officers of

the Dallas police force, and they were all either in the motorcade or in Dealey Plaza on the day of the assassination."

"That is absolutely correct, Mr. Curry, and there were no
tricks. Now that we have established that you know these
men, would you take these four sheets of paper, each of
which contains one of those names, and with this pen, please
write down the names of all their acquaintances?"

"What?" Curry asked, sitting bolt upright.

"Write down the names of those officers' acquaintances,"
Barnes repeated. Matthews wanted to object, but he knew
Curry's earlier answer about Tippitt would be considered
foundation.

"I don't understand what you're getting at."

"Just this, Chief. A few minutes ago, you testified that you
were quite sure that Ruby was not acquainted with Officer
Tippitt. Now, that suggests one of three things: one, that you
know all the acquaintances of a slimy, mob-connected thug
named Jack Ruby, which would be out of place for a chief of
police; second, there is the suggestion in your statement that
you know all your officers and all their acquaintances; or
third, that you know some of your officers and all their acquaintances. Now, you've testified that you know the men
whose names are on those papers. Please either write the
names of all their acquaintances, and demonstrate to this
court that you could honestly say that Mr. Ruby was not
known to Mr. Tippitt, or else let's straighten out the record
on that matter."

Curry pushed the papers and the pen back toward Barnes.
"I don't know who knows whom. On the other hand, I had no
proof that Ruby and Tippitt were connected."

"Chief, you've told us you doubted the veracity of the rifle
on the sixth floor, and you had no witness whatsoever, so it
could be said that you, or your department, had no evidence
concerning the defendant, yet here he is. This suggests odd
behavior on your part, or on the part of Captain Fritz. Either
way, unless Mr. Matthews has further questions, you are excused."

Barnes returned to the defense table, dropped the papers
on the table, and stood behind it, leaning on the table. A few
minutes of silence gave Judge Davis the message that a mo-

tion was coming, and he directed Carson to remove the jury. Barnes then repeated his motion to exclude the weapon, based on the open testimony of the chief of police that a switch was a realistic possibility, as well as his corroboration of earlier testimony that there had been no jurisdictional officer accompanying the weapon when it went to Washington.

"Mr. Matthews?"

"If it please the Court, Your Honor, while recognizing the obvious concerns entered into our record by Chief Curry, it still remains that counsel for the defense stipulated that the defendant purchased an Italian carbine, serial number C2766, and that same gun appears now on the evidence desk with Carl Day's mark on it. Yes, we have heard talk and seen documents about a Mauser, and yes, the FBI removed the weapon, on its own, for twenty-four hours. But when all is said and done, there sits an Italian carbine, serial number C2766, with Lt. Day's mark still on it."

"Mr. Barnes?"

"Your Honor, counsel for the prosecution has just made a most cogent presentation, and under ordinary circumstances, it would perhaps carry reasonable weight. But these are *not* ordinary circumstances. From day one, we have seen a pattern of official ignorance, contempt, and abuse of the principles of evidence. Witnesses' statements were altered to fit a seemingly preordained scenario—as just established by Mr. Curry's acknowledgement that in spite of the savagery that occurred in Dealey Plaza, there were insufficient precautions taken with respect to sealing the building as well as the surrounding city. Evidence was given to the police and it disappeared, as in the case of several key photographic pieces, and bone fragments. Other evidence was treated improperly and rightfully excluded. Other witnesses came forward with stories—even the presidential assistants in the follow-up car, and they were told that their observations did not match up with the official story, and the family's pain was so great. . . . Two dozen certified medical people at Parkland Hospital, simply doing their jobs and stating their observations, as well as almost a dozen support people at Bethesda, mostly the same kind of honest folks, had their entire perspective on the case destroyed when shown one photo of the back of the President's head, which was *totally* at odds with the recollection of more than three dozen witnesses."

Barnes paused, head down, then looked the judge squarely in the eye: "In such circumstances, Your Honor, it is very easy to see how the single most important remaining piece of evidence, that rifle, C2766, designated CE 139, could be tainted without anyone giving such an illegal and deceitful act a second thought. Given that no oil was found, nor any hint or proof that the rifle was fired, nor any eyewitness that identified that rifle, or even saw a telescopic sight on the rifle seen in the window, added to the fact that the FBI could not make the gun work properly without correcting the faults that existed for a left-handed sighted gun, further questions are raised about its pedigree. Add to that the testimony of Boone, Weitzman, and Craig, and the reports typed subsequently, which included the wrong calibers, ranging from seven point sixty-five to six point twenty-five, and then considering that there has been no corroboration that Lieutenant Day did, in fact, mark the weapon at 1:22 when found in the Depository, nor did anyone else mark it, the defense still believes it is the obligation of this court to exclude this piece of evidence."

"If we are agreed that we will be holding a session tomorrow, Saturday, as suggested, I will have a ruling on that motion prior to any testimony tomorrow. Carson, please bring the jury back in so we can conclude what remains of the afternoon. Mr. Barnes, will the remainder of the afternoon's agenda take long?"

"I do not believe so, Your Honor." Barnes then conferred with Dean and Jeffries, asking whether, if he rested the case right now, he could go for a directed verdict, or would that put additional pressure on the motion to exclude? Dean felt the motion to exclude would carry, giving the judge no choice but to issue the directed verdict. Jeffries agreed.

With the jury seated, Barnes looked at his watch—3:29 P.M. of January 22, 1965. Time was about to be suspended.

"Mr. Barnes?" the judge asked, slightly impatiently.

"Your Honor, the defense . . . rests." Dean had been looking over at the prosecution table to gauge their reaction, and it looked like someone had attached powerful electrodes to the three chairs. Carolyn Jeffries had been deputized by Dean to watch the jury, while Barnes watched the judge's reaction. Davis showed no surprise, being the courtroom veteran that he was. The jury was amazed, with several members breaking into mild grins, and the collective being visibly energized, as if their ordeal was nearing its end.

"Mr. Matthews, does the prosecution plan to offer any rebuttal witnesses?"

"Could we have a moment, please?" Matthews answered.

The prosecution team was clearly not ready for what Curry had said, but since he said it, they understood why Barnes cashed in his chips with good cards still to be played: Curry had tied it all up in a pretty ribbon, and probably to cover his own ass. It might cost him his job, but he would avoid jail with his candor. As far as rebuttal witnesses, there was talk of trying to corroborate Day's mark on the gun, and even of trying to find some of those dozen "defendants" and trying to weaken the defense case through their statements. Eaton Graves put it all on the line to Matthews: "Before we consider rebuttal witnesses, who can Barnes put on?"

"How many witnesses are still left on his discovery list?" Matthews asked, knowing the answer would be large.

"Well over one hundred," Earl Vincent answered.

"And who is the biggest name on that list?" Matthews continued.

"John Connally, who insists he was *not* hit with the shot that hit Kennedy," Vincent added, with a sense of finality.

"Still want to rebut?" Matthews asked, rhetorically.

Silence was his answer. "The prosecution does not plan to offer rebuttal witnesses, Your Honor."

"Then we will adjourn until nine A.M. tomorrow," Davis announced, "and we will have an answer to defense's motion, and we will begin closing arguments. Court is adjourned."

As the jury and the defendant were led out, Barnes approached the bench and asked the judge for five minutes in chambers with the prosecution present. Davis agreed, and Barnes went to inform Matthews, who was in ill-humor because he had spent his day giving stipulations and then listening to the Dallas police chief worm his way off the hook and forfeit the case. Barnes, sensing Matthews's discomfort, assured him, "Ray, I didn't know Curry was going to mistake the witness stand for the confessional. Carolyn deposed him, and he stonewalled her in Dallas."

"He pulled the same stunt with Earl," Matthews answered. "Too busy, too much crime, not enough money or men, the old police chief's lament," he concluded.

"Ray, if I had known what he was going to say, would I have held him for today?"

"No. But you have to admit, he made a great final witness for the defense."

"He did that. Come on, I've got to run something by Davis that you need to hear."

Barnes came right to the point in chambers. "Your Honor, with both sides rested and no rebuttal, we have to face the possibility that these proceedings could end very quickly. We've been behind closed doors for a month. Perhaps the bench should give some thought to inviting selected press officers, at least to be on hand if needed."

"I don't want a circus, gentlemen," Davis warned.

"None of us do," Matthews agreed. "But, in the interest of fairness, perhaps one representative from the big three networks, and one from UPI and one from AP. Five people, kept in the corridor until needed, should not make a circus, and will certainly be a way to release a story that has to come out sooner or later."

"But how do we keep it to five once I pick up the phone?" Davis asked.

"Tell each executive to keep it private, and if there's a crowd around the building, or any such, then nobody gets in. That would convince me."

"It's hard to believe we're almost done, Ray, Eddie, and since we may not spend a lot more time together, I must again compliment you both for your conduct, dedication, and labors over the last month. When the history of this case is written—I don't mean what we'll all be reading in the papers about two hours after the verdict—but when all the noise settles down, I think the public will be grateful to all of us, and will obviously see the wisdom of the change of venue. Well, you've got statements to prepare, and I've got phone calls to make. We're almost home. Thank you, gentlemen."

Matthews related the gist of the chambers discussion to Graves and Vincent, concluding, "Now I've got to write a closing argument; anyone have an index card?"

Across the table, the success of the defense's efforts was obvious by the division of labor. Barnes told Bob Dean, who would host the evening's efforts, that a lot of coffee would be required, and that Carolyn would prepare an outline of the opening arguments, to be used at closing, Dean would outline the prosecution's case in the same way, and Barnes would go through the defense's case. "We've got a long night, but in twenty-four hours, with a little luck, we might be done."

# Seventeen

Saturday, January 23, 1965. The start of a normal winter weekend for most Americans, but quite possibly a momentous day for the participants in *The People* v. *Lee Oswald* being conducted in Lubbock, Texas.

Barnes had slept five hours, which was more than he had expected, because the work of putting together a closing argument had been in the capable hands of Bob Dean, who had prepared a summary of the pluses and minuses of each witness as he testified, and each exhibit as it was introduced. Barnes, then, merely had to consult and do some sorting. Still, five hours sleep on Dean's couch was not to be confused with "a good night's sleep." However, it was better than Carolyn Jeffries had done, as she had curled up under a comforter in Dean's recliner, and could hear Barnes snoring and talking in his sleep in the next room. Besides, this was an adventure to her. When she told Barnes, at breakfast, about the racket he had made during the night, Barnes told her he was sorry, "And don't tell my wife."

"I'm sure she already knows, Eddie."

"Of course she does. But what will she think if she hears it from you?"

It was reassuring, upon arrival at the courthouse in Dean's car, that there was no mob outside, but there were a couple of extra cars in the lot. Once inside, there were five individuals already in the corridor, and each introduced himself and asked questions. Barnes, speaking for the defense trio, was direct: "Gentlemen, we've come too far to break silence now. I will be happy to give you a statement and answer *every* question you have, as I am sure Mr. Dean and Miss Jeffries will, but only when the proceedings are concluded, and no, I can't even speculate when that will be. When it happens, I will keep my promise to you. Thank you."

Inside the courtroom, Barnes's first concern was what Matthews looked like, and he looked well rested and relaxed, a sign that perhaps he had not burned the midnight oil for too long. In fact, he hadn't. Assuming the gun would be excluded for all the reasons Barnes had suggested, plus what were now becoming Matthews's own suspicions about something being rotten in Denmark, he knew he had no case. What could he say to the jury to get a conviction? Trust me, he did it? The chief justice believed it, so you should? Let's not acquit and upset the apple cart? All of those scenarios sounded too much like the official version, so for his closer, he simply planned to walk to the jury box, admit that his case, or what he had been presented as a good case, had been tainted, and that each juror should vote his mind with the idea of justice guiding him. He might get one vote for a hung jury, but he doubted it.

The judge and Carson appeared promptly at nine, and called the attorneys—not just the attorneys of record—into his chambers. Carson was the last one in, and closed the door.

"Gentlemen, and Miss Jeffries, first of all, there's no steno here, so what is said in here today is off the record, unless we have been rebugged, which I doubt, since my bulldog bailiff over there has had the place swept twice daily. From now until we walk out into that courtroom, you may speak your minds free in the knowledge that your comments will *not* be transcribed into the official record, nor will they appear in my memoirs. Naturally, I cannot make that promise about each of you. For all I know, Carson is working on a book about famous doors he's opened." That comment broke the ice and tension, at least a little.

"We have before us a motion to exclude the rifle," Davis said, with an ominous sigh that indicated a weariness on his part. "This motion was introduced before, and at that time I was inclined to grant it, but it would have effectively ended the case. For that reason, and to allow further opportunity to bring the whole case before the world, there was an unspoken consensus that the defense would drop the motion, just as the motion to quash was dropped, or at least put in abeyance." Davis paused and looked around for comment, but he clearly still commanded everyone's attention.

"I can assure you all," he went on, "that the rifle out there has given me many problems. If I were still on your side of the bar, lady and gentlemen, I would not want to go within two states of a case that rested on that gun. Through no fault of yours, Ray, and I truly do not want you to take these remarks personally—you didn't find the gun—but we are essentially asked to take that gun, and this case, on faith. Again, off the record, I can tell you that all I ever read about the President's Commission was what made page one from time to time. I have not read those twenty-six volumes out there, but know this—when the gavel comes down for the last time in this case, I fully intend to. Because frankly, what that defendant is doing in our lockup for *this* crime is a total mystery to me. Between us, there's not a snowball's chance in hell that I would preside over his second trial, assuming there is one. But we have all articulated the feeling at one time or another that something really stinks about this whole affair, and I must tell you that the Italian rifle, C2766, is a part of it." Again a pause for comment, which was not forthcoming.

"If this trial had been held in, oh, let's say Delaware, maybe people would say yes, it's a rifle, and rifles kill people, but the simple fact is that this is Texas, where people live, and as we have seen, die with guns, and if one thing has come out of this trial, it is that the gun out there on the table did *not* kill John Kennedy. Ray, you used the experts you were handed, and they said, 'Sure, it's easy.' But nobody came remotely close to doing it, despite repeated tries. Nobody could duplicate the pristine bullet. The weapon needed adjusting to be accurate at fifteen yards. And so on, and so on. I know that doesn't sound very legal, but it's a symptom of the court's frustration with that weapon. I would never put my own prejudices into the record, but I did a little hunting in my younger days, and I spent time one afternoon with that gun, and believe me when I say this, Ray, but Eddie exaggerated the worth of that weapon when he called it junk. If all we have is order forms for it, or for some similar gun, and Carl Day's mark, given the way other evidence was treated, combined with the question of chain of possession and the chief's willingness to say a switch was possible, I have no choice but to rule against that weapon."

The room was silent, and nobody wanted to be the one to break the silence.

"Does anyone have anything else before we go public?"

"Your Honor," Barnes asked, "can the defense ask if your decision to exclude is final?"

"Yes, you may, and yes, it is."

"In that case, Judge, if we walk out there now and bring in the jury, once the weapon is excluded, the defense will request a directed verdict of not guilty, which may bring us right back in here."

Judge Davis thought out loud: "At this point, a directed verdict is tantamount to a repetition to dismiss based on the lack of a *prima facia* case. Naturally, the directed verdict request is preferable and makes more sense at the end of a proceeding than a motion to dismiss. So let's examine the options. Without such a motion, you would make your closing arguments, and I suspect they would reflect two totally different perspectives, and then I would charge the jury. But what with? My charge would essentially be that they could find the defendant guilty if they believed beyond a reasonable doubt and to a moral certainty, that he did it, although there were no eyewitnesses, there is no autopsy report, and there is no weapon, shells, or bullet. I have never made such a charge and I'm not going to start at this point."

After a pause, in which Davis had put his head back and

looked at the ceiling, he continued. "What we have are three options: directed verdict; a charge which tells the jury to acquit; or a lopsided vote to acquit, but not unanimous, in which case the judge can overturn the verdict or leave the case hung, which would create the mind set that there was evidence of guilt, which, to be very honest, I don't see. I don't want to have to overturn a verdict, yet there is always the possibility that one or more of those jurors somehow got through the selection process with a prejudice, either to convict regardless, or to acquit, regardless. That is always a possibility. We can't know the mind of every juror, and there may be just one—one is all it takes—one rabid anti-Communist out there who equates the defendant with Joseph Stalin and his ilk. Okay, I thank you for telling me what's on your mind, Mr. Barnes. Let's hear from you, Ray. You're the judge in this case. What would you do?"

"I'd go out there, exclude the weapon, and tell the reporters that Ray Matthews is one helluva lawyer. Then it would get touchy."

"I appreciate your efforts to break the tension, Ray, but the question was serious."

"I know that, Your Honor. It has been obvious from the first couple days that this case was going from bad to worse from the prosecution standpoint, and there came a time, honestly, when our strategy had to be shifted from conviction to hung jury. The questions you're asking now seem to be 'Would that serve justice?' and 'How would the prosecutor react for the history books if the trial was ended by a directed verdict?' "

"Those seem to be the questions," Davis agreed.

"I can't answer them, Frank," Matthews said. "You are the judge, and heavy is the head that wears the crown. But understand, to date, this case has been politics, at least until my staff, and the defense team, turned it into law. And I agree with you that it stinks. So you go out there, and whatever you decide, I promise you that I will publicly support your decision as being in the best interest of justice."

Carolyn Jeffries felt goose bumps like she had never experienced before.

"Very well said, Ray. Let's go to work, and, Carson, I'll let you know when to bring the reporters in." When Barnes heard that, he knew that in eight hours, he would be the most famous lawyer in America, at least for a while.

When all parties had reclaimed their seats, Oswald was brought in, allowed to sit, and then Carson went to get the jury. During those brief few seconds, Barnes reminded Oswald of the behavior he had suggested on the first day, and told him he better be well behaved today. Oswald started to ask a question, but the judge's gavel cut him off. "Mr. Barnes, I believe we have a motion pending from the close of yesterday's session."

"Yes, Your Honor. The defense moves to have the rifle, CE 139, serial number C2766, excluded from evidence at this time."

"It is the decision of this court that your motion be granted."

"Thank you, Your Honor," Barnes said. Then, continuing slowly, he added, "We therefore . . ." at which time he was cut off by the court.

"Before you go any further, Mr. Barnes, would the officer at the rear door please admit five—and five only—individuals who display valid press credentials from CBS, NBC, ABC, UPI, and AP, and make sure each individual is fully searched for anything out of the ordinary."

Seven minutes, which seemed like seven weeks, later, five journalists, all male, sat in the spectator section of the courtroom. Barnes remained seated while the judge addressed the newly admitted individuals. "Gentlemen, you have been admitted to these proceedings as they conclude. I am instructing the court officer who admitted you to lock the door through which you entered, should anyone get the idea that they want to leave prematurely. I assure you that your stay here will be brief. When the door is opened and you reenter the hallway, you will find telephone accommodations provided for you, and labeled, so you may reach your intended audience with all due dispatch. It is also my understanding that the attorneys of record will be available for statements and some questions. The defendant will not be, however, but he will, for the sake of your reporting, be represented by his counsel, and secondarily through the transcripts of this entire proceeding, which will be furnished to you five—ahead of anyone else, on Monday morning at nine A.M. back in this room. Is there any confusion as to procedure, gentlemen?"

All nodded in agreement, but the man closest to the center aisle, apparently the group spokesperson, rose to thank the court for considering the press and the need to communicate the story to the public.

"Mr. Barnes?" Davis asked.

"Your Honor, at this time, the defense petitions the Court for a directed verdict of 'Not Guilty.' It has become apparently clear in the course of this trial that the prosecution has failed to prove its case, and with the exclusion of the weapon, the bullet, the shells, the autopsy report, and other materials also excluded, there is essentially no longer a case before this court."

"Mr. Matthews?"

"The prosecution must regrettably find agreement with the essentials of the defense attorney's statement, Your Honor."

"In the matter of docket F-154, *The People* v. *Lee Oswald,* the court directs a verdict of not guilty. Inasmuch as the defendant is still charged in another capital case, the murder of a police officer, and in another assault, the attempted murder of the governor of Texas, he is not eligible for bail despite his acquittal in this case."

The journalists were stunned, and looked to each other to try to figure out what the exclusions had meant, but too much else was happening for them to do anything but observe and try to memorize. They saw the defendant extend a sincere handshake to defense attorney Barnes as the judge turned his chair to face the jury. "Members of the jury: I realize you have been here since December, and have not seen your families in the time since then. Sitting here, day after day, while others speak, is often difficult and frequently tedious. But you have done your job. It was your anticipated vote that brought forth the truth in this case, and for that, and your patience, you are to be commended. You will retire one more time to the jury room where I will give you my personal thanks."

As Carson was leading the jury out, the judge thanked the attorneys for their herculean efforts in the case, and told Oswald that it was sad that his name had been linked to this crime when the evidence to convict him did not seem apparent. He added that he would recommend some "well-guarded" release time as part of his continued bail. Oswald thanked him, and was then led away.

The judge then nodded to the court officer, who unlocked the door and avoided a five-man stampede for telephones.

Ray Matthews and his assistants put files in briefcases and headed out to meet the press after shaking hands with the defense team. Carolyn Jeffries gave Bob Dean a bear hug and whispered, "We did it."

Barnes put his head down and wept.

# EPILOGUE

Matthews, Graves, and Vincent walked from the courtroom expecting to be pounced upon by the press, only to find the rotunda empty and the five journalists busy talking into telephone receivers. Matthews looked at his watch: 9:25 A.M. Central Standard Time. Matthews could get some consolation from the fact that the only people learning of Lee Oswald's acquittal at that moment were children on the East Coast watching cartoons, or teenagers who protested when the Beatles' "I'll Follow the Sun" was interrupted on their transistor radios. On the West Coast, early risers were having breakfast.

Although the easy thing to do would have been simply to leave the scene of battle behind, Matthews decided he would face the press and have his say. He suggested to Graves and Vincent that they need not be members of the *Titanic*'s orchestra, but both insisted on remaining.

As Matthews awaited the press, Barnes, Dean, and Jeffries played the roles of "good winners" and stayed behind to allow Matthews a chance to go on the record before they sauntered into the limelight. Congratulations were guarded; they had won, but they had nothing to offer the American public as to where to search for the real killers.

Almost unnoticed, Judge Davis had slipped into the jury room with Carson, and asked the jurors to take places around the table. He then told them how the decision to issue a directed verdict had been one of the most difficult he had ever made, and as he said that, he removed his robe and handed it to Carson, commenting, "I may not be needing this again." He then told the jurors that because of the nature of his decision, he would request their honest thoughts on the case, and the only way that could be done would be to have the jurors vote, as if they were deciding the case. He assured them that the results would never be revealed by him, or Carson, and asked that they take the vote, essentially, because he *had* to know if his decision was in keeping with their interpretation of the evidence.

Carson then picked numbers to see which of the fourteen jurors would be excluded, and jurors nine and ten were chosen. The remaining twelve were given paper ballots and were assured their votes would be anonymous. Each voted and handed the folded slip to Carson, then left with a handshake and the thanks of the judge. Realizing he had twelve slips of paper in his hands and only jurors nine and ten still remained, he asked them for their thoughts. Juror nine said "Not guilty," and departed. Juror ten said, "Guilty as hell," and stormed out. Judge Davis knew at least one juror's face would be on the news that evening.

Two minutes later, Carson and Davis sat alone in the solitude of the judge's chambers. Davis counted the votes: twelve not guilty. "I'll be damned," he told Carson.

"You just might, Your Honor," Carson told him, "but you won't be alone."

The first of the five journalists approached Matthews and began asking questions as fast as he could think of them. Eaton Graves interceded to say that Mr. Matthews would have a statement for the selected pool, when all were present, and then would answer their questions to the best of his ability. Eventually, all five were present and asking questions.

"Gentlemen, please." That seemed to quiet the mini-multitude. "This morning, after hearing fourteen days of testimony and exhibits, the judge issued a directed verdict of not guilty, which was the only proper option, and a verdict which, although I prosecuted the case, I accept the wisdom of and agree with wholeheartedly. I had thought, when I was assigned this case, that it was, as the Dallas authorities had assured me, 'a cinch.' Let me tell you it was—well, obviously it was not. The case presented to us was so flawed that the vast majority of relevant evidence was excluded, and rightly so, and the case was at best circumstantial.

"Although I am not fully aware of the facts in the other prosecution that Mr. Oswald will soon face, I must tell you that even though we learned very little about him in the last three weeks, the evidence as presented to the jury made it day-by-day overwhelmingly clear that he had not pulled the trigger on any rifle in Dealey Plaza on November twenty-second, 1963, and for that, I feel remorse in putting him, and his family, through this ordeal and for having stigmatized him in this way.

"In conclusion, gentlemen, I hope when your papers excerpt the trial transcripts, you print as much as possible, or the entire transcript. Only in that way will the American people truly come to understand how this verdict, the correct verdict, I repeat, came to be. And please, before you editorialize, have your combined resources—the many networks and newspapers you represent—have them hire five top defense attorneys, and have those men spend the time it takes to read the twenty-six volumes of evidence as accumulated by the President's Commission. When they are done, I would virtually guarantee you that none of them would have even considered prosecuting Mr. Oswald based on the absence of real, solid evidence in the case. Now, let's take questions from left to right, and you need not identify yourselves. You, sir."

"Did the defense win this on technicalities or cheap theatrics?"

"Let me assure you that the defense won this case because of thorough scholarship, proper legal ethics, and, I must tell you, a determination to find the truth that transcended their obligation to the client. I'll give you one example: When you read the transcripts, you'll see that we put on a witness who we had been assured was a firearms expert. He said his piece, and then Mr. Barnes put the issue right in his lap: if he, the weapons expert, could duplicate the marksmanship attributed to the defendant, Mr. Barnes promised to change his client's plea to guilty. If the man attempted the duplication and failed—one chance, just as the defendant allegedly had—he would have to resign his commission in the service and forfeit all pension. The guy just didn't back up his words. And that sums up our case. Next?"

"What was the weakest part of the prosecution's case, and the strongest part of the defense's case?"

"That's not easy to answer when there were many prosecution weaknesses and many defense strengths. But I will not evade your question, either. My biggest concern, as we went along, and particularly when testimony began, was the question of motive. People commit crimes for a reason. That may sound oversimplified, but it's true. And try to follow the logic here, because you'll discover this case is an enigma. We just couldn't get a motive for Oswald. Everyone we deposed seemed to indicate he showed admiration for Mr. Kennedy, for his family, and for his civil rights policies. Now, if Oswald had anything to do with this, it was because he had as yet undiscovered ties to intelligence circles, which spells conspiracy with a capital C. And once you say conspiracy, you look over at poor old Oswald and realize that no one is going to stick their neck out and rely on somebody with the track record of failures that he represents. So if you rule out a conspiracy motive, the only reason he would have done the act was to transform a nobody into a somebody. But that never came to pass. In all his time in confinement, in the few days in the public eye at the time of his arrest, he never bragged of having done it—he vehemently denied it. If he was looking for fame, it was right there to grab, but he didn't, and that was a weakness in our case."

Matthews caught his breath and continued, "As for the defense, it can be said that they did their homework. While we were sitting contently on the evidence provided by the Dallas folks, they studied those twenty-six volumes *and* the Dallas evidence, and literally riddled the case with holes. There were just too many inconsistencies, and the President's Commission, well, they let the public down, let's put it that way. Who's next?"

"What will happen to Oswald?"

"I would suspect he will be tried for the murder of the police officer, and I will guarantee you that no court will try him for assaulting Governor Connally, as this case proved he did not fire shots in Dealey Plaza. And given the Dallas mishandling of evidence, it is highly unlikely that the second trial will be in Dallas, and I would doubt it would be here in Lubbock. God knows I don't want to prosecute it, and I'm sure millions of Americans will feel the same way if they do not read the transcripts. Yes—you, sir?"

"Was there ever a time when you felt really confident that you were going to get a conviction in this case?"

"After I made my opening statement to the jury, I felt very confident. Then Mr. Barnes made his statement, and asked many very relevant, thoughtful questions for which I had no answers whatsoever. And we just never caught up. The defense, as you will read, made many of our witnesses on the stand into defense witnesses. That's the kind of case it was. Make no mistake, though. The three men you see before you did their best, but the case wasn't there."

"Are you going to write a book?"

"It's already been done, I'm afraid. It's entitled *The Transcripts in The People* v. *Lee Oswald.* Thank you, gentlemen. I'm sure you will get a wealth of information from Mr. Barnes and his staff, for whom, for the record, I have the utmost respect. Best of luck to you in filing your stories. My office will be available for further comment in the coming days after the transcripts have been released."

And with that classy presentation, Ray Matthews and staff began a fortnight of well-deserved rest, occasionally punctuated with empty bourbon bottles.

The reporters then reentered the courtroom, only to be told that the defense attorneys would make their statement in the hallway and not in a court of law.

Once reassembled in the rotunda, Barnes deflected questions much in the manner that Matthews had. "I do not have a prepared statement, gentlemen, but I will try to tell you what occurred, and I will try to answer your questions. You may also feel free to ask questions of either Mr. Dean, whom I'm sure you know better than me, or of my associate from Minnesota, Miss Carolyn Jeffries."

Having said that, Barnes collected his thoughts, took a deep breath, and began. "Please understand that I will have no comment, nor answer any question with regard to the possible prosecution of Mr. Oswald in the slaying of the police officer. In the trial just concluded, Mr. Oswald was found not guilty primarily because there was a serious insufficiency of evidence to convict him *as charged.* Beyond that, the framework of the case lacked a cohesiveness, which I attempted to demonstrate to the jurors, and frankly I'm curious to see their reactions on newscasts over the next few days. The key to all of it, in my mind, and I believe my colleagues will support this, was the series of actions taken by the defendant after the shots were fired."

Barnes gave the reporters a chance to catch up to his discussion, then continued. "Shots are fired at approximately 12:30; seventy to ninety seconds later, the defendant is on the second floor, and other people who came down the stairs did not see or hear him on the stairs. Then he leaves the building, a curious act. A guilty person might well have stayed put, waited until attendance was taken, then been dismissed. He could then have been hundreds of miles away, or out of the country, before he was missed from work on Monday. But he left, taking a bus and taxi, which are hardly indicative of haste, even offering to let an elderly woman have his cab! But ultimately, he went to get a pistol, and gentlemen, he didn't get that pistol because he was lonely. He got it because at 12:30, he became threatened. If he had known that circumstances would point the finger of guilt at him for the events of 12:30, he would have had that gun with him at 8 A.M. But he didn't, strongly suggesting that events took a turn he had not anticipated. Now, to anticipate some of your questions, there is not much I can tell you about the defendant."

That surprised most of the reporters. "I spoke with him on many occasions, but he was never truly forthcoming. He answered most questions put to him, and I must tell you his answers sounded like the responses of an honest man in a difficult situation. However, he told reporters, folks just like you gentlemen, in the hallway in Dallas, that he was 'a patsy' . . ."

"I was there," one writer commented.

"So then you know what I'm talking about. Well, I asked him about that comment many times, and I never got a shred of an answer. Nothing. No comment. He became a sphinx. I even tried that age-old legal ploy, you know, look, son, if you hold back from me, you may have to get yourself another lawyer. There was a lot behind those eyes of his, but still no answer. He would have cashed me in before he would answer that question. And I'm glad I don't know, to be honest with you."

Barnes paused again for the reporters' sakes, then interrupted his own narrative of events to heap high praise on the other defense attorneys, "without whom this verdict would not have been possible."

"If you believe that," Bob Dean interrupted, "please sit on the jury for the next case I try." There was good-natured laughter all around.

"What are you saying, Mr. Dean?" came the return question.

"I'm saying, for the record, that Eddie Barnes took this case, roped and tied it like a cow in the rodeo, then jumped on the back of the bull—pun *intended*—called the President's Commission and rode it until the animal got tired. I've seen some fine legal work in many a courtroom, but I have never seen anything like the job this man did in that room. You will see the transcripts, but those are just words, and not having heard the way those words were conveyed in that courtroom behind us, you have missed much of the character of those words."

"Now if you believe that," Barnes added, "I want you all on *my* next jury."

"Stop this, all of you," Carolyn Jeffries said. "I want all five of these guys on my next jury." Good-natured laughter again eased the tension.

"The last thing I would like to add before you ask your questions is my admiration for the members of the prosecution team. Few people in the public eye find themselves caught between a bigger rock and a more abrasive hard place, to use the old phrase. They believed they had a case, and who can blame them, when the defendant had already been convicted by local and state authorities, not to mention the head of the FBI and the esteemed members of the President's Commission. Notwithstanding all of that, they too sought the truth, and for that, they deserve the deepest respect and admiration from the citizens of this nation. No individuals won or lost this case. America has begun the process of coming to grips with the truth in a tragedy that has plagued us all in these past many months."

"Do you believe there was a conspiracy?"

"Absolutely. Each of you should insist that your network or wire service be given a clear copy of the motion picture taken by Abraham Zapruder. Warn your audiences that it is not for the squeamish, and then air it. The American people will see for themselves where the shot came from that killed the President."

"Are you at liberty to say if you believe the defendant was part of the conspiracy?"

"At liberty, sure. But it's a tough question. The best estimate I can give you of the defendant's involvement is that he was somehow used—by forces unknown—known perhaps to him, but not as yet to you or me. When he realized he'd been set up, he went home for the gun. I do not believe he was an active part of any group that operated to kill the President. If I did, I would willingly help strap him in the electric chair—believe it."

"If, as the official record now shows, Lee Oswald did not shoot the President, who did?"

"Specifically, I have no idea. However, there was very persuasive evidence that one or more shots were fired from the southeast corner sixth floor window of the Book Depository. There just wasn't any evidence that Oswald did it, and given his mediocre marksmanship abilities, it's very unlikely that anyone would invest in him. All I can offer you about that event is a theory—because if it wasn't Oswald, then who was it? Another Depository employee? Not likely. And my theory is going to hurt many people and their immediate families, and I do not intend that hurt, but it comes down to the old Sherlock Holmes theory that when you eliminate the possibles, you are then stuck with the seemingly impossibles. We know that several Depository employees used the stairs in the time frame immediately after the shots, probably for up to a minute or more. We also know that there were three employees on the floor immediately below who heard noise in the sniper's window but not on the staircase. We also know that the noisy freight elevators never moved. So if nobody came down those stairs in a hurry, who besides a Depository employee would have had the ability to walk casually away from that crime scene a few minutes later—without being stopped?"

One reporter stopped writing and faced Barnes. "What you are about to suggest is unthinkable."

"What am I about to suggest?" Barnes asked the writer.

"That it was a cop," came the reply.

"Not necessarily. But you're close. The witnesses we heard, who saw a figure in the window, identified the person as wearing a light-colored shirt. It could have been a t-shirt for all I know, and we don't have any consensus on the trousers. Shots are fired, but the shooter does not escape down the stairs. He wanders upstairs, dons a police shirt, perhaps to go with blue trousers, and then wanders around until there are enough police present for him to exit very casually. Now that does not imply for a moment that it *was* a cop. God knows, when you read the transcripts of this case, you'll get the clear indication that if the Dallas cops had been intent on killing the President, John Kennedy would be alive and well today. So please don't misquote me that a cop did any shooting. Someone who posed, or later posed as a cop, is a real possibility."

"What about Oswald's marksmanship?"

"Absolute fiction insofar as I could discover. I was curious —hell . . . pardon me, I read the reports. He qualified as a sharpshooter at one point. Other marines said he could not walk and chew gum at the same time. Some people said he lacked the basic coordination to drive a car. He was always being fired from jobs. So everytime I went to talk with him, I took along some item—a tennis ball, something like that—to test his coordination without him knowing he was being tested. For what's it's worth, and I would have to think it bears on his marksmanship ability, Lee Oswald is one very uncoordinated individual. It would probably take him ten minutes to open an aspirin bottle."

"Do you think any government officials will be called on the carpet for these sordid events?"

"I think that if and when the public reads the transcripts of this trial, they're going to demand some justice. Justice in as far as it can be obtained at this late date regarding the President, and justice for those who obstructed justice after the fact. When you see the transcripts, you'll see federal officials falling all over each other to get their hands on evidence that they never had any jurisdiction over in the first place. The Secret Service, which I always had tremendous respect for, was investigating this case, and it's just not their job. Their job is to protect the President, period—and round up counterfeit money—and they could, and should, have let the lawful agencies—Texas authorities—gather the evidence. When all was said and done, they could have learned a great deal about presidential protection from reading the reports of the lawful investigators. They can still learn a great deal about presidential protection, I would like to add, if they, too, read the trial transcripts."

"Are you saying you've lost your respect for the Secret Service?"

"Nothing that happened in Dallas is about to increase my respect for them. Special Agent Hill behaved in a manner of the highest courage and is a model of what other agents' behavior should have been that day. The two in the car are another story. The driver slowed the car down during the ambush, and the front passenger got on the phone. There are also parts of that movie showing them ducking as the bullets are incoming. That's pathetic. On the other hand, Clint Hill performed bravely and risked his life."

"Will we ever learn the truth?"

"I sure hope so, gentlemen, but it won't be from me. I've told you what I know, and the rest is in the transcripts. Just understand this: the truth is buried at the bottom of an immense bureaucratic mine shaft, and it's going to take some incredible digging, in 1965, to find it. I thank you for asking the right questions and I hope we've helped you. The three of us did what we thought justice demanded. Now, it's up to you gentlemen."

Barnes then shook hands and said farewell to Bob Dean, promising to invite him to Minnesota "after the June thaw" and Dean again complimented him on his handling of the case. Dean also took receipt of the keys to the rental cars used by the two Minnesota attorneys. Jeffries and Barnes then reentered the courtroom, and arranged for a departing Wisconsin trooper to take them to their respective hotel rooms, grab suitcases, and ride north with the trooper. Carolyn Jeffries rode all the way to Wisconsin, then caught a local flight to Minneapolis.

Barnes parted company with the trooper and Miss Jeffries

at the first major city on the way north, and exactly which city it was is still unclear in the mind of Carolyn Jeffries, as it was dark and she was drowsy at the time. Barnes then flew directly to Minneapolis where he was reunited with his wife and children.

Any celebrating, however, had to wait a few hours until their next flight touched down, as Amy Barnes, following her husband's guarded instructions, had liquidated their stock portfolio, sold their home at a loss to a realtor, and had stopped at the bank the day before to convert the majority of the money to English pounds. By Monday, January 25, 1965, the Barneses were comfortably settled in a rented farmhouse within thirty miles of Oxford, England.

Barnes never returned to the United States, as he chose not to savor the limelight nor to make himself a target for those who might have had an ax to grind for the job he did in Lubbock, Texas. He lived the life of a country gentleman, dabbling in agriculture while working on a book about the trial, which was published in 1968. There have also been persistent rumors that he did, in fact, have discussions with Oswald which outlined the crime as it happened, and they will eventually be published.

Lee Oswald remained in Lubbock for two weeks before being transferred to a maximum security prison suite in Galveston, Texas, to stand trial for the slaying of Jefferson Davis Tippitt. The trial began in November of 1965 after much legal wrangling, and Oswald was convicted and sentenced to death. The conviction, however, was overturned in late 1966 based on erroneous charges to the jury by the judge. On January 14, 1968, while Oswald was still awaiting retrial, a riot broke out in the prison when the inmates were told that their television sets would be taken away for that afternoon's "Super Bowl" between the Oakland Raiders and the Green Bay Packers. In the confusion of the brief riot, and because some of the prison staff were on the phone to their bookmakers, Lee Oswald was beaten to death. The official cause of death was, ironically, massive brain trauma, and, at autopsy, the weight of his brain was recorded at 1450 grams, another irony, as Kennedy's, although shot out on Elm

Street, had weighed in at 1500 grams. No one was ever charged in the death of Oswald.

Not one law-enforcement officer at either the state or federal level lost their job or was demoted for poor police work during the weekend of November 22–24, 1963. Seventeen FBI agents, including Special Agent James Hosty, were transferred.

Judge Davis remained on the bench, but was never assigned a case with any significance greater than criminal trespass or unlawful assembly. He retired on April 1, 1968, and stayed pretty close to his ranch, which was tended by retired Bailiff Carl Carson.

Ray Matthews kept busy trying the normal run of cases one would expect in a town the size of Lubbock, and, in an irony not lost on him, signed a contract as a consultant for the movie version of the trial of Oswald on March 31, 1968, a few hours before Lyndon Johnson, whose popularity never recovered from its virtual collapse after the acquittal of Oswald, announced he would not seek reelection.

Three days later, in spite of having signed the hefty movie contract, Matthews was found hanging from the beam of his garage. The official verdict was suicide, but the coroner made no mention in his report of the skin particles found under Matthews's nails, nor the extreme contusion on the back of his head. The public took little notice of the story when it "broke" in the papers on April 5, 1968. Most of them were reading about another murder, performed by James Earl Ray, another lone nut, in Memphis, Tennessee, the victim being another one of those individuals who had the vision to make America a better place. And because good stories like that always find a market, there was yet another one, for good measure, in a Los Angeles hotel pantry two months later, only this time, the victim was the one living human being who, had his presidential aspirations not been derailed by an assassin's bullet, would have had the power *and* the courage to find the ultimate solution to his brother's murder.

# EPILOGUE, 1992

What you have read was Lee Oswald *and* history on trial. In reality, Lee Oswald had no judge, and only one juror and executioner. The verdict required only one hour and forty-six minutes, and was pronounced by an attending physician, not a judge or a jury foreman.

Oswald was buried the following day, miles away, under a false name, hours before John Kennedy was laid to rest in a temporary location, since moved, on a peaceful hillside in Arlington, Virginia, that once belonged to Robert E. Lee and overlooks the capital of the nation that vanquished Lee's army. (Little could Robert E. Lee have ever known that 90-odd years after his passing, the son of Robert E. Lee Oswald would be charged with the murder of Jefferson Davis Tippitt . . .)

When Oswald was pronounced dead, autopsied (correctly, and in accordance with Texas law), and buried, America lost its best opportunity to learn the real truth of the events of November 22, 1963, because while Oswald was acquitted in the preceding pages, he confessed to being "a patsy," highly suggestive that he knew something of the other forces that were at work on that awful Friday. Certainly he never knew the whole story, or he would not have been the patsy, but he knew enough to realize at 12:30 that day that he had been cast in that role.

The truth of the event that remained after the murder of Oswald is spelled out in its entirety in the opening few paragraphs of the Prologue to this work. Those few sentences are all we really do know, twenty-nine years later, and the thousands of commentaries that have been written since, a few in support of the official theory, most in opposition, are speculations. That includes this work, although it is hoped, as it was by the writers of the better of the works that preceded this one, that this book has added a good deal to the reader's knowledge of the event and will allow the reader to take a step or two closer, at least in his or her own mind, to the ultimate truth as he or she perceives it.

Other speculations now demand our hindsight focus. If Jack Ruby had not been successful, or had made no attempt, there would of necessity have been a trial . . . but for whose murder?

The evidence that Lee Oswald killed Officer Tippitt is clearly more persuasive than that Oswald killed the President, but that trial, like the one you have just read, would have been an interesting event, and may someday, when other JFK related topics are completed, be the ink that draws this author's quill.

That prospect, however, is again speculative, while Dallas authorities would have faced a real dilemma—which trial would Oswald have faced? Could they have convicted him for the murder, hardly premeditated, of a policeman, and then sold the public on the idea that Oswald was going to prison for a long time, so why waste millions proving what the world already knew, i.e., that Oswald also killed Kennedy, and why cause the family grief, etc., etc.

I don't think so.

On the other hand, one has to suspect that given the rowdy, rough and tumble atmosphere that seemed to characterize Dallas, Texas, at least up to 1963, it would be reasonable to assume that there had been a good number of murders in that city, and that they had obtained a good number of convictions. But there's the catch: when did these Dallas officials, capable of generating murder cases that convinced juries "beyond a reasonable doubt and to a moral certainty" suddenly put on clown suits and throw together such a God-awful sham of a case that a historian with limited legal training could, in layman's terms, point out the quality and quantity of the flaws?

Which raises the question, "What was the Dallas case as of that weekend?" What follows is a ten-item interview with Dallas District Attorney Henry Wade, conducted on November 24, 1963, which appears in Volume 24, pp. 819ff of the *Hearings Before the President's Commission on the Assassination of President Kennedy*. Each point will be questioned as reached, and it should also be noted that this *is* the essence of the Dallas "can't lose" case, and Wade had an extremely high conviction rate in cases he tried.

1. A number of witnesses saw a person with a gun on the sixth floor of the Depository. [Agreed; no one identified Oswald in a lineup, and most, as noted in text, gave rather different descriptions.] Reasonable conclusion: There was a shooter there. But who?

2. The boxes created an ideal sniper's nest and gun rest. [The "hiding place" was created by the flooring crew; part of the gun rest may have been placed by the young black man eating lunch up there at 12:20.] Reasonable conclusion: since point 1 assumes a shooter there, point two is not unreasonable; the question still remains, "Who?"

3. A palm print on a box. [Positive identification of that print, along with the many other, unidentified prints, was sorely lacking; also allow for the fact that the defendant had his fingerprints all over that building—he worked there.] Reasonable conclusion: that palm print would not convict anybody; the other prints should have been run down until they matched up with people in some law enforcement file.

4. Three ejected shells. [As demonstrated by Day's testimony, Sims Exhibit 1, Alyea Affidavit, it's highly unclear who handled them, who bagged them, and where they went. It is clear that they were not marked into evidence until almost eight hours after being found, and that taints evidence and causes its exclusion. Beyond that, there was no "proof" that those shells were fired that day, or by whom. And for all his obviousness in obtaining a rifle and a pistol, the defendant was never linked to the purchase of one cartridge at any time.] Reasonable conclusion: the three cartridges would have been excluded, and if not, their lack of pedigree and mishandling would have given them minuscule weight, except as stage props.

5. The gun found on the sixth floor was linked to Oswald, and although purchased under an alias, that alias was verified by the contents of Oswald's wallet, which carried Hidell identification. [Ownership does not prove that the owner fired the weapon at a given time and place; there was never any proof that the weapon in question *was* fired that day; that "Mauser" problem has never been settled to anyone's

satisfaction; and lastly, the quality of that weapon (and I own one, and as a former firearms expert with the Department of Justice, I can tell you, it is not a weapon you are likely to stake your future upon), its misadjusted, left-handed sights, and its lack of oil make it very questionable.] Reasonable conclusion: the gun so easily traceable to the one defendant *kept* in custody was also a stage prop, and could not be proven to be more.

6. Oswald brought a package to work. [The only persons who saw him with the famous package were adamant that it was several inches smaller than it would have had to have been to have concealed the carbine. Worst case, it was the carbine, but Oswald's proven arrival with it only convicts him as an accessory—it does not put his finger on the trigger at 12:30.] Reasonable conclusion: Oswald brought something to work—he told Wesley Frazier it was curtain rods, when in fact he had gone to see Marina to patch up an earlier quarrel. He could have been carrying a bag of newspaper that he put in the trash at 7:58, to mask the intent of his visit from Frazier, the one person who knew of its "curtain rod" purpose. Beyond that, the failure to match the "bag" to either Depository paper and tape or Paine paper and tape, make it highly questionable. Equally curious is the "second bag" which arrived at Oswald's P.O. Box in Dallas days *after* his death. Too little has been said about that event.

7. The discussion of the President's murder on the bus. [It just never happened as Wade wanted his listeners to believe. He may have believed it, but the bus driver, Cecil McWatters, was insistent that the discussion of JFK's wounds occurred *after* Oswald made his two-block bus trip.] Reasonable conclusion: no jury would buy it, and it proves nothing anyhow —if Oswald was guilty, he certainly was too well "coached," as witnesses indicated, to make such a declaration on public transit.

8. This point involved Tippitt.

9. Fingerprints on the gun. [A palm print, with a limited number of identification points, was found when the gun was disassembled, and Carl Day admitted that his experience taught him it was an *old* print, even when he lifted it on 11/22; the FBI found *nothing*, printwise; a gun that clean

spells one of two words: unused or professional; both exclude Lee Oswald. Also, the FBI privately questioned how Dallas found the print, and Dallas folks mistrusted the FBI about it. Beyond that, it's admitted Oswald owned the gun; what is surprising is that his prints weren't all over it.] Reasonable conclusion: an old print tells nothing about 11/22.

10. Paraffin tests. [Taken seven hours after Oswald's arrest, and after he had been fingerprinted; law enforcement people differ on the validity of these tests, but they tend to suggest the presence of nitrates, which, if Oswald had fired both a rifle and a pistol, he should have tested positive for his hands and face, which he did not. That he tested positive for his hands suggests that he could not have washed the nitrates off his face; that he tested positive for anything suggests an appalling lack of speed in processing a prisoner, and an equally appalling lack of human dignity in not allowing a prisoner, regardless of the charges, a chance to wash himself after he's been tumbled around a theater.] Reasonable conclusion: Don't stake your mortgage on the paraffin test carrying the day.

Would you take that case before the entire world?

Reading it boiled down to its essentials, it is very thin, and not aided much by the subsequent ballistic match of the "magic bullet" (CE 399) to the weapon, as there was absolutely no chain of possession with respect to that bullet, so what really makes it "magic" is that it has generated so many millions of words in spite of its total lack of probity as evidence.

Even today, however, apologists for the official version appear on documentaries and talk shows and proclaim how they could have prosecuted Oswald and gotten a conviction without perspiring. If you ever hear that thought broadcast, write to the speaker, give him the name of the author of this book, ask him to write to me in care of the publisher, and I will debate that person anywhere and at anytime. And I will bring no law books with me; I don't own any. I shall, however, bring "the 26" and sell the Warren Commission its very own Brooklyn Bridge.

It must here be noted that the American judicial system is unique. We have built in so many safeguards, from the inheritance of British common law, through the Bill of Rights, to more recent amendments and court precedents, that our system rests on a philosophy that it is better for ninety-nine guilty individuals to go free than for one innocent person to be convicted. So while the author has never claimed that Oswald was a mere bystander, his guilt, as charged, as the lone gunman who inflicted all the horrible wounds to John Kennedy, could never have been demonstrated beyond a reasonable doubt. He's not as innocent as some would have you believe, nor as guilty as the Warren Commission insisted.

In this narrative, his innocence in the crime of the century was proclaimed on Saturday, January 23, 1965. Had such an event come to pass, it would have been the onset of the long night of the American soul, as our November 1963 agony, frustration, and sense of profound loss would have been revisited upon us in a way that we have never faced in any previous crisis as a nation. Lee Oswald, *innocent?* How could that be? The papers told us . . . the FBI . . . the President's Commission . . .

And who appointed the Warren Commission? Lyndon Baines Johnson, a man whose authority to govern would have collapsed within hours of the nation's receipt of the news of Oswald's acquittal. This is *not* to suggest, or create in any way in the mind of any reader, the idea that Mr. Johnson was an accessory to this crime, recent publications to the contrary notwithstanding. True, his political aspirations, like those of Richard Nixon and many others, seemed blocked for years if John Kennedy's reelection in 1964 signaled the onset of a Kennedy dynasty in American politics. Also true is the notion that few people that have ever gone to Washington were more hungry for, or better at the manipulation of, power than was Lyndon Johnson. In President Nixon's farewell remarks to America, he spoke of mistakes made by his administration, but he was moved to add that they were political mistakes, not errors made for financial gain. Anyone who knows anything about Lyndon Johnson's fiscal portfolio will understand what Mr. Nixon was referring to.

People in Europe take conspiracies, especially those that topple rulers, for granted. In that regard, the acquittal of Oswald would have amounted to little more than an "I told you so" by the European press as regards Oswald, but the commentary would then have turned to what would become of America given the vacuum of leadership created by the onus that Lyndon Johnson would have borne after appointing a commission to investigate a crime, have its results published, accepted by a grateful nation, and then ripped to shreds by a public defender. In the British tradition, such governments collapse and are quickly replaced by ministries that receive votes of confidence in hastily convened elections. But America doesn't work that way, and January 23, 1965, was but the third day of the term to which Lyndon Johnson was elected. The mathematics there alone are enough to provide a hint as to where America would have been with the verdict as suggested in this work. About the only good thing was that it was a Saturday, and the New York Stock Exchange and other markets would have a grace period before facing the inevitable.

The subtitle of this work, "History on Trial," is an attempt to show that if Oswald had lived to go to trial, and had been acquitted, it might have vastly changed the future, and hence, the history of our nation. (In that sense, Lee Oswald was the first televised victim of euthanasia.) Instead, several million young Americans spent some, or the entire remainder, of their youth in Asia; consider the difference in that regard that would have occurred if this work were *not* the *fictional* account of Oswald's acquittal. And given the evidence and the flow of events of the previous narrative, our survival as a nation, and our ability to remain credible in making war to spread our way of "democracy" depended on Oswald's guilt being firmly established. This required two events: Oswald's quick and quiet death, and the creation of the Warren Commission.

The Warren Commission was established on November 29, 1963, by Executive Order 11130, which, among other things, meant that no Senate or House action was necessary, or, for that matter, possible, as both legislative bodies were gearing up to investigate the events of the previous weekend because something smelled very fishy.

The Warren Commission was presided over by Chief Justice Earl Warren, whose liberal decisions as chief justice had made "impeachment" a household word well before 1963 (which makes it laughable to see commission apologists put forth the "unimpeachable" integrity of the members of the commission, hence its unimpeachable correctness).

The commission also included Allen Dulles, who had been fired as the head of the CIA by John Kennedy, an odd choice at best to investigate a very suspicious murder. Another member was Gerald Ford (the only living member at the time of this writing), who made conspiracy bashing such a fine art that he kept in shape by running to the FBI with rumors they could somehow sweep under the carpet, then affixing his name to a book about Oswald, "the lone assassin," which drew from source material that was subsequently sealed until the year 2039. As Earl Warren commented, "There are things you will not learn in your lifetime." Well, he was right on that one.

Gerry Ford continued his "there is no substance to the charges" one-man show in his brilliant career as vice-president, when he proved to be one of Richard Nixon's most able defenders, to the point where he had to be called home and told to cancel his "Nixon is innocent" world tour in August 1974 because the smoking gun had been found. Two years later, in a televised debate with a peanut farmer, President Ford, having received the ultimate promotion for his Warren Commission labors, assured Americans that Poland was *not* a Communist country, and he did so with the same conviction as when he told us of Oswald's "lone nut" status. Believe what you will, but the peanut farmer ran him out of town.

The remainder of the Warren Commission were generally people that John Kennedy would *not* have appointed to key positions involving trust, not that they could not be trusted—as Hale Boggs and Richard Russell were men of very high integrity. But they weren't the right people—men with an unquenchable fire in their gut to find out what really happened in Dallas. They were more typified by the character of John J. McCloy, portrayed in a recent biography as the "ultimate establishment man." Before their deaths, both Boggs and Russell expressed public doubts about what they had affixed their signatures to on September 24, 1964.

For the record, the Warren Commission *did not* cover up

any evidence of any bizarre conspiracies, or multiple shooters, or plots within the government or beyond our national
borders. The simple truth is that they did not look hard
enough, or beyond the shadow of Lee Oswald, one rifle, three
slugs, one palm print, a Russian wife, and a fake Selective
Service card, to find any of those things. It has been suggested that Lyndon Johnson's hole card in twisting Earl Warren's arm to head the commission, and thereby commit political suicide, was the threat of nuclear war should it be
revealed that a foreign power (USSR, Cuba) was behind Oswald.

The thesis is ludicrous. No American had the power, or the
desire, to push the button. John Kennedy was dead. I would
wager that Americans would have been satisfied with any
*truth* in lieu of what they got.

So what did they get? A grand cover-up? No. They got the
ultimate "white lie." Just as a young child might not be able
to cope with the loss of his favorite grandpa, mom and dad
tell little Billy that Grandpa Hopkins "went away." Sooner or
later, when the little tyke gets his driver's license, he's going
to tumble to the fact that he's been scammed, but by then
he'll know that's how the system works sometimes.

Enter the Warren Commission. No interviews of the other
twelve people arrested in Dallas. No interest in stories that
the plain folk of Texas were willing to tell under oath. One of
today's most vocal surviving witnesses is Jean Hill, who
claims to have seen a shot fired from the knoll. Discover for
yourself where she was interviewed by now-Senator Arlen
Specter, another man well-promoted for his labors. When
you learn where she was interviewed, ask yourself how *you*
would have answered the tough questions.

The concept of the Warren Commission itself is misleading.
They (the seven commissioners) rarely met as a group and
only were present for a small portion of the testimony, and
then in groups usually much less than seven. The remainder
of the work was compartmentalized, so the staff lawyers, who
wrote the report, never really saw all the evidence from the
other areas. I would not want to spend much time in a 747
airliner constructed in the manner in which the Warren
Commission accomplished its task.

If you cannot obtain the twenty-six, read the report carefully. Look for key words that subconsciously lead the reader down the path to the lone assassin. Over fifty people were willing to come forward and say that a shot or shots were fired from places other than the sixth floor window. The report concludes there was no "credible" evidence. Translation: there was no gun, shells, or palm print found on the knoll, so it didn't happen. Many people ran into clearly fraudulent individuals posing as Secret Service men on the knoll. An allegation such as this is answered with the statement that it can be proven that there were no agents on the knoll, so therefore the witnesses are all wrong. Another key word is "persuasive." It means, "We want to believe it, and we hope you do, too."

In a time of national agony, it was ultimately proved that Americans will cave in to name-dropping and statistics. The author still has a very clear visual image of then Attorney General Richard Kleindienst on television during the height of the Watergate controversy, telling how the FBI had investigated *every* possibility, and could find no ("credible or persuasive" would have been good adjectives) evidence of wrongdoing by anyone in the White House. Mr. Kleindienst then went on to tell how exhaustive the investigation was, similar to Kennedy assassination rhetoric. When I heard that sentence, I knew America was in for another crisis. As for Mr. Kleindienst, one year, as a VIP, he received a fancy license plate. A year later, he was in a position to manufacture them.

The author must state as we near the end of our text that he is *not* a believer in the conspiracy/paranoia school of history. But that is not to deny that there have been conspiracies. At a very early session of the Warren Commission, former super-spy Allen Dulles gave the other members of the commission a small monograph detailing how American political murders were the work of lone crazed individuals (the chapter on Lincoln must have been very brief). Imagine, five hundred pages ago, if Prosecutor Matthews had tried to hand that same book to the jurors in Lubbock, Texas. That about epitomizes all that can be said on the positive side for the Warren Commission. No doubt, had they been given Executive Order Number 11131, to investigate the murder of Julius Caesar, they would have singled out Brutus as the sole assassin (he actually stabbed Caesar just above the knee) and insisted that rumors of a "second dagger" were not "credible."

The paranoia school of history, however (for its adherents), began on November 22, 1963. After eight years of the grandfatherly Eisenhower, America began to march down a new road under JFK, only to have Camelot aborted before its second trimester. The government, in this scenario, did itself in, "in a military style ambush . . . it was a coup d'etat," to paraphrase Kevin Costner. LBJ was undone when intelligence failures destroyed his Vietnam credibility in the face of the Tet Offensive. His successor, Richard Nixon, ultimately lost possession of the White House because former CIA expert operatives did not know how to tape a door properly, and a lowly security guard toppled all the President's men. Gerry Ford made his exit when intelligence experts failed to brief him on the sudden rise of Communism in Poland, beginning with the covert influx of Red Army tanks in the mid 1940's. Jimmy Carter lost the White House when the CIA's need for listening posts in Iran exceeded common sense in the face of a revolution there, and military plans to free the hostages collapsed in the desert because the operation was essentially a fiasco from the beginning. Ronald Reagan narrowly missed assassination, and if the bullet had been a few millimeters to the left, George Bush, former head of the CIA, would have been President after ten weeks of Ronald Reagan's first term. Watergate, Contragate, the "October Surprise" . . . the children of Dallas?

In a companion volume, the author plans to demonstrate how the Warren Commission told its white lie. Oh, they asked tens of thousands of questions, but they were never the right questions. One witness was being asked if Oswald, at seven P.M. on Friday night, had the appearance of having been beaten by police. The witness, a detective, told that he left the interrogation of Oswald to take a phone call in which the caller detailed to the detective how a conspiracy had killed John Kennedy a few hours earlier. The witness told the Warren Commission of the conspiracy allegation, and the

Warren Commission member repeated his question about Oswald's appearance.

The best single exchange, in terms of sheer failure to understand, was between Commissioner Ford and Dr. Charles Carrico of Parkland Hospital: Dr. Carrico: (discussing the wound he saw *above* the President's tie in the front of the neck) "Yes. And this wound was fairly round, had no jagged edges, no evidence of powder burns, and so forth." Representative Ford: "No evidence of powder burns?" (III, 362.)

No, Gerry, not unless Mrs. Kennedy shot him.

Ninety-nine percent of what all of us ever needed to know happened in 5.6 seconds at approximately 12:30 C.S.T. on November 22, 1963, in Dallas, Texas: John Kennedy was for all practical purposes killed instantly when hit in the head by a bullet.

The other one percent of the story has nagged people like me, and readers like you, for the last three decades. And it won't end with this book, or the next one, or the one after that. Every time I visit John Kennedy's grave at Arlington, the same deep abiding admiration I had for the man fights back the nagging doubts I have in my mind about what happened during those awful few seconds.

He is lying there now, under the earth and the stones that cover him, next to a daughter and a son that never knew the joys of life, nor the pain he suffered in losing them, like the pain we suffered in losing him.

Above him is the eternal flame. All around him is the eternal doubt.

# APPENDIX A

The following is an alphabetical list of witnesses who were subpoenaed but not called in the case of *The People* v. *Lee Harvey Oswald*. For the sake of space, abbreviations are used where possible: "LHO" is the defendant; "JFK," the victim; "LBJ," his successor; "WC" for Warren Commission; "USMC" for U.S. Marine Corps; FBI, SS, CIA for those respective agencies; ONI for Office of Naval Intelligence; TSBD for Depository.

Ables, Don. Was a Dallas jail janitor used in some of the lineups involving LHO.

Adamcik, John P. A Dallas detective who participated in the searches of the Paine residence.

Adams, Victoria E. Viewed motorcade from 4th floor of TSBD; believed shots came from right and below rather than left and above.

Agers, Bradley. CIA agent; told a researcher, subsequent to 1965, that LHO had some connection to the CIA.

Akin, Dr. Gene C. Parkland Hospital. Made observations of JFK's wounds and told WC that exit wound was large wound in the back of the head.

Alderson, Dr. Lawrence. Dentist. Had met Jean Soutre in 1953; as Soutre was a suspected assassin for hire, Dr. Alderson found himself under FBI surveillance after 11/22/63.

Alexander, William. Dallas Deputy D.A. Expressed surprise at LHO's self-control during interrogation; under the impression that LHO rather liked JFK.

Anderson, William C. Dallas resident in '63; had a curious story to tell in Decker 5323, XIX, 501, in which a group of transients came and went from his neighborhood before and after 11/22; found evidence—shell casings, photos, and took them to Dallas sheriff—here the narrative ends.

Anderton, James. Dallas FBI; part of chain of possession of "Harper Fragment"; told to get it to DC, and with no publicity.

Andrews, Dean. New Orleans attorney. Allegedly asked to defend LHO, as he had represented him before; perhaps correct to say that only "Deano" truly knows his story.

Atwood, William. Special advisor to US United Nations delegation;

was privy to negotiations, in progress, between emissaries of US govt and Castro, to normalize relations, which ended on 11/22; if LHO was pro-Cuban, Atwood's testimony would give LHO and JFK much in common.

Austin, Sgt. Horace. N. Orleans police; believed that LHO was being used by unknown forces at the time of the leaflet fracas.

Azcue, Eusebio. Employee at Cuban, Embassy in Mexico City, where "LHO" presented himself—but differed greatly in description from the LHO in this narrative.

Ballen, Samuel B. Potential employer of LHO, who found LHO to be negative about US and USSR, though formed the subjective impression that LHO liked JFK; recognized that LHO was skilled in secretive photo techniques.

Bargas, Tommy. Employee of Leslie Welding Co., where LHO was employed, 7/17–10/8/62—but could not identify LHO to WC.

Barger, Dr. James. Acoustics expert employed by Bolt, Beranek & Newman; told '78 House panel that acoustic evidence was highly suggestive of knoll gunman.

Barnes, W. E. Dallas p.d. Paraffin test on LHO.

Barnett, Welcome E. Dallas p.d. On duty at Elm and Houston yet looked up and saw nothing in windows—thought shots coming from top of building.

Beaty, Buford Lee. Fifteen-year Dallas detective. Told WC that "Everybody knew Jack Ruby."

Beers, Ira Jefferson. Photographer, *The Dallas Morning News*. Saw officers bring a suspect out of the TSBD and took a photo of suspect. Did not see suspect or photo again.

Bell, Audrey. Parkland nurse. Received bullet fragments taken by surgeons from Governor Connally that could not have come from the pristine "Magic Bullet"; also saw JFK on emergency gurney and did not see damage until Dr. Perry indicated the back of the head.

Bennett, Glen. SS—follow-up car; saw shot strike JFK 4 inches down from the right shoulder.

Bertram, Lane. SS agent—Houston; filed report indicating that several people had seen Ruby in the vicinity of JFK's hotel in Houston on 11/21.

Betzner, Hugh W. Motorcade eyewitness, photographer. Saw JFK's car come to virtual halt; saw police officials digging in plaza for a bullet.

Bledsoe, Mary E. Rented a room to LHO for five days, Oct. '63; Was on the bus driven by McWatters that LHO was on; yet her story is wild and disjointed and includes the sighting of someone being arrested.

Bolden, Abraham. SS—Chicago; threats vs. JFK in Chicago shortly before the events in Dallas.

Bookhout, James W. FBI—Dallas; sat in on interrogations of LHO, who vehemently denied shooting JFK.

Botelho, James A. USMC with LHO; LHO in Russian posture, but spoke of Marxism, not Russian Communism. Considered subsequent investigation into LHO's defection to be a charade.

Boyd, Elmer. Dallas p.d. Searched LHO at 4:05 and found revolver shells; "I never saw a man that could answer questions like he [LHO] could" (VII, 135).

Brading, Eugene, a/k/a Braden, Jim. Detained for suspicious behavior in Dealey Plaza. N. Orleans address was the same room as the one used by Carlos Marcello's private investigator, a man named David Ferrie.

Brehm, Charles. Dealey Plaza eyewitness. Shots close together, came from one of two buildings behind JFK.

Breneman, Charles. Dallas surveyor. Conducted two re-creations of 11/22—one for WC proved their hypothesis wrong; WC changed their figures, but not called before WC again.

Brewer, E. D. Dallas motorcycle officer. Far ahead of JFK in motorcade. Given info about gun in 2nd floor window of TSBD—but from whom?

Brewer, Johnny. Shoe salesman who alerted Julia Postal that LHO, looking suspicious, had entered Texas Theater.

Brian, V. J. Dallas Detective. Told WC that J. Hill found the two cartridges in sniper's nest, later amended to three; was earwitness to FBI S/A Hosty's comments about LHO in basement of Dallas p.d. on afternoon of 11/22.

Bringuier, Carlos. Pro-Cuban activist who punched LHO, for which LHO was fined $10.

Bronson, Charles. Photographed motorcade. Eighty-plus frames of movie strongly suggest two figures moving in sixth floor, TSBD, as JFK's car is directly underneath.

Burkley, George. JFK's physician. The US Navy death certificate he signed gave a more accurate description of the wounds than the autopsy report.

Cabell, Earle. Mayor of Dallas, brother of CIA exec fired by JFK. He and Mrs. Cabell told almost identical story to WC, except she distinctly smelled gunpowder as the car was well down Elm St.

Cairns, Dr. A. B. Methodist Hospital, Dallas. Examined the "Harper

Fragment" and found it to bear the greatest resemblance to occipital bone.

Carlin, Karen, a/k/a "Little Lynn." Ruby stripper. Hedged on positively identifying LHO at Ruby club.

Caster, Warren. TSBD employee. Brought two guns into TSBD on Wed., 11/20/63. Took them home the same day. One was a Mauser.

Chaney, James. Dallas motorcycle officer. Some shots from right rear; yet saw JFK struck in the face by bullet.

Chayes, Abraham. State Dept. legal advisor. Claimed he'd never heard of LHO before 11/22; admitted LHO never gave up US citizenship; when asked why LHO got passport in '63 after promising secrets to Russians, answered, "Of course, we know he didn't have very much information" (V, 373).

Cheramie, Rose. Transient found on La. roadside on 11/20 who professed to know of a plot in progress to kill JFK in Dallas; information ignored by Dallas; later killed on highway on 9/4/65 under questionable circumstances.

Conforto, Janet Adams, a/k/a "Jada." Ruby stripper. Saw LHO at Ruby's Carousel Club.

Connally, John. Governor of Texas. Believed then, and believes now, that he and JFK were hit by separate bullets. Corroborated by wife, Nellie.

Contreras, Oscar. Mexican. Met "LHO" in cafe; LHO was too obvious in a casual introduction, suggesting the impostiture; described LHO as short, and witness is 5'9."

Cooley, Sherman. USMC. Expert shot; if he had to be shot at by anyone on earth, he would have chosen LHO; too uncoordinated to be good with guns; Cooley did not think *he* could have duplicated Dealey Plaza.

Crafard, Larry. Ruby-Carousel Club hanger-on. Left Dallas on 11/23; found in Michigan by FBI. Sudden departure from Dallas unexplained.

Crowe, William D. a/k/a "Billy DeMar." Ruby emcee. Thought he had seen LHO at Carousel Club. Told to keep quiet.

Cummings, Raymond. Dallas cabbie. Reportedly drove LHO and David Ferrie to Carousel Club some time in '63.

Currington, John. Special Asst. to H. L. Hunt. Allegedly reported to Hunt that security around LHO, in custody, was lax; also claimed to have seen Marina Oswald in Hunt's office suite weeks after 11/22.

Daniel, Jean. French journalist. Part of US effort to normalize relations with Castro; was with Castro when news came from Dallas—Castro repeated what bad news it was.

Dannelly, Mrs. Lee. Austin, Texas, Draft Board. Saw "LHO" trying to get his discharge upgraded at a time when he could not have been anywhere near Austin (9/25/63).

Davis, Floyd. Rifle range owner. Unable to i.d. LHO. Corroborated by wife.

Dean, Patrick. Dallas p.d. Put on hot seat by WC counsel. Told of Canadian journalist with film, including TSBD.

Decker, Bill. Dallas county sheriff. Ordered men into r.r. yards; allegedly saw one bullet strike pavement; also alleged to have shady ties to suspicious characters well before 1963.

Delgado, Nelson. USMC buddy of LHO; LHO not a good shot and did not maintain rifle; much to tell about LHO.

de Mohrenschildt, George. Oil geologist and probably much more. Upper-crust aristocrat who befriended the downtrodden LHO. Suicide prior to House panel questions.

Dhority, C. N. Dallas policeman kept busy on 11/22.

Duran, Silvia. Cuban embassy. Described "LHO" as 5'3," thin, blond, and with blue or green eyes.

Eberhardt, A. M. Dallas cop. Knew Ruby well—JR had sent a christening card for A.E.'s child. "What cops did Ruby know best?" "He knew just about everybody" (XIII,195).

Edwards, Robert E. Dealey Plaza. Saw figure in upper window. "How many shots?" "Well, I heard one more than was fired, I believe" (VI, 205).

Faulkner, Jack W. Dallas p.d. Dealey Plaza. Got reports from several witnesses—none named. Interviewed unknown w/f; "I asked her where the shorts [sic] came from" (XIX, 511).

Ferrie, David. New Orleans individual of less-than-great morality who was involved with right-wing causes, mob figures, and LHO. Alleged that LHO had Ferrie's library card in his pocket when arrested 11/22, which was the cause for Ferrie's subsequent interrogation. Ferrie began that session, before being asked, by telling the authorities he did not know how the card got to LHO.

Fischer, Ronald B. Elm and Houston eyewitness. Got a very good look at somebody in TSBD upper floor window; had interesting comments for WC.

Flynn, Charles W. FBI agent. Opened a criminal informant file for Ruby in 1959; Ruby met with FBI in this role several times in that year.

Fritz, Will. Dallas Homicide Bureau chief. Warned LHO of his rights regularly, then did not record LHO's answers so they could be used against him.

Gallagher, John F. FBI neutron activation analysis.

Gaudet, William G. CIA operative; In one of the "several" coincidences that run through this narrative, he just happened to be just about everywhere LHO was on the Mexican trip; admitted, however, that he believed LHO was the patsy.

Grammer, Billy. Dallas p.d. switchboard. Took a call in the early hours of 11/24 strongly suggesting that LHO would be killed; tried to reach Curry and couldn't, as Curry had his phone off the hook. When awakened and told that Ruby had shot LHO, he then remembered whose voice had made the call.

Greener, Charles W. Gun shop owner. Aware of weapons' capabilities and the need for them to be sighted in.

Gregory, Dr. Charles F. Parkland surgeon—Connally. Would be able to shed much light on how much metal was removed from the governor.

Haire, Bernard J. Owned business adjacent to Texas Theater. Believed he saw an individual in custody removed from side door of theater.

Harbison, Charles. Texas state trooper. Stationed at door of Connally's operating room, handled fragments. Given to someone . . . ?

Harper, William. Dallas medical student. Found "Harper Fragment" in plaza, late afternoon, 11/23.

Helpern, Dr. Milton. NYC medical examiner. Had done over 10,000 autopsies by '63, and had many reservations about JFK "autopsy."

Hemming, Gary. USMC. Recruited by ONI; felt LHO was in similar capacity.

Hickey, George. SS agent, follow-up car; would have been a good witness, as he reacted quickly to events in Dealey Plaza; however, he was accused in a recent work of accidentally killing JFK, an absurd charge, so he was not called as a witness in this case. The man has been through enough.

Hill, Jean. Dealey Plaza eyewitness. A very courageous lady who has been through a lot for her honesty. She was not called in this trial as she is publishing a book of her recollections, and she can tell the story far better from that vantage point. If she is correct in saying she was questioned on an upper floor of a building by counsel for the WC, somebody's fibbing, as the WC had her in the Dallas Post Office.

Hill, Jimmy. Manager of after-hours club, the Cellar. Saw SS drinking on duty.

Hodge, Alfred D. Gun shop owner. Asked to come to police H.Q. on evening of 11/22 and look at "guns," plural.

Holmes, Harry. Postal inspector, Dallas. Could have told about LHO's peculiarities with respect to having p.o. boxes everywhere in his travels—an oddity for a cheapskate like LHO.

Holly, Harold B., Jr. Dallas police reserve. Testified to WC that many Dallas cops and reserves knew Ruby.

Hosty, James P. FBI Dallas. Case officer for LHO. Admitted to destruction of evidence, but well after the event.

Hoover, J. Edgar. FBI Director, 1924–1972. Took many secrets to his grave, even if, as he suggested to close friends, he would only be there for three days.

Jacks, Hurchel. Texas state highway patrol. Drove LBJ in motorcade. Saw JFK wound at Parkland. Has the distinction of being the last non-SS commoner to drive LBJ.

Johnsen, Richard. SS agent who was handed CE 399, or "Magic Bullet" by O. P. Wright at Parkland. Unable to i.d. it positively to FBI.

Johnson, Gladys. Owner of 1026 N. Beckley. Told how she read that LHO had been at a rifle range at a time when she knew he was in her residence.

Jones, Col. Robert E. 112th Military Intelligence, San Antonio, Texas. Had an intelligence file on A. Hidell, which identified A.H. as LHO.

Kantor, Seth. Journalist in motorcade. Highly respected in his field, Kantor insists to this day that he had a conversation with Ruby at Parkland, c. 1:30 on 11/22. WC suggested he was wrong.

Kay, Kathy. Carousel Club "entertainer." Claimed she saw, and danced with, LHO at Carousel Club.

Kirkwood, Pat. Owner of the Cellar—SS drinking, 11/21–22.

Levchenko, Stanislav. KGB defector to US. Told how Soviet intelligence was desperate for *any* US military info; this would suggest that either they picked the brains of the defector, LHO, or they avoided the spy, LHO.

Marchetti, Victor, CIA. Had knowledge of extensive CIA use of ONI personnel; indicated CIA got very tense when Jim Garrison brought Ferrie's name into case.

McIntyre, William. SS, follow-up car. Three shots, five seconds; agents' discussions at the time demonstrated nobody could pinpoint the source of the shots.

Mercer, Julia Ann. Dealey Plaza A.M. witness. Claimed to see rifle unloaded from pickup truck up on curb by knoll with Ruby behind the wheel. Saw police nearby.

Millican, A. J. Dealey Plaza eyewitness and H. Brennan coworker. Heard eight shots, from different locations, and from either a handgun or a rifle.

Molina, Joe R. TSBD employee. Suspected as subversive, had name broadcast in connection with 11/22 events. Then unceremoniously fired from TSBD after sixteen years.

Moorman, Mary. Dealey Plaza. Took famous Polaroid photo at time of Z313; also took two photos as car came down street, with TSBD clear in background. Cops got them and kept them.

Nix, Orville. Dealey Plaza. Took a home movie, of which a few frames have appeared in public. As of 7/15/91, Gayle Nix Jackson and David Nix are still seeking the return of the original print so it can be optically enhanced.

Norwood, Hal. Immigration and Naturalization Inspector. Reportedly received urgent phone calls on 11/22 to pick up a foreign national. Order quickly rescinded.

Odio, Sylvia. Cuban living in Dallas. Seen as the patsy in an LHO look-alike scam. Gave the WC fits with her testimony.

Olds, Gregory. Journalist. Allowed into LHO midnight press-conference with no questions asked, and had never been in the building before.

Oliver, Betty. "Babushka lady" in Dealey Plaza. Also lost home movies to authorities. Claims also that she met LHO at Ruby's club.

Oswald, Lee Harvey. Defendant. No doubt had, at minimum, some knowledge of certain events which were to transpire on 11/22; unlikely he had knowledge that anyone was going to expire that day; self-proclaimed "patsy," a confession which may have caused the events of 11/24.

Otepka, Otto. Chief Security Officer, State Dept. Claimed there was uncertainty, as late as June '63, as to whose side LHO was on.

Paine, Michael. Owner, Irving St. residence. Spent enough time with LHO to be able to form character opinions. Was separated from wife shortly before Marina arrived, came back to wife shortly after Marina departed . . .

Palmer, Henry. Voter registrar in Clinton, La. Convinced LHO waited in line to register in 9/63; LHO unable to register, then returned to Cadillac with two other w/m.

Pickard, Major John. Commander, Photo Dept., Canadian Def.

Dept. Studied "backyard photos"—seen as fakes in many regards.

Piper, Eddie. TSBD employee. Saw Roy Truly and Officer Baker hastily go up TSBD stairs, and nobody had come down them. Police then sent TSBD employees home after taking names and addresses.

Price, Jesse. Dealey Plaza. Shots from other than TSBD; saw someone flee in direction of railroad yards.

Quigley, John L. N. Orleans FBI. Interviewed LHO after leaflet embroglio; may have had other contacts.

Randle, Linnie Mae. Paine neighbor. Helped LHO get job at TSBD. Other witness to 27" bag, 11/22 A.M.

Reid, Mrs. Robet A. TSBD. Saw LHO leave building, with Coke in hand—in no hurry.

Revill, Lt. Jack. Dallas Criminal Intelligence. Told by FBI S/A Hosty early P.M. 11/22 that a Commie killed JFK, and that FBI knew of LHO, but couldn't reveal what they knew.

Rich, Nancy. Ruby employee. Had knowledge of regularity of police contacts at Carousel Club.

Rose, Dr. Earl. Dallas County Coroner. Might have had some thoughts on "chain of possession" as JFK left Texas without the benefit of an autopsy.

Shaw, Dr. Robert R. Connally surgeon, Parkland. Fragments?

Shorman, Robert. Carousel Club musician; saw hundreds of police at Ruby's club, including Will Fritz.

Sibert, James. FBI at JFK autopsy. Saw something which inspired him to write "surgery of the head area" at Bethesda. Gagged by FBI thereafter.

Similas, Norman. Canadian journalist. Claimed to have photographed TSBD, including a rifle barrel, with two figures in picture. Photo never printed by editor; received all materials except that picture back, plus hefty remuneration.

Soutre, Jean. Suspected foreign assassin. Believed to be in Dallas/Ft. Worth area, 11/22; from there, stories differ.

Speaker, Sandy. H. Brennan's foreman; told of five shots, from different locations. Also believed Brennan had been so grilled by the Feds that he became a changed person.

Steele, Charles H., Jr. New Orleans student. Hired by LHO to hand out leaflets for a few minutes, until incident was completed.

Styles, Sandra K. TSBD. Was with Victoria Adams on fourth floor and then went down the stairs and heard nobody.

Terry, L. R. Dealey Plaza. Saw rifle in sixth floor, TSBD. Two individuals with it.

Thornley, Kerry. USMC. With LHO in California. No rifle practice at all for their unit; LHO occasionally given special treatment. Later wrote a book about LHO—not as assassin, but just as an oddball.

Tomlinson, Darrell C. Parkland Hospital. Found "Magic Bullet." Not comfortable in telling WC that it came from Connally's stretcher to the exclusion of all others. Could not positively i.d. bullet.

Walker, Edwin. General of US Army, resigned. Had some interesting theories before WC, almost as if it was his case. Further study here.

Walter, William. FBI security clerk, New Orleans. Said to have seen documents indicating LHO was FBI informant; also received teletype, 11/18/63, re: threat vs. JFK in Dallas. Memo signed "Director."

Warner, Roger C. SS—Love Field. Left to question "suspect" Donald Wayne House, caught in Fort Worth . . .

Weiss, Dr. Mark. Acoustics expert for '78 House inquiry. Found fourth shot on police tape, within four to five feet of knoll "suspect" location; at least two other impulses on tape and possibly as many as nine shots.

Wilcott, James. CIA finance officer. Claimed to have handled payments to LHO, despite LHO's inability to do anything positive for agency.

# APPENDIX B

Re: LEE HARVEY OSWALD   Rifle Bullet, C1

On June 12, 1964, Darrell C. Tomlinson, Maintenance Employee, Parkland Hospital, Dallas, Texas, was shown Exhibit C1, a rifle slug, by Special Agent Bardwell D. Odum, Federal Bureau of Investigation. Tomlinson stated it appears to be the same one he found on a hospital carriage at Parkland Hospital on November 22, 1963, but he cannot positively identify the bullet as the one he found and showed to Mr. O. P. Wright. At the time he found the bullet, the hospital carriage was located in the Emergency Unit on the ground floor of the hospital.

On June 12, 1964, O. P. Wright, Personnel Officer, Parkland Hospital, Dallas, Texas, advised Special Agent Bardwell D. Odum that Exhibit C1, a rifle slug, shown to him at the time of the interview, looks like the slug found at Parkland Hospital on November 22, 1963, which he gave to Richard Johnsen, Special Agent of the Secret Service. He stated he was not present at the time the bullet was found, but on the afternoon of November 22, 1963, as he entered the Emergency Unit on the ground floor of the hospital, Mr. Tomlinson, an employee, called to him and pointed out a bullet, which was on a hospital carriage at that location. He estimated the time as being within an hour of the time President Kennedy and Governor Connally were brought to the hospital. He advised he could not positively identify C1 as being the same bullet which was found on November 22, 1963.

On June 24, 1964, Special Agent Richard B. Johnsen, United States Secret Service, Washington, D. C., was shown Exhibit C1, a rifle bullet, by Special Agent Elmer Lee Todd, Federal Bureau of Investigation. Johnsen advised he could not identify this bullet as the one he obtained from O. P. Wright, Parkland Hospital, Dallas, Texas, and gave to James Rowley, Chief, United States Secret Service, Washington, D. C., on November 22, 1963.

On June 24, 1964, James Rowley, Chief, United States Secret Service, Washington, D. C., was shown Exhibit C1, a rifle bullet, by Special Agent Elmer Lee Todd. Rowley advised he could

2

COMMISSION EXHIBIT No. 2011—Continued

Re: LEE HARVEY OSWALD

not identify this bullet as the one he received from Special Agent Richard B. Johnsen and gave to Special Agent Todd on November 22, 1963.

On June 24, 1964, Special Agent Elmer Lee Todd, Washington, D. C., identified C1, a rifle bullet, as being the same one he received from James Rowley, Chief, United States Secret Service, Washington, D. C., on November 22, 1963. This identification was made from initials marked thereon by Special Agent Todd at the Federal Bureau of Investigation laboratory upon receipt.

3

COMMISSION EXHIBIT No. 2011—Continued

FIGURE ONE: CE 2011, a report on the "magic bullet" indicates that none of the individuals who allegedly saw the bullet was able to identify it positively. The inability to maintain the integrity of the chain of evidence among witnesses renders the bullet worthless as evidence. This document shatters it. (*Hearings*, XXIV, 412.)

UNITED STATES DEPARTMENT OF JUSTICE

FEDERAL BUREAU OF INVESTIGATION

*In Reply, Please Refer to*
*File No.*

WASHINGTON 25, D. C.

June 16, 1964

LEE HARVEY OSWALD

On June 16, 1964, the confidential source
abroad which had furnished information classified
Secret on March 16, 1964, concerning the C-14 rifle,
Serial No. C-2766, which information was incorporated
into a memorandum dated March 17, 1964, captioned as
above, gave permission to declassify all of the information it had provided on March 16, 1964, concerning
the C-14 rifle.

## COMMISSION EXHIBIT No. 2559—Continued

Memo for the Record

Mr. Eisenberg

Telephone message received from Mr. Meade Werner of the BRL
of the Aberdeen Proving Ground on April 6, 1964:

"There were three pieces in the scope examined by the
BRL gunsmith. Two pieces were .015 inches thick so placed
as to elevate the scope with respect to the gun. One piece
was .020 inches thick so placed as to point the scope
leftward with respect to the gun. The gunsmith observed
that the scope as we received it was installed as if for
a left-handed man."

## COMMISSION EXHIBIT No. 2560

FIGURE TWO: CE 2560, a document "buried" in the lower corner of
the page, which offhandedly states, "The gunsmith observed that the
scope as we received it was installed as if for a left-handed man."
(*Hearings,* XXV, 799.)

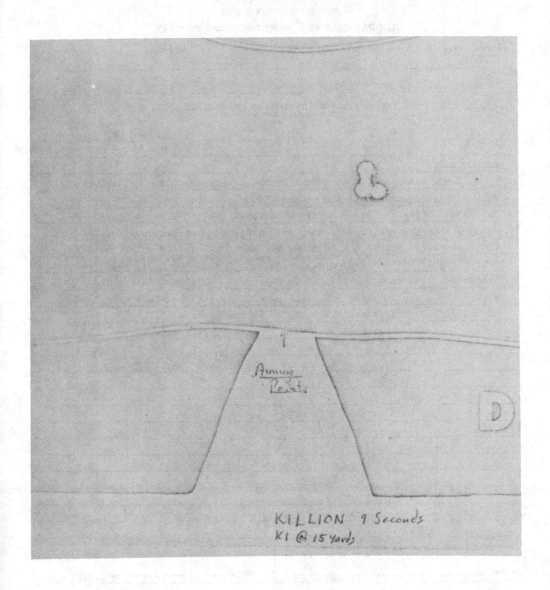

**FIGURE THREE: CE 549, a sample of the FBI's test firings of the Mannlicher-Carcano. This exhibit shows that a firearms expert named Killion, given nine seconds, could not hit the notch of the target with the weapon stationary from a distance of *fifteen yards*. (*Hearings*, XVII, 245.)**

FORM 114 SUP. INV.

## COUNTY OF DALLAS
### SHERIFF'S DEPARTMENT
## SUPPLEMENTARY INVESTIGATION REPORT

Name of Complainant                               Serial No.

Offense
_____

DETAILS OF OFFENSE, PROGRESS OF INVESTIGATION, ETC.:
(Investigating Officer must sign)

Date **Nov. 22, 1963** 19___

Mr. Decker;

     I was assisting in th search of the 6th floor of the Dallas County
Book Depository at Elm st and Houston St. proceeding from the Nartkxxtxx
East side of the building . Officer Whiteman DPD and I were together as
we approched the Northwest corner of the building xxxxxxxxtxx I was the
rifle partially hidden behind a row of books with two (2) other boxes of
books against the rifle. The rifle appeared tb be a 7.65mm Mauser with a
telescope sight on the rifle. Capt. Fritz was called to the scene and also
someone from the ID ENXXX pictures were taken and then Capt Fritz picked
up the rifle. I first saw the rifle at 1:22pm date.


                             E. L. Boone. 240 DSO

I recommend this case be declared { Unfounded / Inactive (not cleared) ☐ / Cleared by Arrest ☐ }     Case declared { Inactive (not cleared) ☐ / Unfounded ☐ }

Signed_____          Signed_____

                  Investigating Officer                Commanding Officer

DECKER EXHIBIT No. 5323—Continued

**FIGURE FOUR: Part of DECKER 5323, this document, which
appears in two different forms but with the same information, shows
that Deputy Eugene Boone, who found the "assassination rifle" on the
sixth floor of the Depository, identified it in writing as something quite
different than what we have been led to believe. (*Hearings*, XIX, 507.)**

MISCELLANEOUS CRIME REPORT

Form 111.

# COUNTY OF DALLAS
## SHERIFF'S DEPARTMENT

ASSAULT WITH INTENT TO COMMIT MURDER
Classification of Crime

Report 400 Block of Elm Street   Serial No. 1A-20-63

Name of injured party **John B. Connally**

Res. Address **Austin, Texas**

Phone

Date Committed **November 22, 1963**

Time Committed

Person Attacked
**John B. Connally W/M**

Property Attacked **6.25 Italian rifle**

How Attacked

Means of Attack

Object of Attack

Trademark

Vehicle Used

Where Committed **Dallas, Texas**

Reported by

Address

Time Reported **November 22, 1963**

Reported to

Investigating Officers

Persons Arrested **Lee Harvey Oswald W/M 24** Arrest No.

Arrest No.

Arrest No. Date **11-24-63**

By

Suspect

Hair Color                    Eye Color

Height            Weight                Age

Nationality                    Build

Occupation                    Marks

Dress

The complainant, THE GOVERNOR OF THE STATE OF TEXAS, was riding in a motorcade with JOHN KENNEDY, PRESIDENT OF THE UNITED STATES and their wives. 3
shots rang out coming from the Texas School Book Depository building located
at the corner of Elm and Houston Streets.

| QUANTITY | DESCRIPTION OF PROPERTY STOLEN | ESTIMATED VALUE | RECOVERED Quantity | Date |
|---|---|---|---|---|
| | | | | |
| | | | | |
| | | | | |
| | | | | |
| | | | | |
| | | | | |

I hereby acknowledge receipt of the above recovered articles delivered to me by

Date _____ (Signed) _____

TO INVESTIGATION OFFICER: Complete this report by writing in missing data: if available. Write on reverse side details of your investigation and names and addresses of witnesses.

November 22, 1963

—Case Filed—          Inactive (not cleared) ☐   Date

Yes ☒ No ☐   This offense is   Unfounded ☐

Cleared by arrest ☒

Arresting Officer.

DECKER EXHIBIT No. 5823—Continued

**FIGURE FIVE:** Another document from DECKER 5323, which charges the defendant with killing the President with a "6.25 Italian rifle." A document such as this could, by itself, ruin a prosecution's case, or, at worst, reflect a sloppiness on the part of Dallas authorities who were not concerned that there would be a trial. Either way, when coupled with the data in Figure Four, it gives one pause about the rifle(s) found. (*Hearings,* XIX, 456 and 457.)

COMMISSION EXHIBIT 479

**FIGURE SIX: Howard Brennan's "confusion". In the top photo, CE 477, he is posing on March 20, 1964 to show the Warren Commission what a perfect view he had of the crime in Dealey Plaza. In the bottom photo, CE 479, one frame from the Zapruder film, Mr. Brennan is shown in the actual position he was on November 22, 1963. The Warren Commission noticed the obvious discrepancy, as Counsel David Belin asked, "Your legs, in this picture, Exhibit 479, I notice, are not dangling on the front side, is that correct?" Brennan answered that Belin's comment was correct, and then the subject was changed. (Exhibits are from *Hearings,* XVII, 197–8; the testimony appears in III, 142.)**

Commission Exhibit No. 391

SUPPLEMENTARY REPORT OF AUTOPSY NUMBER A63-272
PRESIDENT JOHN F. KENNEDY

PATHOLOGICAL EXAMINATION REPORT          No. A63-272          Page 1

GROSS DESCRIPTION OF BRAIN:

Following formalin fixation the brain weighs 1500 gms. The right cerebral hemisphere is found to be markedly disrupted. There is a longitudinal laceration of the right hemisphere which is para-sagittal in position approximately 2.5 cm. to the right of the of the midline which extends from the tip of the occipital lobe posteriorly to the tip of the frontal lobe anteriorly. The base of the laceration is situated approximately 4.5 cm. below the vertex in the white matter. There is considerable loss of cortical substance above the base of the laceration, particularly in the parietal lobe. The margins of this laceration are at all points jagged and irregular, with additional lacerations extending in varying directions and for varying distances from the main laceration. In addition, there is a laceration of the corpus callosum extending from the genu to the tail. Exposed in this latter laceration are the interiors of the right lateral and third ventricles.

When viewed from the vertex the left cerebral hemisphere is intact. There is marked engorgement of meningeal blood vessels of the left temporal and frontal regions with considerable associated sub-arachnoid hemorrhage. The gyri and sulci over the left hemisphere are of essentially normal size and distribution. Those on the right are too fragmented and distorted for satisfactory description.

When viewed from the basilar aspect the disruption of the right cortex is again obvious. There is a longitudinal laceration of the mid-brain through the floor of the third ventricle just behind the optic chiasm and the mammillary bodies. This laceration partially communicates with an oblique 1.5 cm. tear through the left cerebral peduncle. There are irregular superficial lacerations over the basilar aspects of the left temporal and frontal lobes.

In the interest of preserving the specimen coronal sections are not made. The following sections are taken for microscopic examination:

   a.  From the margin of the laceration in the right parietal lobe.

   b.  From the margin of the laceration in the corpus callosum.

   c.  From the anterior portion of the laceration in the right frontal lobe.

   d.  From the contused left fronto-parietal cortex.

   e.  From the line of transection of the spinal cord.

   f.  From the right cerebellar cortex.

   g.  From the superficial laceration of the basilar aspect of the left temporal lobe.

COMMISSION EXHIBIT 391

**FIGURE SEVEN: CE 391, the supplemental Autopsy Report on John F. Kennedy, No. A63-272. "Following formalin fixation the brain weighs 1500 gms." Most standard texts on the brain suggest the average brain weighs 1350 grams. Oswald's brain at autopsy weighed 1450 grams; JFK's, which lost cortical substance in Zapruder frame 313, some of which sprayed the car, its occupants, and the police escort, and some which wound up on the floor at Parkland, is shown in this document, signed on page 2 by James J. Humes, to weigh 1500 grams, an *impossibility*. I know of no one present in the morgue at Bethesda, with the possible exception of Dr. Humes, who would ascribe such weight to what remained of the President's brain. (*Hearings*, XVI, 987.)**

FORM 114 SUP. INV.

### COUNTY OF DALLAS
#### SHERIFF'S DEPARTMENT
#### SUPPLEMENTARY INVESTIGATION REPORT

Name of Complainant                                Serial No.

    Page 3 - continued

Offense

____Allan Sweatt, Chief Deputy Sheriff, Dallas County, Texas.____

DETAILS OF OFFENSE, PROGRESS OF INVESTIGATION, ETC.:
(Investigating Officer must sign)

Date_____19____

During this time, Deputy Bill Wiseman brought in two girls to me with some pictures they had taken. 1 picture was taken just shortly before the shooting of the President which showed the Sexton Building in the background. This picture was turned over to Secret Service Agent Patterson, who gave this woman his card, advising her that the picture would be returned to her.

I also received copies of pictures taken from a witness by name of "Betzner, Jr.", which have been included in the files of this case.

I have contacted all Deputies to come in this date and make their supplements of activities during the day of November 22nd, 1963.

I still have in my custody all original statements, supplements and copies of pictures by Betzner subject.

                                        Allan Sweatt

I recommend this case be declared {Unfounded ☐ / Inactive (not cleared) ☐ / Cleared by Arrest ☐}    Case declared {Inactive (not cleared) ☐ / Unfounded ☐}

Signed_____ Investigating Officer    Signed_____ Commanding Officer

DECKER EXHIBIT No. 5323—Continued

**FIGURE EIGHT: Another document from DECKER 5323, a photo taken by Mary Moorman, showing the Depository in full during the shooting, was confiscated by local authorities and passed to a Secret Service agent, who had no jurisdiction whatsoever, again suggesting that local authorities were not overly concerned about the possibility of a trial. Of equal interest in this document is the notation of the "Sexton Building" which is in fact the Depository. Only with regard to threatening evidence such as this photo, which has never been seen since, is the Book Depository's old name invoked. (*Hearings,* XIX, 533.)**

Standard Form 600
Promulgated Nov. 1962
By Bureau of the Budget
Circular A-23

| HEALTH RECORD | CHRONOLOGICAL RECORD OF MEDICAL CARE |
|---|---|
| DATE | SYMPTOMS, DIAGNOSIS, TREATMENT, TREATING ORGANIZATION (Sign each entry) |

USNAS, Navy #3835, c/o FPO, San Francisco, California

9/16/58

Diagnosis: Urethritis, Acute, due to gonococcus #0303
Origin: In line of duty, not due to own misconduct.
CC: Urethral discharge

PI: Patient complains of a slight discharge and a stinging
sensation on urination.

PH: Previous V.D.:

PE: Essentially negative except for a thick mucopurulent
discharge from the urethra.

LAB: Smear reveals gram negative intra-and extracellular
diplococci having the morphology of N. Gonorrhea.

RX: Procain Penicillin 900,000 Units I.M. X 3 days

9/16/58 To duty under treatment and observation:

PES-1421(VD) submitted: No B 754

SUBMITTED P. DERANIAN
CAPT.MC USN

APPROVED:

P. DERANIAN
CAPT MC USN
SENIOR MEDICAL OFFICER

| SEX | RACE | GRADE, RATING, OR POSITION | ORGANIZATION UNIT | COMPONENT OR BRANCH | SERVICE, DEPT. OR AGENCY |
|---|---|---|---|---|---|
| M | C | PVT | MACS 1 MAG 11 | USMC | |

| PATIENT'S LAST NAME—FIRST NAME—MIDDLE NAME | DATE OF BIRTH (DAY-MONTH-YEAR) | IDENTIFICATION NO. |
|---|---|---|
| OSWALD, Lee Harvey | 10/18/39 | 1653230 |

CHRONOLOGICAL RECORD OF MEDICAL CARE
Standard Form 600.

DONABEDIAN EXHIBIT No. 1—Continued

**FIGURE NINE: Donabedian Exhibit #1, which shows that Oswald, while a Marine, contracted gonorrhea, *in the line of duty*. (*Hearings*, XIX, 605.)**

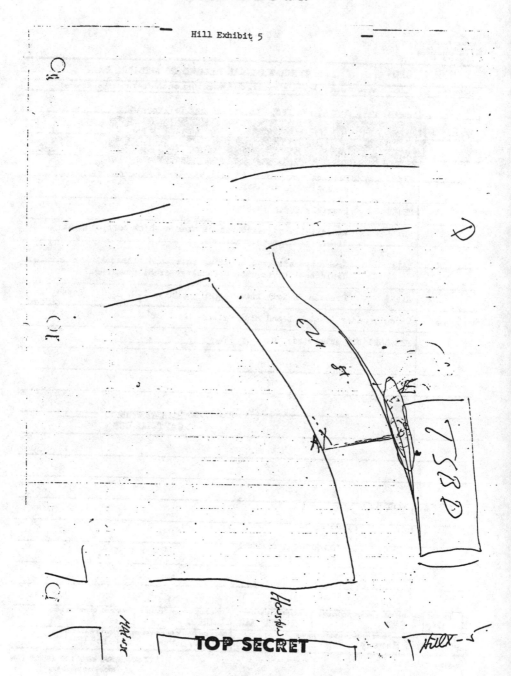

Hill Exhibit 5

HILL (JEAN) EXHIBIT No. 5

**FIGURE TEN: Hill Exhibit #5. In this hastily executed sketch, a key eyewitness has drawn her location in Dealey Plaza. The ever-vigilant authorities have wisely stamped it "TOP SECRET" lest America's enemies secure it. (*Hearings,* XX, 158.)**

Mr. CARR. I am Waggoner Carr, attorney general of the State of Texas.

Mr. RANKIN. And you are a practicing lawyer, are you?

Mr. CARR. Yes, sir; before I was elected, I was practicing law in Lubbock, Tex. Now, of course, being attorney general, this has taken me out of the private practice. Prior to that I graduated from law school at the University of Texas, had my pre-law with a BBA degree from Texas Tech. I have been an assistant district attorney for the 72d judicial district in Texas; county attorney of Lubbock County for 2 years; served in the Texas House of Representatives for 10 years, the last 4 of those years being as Speaker of the House, and was elected attorney general in 1960.

Mr. RANKIN. You are the same Waggoner Carr who has participated from time to time in observing these hearings and cooperating with the Commission regarding its work?

Mr. CARR. Yes.

Mr. RANKIN. Insofar as the State of Texas is concerned?

Mr. CARR. Yes.

Mr. RANKIN. Were you here when Henry Wade was testifying with regard to a conversation between himself and yourself, this morning?

Mr. CARR. Yes, sir.

Mr. RANKIN. Would you relate to us that conversation as you recall it, both what you said and what he said?

Mr. CARR. As I recall, it was around 8 or 9 o'clock at night on November 22, 1963, when I received a long-distance telephone call from Washington from someone in the White House. I can't for the life of me remember who it was.

A rumor had been heard here that there was going to be an allegation in the indictment against Oswald connecting the assassination with an international conspiracy, and the inquiry was made whether I had any knowledge of it, and I told him I had no knowledge of it.

As a matter of fact, I hadn't been in Dallas since the assassination and was not there at the time of the assassination.

So the request was made of me to contact Mr. Wade to find out if that allegation was in the indictment.

I received the definite impression that the concern of the caller was that because of the emotion or the high tension that existed at that time that someone might thoughtlessly place in the indictment such an allegation without having the proof of such a conspiracy. So I did call Mr. Wade from my home, when I received the call, and he told me very much what he repeated to you today, as I recall, that he had no knowledge of anyone desiring to have that or planning to have that in the indictment; that it would be surplusage, it was not necessary to allege it, and that it would not be in there, but that he would doublecheck it to be sure.

And then I called back, and—as I recall I did—and informed the White House participant in the conversation of what Mr. Wade had said, and that was all of it.

Mr. RANKIN. Was there anything said to you at any time by anybody from Washington that if there was any evidence that was credible to support such an international conspiracy it should not be included in the indictment or complaint or any action?

Mr. CARR. Oh, no; absolutely not. There was no direct talk or indirect talk or insinuation that the facts, whatever they might be, should be suppressed. It was simply that in the tension someone might put something in an indictment for an advantage here or disadvantage there, that could not be proved, which would have very serious reaction, which the local person might not anticipate since he might not have the entire picture of what the reaction might be.

Mr. RANKIN. Thank you. That is all I have, Mr. Chief Justice.

The CHAIRMAN. Mr. Attorney General, I don't know whether you will be testifying on any other subject before the Commission or not, but in the event that you do not, and both of us are not here in the Commission again at the same time, I want to say to you for the record that from the very beginning of our investigation your cooperation has been complete, it has been enthusiastic, and it has been most helpful to the Commission.

The Commission and I all appreciate it very much indeed.

**FIGURE ELEVEN: Testimony by Waggoner Carr, the Attorney General of Texas, clearly states that officials within the White House were attempting to dictate on the evening of November 22, 1963 the wording of Oswald's indictment. The testimony shows that Carr cannot recall the name of the caller, yet he returned the call. (*Hearings*, V, 259.)**

Form 141- AFFIDAVIT—General    David Johnston Exhibit 3

*IN THE NAME AND BY THE AUTHORITY OF THE STATE OF TEXAS.*

    PERSONALLY APPEARED before me the undersigned authority this affiant, who after being by me duly sworn, deposes and says your Affiant has good reason to believe and does believe that one

    *Lee Harvey Oswald*

hereinafter styled Defendant, heretofore on or about the *22nd* day of *November* A. D. 19*63* in the County of Dallas and State of Texas, did unlawfully *then and there* *voluntarily* *and* **With Malice Aforethought** *kill* *J.D. Tippitt by shooting him with a gun*

Against the peace and dignity of the State.

David Johnston Exhibit No. 3

Sworn to and subscribed before me this the

*22nd* day of *NOVEMBER* A. D. 19*63*

*W. F. Alexander*

Assistant Criminal District Attorney of Dallas County, Texas.

*J.W. Fritz*

Affiant

JOHNSTON EXHIBIT NO. 3

**FIGURE TWELVE: David Johnston Exhibit #3.** An unnoticed postscript to the events of November 22, 1963. In this document, Oswald was arraigned before Magistrate Johnston for the Tippit murder. However, the charge, as shown, was premeditated murder, suggesting either that Oswald went to Tenth and Patton to kill a specific police officer that day, or that it did not matter, as it would never reach a courtroom. As we now know, it did not. (*Hearings*, XX, 319.)

# SELECT BIBLIOGRAPHY

Anson, Robert S. *They've Killed the President! The Search for the Murderers of John F. Kennedy.* New York: Bantam Books, 1975.

Ashman, Charles. *The CIA-Mafia Link: The Inside Secrets of Assassination, American Style.* New York: Manor Books, 1975.

Bamford, James. *The Puzzle Palace: A report on NSA, America's Most Secret Agency.* Boston: Houghton-Mifflin, 1982.

Belin, David W. *November 22, 1963: You Are the Jury.* New York: Quadrangle Press, 1973.

Blakey, G. Robert, and Billings, Richard N. *The Plot to Kill the President: Organized Crime Assassinated J.F.K.* New York: Times Books, 1981.

Bloomgarden, Henry S. *The Gun: A Biography of the Gun That Killed John F. Kennedy.* New York: Bantam Books, 1976.

Blumenthal, Sid, and Yazijian, Harvey. *Government by Gunplay: Assassination Conspiracy Theories from Dallas to Today.* New York: New American Library, 1976.

Bringuier, Carlos. *Red Friday: November 22, 1963.* Chicago: C. Hallberg, 1969.

Brook-Shepherd, Gordon. *The Storm Birds: Soviet Post-War Defectors.* London: Weidenfeld and Nicolson, 1988.

Buchanan, Thomas G. *Who Killed Kennedy?* New York: G.P. Putnam's Sons, 1964.

Canfield, Michael, and Weberman, Alan J. *Coup D'Etat in America: The CIA and the Assassination of John F. Kennedy.* New York: The Third Press, 1975.

Clarke, James W. *American Assassins: The Darker Side of Politics.* Princeton, N.J.: Princeton University Press, 1982.

Crenshaw, Dr. Charles A., with Hansen, Jens, and Shaw, J. Gary. *JFK: Conspiracy of Silence.* New York: Signet, 1992.

Curry, Jesse E. *JFK Assassination File.* Dallas: By Author, 1969.

David, Jay, ed. *The Weight of the Evidence: The Warren Report and its Critics.* New York: Meredith Press, 1968.

Davidson, Jean. *Oswald's Game.* New York: W.W. Norton, 1983.

Davis, John H. *Mafia Kingfish: Carlos Marcello and the Assassination of John F. Kennedy.* New York: McGraw-Hill, 1989.

DeLillo, Don. *Libra.* New York: Viking, 1988.

Eddowes, Michael. *The Oswald File.* New York: Clarkson Potter, 1977.

Epstein, Edward Jay. *Counterplot.* New York: Viking Press, 1959.

———. *Inquest: The Warren Commission and the Establishment of Truth.* New York: Viking Press, 1966.

———. *Legend: The Secret World of Lee Harvey Oswald.* New York: Reader's Digest Press, 1978.

Feldman, Harold. *Fifty-one Witnesses: The Grassy Knoll.* San Francisco: Idlewild, 1965.

Fensterwald, Bernard, and Ewing, Michael, eds. *Coincidence or Conspiracy?* New York: Zebra Books, 1977.

Flammonde, Paris. *The Kennedy Conspiracy: An Uncommissioned Report on the Jim Garrison Investigation.* New York: Meredith Press, 1969.

Ford, Gerald R., and Stiles, John R. *Portrait of the Assassin.* New York: Ballantine Books, 1966.

Fox, Sylvan. *The Unanswered Questions about President Kennedy's Assassination.* New York: Award Books, 1965.

Garrison, Jim. *A Heritage of Stone.* New York: G.P. Putnam's Sons, 1970.

———. *On the Trail of the Assassins: My Investigation and Prosecution of the Murder of President Kennedy.* New York: Sheridan Square Press, 1988.

Giancana, Sam and Chuck. *Double Cross: The Explosive, Inside Story of the Mobster Who Controlled America.* New York: Warner Books, 1992.

Groden, Robert J., and Livingstone, Harrison Edward. *High Treason: The Assassination of President John F. Kennedy: What Really Happened.* New York: The Conservatory Press, 1989.

Hepburn, James. *Farewell America.* Belgium: Frontiers Publishing Company, 1968.

Hougan, Jim. *Secret Agenda.* New York: Random House, 1984.

———. *Spooks.* New York: William Morrow, 1978.

Houts, Marshall. *Where Death Delights: The Story of Dr. Milton Helpern and Forensic Medicine.* New York: Coward-McCann, 1967.

Hurt, Henry. *Reasonable Doubt: An Investigation Into the Assassination of John F. Kennedy.* New York: Holt, Rinehart, and Winston, 1986.

Israel, Lee. *Kilgallen.* New York: Delacorte Press, 1979.

Joesten, Joachim. *Oswald: Assassin or Fall Guy?* New York: Marzani and Munsell, 1964.

Jones, Penn Jr. *Forgive My Grief.* 5 Volumes. Midlothian, Texas: Midlothian Mirror, 1966ff.

Kantor, Seth. *Who Was Jack Ruby?* New York, Everest House, 1978.

Kirkwood, James. *American Grotesque: An Account of the Clay Shaw—Jim Garrison Affair in the City of New Orleans.* New York: Simon and Schuster, 1970.

Lane, Mark. *A Citizen's Dissent: Mark Lane Replies.* New York: Holt, Rinehart and Winston, 1968.

———. *Plausible Denial: Was the CIA Involved in the Assassination of JFK?* New York: Thunder's Mouth Press, 1991.

———. *Rush to Judgment.* New York: Holt, Rinehart and Winston, 1966.

Lattimer, Dr. John K. *Kennedy and Lincoln: Medical and Ballistic Comparisons of Their Assassinations.* New York: Harcourt Brace Jovanovich, 1980.

Lifton, David S. *Best Evidence: Disguise and Deception in the Assassination of John F. Kennedy.* New York: Macmillan, 1980.

Livingstone, Harrison Edward. *High Treason 2.* New York: Carroll and Graf, 1992.

McDonald, Hugh C. *Appointment in Dallas: The Final Solution to the Assassination of JFK.* New York: H. McDonald Publishing Co., 1975.

McMillan, Priscilla Johnson. *Marina and Lee.* New York: Bantam Books, 1978.

Manchester, William. *The Death of a President: November 1963.* New York: Harper and Row, 1967.

Marchetti, Victor, and Marks, John. *The CIA and the Cult of Intelligence.* New York: Alfred A. Knopf, 1974.

Marcus, Raymond. *The Bastard Bullet: A Search for Legitimacy for Commission Exhibit 399.* Los Angeles: by author, 1990.

Marrs, Jim. *Crossfire: The Plot that Killed Kennedy.* New York: Carroll and Graf, 1989.

Meagher, Sylvia. *Accessories After the Fact: The Warren Commission, the Authorities, and the Report.* New York: Vintage Books, 1976.

Melanson, Philip H. *Spy Saga: Lee Harvey Oswald and U.S. Intelligence.* New York: Praeger, 1990.

Menninger, Bonar. *Mortal Error: The Shot that Killed JFK.* New York: St. Martin's Press, 1992.

Model, F. Peter, and Groden, Robert J. *JFK: The Case for Conspiracy.* New York: Manor Books, 1976.

Morin, Relman. *Assassination: The Death of President John F. Kennedy.* New York: New American Library, 1968.

Newman, Albert H. *The Assassination of John F. Kennedy: The Reasons Why.* New York: Clarkson N. Potter, 1970.

North, Mark. *Act of Treason: The Role of J. Edgar Hoover in the Assassination of President Kennedy.* New York: Carroll and Graf, 1991.

O'Neill, Tip, and Novak, William. *Man of the House: The Life and Political Memoirs of Speaker Tip O'Neill.* New York: Random House, 1987.

Oswald, Robert, with Land, Myrick and Barbara. *Lee: A Portrait of Lee Harvey Oswald.* New York: Coward-McCann, 1967.

O'Toole, George. *The Assassination Tapes: An Electronic Probe Into the Murder of John F. Kennedy and the Dallas Coverup.* New York: Penthouse Press, 1975.

Popkin, Richard H. *The Second Oswald.* New York: Avon Books, 1966.

Prouty, L. Fletcher. *The Secret Team: The CIA and Its Allies in Control of the United States and the World.* Englewood Cliffs, N.J.: Prentice-Hall, 1973.

Roffman, Howard. *Presumed Guilty.* S. Brunswick, N.J.: A. S. Barnes, 1976.

Sauvage, Leo. *The Oswald Affair: An Examination of the Contradictions and Omissions of the Warren Report.*Cleveland: World Publishing, 1966.

Scheim, David E. *Contract on America: The Mafia Murder of President John F. Kennedy.* New York: Shapolsky Books, 1988.

Scott, Peter Dale; Hoch, Paul L.; and Stetler, Russell. *The Assassinations: Dallas and Beyond: A Guide to Cover-ups and Investigations.* New York: Random House, 1976.

Shaw, J. Gary, and Harris, Larry R. *Cover-Up: The Governmental Conspiracy to Conceal the Facts About the Public Execution of John Kennedy.* Cleburne, Texas: by authors, 1976.

State of Texas. Attorney General's Office. *Texas Supplemental Report on the Assassination of President John F. Kennedy and the Serious Wounding of Governor John B. Connally, November 22, 1963.* Austin: Attorney General's Office, 1964.

Sullivan, William C., with Brown, Bill. *The Bureau: My Thirty Years in Hoover's FBI.* New York: W.W. Norton, 1979.

Summers, Anthony. *Conspiracy.* New York: McGraw-Hill, 1980.

Thompson, Josiah. *Six Seconds in Dallas: A Micro-Study of the Kennedy Assassination.* New York: Bernard Geis, 1967.

Thornley, Kerry. *Oswald.* Chicago: New Classics House, 1965.

United States. House of Representatives. *The Final Assassinations*

*Report: Report on the Select Committee on Assassinations.* New York: Bantam Books, 1979.

————. House. Select Committee on Assassinations. *Hearings Before the Select Committee: Investigation of the Assassination of President John F. Kennedy.* 95th Cong., 2nd sess. 5 vol., 1978.

————. House. Select Committee on Assassinations. *Investigation of the Assassination of President John F. Kennedy: Appendix to Hearings Before the Select Committee on Assassinations.* 95th Cong., 2nd sess. 7 vol., 1979.

————. Rockefeller Commission. *Report to the President by the Commission on CIA Activities Within the United States.* New York: Manor Books, 1975.

————. Senate. "Church Committee." *Final Report of the Select Committee to Study Governmental Operations: Book V—The Investigation of the Assassination of President John F. Kennedy; Performance of the Intelligence Agencies.* Washington, D.C.: Government Printing Office, 1976.

————. Warren Commission. *Hearings Before the President's Commission on the Assassination of President Kennedy.* 26 Volumes. Washington, D.C.: Government Printing Office, 1965.

Weisberg, Harold. *Oswald in New Orleans: Case for Conspiracy with the C.I.A.* New York: Canyon Books, 1967.

————. *Whitewash—The Report on The Warren Report.* New York: Dell Publishing Co., 1966.

————. *Whitewash II: The FBI-Secret Service Cover-up.* New York: Dell Publishing Co., 1967.

————. *Photographic Whitewash: Suppressed Kennedy Assassination Pictures.* Hyattstown, Maryland: by author, 1967.

————. *Whitewash IV—JFK Assassination Transcript.* Frederick, Maryland: by author, 1974.

————. *Post Mortem: JFK Assassination Cover-up Smashed!* Frederick, Maryland: by author, 1965.

Wilber, Charles. *Medicolegal Investigation of the President John F. Kennedy Murder.* Springfield, Ill.: Charles Thomas and Sons, 1978.

Youngblood, Rufus W. *20 Years in the Secret Service.* New York: Simon and Schuster, 1973.

Zirbel, Craig I. *The Texas Connection: The Assassination of John F. Kennedy.* Scottsdale, Arizona: The Texas Connection Company, 1991.

Excepting the rash of recent titles cited above, and those worthy of reprinting *because* of the rash of recent titles, most of the works cited above are long out of print, and some are in the category of "downright hard to find." Where the publication is listed "by author," some titles may still be available "from author." If not, two excellent—and reasonable—booksellers on assassination and related ephemera are The Last Hurrah Bookshop, 937 Memorial Avenue, Williamsport, Pa. 17701 (717) 327-9338; and The President's Box Bookshop, PO Box 1255, Washington, DC 20013 (703) 998-7390.

# INDEX

Aberdeen Proving Grounds, 344–345, 346

Ables, Don, 613

Adamcik, John P., 226, 229, 230, 613

Adams, Victoria E., 613

Agers, Bradley, 613

*Air Force One*, xvi, 534, 546, 553, 556

Akin, Gene C., 613

Alaska, 512, 513

Alba, Adrian T., 130–136, 206, 374–375

Alderson, Lawrence, 613

Aleman, Jose, 545–546

Alexander, William, 613

Allright Parking Systems, 482, 483

Altgens, James, 528–530

Alyea, Tom, 182, 183, 202

*American Rifleman*, 142

Anderson, Eugene D., 354–358, 378

Anderson, William C., 613

Anderton, James, 613

Andrews, Dean, 613

Andrews Air Force Base, 534, 546

Applin, George, 549

Arce, Danny G., 470–471

Army, U.S., evidence as handled by, 345–362

Arnold, Carolyn, 525–527

Arnold, Gordon, 512–514

assassination, ix, xi, xiii, 23, 27, 29, 41, 84, 106, 210, 212–213, 386
  historical lessons of, 601–612
  photographs of, 528–529; *see also* Zapruder film
  Secret Service and, xiii, xvi, 46, 157, 213, 277, 353, 400–428, 464, 466, 474, 506, 525, 529, 555
  shooting sequence in, 466–476, 501–520, 523–530
  weapon in, *see* Mannlicher–Carcano rifle; Mauser rifle
  *see also specific incidents and individuals*

Associated Press, 529

Atkins, Thomas, 470

Atlanta, Ga., 398

Atwood, William, 613–614

Ault, Cecil, 470

Austin, Horace, 614

Austin, Tex., 509

autopsy, 41, 45, 64, 245, 256–258, 260–262, 264–276, 282–290, 292–299, 372, 377–378, 425, 464, 531, 533
  eyewitness conflict with, 413–414, 423, 430–434, 436–437, 446, 536
  pathological evidence and, 255–299, 372, 430–447, 535–537
  Texas legal requirement for, xvi, 46, 49

Azcue, Eusebio, 477, 614

Baker, Marrion L., 69, 164–167, 170, 181, 311, 374, 375, 412, 574

Baker, Virginia Rachley, 470

ballistic evidence, 335–362, 371

Ballen, Samuel B., 614

Banister, Guy, 550

Bargas, Tommy, 614

Barger, James, 614

Barnes, Edward, 22, 23, 25, 27, 29, 35–36, 37, 38, 75, 113, 180–181, 236, 329–334, 348
  background of, 31–33
  conspiracy theory of, 156–157
  dismissal rationales offered by, 324–326, 370–379
  further career of, 599–600
  opening rebuttal by, 43–73
  strategies adopted by, 138, 159, 205–206, 313–314, 366–368
  witnesses called by, 383–577
  witnesses cross–examined by, 78–86, 87–90, 91–92, 93–96, 98–100, 101–102, 103, 104–105, 106, 110–112, 114–117, 124–130, 132–136, 139–141, 143–145, 147–149, 150–152, 160–163, 165–167, 168–172,

175–178, 179–180, 181–183, 189–
202, 209–211, 212–215, 216–220,
224–225, 227–234, 251–253, 301–
302, 305–308, 310, 316, 320, 323–
324, 326–327, 338–343, 345–347,
349–358, 360–362
Barnes, W. E., 236, 238, 614
Barnett, Welcome, 614
Baxter, Charles R., 446
Bay of Pigs, 61
Beaty, Buford Lee, 614
Beers, Ira J., 614
Bell, Audrey, 614
Bennett, Glen, 614
Bentley, Paul, 223–225, 376–377
Berger, Andrew, 420–421
Bertram, Lane, 614
Bethesda Medical Center, 41, 64, 246,
546
Bethesda Naval Hospital, 49, 257, 258,
266, 287, 297, 414, 424, 530, 533
evidence by personnel of, 535–537
Betzner, Hugh W., 614
Blake, Arthur W., 169
blanket, at Paine residence, 227, 230,
309–311
Bledsoe, Mary E., 614–615
Bogard, Albert G., 478–482
Boggs, Hale, 608
Bolden, Abraham, 615
Bolivia, 153, 375
Bookhout, James W., 615
Boone, Eugene, 208–211, 212, 214,
376, 562, 577
Boswell, Thornton, 256, 264, 289,
292–295, 298, 377, 533
Botelho, James A., 615
Bouck, Robert I., 400–404
Bowers, Lee, 523–524
Bowron, Diana H., 439–440
Boyd, Elmer, 615
Braden, Jim (Eugene Brading), 570,
571, 615
brain, of Kennedy, 289–290, 433, 447
Brehm, Charles, 615
Breneman, Charles, 615
Brennan, Howard, 102–103, 109, 113,
119–130, 374, 410, 411, 621
Brewer, E. D., 615
Brewer, Johnny, 548, 615
Brian, V. J., 615
Bringuier, Carlos, 615

Bronson, Charles, 615
Brown, Charlie, 487
Brown, Earle V., 470
Brown, Walt, ix–xi
Bryant, Martin, 24, 26, 36
bullet:
    CE 399, 251–255, 273, 316–317,
    318
    fragments of, 514–516
    "magic," 251–255, 273, 316–317,
    318
    path of, 51–52, 271–276, 285, 289,
    293, 295, 298
Burkley, George, 615
Burroughs, W. H. "Butch," 548, 549
Bush, George, 611

Cabell, Earle, 615
Cadigan, James, 145–150, 205, 375
Cairns, A. B., 615–616
Campbell, O. V., 469–470
Carlin, Karen, 616
Carr, Richard Randolph, 395–399
Carr, Waggoner, 237, 386–390, 395,
568
Carrico, Charles, 270, 430, 444–446,
612
Carro, John, 162
Carson, Carl, 22, 23, 26, 35, 43, 98,
108, 109, 126, 127, 155, 248, 250,
276–277
Carter, Cliff, 388
Carter, Jimmy, 611
Carter, William N., 87
cartridges, *see* hulls
Caster, Warren, 171, 616
Castro, Fidel, 617
Central Intelligence Agency (CIA), 61,
151, 277, 420
CE 399 bullet, 251–255, 273, 316–317,
318
chain of possession, 194, 202–203,
220, 327, 371, 376, 377, 605
Chaney, James, 616
Chayes, Abraham, 616
Cheramie, Rose, 549, 616
Chicago, Ill., 402, 509, 510
Chism, John, 469
circumstantial evidence, 77–96, 101–
102, 104, 167–172, 373–376, 466–
476, 501–520, 523–530
Clark, Kemp, 440–441

Clifton, Chester, 546
clothing:
    of assassination suspect, 166, 217,
        219, 223–225, 309, 311, 377
    of Kennedy, 266–267, 270, 288–289,
        337, 342
Cole, Alwyn, 299–300, 378
Communists, xvii, 61, 278, 385, 387,
    449–450
concrete pergola, 170, 467
Conforto, Janet A., 616
Connally, John, xiii, 38, 52, 53, 245,
    272, 337, 343, 423, 427, 509, 519,
    529, 573, 578, 616
Connally, Nellie, xiii, 423, 616
consistency of evidence, 47–48, 62–63
conspiracy evidence, xviii, 68, 156–
    157, 278–279, 387, 389, 391–394,
    531–532, 537, 539–580, 601–612
Constitution, U.S., xiv, 229
Contreras, Oscar, 477, 616
Cooley, Sherman, 616
Corcoran, Poole, and Hubbard, 189
Costner, Kevin, 611
Couch, Malcolm, 103, 374
court exhibits (CEs), see specific items
Court House, Dallas, 470
Crafard, Larry, 616
Craig, Roger, 179, 495–498, 571, 577
Crawford, James N., 469
Crescent City Garage, 131, 132, 135
Crescent Firearms Company, 140
Crichton, Jack, 521
Crowe, William D. (Billy DeMar), 616
Cummings, Raymond, 616
Cunningham, Cortlandt, 300–302, 378
Currington, John, 616
Curry, Jesse, 129, 179, 207, 237, 314,
    331, 405, 409, 552–575
Curtis, Mr., 265
Custer, Jerrol, 265, 535
cut–down procedure, 287

Dallas, Tex., xiii, 21, 84, 189, 221,
    278, 345, 384, 549
Dallas County, 386
Dallas County Records Building, 514
Dallas County Sheriff's Office, 36
Dallas Morning News, 113, 471
Dallas Police Department, xiii, 36, 50,
    84, 109, 174, 240, 277, 327, 331,
    385, 386, 397, 487, 552–575

investigation by, 181–203, 208–220,
    223–236, 303, 306, 464, 496, 497–
    498, 552–575
    radio transmissions by, 563–566
    reduced manpower of, 559
Dallas Police Headquarters, 60, 219,
    220
Dallas Times Herald, 201
Dallas Transit Company, 172, 173
Daniel, Jean, 616–617
Dannelly, Lee, 617
David, Dennis, 535
Davis, Avery, 469
Davis, Floyd, 617
Davis, Franklin W., 22–30, 33, 35, 36,
    42, 43, 45, 66–67, 72, 76, 83, 85,
    96, 102, 120, 173
    prosecution and defense conferences
        with, 106–108, 124–127, 141–142,
        149–150, 222–223, 234–236, 248–
        249, 276–279, 290–291, 324–326
    trial as managed by, 112–113, 153,
        174, 184, 195, 202–203, 215, 220,
        226–227, 239, 250–251, 253–254,
        255, 294–295, 327, 331–334, 362–
        363, 380–381, 581–588
Davis, Jack, 548, 549
Day, J. C., 183–202, 223, 236, 237,
    240, 303, 307, 376, 576, 577–578,
    603, 604
Dealey Plaza, 32, 49, 63, 67, 103, 213,
    358, 393, 406, 409, 410, 412, 467,
    469, 473, 476, 495, 514–515, 570,
    575
Dean, Patrick, 617
Dean, Robert Bennett, III, 24, 35, 36,
    38, 42, 56, 62, 72, 73, 81, 82, 86,
    92, 93, 96, 101, 103, 108, 120,
    124, 136–138, 139, 154, 183, 236,
    250, 359
    Barnes aided by, 210, 221, 223, 234,
        236–237, 250, 251, 366–367, 382–
        383
    witnesses cross–examined by, 264–
        276, 281–290, 293–299
Decker, William, 129, 181, 183, 207,
    209, 331, 460, 496, 554, 555, 556,
    562, 617
defense:
    case discussed by, 205–206, 382–
        383, 476–477

conspiracy claims bolstered by, 539–
580
cross–examinations conducted by,
78–362
motions to dismiss requested by,
324–326, 362–381
motions to exclude requested by,
234, 318–319, 326, 334
witnesses called by, 383–577
Delgado, Nelson, 617
DeMar, Billy (William D. Crowe), 616
Democratic party, 384
de Mohrenschildt, George, 617
Dhority, C. N., 201, 617
discovery process, 543
dismissal of case, 581–589
rationales for and against, 370–381
Drain, Vincent, 224, 225, 314, 323–
327, 329, 332, 369, 378, 420, 567
drawings:
of Dealey Plaza, 467
of Kennedy's wounds, 267–268
Dulles, Allen, 608
Duran, Silvia, 617

Eberhardt, A. M., 617
Ebersole, John, 535
Edgewood Arsenal, Md., 349, 351
Edwards, Robert E., 617
Eisenhower, Dwight D., 241
Ellis, Stavis, 544
Elm Street, Dallas, 170, 175, 193, 213,
217, 284, 324, 354, 421, 426, 465,
471, 472, 475, 554
location of, 87, 92, 101, 112, 172,
178, 181, 185, 197–198, 405, 409,
411, 420, 467, 469, 472, 496, 502,
508, 516
photograph taken on, 528–529
shots fired from, 474, 507
Enfield rifle, 503
epileptic seizure, at time of motorcade,
516–517
Euins, Amos Lee, 97–100, 373, 410
evidence:
of alibis, 448–461
ballistic, 335–362, 371
chain of possession and, 194, 202–
203, 220, 327, 371, 376, 377, 605
circumstantial, 77–96, 101–102, 104,
167–172, 373–376
consistency of, 47–48, 62–63

of conspiracy, xviii, 68, 156–157,
278–279, 387, 389, 391–394, 531–
532, 537, 539–580, 601–612
defense assessments of, 370–379
FBI's handling of, 96, 145–150, 161,
205, 207, 223, 238, 250–255, 299–
312, 314–328, 335–344, 361, 386,
398–399, 471, 474, 475, 478, 481,
487, 494, 505, 509, 510–511, 521–
522, 550–551, 569
origins of shots and, 466–476
of Oswald impersonators, 478–498,
549
pathological, 255–299, 372, 430–
447, 535–537
police handling of, 185–203, 223–236
prosecution assessments of, 379–380
by Secret Service, 400–428
of shooting sequence, 466–476, 501–
520, 523–530
expert witnesses, 50, 109, 146, 159,
184, 255–258, 296, 303, 315, 336,
344, 354, 359, 415, 429

Fair Play for Cuba Committee, 59, 149,
373
Faulkner, Jack W., 617
Federal Bureau of Investigation (FBI),
xvii, 31, 37, 54, 59, 60, 81, 88–89,
135, 145, 154, 166, 189, 194, 214,
240, 277–278, 410, 411, 420, 451,
460, 546, 610
evidence as handled by, 96, 145–
150, 161, 205, 207, 223, 238,
250–255, 299–312, 314–328, 335–
344, 361, 386, 398–399, 471, 474,
475, 478, 481, 487, 494, 505, 509,
510–511, 521–522, 550–551, 569
Oswald as paid informant of, 135,
389, 453, 550
fence area, shots fired near, 471, 473,
507, 513
Ferrie, David, 550, 617
film, Zapruder, 67, 125, 261, 284–285,
316, 337, 404, 468, 474, 528, 529,
563
Finck, Pierre, 256, 264, 289, 296–299,
377, 423, 533
fingerprinting, 188–189, 238, 303,
305–308
Firearms Investigation, Identification,
and Evidence (Hatcher), 335–336

Fireman's and Policeman's
Benevolence, 501–502
Fischer, Ronald B., 617
Florida, 390, 391, 403, 509, 510
Flynn, Charles W., 617
Folsom, Allison G., 356, 357, 551
Fonville, A. O., 59
Ford, Gerald R., 608, 611, 612
Fort Worth, Tex., 406
Frazier, Buell Wesley, 38, 76–86, 121,
133, 228, 229, 371, 373, 451, 571,
574, 604
Frazier, Robert A., 322, 323, 335–343,
378
Freeman, H. R., 544–545
Fritz, Will, 181, 182, 183, 187, 207,
209, 211, 237, 314, 331, 460,
549–550, 557, 558, 560, 562–563,
565, 574, 575, 617
Fruge, Francis, 549

Gallagher, J. F., 337, 618
Galveston, Tex., 564
Gaudet, William G., 618
Gibson, John, 548
Grammer, Billy, 618
grassy knoll, 217, 407, 409, 411, 412,
514, 529, 555
shots heard near, 467, 468, 473, 501
Graves, Eaton, 24, 35, 37, 62, 72, 73,
75–76, 79, 86, 90, 97, 102, 103,
105, 108, 119, 138, 144, 162, 163,
178, 196, 232, 255, 290–291, 299,
313–314, 354
Matthews aided by, 206–208, 211,
215, 236–238, 261, 364–366
Green Bay Packers, 599
Greener, Charles W., 618
Greer, William, 47, 415, 418, 419, 423,
426–427
Gregory, Charles F., 618
Griffin Street, Dallas, 172
Guinn, Vincent, 318, 319–322, 337,
378
guns:
Oswald's knowledge of, 131–133,
135–136, 206
testimony concerning, 345–362
in Texas Theater arrest, 215–223
*see also* Mannlicher–Carcano rifle;
Mauser rifle

Haire, Bernard J., 618
Harbison, Charles, 618
Hargis, Bobby W., 467–469
Harkness, D. V., 574
Harper, William, 618
Hartman, Edna, 474
Hartogs, Renatus, 146, 156, 157, 158–
163, 240, 314, 375
Hatcher, Julian S., 335
Hathaway, Philip B., 546–547
Haygood, Clyde, 504, 527–528, 574
Helpern, Milton, 377, 618
Hemming, Gary, 618
Henchcliffe, Margaret, 442
Henderson, Ruby, 474
Hester, Beatrice, 475
Hester, Charles, 475
Hickey, George, 618
Hicks, Officer, 236, 238
Hidell, Alek J. (Oswald's alias), 138,
144, 145, 147, 228, 299–300
Hill, Clint, 412–416, 419, 423
Hill, Jean, 609, 618
Hill, Jimmy, 619
Hine, Geneva L., 100–102, 374
Hodge, Alfred D., 619
Hoffa, James, 545, 546
Hoffman, Ed, 475–476
Holland, S. M., 474
Holly, Charles Hardin "Buddy," 31
Holly, Harold B., 619
Holmes, Harry, 308, 619
Hoover, J. Edgar, xvii, 61, 68, 96, 238,
278, 326, 385, 386, 551, 619
Hosty, James P., 619
House, Donald Wayne, 569, 571
Houston Street, Dallas, 113, 178, 197,
393, 405, 475, 509, 514, 529, 554
location of, 92, 112, 127, 172, 193,
198, 426, 471, 474, 502, 507, 515,
516
Howard, James, 569
Hudson, Emmett J., 473
hulls (cartridges):
from sniper's nest, 190–191, 199–
200
from Texas Theater arrest, 220, 223
Humes, James J., 238–239, 240, 242–
246, 247, 250, 254, 294, 295, 296,
298, 377, 433, 531, 533, 537
on Kennedy autopsy, 255–262, 264–
276, 281–290

Hunt, Jackie, 441–442
Hunter, Gertrude, 485
Hurt, Henry, xiv
Hutchinson, Leonard, 483–484
Hutton, Patricia, 437–438

impersonators, of Oswald, 465–466,
    478–498, 549
Internal Revenue Service (IRS), 55–56,
    59
investigations:
  ballistic, 335–362
  by FBI, 96, 145–150, 161, 205, 207,
    223, 238, 250–255, 299–312, 314–
    328, 335–344
  by police, 185–203, 208–220, 223–
    236, 303, 306, 464, 496, 497–498,
    552–575
  by Warren Commission, *see* Warren
  Commission
Iran, 611
Irving, Tex., 77, 82, 84, 179, 226, 230,
    233, 492
Irving Sports Shop, 488

Jacks, Hurchel, 619
Jackson, Robert Hill, 109, 113–117,
    374
Jaggers–Chiles Stovall, 551
Jarman, James "Junior," 87, 90–91,
    93, 96, 97, 373
Jefferson Street, Dallas, 547
Jeffries, Carolyn, 24, 35, 42, 49, 86,
    92, 103, 108, 111, 130, 136, 221,
    222, 236, 279, 313
  Barnes aided by, 205–206, 318, 320,
    354, 363–364, 367–368, 382–383,
    431, 435, 436, 438
  witnesses cross–examined by, 300
Jenkins, James, 535
Jenkins, Marion T., 442
*JFK*, ix, xviii
John Birch Society, 402
Johns, Lem, 557
Johnsen, Richard, 253, 254, 318, 319,
    619
Johnson, Gladys, 619
Johnson, Lady Bird, 555
Johnson, Lyndon B., xiii, xiv, 61, 107,
    384, 388, 419, 463, 534, 555,
    556–557, 606, 611
Jones, Robert E., 619

Jones, Ronald C., 438–439
Justice Department, U.S., 61, 545

Kantor, Seth, 619
Kay, Kathy, 619
K–BOX radio station, 210
Kellerman, Roy, 404, 421–425, 427
Kennedy, Jacqueline, *see* Onassis,
    Jacqueline Bouvier Kennedy
Kennedy, John F., 40, 120, 505–506,
    512, 545–612
  assassination of, *see* assassination
  autopsy on, *see* autopsy
  ballistic evidence on, 335–362
  brain of, 289–290, 433, 447
  burial place of, 612
  clothing worn by, 266–267, 270,
    288–289, 337, 342
  distrust for policies of, 60–62
  removal of remains of, 534–537
  threats against, 391, 400–403
  wounds of, 413–414, 423, 430–447,
    520–521, 529
Kennedy, Robert F., 61, 545
Khrushchev, Nikita Sergeyevich, 40
Kingston, John, 365
Kinney, Sam, 418–420
Kirkwood, Pat, 406, 619
Kleindienst, Richard, 610
Klein's Sporting Goods, 140, 142, 143–
    144
Knight, Frances G., 550
Kounas, Dolores, 471

Landis, Paul, 416–418
Latona, Sebastian F., 302–308, 378
Lawrence, Jack, 569, 571
Lawson, Winston, 129, 401, 404–407,
    409, 554
Leavelle, James, 569
Lee, Robert E., 601
Lester, Richard, 515–516
Levchenko, Stanislav, 619
Lewis, C. L., 495
Lincoln, Abraham, 243, 259
Lincoln conspiracy, xiv
Lincoln convertible:
  fragments found in, 319–322, 332,
    342
  Kennedy in, 317, 337, 342
  *see also* motorcade, presidential
Louisiana state police, 549

Love Field, Dallas, 406, 534, 553, 555, 565, 571
Lovelady, Billy, 465–467
Lubbock, Tex., xv, 21, 28, 31, 76, 221
Lubbock County, Tex., 27
Lumpkin, Chief, 521
Lutenbacher, David, 49

Mabra, W. W., 475
McBride, Palmer, 157, 241–242
McClelland, Robert, 435–437
McCloy, John J., 608
McDonald, M. N., 215–220, 222, 376
McGraw–Hill Book Company, 471
McIntyre, William, 619
McKinnon, Cheryl, 473
McVickar, John A., 152–153, 375
McWatters, Cecil J., 172–178, 375, 604
Mafia, 61–62, 545
"magic" bullet, 251–255, 273, 316–317, 318
Main Street, Dallas, 172, 212, 405, 412, 470, 475, 495, 506, 507, 529
Mamantov, Ilya A., 521–523
Mannlicher–Carcano rifle, 57, 140, 320, 324, 326, 332–334, 336, 338, 344, 352, 356–357, 360
  as assassination weapon, 79–82, 103, 115, 128, 129, 133–134, 142, 166, 195, 209, 211, 212, 214, 215, 228, 278, 309, 323–327, 349–350, 486, 487–488, 489–490, 494, 496, 503, 532, 562, 569, 576
  evaluation of, 50–51, 136
  inaccuracy of, 341, 343, 345, 358, 370–371
Marcades, Melba Christine, 549
Marchetti, Victor, 619
Marine Corps, U.S., 39, 47, 133, 150, 242, 347, 355, 357
Martinez, Anita, 23, 30, 126, 236, 253
Matthews, Raymond, Sr., 21, 24, 29, 32, 35, 62, 72–73
  background of, 30–31, 330
  cross–examinations conducted by, 386, 390, 394–395, 397–398, 399–400, 403, 404, 407, 411–412, 416, 417, 418, 419–420, 425, 428, 434, 436–437, 438, 439, 441, 446, 456–458, 461, 467, 468–469, 482, 487, 492–493, 497–498, 503–504, 505,

509, 511–512, 514, 515, 524, 525, 526–527, 530, 537, 573–575
  dismissal rationales rebutted by, 324–325, 379–380
  further career of, 600
  opening argument of, 36–42
  strategies adopted by, 75–76, 90–91, 97, 102–103, 109, 113, 119, 145, 146, 206–208, 236–246, 330–331, 363–366
  witnesses called by, 76–362
Mauser rifle, 51, 57, 171, 194, 195, 200, 209, 211, 212, 214, 339, 376, 486, 497, 504
  police identification of, 210, 496, 562
Mercer, Julia Ann, 620
Mexico City, 477
Miami, Fla., 403
Michaelis, Heinz, 138–139, 145, 220, 375
Millican, A. J., 620
Milteer, Joseph, 391–394
Minox camera, 398–400
Minsk, 38, 39, 40, 59
mock–up, of sniper's nest, 189–190, 195–198
Molina, Joe R., 620
Monterey, Calif., U.S. Army School at, 551
Mooney, Luke, 181–183, 202, 376
Moorman, Mary, 552, 620
Morgan, Dean, 514–515
Morrow, Hubert, 482–483
motions to dismiss, defense, 324–326, 362–381
motions to exclude, defense, 234, 318–319, 326, 334
motive, xiv, 47, 60–62, 372
motorcade, presidential, x, xiii, 67, 84, 91, 101, 109, 122–123, 170, 392–393, 468, 470, 472, 500, 514, 516–517
  to Bethesda Naval Hospital, 534–535
  presidential limousine in, *see* Lincoln convertible
  route taken by, 404–405, 408–409, 413, 418–419, 420, 426–427, 514, 515, 554–555
  security personnel in, 405–406, 554, 575
  vulnerability of, 509–510
Murphy, Thomas J., 473

Navy Intelligence, U. S., 135
Nelson, Doris, 434–435, 534
neutron activation analysis, 55, 319, 320
New Frontier, 509
Newman, Jean, 473
Newman, William, 472–473
New York City Board of Education, 162
Nix, Orville, 620
Nixon, Richard M., 55, 120, 383–386, 388, 606, 608, 611
Nixon–Kennedy debates, 120
Norman, Harold, 86–90, 91, 93, 96, 97, 373
North Beckley Street, Dallas, 178, 179, 180, 459, 549
Norwood, Hal, 620

Oak Cliff, Dallas, 459, 492
Oakland Raiders, 599
Oak Ridge, Tenn., 55
O'Connor, Paul, 265
Odio, Sylvia, 477, 620
O'Donnell, Kenneth P., 509–512, 519
Odum, Bardwell, 318
Ofstein, Dennis H., 551
oil depletion allowance, 61
Olds, Gregory, 620
Oliver, Betty, 620
Olivier, Alfred G., 349–354, 378
Onassis, Jacqueline Bouvier Kennedy, xiii, 106, 413, 424, 425, 534–535, 554
O'Neal Ambulance Service, 517, 534
Oswald, Lee Harvey:
  aliases of, 138, 144, 145, 147, 228, 241–242, 299–300
  alibis of, 448, 453, 456
  alleged impersonators of, 465–466, 478–498, 549
  arrest of, xvii
  charges against, 23, 27–28, 41
  defense's portrayal of, 47–71
  domestic habits of, 459–460, 461
  espionage attributed to, 39–40, 47, 54, 150–153
  FBI connections of, 135, 389, 550
  guns discussed by, 131–133, 135–136, 206
  Kennedy discussed by, 450
  marksmanship of, 53–54, 354–358
  motives attributed to, xiv, 372

"not guilty" plea of, 23
official grounds for case against, 602–605
Paine residence visited by, 451–454
"patsy" claim of, xviii–xix, 60, 61, 66, 392, 533, 601
political beliefs of, 449–450
proof lacking against, 370–379
prosecution's portrayal of, 36–42
psychiatric reports on, 159–163
shooting of, xiii, xv, xvi, 207, 237, 601
witness identifications of, 176–177, 178, 179, 216, 228, 459, 526
Oswald, Marina, 226–227, 229, 230, 449, 450, 452–453, 455, 458, 484, 521–523, 604
Oswald, Robert E. Lee, 601
Otepka, Otto, 620
Owens, Ernest Jay, 547
Oxford, J. L., 226, 229, 231

Paine, Michael, 227–228, 230, 234, 453, 620
Paine, Ruth, 77, 226, 227, 229–230, 232–233, 448–458, 477, 478, 480–481
Paine residence, xviii, 58, 65, 226–228, 230–232, 233–234, 398, 572
  blanket at, 227, 230, 309–311
Palmer, Henry, 620
palm prints, 188–189, 303–304, 305
paraffin test, 238, 301, 302, 378, 605
Parkland Hospital, xvi, 46, 52, 129, 270, 271, 410, 412, 413, 420, 422, 428, 505, 517, 555, 558
  evidence by personnel of, 430–447, 531, 534
  Ruby observed at, 506
Partin, Edward, 545
Passport Office, U.S., 550
pathological evidence, 255–299, 372, 430–447, 535–537
"patsy" claim, of Oswald, xviii–xix, 60, 61, 66, 392, 533, 601
Patterson (Secret Service agent), 552
Pearl Harbor, 386
People of Texas v. Lee Harvey Oswald:
  courtroom bugged in, 249, 255, 262–263, 279, 291–292, 299, 334
  defense discussions of, 205–206
  defense rebuttals in, 43–73

defense witnesses in, 383–577
facts of, xiii, 601–612
fictional events in, xvii
motions to dismiss in, 324–326,
    362–381
post–trial interviews on, 589–598
process of, 21–33
prosecution arguments in, 36–42
prosecution discussions of, 206–208
prosecution witnesses in, 76–362
verdict in, 581–589
Perry, Malcolm, 271, 429–434, 440
Peters, Paul, 443
photographs:
    of assassination, 528–529; see also
        Zapruder film
    destruction of, 266
    FBI testimony about, 314–318
    of Kennedy's corpse, 259–262, 265–
        266, 273, 274, 282
Pickard, John, 620–621
Piper, Eddie, 621
Pizzo, Frank, 482
Poland, 608, 611
police, see Dallas Police Department
possession, chain of, 194, 202–203,
    220, 327, 371, 376, 377, 605
Postal, Julia, 547–548
Powell, John, 472
Powers, Dave, 509, 519–521
presidential motorcade, see motorcade,
    presidential
Price, Jesse, 621
Price, Malcolm, 485–487
prosecution:
    case discussed by, 97, 102, 108–109,
        206–208, 236–246
    witnesses called by, 76–362
    witnesses cross–examined by, 461–
        575
Protective Research Section, of U.S.
    Secret Service, 400–401, 402, 404
PT–109, 60
Public Safety, Department of, 529

Quakers, 449
Quigley, John L., 550, 621

radio transmissions, Dallas police,
    563–566
railroad area, 555, 556, 570

shots fired near, 170, 182, 469–470,
    471, 472, 508, 523
transients observed in, 524
Randle, Linnie Mae, 36, 228, 621
Rankin, Lee, 389
Reagan, Ronald, 611
Reed, Edward, 535
Reibe, Floyd A., 265, 535
Reid, Robert A., 621
Reilly, Frank E., 472
Republican party, 384
Revill, Jack, 621
Rex v. Preston, xiv
Rex v. Wemms, xiv
Rich, Nancy, 621
rifles, see Mannlicher–Carcano rifle;
    Mauser rifle
Rike, Aubrey, 517, 534
Roberts, Delphine, 550
Roberts, Earlene, 458–461, 477, 478,
    549
Roberts, Emory, 418, 423
Roberts, Raymond, 472
Roosevelt, Franklin D., 386
Rose, Detective, 226, 229, 230
Rose, Earl, xvi, 46, 534, 556, 621
Rose, Guy F., 398–400
Rosenberg case, xiv
Rowland, Arnold, 410, 507–509
Rowley, James, 251, 253, 254, 318,
    319, 407–408
Ruby, Jack, xi, xiv, xv, 153, 506, 574,
    575, 602
Russell, Richard, 608
Russia, 458
Russian emigré community, in Texas,
    449, 457, 458
Ryder, Dial, 488–491

sabots, 339–340, 514
Sacco and Vanzetti case, xiv
St. Paul Street, Dallas, 172
Sanders, Pauline, 104–105, 374
Sawyer, J. H., 236, 238
Scibor, Mitchell J., 139–141, 375
Scott, Dred, xiv
Secret Service, U.S., 37, 87, 88, 109,
    128, 135, 314, 393, 432, 433, 447,
    456, 460, 513, 518–519, 531, 554
assassination as handled by, xiii, xvi,
    46, 157, 213, 277, 353, 400–428,
    464, 466, 474, 506, 525, 529, 555

Kennedy's corpse removed by, xvi, 534–535

police precautions rejected by, 559

Protective Research Section of, 400–401, 402, 404

Shaneyfelt, Lyndal, 314–318, 378

Sharp, William, 144, 569, 571

Shaw, Robert R., 621

shims, 340–341, 361

shooting sequence, circumstantial evidence on, 466–476, 501–520, 523–530

Shorman, Robert, 621

Sibert, James, 621

Similas, Norman, 621

Simmons, James, 472

Simmons, Ronald, 343–347, 378

Sims, Richard, 183, 190, 200, 202

Sitzman, Marilyn, 472, 501

Slack, Garland, 487–488

Smith, E. L., Jr., 471

Smith, Joe Marshall, 516–517

Smith, L. C., 506–507

sniper's nest, 97, 315, 474

  mock–up of, 189–190, 195–198

  police testimony about, 185–188, 198, 202, 376

Snyder, Richard E., 150–152, 375

Somersett, Willie, 390–395

Sorrels, Forrest V., 124, 128, 129, 213, 405, 408–412, 518, 554

Southland Hotel, 482

Soutre, Jean, 621

Soviet Union, 39, 40, 54, 146, 150, 450, 457, 458, 522, 551

Speaker, Sandy, 125, 621

Specter, Arlen, 349, 609

Sports Drome Rifle Range, 486, 491, 492, 493

spy camera, 399–400

Staley, Mr., 346

Stamps, Roy, 505–506

State Department, U.S., 54, 151, 152

Steele, Charles H., 621

Stevenson, Adlai E., 384, 401, 408

Stombaugh, Paul, 308–312, 378

Stone, Oliver, xviii

Stovall, Richard S., 225–236, 377

Stover, John, 535, 537

Stringer, John, 265, 535

Studebaker, R. L., 186, 236–237, 303, 304

Styles, Sandra K., 621

Summers, Malcolm, 524–525, 532

Sweatt, Alan, 552

Tague, James Thomas, 338, 496, 504–505, 621–622

Taylor, Charles, 544

Teamsters, 545

Terry, L. R., 622

Tet Offensive, 611

Texas Rangers, 36

Texas School Book Depository, 546, 547, 554, 566

  assassin alleged to have fired from, xviii, 37, 38, 41, 52, 76, 103, 105, 106, 109, 112–114, 116, 120, 129, 164, 165, 167, 180, 181, 284, 345, 361, 371, 395–396, 409, 464, 468, 469, 482, 496, 502–504, 507–508, 509, 523, 527, 552

  evidence by employees of, 77–96, 101–102, 104, 167–172, 373–374, 469, 470, 471, 525–526

  location of, 517

  Oswald employed by, 65–66, 69, 168–170, 452, 455, 458

  Oswald look–alike at, 465–466

  police investigation in, 181–203, 208–220, 577

  Secret Service investigation at, 410–412, 417

  sixth floor of, 65, 67, 182–183, 303, 307, 309, 346–347, 372–373, 400, 572

  sixth floor window of, 44, 51, 130, 316, 357, 397, 472, 515

Texas State Police, 36

Texas Theater, 49, 216, 217–218, 220, 547–548

Thornley, Kerry, 622

Time–Life, 501

Tippitt, Jefferson Davis, 574, 575, 601

Todd, Elmer Lee, 250–255, 318, 319, 377

Tomlinson, Darrell, 253, 254, 318, 319, 622

tracheostomy procedure, 271–272, 286, 287, 430, 431, 432, 434, 445–446

Trade Mart, 405, 406, 417, 554, 565

Trafficante, Santo, 545

triangulation of fire, 68

Truly, Roy, 164, 167–172, 375, 396, 477, 478
Twin Cities Arsenal, 514

U–2 reconnaissance planes, 40, 59
underpass, shots fired near, 406, 407, 469, 470, 472, 475, 520, 523

Valachi, Joe, 61
Vallee, Thomas, 402
viaduct, shots fired near, 469, 470, 471
Vietnam War, 61, 357, 611
Vincent, Earl, 24, 35, 73, 75–76, 79, 86, 97, 102, 105, 108, 119, 139, 143, 155–157, 163, 232, 255, 299, 313, 331–332
  Matthews consulted by, 206–208, 211, 215, 236, 238, 240, 241–242, 364–366

Wade, Henry, 237, 314, 331, 387, 558, 602, 604
Waldman, William J., 141–145, 375
Walker, Edwin A., 371, 571, 573, 622
Walter, William, 550, 622
Walter Reed General Hospital, 546
Walther, Carolyn, 502–504
Walthers, Buddy, 226, 229
Warner, Roger C., 569, 622
Warren, Earl, 607–608
Warren Commission, ix, xvii, 27–28, 136, 165, 295, 389, 394–395, 602–605
  Oswald as viewed by, xiii–xiv
  political purpose of, 606–612
  testimony before, xvii, 88, 91, 100, 126, 127, 153, 163, 237, 298, 315, 341, 349–350, 414, 440, 453, 470, 473, 478, 493, 497, 510, 523–524, 528, 529, 533, 548, 550, 572
Watergate scandal, xviii, 610
Weatherford, Harry, 226, 229
Weiss, Mark, 622
Weitzman, Seymour, 208, 211–215, 240, 376, 562, 577

Westbrook, W. R., 547
WFAA–TV, 182
Whaley, William, 178–180, 374–375
Whitworth, Edith, 484–485
Wilcott, James, 622
Williams, Bonnie Ray, 87, 91, 92–96, 97, 373
Willis, Phillip L., 105–108, 374
Wilson, Steve, 471
Wiseman, Mary, 552
witnesses:
  for defense, 383–577
  defense categorization of, 49–50, 367
  expert, 50, 109, 146, 159, 184, 255–258, 296, 303, 315, 336, 344, 354, 359, 415, 429
  hostile, 553
  Oswald identified by, 176–177, 178, 179, 216, 226, 459, 526
  perjury by, 111–113, 125, 154, 244, 246, 268, 339
  for prosecution, 76–362
  threats against, 396–397, 455
Wood, Homer, 491–493
Wood, Sterling C., 493–494
Woodward, Mary, 471
World War, II, 51, 143
Worrell, James R., 109–113, 370, 374
Wright, O. P., 253, 254, 318, 319

X–rays, of Kennedy's corpse, 265, 266, 274–275, 372

Yarborough, Ralph W., 513–514
Youth House, 159, 160

Zahm, James A., 359–362, 378
Zapruder, Abraham, 63, 284, 472, 500–502
Zapruder film, 67, 125, 261, 284–285, 316, 337, 404, 468, 472, 474, 528, 529, 563
Zenger, John Peter, xiv